Globalization and After

Globalization and After

Edited by

SAMIR DASGUPTA

AND

RAY KIELY

Sage Publications
New Delhi / Thousand Oaks / London

First published in 2006 by

Sage Publications India Pvt Ltd
B-42, Panchsheel Enclave
New Delhi 110 017
www.indiasage.com

Sage Publications Inc	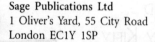	**Sage Publications Ltd**
2455 Teller Road		1 Oliver's Yard, 55 City Road
Thousand Oaks, California 91320		London EC1Y 1SP

Published by Tejeshwar Singh for Sage Publications India Pvt Ltd, typeset in 10/12 Minion at Excellent Laser Typesetters, New Delhi, and printed at Chaman Enterprises, New Delhi.

Library of Congress Cataloging-in-Publication Data

Globalization and after/edited by Samir Dasgupta & Ray Kiely.
    p. cm.
Includes bibliographical references and index.
    1. Globalization. 2. Globalization—Social aspects. 3. Anti-globalization movement. I. Dasgupta, Samir, 1949–. II. Kiely, Ray, 1964–.

JZ1318.G578624   303.48'2—dc22   2006   2006014024

ISBN: 10: 0–7619–3506–1 (PB)   10: 81–7829–661–6 (India-PB)
              13: 978–0–7619–3506–3 (PB)   13: 978–81–7829–661–6 (India-PB)

Sage Production Team: Swati Sahi, Anindita Majumdar, Girish Sharma and Santosh Rawat

Mani, Jenny, Manu, Lynn, Tanu and Shani
for their encouragement and too much caring.

CONTENTS

LIST OF TABLES

PREFACE AND ACKNOWLEDGEMENTS

Globalization and After is a collection of essays from scholars who are excellent in the field of globalization theory. From the late 1980s or the early 1980s some prime incidents started to happen in the world's socio-political, cultural, and economic arenas. The fall of the Soviet Union and the subsequent termination of the "Cold War," demolition of the Berlin Wall, the "Asian Crisis" are some of the major events that accelerated the rejuvenation of globalization at the beginning of the New Millennium.

In the unending debates that are raging about globalization, it is often found that people take extreme views, like the two end points of a pendulum. One side supports it to the extent that it is ready to swallow it, hook, line and sinker. The other side is equally ardent to reject it, viewing it like an ogre, ready to swallow the poor countries. It is quite a tough task for a social scientist to find the exact point along the swinging track of the pendulum. For some, it implies the concrete structuration of the world as a whole—emergence of a single social system—the process which is hastened by a worldwide network of ecological, economic, political, cultural, and social relationships that produce a unique social order. For others, it implies the hegemonic threat of the globalists—emergence of a shrinking world, "the west and the rest" dichotomy, globalization anarchy, and the exhibition of immense power of the increasingly global capitalist class over the direction of change. This volume examines the impact of global capitalism on anti-global solidarity and resistance.

Our present situation is not favorable. Many questions therefore arise. Does globalization create a situation of "Civilization clash" or "end of history"? The rhetoric of debate often suppresses more than it expresses. So the debate over merits and demerits of globalization continues. And the concept demands revision, reassessment, and re-projection. This book examines the manifestation of meanings and related issues by blending theories with empirical realities with reference to topical issues and examples, which cut across the world. The authors also explore the potentials of globalization discourse on the one hand and its limitations on the other. The book captures the essence of both the empirical and conceptual reflection, which leads one to conclude that the process of globalization is far from unilinear and there is no turning back the clock.

We are very much indebted to Professor Arabinda Kumar Das, the Vice-Chancellor of University of Kalyani, Professor Surendra Munshi, Debjani Majumdar, Mimi Chaudhury, Professor Pabitra Sarkar, Professor Pujan Kumar Sen and Professor Swapan Bhattacharyaya, Sumitra Dasgupta, Dibakar Dasgupta, Dr Kaushik Chattopadhyay, Sanjoy Sarkar and especially the Scholars, students and activists for their good wishes and academic support. We are also indebted to all the contributors of this volume for their chapters. We want to thank them for their constant encouragement.

Thanks are also due to Distinguished Professor Immanuel Wallerstein, George Ritzer, Professor Amitai Etzioni, Leslie Sklair, Jay Weinstein, Edward Lehman and Andre Gunder Frank for their unflagging inspiration and academic support to this volume. It has been our pleasure to work with Sage.

Samir Dasgupta

Special acknowledgement from **Ray Kiely**:
To Samir
Just be your good self!

THE TURNING OF THE TIDE*

BARRY K. GILLS

Over two centuries ago, in the year 1776, the historian Edward Gibbon published the first volume of his *History of the Decline and Fall of the Roman Empire*, which he entitled *The Turn of the Tide*. In this epic work, Gibbon analyzed the historical processes by which the prosperity, peace, and stability of the Roman world order gradually came to an end, ushering in a new epoch defined by first the disintegration, and subsequently the rebuilding of Western civilization over the course of many centuries. Today, in our own era, we have witnessed the end of the Cold War, the fall of the Soviet Union and communism in Eastern Europe, the rise and apparent demise of the Washington Consensus, the impact of the events of 9/11 and their aftermath, a host of conflicts and humanitarian crises around the globe, and the dramatic entry of new social forces of protest and civil activism onto the stage of global politics. All these have given us reason to question whether we also are now "at the turn of the tide," at a juncture in world history where one order passes away and a new order comes into being.

It is at such moments in history that new concepts, new ideas, bearing new paradigms and new understandings and perspectives on human experience will make their entry into public consciousness. Now is such a moment. It is in this context that Globalizations appears. It is a reflection of the central role this new concept has already established in the pivotal debates of our time and a strategic recognition of the need to further develop this concept and the new paradigms surrounding it.

A concept such as "globalization" needs a definition. But it is our founding premise, as expressed in the plural form of our title (Globalizations) that the problem is not one of finding a singular definition, but rather of finding plural definitions; i.e., defining not one globalization, but many globalizations. The move from the singular to the plural is deliberate and implies deep skepticism

---

* Previously published as, Editorial, *Globalization*, 2004, 1(1): 1–6, Taylor & Francis Ltd.

of the idea that there can ever be a single theory or interpretation of globalization. By beginning from the premise that there are many globalizations, we open
the door to exploration of multiple processes and multiple interpretations and
perspectives that may constitute many possible alternative globalizations, many
possible paradigms. There is already a tendency to polarize the discussion of
globalization around the opposition: Globalizations between a "corporate" globalization versus a "people's" globalization, or "globalization from above" (elite)
versus "globalization from below" (popular). But even the mis-labeled "anti-
globalization" movements are more often than not in fact advocates of an
alternative globalization, or "alter-globalization," inspired by the belief that
"another world is possible," the global slogan of the World Social Forum and
its supporters. Thus, even so-called "resistance" to globalization is not external
to the processes of globalization, not merely reactive, but very much an integral
and "internal" part of the historical processes of change that we call
"globalizations."

It is with this perspective that we hope to widen the debate on globalization
beyond a narrow definition of the processes as simply economic, or even worse,
as merely about "free trade" and liberalization. The central debate is not framed
as an either-or question, to either accept or reject "globalization." The problem
of the reversibility or irreversibility of globalization is not therefore so simple
as some would have us believe. It is not a matter of somehow stopping altogether
the historical processes of globalization, but rather of understanding and engaging with the very complex processes of shaping the historical direction of
globalization.

Moving from singularity to multiplicity is not to speak of any single or
inevitable globalization, or even of a set of processes of a single globalization,
but rather, to accept "multiple globalization processes" and indeed "multiple
globalizations." This in itself signifies something of a paradigm shift from the
type of thinking that dominated the first phase of the globalization debate. This
move is intrinsically inclusive both intellectually and politically or socially.

It is therefore evident that the debate addressing such a range of perspectives
and issues must be potentially as open as possible, encompassing all fields of
knowledge rather than founded in any single disciplinary or theoretical tradition. A concept as inclusive as globalizations requires and indeed encourages
openness to enquiry in multiple fields of knowledge, and it benefits by their
mutual contact and interaction. Globalizations' academic intention will therefore be to encompass as many perspectives as possible, including not only the
traditional social sciences and humanities, but including contributions from the
natural, environmental, medical, and public health sciences as well. We should
encourage new types of multidisciplinary research and transnational research
involving participants from more than one field or country. In this respect, we
see our role as contributing to the emergent field of critical Globalization

Studies, or Global Studies, and to the pursuit of new modes of global education and the "globalization of education." There is a necessary link between this new model of global research and education and the realm of practical action, politics, and policy. It will seek to engage with social, cultural, political, and ideological debate on the nature and practices of global change. In doing so, it is necessary to establish a real bridge between the academic world and the world of practice, the world of action. To publish work that is relevant and accessible to a wide public, including academics and students, non-governmental organizations and policymaking communities, and bring them actively into direct dialog wherever possible is also demanded that may forecast the current and the future trend. It is that commitment which should encourage us to publish work by the new generation of younger scholars, who have already embraced the new research agenda of Globalizations, as well as by practitioners and activists in as many fields as possible. By encouraging the development of this emerging global community of globalization scholars and activists, the published resources will seek to become part of its own times, as aspect of "the turning of the tide." We hope to bring new meanings and fresh ideas to the concept, broadening its scope and contributing to the debates that will shape our common future.

"The turning of the tide" implies a sense of history, an understanding of human development in the long-term and the evolution of the global human community as the main subject of understanding. That is why you will see in these pages a deliberate concern for history, for "global history" and the "historicization of globalization" as well as the "globalization of history." All of this is intimately related to the remaking of global education, escaping the parochial confines of nineteenth century inspired nationalism and national historical narratives. It also contributes to the shaping of contemporary "global consciousness" or "world consciousness," which in fact is not unique to our present age, but itself has a long "history." The true meaning of "globalization," in its deepest and most generic sense, has everything to do with "global history" and with the perception as well as the ultimate reality of the "unity of humanity" as a central fact of global history. This (re)-awakening of world-consciousness recaptures in our own time what is perhaps the oldest and most simple truth of history, as recorded in the oldest extant literary tradition from Sanskrit, that is, that "In truth, the whole world is indeed one family." We are witnessing, in our own time, a renewed impetus to the formation of world consciousness, as globalization processes bring all of humanity into greater physical and communicative proximity to one another. These same processes are rapidly altering the social relations and social networks that compose the basis of the human community.

The global level of reality is now becoming increasingly proximate to every human being in one manner or another, and therefore "globality" or "globalization" is something everyone has to deal with. This implies recognizing human unity at some levels while simultaneously maintaining and adapting identity and social relationships at the individual, family, community (or "local"), national, and regional levels, thus ensuring the continuation of human and cultural diversity. However, in so far as the "unity of humanity" is a truth, it is based on two fundaments, two "facts" of nature. The first is our genealogy, the fact that we are in truth all members of one species, all related to one another, all sharing the common heritage of our remote ancestors, despite millennia of migration and the formation of myriad groups. The second fact is our mutual inhabitancy of a single, integrated common natural environment, our planet and its single biosphere, which knows in reality no political, territorial, ideological, or other artificial human imposed boundaries, yet all within a continuum of planetary and human history. The evolution of world-consciousness, awareness of the world-as-a-single-place, and the evolution of world or "global civilization" are all intimately related historical processes, the inheritors of all that have come before down the ages and combining all the streams that have fed the great river we call human history.

It is thus that today we have established new concepts such as "global governance" and "sustainability" in relation to the evolution of the human polity and to its relationship with the natural environment. It is to the first of these, the evolution of the polity, as it approaches truly global level, that the concepts and practices of globalization will perhaps play the most important part. The enduring idea of a universal humanity implies an evolution towards some form of universal polity, in turn premised on some manifestation of universal or world consciousness. Perhaps, in this sense, "globalization" is a way of expressing our present stage of evolution or historical development towards a world polity and world consciousness. This is not a new phenomenon, but in fact a feature of human history extending back many millennia until the present. There may in fact be a fundamental desire for an international or global order that brings unity, peace, prosperity and stability. In times of disintegration, confusion, or strife, the longings of many wise as well as ordinary souls may be for a type of unity that brings peace and the benefits of law to all. Despite many historical attempts to build such enduring orders, often accompanied by aspiring universal ideologies or religious visions, none have so far been truly world encompassing and none has been more than temporary. Perhaps all hegemonies, all empires, and all states and their universalisms are only temporary. Why should our present time be an exception? Yet, the deep desire for unity, peace, and stability still remains a potent force in history. Even as the idea of the Roman Empire persisted in the West for more than a thousand years after its actual historical unravelling, as Gibbon so adeptly analyzed, in its absence the idea of unity persisted in that of the universal church, as Augustine outlined in his *De Civitate Dei*. There are counterparts to this history in many other traditions and civilizations, such as the institution of the Caliphate in Islam, which persisted for many centuries, and in the idea of a unified state that has influenced the history of China and India from antiquity to the present. In all these expressions, and many others not mentioned here, the idea of the experience of unity, of integration in a single community rather than separateness and fragmentation, is deeply implanted in the human mind. Today, it finds at least partial expression in modern institutions such as the United Nations and the Olympic Games, where divisions are to be at least temporarily set aside, in the pursuit of the experience of unity. However, it is unclear how far, or how fast, humanity will progress towards a true world polity, or what form world consciousness will take in the future. None of these matters are to be taken as givens nor are they inevitable. It is clear, however, that a form of global governance is being sought by many that does not rely on exclusiveness, that does not merely perpetuate the power and privileges of a few. An order based on such exclusiveness cannot deliver lasting peace and justice or meet the deep desire for unity. We are in danger of repeating the mistakes of the past and of lapsing or sleepwalking into nightmarish repetition scenarios, whereby great power politics pursues domination rather than integration, and fosters violent fragmentation and mutual enmities rather than the experience of unity and concord.

Collective fear is again reverberating and with it the danger of rising hatred and suspicion between peoples and their rival political, ideological, or religious belief systems. The so-called "clash of civilizations" is not a new phenomenon, but rather an example of the re-emergence and persistence of historical divisions that threaten to destabilize our chances of a peaceful world order. It is also another name for "business as usual," signifying the changes brought by the onset of a new age of chaos, barbarism, and human suffering as the old order slowly disintegrates and the center cannot hold. We cannot meet these challenges by a resort to conservatism, a return to tradition, a selective manipulation of historical memories that rekindle old enmities, or by an attempt to reinforce the reigning exclusiveness of the dominant powers and interests. Only by innovation, bold change, and new responses can we hope to effectively meet the challenges of our contemporary global crisis. The status quo is not really an option. Only the willingness to make fundamental, perhaps sweeping changes, can offer us the possibility of avoiding the worst consequences of the present order and the opportunity to consolidate a new and better world order. Whether globalization means utopia or dystopia in the future will largely depend on what this generation does today, on how this generation and its children responds to the present global crisis. Perhaps the time has come to recognize that the only good use of power is the power to do good. Only by abandoning the pursuit of power and by embracing an alternative culture of mutual assistance, empathy, and non-violence can humanity hope to construct a world order realizing the ideals of peace, prosperity, stability, and unity for the majority of the world's people. Competition is promoted by some—both political realists and economic liberals—as the right central organizing concept for human affairs, or even as a form of natural law. Yet biological, zoological, anthropological and sociological research tells us that real and lasting success is perhaps more a consequence of cooperation and mutual assistance among a species rather than a ruthless Social Darwinism or a quest for domination where inevitably some are "winners" and others are "losers." While competition is held by some to offer benign consequences and even the achievement of efficiency and security, others question its efficacy and its status as natural law, and see it as an ideology masking a set of material interests. Similarly, while many favor some version of "free trade" in principle, many more people are rationally suspicious of taking the principle (as with competition) to extremes. Most people would actually prefer a set of more pragmatic compromises that preserve a complex balance of social interests and, which do not sacrifice all on the altar of a single-minded goal such as free trade for its own sake. This set of circumstances is very evident today in the (lack of) progress of the Doha Round of global trade talks. The reaction of the developing world at the Cancun ministerial, and the WTO's subsequent abandonment of all of the so-called Singapore Issues with the sole exception of "trade facilitation" (which is simply easing of customs procedures) indicates that much greater compromise is needed in the direction of meeting the needs of the majority of people in the world, if there is to be a real prospect of preserving multilateralism and the rule of law in global economic relations.

Likewise, while the post-9/11 politics of American global power seem to indicate a retreat from genuine multilateralism, there are many people in the world who are convinced that multilateralism is an objective trend and indeed a requirement of effective global governance in an era of globalization. These people, who may indeed represent the global majority, may move ahead with this agenda regardless of the (temporary?) tendencies in Washington. The great dangers to be avoided and opposed at the present conjuncture of global history are a reversion to power politics and the naked pursuit of power and interests, domination and thus the "clash of civilizations" as a self-fulfilling prophecy. The rekindling of ancient enmities will only fuel a new phase of global conflicts, with a never-ending spiral of violence and revenge. We must, therefore, abandon the culture of militarism, of dogmatic self-assertion, of ego-centrism and arrogance, in favor of the creation of a new global culture based on mutual cooperation, political rather than military settlement of conflicts, and global dialog and toleration rather than single-minded missionary or crusading zeal. To begin, an urgent global effort is needed to finally ban all weapons of mass destruction, including the nuclear weapons (in all categories) of all the powers, and all other biological and chemical weaponry. These standards must be universal and applied without exception, even to the most powerful. Beyond this, it is also necessary to resume the trajectory initiated immediately following the end of the Cold War to make new and hopefully rapid progress towards more general disarmament and arms control, and reverse the present dangerous trend to initiate yet further expensive and potentially dangerous arms races. In principle, the world may see the long-term wisdom of reversing the present priorities of spending on military versus development needs, which at present stands at something like $900 billion for the former and a mere $50 billion for the latter. Finally, the idea of national sovereignty stands out to some as their last bastion in a time of great uncertainty and perceived threat. However, to many others it is perhaps more of a last great obstacle to human unity and integration and must therefore, rather than being reinforced, be gradually circumscribed with limitations, thus strengthening a supra-national world order, based on universal human rights and the rule of law. By effectively limiting the power of the states, especially the Great Powers, by a host of means, including the increased participation of "global civil society" in global governance, the global community insures its own stability and future viability. The ultimate question is whether the status quo will be allowed to re-assert itself and thus perpetuate the gross inequalities of the present world order, between North and South, East and West, male and female, rich and poor, and myriad other categories of division that beset our present world. Or, whether this status quo will be directly and effectively challenged by new social forces and new ideas, that seek to radically restructure and reform both global capitalism, as we know it, and the inherited international political system. The challenge is to dissolve the entrenched hierarchies of wealth, power, knowledge, and wellbeing that characterize the present world order. We must make these give way to a new set of structures and relationships that will serve the needs of the majority of humanity, and by doing so, guarantee our best chance for a real and lasting global consensus. Global governance, and indeed globalization itself, should be, must be, more than a mere condominium of vested interests and power, more than a perpetual oligarchy. If we are indeed to move towards a world of shared responsibilities and shared benefits, of a "fair globalization," and to an ethics of "global justice," then this can only be accomplished by actually serving the interests of all of the world's peoples, and those of its poorest and most disenfranchised as the highest priority. Only then, and by the active engagement of the world's people in the processes of protest and challenge to the status quo, can our future globalizations be made truly positive.

Policies and practices at the global level must be made to correspond to the needs of the global majority, whether this relates to the need for peace, material prosperity, human security and dignity, gender equality, health and welfare, or the protection and preservation of the common environment. It is our challenge to overcome the obstacles inherited from centuries of conflicts, divisions, and enmities, and replace these with a new global ethos based upon profound empathy for our fellow humanity, compassion for their suffering, and the will for unity.

Globalization is not about a set of predetermined historical outcomes, already set in stone by the laws of nature or history. Our common history remains open, and it is up to all of us to shape its ultimate outcomes. In the rich tapestry that is our common global history, it is by finally embracing the positive potential of globalizations, and the humanocentric rather than egocentric perspective that this move entails, that we will come to see all history as our own, and the future as one common destiny. To me, this is the real meaning of Globalizations. It is the acceptance of a collective human identity, the forging of a collective human will, and the fulfilling of collective responsibilities for the welfare, peace, prosperity, and security of all human beings. This, then, is the "turning of the tide" in human history. Where we go from here is entirely up to us.

INTRODUCTION

SAMIR DASGUPTA AND RAY KIELY

"Anyone who would confidently chart the future today would be a fool, but the first thought that struck me when thousands of casualties resulted from an attack on the American mainland, for the first time since the civil war, was that over the long pull the American people may exercise their longstanding tendency to withdraw from a world deemed recalcitrant to their ministering, and present Washington with a much different and eminently more difficult dilemma...: how to rally the citizens for a long twilight struggle to maintain an ill-understood American hegemony in a changed world."

—**Bruce Cumings**, *"Some Thoughts Subsequent to September 11th"*

We are not global pessimists. Global pessimists are those who claim that the gains of global capitalism are unevenly distributed. They suggest that large disparities of wealth feed international terrorism and worry about the impact of a technological and consumerist society. Masters of alarm and anxiety, they prey on fear of the future and have authored one of the great narratives of our time: globalization is bad. We are not going to call globalization bad. Rather our aim is to describe and explore the future of globalization. Peter Heslam in his book review states that, along with many others, Stiglitz insists that globalization can be a force for good. It has the potential to enrich all, including the poor. The problem is that this potential is not being fully realized, partly as a result of the "free trade" policies that dominate international trade agreements. We are not going to measure the rate and intensity of goodness or badness of globalization because the future is difficult to predict. This volume attempts to analyze causes and consequences of the downsizing of globalization and explore the hiddens of globalization deviation, which may help increase awareness in readers of the dangers we live in at the highest levels of society. But it is doubtful that such awareness will improve matters without a powerful impulse for change from below. The outcome of the dilemma between globalization from above and globalization from below perhaps may show some signs of the future of globalization. Beck descried "the capitalist fundamentalists" as "a dangerous illusion," and called for a reinvigoration of the state. "We need", he wrote, "to combine economic integration with cosmopolitan politics. Human dignity, cultural identity and otherness must be taken more seriously in the future." It is the reality that the economic malaise deepens; the ecological problem is bound to worsen. And in either case, the deprived majorities of "the rest" will continue to be trapped in a downward trajectory that engenders bitterness and hatred against global capitalists. The struggle against this widening gulf between the winners and the insecurity and misery of the losers has been going on since the mid-nineties. The losers tardily, appeared to react against economic, environmental and moral and humane disasters triggered by the gospel of progress. The problems of impending environmental catastrophe, economic malaise, cultural imperialism, technological hazards, loss of traditional identity and sense of local patriotism loom before us as a double wall blocking the future. The world is becoming smaller, but people from all spaces of the world is not coming together close. Indeed as economies are drawn closer, nations, cities, and neighborhoods are being pulled apart. The processes of global economic integration are stimulating political, cultural, and social disintegration.

Arthur Mitzman (2003) views that environmentally, our spoliation of the earth's resources and our poisoning of air, earth and water may have led us to a point of no return. The results of a social order founded on technological hubris and on individual and collective avarice are already being felt: the steady destruction of the earth's rainforests by huge lumber and agricultural combines, the acid rain denuding woodlands throughout Europe, and the warming trend which, if unreversed, will probably lead to the inundation of the earth's coastal areas and the death or homelessness of hundreds of millions of people by the middle of the present century. In the enormous land mass of the former Soviet Union, nuclear and other varieties of pollution have diminished life expectancy by ten years in the last generation, proof that the rape of nature by the capitalist state can be as traumatic as that by the private capitalist. A renowned economic commentator of the World Bank found that the richest 1 percent in the world get as much income as the poorest 57 percent. The richest 5 percent had in 1993 an average income 114 times greater than that of the poorest 5 percent; the ratio was 78 times in 1998. The poorest 5 percent grew poorer, losing 25 percent of the real income, while the richest 20 percent saw their real incomes grow by 12 percent, more than twice the average world income. World inequality grew because inequality grew between countries. The rich nations grew richer at the expense of the poor ones.

It is evident from the United Nations Development Programme's Human Development Report 2003 that the income of the richest 25 million Americans was equivalent to that of nearly 2 billion of the world's poorest. In 1920, per capita income in Western Europe was three times that in Africa; by the 1990, it was more than 13 times as high. Adding human meaning to these numbers, the report said, "the statistics today are shaming; more than 13 million children have died through diarrhoea disease in the past. Every year over a half million women, one for every minute of the day, die in pregnancy and childbirth. More than 800 million suffer from malnutrition" (Cited in Sukomol Sen 2004). Fidel Castro imagines a new type of social and economic order as an alternative to present globalization:

> The world needs an order. There is a need for universal, global, just and democratic order. There is an order coming, one that can be seen coming at a full speed, unstoppable—it's the neoliberal globalisation, going global. We have to start thinking about an order of a different kind and, in the meantime, denounce and struggle.

✗ The idea of a global village was predicated on the promises of widespread prosperity and economic globalization, and the further belief that this prosperity went hand in hand with delivering the fruits of liberal democracy. The betrayal of these promises, however, is evident in growing inequalities and increased poverty. It may now be argued that the globalization paradigm is no✗ longer operative because its potential to liberate was never realized. Some see the ever-increasing economic inequality and degeneration of cultural localism, and traditional belief and values as symbol of the failure of globalization and the triumph of the local frustrations that it engendered. Indeed, the euphoric ideal of global freedom has been replaced by the very real challenges posed by globally unbounded and unrestrained "others" that belong to "the rest." So we may argue that post-globalization or "after globalization" does not necessarily mean abandoning globalization, but to move beyond its discursive limitations. Some say that post-globalization is not an end to globalization but the emergence of a different kind of engagement that is sharply at odds with the visions of liberal, multicultural globalization. Here, both religious fundamentalism and imperial hegemony begin to emerge as new forms of global engagement (source: Report of IASTE conference 1996). The critics, who hold the negative view, assert that globalization produces an undermining of democracy, a cultural homogenization, and increased extinction of natural species and the increasing loss of biodiversity and environmental hazards. Some imagine the globalization agenda—whether viewed positively or negatively—as inevitable and beyond human control and intervention. Others view globalization as generating new conflicts and spaces for clash and upsurge, distinguishing between globalization from above and globalization from below (Brecher, Costello, and Smith 2000). Kellner, while arguing the fate of globalization, states,

> I want to argue that in order to properly theorize globalization one needs to conceptualize several sets of contradictions generated by globalization's combination of technological revolution and restructuring of capital, which in turn generate tensions between capitalism and democracy, and 'haves' and 'have nots'... Globalization is thus a contradictory amalgam of capitalism and democracy, in which the logic of capital and the market system enter ever more arenas of global life, even as democracy spreads and more political regions and spaces of everyday life are being contested by democratic demands and forces. But the overall process is contradictory. Sometimes globalizing forces promote democracy and sometimes

inhibit it, thus either equating capitalism and democracy, or simply opposing them, are problematical. These tensions are especially evident, as I will argue, in the domain of the Internet and the expansion of new realms of technologically-mediated communication, information, and politics.

The processes of present-day globalization are highly turbulent and lead to anti-globalization movements throughout the world. The theorists often describe the strife between homogenizing, commercialized, and Americanized ways of the global economy and culture with traditional cultures and economy, which appears resistant to globalization. Kellner (1997) argues that "Globalization from below" refers to the ways in which marginalized individuals and social movements resist globalization and/or use its institutions and instruments to further democratization and social justice. While on one level, globalization significantly increases the supremacy of big corporations and big government, it can also give power to groups and individuals that were previously left out of the democratic dialog and terrain of political struggle.

The term globalization has received emotive force. It is, some view, as a process that increases future global economic development and others regard it as the process that expresses the upsurge of ethnic violence, cross border terrorism, dissonance, discrimination, and inequality. It sometimes offers opportunity for actual development for the winners of the North but mostly it is a threat to "the rest". So we see the birth of neo-nomological paradigms in the field of globalization. But what would be the future of globalization? Globalization of globalization or localization of globalization? And the dispute over the *globalization and after* begins to continue.

For a decade the term "globalization" has played a seminal role and become an all-purpose catchword in social science discourse. It is necessary to further evaluate and review continuities and transformational changes. It is also important to present theoretical and empirical evidences for reassessing the recent issues and consequences of globalization on the one hand and anti-globalization on the other. Globalization now has two contradictory and inevitable bearings: it is a new historical period with hope and opportunities as well as fragmented *de-globalization* and a *threat*. The rhetoric discourse of globalization began in the period 1870–1914 when Britain ruled hegemonic power over the globe and when the first technological revolution took place. During the 1950–1960s the hegemonic economic and political power had shifted to the US. The game at the beginning was dominated by imperial nation-states. Now MNCs and TNCs have taken over the world.

EXISTING GLOBALIZATION: CHALLENGES AND ALTERNATIVES

An old Chinese proverb catches the paradoxical flavor of our modern times: "To prophesy is extremely difficult—especially with respect to the future." Our volume is about the future study of globalization but we are not futurologists. And it is very difficult for social scientists to make accurate prophesy about the future society. We can only dissect the problems of our present-day globalization and comprehend its projective versions. The introduction aims to unravel the meaning of the two key words in the title—*globalization* and *after*—and then uses this discussion to introduce, and at times critically reflect on, the chapters that follow. Clearly, globalization is the key term. But before examining what is meant by globalization a few words are necessary concerning the use of the word "after". On the face of it, this may seem a somewhat back-to-front way of proceeding, but we will suggest that the term "after" has some implications for understanding globalization, and this will become clear in due course. Hereafter means "post" or more clearly the future of globalization. In this book, *after* broadly refers to three (related) ideas. *First,* that since September 11, 2001, we have moved beyond globalization, and (back?) into an era where state sovereignty, and above all the dominance of one nation-state, the United States, is visible. This theme is taken up in a number of chapters. *Second,* the volume also refers to the potential challenges and alternatives to actually existing globalization proposed by the commentators of anti-globalization movements, or perhaps more accurately, the movement(s) for global justice. *Third,* the book estimates the future form of society on the basis of the theoretical and empirical propositions and sweeping criticisms of the existing globalization that is now in trouble. On the face of it, of course, if we have moved beyond globalization then how can we analyze the challenge to globalization? The immediate answer—and one that we will unravel in the rest of this introduction—is that we have not moved beyond globalization, and that there is substantial continuity—as well as important change—in the international order, both before and after "September 11". Moreover, this has implications for so-called (!) anti-globalization movements, because they continue to challenge "actually existing globalization," while responding to the challenge of the more overt militarism of the dominant state.

These points are perhaps best illustrated by further examining the concept of globalization, and particularly the (fallacious) claims of mainstream globalization theory. Anthony Giddens' *The Consequences of Modernity* (1990: 64) is one of the most important sociological works that attempts to construct a theory of globalization. He defines globalization as "the intensification of worldwide social relations which link distant localities in such a way that local happenings are shaped by events occurring many miles away and vice versa." In what is probably the most comprehensive examination of globalization to date. David Held and his co-authors similarly define it as "the widening, deepening and speeding up of worldwide interconnectedness in all aspects of contemporary social life, from the cultural to the criminal, the financial to the spiritual" (Held et al. 1999: 2). They further claim that globalization is "(a) process (or set of processes) which embodies a transformation in the spatial organization of social relations and transactions—assessed in terms of their extensity, velocity and impact—generating transcontinental or interregional flows and networks of activity, interaction, and the exercise of power" (Held et al. 1999: 16).

On the face of it, there is nothing wrong with these definitions. They rightly point to the extension and expansion of social relations beyond the nation-state. But this is where the problems begin. First, there is the question of whether such an expansion is as new as is sometimes implied. Indeed, much of the mainstream literature tends to take realist theories of international relations at face value for the era before "globality," arguing that the era of state autonomy or sovereignty has only recently ended. But this tends to conflate sovereignty and autonomy, with a number of results. First, it ignores the fact that state sovereignty for much of the world has only been universalized since 1945; in this respect, it has only just *begun*. In this respect, and quite typically, mainstream globalization theorists tend to ignore the experience of much of the developing world. Second, it ignores the fact that there has always been a tension between state sovereignty and the international expansion of capitalist social relations, which are not necessarily territorially fixed in the way that, say, feudal social relations were. Third, mainstream globalization theory rightly points to the expansion of such social relations, but it tells us nothing about the form and character of such relations. The capitalist and neoliberal character of globalization is therefore ignored and underestimated or supported. This results in a number of problematic contentions: first, the idea that "the global" must be embraced, without necessarily telling us the specifics—and the politics—of what this concretely means; second, the idea that state autonomy has been reduced, which at the same time ignores the hierarchical and unequal ways in which this affects different states. In other words, much of the literature on globalization ignores the unequal and uneven character of actually existing globalization, and the ways in which this is intrinsic to the way that such globalization operates. In particular, this manifests itself in the ways in which neoliberal capitalism intensifies the unevenness and inequalities of the international capitalist economy *and* the international state system. It is these manifestations of contemporary— capitalist, neoliberal—globalization that movements for global justice resist and not globalization per se. Indeed, the global justice movement is explicitly concerned with issues of transnational solidarity, and so cannot be described as being against all forms of globalization. In this respect mainstream globalization acts as an ideology, as it allows today's neoliberals (third way and neoconservative) to accuse activists of being parochial, and backward looking. This may be true of some factions within the movement, but in fact the bulk of the global justice movement itself claims allegiance to a cosmopolitanism, which rejects the violence and war interests of the state and the inequalities, exploitation, and environmental destruction of neoliberalism.

GLOBAL INTEGRATION OR REVERSAL?

The gap between the rich and the poor countries has widened considerably. Amartya Sen (2002) comments: "To see globalization as merely Western imperialism of ideas and beliefs (as the rhetoric often suggests) would be a serious and costly error." Sen links issues related to globalization to imperialism. But it would be a great mistake "to see globalization primarily as a feature of imperialism. It is much bigger—much greater—than that."

One can now easily claim that we are living in dangerous times, with the entire "post war edifice of multilateralism and cooperation crumbling. The danger today arises particularly on the economic front. If the root is the attempt to repeat history, with active neo mercantilism of the powerful countries lurking behind the rhetoric of neo liberalism and globalization" (Raghavan 1998).

The neoliberalists view globalization as a deregulated freedom for economic activities, whereas the opponents use it as an institutional process to maximize profit. This particular *dilemma-paradigm* invites a clash between global initiators and anti-globalization protestors. What to some is the indispensable condition of progress and prosperity appears to others as a cancerous affliction of society. Wiseman (2000) ascertains only one way to approach the dilemmas of globalization. He argues that the starting point is to begin with a grounded critique of real cost and dangerous taken-for-granted forms of unregulated free market globalization. He notes, "A sustained critique of the dominance of neoliberal economics needs to be linked to the articulation of a language which conveys the possibility of more desirable relationships between individuality and mutuality; solidarity and difference" (224). Examining some of the economic and social traits of neoliberal globalization, it should be pointed out that neoliberal globalization has expanded; the world-economy has grown more sluggishly. Consequently, economic growth promised by the neoliberal ideology is, in actual practice, shrinking. While between 1950 and 1973, the world product grew at an almost 5 percent, between 1974 and 1980, it dropped down to 3.5 percent; between 1981 and 1989, the growth rate was only 3.3 percent and in more recent years, between 1990 and 1996, the rate was extremely low— only 1.4 percent (Martinez 1997).

The unevenness of globalization compounds such disparities since it would appear that the strong are becoming stronger and the weak weaker. The benefits of globalization accrue to a relatively small proportion of the world's population while global inequality and social exclusion continue to increase. So the intellectual discourse and consequences of globalization remain hotly controversial. Globalization, undeniably covers wide-ranging debates and contrasts, which sometimes provide opportunities and other times threat. Berger (2002) observes: "For some, it implies the promise of an international civil society, conducive to a new era of peace and democratization. For others it implies the threat of an

American economic and political hegemony…" (2) Behind the architecture of New World order (benign globalization?) the malignant globalization creates a three-tier structure across national boundaries. Hoogevelt (1997) views that the globalists reside in the core of the circle. In the second circle we find the people who "labour in insecure forms of employment and thrown into cut-throat competition in the global market". The outer ring represents these excluded. To some observers, the process of globalization is linear and unidirectional. But this is not fully true. Inconsistencies and disharmony characterize the mainstream globalization process. At the root, there are profound contradictions between *globalization in progress* and *globalization in conflict*. One may raise the key question: Is globalization bringing people a new freedom to act or does it portend an uninvited, unwanted and cruel fate for the deprived majorities? For the clash continues between fear, anxiety and uncertainty for the dejected majority, and freedom, comfort, and happiness for the few elites (Dasgupta 2004).

The report of International Labour Organization acknowledges that globalization's potential has opened the door to many opportunities and benefits. It has promoted open societies and open economies and encouraged a freer exchange of goods, ideas, and knowledge. The report states that a truly global conscience is beginning to be sensitive to the inequalities of poverty, gender discrimination, child labor and environmental degradation. But the deep-seated and persistent imbalances in the current realities of the global economy, global morality, sense of altruism, justice and global ethics have created a worldwide impasse. These imbalances may be assumed as capitalistic implosion. And the reflective thinking and debate towards protest movement against such a deviant globalization begin, which assumed a new intensity after Seattle. This worldwide protest movement is the part of the international mobilization against the growing concentration of neo-capitalist forces and the ravages of their capitalist globalization. It is not organized around a single issue, identity based, or somehow "implicitly" radical. On the contrary, this movement directly attacks global capital's economic and political infrastructure with a radically democratic politics and a strategy of confrontation. It is bold, anti-authoritarian, and truly global. But a section of the reformers now claim the anti-globalization movement as a part of globalization because most of the protestors come to join across the world where there is no border and they claim this anti-globalization movement as global justice movement or global liberation movement.

In a report of ILO (2004) it is also stated that there is a growing concern about the direction globalization is currently taking:

Its advantages are too distant for too many, while its risks are all too real. Corruption is widespread. Open societies are threatened by global terrorism, and the future open markets are increasingly in question. Global governance is in crisis. We are at a critical juncture, and we need to urgently rethink our current policies and institutions. (Report of ILO 2004)

The protestors of anti-globalization movement seek to have a break from capitalist control and dominance, hegemony and subjugation, and oppose privatization and disinvestment policies of the capitalist government, reject foreign debt and call for unilateral liquidation. The resistant movements stand with the people of Iraq, Afghanistan and Palestine that are being crushed under the jack-boots of US-led capitalist or Zionist aggression (Mumbai Resistance 2004). The emergence of the anti-globalization movement, Naomi Klein feels, has produced a feeling of near euphoria among anarchists.

Not only are our commitments to direct action and decentralization shared broadly in the movement as a whole, but we are also enjoying a political legitimacy that has eluded us for decades. We can now articulate our anti-statist, utopian message to activists around the world and we are no longer dismissed as terrorists or cranks. In many respects it seems like we should just mobilize, mobilize, and mobilize. Unfortunately this would be a grave mistake. The movement's anti-authoritarian, revolutionary character is currently under attack by an informal network of reformists, who want nothing more than to see this movement accommodate itself to the basic structures of the present world. They are not waging a direct assault upon revolutionaries in the movement: they recognize that this would alienate them from the movement's base. Instead, they are fighting us indirectly, in the realm of ideas. In particular, they hope to define the movement in a way that renders its most expansive, utopian potentials literally unthinkable. (Quoted from an interview with Naomi Klein)

Klein observes: "As important as it is to mobilize, anarchists will have to respond to this challenge on the theoretical terrain: we cannot afford to lose the battle of ideas." Above all, Klein observes, "We must link the anti-globalization movement to a broader revolutionary project in a way that is coherent, concrete, and irrefutable. However, as a defensive measure, we should expose the reformist's attempt to sever this link and reveal their designs to the movement as a whole."

Our title, *Globalization and After*, raises the question: Will it be a continuation of recent trends, a levelling off of global integration, or a reversal? Will the marketization, privatization, and deregulation of the economy increase, or will there be a reaction against these developments? And if there is a reaction, what forms will it take? Will there be a return to economic nationalism or, will new forms of global governance emerge that can ameliorate the disparity and dejection that have been expanded by corporate globalization? What will be the alternatives to globalization? Will it be found in the local projects of insurgent groups or in the programmatic transformation of movements in struggle? (Petras and Veltmeyer 2001). Are we entering into an anarchic transition from the existing world-system to a different one? Are we waiting for an uncertain alien future? Will we suffer from postmodern vertigo? What will be the condition of health, mentality, environment, and other traditional and local cultural forms, behavior patterns and mindset of the people in the Third World? Are we waiting for a doomsday or entering into a brighter tomorrow? The answer to the questions may refine our understanding of global integration–reversal dilemma. *Naming the Enemy* and *Globalization from Below* are exemplary documents of the reformist wing of the anti-globalization movement. These documents focus on the deeper questions upon which its identity hangs. These two works celebrate the movement's radicalism emphatically, but in terms that make the revolutionary transformation of the social order inconceivable.

In *Globalization from Below*, Jeremy Brecher, Tim Costello, and Brendan Smith (2000) argue that the economic, political, and cultural interconnectedness signified by globalization is irreversible and possibly a good thing: this interconnection, they assert, could potentially serve the interests of people and the earth, not just the elites. Although the rich and powerful have shaped globalization in their interest thus far ("globalization from above"), there is a countermovement that seeks to reshape the interconnected world in the interests of people and the planet ("globalization from below"). They believe that the movement for "globalization from below" is disparate but growing, and their book is meant to provide a framework for uniting it into a common, grassroots struggle. They want to build a world structured by "human values other than greed and domination," one "less dominated by the culture and values of global capital, even if it is still constrained by them." They believe that the movement for "globalization from below" can transform the world by leading people to withdraw their consent from dominant social relationships, which will prevent the reproduction of the social order, and thus create a situation in which the movement can impose different, more just norms upon society as a whole. The anti-globalizers criticize global capital and the types of alternatives they envision. Some scholars offer a critical view of the movement structured around three responses to global capital: "restraining it, democratizing it, or building local alternatives to it". The anti-corporate scholars examine anti-globalization movement that want to restrain global capital through state regulation. They treat movements against structural adjustment, peace and human rights groups, land reform, debt relief, cultural localism, steady employment generation, creation of local and national labor market, and rebirth of nation-states—the explicitly anti-corporate movement. The movement for "globalization from below," or democratization of globalization, mean making governments and corporations accountable to common people instead of a few elites or corporate managers and global traders. So they look at the "environmental and labour movements, socialist movements, anti-free trade movements, and the Zapatistas." Here, the concept of "delinking" comes to the fore that wants to separate from global capital and build locally based alternatives.

Of course, many leaders in the West support the advent of globalization through free trade and political cooperation. "By the late 1990s, cheerleading turned into jeremiads, a banner became a bull's-eye." Globalization is not only the buzzword, rather, it is the catchword relating to the consequences of global change for the wellbeing of various classes, the sovereignty and identity of the states, the inequalities among peoples, and the health of ecology. The mental mapping of the World in 2020 as projected by National Intelligence Council declares that the traditional geographic groupings will increasingly lose salience in international relations and the increasing power on the world scene of traditionally non-Western powers will be in the forefront.

The projection report states that as with the East–West divide, the traditional North–South fault line may not be a meaningful concept for the world in 2020 owing to globalization and the expected rise of China and India, which have been considered part of the "South" because of their level of development.

Divisions other than economic may also shape how we view the world. We anticipate that religion will play an increasing role in how many people define their identity. For many societies, divisions between and within religious groups may become boundaries as significant as national borders. Globalization above all will have replaced the former divide among the industrialized West; Communist East; and the developing, non-aligned, or Third World. New alignments instead will be between those countries, or even parts of countries or hubs, that are integrating into a global community and those that are not integrating for economic, political or social reasons. The international order is in the midst of profound change: at no time since the formation of the Western alliance system in 1949 have the shape and nature of international alignments been in such a state of flux as they have during the past decade. As a result, the world of 2020 will differ markedly from the world of 2004, and in the intervening years the United States will face major international challenges that differ significantly from those we face today. The very magnitude and speed of change resulting from a globalizing world—regardless of its precise character—will be a defining feature of the world out to 2020. (Report of NIC)

The future of globalization as described by the experts of NIC includes: The contradictions of globalization; rising powers: the changing geopolitical landscape; new challenges to governance; a more pervasive sense of insecurity; the expanding global economy; the accelerating pace of scientific change and the dispersion of dual-use technologies; lingering social inequalities; emerging powers; the global aging phenomenon; halting democratization; a spreading radical Islamic ideology; the potential for catastrophic terrorism; the proliferation of weapons of mass destruction; and increased pressures on international institutions.

In addition to the pivotal role of the United States, different international organizations, multinational corporations, non-governmental organizations (NGOs) and others can mitigate distinctly negative trends, such as greater insecurity, and advance positive trends. The discourse of such a projection contradicts with the reality. The increasing disparity and the rise of the capitalist implosion derail globalization. A large section of the experts believe that the process of globalization, powerful as it is, could be substantially slowed or even stopped.

Hirst and Thompson consider the future of "globalization", as the processes promoting international interconnectedness. They have examined three questions regarding the future of globalization: (1) Is contemporary globalization unusual compared to past episodes such as 1850–1914? Then there was rapid growth in trade, capital flows, and migration comparable to or greater than today. There was also a policy backlash and the widespread adoption of protectionist policies. (2) Are contemporary globalization processes undermining national economies and thus hollowing out states? On the contrary, the major states are reinforced in their role of international actors. However, both the global economy and national governments will face crucial challenges during this century. Such changes will tend to foster conflict and thus reinforce the role of the state, but in a context where governance at every level will be harder to achieve. (3) Is economic globalization likely to increase or decrease? Evidence about the effects of borders and the limits to trade expansion are presented, which indicate that we could be close to the limits of feasible globalization.

David Korten in an interview taken by Alexander M. Duke refers to globalization as many different things to different people: the world becoming smaller through means of communication; a spreading of Western influenced entertainment and capitalistic culture; but also, environmental issues such as global warming and a widening gap between rich and poor, North and South. He refers to global economy as "out of control and performing contrary to basic principles of market economics. It is certainly against any political vision of a just world." Korten clearly says,

We are being told that globalism is the key to economic progress and efficiency and the triumph of the market over communism. My claim is that we do not have a market economy, but a capitalist economy. Capitalism and the market are presented as synonymous, but they are not. Capitalism is both the enemy of the market and democracy. Capitalism is not about free competitive choices among people who are reasonably equal in their buying and selling of economic power. It is about concentrating capital, concentrating economic power in very few hands, using that power to trash everyone who gets in their way.... This is not a market, and definitely not a democracy. The basic principle of democracy is "one person one vote" and in the capitalistic society, we have "one dollar one vote."

If you look internationally over the last fifty years, Korten continues, there have been improvements in the Third World, but in the last twenty years the reverse has happened, with increased debt crises and poverty.

We are consuming more than we are producing. And what we are producing are predominantly financial assets, i.e., bubbles as we have seen in the Asia crisis and with the Internet and technology crash. When the bubble bursts, liabilities remain and a crisis starts. Some of the politicians opposed to US hegemonic influence, and social and political activists opposed to the disparity of oppressive global capitalism now portray globalization as dangerous. *Globalization, anti-globalization dilemma* has thus become an issue in a wide-ranging global debate. President Halonen of Finland declares, "we believe that globalization could and should be a force for a brighter future for all people. Unfortunately, today's globalization falls far short of this promise and actually is morally wrong and politically unsustainable."

The unbalanced outcome between and within countries, the upsurge of insecurity, inequality, political turbulence, conflicts and wars, and vulnerability to uncontrolled changes are signalling a new transformation. So, the question arises: what would be the next to globalization? The result of the clash of *hegemony and counter-hegemony* can only locate the module of such a transformations. Gramsci (1971) notes, "Anybody who makes a prediction has in fact a 'programme' for whose victory he is working, and his prediction is precisely an element contributing to that victory.... Indeed one might say that only to the extent to which the objective aspect of prediction is linked to a programme does it acquire its objectivity" (171). It means that we can predict the future to the extent that we are involved in making it happen (Katz 1995). The rhetoric discourse can only explore the possibility of intellectual prediction. But the actual prediction comes from the voices of participants. The agitated anti-globalizers come from intellectual and practical directions. They belong to different political ideologies and different spatial origins. But all of them form an "ethos conferred of an anti-capitalist, anti-globalization, and acute anti-corporation mindset" (Bhagwati 2004: 4). Now the debate on globalization is overlaid by another fallacy that raises the question: will the present globalization process perish? If the answer is "yes" then what would be the alternative to globalization? Joseph Stiglitz (2002) rightly states, "Rarely did I see thoughtful discussions and analyses of the consequences of alternative policies" (14). He continues, "World leaders want to get together to discuss a new trade deal, they will need to build a modern-day fortress to protect themselves from public rage, complete with armoured tanks, tear gas, water cannons and attack dogs" (24).

Are they "enemies" to the world leaders? Is it the truth that the politics of hegemonic domination are being replaced by the politics of communication, interfacing and collaboration? The reality depicts rather a very sordid picture. Perhaps so the fearful *malignant-impact* ideas have come to haunt the world leaders. So they often claim, "To those who may belittle and even ridicule us for trying to go beyond the world of 'us' and 'them', of governance through exclusion of 'enemy' as part of human nature, the young generation may wish to respond that such ridicule is simply the consequence of arrogance" (Picco 2001: 25). But what is the lived reality? Does globalization really foster equal footing, interfacing, economic equality, freedom, and real democracy? The defaced globalization does not support the so-called rhetoric fair deal (!) of globalization. "Globalization today is not working...for many of the World's poor...for much of the environment...for the stability of the global economy" (Stiglitz 2002). Whatever may be the theoretical puzzles, it is the lived reality that the rules of globalization do not reflect a proportionate sense of distributive social justice. So the protest against globalization anarchy. The question rises: What would be the future of globalization? What comes after neoliberalism? To answer that question we must ask a more fundamental question: What do neoliberalism and neoconservatism have in common with the anti-globalization and antiwar movements? The answer is that all ostensibly share a focus on redefining democracy in the contemporary world-system. "Spreading democracy" is the rallying cry of both the Washington Consensus and the Bush Doctrine. The "Washington Consensus" is the claim that global neoliberalism and core finance capital's economic control of the periphery and the entire world by means of the International Monetary Fund (IMF) and the World Trade Organization (WTO) is the only realistic alternative to misery and disaster. The "Bush Doctrine" is the bald neoconservative justification of US global military domination and pre-emptive war—as part of a renewed attempt to make the world safe for democracy. For the anti-globalization and antiwar movements, these establishment doctrines, in so far as they profess to be "spreading democracy," are nothing but window dressing for the global dictatorship of the US and core corporate governing elites. While focusing their attack on the institutions that enforce this dictatorship, these movements also strive to create an alternative, a genuine participatory democracy.

THE FAILURE OF MAINSTREAM GLOBALIZATION

The concept of de-territorialization, growth of interconnectedness, speed of social and economic activity, a long-term process with sudden or recent events in social, economic, political and cultural life, the emergence of "around-the-world, around-the-clock" economic market, liberalization of market, rapid-fire communication technologies—all mean mainstream globalization. The failure of mainstream globalization was a sudden trauma to the global initiators. The ever-increasing economic disparity between "the West and the Rest," between "the North and the South," the global–local cultural conflict, the upsurge of ethnic conflict, the vibrant intensity of terrorism, communalism, fanaticism, and increasing inequality within and between nations threaten the rationale of globalization process. The crisis in the emerging markets has made it evident that globalization opportunities come with high uncertainty. Secondly, the vicious circle of poverty dominates over technology and communication in the Third World. The movement of the global economy, in the words of Chossudovsky is "regulated by a worldwide process of debt collection which constricts the institutions of the national state and contributes to destroying employment and economic activity" (14). Entire countries have been destabilized as a consequence of the debt burden, of the collapse of national currencies, often resulting in the outbreak of social strife, ethnic conflict and civil war. Structural reformers promote trade liberalization, whose main result is closure of domestic manufacturing in the Third World countries—and thus exacerbation of their debt burden. The unspoken motive of the trade-liberalization agenda was quick disbursement of loans to the Third World that would allow them to continue importing goods and commodities from the international market. This has led to complete economic stagnation, development crises, and the destruction of entire domestic economies.

The World Commission expresses divergent views in convergent voices. The report states, "The current process of globalization is generating unbalanced outcomes, both between and within countries. Wealth is being created, but too many countries and people are not sharing in its benefits." It notes that work and employment widen the benefits of globalization. But the reality depicts a more sordid picture. It is evident from the data that over 185 million are globally unemployed. The informal economy also continues to increase. Today, the TNCs enjoy an enviable 50 percent share of the world's largest economic sales units. Seizing the opportunities provided by this type of globalization process, the giant companies entirely or partly control national economies all over the globe, and are now able to move capital freely across national boundaries. Pieterse (2001) rightly states, "We inhabit a global theatre of the absurd, a winner-takes-all world in which the wealthiest billionaires own as much as approximately half the world population" (165). No one can deny globalization divides the world into hegemony and domination at one end, and exclusion and threat at the other. The neoliberalism that has dominated globalization policy during the past quarter century is characterized by its emphasis on deregulation, privatization and free competition. But its hidden aim is to de-politicise the state. And the local populations' claims on the state's resources were treated as an unfortunate burden on the grand designs of global economic growth.

The political agenda dictated by the World Bank, IMF and the WTO is essentially globalization from above. In response, a movement has emerged to resist this agenda: *anti-globalization*. The Earth Summit in Rio de Janeiro in 1992 directed international attention to the need to control greenhouse gases. The slogan, "Fifty years is enough," echoed by the anti-globalization campaigners in 1994 and the anti-globalization campaigns again landmines, Nike shoes, Nestle, Enron, etc., served to articulate the movement's program. The 1999 "Battle in Seattle" against the WTO was the first major victory for the movement. Since these events, the movement has sought to lay the foundation of a global civil society that can derail globalization.

So the neo-globalization initiators changed the track and developed a variety of nomological paradigms like "civil society," "good governance," uncorrupted privatization, government's transparency, etc. When anti-globalizers are protesting against corporate capitalism replacing its neoliberal principles and call for an alternative architecture, then the global initiators are speaking about "fair globalization" with the mission of "good governance." And the wave of debate over such a discourse continues. Amartya Sen has argued that "public action that can radically alter the outcome of local and global economic relations." For him: "The central issue of contention is not globalization itself, nor is it the use of the market as an institution, but the inequity in the overall balance of institutional arrangements—which produces very unequal sharing of the benefits of globalization. The question is not just whether the poor, too, gain something from globalization, but whether they get a fair share and a fair opportunity" (Sen 2002).

The earlier popular discourse on globalization suggests that globalization and "world economic growth occur in tandem." The reality is that despite several nations with remarkable growth in the 1980s and 1990s, overall polarization in the world did not shrink but increased in the latest era of globalization. So the refreshed academic discourse need for theoretical clarity and empirical transparency. For the purpose the distinguished commentators on globalization from different Continents attempt to examine the diverse phenomenon of "globalization" in order to shape "a less polarized and more peaceful social world." This book examines the links between neoliberal, capitalist globalization, and the ways in which this is being challenged by the global justice movement. This is the unifying theme of all the chapters. Some chapters mainly focus on theoretical debates related to globalization, while others on the politics of global justice movements. There are specific disagreements, or at least differences of emphases on the part of different writers.

For instance, Wallerstein's chapter essentially rejects "globalization talks" outright. Wallerstein claims that the rhetoric discourse that we are now living, and for the first time, in an era of globalization that has changed everything: the sovereignty of states has declined; everyone's ability to resist the rules of the market has disappeared; such a discourse, is in fact, a gigantic misreading of current reality—a deception imposed upon us by powerful groups, and even worse one that we have imposed upon ourselves, often despairingly. It is a discourse that leads us to ignore the real issues before us, and to misunderstand the historical crisis within which we find ourselves. We do indeed stand at a moment of transformation. The future, far from being inevitable and one to which there is no alternative, is being determined in this transition that has an extremely uncertain outcome.

US HEGEMONY IN THE WORLD-SYSTEM AND TERMINAL CRISIS

The end of the Cold War brought to an end a period of international bipolarity. Academics, social activists and policymakers have since then tried to explore exactly what kind of power structure would replace it. "There were two main views: first that the United States would withdraw from international entanglements since there was no longer any great enemy, no global cause to structure US foreign policy, nor any clear reason for the US to continue to spend so much money acting as world policeman. Add to this the changing nature of US internal politics, and specifically the shifts within its ethnic mix. The opposite view was that the US would be able to influence world politics like never before: it was a unipolar moment, in which the US was the world's only remaining superpower. According to this view, no one power or group of powers could challenge US hegemony for the foreseeable future. And, of course, there were those who saw some kind of self-interested combination of these two positions being the likely outcome, with the US pulling back from international commitments that were not seen as central to its interests while aggressively pursuing other interests through its overwhelming economic, political, cultural and military power" (Smith 2002). We may have these views in Samuel Huntington's *The Clash of Civilizations and the Remaking of World Order* (1993), Benjamin Barber's *Jihad vs McWorld* (1996) and Francis Fukuyama's *The End of History and the Last Man* (1992). Barber's (1996) vision of the future world order seems most in accord with the world order that is most likely to emerge from the current crisis. Barber (1996) visualizes a world in which two forms of international order co-exist: "The first 'rooted in race holds out the grim prospect of a re-tribalization of large swaths of humankind... in which culture is pitted against culture... a Jihad... against modernity itself." The second is "a busy portrait of onrushing economic, technological, and ecological forces that demand integration and uniformity... one McWorld tied together by communications, information, entertainment, and commerce" (1996: 4).

What are the main consequences of the events of September 11 for future world order? The social scientists as yet have analyzed the following implications: "First, the United States has abruptly ended its brief experiment with unilateralism because the US was simply not interested in developing multilateral responses to world problems. The events of September 11 shatter the key assumption of many proponents of globalization that the conveyor belt of economic development and the spread of liberal democracy were in some way inevitable, irreversible and universal." The radicalists, in terms of some rhetoric coinages like truism, humanism, liberty and justice, wisdom, civility try to promote new globalization paradigm. So they claim, "History has not ended and civilizations have not clashed, even after September 11, 2001" (Picco 2001). They claim that globalization may lead to faceless homogenization that is ignorant about differences and arrogant about hegemonic power and quest for identity; through dialog, it may also lead to a genuine sense of global community and global communication. But the elements of the new paradigm like equal footing, reassessment of the enemy (?), dispersion of power, deregulated market, neoliberal economic relations appear as completely rhetoric. Our world has not yet crossed the divide. So globalization is now on trial (Klein 2002). And the anti-globalization protestors are now becoming more and more able to pore a direct challenge to the "seductive rhetoric of the borderless world." Participants at the 2nd Cairo Conference observed,

the US continues its efforts to strengthen its control over the world, using its increasing control over the world-economy and its major military powers, seeking to prevent the recreation of a multipolar world, which might undermine its increasing influence and powers. It is stated in the declaration: "It is therefore important for the international movement against capitalist globalization and US hegemony to challenge that tendency, which includes:

(1) The increase and spread of US military presence in new areas of the world such as the Arab World and middle and Eastern Europe in addition to Afghanistan, constituting a direct threat to the peoples of the world. (2) The use of international capitalist institutions in achieving more control over the world-economy and the reformulation of international economic relations within the framework of free trade agreements, conditioned loans and aid and the international financial and monetary policies, the creation of new relations that are opposed to the previous tendencies with a view to establish a new economic world order that can achieve justice and allow for the advancement of developed nations. (3) The insistence of the US to launch war against Iraq, despite the objection of the UN and its continued use of pressure on the UN to rationalize the war and the obstruction of any security council resolution that may condemn the Israeli aggression on Palestine, Syria and Lebanon, thereby clearly falsifying international legitimacy against the interests of the peoples and creating a double standard in international criteria which contradicts the charter of the UN. (4) To impose an American model for democracy on people and to advocate for a false democratic model in the Arab World, which ignores the most basic characteristic of real democracy represented in its social content and its acknowledgement of national sovereignty and the political freedoms and rights that are derived from the will of the peoples themselves and the use of that false democratic proposal to force Arab countries into the acknowledgement of the legitimacy of the racist Zionist entity, to accept its leadership role in the region and to submit to the agenda of neoliberal globalization. (2nd Cairo Declaration, 2003)

Wallerstein refers to the period from 1945 to today saying it is of a typical Kondratieff cycle of the capitalist world-economy, which he divides into two parts: an A-phase or upward swing or economic expansion that went from 1945 to 1967/1973, and a B-phase or downward swing or economic contraction that has been going from 1967/1973 till today and probably will continue on for several more years. Its period of normal development has currently entered into its period of terminal crisis which coincides with the high point of United States hegemony in the world-system. Samir Amin (1997) refers to the concept of global hierarchy in the context of world-system which he views as the successive stages of "five monopolies", i.e., technological monopoly, financial control of world-wide financial markets, monopolistic access to natural resources, media and communication monopolies, and monopolies over weapons of mass destruction.

Amin notes, "What results is a new hierarchy, more unequal than ever before, in the distribution of income on a world scale, subordinating the industries of the peripheries and reducing them to the role of subcontracting. This is a new foundation of polarization, presaging its future forms"(5).

Wallerstein feels interest to discuss the historicity of world-economy mentioning the relation between the Kondratieff cycles and the systemic crisis and then seeks the political way out of what kind of social action is possible and desirable during a systemic transition. Kondratieff cycles are part of the "normal" functioning of the capitalist world-economy, which enters into a new period of expansion; it will thereby exacerbate the very conditions, which have led it into a terminal crisis. And the fluctuations will get wilder and wilder, or more "chaotic," and the direction in which the trajectory is moving ever more uncertain, as the route takes more and more zigzags with every greater rapidity. And this will no doubt increase the amount of day-by-day violence in the world-system. US is unquestionably the hegemonic power in the world-system possessing a combination of economic, military, political, and cultural advantage over, any and all other states (Wallerstein 2003). He distinguishes the three axes, i.e., "the internal competitive struggles of the major loci of accumulation of the capitalist world-economy; the "North–South" struggle; and the battle to determine future world-system" within the period of the postwar apogee of US hegemony, the late summer glow (1967–2001) and the stage of anarchy (2001–2025 or 2050). As a result the people in the Third World feel very scared of the future of the present world-system: "We move into the uncertain immediate future and in moments of systemic anarchy such as the present anything can happen.... We have entered an anarchic transition—from the existing world-system to a different one" (Wallerstein 2003).

Ray Kiely examines the relationship between US hegemony, contemporary imperialism and globalization. The more belligerent foreign policy of the US state since the terrorist attacks in September 2001 constitutes a significant departure from "globalization." In order to address this question, Kiely considers the practices of the Bush administration and relates these to claims made concerning the nature of globalization, and deliberate on the extent to which these constitute a break from globalization. In order to address these questions he considers the claims made concerning globalization, and a critique of some of these claims are central to the chapter's overall argument. Kiely's arguments challenge the claims made by a body of thought that can be called globalization theory, focusing on the flawed methodology of this theory and its problematic interpretation of the decade of globalization in the 1990s. This critique is then used to challenge the argument that post-September 11, US foreign policy represented an unambiguous and regressive retreat from the potential of globalization. While there are crucial differences between the 1990s and post-2001, there are also considerable continuities. Crucial to these continuities is the neoliberal character of contemporary globalization. In making these arguments, the relationship between the US state and imperialism will also be addressed. It is generally argued that US foreign policy from 2001 represents a significant break from the 1990s. Second, these arguments are subject to a critique based on a rejection of globalization theory and its claims concerning international relations in the 1990s, and the proposition that Bush II was characterized by significant continuity (as well as considerable change) in the nature of US foreign policy. Third, the implications of these arguments are addressed through a consideration of the wider relationship between the US state, and the character of contemporary "globalization" and "imperialism."

CAPITALIST GLOBALIZATION AND TRANSNATIONAL POLITICS

In talking about globalization and neoliberalism, we are told over and over that we live in a globalized space, in a world-economy in which nation states have been virtually dissolved and national sovereignty has lost its identity. This view supposes that this is the only possible world that can witness the end of history, which is perceived as something different from capitalism and in which different forms of social stratification, imperialism, and ideologies come to an end. Whereas Sklair is committed to understanding globalization as something that is not just ideological, but which refers to a specific, novel period of capitalism led by a transnational capitalist class—a position in turn briefly challenged by Steger. Although bearing a close resemblance to Frank and Wallerstein, Sklair's theoretical paradigm has built on the issue of transnational relationships that emerge under globalization (Waters 1995). He is equivocal about the balance of effectivity between transnational practices and nation-states. Malcolm Waters writes that Sklair reifies "a global capitalist class that effectively runs the planet on its own behalf." The events of September 11, 2001 have understandably dominated the media and politics in many parts of the world. To locate the period from 1995 to the first decade of the twenty-first century as a turning point for capitalist globalization and for humanity is the claim of the social scientists. The institutional movements that have so far happened, were meant to promote capitalist globalization, those who own and control the transnational corporations and their allies in state, international and transnational politics and bureaucracies, the professions, and consumerist elites. These initiatives of what Sklair has termed the transnational capitalist class stimulated renewed efforts of counter-movements, the origins of which are traced back to protectionism, New Social Movements, and Green movements. While none of these counter-movements mounted a coherent challenge to capitalist globalization, all contributed to what is now a variety of anti-globalization movements with the potential to becoming a serious movement, offering a serious alternative to capitalism. He strongly believes that the struggle to resist globalization from above through globalization from below has begun. The neoliberal globalization, some argue, has globalized exclusion, exploitation and social malaise. Osvaldo Martinez (1997) declares in a convention: "We must globalize resistance against it. The system operates at a higher level of internationalization and even transnationalization. Therefore, our response requires a high level of coordination and international unity around a minimum program of action against neoliberal globalization." He continues, "This neoliberal globalization has been and continues to be like a storm" that is sweeping over the planet, affecting all countries to a greater or lesser extent, creating economies and societies increasingly exclusive and polarized.

The focus of most contemporary social movements has been on either polarization issues (primarily class, ethnic and gender polarization) or ecological issues. But the greatest challenge remains to make viable connections between them. Many of the successes of the anti-globalization movement, in the short time since its emergence, Sklair claims, have been due to its capacity to make these connections. The future success of the movement against capitalist globalization and the viability of alternatives to it ultimately depend on the victory of non-violence as a universal principle. The growing influence of the globalization of human rights—in particular taking economic and social rights as seriously as civil and political rights—in movements against global capitalism is a positive contribution to these ends.

Wallerstein argues that US hegemony is in decline, whereas some other commentators argue that there are both signs of strength and weakness in the US-led international order. There are also differences of emphases in understanding global capitalism, with Wallerstein and De Zolt all committed to a *"third worldist,"* core-periphery approach. Other views on the other hand suggest that core and periphery may be useful ways of capturing some features of international capitalism, but these must be regarded as ultimately being determined by the uneven development of international capitalism. For all these and other disagreements, the chapters reject optimistic apologies for actually existing globalization, and particularly the claims that it is both inevitable and desirable.

Immanuel Wallerstein rejects the idea that the "globalization discourse" that dominated the 1990s represented a new development in human history. Instead, he argues that recent changes can be better explained through an analysis of the cyclical ups and downs of the world capitalist economy since 1450, and that the current era is part of a downturn in the world-economy reflected in US hegemonic decline and the resurgence of neoliberalism. These manifest themselves through inter-imperialist competition, the massive US trade and budget deficits, the restructuring of industries and liberalization of finance.

ANTI-GLOBAL SOLIDARITY AND
POLITICS OF RESISTANCE

Michael Albert (2001) in his speech says,

We do not oppose global entwinement. We do not oppose trade. We oppose global relations that increasingly empower huge corporations and weaken whole nations and populations. Our upsurge of activism has emerged from and added to already growing awareness in dozens of countries around the world. Our dissent has focused not solely on poverty, privatization, profit-seeking finance, and trade imbalance, but also on very specific institutions such as the IMF, the World Bank, and the WTO. Focusing on these has in turn caused us to rally not just against injustice, but against important institutional causes of injustice, which, in thinking about them, is leading us inexorably to also think about critical relationships of capitalist ownership, market allocation, distribution of income, and undemocratic decision-making.

The emerging and growing anti-globalization movement is, some say, a radical movement with the potential to address the roots of centrally important economic and social problems. And not only do we have a growing anti-IMF, anti-WTO, anti-World Bank, and anti-corporate awareness we also have a growing militancy, anger, and commitment to dissent aggressively about that awareness, and a growing solidarity even across countries and whole continents. Albert continues,

Witness your conference and its diverse attendance not only from Greece, but also from France, Italy, and other European countries. And witness Porto Alegre with upwards of ten thousand activists in attendance, from a thousand organizations, from all over the world. This is all very powerful. It is very promising. And of course it is very welcome. It has been a long time coming. And we should celebrate and build upon it.

Against capitalist implosion from above, there have been a significant upsurge of forces and of resistances that have attempted to preserve specific forms of culture and society against globalization and homogenization, and to create alternative forces of society and culture, thus exhibiting resistance and globalization from below (Kellner 1997). The protest movements have resisted capitalist globalization and the backlash against existing globalization is quite visible across the globe.

    Let us mention the realities of expansion of protest movement across the world, which will shed light on the intensity and degree of turbulence of such New Social Movements, and let us imagine the volcanic eruption of present day globalization. The protestors gathered in New York, Washington, Chicago, Berlin, Paris, Madrid, Lisbon, Stockholm, Helsinki, Amsterdam, Berne, Egypt, Gaza, Nouakchott, Stuttgart, Frankfurt, Heidelberg, Mannheim, Cologne, Dusseldorf, Vienna, Switzerland, Finland, Sweden, Oslo, Dublin, Indonesia, Malaysia, Kolkata, New Delhi, Dhaka, Seoul, New Zealand and Australia. Thousands of small and large global protests against war on Iraq were held in 2003, voicing popular opposition to war on Iraq. On January 18, demonstrations against war took place in villages, towns and cities around the world, including Tokyo, Moscow, Paris, London, Dublin, Montreal, Ottawa, Toronto, Cologne, Bonn, Gothenburg, Florence, Oslo, Rotterdam, Istanbul and Cairo, in Washington D.C. and San Francisco, California. In San Francisco, between 150,000 and 200,000 people attended the demonstration. The San Francisco police had originally estimated the crowd size at 55,000, but admitted later that they had badly underestimated the number and changed their estimate to 150,000. The millions of protestors throughout the world gathered voicing anger and hatred against capitalist expansionism. The antiwar demonstrators were chanting "No blood for oil" which sounds like globalization for war. Noam Chomksy points out the significance of current antiwar movement as compared to the nature of movement that happened during the time of Vietnam War. He views,

Even in the United States there is overwhelming opposition to the war and that corresponding decline in trust in the leadership that is driving the war...that never happened before. If you compare it with the Vietnam war the current stage of the war with Iraq is approximately like that of 1961—that is before the war actually was launched, as it was in 1962 with the US bombing of South Vietnam and driving millions of people into concentration camps and chemical warfare and so on, but there was no protest. In fact, so little protest that few people even remember (cited in Tempest 2003).

The present-day protest movement against war perhaps indicates the positive sign of fair globalizations. The people here have compressed spatially, morally and humanely and such a global protest, we can easily perceive, threatens the vulnerable globalization process of the neoliberal capitalists. The Tsunami of new voices of another globalization is about to engulf the existing hegemonic and regimental globalization. In the second annual World Social Forum at Rid-Grande do sul, held in January 2002, near about 1.3 million people had voiced the slogan "Another World is Possible" and the protestors proclaimed battle against the "profound dehumanization and systematic banalization of civilization." The protest movement is very much against the selling of humanity as commodity. Lori Wallach notes, "We are labelled as anti, anti, anti we need to change that perception. It's they who are anti. We are a movement for democracy. For equity. For the environment. For health. They are for a failed status" (cited in Cooper 2002). The globalization protestors view that globalization handed two cunning and inscrutable boon: neo-capitalistic exploitation and war. They have given us poverty, environmental risk, health hazard, unemployment, debt burden, technological hazards and agonizing death. The Mumbai Resistance 2004 is a significant mark of a strong anti-capitalist and antiwar movement. Here antiwar protest got an added significance. It indicates that the double edges of a single razor are imperialist wars and neoliberal capitalism. The

MR 2004 considers itself as a continuation of the militant traditions set in the anti-globalization and antiwar movements that assumed a new intensity after Seattle. The Mumbai Resistance seeks to take the anti-imperialist movement in India one step forward as part of the international mobilization against the growing concentration of neoliberal capitalist forces across the world and the ravages of the "imperialist globalization," which is very alarming from the socio-economic development of the deprived majorities. The movement calls for "Another Possible World."

The aims of the resistance movements across the world are: To locate and identify an alternative, self-reliant socioeconomic structure free from hegemonic domination and institutionalized capitalistic subjugation; to oppose the rapacious plunder of the underdeveloped countries of the world—their local resources, natural potentials, agriculture and the talents of the people; and to oppose privatization and disinvestments policies. The movements have values that protestors aspire to—justice, equality, solidarity, democracy and participation. But the protestors don't know what they want in place of existing globalization. To continue, the movements aim to free the world from debt trap and call for its unilateral liquidation; to oppose attack on the working masses and the innocent particularly in Afghanistan and Iraq under the banner of globalization; to protect eco-balance and environmental hazards caused by the commodification of natural resources and "corporate greed"; to protect democratic values and culture traditions from the demonic grip of silver-lining consumer culture, fundamentalism, religious bigotry, terrorism, separatism, and religious fascism caused by the intensified market fetishism of globalization; to stand against oppression and negative exposure of women, to dislocate them from the arena of vulgar and obscene hybrid culture, and to open more liberal avenues of human senses and socioeconomic facilities for making them more empowered.

Mumbai Resistance especially opposes the intervention of the US and stands for the "unilateral withdrawal" of all US bases from various countries in the world. The anti-globalization movement mainly emerges against regimentalism of the capitalists and the capitalism expansion throughout the world in the guise of rhetoric humanism. Precisely, the movement spreads to stop deviant globalization. The anti-globalization movements across the world have a very "unique" political bearing. The protestors do not consistently make any political or ideological homogeneity. It is a heterogeneous body of communists and non-communists, social activists and intellectuals, NGO workers and environment scientists, religious leaders and the nationalists. The protestors only pinpoint that a change is needed in the very "structural principle" (Saroj Giri 2004). But who will be the leaders of such anti-globalization movements? Will the movements follow the left line or radical line or right wing is of deep concern. We could only perceive that it indicates a trend of structural-political-pluralism, which is a new phenomenon in the history of politics and resistance movements.

Those who speak on contemporary radical politics, whether mainstream or activist, agree that something new was born at the Seattle protests against the World Trade Organization (WTO) in December 1999. This was a global movement variously termed "anti-capitalist," "anti-globalization," "anti-corporate," and "anti-neoliberal." Now the movement is termed as the "Movement for Global Justice" or the "Global Justice and Solidarity Movement". Chomsky writes: "The rich people are going to have a nanny state protecting and subsidizing them. The neoliberal reforms used by the global system are clearly meant to trick people into thinking that the West is using democratic principles to usher in an environment of freedom and equality." It appeals to the predisposition of distrust that drives the thinking in the Third World.

The political economy of the modern world, with its faith on globalization, has contributed to an increasingly complex arrangement of relations between governments, corporations, and indigenous peoples of semi-peripheral and peripheral nations. Zolt's work empirically examines the impact of global capitalism on the sponsorship of anti-global solidarity and resistance, by examining ten cases of transnational resistance between 1994 and 2003. The focus of his paper is to examine the adverse effects of global economic expansion on semi-peripheral and peripheral nations through an assessment of both theoretical assumptions and actual case studies; and the efforts of organized resistance to oppose global economic expansion. A review of ten cases of global confrontation over labor and resources suggests that a primary and intricate relationship exists between global economic expansion and organized resistance.

The theme of change and continuity before and after September 11 is taken up in the chapter by Jarrod Wiener and Jessica Young, who contrast the discourse of globalization—which encourages a passive acceptance of the logic that there is no alternative—to the discourse on the war on terror, in which the dominant state power takes action to determine its fate. Nevertheless, despite such a contrast, the war on terror is still embedded within a globalizing order. Jarrod and Young interrogate whether the discourse of globalization has been overtaken by a new political rhetoric, in particular the War on Terror. They begin by outlining different conceptualizations of globalization, in particular the main objective and inter-subjective understandings that dominate the literature in International Relations and find that the empirical evidence continues to support the increasing internationalization of world politics. The discourse on globalization not only continued after September 11, 2001, but it has increased markedly. Interestingly, far from having been overshadowed, the rhetoric of globalization has gained momentum and they argue that both the discourse on globalization and the War on Terror share key components of state authority and responsibility, and that the US government has been extremely adept at shaping both discourses to its political agenda.

The chapters by Nederveen Pieterse, Kiely and Steger also focus on change and continuity. Pieterse locates the origins of neoliberalism in the theories of the Chicago School. He argues that the policies of the Reagan and Thatcher governments overlooked the economic policies that shaped "real neoliberalism" already in place before the Reagan era. According to the popular neoliberalists, the benefits of globalization are threefold: (1) Both the nations comprising the world-economy's industrial core and those in the developing periphery benefit massively when the capital-rich core (where interest rates are low) gives loans to the capital-poor periphery (where interest rates are high); (2) Consumers benefit when lower transport costs and reduced tariffs make goods produced far away more affordable. Producers of goods that are exported gain as well because they sell a wider market. Producers of goods for home consumption do not gain, but there is nothing like competition from abroad to keep them on their toes, alert them to ways in which they can improve efficiency and better satisfy their customers; (3) The more internationalized the world-economy, the more use producers in each country can make of commodities and production processes invented elsewhere. Faster diffusion of knowledge raises the level of productivity and technology worldwide. Thus, globalization leads to a richer world, and to a more vibrant and tolerant world as well. Governments should not fight globalization, neoliberals contend. Instead they should embrace it.

Some others seek to point out the ways in which the idea of globalization has been over-hyped. "Globalization theories are always in danger of falling victim to grandiosity. Yet there remains a sense in which debunkers of globalization run the risk of missing the forest for the trees. They focus on the minutiae of the present, at the expense of the trends that would allow them to forecast the future" (Source: Bradford www.j-bradford-delong.net). The low-taxes, low-services regime envisioned by the advocates of the free market economy already existed in the American South. Real neoliberalism in the United States in the 1970s and 1980s meant the implementation of the low-wage, low-tax model of Southern economics or Dixie capitalism. Steger's chapter considers how this has come about and focuses on the economic and political shift within the United States to the South (and the Southern conservatives and "red states"), the connection between the Cold War and neoliberalism, and the role of the Washington Consensus.

Steger searches the historical root of *globalization–anti-globalization* dilemma and cites the nomology of enthusiastic "neoliberal free market" on the one hand and high-risk zone of social and economic inequality and disparity on the other. Here we may get the trace of wealthy Northern Hemisphere (winners) and impoverished and exploited global South. Regardless of whether one agreed or disagreed with the world view of globalists, one thing seemed certain: President Bush would have to focus on many of the same issues related to world trade, economic development, and political multilateralism that preoccupied his predecessor in the White House throughout the 1990s. It sounds like a cliché to say that on the day of the terrorist attacks of September 11, 2001 "the world changed forever"—but even clichés can sometimes capture momentous histori-cal shifts. Steger in his chapter views that the anticipated joys of an interdepen-dent world turned into the dark fears of an interdependent world and ultimately the *ideological* struggle over the meaning and the direction of globalization begins. The American President and his Cabinet members reminded their audiences around the world that the War on Terror would be a lengthy conflict of global proportions. By 2005, this struggle had expanded from the initial limited war against the Taliban regime in Afghanistan to the massive war in Iraq waged by an American-led "coalition of the willing" against Saddam Hussein's regime. This new historical context may be the indicator of the future of globalization. While analyzing his chapter Steger puts the question: Will the global War on Terror lead to more intensive forms of international cooperation and exchange or will it fortify existing borders and divisions? Will the rise of the American empire be the harbinger of a benign global order or will it breed furious resistance that might stop the powerful momentum of globalization? He discusses how the new political realities created by 9/11 and its aftermath has impacted what he identified as the three most likely future trajectories of globalization. In the years following the terrorist attacks on American soil; the dominant 1990s neoliberal version of globalization has been giving way to a more militaristic, neoconservative model supported by the current American government. Given the re-election of George W. Bush, Steger expects that in the near future a further strengthening of this tendency towards an "imperial globalism" anchored in the unilateralist and militarist policies of the Bush administration. They all derive from alternative radical traditions from that of Wallerstein and Frank, but share similar concerns. All would hesitate to use the fascist analogy utilized by Frank, and would no doubt not share Frank's flirtation with conspiracy theories that purport to explain September 11. In terms of theoretical traditions, these three chapters draw on open Marxist traditions based on analyzing relations of production as a *starting point* for analysis (though the authors would probably disagree over the extent of the limitations of this open Marxist method). These three chapters are united by an assessment of neoliberal globalization, both before and after September 11 and the rise of neoconservatism. All see areas of continuity as well as change, with the neocon-servative turn, and all point to the strengths and weaknesses of US hegemony and contradictions of neoliberalism. Thus, despite their different theoretical starting points, these chapters share with Frank and Wallerstein the argument that actually existing globalization is exploitative, environmentally destructive, hierarchical, uneven, and unequal.

Mehdi, Dasgupta, and Sing Chew take up these themes in various ways in their chapters. Mehdi and Dasgupta argue that much globalization talk neglects the questions of the South and development, and in particular continued North–South inequalities. The standard "pro-(neoliberal)-globalization" response is that countries are poor because they are insufficiently globalized, a view that unites George W. Bush, Tony Blair, the World Bank and IMF, and not a few leaders in the "Third World." The problem with this mainstream argument is that it ignores the fact that for twenty years, all developing countries have made themselves open to investment and competition through free trade, but few have achieved any developmental benefits. Indeed, those who have experienced rapid growth, particularly China and India, still have comparatively interventionist states, even if they have in some respects liberalized. It is stated in the report of National Intelligence Councils (2020 Project) that the reach of globalization was substantially broadened during the last twenty years by Chinese and Indian economic liberalization, the collapse of the Soviet Union, and the worldwide information technology revolution. Through the next fifteen years, it will sustain world economic growth, raise world living standards, and substantially deepen global interdependence. At the same time, it will profoundly shake up the status quo almost everywhere—generating enormous economic, cultural and consequently political convulsions. The report states, "*India and China probably will be among the economic heavyweights or 'haves.'*"

Moreover, it is evident from the report that the character of globalization probably will change just as capitalism changed over the course of the nineteenth and twentieth centuries.

While today's most advanced nations—especially the United States—will remain important forces driving capital, technology and goods, globalization is likely to take on much more of a "non-Western face" over the next 15 years. Most of the increase in world population and consumer demand through 2020 will take place in today's developing nations—especially China, India, and Indonesia—and multinational companies from today's advanced nations will adapt their "profiles" and business practices to the demands of these cultures. (National Intelligence Council's Report, 2020 Project)

Just as earlier development occurred—in East Asia, and indeed Japan, Europe and the United States—with states pursuing policies that challenged neoliberalism, so too have contemporary developers. Moreover, the development that has occurred, even in those countries experiencing growth, has a lot of downsides. What globalization stands for seems so clear that it can compete with crystal. That's the impression the concept radiates with the first encounter. It has the halo of a tree with an all-encompassing girth whose branches spread everywhere. Problem begins with the question about the implications of its economic, political and cultural presence to the world. At that point it turns into the proverbial elephant, which, to those who hold its tusk, it is a spear, to those who hold the swinging tail, a rope while the true picture, what it really is, remains ever so elusive. Indeed, globalization shares a lot with the proverbial elephant.

If one takes the popular meaning of the concept as propagated by its supporters and one relates this to the conditionalities of the International Monetary Fund to the developing countries, one comes off with globalization as another word for globalizing the IMF conditionalities, this time, without the strings of loans to the economies in trouble. Let us liberalize. Let us remove trade barriers. Let us allow the goods to pour in from everywhere. If these don't solve the problem, one should throw the doors of the market completely open; again liberalize. What this means is uncontrolled influx of goods from the producers to the consumers without economic control mechanisms or strict and effective political management. It is easy to predict the loser of this game: the developing countries that have little to offer the world market. That's not what globalization is all about, contend its advocates. That's what it is, say the critics. There seems to be a problem of meaning and implication, somewhere. So, what is globalization really? This answered, are its benefits global as it promises or are they reserved for the few? Indeed, whose benefit, globalization?

And it is the claim that globalization does not take that road to the world. Someone, at present, discloses the contents of the globalization package because it encourages nations to rapidly dismantle barriers to international trade of goods and services and the mobility of capital. Unlike development, on which everybody knows what is being talked about and could make prediction on the future, the mention of the word "globalization" rakes up, on the side of the developing countries, the devastating effects of structural adjustment program on their economies in which their currencies are freewheeled to duds and crashed in the valley of devaluation. Mehdi puts his question: Is globalization then another word for structural adjustment program at a global scale? The central problem with globalization is the identity crisis that stems from its meaning and the vagueness of its implications. Globalization is in search of an identity that will in turn have an impact on international trade and relations. But if we agree on the common understanding, the losers of the global economic game are the developing economies that hardly know the rules. For as long as there is no room for "glocalization", for that long shall the intellectual debate continue between those who favor it, for the benefits the confusion of its meaning offers, and those who would like to abort it right away to avoid, before it is too late, the birth of the monster of injustice and exploitation, once again, unto the world. However, as soon as one remembers what the anti-globalization movement was calling for and does not stop doing so, the romance with globalization becomes sour. It is always the case that when a word or term has been bandied about for so long with fanfare, it arrogates to itself a mythical halo that neutralizes its existential reality. Globalization belongs to such a class of words or terms whose importance is inflated by the press to the extent that while jubilating, the celebrators, dazzled by its external glamor, forget or are diverted from inspecting its internal constitution. Mehdi through inspection of this constitution shows that globalization is not as innocent as its public relations drummers have sold it to the developing countries in the name of liberalization, free trade, and life in abundance. Nor is it a mega state in the robe of a dandy lady with a duty to seduce the unwary economies into budget deficits and trade imbalance. What globalization really is or would turn out to become, depends on how it is managed. It is now important to re-explore how the managers of globalization puppeteered the developing economies by turning the wheel of globalization against them. What can then be done to make the distribution of resources and their access to the world markets more widespread without encountering the bottleneck of protectionism or pampering nationalist interest so that it can fulfill its mission of prosperity for all. And Mehdi has reexamined such a discourse.

Dasgupta explores the realities of new global order, which is facing a tremendous identity crisis and which is very dangerous for our economic growth, cultural integration, social solidarity, identity of tradition, environmental balance, and mental and physical health. He contextually puts some basic questions: Is globalization a dream of a world without poverty, ethnic cleansing and cross-border terrorism? Is it a dream of a world without economic inequality, religious bigotry, fanaticism and separatism? Is it a dream of a world with no war and no holocaust? These are the challenges to the dreams of global equality and globalization with a human face. The world is divided into the West and the East. The capitalism of the West was disposed to the people in the East: a new type of capitalism (flexible or managerial) in the guise of globalization. The space is shrinking but not the economy. And "the West and the East" dilemma is exerting tremendous pressure on globalizers. The ever-growing disparity makes globalization gloom darker and it will be more difficult to address in the future. In this ambiguous global system, problems for the relatively poorer countries are not empirical domination but sheer rejection and exclusion. The hegemonic domination remains unchanged. And globalization begins as an offshoot of neocapitalism. The hegemony of the West in globalization, one may call it either real or rhetoric, fails to honor the importance of the local, regional, or national, thus, intensifying uneven development. The neoliberal capitalism compels the people in the Third World to be delocalized, detraditionalized, disempowered and disenchanted. The newly introduced "free market" gospel thus resists the ethics (imaginative or motivated!) of globalization, which deface common humanity. The protest movement thus begins. Dasgupta also examines the causes and consequences of postmodern shocks and crises related to physical health, mental stress, and strain due to technological and digital juggernaut, moral and ethical mindset of the common people, and loss of traditional and community identity, and environmental risks.

The consciousness of the world as a single place (Robertson 1992) perceives the globe as a natural phenomenon. The biophysical reality shapes social reality that creates a diverse but balanced ecosystem. The differences between the climates and topographical differentiation appear to deny the possibility of globalization. Environmental disharmony and loss of ecological diversity appears to reject the possibility of global culture, economy, and humanism. Contemporary social scientists who fear threats to the global environment, especially after the tragic Tsunami in South Asian Countries, now seek a global environmental identity for survival and feel the need to study globalization-environmental problems in terms of species threatening phenomena. Ecological modernization, it is undeniable, appears as a threat to a balanced future and biological security. Ulrich Beck (1992), in his excellent work, *Risk Society*, examines the impact of dominant global economic forces and postmodern culture. According to him, these will lead to uncertainty and loss of control. Beck observes that

Forests have also been dying for some centuries now—first through being transformed into fields, then through reckless over-cutting. But the death of forests today occurs globally, as the implicit consequence of industrialization.... It is nevertheless striking that hazards in those [early] days assaulted the nose or the eyes and were thus perceptible to the senses, while the risks of civilization today typically escape perception and are localized in the sphere of physical and chemical formulas.... In the past, the hazards could be traced back to an under supply of hygienic technology. Today they have their basis in industrial overproduction. The risks and hazards of today thus differ in an essential way from the superficially similar ones in the Middle Ages through the global nature of their threat. They are risks of modernization.

In the Dark Ages the people lived with environmental hazards, threat and uncertainty. Even today the influence of globalization has also threatened their biological security. Sing Chew observes that the past can help us understand the future. Ecological modernization is a concept developed by the global initiators but recent occurrence of Tsunami in South Asian countries does not support the view. Beck observes that the quest for ecological modernization becomes a global imperative, which results in ecological disaster as well as repair. It means the work of repairing is in the hands of global initiators. But the recent tragic happening of Tsunami, which killed more than 100,000 people in South Asian countries did not escape. Does it signify the failure of the capitalist's ecological modernity project or neoliberal globalization? Is environmental deterioration, a worldwide problem of top importance? Neoliberal globalization today, with its vast possibilities of action on a world scale, has the means to devastate the environment anywhere in the world by universalizing technologies or exporting pollution.

The South Commission (1990) in its report states: "The countries of the South are today victims of the delirious environmental effects of policies and patterns of development in the North. These include such global phenomena as the thinning of the Ozone layer, nuclear radiation and the Greenhouse effects, as well as such direct acts as the dumping of hazardous wastes and the location of polluting industries in the South. Attempts by the developing countries to bring the global commons-in particular the oceans and outer-shape-under effective international jurisdiction have been defeated in practice by the lack of cooperation of the developed countries" (218). Sing Chew mentioned, "Dark Ages" as a period of not only socioeconomic and political decline but also one of ecological degradation and climate changes, which is proposed to understand the course of world history and system evolution. Because of the repetition of Dark Ages over world history, it is examined in his chapter that we can learn from the past and project some possible ecological futures. Historical trends of deforestation, climate changes and natural disturbances, along with socioeconomic and political ones are presented to project ecological futures. Sing Chew throws light especially on the issue of global ecological future. His work represent the historicity of environmental prophesy but we should be more concerned with the reality. How to combat environmental disaster and how to save millions of people from earthquakes, Tsunamis, volcanic eruptions, floods and twisters, etc., should be the prime agenda of the global environment project. The emission of gases, ozone-depleting chemicals, the dumping of ash, the poisonous organic compounds, the deposits of waste products and warfare chemicals in the ocean not only create biodiversity disequilibrium but also exert heavy pressure on the soil of the earth. All these technological hazards present risks of natural catastrophe and environment disturbances. To maintain ecological balance arrests for illegal dumping should be prohibited. The causes of such environmental threat are global and are the gifts of modernization that results in the threat to animals and plant life. For example, after the recent Tsunami, 19 sperm whales, sharks, dolphins, rare species of sea turtles and 20,000 eggs were washed away. It wreaked havoc on the coral reefs.

The endangered species of Dugong, the grass-eating underwater mammals, also known as the legendary mermaids due to their half-woman, half-fish looks, have lost the grasslands that were their habitat in the Andaman Islands. Mangroves—tropical inter-tidal forests that support a huge variety of marine organism and are considered vital nursery areas for many species of fish and crustaceans have also been severely inundated by the Tsunami. (Chakrawertti 2005)

The sense of consciousness is necessary to protect local disaster from such an environmental threat and malignant downsides. It is, we should remember, very much concerned with humanity, altruism, and local economic restructuring. But ecological disequilibrium as a universal phenomenon appears to deny the possibility of global culture and humanism.

CULTURAL IMPERIALISM AND FUTURE CULTURE

Globalization entails cultural imperialism. Lechner and Boli (2000) argue that globalization displaces local and folk culture traditions and languages. The "great and little traditions" have already lost their identity. The West set global cultural values on local ethos and tradition of the rest. Global media has already touched the inner courtyard of the Third World countries to make local people global. For instance, the popular culture of "McWorld" is of American origin. Globalization of culture and art has recently taken a new shape. Someone calls it consumer globalization that bears the testimony of "selling globalization." The anti-globalizers call consumer globalization as the bi-product of Americanization. The late modernized consumer culture experiences hyper commodification (Crook et al. 1992) in which consumption is differentiated on the basis of the signifiers known as "brand names." "It is hyper stimulated having a life of its own that is beyond the control of any particular group"(Waters 1995). The cultural hegemony that the functionalists call cultural homogenization, affects even the dietary consumerism pattern of the "the East and the Rest." The art form of McDonaldization, it is undeniable, has spread its US-based anti-art form (commercial and capitalistic) to most countries of the world. And the import of such an art entrepreneurship offers a threat to the loss of identity of local, traditional, and mundane culture. Sklair (1991) and others argue that capitalism turns people into consumers. Some call McCulture non-sacramental. Paraphrasing Freud, Berger notes, "Sometimes a hamburger is just a hamburger. But in other cases, the consumption of a hamburger, especially when it takes place under a golden icon of a McDonald's restaurant, is a visible sign of the real or imagined participation in global modernity"(7) Sklair (1991) considers that cultural globalization exports "culture–ideology–consumerism." Secondly, we want to say that cultural or art imperialism dissolve the core and extend its intensified network to the nook and corner of the periphery through transnational linkage. Jeremy Sklarsky (2002) views: "Globalization is not an enemy. It is an international, socioeconomic-political system. Due to advances in information technology, the rise of a postindustrial economy and the collapse of the bipolar Cold War world, a system has arisen in which the interests of individuals and governments around the world are intertwined. The overlap of people's interests has led to increased global cooperation. It can even be argued that the motivation for acts of international terrorism like September 11 is actually a categorical rejection of the globalization system. The young men who crashed airplanes into the World Trade Center were born and raised in some of the countries that are the least globalized." Globalization is not trying to unite the planet in blanket sameness. Actually, some argue McDonald's is a notorious symbol of globalization. A further feature of the globalization debate relates to culture and "community," and the extent to which these may be breaking down in the face of globalizing tendencies.

The above aspects are explored in Ritzer's discussion of the relationship between art and globalization, and how it relates to his Weber-inspired concepts of McDonaldization and "grobalization." In an interview, Jeremy asked Ritzer:

"You have described the McDonaldized society as a system of 'iron cages' in which all institutions come to be dominated by the same principle. So what sort of world would you like us to be living in?" Ritzer: "Well, obviously (laughter)...a far less caged one. I mean the fundamental problem with McDonaldized systems is that it's other people in the system structuring our lives for us, rather than us structuring our lives for ourselves. I mean, that's really what McDonald's is all about. You don't want a creative person clerk at the counter—that's why they are scripted. You don't want a creative hamburger cook—you want somebody who simply follows routines or follows scripts. So you take all creativity out of all activities and turn them into a series of routinized kinds of procedures that are imposed by some external force. So that's the reason why it is dehumanizing.

Humanity is essentially creative and if someone develops these systems that are constraining and controlling people he can't be creative, can't be human. The idea is to turn humans into human robots. This is the sign of postmodern trauma. The next logical step is to replace human robots with mechanical robots. And I think we will see McDonaldized systems where it is economically feasible and technologically possible to replace human robots with non-human robots." In the modern era, the global consumer culture influences the lifestyles and enforces local people to adopt Western patterns of behavior. But side by side, traditional consumer behavior also prevails. This dilemma creates a global–local administrative clash. Ritzer introduces a new concept like "culturepreneur," in the art world. In the postmodern era with imbibed capitalistic globalization, art turns into a homogeneous, saleable commodity, which is the focus of Ritzer's discussion of nothing in the art world. Theoretically, the artist cares little about the efficiency of the production process, but mainly about *producing a high-quality, and qualitatively unique, end-result, no matter what it takes to achieve such goals.* Secondly, at McDonald's, the emphasis is on the size of products rather than on the quality of those products. Art, of course, is defined by qualitative characteristics. On the one hand, Ritzer continues, "great art is distinguished from the mundane by its high-quality." But commodification of any art form does not depend on quality. And McDonaldization deviates from the philosophy of high-quality art. Predictability is just about a death sentence for a work of art. This often involves a deskilling whereby skills are extracted from humans and built into technologies that then exercise control over them. It can be assumed from Ritzer's view that McDonaldization is either the symbol of postmodern culture where absence, rhizome, decentralization, antiform, artistic anarchy, happening and chance are the favorable compositions, or it is the capitalistic anti-art form which can accumulate more and more capital. So Ritzer feels that the major force in the McDonaldization of art is commercialization, especially the desire of artists to be global commercial successes. The makers of the McDonald food are the cheap labors not artists. They are very much associated with the unrestricted growth of multinational corporations.

His excellent work on globalization and culture can be interpreted in a way that leads to a romantic attachment to closed, fixed "communities". It celebrates the local against the global, and it discriminates against outsiders and ignore inequalities within such "communities." Douglas Kellner criticizes that Ritzer could better contextualize the phenomenon within the framework of a restructuring of capitalism, aiming at the increase of productivity and profit through rationalization of production and consumption. For, in addition to being part of a rationalization process, McDonaldization is part of a new global form of techno-capitalism in which world markets are being rationalized and reorganized to maximize capital accumulation.

GLOBAL CIVIL SOCIETY AND ANTI-GLOBALIZATION POLITICS

Moreover, community does not have to be territorially fixed. Some "cosmopolitan" writers, who do not necessarily sympathize with actually existing globalization, have argued that increased connectedness provides some basis for a global community or global civil society. These themes are addressed in the chapter by Driskell, who usefully examines the ways in which "communities" are constructed.

Everywhere in the world, political and administrative devolution of power to local authorities is leading to a revival of local roots. At the same time, the world-economy and the world polity are increasingly interconnected and interdependent. This leads to a growing duality and sometimes clash, between the desire to reaffirm local identities and develop local economies, and the globalization of trade, investment, knowledge and workforces.

The theories of globalization assess the changes in the economy and political system, and sometimes cultural and technological advances. One of the most important impacts of globalization has been on the community. The influences on community and local development are often derived from the global level. Important economic and political powers can come from the local community, creating a change. The community changes can be seen in the "mass society" phenomenon, the "great change" towards extra-community systems, and post-globalization societies. Critiques of modern global societies often include the "loss of community." The idea that community is lost with the process of globalization has been part of sociology since the early writings of Tönnies, Simmel and Wirth. Driskell's empirical searching assesses the loss of the territorial community and the psychological community and explores avenues for finding community in the neighborhood, voluntary associations, and cyberspace. Community continues to evolve with globalization as the traditional memberships in voluntary associations shift and the Internet expands; yet the territorial community continues to provide the basis for much psychological community in our global society.

The argument that "global civil society" is in formation ignores the inequalities and conflicts, and the very different politics espoused by social and political movements within this "global space." These, of course, have been exacerbated by neoliberal capitalism, and at its worst, the idea of global civil society is guilty of wishful thinking. Having said that, progressive alternatives to neoliberal capitalism do have to address the issue of international solidarity, but without ignoring local and national questions, and it is these issues which are crucial to the discussion in the second half of the book. Critics of the neo-classical approach reform international regimes to take them comfortably to the under-developed countries by protecting local producers and the autonomy of local governments so that international exchange is truly based on mutual consent and fairness. The issue is: How is this to be done? Is reform of existing structures and institutions possible? Or, is more fundamental change based on transforming class relations essential?

These questions bring us to a criticism, which comes from NGOs, and civil society groups that offer a more basic critique of corporate globalization and capitalism. William K. Tabb (2003) states,

To the social justice movements, class power and imperialism are at the core of the problem. These movements oppose the domination of social needs by market criteria, and the power of transnational capital and the most powerful governments (above all, the United States) to establish rules for their own benefit at the expense of the weaker, subordinate nations and classes. From this critical perspective, it is obvious that the reforms being suggested are reinforcing the system of class rule and imperial domination, which must be replaced. The growing strength of what is called the anti-globalization movement, or better, the alternative globalization movement, is testament to this critique, which is becoming a material force in the international political economy.

Elvira Del Pozo Aviñó examines "anti-globalization" politics as an instance of the rise of global civil society. The globalization discourse declares the end of the chapter of nation-state and brings up the concept of civil society or good governance. It is imagined that civil society has developed from a rather vague conglomerate of individual households and good governance is linked to the "local or community synergy between political, cultural and economic actors." But calling of civil society with so-called "good governance," ignoring the importance of the nation-state and local community is just a speculative spell. Contemporary alternative globalization initiators invite "renationalization" instead of global civil society. Edwards and Hulme (1995) comment that in the New Policy Agenda, which combines market economies and liberal democratic politics, NGOs are simultaneously viewed as market-based actors and placed in a central position as components of "civil society." At present, NGOs are an influential social force and play a big role in stimulating public awareness. They frequently act as "Watchdogs" (Steven Yearley 1996). The NGO activists pretend that they act as the vanguard of "civil society" operating in the interstices of the global economy. Petras and Veltmeyer (2001) notes, "The phrase-mongering about "civil society" is an exercise in vacuity. Civil Society is not a unitary virtuous entity—it is made of classes probably more profoundly than ever in the century. Most of the greatest injustices against workers are committed by the wealthy bankers in civil society" (p. 130). Petras and Veltmeyer also argue that the NGO plays a double role of criticizing social and economic anarchy and human rights violations and, secondly, to act as radicalist and to launch popular movements "Collaborative relations with dominant neoliberal elites". They call them petit bourgeoisie that forms radical wing of the neoliberal establishment. Aviñó puts the question: Are social movements influencing the course of globalization and its pervasiveness for humanity?

Since the 1980s, and especially since 2001, literature in both academic and non-academic circles indicates that they certainly do. In 2001, the world witnessed the commencement of the World Social Forums. As a result, we are learning that theorists and activists are meeting to plan the role social movements play in the definition of our future. The Forums mostly offer a magnificent opportunity for activists to attract the attention of the media internationally. However, social movements lag behind the structural contexts in which they operate. Even though they exert a huge impact on the world community, the relationships they have with nation-states are restricted to a limited role within the United Nations system. Thus, their role in the international community needs to be redefined by larger international and governmental institutions. Del Pozo's observation of anti-globalization protest as an instance of the rise of global civil society echoes the argument of De Zolt's assessment of the politics of "anti-globalization" protests at various international summits. Sklair mirrors this focus in his assessment of transnational resistance to transnational capitalism. Unlike Del Pozo Aviñó, Sklair also examines the local and national spaces of resistance, an argument developed further by Mac Sheoin and Yeates.

Mac Sheoin and Yeates most explicitly problematize the argument that movements for global justice have developed new, transactional networks that transcend the nation-state. The burgeoning literature on transnational social movements and activism seeks to explain what are considered to be "new" politics occurring "above" and "beyond" the national sphere, and draws on the anti-globalization movement to illustrate the "new" global politics. Their chapter critically examines the assumptions and conclusions of this literature. It may be contended that the anti-globalization movement has much in common with previous social movements, whether "old" or "new." They argue that an overemphasis on the transactional elements of the anti-globalization movement ignores the importance of its local and national bases. They emphasize the continuation of "old" forms of politics in the resistant movement. They compare two contrasting organizations within the movement—the Social Forum and Indymedia—as a means of exploring issues of coalition and conflict between "old" and "new" forms of politics within the anti-globalization movement.

GLOBALIZATION AND LABOR INSURGENCY

Globalization is seen as offering capital a way of escape from negotiation from organized labor. (McBride 2000). Capital mobility and technological know-how for production maintains the balance of power between capital and labor. Globalization has changed the modus operandi, deregulated the labor conditions and opened its access to the market. McBride (2000) argues, "The globalization era is one in which national Fordism and Keynesianism has been displaced by global post-Fordism and neoliberalism" (25). So one should clearly understand that the neoliberal discourse has some say about the labor market. It is said that, like any other market, a balanced price is generally being created for wages.

This price is the highest the buyers are able to pay and sellers are able to collect, with everyone satisfied with the result. Workers go to the market to offer a service, labour, in exchange for wages, which according to this concept, is the price of labour. Workers would be force to opt between laziness and work. Wages would be the price for which workers would be willing to give up work apathy and, allegedly, a break-even point, or wage level, would be reached where everyone would be satisfied. (Martinez 1997)

But a question rises in the mind: Will there be any unemployment in this "idyllic theoretical construct?" The neoliberal answer to this question is:

At a sufficiently low wage level, everyone should be able to find employment, although it could happen that, if wages are too low, some would opt for idleness. This option would be a sovereign decision adopted by the workers who go to the labour market as free and equal economic agents. (Martinez 1997)

A comparison between rhetoric discourse and the reality of the workers reveals that the situation of the world-economy today is really pathetic. It should be pointed out that the world-economy has grown more sluggishly with the expansion of the neoliberal globalization. Consequently, economic growth, promised by the neoliberal ideology, is shrinking. While between 1950 and 1973, the world product grew at almost 5 percent, between 1974 and 1980 it dropped down to 3.5 percent; between 1981 and 1989, the growth rate was only 3.3 percent and in more recent years, between 1990 and 1996, the rate was extremely low—only 1.4 percent.

The process of deregulation has increased with the ever slower economic growth, that is, market forces remain unrestricted and uncontrolled. And this deregulation operates in the monetary, financial trade and, by the way, the labor spheres. Martinez discusses that as to the role of trade unions in this neoliberal scheme, it is to be deduced that in this perfect balance in the labor market, no forces outside the market should intervene in the free individual decision of the worker to opt for work or idleness. Trade unions would then become a distorting, anti-natural factor in their efforts to establish wages that do not respond to free-market actions. Neither should there be minimum wages fixed by legislative action, since this would also impinge on the infallible dictates of the market. He puts forth a prime question: How is this perfect abstract and theoretical neoliberal balance reflected, in real terms, in present-day neoliberal globalization? Does it signify the rhetoric version only? The reality depicts the other face of such a theoretical puzzle. "Of the 5.6 billion people that inhabit the planet, some 2.8 billion make up the economically active population, that is, people of working age. Of them, 1.14 billion (41 percent of the economically active population) are unemployed or underemployed throughout the world" (Martinez 1997).

It is evident from his observation that the anti-human and defaced neoliberal globalization keeps 40 percent of the world's economically active population subjected to unemployment and underemployment. It is the view of the globalization protestors and intellectuals that globalization launched a direct assault on labor in terms of wages, conditions and benefits, as well as its capacity to organize and negotiate (Petras and Veltmeyer 2001: 17). In the report of UNCTAD (1995/1996) it is estimated that near about 120 million workers are now officially unemployed. Petras and Veltmeyer, of course, have explored a new dimension of labor force that they refer to as "mobile labour force." And near about "80 million expatriate labourers have formed to constitute new world labour markets" (17). It is undeniable that in a period of neoliberal globalization labor is disempowered on several dimensions and agenda. New Social Movements' theorists, despite their substantial differences, argue that the traditional response of the labor movement to global capitalism, based on class politics, has generally failed, and that a new analysis based on identity politics (of gender, sexuality, ethnicity, age, community, belief systems) is necessary to mount effective resistance to sexism, racism, environmental damage, warmongering, capitalist exploitation, and other forms of injustice (Sklair 1999).

Kaxton Sui, of course, deviates from rhetoric discourse and focuses on national resistance through an examination of labor in the context of restructuring in Hong Kong. He claims that the rise of globalization by the late 1980s has changed industrial relations and class politics by imposing flexible employment in local economies worldwide. He compares four features between traditional and flexible employments: employment patterns, gender distributions in labor market, work arrangements and employment relationships. The World Commission (2004) in its report examined the current process of globalization that generates an unbalanced outcome both between winners and losers. Wealth is being created but the people in the Third World are not getting its benefit. Work and employment are the prime rationales of fair globalization mission but the reality contradicts with the rhetoric. It is evident from the report of ILO that global unemployment has reached over 185 million people, along with the speedy growth of "informal economy." The Commission's report also emphasizes that the benefit of globalization can only reach all people if the huge informal economy is brought into the economic mainstream "by establishing and respecting property rights and the rights of workers, and by increasing productivity and access to market." If the vision of globalization is anchored at the local level then the labor market should be locally, regionally, and nationally oriented. As yet globalization fails to promote employment and labor interest in global production system. Not only that, the distinguishing features of flexible employment are suppressive to workers and labor movements, so the labor insurgency emerges at the local and national levels as a result of global–local labor market transition. Kaxton examines the new pattern of labor insurgency under flexible employment conditions, through empirically investigating the Student–Worker Mutual Aid Campaign launched in Hong Kong. But Kaxton's empirical evidences suggest how local organizations learn, equip and transform their mobilizing strategies in organization and resources terms in responding to the suppressive globalization forces. Finally, he returns to rethink the nature of flexible employment by exposing its inherent rigidity, uncertainty, and dilemma.

SOUTH EAST ASIAN DILEMMA

The East Asian crisis is not an isolated phenomenon; it is a symptom of general weakness in global capital markets. This is the comment of UN development experts. Jagdish Bhagwati (2004) on the other hand notes, "The Asian crisis cannot be separated from excessive borrowings of foreign short-term capital.... It has become apparent that crises attendant on capital mobility cannot be ignored." The South Asian countries experienced the entrance of short-term investment money. Most of the countries including Indonesia, Thailand, Philippines and Malaysia accepted the open-door policy to foreign investments (Ellwood 2001). Sisir Jayasuriya (2002) observes that despite a history of political activism and deep-rooted egalitarian ethos in socio-political discourse, pre-reform South Asia had relatively little success, at least compared to East Asia, in growth, poverty eradication or reduction of inequality. South Asia remains one of the poorest regions in the world, with 40 percent of its 1.3 billion people living below the poverty line, and its share of global gross products is less than 2 percent. It is revealed from his findings that "globalization has caused a decline in the income of 515 million poor people of South Asian countries with the subsequent weakening of social safety nets for them, according to the Human Development Report in South Asia—2001. The report paints a gloomy performance of the region in terms of poverty reduction, integration of regional economy to the world-economy, intra-regional trade and the slow reform process, especially during the recent years of globalization." It is undeniable that most of the South Asian countries could not bridge a link between economic and social development policies during the era of neo-globalization. Not only that. The countries were facing more challenges against democracy, in the form of ethnic conflict, religious fundamentalism, regional secessionism, environmental hazard and terrorism. Very recently, the global–local dilemma in South Asian countries has created globalization morbidity. The emerging new social movements pinpoint the issue of re-emerging nation-states or renationalization process. Barry Gills challenges the strong assumption in the intellectual and political discourse that we are witnessing an historical global advance of both capitalism and liberal democracy. According to Gills, this assumption is a misconception because the majority of the people in the "modern democracies are continuously facing repression and disempowerment for the sake of maintaining the dominance of the wealthy classes." The author believes that the point is already reached for the emergence of new social movements as a new political counter.

Wignaraja examines the relationship between local and regional resistance through an examination of debates over the contested meanings of participatory development in South Asia. His argument goes beyond the critique and inadequacy of mainstream development thinking and action, as a response to the challenge of globalization, poverty, and youth employment in South Asia. It draws the lessons from innovative new social movements on the ground and macro–micro policies and actions, for identifying undogmatic critical elements, which form the basis of a value-led, culturally-rooted pattern of sustainable development and participatory democracy. The underlying fundamentals are then knit together into a school of thought, which can inform good governance issues in South Asia. The evolution of this school of thought involved interdisciplinary analysis, collective creativity, and social praxis. It was not based on a priori theorizing or on conventional Cartesian social science methodologies. A number of empirical studies are analyzed by Wignaraja to demonstrate the process of this pioneering intellectual quest over a period of three decades, and shows how the new social movements provided the material basis for the theoretical insights and transitional pathway through relevant practice. These insights and practice provide the guidelines not only for national policy but also for revisioning South Asian regional cooperation and political stability in the current era of globalization.

The book is intended to put such global crisis and global anarchy in perspectives by drawing on theoretical and empirical tools of sociological, economic, cultural, and political analyses. It takes stock of the discourse about pending crises, dilemmas and the prognosis for the future. The selections compiled in this volume aim to describe and explain the course of present-day globalization and consideration of a new world society and to imagine its future forms.

The authors of this volume have challenged the influential perspective on globalization and most of them see globalization as a "juggernaut of untrammelled capitalism." They fear and see economic interdependence as making Third World countries more vulnerable to the destructive impact of capitalistic implosion. Globalization, as most of them suggest, not only helps to increase economic inequality and social disparity but also narrows the space for moral and ethical judgements and undermines people's humaneness. It also undermines cultural and moral integrity, destroys traditional and community value system, threatens health, environment and nature, creates overstrain, encourages rat race and striving for a particular lifestyle, invites virtual realities and hyper real off world images, privatizes all economic sectors, and is, therefore, repressive, exploitative, and harmful to the vast majorities of "the rest."

Immanuel Wallerstein rejects the idea that the "globalization discourse" represented a new development in human history. The chapters by Nederveen Pieterse, Kiely and Steger also focus on change and continuity. They all derive from alternative radical traditions from that of Wallerstein and Frank but share similar concerns. All would hesitate to use the fascist analogy utilized by Frank, and would no doubt not share Frank's flirtation with conspiracy theories that purport to explain September 11 (though this is not to deny that the US administration was focused on other issues and has covered up links between the US and Saudi Arabia). In terms of theoretical traditions, these three chapters all draw on open Marxist traditions based on analyzing relations of production as a starting point for analysis (though the authors would probably disagree over the extent of the limitations of this open Marxist method). These three chapters are united by an assessment of neoliberal globalization, both before and after September 11, and the rise of neoconservatism. All see areas of continuity as well as change, with the neoconservative turn, and all point to the strengths and weaknesses of US hegemony and contradictions of neoliberalism. Thus, despite their different theoretical starting points, these chapters share with Frank and Wallerstein the argument that actually existing globalization is exploitative, environmentally destructive, hierarchical, uneven and unequal. These themes are taken up in various ways in the chapters by Mehdi, Dasgupta and Sing Chew. The first two argue that much globalization talk neglects the questions of the South and development, and in particular continued North–South inequalities. Moreover, the development that has occurred, even in those countries experiencing growth, has a lot of downsides, as some commentators remind us. A further feature of the globalization debate relates to culture and "community," and the extent to which these may be breaking down in the face of globalizing tendencies. This is explored in Ritzer's discussion of the relationship between art and globalization. His excellent work on globalization and culture can be interpreted in a way that leads to a romantic attachment to closed, fixed "communities" that celebrate the local against the global, discriminate against outsiders and ignore inequalities within such "communities." Moreover, community does not have to be territorially fixed, and some "cosmopolitan" writers, who do not necessarily sympathize with actually existing globalization, have argued that increased connectedness provides some basis for a global community or global civil society. These themes are addressed in the chapter by Driskell, who usefully examines the ways in which "communities" are constructed. The argument that "global civil society" is in formation ignores the inequalities and conflicts, and the very different politics espoused by social and political movements within this "global space." These, of course, have been exacerbated by neoliberal capitalism and, at its worst, the idea of global civil society is guilty of wishful thinking. Having said that, progressive alternatives to neoliberal capitalism do have to address the issue of international solidarity, but without ignoring local and national questions. It is these issues, which are crucial to the discussion in the book. Finally, some sections finish by returning to the question of change and continuity within globalization in the context of the resurgence of US neoconservatism. Weiner and Young provide a detailed and valuable contrast of the supposed passivity of the state in the context of globalization, and the more directive policies promoted by the so-called war on terror.

The volume also largely focuses on the questions of resistance in the age of globalization, and questions of solidarity, political alternatives, and anti-imperialist politics. Elvira examines "anti-globalization" politics as an instance of the rise of global civil society, as does De Zolt in his assessment of the politics of "anti-globalization" protests at various international summits. Sklair mirrors this focus in his assessment of transnational resistance to transnational capitalism. Unlike Elvira, Sklair also examines the local and national spaces of resistance, an argument developed further by Mac Sheoin and Yeates. Kaxton Sui focuses on national resistance through an examination of labor in the context of restructuring in Hong Kong, while Wignaraja examines the relationship between local and regional resistance through an examination of debates over the contested meanings of participatory development in South Asia. Mac Sheoin and Yeates most explicitly problematize the argument that movements for global justice have developed new, transnational networks that transcend the nation-state. They argue that most movements remain nationally focused, even while making substantial movements towards establishing solidarity with other national movements, which may be expressed at various local, national, regional, and world social forums. This implies that questions of the spontaneous resistance of the "transnational multitude," fashionable in some academic and political circles in the North, evade concrete issues of political strategy.

We can summarize the discourse of *globalization-anti-globalization dilemma* after Pieterse (2001) who viewed anti-development and anti-globalization as the dual aspects of the same process. He has developed a paradigm of globalization/ development and future options. Problems with Structural Adjustment Plan which has already defaced humanity with "safety nets and poverty alleviation," remodelling of good governance and civil society, orthodox globalization–fair globalization dilemma, uneven distribution of wealth, taking over the world by multinational corporations, failure of neoliberalism, growing intensity of capitalism, revised hegemony of US, and rejuvenation of imperialism—all invite global politics of resistance. The essays in this book abound with rethinking of concepts; problems and theories help to assess the prediction of future globalization. Some chapters finish by returning to the question of change and continuity within globalization in the context of the resurgence of US neoconservatism while some largely focus on the questions of resistance in the age of globalization and that of solidarity, political alternatives and anti-imperialist politics.

All authors share a scepticism towards the claims made for the benefits of globalization and emphasize the fact that globalization is overwhelmingly led by neoliberal social and political forces. The dominant forms of globalization are therefore uneven, unequal and environmentally destructive. These basic differences have received serious attention, but we feel necessity to further clarify and review the issues of continuities and transformational changes, and to present theoretical and empirical evidences for evaluating the recent issues of globalization and anti-globalization. It is for these reasons that global justice movements oppose and resist globalization, and the book goes on to explore the tensions, dilemmas and debates within a variety of global, national, and local movements. Central to these debates is the attempt to re-politicize the debate over globalization, the agencies that resist neoliberalism, alternatives to globalization, and the forms that more desirable globalizing processes should take. The theoretical knowledge and empirical evidences of the chapters examine the downsides of globalization that have occurred in the winning countries. Their chapters largely focus on the questions of resistance in the age of globalization, questions of environmental equilibrium and protectionism, local and community development, and questions of anti-global solidarity, political alternatives and anti-capitalist politics. Finally, the contributors argue that most movements remain nationally focused even while making substantial movements towards establishing solidarity with other national movements, which may be expressed at various local, national, regional, and world social forums. There is nothing intrinsically progressive or reactionary about global, national or local resistance—rather than focus on such global, national or local "spaces," the focus should be on the political alternatives promoted both within and between such spaces.

Whatever is happening across the world will contain an alternative to the existing free market, cultural world order, neoliberal economic policy with deregulated trade, postmodern virtual realities, environment, and intellectual hegemony as we know it today. But it does not provide a satisfactory home for the humanity. The market is global, communication is global, the technology is global, the philosophical discourse is postmodern and accordingly global, and the culture is global but not humane. Human beings need a place, need food, need a secure job, a language of their own, a story, a tradition, the feeling of belonging to a community, a sense of local patriotism, and a set of face-to-face relationships where *e-interaction* will not get the prime priority. This is why ethnicity, terrorism, communalism, fundamentalism, separatism, and global protest movements are emerging as powerful counter-forces to globalization today.

References

Albert, M. 2001. *The Movements Against Neoliberal Globalization from Seattle to Porto Alegre.* A speech delivered electronically in lieu of Athens Conference, March 9.

Amin, S. 1997. *Capitalism in the Age of Globalization.* London: Zed Books.

Barber, B.R. 1996. *Jihad vs McWorld.* New York: Ballantine.

Beck, U. 1992. *Risk Society: Towards a New Modernity.* London: Sage.

Berger, P.L. 2002. Introduction: The Cultural Dynamics of Globalization, in P.L. Berger and S.P. Huntington (eds), *Many Globalizations—Cultural Diversity in the Contemporary World.* New York: Oxford University Press.

Bhagwati, J. 2004. *In Defence of Globalization.* Oxford: Oxford University Press.

Brecher, J., T. Costello and B. Smith (eds). 2000. *Globalization from Below.* London: South End Press.

Chakrawertti, S. 2005. *The Times of India*, March 9.

Cooper, M. 2002. From Protest to Politics—A Report from Porto Alegre. *The Nation Magazine.* March 11.

Crook, S., J. Pukulski and M. Waters. 1992. *Postmodernization.* London: Sage.

Dasgupta, S. (ed.). 2004. *The Changing Face of Globalization.* New Delhi: Sage.

Edwards, M. and D. Hulme (eds). 1995. *Non-Governmental Organizations: Performance and Accountability: Beyond the Magic Bullet.* London/West Hartford: Earthscan/Kumarian.

Ellwood, W. 2001. *No-Nonsense Guide to Globalization.* London: New International Publishers Limited.

Fox, J. 2001. *Chomsky and Globalization.* London: Icon Books.

Fukuyama, F. 1992. *The End of History and the Last Man.* New York: Free Press.

Giddens, A. 1990. *The Consequences of Modernity.* Cambridge: Polity.

Giri, S. 2004. The Old Left for another World. Lecture delivered at the World Social Forum, January 10, Mumbai.

Gramsci, A. 1971. *Selection from the Prison Notebooks.* Ed. and trans. by Q. Hoare and G. Nowell Smith. New York: International Publishing.

Held, D., A. McGrew, D. Goldblatt and J. Peterson. 1999. *Global Transformations: Politics, Economics and Culture.* Stanford: Stanford University Press.

Hirst, P.Q. and G. Thompson. 2002. The Future of Globalization. *Cooperation and Conflict* 37(3): 247–65.

Hoogevelt, A. 1997. *Globalization and the Post Colonial World: The New Political Economy of Development*. London: Macmillan.

Huntington, S. 1996. *The Clash of Civilizations and the Remaking of World Order*. New York: Simon and Schuster.

International Labour Organization. 2004. *Press Release*, February.

Jayasuriya, S. 2002. Global Development Network (GDN).

Katz, C. 1995. Major/Minor: Theory, Nature, and Politics. *Annals of the Association of American Geographers*, 85(1).

Kellner, D. 1997. Globalization and the Postmodern Turn. Available online at http://www.gseis.ucla.edu/courses/ed253a/dk/GLOBPM.html

Klein, N. 2002. *Fences and Windows*. New Delhi: Left Word Books.

Lechner, F.J. and J. Boli (eds). 2001. *The Globalization Reader*. London: Blackwell.

Martinez, O. 1997. Speech delivered at the International Meeting of Workers Against Neoliberalism and Globalization. Havana Convention Center, Cuba, August 6. Available online at http:/www.lalabor.org

McBride, S. 2000. The Politics of Globalization and Labor Strategies, in S. McBride and John Wiseman (eds). *Globalization and Its Discontents*. London: Macmillan Press.

Mitzman, A. 2003. *Prometheus Revisited: The Quest for Global Justice in the 21st Century*. Mass.: University of Massachusetts Press.

National Intelligence Councils Report (2020 Project). Available online at http://www.cia.gov/nic/NIC

Petras, J. and Veltmeyer. 2001. *Globalization Unmasked*. Delhi: Madhyam Books.

Picco, G. (ed.). 2001. *Crossing the Divide*. New Jersey: School of Diplomacy and International Relations.

Pieterse, J.N. 2001. *Development Theory*. New Delhi: Vistaar Publications.

Raghavan, C. 1998. Text from Speech on accepting the 1997 G-77/UNDP Award for TCDC/ECDC, January 12.

Ritzer, G. 1996. *Modern Sociological Theory* (Fourth Edition). New York: McGraw-Hill.

————. 2001. *Explorations in the Sociology of Consumption*. New York: Sage.

Robertson, R. 1992. *Globalization: Social Theory and Global Culture*. London: Sage.

Sen, A. 2002. How to Judge Globalization. *The American Prospect Online*.

Sen, S. 2004. The Fantasy of 'Fair Globalisation'. *People's Democracy*, July 15.

Sklair, L. 1991. *Sociology of the Global System*. Hemel Hempted: Harvester Whearsheaf.

————. 1999. Competing Conceptions on Globalization. *Journal of World-Systems Research* 5(2): 143–62.

Smith, S. 2002. Europe, The United States and International Security. Jean Monnet Lecture 2000 delivered at the Royal Irish Academy. April.

South Commission. 1990. *Challenge to the South*. The Report of the South Commission. Oxford: Oxford University Press.

Stiglitz, J. 2002. *Globalization and Its Discontents*. Great Britain: The Penguin Press.

Tabb, W.K. 2003. After Neoliberalism? *Monthly Review* 55(2). Available online at http://www.monthlyreview.org

Tempest, M. 2003. Noam Chomsky on the Anti-War Movement (An Interview). Available online at gpf@globalpolicy.org

Wallerstein, I. 2003. Entering Global Anarchy. *New Left Review* 22, July–August.

Waters, M. 1995. *Globalization*. London: Routledge.

Wiseman, J. 2000. Alternatives to Oppressive Globalization, in S. McBride and J. Wiseman (eds), *Globalization and Its Discontents*. London: Macmillan Press.

Yearley, S. 1996. *Sociology, Environmentalism, Globalization*. London: Sage.

1

GLOBALIZATION OR THE AGE OF TRANSITION?

A Long-Term View of the Trajectory of the World-System

IMMANUEL WALLERSTEIN

The 1990s saw a deluge of talk about globalization. We were told by virtually everyone that we are now living, for the first time, in an era of globalization. We were told that globalization has changed everything: the sovereignty of states has declined; everyone's ability to resist the rules of the market has disappeared; our possibility of cultural autonomy has been virtually annulled; and the stability of all our identities has come into serious question. This state of presumed globalization has been celebrated by some, and bemoaned by others.

This discourse is in fact a gigantic misreading of current reality—a deception imposed upon us by powerful groups, and even a worse one that we have imposed upon ourselves, often despairingly. It is a discourse that leads us to ignore the real issues before us, and to misunderstand the historical crisis within which we find ourselves. We do indeed stand at a moment of transformation. But this is not that of an already established newly globalized world with clear rules. Rather we are located in an age of transition—transition not merely of a few backward countries that need to catch up with the spirit of globalization, but a transition in which the entire capitalist world-system will be transformed into something else. The future, far from being inevitable and one to which there is no alternative, is being determined in this transition that has an extremely uncertain outcome.

THEORIZING GLOBALIZATION

The processes that are usually meant when we speak of globalization are not in fact new at all. They have existed for some 500 years. The choice we have to make today is not whether or not to submit to these processes, but rather what to do when these processes crumble, as they are presently crumbling. One would think, reading most accounts, that "globalization" is something that came into existence in the 1990s—perhaps only upon the collapse of the Soviet Union, or perhaps a few years earlier. The 1990s were not, however, a significant time marker to use if one wants to analyze what is going on. Rather, we can most fruitfully look at the present situation in two other time frames, one going from 1945 to today, and the other going from circa 1450 to today.

The period 1945 to today is that of a typical Kondratieff cycle[1] of the capitalist world-economy, which has had as always two parts: an A-phase or upward swing or economic expansion that went from 1945 to 1967/1973, and a B-phase or downward swing or economic contraction that has been going from 1967/1973 to today and probably will continue for several more years. The period 1450 to today, by contrast, marks the life cycle of the capitalist world-economy, which has had its period of genesis, its period of normal development, and has now entered into its period of terminal crisis. In order to comprehend the present situation, we need to distinguish between these two social times, and the empirical evidence for each of them.

In many ways, the Kondratieff cycle in which we find ourselves is the easier of the two social times to understand, since it resembles all previous Kondratieff cycles, which have been much studied. The A-phase of the present Kondratieff was what the French aptly called "les trente glorieuses." It coincided with the high point of United States hegemony in the world-system, and occurred within the framework of a world order that the US established after 1945. The US, as we know, emerged from the Second World War as the only major industrial power whose industries were intact and whose territories had not been badly damaged by wartime destruction. US industries had, of course, been perfecting their efficiencies for over a century. This long-term economic development combined with the literal collapse of the economic structures of the other major loci of world production gave the US a productivity edge that was enormous, at least for a time, and made it easy for US products to dominate the world market. It made possible furthermore the largest expansion of both value and real production in the history of the capitalist world-economy, creating simultaneously great wealth and great social strain in the world social system.

As of 1945, the US had two major problems. It needed a relatively stable world order in which to profit from its economic advantages. And it needed to re-establish some effective demand in the rest of the world, if it expected to have customers for its flourishing productive enterprises. In the period 1945–55, the US was able to solve both these problems without too much difficulty. The problem of world order was resolved in two parts. On the one hand, there was the establishment of a set of interstate institutions—notably, the United Nations, the IMF and the World Bank—all of which the US was able to control politically, and which provided the formal framework of order. And on the other hand, and more importantly, the US came to an arrangement with the only other serious military power in the post-1945 world, the USSR—an arrangement to which we have come to refer by the code-name "Yalta."

Yalta was an agreement, worked out in detail over a period of a decade, that basically had three clauses. First, the world was to be divided *de facto* into a US zone (most of the world) and a Soviet zone (the rest), the dividing line to be where their respective troops were located when the Second World War ended, and both sides would agree to remain militarily within these boundaries. Second, the Soviet zone could, if it wished, pursue collectively a mercantilist policy, that is, reduce to minimum trade transactions with the US zone until it strengthened its own productive machinery, but this involved, however, as a counterpart that the US would not be expected to contribute to the economic reconstruction of this zone. And third, both sides were free, indeed encouraged, to engage in vigorous, reciprocally hostile rhetoric, whose chief function seemed to be to consolidate the political control of the US and the USSR over their respective zones. The Berlin Blockade and the Korean War, both of which ended in truces reaffirming the original lines of partition, were the final capstones of this global agreement.

The problem of creating enough world effective demand for US production was solved by means of the Marshall Plan for western Europe and equivalent economic assistance to Japan, the latter occurring particularly after the outbreak of the Korean War and on the excuse of the war. The US took advantage of the Cold War tensions to reinforce these economic links with military ties—NATO plus the US–Japan Defence Pact—which ensured that these zones would follow faithfully the political lead of the US on all major issues in the international arena.

To be sure, not everyone was happy with these arrangements. There were, after all, those left out of the benefits of Yalta—the Third World as a whole, the least favored groups within the Western world, and the Soviet satellite states of east/central Europe who endured their yoke but did not celebrate it. Those left out erupted with some regularity, and on occasion with particular force: China in 1945–48, Vietnam, Algeria, Hungary in 1956, Cuba and southern Africa. These successive eruptions posed problems for the US-led world order, and indeed for the Soviet Union as well. But they were like punches to the stomach of a strong boxer; the punches could be absorbed, and they were. The big exception was the Vietnam War, which began to bleed the United States, both in terms of finance and lives lost, and therefore, in terms of the US national morale.

But the biggest blow to the US, the hardest to absorb, was the economic recovery and the then flourishing of western Europe and Japan. By the 1960s, the productivity gap between these countries and the US had been more or less eliminated. The west European countries and Japan recovered control over their national markets, and began to compete effectively with US products in the markets of third countries. They even began to be competitive within the US home market. The automaticity[2] of US economic advantage had, thus, largely disappeared by the late 1960s.

The increase in world production resulting from the recovery and expansion of west European/Japanese production led to a glut on the world market and a sharp decline in the profitability of many of the principal industrial sectors, such as steel, automobiles, and electronics. The consequent downturn in the world-economy was marked by two major events: the necessity for the United States to go off the gold standard, and the world revolution of 1968. The first was caused by the fact that the politico-military expenses of enforcing US hegemony plus the lessened competitivity in world markets turned out to be quite expensive and thus drained the US financial surplus. The US had to begin to work hard politically to maintain the economic advantages it had had so easily in the A-phase, and began by pulling in its monetary belt somewhat.

The world revolution of 1968 was triggered by the discontents of all those who had been left out in the well-organized world order of US hegemony. The details of the 1968 uprisings were different in the various arenas of the world-system, but such uprisings did occur everywhere: in addition to the obvious 1968 events in the Western world and Japan, usually noted, I include the cultural revolution in China beginning in 1966 and the turn to "socialism with a human face" in Czechoslovakia in 1968, as well as the diverse happenings in Mexico, Senegal, Tunisia, India, and many other countries of the Third World. In all of them, however different the local situation, there was a recurrent double theme. The first was opposition to US hegemony, *and* to Soviet collusion with that hegemony (the Yalta arrangements between what the Chinese called the "super-powers"). And the second was disillusionment with the Old Left in all its forms (Communist, Social–Democrat, movements of national liberation). The latter disillusionment was the unpredicted consequence of the very success of these movements. All these movements had constructed in the late nineteenth century an identical two-step strategy of struggle—first conquer state power; then transform society. The fact is that, in the period of US hegemony, paradoxically (or perhaps not so paradoxically) the movements of the Old Left had indeed come to power almost everywhere: as Communist parties in the socialist countries (running from the Elbe to the Yalu); as Social–Democratic parties (or their equivalents) in the pan-European world (western Europe, North America and Australasia); and as national liberation movements in the Third World (or equivalently as populist movements in Latin America). They had come to power but they had not been able to achieve the second step they had envisaged, the transformation of society, or so the revolutionaries of 1968 believed. The movements in power were seen as having failed to deliver on their historic promises.

THE WORLD-ECONOMY IN CRISIS

It is just at this point that the world-economy entered into its long period of stagnation. The crucial measure of a stagnation in the world-economy is that profits from production drop considerably from the levels at which they were in the preceding A-phase. This has a series of clear consequences. People with capital shift their primary focus of seeking profit from the productive sphere to the financial sphere. Second, there is significantly increased unemployment worldwide. Third, there occur significant shifts of loci of production from higher-wage areas to lower-wage areas (what used to be called the phenomenon of "runaway factories"). This trio of consequences can be seen to have occurred worldwide since circa 1970. We have had endless escalation of speculative activity, which is, of course, very profitable for a relatively small group of people, at least until the point when the bubble bursts. We have had very large shifts of production from North America, western Europe, and even Japan to other parts of the world-system, which have consequently claimed that they were "industrializing" and, therefore developing. Another way of characterizing what happened is to say that these semiperipheral countries were the recipient of what were now less profitable industries. And we have had a rise in unemployment everywhere—in most countries of the South to be sure, but in the North as well. To be sure, unemployment rates do not have to be uniform in all countries. Far from it! Indeed, one of the major activities of the governments of all states during this period has been to try to shift the unemployment burden to other states, but such shifts can be only momentarily successful.

Let us rapidly review how this scenario has been played out.

The most striking economic happening of the early 1970s, now almost forgotten but at the time one that absorbed the newspaper headlines of the entire world, was the OPEC oil price rise. All of a sudden, the major oil-producing countries created in effect a serious cartel and raised the price of oil on the world market considerably. Originally, this was hailed by some as an intelligent political move by Third World states against the principal states of the North. But observe right away something strange. The decision of OPEC, a decision that had been advocated for a long time by the so-called radical states such as Libya and Algeria, was only made possible now by the suddenly acquired enthusiastic support of the two closest friends of the US in the Middle East— Saudi Arabia and Iran under the Shah. How curious!

The effect of the oil price rise was immediate. It raised prices of virtually all other products, but unevenly. It led to a reduction in production of many commodities, useful given the glut. Countries which relied on income from the export of raw materials saw their income go down at the very moment that their imports went up in price; hence there were acute difficulties in balance of payments. The increased income from the sale of oil went first of all to oil-producing countries, and of course, to the so-called Seven Sisters, the great transnational megastructures in the petroleum industry. The oil-producing countries suddenly had a monetary surplus. Some of it went toward increased expenditures on their part, largely imports from the North, which helped restore demand in the latter countries. But another part went into bank accounts, largely in the US and Germany. The increased funds in the banks had to be lent to someone. These banks aggressively peddled loans to the finance ministers of poorer countries suffering from balance of payment difficulties, acute unemployment, and consequent internal unrest. These countries borrowed extensively, but then found it difficult to repay the loans, which thus cumulated until debt payments rose to intolerable levels. It was just at this point that the Japanese competitive advantage suddenly blossomed, although western Europe was also not doing badly, whereas the US was suffering from so-called stagflation.

In the meantime, the US sought to maintain its political hold on western Europe and Japan by erecting a pastiche of consultative structures: the Trilateral Commission, the G-7 (which, be it said, was an idea of Valéry Giscard d'Estaing, that he thought might limit US power, but which turned out to do the opposite). The US reacted politically to the Vietnam fiasco by adopting for a time of "low posture" in the Third World—becoming more flexible in zones like Angola, Nicaragua, Iran and Cambodia. But not everyone was ready to respond to such flexibility by lowering their demands. The new revolutionary government of Iran, under Ayatollah Khomeini, refused to play by the rules of the interstate game, denouncing the US as the Great Satan (and the Soviet Union as the number two Satan) and imprisoning US diplomats. Liberal centralism and Keynesian economics suddenly went out of fashion. Margaret Thatcher launched so-called neoliberalism, which was, of course, really an aggressive conservatism of a type that had not been seen since 1848, and which involved an attempt to reverse welfare state redistribution so that it went to the upper classes rather than to the lower classes.

If the 1970s thus ended with a bang, the 1980s was not far behind. The loans to the poorer states had gotten out of hand, and the debt crisis began. It began, not in 1982 as usually argued when Mexico announced it could not repay its debt, but in 1980, when the Gierek government of Poland decided to try to meet its debt problems by squeezing its working class, a move that met spectacular resistance with the emergence of Solidarnosc[3] in Gdansk. The events in Poland marked the death knell of the Soviet satellite system in east/central Europe, a key linchpin in the Yalta arrangements, although it would still take a decade for the disintegration to be fully accomplished. This was the same moment that the USSR made the crucial tactical error of going into Afghanistan, and would thus bleed itself in the same way the US had done in Vietnam, with less social resilience to permit it to survive the consequences.

The 1980s can be summed up in a few code words. The first was the "debt crisis," which brought down not only most of Latin America (not to speak of Africa), but also east/central Europe. The debt crisis revealed the degree to which the economic realities of east/central Europe were not essentially different from those of the Third World. The second was the "flying geese" of East Asia–Japan's amazing economic romp through the world-economy, followed by and dragging along first, the four dragons (South Korea, Taiwan, Hong Kong and Singapore), and eventually south-east Asia and mainland China as well. The third was the "military Keynesianism" of the Reagan administration that overcame US recession and high unemployment by enormous government borrowing, in particular from Japan, on the excuse of the reinforcement of military structures, and whose single biggest consequence was the creation of an incredible US national debt. The fourth was the flourishing of "junk bonds" on the US stock exchange, which essentially meant enormous borrowing on the part of large corporations in order to make short-run speculative profits at the expense of productive machinery, and causing in turn so-called "downsizing," which meant forcing middle-income strata into lower-paying jobs in the economy.

In the 1980s, the whole world-economy appeared in bad shape except for East Asia, although that did not prevent financial speculators from making astounding profits. And along with this, and for a time, a certain stratum of the upper middle class, the so-called yuppies, prospered, causing inflationary pressures in the luxury market and in real estate worldwide. But most of the world suffered loss of income and deflation through the collapse of currencies. In the wake of these worldwide difficulties, the Soviet Union came apart. Or rather, Gorbachev made a spectacular attempt to prevent this by throwing ballast overboard. He unilaterally disarmed, forcing US reciprocity. He abandoned Afghanistan and, in effect, east/central Europe. And he sought cautiously to reform the internal political system. His downfall was due to the fact that he grievously underestimated the emergent forces of nationalism within the Soviet Union itself, and most of all that of Russian nationalism.

The tensile strength of the Yalta agreements came undone, as much because of US as because of Soviet weakness. Neither the US nor Gorbachev wanted the arrangements to come apart. But the long stagnation in the world-economy had undone them. And Humpty Dumpty could not be put together again.

Since 1970, the world-economy had gone through three debt cycles, which were all attempts to maintain the spending power of the world-system: the oil money loans to the Third World and to the socialist countries; the borrowing of the US government; and the borrowing of the large corporations. Each artificially raised prices in some areas beyond their market value. Each led to great difficulties about repayment, handled by various kinds of pseudo-bankruptcies. Finally, in 1990, the Japanese real estate bubble burst, reducing paper value enormously.

The last bulwark of productive economic strength in the world-economy had come under assault. This was to be the story of the 1990s.

The US political position now came under severe attack, not despite but precisely because of the collapse of the Soviet Union. Saddam Hussein decided to take advantage of the post-Yalta reality, directly challenging the United States militarily by invading Kuwait. He was able to do this because the USSR was no longer in a position to restrain him. He did this because, in the short run, it promised to solve the problems of Iraq's debts (heavily owed to Kuwait) and increase its oil income. And he did this because he hoped to use this invasion in the middle run as the basis for a military unification of the Arab world under his aegis—a unification that he saw as a necessary step in a direct military challenge to the North in general, and to the United States in particular.

There were two possibilities for Saddam, that the US would back down or that it would not. If the first occurred, his victory would be immediate. But he counted on the fact that, even if the second occurred, he would gain over the longer run. For some time, this appeared to be a correct calculation. The US of course did mobilize the necessary military force to drive the Iraqis out of Kuwait and to place Iraq under severe international constraints thereafter. But the price proved high for the US. It demonstrated that it could not financially afford to conduct such operations. The entire military bill of the US was borne by Saudi Arabia, Kuwait, Japan and Germany. And it demonstrated that it could not remove Saddam from inside Iraq because the US was unwilling to send troops into its interiors. The two constraints—financial and military—were both dictated by US public opinion, which was ready to applaud nationalist victory, provided it cost no money and no lives. This changed with the rise of the neoconservatives in the US, but the 2003 war in Iraq has also imposed considerable costs on the US, in terms of finance and international legitimacy. Indeed, this war may come to be seen as the last throw of the dice for US primacy in the international order.

In the 1990s, western Europe took the essential step forward in its unification, with the creation of the euro, and thus achieved the financial underpinning necessary to pull away from its close political links to the United States. This will no doubt lead in the coming decade to the creation of a real European army, and thereby a military disjunction from the US. The disintegration of the Balkan zone has demonstrated clearly the very limited effectiveness of NATO as a political force, and has managed to strain even further US–western European relations.

And in the midst of all this came the so-called "Asian crisis." The financial collapse of the south-east Asian states and the four dragons was followed by the disastrous interference of the IMF, accentuating both economic and political consequences. What we should note essentially about this collapse is that deflation has at last hit East Asia and its derivative zone, followed as we know by

Russia and Brazil. The world holds its breath, waiting for it to hit the United States. We shall then enter into the last subphase of this Kondratieff downturn.

WAYS OUT OF THE CRISIS

After that, will we at last see a new Kondratieff A-phase? Yes, assuredly, but one within a secular deflation as in the seventeenth and nineteenth centuries, and not one within a secular inflation as in the sixteenth, eighteenth, and twentieth centuries. But we shall also see something different. We must now turn our attention away from the Kondratieff cycles and onto the long-term development of the modern world-system as an historical system.

The capitalist world-economy has long maintained itself, as any system does, by mechanisms that restore equilibrium every time its processes move away from it. The equilibrium is never restored immediately, but only after a sufficient deviation from the norm occurs, and of course, it is never restored perfectly. Because it requires that deviations go a certain distance before they trigger counter-movements, the result is that the capitalist world-economy, like any other system, has cyclical rhythms of multiple kinds. We have been discussing one of the principal ones it has developed that are called Kondratieff cycles. They are not the only ones.

The equilibrium is never restored to the same point because the counter-movements require some change in the underlying parameters of the system. Hence, the equilibrium is always a moving equilibrium, and therefore the system has secular trends. It is this combination of cyclical rhythms and secular trends that define a system that is functioning "normally." However, secular trends cannot go on forever, because they hit asymptotes. Once this happens, it is no longer possible for the cyclical rhythms to bring the system back into equilibrium, and this is when a system gets into trouble. It then enters into its terminal crisis, and bifurcates—that is, it finds itself before two (or more) alternative routes to a new structure, with a new equilibrium, new cyclical rhythms and new secular trends. But which of the two alternative routes the system will take, that is, what kind of a new system will be established, is intrinsically not possible to determine in advance, since it is a function of an infinity of particular choices that are not systemically constrained. This is what is happening now in the capitalist world-economy.

To appreciate this, we must look at the major secular trends that are approaching their asymptotes. Each of them is thereby creating limits to the accumulation of capital. But since the endless accumulation of capital is the defining feature of capitalism as an historical system, the triple pressure tends to make unfeasible the primary motor of the system and hence creates a structural crisis.

The first secular trend is the real wage level as a percentage of costs of production, calculated as an average throughout the whole world-economy. Obviously, the lower this is, the higher the profit level, and vice versa. What determines the real wage level? Quite clearly, the answer is the *rapport de forces* between the labor force in a given zone and sector of the world-economy and the employers of such labor. This *rapport de forces* is a function primarily of the political strength of the two groups in what we call the class struggle. When one speaks of the market as the constraining element in determining the wage levels, it is deceptive, since the market value of labor is a function of the multiple *rapports de force* in the various zones of the world-economy. These varying political strengths are in turn a function of the efficacy of political organization in one form or another of given work forces and the real alternatives of the employers in terms of relocating their operations. Both of these factors constantly change.

What one can say is that, over time, in any given geographical/sectoral locality, the work force will seek to create some form of syndical organization and action that will enable them to bargain more effectively, either directly with the employer or indirectly via their influence on the relevant political machinery. While no doubt such political strength can be set back in given localities through political counter-offensives of capitalist groups, it is also true that the long-run "democratization" of the political machineries throughout the history of the modern world-system have served to make the curve of the political strength of the working classes an upward one over the *longue durée* in virtually all states in the world-system.

The principal mechanism by which capitalists worldwide have been able to limit this political pressure has been the relocation of given sectors of production to other zones of the world-economy that are on the average lower-wage areas. This is a difficult operation, politically as well as one dependent on skill levels in the calculations of eventual profits. Hence, it tends to be done primarily during Kondratieff B-phases, as we suggested earlier. Nonetheless, it has been done repeatedly during the historical development of the modern world-system. But why are the areas into which the sectors are relocated lower-wage areas? It solves nothing to say that this is the consequence of "historical" wage levels. And whence this history?

The primary source of truly low-wage labor has always been newly-recruited migrants from rural areas, often entering the wage-labor market for the first time. They are ready to accept what are, by world standards, low wages for two reasons. The net income they are receiving is in fact higher than the net income they previously received in their rural activity. And since they are socially uprooted, and consequently politically somewhat in disarray, therefore unable to defend well their interests. Both explanations wear out over time, certainly after say, thirty years, and such workers begin to exert pressures on wage levels parallel to those of workers in other regions of the world-economy. In this case, the major option for capitalists is further relocation.

As one can see, such a mode of conducting the class struggle is dependent on always new areas of the world-system into which to relocate, and this is dependent on the existence of a significant rural sector not yet engaged in the wage-labor market. But the latter is precisely diminishing as a secular trend. The de-ruralization of the world is on a fast upward curve. It has grown continuously over 500 years, but most dramatically since 1945. It is quite possible to foresee that it will have largely disappeared in another 25 years. Once the whole world-system is de-ruralized, the only option for capitalists is to pursue the class struggles where they are presently located. And here the odds are against them. Even with the increased polarization of real income, not only in the world-system as a whole but within the wealthiest countries, the political and market sophistication of the lower strata continues to grow. Even where there are large number of people who are technically unemployed and deriving their income, such as it is, from the informal economy, the real alternatives available to workers located in the *barrios* and *favelas* of the world-system are such that they are in a position to demand reasonable wage levels in order to enter the formal wage-economy. The net result of all of this is a serious pressure on profit levels that will increase over time.

The second secular trend disturbing to capitalists is rather different. It has to do not with the cost of wage-labor but with the cost of material inputs. What is involved in the cost of inputs? It is not only the price at which they are bought from a different firm but also the cost of treating them. Now while the cost of purchase is normally borne entirely by the firm that will eventually get the profits, the costs of treating the materials is often partially borne by others. For example, if in treating the raw materials, there is toxic or cumbersome waste, part of the cost involved is getting rid of such waste, and if toxic, in a safe manner. Firms, of course, desire to minimize these costs of disposal. One way they can do thus, a way very widely practiced, is by placing the waste somewhere away from the factory site after minimal detoxification, for example, by dumping chemical toxins into a stream. This is called by economists "externalizing the costs." Of course, this is not the end of the costs of disposal. To stick to the example, if toxins are dumped into a stream, this may poison the stream, and eventually (perhaps decades later) there will be damage to people or to other matter (at costs that are real, if difficult to calculate). And there may be a social decision to clean up the toxins, in which case, the body that undertakes the clean-up—often the state—is bearing the cost. Another mode of reducing costs is to utilize raw materials, but not to provide for (that is, pay for) their renewal, a problem especially true of organic matter. Such externalization of costs significantly reduces the costs of raw materials to given producers and, hence increases the margin of profit.

The problem here is akin to that of relocation as a solution to wage costs. It works as long as there are previously unutilized areas in which to dump waste. But eventually there are no more streams to pollute, or trees to cut down—or at least, there are no more without serious immediate consequences for the health of the biosphere. This is the situation in which we find ourselves today after 500 years of such practices, which is why today we have an ecology movement that has been growing rapidly throughout the world.

What can be done? Well, the governments of the world can undertake what amounts to a vast clean-up campaign and a vast campaign of organic renewal. The problem is the cost of an effective operation, which is enormous, and thus must be paid by someone via some form of taxes. There are only two someones: either the firms that are considered to have been the perpetrators of the waste, or the rest of us. If it is the former, the pressure on the profit margins will be impressively high. If it is the latter, the tax burdens will mount significantly, a problem to which we will now refer. Furthermore, there is not much point in clean-up and organic renewal if the practices remain as at present, since it would amount to cleaning an Augean stable. Hence, the logical inference is to require the total internalization of all costs. This, however, would add still further to the pressure on the profits of individual firms. I do not see any plausible solution for this social dilemma within the framework of a capitalist world-economy, and hence I suggest that this—environmental costs—is the second structural pressure on the accumulation of capital.

The third pressure lies in the realm of taxation. Taxation is, of course, a payment for social services, and therefore is accepted as a reasonable cost of production, provided it is not too high. Now what has determined the level of taxation? To be sure, there has been the constant demand of security (the military, the police). This has, as we know, steadily risen over the centuries because of the increasing relative costs of the means of security, the scope of military actions, and the perceived need of police actions. The second steady rise has been in the size of the civil bureaucracies of the world, a function first of all of the need to collect taxes, and second of all to perform the expanding functions of the modern states.

The major expanding function has been in providing for certain popular demands. This has not been an optional expense. The growth of these provisions has been a principal means of ensuring relative political stability in response to growing discontents of the lower strata, concerning the increasing polarization of real income, which has been a steady feature of the world-system. Social welfare efforts by governments have been the pay-off utilized to tame the "dangerous classes," that is, to keep the class struggle within limited bounds. We call the response to these popular demands "democratization," and it has also been a very real secular trend. There are three principal varieties of such popular demands: educational institutions, health facilities, and guarantees of income across the lifetime of individuals (especially, unemployment insurance and social security for the aged). There are two things to be noted about such demands. They have been made in more and more zones of the world-system, and are today nearly universal. And the levels of the demands have risen steadily within each country, with no clear limit in sight.

This has meant, has had to mean, steadily rising tax rates in virtually every country, with at most, occasional slight reductions. But, of course, at a certain point, such redistributive taxation reaches levels where it interferes seriously with the possibility of accumulating capital. Hence the reaction today to what is perceived as the "fiscal crises of the states," is for capitalists to demand a rollback, and to seek popular support on the grounds that individual taxation is also rising sharply. The irony is that while there is often popular support for limiting taxes, there is zero popular support for cutting back welfare provisions (either of education or of health or of income guarantees). Indeed, at the very time that there are clamors about high taxation, the levels of popular demand on government services are growing. So here too, we have a structural pressure on the accumulation of capital.

So there we are—three major structural pressures on the ability of capitalists to accumulate capital, the result of secular trends that continuously ratchet upward. This crisis, not in growth but in capital accumulation, is further complicated by a different phenomenon, the loss of legitimateness of the state structures. States are a crucial element in the ability of capitalists to accumulate capital. States make possible quasi-monopolies, which are the only source of significant profit levels. States act to tame the "dangerous classes," both by repression and by appeasement. States are the principal source of ideologies that persuade the mass of the population to be relatively patient.

The major argument for patience has been the inevitability of reform. Things will get better—if not immediately, then for one's children and grandchildren. A more prosperous, more egalitarian world is on the horizon. This is, of course official liberal ideology, and has dominated the geoculture since the nineteenth century. But it has also been the theme of all the anti-systemic movements, not least those that have proclaimed themselves most revolutionary. These movements have particularly emphasized this theme when they occupied state power. They have said to their own working classes that they were "developing" their economies, and these working classes must be patient while the fruits of economic growth eventually improve their life situations. They have preached patience about standards of living, but also about the absence of political equality.

As long as such anti-systemic movements (whether they were Communist, or Social–Democrat, or national liberation movements) were in their mobilizing phase against inegalitarian, militaristic, dictatorial, fascist, colonial, or even simply conservative regimes, this theme was muted and did not interfere with the ability of anti-systemic movements to secure extensive popular support. Once, however, such movements came to power, as they did extensively throughout the world during the period 1945–70 (the Kondratieff A-phase of which we have been speaking), they were put to the test. And worldwide they have been found wanting. The record of post-"revolutionary" regimes has been that they have not been able to reduce worldwide or even internal polarization to any significant degree, nor have they been able to institute serious internal political equality. They have no doubt accomplished many reforms, but they promised far more than reforms. And because the world-system has remained a capitalist world-economy, the regimes outside the core zone have been structurally unable to "catch up" with the wealthy countries. This is not merely a matter of academic analysis. The result of these realities has been a monumental disillusionment with the anti-systemic movements. To the extent that they retain support, it is as most as a *pis aller*, as a reformist group better perhaps than a more rightwing alternative, but certainly not as a harbinger of the new society. The major result has been a massive disinvestment in state structures. The masses of the world, having turned towards the states as agents of transformation, have now returned to a more fundamental skepticism about the ability of the states to promote transformation, or even to maintain social order.

This worldwide upsurge of anti-statism has two immediate consequences. One is that social fears have escalated, and people everywhere are taking back from the states the role of providing for their own security. But of course, this institutes a negative spiral. The more they do so, the more there is chaotic violence, and the more there is chaotic violence, the more the states find themselves unable to handle the situation, and therefore the more people disinvest the state. This further weakens the ability of the states to limit the spiral. We have entered into this spiral at varying paces in the various countries of the world-system, but at a growing pace virtually everywhere.

The second consequence is one for the capitalists. States that are de-legitimated find it far more difficult to perform their function of guaranteeing the quasi-monopolies capitalists need, not to speak of their ability to tame the "dangerous classes." Thus, at the very moment that capitalists are faced with three structural squeezes on the global rates of profit, and hence on their ability to accumulate capital, they find that the states are less able than before to help them resolve these dilemmas.

It is thus that we can say that the capitalist world-economy has now entered its terminal crisis, a crisis that may last up to fifty years. The real question before us is what will happen during this crisis, this transition from the present world-system to some other kind of historical system or systems. Analytically, the key question is the relation between the Kondratieff cycles I first described and the systemic crisis of which I have been talking now. Politically, there is the question of what kind of social action is possible and desirable during a systemic transition. Kondratieff cycles are part of the "normal" functioning of the capitalist world-economy. Such so-called normal functioning does not cease because the system has entered into a systemic crisis. The various mechanisms that account for the behavior of a capitalist system are still in place. When the present B-phase has exhausted itself, we shall undoubtedly have a new A-phase. However, the systemic crisis interferes seriously with the trajectory. It is a bit as though one tried to drive a car downhill with a motor still intact but with a damaged body and wheels. The car would no doubt roll forward but surely not in the straight line one would have previously expected nor with the same guarantees that the brakes would work efficiently. How it would behave would become rather difficult to assess in advance. Supplying more gas to the motor might have unexpected consequences. The car could crash.

Schumpeter accustomed us a long time ago to the idea that capitalism would not collapse because of its failures but because of its successes. We have tried to indicate here how the successes (modes of counteracting downturns in the world-economy, modes of maximizing the accumulation of capital) have, over time, created structural limits to the very accumulation of capital they were intended to ensure. This is concrete empirical evidence of the Schumpeterian assumption. No doubt, to continue the analogy of the damaged automobile, a wise chauffeur might drive quite slowly under these difficult conditions. But there is no wise chauffeur in the capitalist world-economy. No individual or group has the power to make the necessary decisions alone. And the very fact that these decisions are being made by a large number of actors, operating separately and each in his/her own immediate interests, virtually ensures that the car will not slow down. Probably, it will start to go faster and faster. Consequently, what we may expect is recklessness.

As the world-economy enters into a new period of expansion, it will thereby exacerbate the very conditions that have led it into a terminal crisis. In technical terms, the fluctuations will get wilder and wilder, or more "chaotic," and the direction in which the trajectory is moving ever more uncertain, as the route takes more and more zigzags with even greater rapidity. At the same time, we may expect the degree of collective and individual security to decrease, perhaps vertiginously, as the state structures lose more and more legitimacy. And this will no doubt increase the amount of day-by-day violence in the world-system. This will be frightening to most people, as well it should be.

Politically, this situation will be one of great confusion, since the standard political analyses we have developed to understand the modern world-system will seem not to apply or will seem to be outdated. This will not really be true. But these analyses will apply primarily to the ongoing processes of the existing world-system and not to the reality of a transition. This is why it is so important to be clear on the distinction between the two and on the ways in which this double reality will be playing itself out. In terms of the ongoing reality, it will be almost impossible for political action to affect it very much. To return to the analogy of the damaged car going downhill, we may correctly feel somewhat helpless, and the most we may be able to do is to try to maneuver so as to minimize immediate harm to ourselves. But in terms of the transition as a whole, the opposite is true. Precisely because its outcome is unpredictable, precisely because its fluctuations are so wild, even the slightest political action will have great consequences. I like to think of this as the moment in historical time when free will truly comes into play.

We can think of this long transition as one enormous political struggle between two large camps: the camp of all those who wish to retain the privileges of the existing inegalitarian system, albeit in different forms, perhaps vastly different forms; and the camp of all those who would like to see the creation of a new historical system that will be significantly more democratic and more egalitarian. However, we cannot expect that the members of the first camp will present themselves in the guise that I used to describe them. They will assert that they are modernizers, new democrats, advocates of freedom and progressive. They may even claim to be revolutionary. The key is not in the rhetoric but in the substantive reality of what is being proposed.

The outcome of the political struggle will be in part the result of who is able to mobilize whom, but it will also be in large part the degree to which who is able to analyze better what is going on, and what are the real historical alternatives with which we are collectively faced. That is to say, it is a moment at which we need to unify knowledge, imagination, and praxis. Or else we risk saying, a century from now, *plus ça change, plus c'est la même chose*. The outcome is, I insist, intrinsically uncertain, and therefore precisely open to human intervention and creativity.

Notes

1. The Kondratieff Cycle is a theory based on a study of nineteenth century price behavior, which included wages, interest rates, raw material prices, foreign trade, bank deposits, and other data. Kondratieff, like R.N. Elliott, was convinced that his studies of economic, social, and cultural life proved that a long-term order of economic behavior existed and could be used for the purpose of anticipating future economic developments.

   He observed certain characteristics about the growth and contractionary phase of the long wave. Among them, he detailed the number of years that the economy expanded and contracted during each part of the half-century long cycle, which industries suffer the most during the down wave, and how technology plays a role in leading the way out of the contraction into the next up wave.

   The fifty to fifty-four year cycles of catastrophe and renewal had been known and observed by the Mayans of Central America and independently by the ancient Israelites.

Kondratieff's observations represent the modern expression of this cycle, which postulates that capitalist countries tend to follow the long rhythmic pattern of approximately half a century.

2. Automaticity is the ability to effortlessly complete everyday tasks with low interference of other simultaneous activities and without conscious thought to step-by-step process. When the brain recognizes familiar tasks it processes the information and applies the correct rules to the procedure in order to reduce the demand on the working memory and allow for higher order processing of information.

3. Solidarity (Polish: *Solidarność* full name: Independent Self-governing Trade Union "Solidarity. Lech Walesa, along with some of his friends in the anti-communist trade union movement, founded Solidarnosc (Solidarity). It was not long before the organization had 10 million members and Walesa was its undisputed leader. In August 1980 Walesa led the Gdansk shipyard strike, which gave rise to a wave of strikes over much of the country. Walesa, a devout Catholic, developed a loyal following and the communist authorities were forced to capitulate. The Gdansk Agreement, signed on August 31, 1980, gave Polish workers the right to strike and to organize their own independent union.

2

NEOLIBERAL GLOBALIZATION

JAN NEDERVEEN PIETERSE

During the past two decades the dominant approach has been neoliberal globalization, not in the sense that it is all there is to globalization but in the sense that it became a global regime. Most protests against globalization concern neoliberal globalization and this is the actual problem, rather than globalization per se. Contemporary globalization can be described as a package deal that includes informatization (applications of information technology), flexibilization (de-standardization in the organization of production and labor), and various changes such as regionalization and the reconfiguration of states. Since the 1980s, the growing impact of neoliberal policies adds to the globalization package, deregulation (liberalization, privatization), marketization (unleashing market forces), financialization and securitization (conversion of assets into tradable financial instruments), and the ideology of lean government. This essay considers how this has come about and focuses on the economic and political shift within the United States to the South, the connection between the Cold War and neoliberalism, and the Washington consensus.

Studies generally explain the onset of neoliberalism as the confluence of the economic ideas of the Chicago school and the policies of Ronald Reagan and Margaret Thatcher. A further strand is the Washington consensus, the economic orthodoxy that guided the IMF and World Bank in their policies through the 1990s and turned neoliberalism into global policy.

Adding detail to this account, Adam Tickell and Jamie Peck (2003) discuss the development of neoliberalism in three phases: an early phase of *proto-neoliberalism* from the 1940s to the 1970s in which the main ideas took shape; a phase of *roll-back neoliberalism* in the 1980s when it became government policy in the US and UK; and *roll-out neoliberalism* in the 1990s when it became hegemonic in multilateral institutions.

Like many accounts, this focuses on economic ideas (of the Mont Pèlerin Society, Friedrich von Hayek and Milton Friedman) and the policies of Reagan and Thatcher. But by locating the origins of neoliberalism in the realm of ideas and the theories of the Chicago school, this overlooks the actual economic policies that shaped "real neoliberalism" already before the Reagan era. The low-taxes, low-services regime envisioned by free market advocates already existed in the American South. Real neoliberalism in the United States in the 1970s and 1980s meant the implementation of the low-wage, low-tax model of Southern economics. The political muscle of the Southern conservatives and the welcome mat of the anti-union South for corporations fleeing the Northeast is what gave the "Reagan revolution" its depth and punch. Eventually, this led to the roll-back of the regulatory and social functions of the state as a national trend.

This is worth considering for several reasons. Just as we don't analyze Soviet society by reading the texts of Marx but by examining "real existing socialism," we should look at the material political economy of neoliberalism and not just its theoretical claims. Had the American South with its low wages, high exploitation and reactionary culture been upheld as the model of economic growth, it would never have exercised the glossy appeal that the "free market" did in theory. The Chicago school provided an economic rationale and intellectual gloss to what was and remains a backward and impoverished economic condition. Revisiting Chicago economics in order to understand neoliberalism is largely revisiting smoke and mirrors. A further omission in most accounts of neoliberalism is that it ignores the setting of the Cold War and glosses over the affinities it shared with neoliberalism. Both these elements are fundamental to understanding the actual character of neoliberal globalization and its subsequent metamorphoses.

DIXIE CAPITALISM

American politics has undergone a long conservative trend that has recently taken an aggressive turn; to understand this trend we must go back several decades in American history. When in response to stagflation in the 1970s the US Federal Reserve raised interest rates, it prompted the onset of the debt crisis in the global South, which led to the IMF imposing its financial discipline and eventually the regime of structural reform. Meanwhile in the United States, corporations sought to retain their profitability by moving to low-wage areas of operation, which they found first in the American South.

The economic strategy of the American South was "based on low-wage, labor-intensive, high-exploitation production, and hostility to unions" and has its roots in the period following Reconstruction. During the New Deal in the 1930s the agricultural South and West had been modernized through vast state-capitalist projects, of which the Tennessee Valley Authority is best known. But its tax structures, labor laws and institutions did not change and remained as conservative and non-liberal as during the days of post-Reconstruction. In the

1970s, its industrial policy consisted of providing "a safe haven for 'footloose' capital seeking refuge from the regulatory and industrial relations regime and tax structures of the Northeast and Midwest." The South was committed to low taxes on capital and limited social services and had "a long tradition of using the law as a tool to build and protect a racialized political and economic order" (Wood 2003: 24). This was the land of Jim Crow law.

During the liberal 1960s, the expectation was that Fordism would spread southward and this would result in the "Americanization of Dixie." What happened instead was the "Dixiefication of America." The Southern model not only survived but became the way out of the 1970s economic crisis and the template for the Reagan revolution: "the economic development policies that we have implemented in the United States over the past three decades have taken on the characteristics of an up-to-date, modified version of those that have been in effect in the American South for decades" (Cummings 1998: x). Southern economics has its roots in plantation economics with rural oligarchies and a low-cost workforce that performs manual labor—slaves, segregated blacks, rightless migrant workers from Mexico under the Bracero program, and after 1964, many illegal immigrants. According to Stephen Cummings, it is "the export of Southern and Republican conservative economic values to the nation that replaced the northern liberal values of the New Deal and the Great Society programs that set the country on the path to economic insecurity" (ibid.: 6).

The Reagan reforms came with an anti-democratic cultural and racial backlash that had its beginnings in the 1960s with George Wallace in the South: "it was no accident that the groups Wallace attacked were the least powerful in society, such as welfare mothers and aliens—easy targets to scapegoat" (ibid.: 10). In 1971 the prison population in the South was 220 percent higher than in the Northeast; now nationwide incarceration rates began to approximate those that had long prevailed in the South. Within corporations, management became punitive—all elements that feed into a low-wage, high-exploitation accumulation strategy.

If the American South provided the material matrix, Chicago school economics provided the intellectual sheen. At a time of rapid technological change, a return to neoclassical economics offered a gloss of modernist minimalism. Hayek added a cybernetic twist by claiming that market forces, in contrast to state planning, provide superior circulation of information. Friedman's monetarism attacked Fordism and New Deal capitalism. The Laffer curve (tax cuts stimulate the economy and will yield more tax revenue) provided a rationale for rolling back government. Deregulation and tax cuts became bywords for achieving "competitiveness" and "flexibility," while in effect they converged on creating a low-wage, high-exploitation regime. As Will Hutton points out, the origin of what became the Washington consensus lies in a Southern conservative campaign.

By 1979, when the Business Roundtable published its manifesto, essentially arguing for what was later to be dubbed the "Washington consensus" (balanced budgets, tax cuts, tight money, deregulation, anti-union laws), with the Moral Majority and the NRA campaigning hard on conservative social issues, the conservatives…were on the move…. The centre of political and economic gravity was moving to the south and west. (Hutton 2002: 106)

Another variable is Wall Street, which had played a destructive role in the 1920s, leading to the 1929 crash. The Reagan Administration dismantled the New Deal regulatory structure that had been put in place precisely to counteract the speculative financial practices of the 1920s and unleashed the financial sector. With the institutional restraints gone, the Wall Street-driven preoccupation with short-term stock value gradually transformed the character of American corporations. Since corporations needed to show profits at the end of each quarter, the organizational weight within firms shifted to the financial department and elevated the status of financial overproductive operations. The institutionalized obsession with earnings led to fraud, and eventually culminated in Enron and the cascade of related scandals. Both forms of capitalism, the high-exploitation capitalism of the South and Wall Street financial engineering, are essentially predatory and profoundly different from the productive capitalism that had originally been the basis of American economic success.

The Bush II Administration adds a Texan chapter to the magnolia model and reflects an ethos unlike any previous administration, which Michael Lind describes thus: "Although Bush's ancestors were Northeastern, the culture that shaped him was made in Texas—a culture that combines Protestant fundamentalism and Southern militarism with an approach to economics that favors primitive commodity capitalist enterprises like cotton and oil production over high-tech manufacturing and scientific R&D" (2003: 80).

While this sheds light on the Bush II Administration, Lind easily lapses into schematic judgments, at times essentializes the South, assumes sweeping continuities over time, and dichotomizes Texas elites into modern and pre-modern factions. Peter Applebome notes that "the South's stock in trade has been the myth and reality of its distinctiveness: the only part of the nation with institutionalized apartheid; the only part of the nation to know the crushing burden of losing a war" (1996: 10).

There is an American "Dixie industry" that produces a "Southern mystique," which operates as an "internal orientalism" within the United States (Zinn 1964; Jansson 2003). This comes with the usual North–South dichotomies of modern–traditional, rational–irrational, secular–fundamentalist, urban–rural, tolerant–racist that are familiar from other regions of the world. So while tucked within American exceptionalism there is a "Southern exceptionalism," this is not a straightforward matter. The South is internally differentiated and quite dynamic; for decades it has led the United States in population growth and economic growth. Traditional Southern elites represent a different political economy, but to classify it as "premodern" is too easy; it may well be considered an alternative modernity. This means to acknowledge that it has dynamics of its own and is not simply locked in a premodern pattern. So assessing the significance of the American South is not simply a matter of adding up stereotypes and indicators of regional uneven development, but of navigating representations and deciding what kernels to keep.

While avoiding the trap of "internal orientalism," a few points stand out when we seek to understand the ongoing changes in American policies. One is the empirical circumstance of the American South as a low-tax zone. The second is the leadership of Southern conservatives in American politics virtually since the 1970s. While Republicans also lead in the West and Northwest, the demographic center of the GOP (Grand Old Party—another name for the Republicans) is the much more densely populated South. The third circumstance is that over a long period Southern conservatives have consistently resisted the politics of the New Deal. "The Bush II administration was also the culmination of seventy years of a counter-revolution against the New Deal, in both domestic policy and foreign policy" (Lind 2003: 81–82). Today the American South "has the largest concentration of low-wage jobs, its economy is dominated by externally owned branch plants...and is still dependent on natural resources, particularly oil and gas, just as it was a century ago" (Cummings 1998: 117).

The United States has been subject to three decades of non-stop conservative onslaught coming from multiple sources. Southern conservatives pushed for dismantling the New Deal, bringing the country to the low-taxes, low-wages and low productivity level of the South. Chicago economics advocated the virtues of free markets and deregulation. Both agree on the conservative equation that "less regulation = more growth = more employment" (Cummings 1998: 75). These socially reactionary changes were pushed through at a time of rapid technological change and presented as progressive measures, in keeping with the information society. New technologies were harnessed to achieve a fundamental change in the balance of forces between capital and labor, duly amplified by the spin of business media.

In Britain, during the Thatcher years, the neoliberal package was welcomed as an attack on trade union power and New Labour continued this realignment. New Democrats in the United States accepted the tenets of the post-industrial society, flexibility and the new economy, abandoned the commitment to Fordism and the New Deal, and went post-Fordist. The Democratic Party moved to the center right and, albeit for different reasons than the Southern conservatives, accepted major parts of Reaganomics. The Clinton Administration institutionalized strands of Reaganomics as a bipartisan agenda—business deregulation, welfare reform, the "three strikes and out" regime—and exported it on an international scale. Instead of a democratic approach of stakeholder capitalism, New Democrats and New Labour adopted an authoritarian version of "flexibility."

How does Southern economics travel? The low-wage model increased the number of American families with two-wage earners and lengthened working hours without a proportional increase of incomes. The single-minded pursuit of short-term profits and shareholder revenue eroded economic capacities to the extent that the main product of leading American enterprises has become financial engineering or paper entrepreneurialism: making sure that the books show higher numbers at the end of each quarter. The conservatives have been so busy dismantling the government and the New Deal that they have paid little attention to the actual American economy, which has experienced a thirty-year decline. Long-term trends include massive de-industrialization, shrinking or inadequate investments in plants and equipment in many sectors, decline in research and development, and the growth of service jobs with low productivity, low wages, low job security and long working hours. Downsizing corporations has resulted in employee alienation and low morale. Income inequality has grown steadily.

The result of trying to be competitive on the cheap is that American industries have lost international competitiveness in several sectors (cf. Porter 1990). This is reflected in the US trade deficit and growing indebtedness at every level of the American economy, in households, corporations, cities, states and the federal government. The bottom line is a current account deficit that has grown to unsustainable levels.

From time to time, various circumstances have boosted the numbers, such as financial crisis in other parts of the world (in part as an effect of American-induced liberalization of capital markets) and the new economy bubble of the Clinton years. What keeps the American economy going in a structural fashion is a combination of expansion, government deficit spending and the influx of foreign funds. Expansion takes the form of corporations branching into other areas of business (as in conglomerates, frequently leading to business failure), waves of mergers and acquisitions (spinning fortunes in Wall Street while usually leading to less productive combinations), and opening up other markets by means of free trade agreements that liberalize capital markets and export American financial engineering overseas. The main form of government funding is the military-industrial complex. The inflow of foreign funds is a major cornerstone of the American economy. The influx of low-priced goods from China and Asia (and increasingly also services) keeps prices low as American incomes stagnate; also significant is the steady inflow of cheap migrant and immigrant labor, in particular from Mexico.

THE COLD WAR AND NEOLIBERALISM

The postwar period of "proto-neoliberalism" coincides with the Cold War era. During these years the infrastructure of neoliberalism was built in economic thinking and ideology (free market), think tanks, and economic policy (the "Chicago boys" in Chile and Indonesia). In fact, could we consider neoliberalism as the sequel to the Cold War?

Founding texts such as Friedrich von Hayek's *The Road to Serfdom* and Walt Rostow's *The Stages of Economic Growth* (subtitled *An Anti-Communist Manifesto*) were originally anti-communist tracts. Over time, anti-communist critique became "Free World" policy, Cold-War geopolitics was converted into a global financial regime, and the erstwhile anti-communist alliance morphed into a free-market hegemonic compromise. Since the spoils come to the victor, the kind of capitalism that triumphed was Anglo-American "free enterprise" capitalism. As part of anti-communism, the United States actively undermined socialist forces throughout the world, pressured international labor unions, and blocked global alternatives such as a new international economic order. European social democracy and Asian state-assisted capitalism were similarly disparaged.

The affinities between the Cold War and neoliberalism take several forms. The postwar modernization of Dixie capitalism in the non-union Sunbelt was made possible by military tax dollars, so Dixiefication and the Cold War were tandem projects. The American Sunbelt is now the most dependent on military contracts. The overseas network of security alliances built during the Cold War was reproduced under the neoliberal dispensation with a new inflection. From the "Washington connection" it was a small step to the Washington consensus. Now, IMF conditionalities and World Bank structural adjustment programs disciplined unruly states. Applied to the USSR, Fred Halliday (1986) refers to this process as the "second Cold War." By undermining trade unions and nationalist governments in much of the global South, US foreign policy helped create a favorable investment climate for American capital. American capital flight in turn, weakened the hold of the New Deal within the US, thus establishing an elective affinity between a domestic and transnational hegemony of similar inclination.

During the Cold War, economic and security interests mingled in the military-industrial complex. If the Soviet Union had been economically exhausted by the arms race, so arguably was the United States, though this was masked by economic achievements. For the US, the real burden of the superpower arms race was its growing path of dependence on the military-industrial complex. American economics, politics and institutions have been huddled around the military-industrial complex for so long that it has become a functionally autonomous logic. American militarism has become entrenched in policy; as Chalmers Johnson (2002) notes, this entails the formation of a professional military class, the preponderance of the military and the arms industry in administration policy, and military preparedness as the main priority of government policy. The end of the Cold War, then, created an "enemy deficit," for how to sustain this gargantuan apparatus in the absence of a threat?

With the waning of the Cold War, security interests slipped into the background and the Treasury and Commerce became the most salient government agencies, in cooperation with Wall Street and with the international financial institutions based in Washington. So, in the shift from the Cold War to neoliberalism some elements remained constant—such as a strong US military and support for strategic allies, such as Israel—while in other respects there were marked shifts of emphasis (see Table 2.1).

Table 2.1: Continuities/Discontinuities between Cold War and Neoliberal Globalization

Dimensions	Cold War	Neoliberalism
Ideology	Free world	Free market
	Open door	Free trade
	Anti-communism	Pro-American capitalism
Key state agencies	Pentagon, CIA	Treasury, Commerce
Economic center	Military-industrial complex, MNCs	MNCs, banks, Silicon Valley, telecommunications, media
Pressure on developing countries	Join Free World	Structural adjustment
Means of pressure	National security and economic incentives	Financial discipline and economic incentives
Agents of pressure	US government, Pentagon	IMF, World Bank, WTO
Investments	Sunbelt	Third World made safe
Security	Strong US military	Strong US military
Politics of containment	Military intervention, covert operations	Humanitarian intervention, nation-building
Allies	NATO, Israel, etc.	NATO, Israel, etc.
	Religious movements (Mujahideen, Hamas, etc.)	"Clash of civilizations": Islam as opponent.

THE WASHINGTON CONSENSUS

Postwar American development policies in the global South favored nation-building, "betting on the strong," Community Development that matched the American voluntary sector, and the instilling of achievement orientation—all strands of modernization theory, in which modernization equals westernization equals Americanization. Policies such as the Alliance for Progress interacted with Cold War strategies and the "Washington connection."

The Washington consensus that took shape in the late 1980s as a set of economic prescriptions for developing countries, echoes the core claim of Cold

War ideology: that free market and democracy go together. The main tenets of the Washington consensus are monetarism, reduction of government spending and regulation, privatization, liberalization of trade and financial markets, and the promotion of export-led growth. A difference is that postwar modernization was a *rival* project, a contender in the Cold War, while the Washington consensus no longer looks to national security states to withstand communist pressure. Hence, if modernization theory was state-centered and part of the postwar, governmental Keynesian consensus in development thinking, the Washington consensus turns another leaf, to government roll back and deregulation, now elevated from domestic policy to international program. In this sense, the Reagan era was a foretaste and then consummation of American Cold War victory, acknowledging no rival, no competition. This imprint shows in the policies of the international financial institutions: "the end of the Cold War has been associated with the increasing politicization of the IMF by the US. There is evidence that the US has been willing to reward friends and punish enemies only since 1990" (Thacker 1999: 70).

The 1990s has been described as a time of contestation between American and Asian capitalism in which American capitalism won (Hutton and Giddens 2000). Speculative capital and hedge funds unleashed by Reagan's deregulation played a major part in the Asian crisis of 1997 and subsequent financial crises. In the United States, the Asian crisis was hailed as an opportunity for the further Americanization of Asian economies (Bello 2003).

The Washington institutions have been governed by the Wall Street–Treasury–IMF complex in accordance with American economic orthodoxy, so a shorthand account of neoliberal globalization is American economic unilateralism. These policies resulted in a roll back of developing country government spending and the growth and mushrooming of NGOs.

Amid all the criticism of neoliberalism, little attention is given to the counter-revolution in the United States that prefigured the "counter-revolution in development." Changes in the US prefigure those undertaken in the global South in the name of structural reform; in both, there is an attempt to dismantle the regulatory state. In the United States government cutbacks were implemented through Reaganism; on a world scale the drive to liberalize and privatize economies was implemented by means of IMF stability in lending and World Bank structural adjustment.

Through structural reform, the combination of Dixie capitalism and Wall Street financial engineering has been extrapolated on a global scale. Southern economics and its depth of structure of plantation economics shed light on the realities of structural adjustment in the global South. Real neoliberalism, on display in the American South, is also known as "the Haitian road of development." So it's no wonder that during neoliberal globalization, development policies were a paradox, which is politely referred to as "policy incoherence":

institutions matter, but governments are rolled back; capacity building is key, but existing public capacities are defunded; accountability is essential, but privatization eliminates accountability; the aim is "building democracy by strengthening civil society," but NGOs are professionalized and depoliticized. (cf. Nederveen Pieterse 2001)

Neoliberalism sought to do away with "development economics" and instead presented the unfettered market as the answer to all economic questions. If we would only consider the economic theories of the free market advocates, there might be a rationale to this, even if at best half-true; enough of a rationale to serve for a while as the basis of a transnational hegemonic compromise. During the Clinton years, the WTO became the overarching framework of neoliberal globalization. But neither structural reform nor multilateral trade would conceal the actual character of neoliberalism as a high-exploitation regime. Stepping in as a debt collector for western lenders and investors, the IMF weakened states in the South. This is frontier capitalism that thrives on low wages and high exploitation.

Commenting on 9/11, Ulrich Beck (2001) observes that

The terrorist attacks on America were the Chernobyl of globalization. Suddenly, the seemingly irrefutable tenets of neoliberalism—that economics will supersede politics that the role of the state will diminish—lose their force in a world of global risks.... America's vulnerability is indeed much related to its political philosophy.... Neoliberalism has always been a fair-weather philosophy, one that works only when there are no serious conflicts and crises.

September 11 has shaken the "animal spirits" of late capitalism. An economy driven by replacement demand and consumer spending on status goods, kept going by marketing mood-making, comes tumbling down like a house of cards once consumer confidence fades. Aviation, tourism, retail, stocks, banks, insurance, advertising, Hollywood, fashion, media—all sectors have been trembling and repositioning under the impact of 9/11. Global capitalism turns out to be as interconnected as network analysis has suggested, and as vulnerable. With the exception of insurance rates, the economic impact of 9/11 has been temporary; the impact of the Enron episode is probably far more significant.

That neoliberalism is crisis-prone rather than crisis-proof is no news to most of the world, but a novel experience for the United States. There is a glaring inconsistency between federal government support for sectors hit by the 9/11 crisis—especially airlines and insurance—and the Washington consensus which has been urging all governments, crisis or no, to liberalize economies and cut back spending. If the insurance industry would not receive government support, rates would increase, delaying economic recovery. Countries that have been lectured by Washington and the IMF on economic sanity may be surprised to learn that the United States does not follow its own counsel.

This raises the wider question whether the Washington consensus applies to Washington.

John Williamson (1990) originally formulated the Washington orthodoxy in ten points. The first is *fiscal discipline*. In Washington this applied during the 1990s, but not before or after. The second point is *reordering public expenditure priorities in a pro-poor way*. This has not been a Washington priority since the New Deal. Like the Reagan Administration, the Bush II government uses deficit spending as a political instrument to cut back social spending (eventually heading for the privatization of social security). The third point is *tax reform towards a system that combines a broad tax base with moderate marginal tax rates*. The Bush II Administration scrapped estate and dividend taxes and gives tax cuts disproportionally to the very affluent. States and cities are in financial crisis; cut support for education and services and raise taxes. And so forth. Thus, of the ten points of Washington orthodoxy, it is practically only in privatization and deregulation that Washington follows the Washington consensus.

For some time the neoliberal project has been unraveling, and the Washington consensus faces mounting problems. The IMF handling of financial crises has lost credibility even in Washington and on Wall Street (e.g., Soros 1998). Its reputation is now that of a "Master of Disaster" (Cassidy 2002) and in Argentina it is the International Misery Fund. Congress has pressed the IMF for reforms of its operations since its recurrent failures in crisis management. In 2000, the Meltzer Commission examined the World Bank on behalf of the US Congress and found that most of its projects have been unsuccessful, and the bulk of its lending has gone to higher-income developing countries (which ensure a higher return on investment), so its impact on global poverty has been close to nil (Bello 2003). Subsequently the World Bank made combating poverty its priority, but this does not sit well with the neoclassical orthodoxies of the Treasury, which has pressured the World Bank to the point of weakening its credibility.

The WTO is stalled by mounting public criticism and seesawing American policies. It is no longer merely a tool of American power but also monitors the US (on tax breaks, steel tariffs and farm subsidies). Growing worldwide mobilization against the WTO, from the battle of Seattle to the World Social Forum, has made this an increasingly difficult and high-risk option. Earlier international NGOs blocked the Multilateral Agreement on Investments.

Arguably, there is no more Washington consensus; what remains is a disparate set of ad hoc Washington agendas. In view of the disarray of the international financial institutions, the idea of a "post-Washington consensus" papers over incoherence and improvization (Stiglitz 2002). In economics, the neoliberal orthodoxies are no longer broadly accepted; attention has long shifted from state failure to market failure, the importance of institutions, and themes such as social capital. After decades of structural adjustment, most developing countries are worse off. As a development policy, neoliberalism has been an utter failure—not surprisingly because it is a regime of financial discipline.

Since the Washington consensus followed the compass of American neoliberalism, its status rises and falls with the success or failure of the American economy, which has been losing points in its own right. Signals of failure are the collapse of the new economy, followed by the Enron series of corporate scandals, Wall Street decline, and recession. A reorientation of US policies would be in the cards at any rate. The decomposition of the neoliberal order sheds light on the subsequent American turn to "permanent war."

Twenty years of rampant neoliberalism created a culture and habitus of neoliberalism. An anthropological study of the "meanings of the market" in western culture finds as the basic assumptions of the market model that the world consists of free individuals, who are instrumentally rational and operate in a world that consists only of buyers and sellers (Carrier 1997). The peculiar ethos of casino capitalism that neoliberal globalization unleashed on the world is ultimately an occidental cargo cult. Its secret rituals include Dixie capitalism, Wall Street wizardry and Cold War strategy.

References

Applebome, P. 1996. *Dixie Rising: How the South is Shaping American Values, Politics and Culture*. New York: Times Books.

Beck, U. 2001. The Chernobyl of Globalization. *Financial Times*, November 6.

Bello, W. 2003. *Deglobalization: Ideas for a New World-Economy*. London: Zed Books.

Carrier, J. (ed.). 1997. *Meanings of the Market: The Free Market in Western Culture*. Oxford: Berg.

Cassidy, J. 2002. Master of Disaster. *The New Yorker*, July 15.

Cummings, S. 1998. *The Dixiefication of America: The American Odyssey into the Conservative Economic Trap*. Westport, CT: Praeger.

Halliday, F. 1986. *The Second Cold War*. London: Verso.

Hutton, W. 2002. *The World We're In*. London: Little, Brown.

Hutton, W. and A. Giddens (eds). 2000. *Global Capitalism*. New York: New Press.

Jansson, D. 2003. Internal Orientalism in America: W.J. Cash's *The Mind of the South* and the Spatial Construction of American National Identity. *Political Geography* 22: 293–316.

Johnson, C. 2002. American Militarism and Blowback: The Costs of Letting the Pentagon Dominate Foreign Policy. *New Political Science* 24(1): 21–38.

Lind, M. 2003. *Made in Texas: George W. Bush and the Southern Takeover of American Politics*. New York: Basic Books.

Pieterse, J.N. 2001. *Development Theory: Deconstructions/Reconstructions*. London: Sage.

Porter, M. 1990. *The Competitive Advantage of Nations*. New York: Free Press.

Soros, G. 1998. *The Crisis of Global Capitalism*. New York: Public Affairs.

Stiglitz, J. 2002. *Globalization and its Discontents*. New York: Norton.

Thacker, S. 1999. The High Politics of IMF Lending. *World Politics* 52(1): 38–75.

Tickell, A. and J. Peck. 2003. Making Global Rules: Globalisation or Neoliberalisation? in J. Peck and H. Cheung (eds), *Remaking the Global Economy: Economic-Geographical Perspectives*. London: Sage.

Williamson, J. 1990. What Washington Means by Policy Reform, in J. Williamson (ed.), *Latin American Adjustment: How Much Has Happened?* Washington, D.C.: Institute for International Economics.

Wood, P. 2003. The Rise of the Prison-Industrial Complex in the United States in A. Coyle, A. Campbell and R. Neufeld (eds), *Capitalist Punishment: Prison Privatization and Human Rights*. Atlanta, GA and London: Clarity Press and Zed, pp. 16–29.

Zinn, H. 1964. *The Southern Mystique*. New York: Knopf.

3

Business as Usual or Radical Shift?

Theorizing the Relationship between US Hegemony and Globalization

Ray Kiely

The purpose of this essay is to examine the relationship between US hegemony, contemporary imperialism and globalization. It specifically examines the claims that the more belligerent foreign policy of the US state since the terrorist attacks in September 2001 constitutes a significant departure from "globalization." In order to address this question, we need to examine what is (or was?) meant by globalization, consider the practices of the Bush Administration and relate these to claims made concerning the nature of globalization, and deliberate on the extent to which these constitute a break from globalization. In order to address these questions, we need to consider in detail the claims made concerning globalization, and a critique of some of these claims are central to the essay's overall argument. Specifically, this chapter challenges the claims made by a body of thought that can be called globalization theory, focusing on the flawed methodology of this theory and its problematic interpretation of the decade of globalization in the 1990s. This critique is then used to challenge the argument that post-"September 11," US foreign policy represented an unambiguous and regressive retreat from the potential of globalization. While there are crucial differences between the 1990s and post-2001, there are also considerable continuities. Crucial to these continuities is the neoliberal character of contemporary globalization. In making these arguments, the relationship between the US state and imperialism will also be addressed.

The chapter is divided into three sections. First, globalization and globalization theory are considered, along with the argument that US foreign policy from 2001 represents a significant break from the 1990s. Second, these arguments are subject to a critique based on a rejection of globalization theory and its claims concerning international relations in the 1990s, and the proposition that Bush II was characterized by significant continuity (as well as considerable change) in the nature of US foreign policy. Third, the implications of these arguments are addressed through a consideration of the wider relationship between the US state, and the character of contemporary "globalization" and "imperialism."

THE END OF GLOBALIZATION? THEORY, POLITICS AND THE 2001 "BREAK"

Globalization was undoubtedly central to political debate in the 1990s. This was true in the academic social sciences, but equally in mainstream (and alternative) political discourse. But as the introduction to this book has already shown, precise definitions of globalization were less than clear. Giddens' definition (see Introduction) was often accepted, but this amounted to little more than a description of certain very general trends. There was actually little agreement on the extent, different ways of measuring, and the desirability of globalization. Often these debates cut across each other precisely because of this lack of clarity. It will become clear in due course that this is an important part of the argument of this chapter, but first we need to consider the claims made for the idea of globalization.

In what remains the most comprehensive text on globalization, Held and his collaborators defined it as "the widening, deepening and speeding up of world-wide interconnectedness in all aspects of contemporary social life, from the cultural to the criminal, the financial to the spiritual" (Held et al. 1999: 2). They go on to refer to "(a) process (or set of processes) which embodies a transformation in the spatial organization of social relations and transactions—assessed in terms of their extensity, velocity and impact—generating transcontinental or interregional flows and networks of activity, interaction, and the exercise of power" (ibid.: 16). Briefly then, globalization appears to refer to a set of processes that have increased interconnectedness across the globe, and that crucially, these connections in many respects transcend the narrow boundaries of the nation state. Central to this argument is the idea of a widening of "spatiality" through the severing of the intrinsic connection between territoriality and polity. Globalization, thus, refers to de-territorialization, or "a far reaching change in the nature of social space" (Scholte 2000: 46). Whereas previous eras had seen a compression of time and space that reduced the impact of location, globalization is "supra-territorial," in which the only limit is planetary or global.

These contentions have enormous political implications, for globalization is said to have given rise to such far-reaching changes that the "international," or relations between nation-states, may be potentially a thing of the past. Certainly, no globalization theorist actually argues this point, and most qualify statements such as Giddens' (1999: 18) contention that "following the dissolution of the Cold War, most nations no longer have enemies," or indeed, Scholte's (2000: 61) claim that "(w)e no longer inhabit a territorialist world." Nevertheless, some globalization theorists[1] drew particular, optimistic conclusions from the deepening and stretching of social relations that was said to characterize globalization. In particular, the argument was made that the stretching of social relations across national borders provided the basis for a new cosmopolitanism, in which a genuinely global, universal interest could result (Held and McGrew 2002). This was linked not only to the end of the Cold War, but also to the idea that there are genuinely global problems that require cooperation between states, the rise of various institutions of multilateral global governance, and the emergence of a transnational civil society, in which global, non-state actors could put pressure on nation-states and international institutions in order to facilitate "global justice." This relatively optimistic perspective was usually separated from the dominance of neoliberal economic policies (Held et al. 1999), although in some cases the claim was made that the 1990s represented a shift towards a post-neoliberal world (Giddens 2000). This was usually associated with the "third way" of the Clinton and Blair governments in particular, but also to many governments in the South that supported market expansion alongside appropriate institutional changes that could facilitate such expansion. This was linked to World Bank and IMF policies that supported "good governance," "market friendly intervention," the promotion of "social capital," and "poverty reduction." Even for those writers that remained critical of the World Bank and IMF, there was considerable hope that the extension of multilateral institutions could provide the potential for democratization of such institutions. Much was therefore made of the new post-Cold War extension of the principles of "liberal internationalism" through expansion of the European Union, the creation of the World Trade Organization, and the creation of new regional agreements, such as the North American Free Trade Agreement. While these were considered to be far from perfect vehicles of global democratization, they were also said to have some potential in that they were at least preferable to an international order composed of self-interested nation-states.

For globalization theory, the terrorist attacks of September 11 undermined this potentially better future. The attacks themselves were, of course, atrocities carried out by reactionary political forces that would have little sympathy with the liberal cosmopolitanism advocated by globalization theorists. But equally, the response of the Bush Administration to these attacks laid the basis for what some globalization theorists have called a "regressive globalism" associated with the Bush II Doctrine. In this account, regressive globalizers "are individuals, groups, firms, or even governments that favour globalisation when it is in their particular interest and irrespective of any negative consequences for others" (Kaldor et al. 2003: 5). Globalization theorists reject the Bush II Doctrine on the grounds that it breaks with the expansion of multilateral governance, using the United Nations (UN) as a simple tool of US state interests. This is most visible in the cases of the wars in Afghanistan and especially Iraq. Held (2003) and Archibugi (2000) thus, both criticize the war in Afghanistan as it attacked a state rather than using the forces of international law and international policing cooperation to undermine the Al-Qaeda terrorist network. In the case of Iraq, globalization theorists generally reject the contempt that the Bush II Administration (among others) showed for the UN, and regard the war as an affront to the principles of international law and multilateral cooperation. Not all globalization theorists agree, and Anthony Giddens for one has supported the actions of British Prime Minister Tony Blair in supporting the war in Iraq. Below, I return to the question of Tony Blair in the context of a wider discussion of globalization. For the moment though, we need to return to the question of the Bush II Administration. Essentially then, most globalization theorists regard world events since 2001 with dismay, arguing that the limited but real advances in "global governance" have been reversed by the actions of the Bush Administration. Indeed, this applies not only to the question of military action, but also to issues such as non-cooperation on arms limitation, the international criminal court, environmental regulation, and protection of US industries from foreign competition. The potential for progressive globalization has thus given way to the self-interested "realist" foreign policy of the Bush II government.

GLOBALIZATION THEORY AND GLOBALIZATION AFTER 2001: QUESTIONING THE BREAK

There is plenty of evidence to support the idea of a radical break in US foreign policy from 2001 onwards. The Bush Administration has undoubtedly been more unilateralist than its predecessor. Moreover, the neoconservative defeat of the Democrats did represent an important shift away from Clintonite policies. This was rooted not only in the more overt unilateralism of Bush II, but was also the product of an America-first strategy that combined the idea of saving the promotion of forward thinking Americanization abroad, while simultaneously restoring the values of a mythical America at home (Lieven 2004). These ideas are far from novel in US political culture, but they were central to the Bush II Administration's critique of Clinton, who was accused of not pursuing primacy with enough vigor abroad (see below), and who was regarded as a decadent liberal at home.

But this section suggests that the extent of the break may not be as great as is often suggested, and that indeed there are areas of substantial continuity and convergence between Democrats and Republicans. This is not the place to discuss this in anything like sufficient detail, but some areas of crossover in foreign policy will be discussed, not least because they are central to understanding the reality of "actually existing globalization." In particular, I will suggest that Clinton was not as multilateral, and equally, Bush II was not as "anti-globalist" as is sometimes suggested. I will then move on to suggest that these observations have implications for understanding the reality of globalization, under both Clinton and Bush II, and that the central continuity is based on an intrinsic link between US hegemony and the *neoliberal* nature of contemporary global capitalism. This issue is taken up further in the third and final section, but the implications of this point are first examined through a critique of globalization theory, which completes this section.

The first point then relates to the multilateralism of Clinton and unilateralism of Bush II. Certainly the neoconservatives that were influential in the Bush Administration were critical of Clinton's multilateralism and (comparative) reluctance to fully utilize hard, military power against perceived enemies. Whether or not this is an accurate representation of those presidencies is debatable, and some commentators have argued that Clinton was particularly effective in strengthening US interests against potential competitors (Bacevich 2002). However, it would be mistaken to draw the conclusion that this was sufficient to constitute a radical break. Indeed, the much cited neoconservative Project for the New American Century, founded in 1997, sees itself as continuing the project of liberal internationalist expansion. Indeed, it was actually more *optimistic* concerning the expansion of liberalism than its predecessors. In 2000, for instance, the Project argues that there was a need for substantial military presence in the Gulf, and that this issue transcended "the issue of the regime of Saddam Hussein," and must be linked to a broad project to democratize the whole of the Middle East (Project for the New American Century 2000). Perhaps the most prominent neoconservative thinker/official, Paul Wolfowitz (2000) has argued that "nothing could be less realistic than the version of the 'realist' view of foreign policy that dismisses human rights as an important tool of American foreign policy...(W)hat is most impressive is how often promoting democracy has actually advanced American interests." The US' National Security Strategy for 2002 stated that "(t)he United States will use this moment of opportunity to extend the benefits of freedom across the globe.... We will actively work to bring the hope of democracy, development, free markets, and free trade to every corner of the world" (NSS 2002). Neoconservatives themselves, therefore, partially endorse Wilsonian liberal internationalism, albeit in ways in which they are more prepared to use military power to promote American liberalism abroad (Kagan and Kristol 2000).

These principles were of course applied inconsistently, in part because unilateralism itself involves considerable compromise with democratic principles. Moreover, neoconservatives do often betray a straightforward "realist" fear of the rise of rival powers to US dominance, and this is particularly applied to the rise of China. Indeed, Wolfowitz had argued for preventive policies against potential competitors in 1992, an argument treated with considerable hostility at the time (see Bacevich 2002: 44). Neoconservative foreign policy therefore, is based on an uneasy combination of liberal cosmopolitanism and realism. But is this so different from the Clinton Administration? Advocates of US unilateralism like Philip Bobbit (2002: 228) admired (and worked for) Clinton's presidency, arguing that the Clinton years constituted a sea change in international relations, as the principle of national sovereignty was challenged, and intervention justified on the basis of defence of human rights, anti-terrorism and to block nuclear proliferation. The long-term goal of such interventions was incorporation into the liberal sphere through the extension of the market state (ibid). While multilateralism may be preferable, unilateralism is regarded as inevitable given the role of the US state in the international order, where "it is simply not in the same position as other states, and therefore should not be shamed by charges of hypocrisy when it fails to adopt the regimes that it urges on others" (ibid.: 691). This continuity is even recognized by some of Clinton's fiercest neoconservative critics, including Wolfowitz (2000) himself, who argues that even prior to September 11, many had come round to the arguments that he had made in 1992. His disagreement with Clinton was not that this strategy for US primacy had been rejected, but that it had not been pursued with sufficient clarity and zeal. Moreover, post-"September 11", it was not only neoconservatives who were openly advocating the use of "hard" power, in part to deter potential rivals (though it is far from clear how military power could be used against China). This more open advocacy of military power was one of the reasons why neoconservatives were so critical of Clinton's policy of giving less priority to military spending (from 1992 to 2000, military spending as a percentage of GDP fell from 4.72 percent to 2.99 percent—Pollin 2003: 29). Neoconservatives called for renewal of the Reagan Doctrine (Project for the New American Century 2000) and the more overt use of US hard power.

But equally, before the fiasco of the war and its aftermath in Iraq, neoconservatives were very optimistic about the capacity of the US to expand democracy in the Middle East. Indeed, neoconservative advocacy of the democratization of the Middle East is a major source of concern to traditional realists in the Republican Party (Halper and Clarke 2004; Hulsman 2004). Neoconservative commentator Thomas Barnett (2003) divides the world into a "functioning core" and a "non-integrating gap," and bases the divide in terms of the degree of states' incorporation into "globalization." Mazarr (2003: 509), a senior official at the Department of Defense and admirer of Bush's "idealism," goes as far as suggesting that it represents an idealism worthy of the liberal internationalism of Woodrow Wilson. What is crucial here is the belief that the world can be re-made in the US' own self-image, and therefore, in the process human rights, democracy and freedom can be universalized. As two prominent

neoconservatives argued, "democracy is a political choice, an act of will...
(h)istory suggest it comes most effectively from the United States" (Kaplan and
Kristol 2003: 108–9) In this argument, liberal cosmopolitan ideals can be unilaterally promoted by the US state, rather than say, through the United Nations.
This may of course be contradictory, "since such principles and ideals are
incompatible with the imposed, unelected global dominance of any single
nation" (Singer 2004: 192). But it is also a policy committed—however selec-
tively, hypocritically and counter-productively—to liberal expansion.

Of course, it is liberal expansion through unilateral means, but was Clinton
as committed a multilateralist as is sometimes implied? We have already noted
the similarity in terms of dealing with potential competitors between Clinton
and Bush. But equally, Clinton was involved in the exercise of military adven-
tures in the former Yugoslavia, Sudan, Afghanistan and Iraq, none of which had
UN backing (although retrospective approval was given in the first case). It was
also under Clinton—though admittedly at times because of Congress—that the
US stalled on decisions concerning the International Criminal Court, arms
reduction and enhanced international environmental regulation. Clinton—and
the Democratic Party more generally—supported the wars in Afghanistan and
Iraq (Cockburn 2004). Indeed, it could be argued that this support provides
some clue as to the thinking behind the Bush–Blair alliance in the run-up to
war in Iraq. Both the neoconservatives and Blair's Third Way support the
expansion of liberal democracy and the "free market" in the developing world,
and both are hopelessly optimistic about the ease with which such an imposition
can have the desired, and expected outcomes. This may involve double standards
as both Bush II and Blair have been more than prepared to support authoritarian regimes, including many in the coalition against terror. But what is more
relevant to our concerns here is that both believe that US hegemony is good for
the whole world, and both are basically prepared to utilize hard power in order
to achieve this aim. In his speech to the US Congress on July 18, 2003, Blair made
the following statements:

Ours are not western values. They are the universal values of the human spirit...What you
can bequeath to this anxious world is the light of liberty...Why America?...(B)ecause destiny
puts you in this place in history, in this moment in time, and the task is yours to do. And
our job, my nation...our job is to be there with you. You are not going to be alone. We'll
be with you in this fight for liberty. (Quoted in Coates and Krieger 2004: 9)

Clearly, Blair is committed to the notion that the national interest of the United
States and the universal interest of humanity is inseparable, an argument
ironically with deep roots in old Labour policies (Coates and Krieger 2004).
What is different from old Labour, but fully compatible with Bush II and
Clinton, is the belief that the path to prosperity is through the adoption of
"market friendly" policies accompanied by liberal democratic government. The

theme that above all unifies Clinton, Blair and Bush II, then, is the project of liberal expansion. This liberal internationalism has a long history, and has been applied to the Cold War era. In practice, this liberalism was selective and often meant support for authoritarian regimes. But the crucial difference is that the period from 1945 until the 1980s was one in which "liberal internationalism" was based on "neo-Keynesian liberal internationalism," and since then we have seen the expansion of neoliberal internationalism. The grounds for optimism that pervades the work of among others, globalization theorists, is based on the fact that the post-Cold War period could be a genuine era of liberal internationalism, as there is no longer any conflict between capitalism and communism. More critical globalization theorists, such as Held and McGrew, attempt to separate this optimism from the reality of neoliberal globalization, and call for reforms that effectively globalize social democracy (Held 1996). This position certainly does not deserve outright rejection, but it is still subject to the charge of overoptimism concerning the reality of the 1990s and, as a result, an exaggeration of the break in US policy before and after 2001.

The Cold War was characterized not only by a strategy of "containment," which aimed to limit the expansion of communism, often through military and other support for authoritarian regimes, but also by one of "enlargement," which meant the expansion of capitalism and world markets. This expansion became the key strategy of the Clinton Administration. Clinton's National Security Adviser Anthony Lake (1993) argued for a strategy of "enlargement of the world's free community of market democracies." This was linked to the idea of democratic peace between liberal states (Doyle 1983) and enhanced prosperity through the expansion of "free markets." In practice, democratic expansion of a kind did take place but was limited, as were the results of market expansion, but more important for the moment is the fact that this commitment was fully endorsed by the Bush II Administration. Thus, Chapter 6 of the 2002 National Security Strategy of the United States was entitled "Ignite a New Era of Economic Growth through Free Markets and Free Trade." Similarly, in 1999, Tony Blair explicitly linked market expansion and globalization, arguing that

(w)e are all internationalists now whether we like it or not...We cannot refuse to participate in global markets if we want to prosper. We cannot ignore new political ideas in global markets if we want to prosper...Globalisation has transformed our economies and our working practices...Any government that thinks it can go it alone is wrong. If the markets don't like your policies they will punish you. (Blair 1999)

In this account, globalization is regarded as a purely external force, beyond the power of individual states, with the implication that because of the unquestioned power of "the markets," governments must adjust accordingly. Al Gore (1999) made the same point, arguing that "(i)n this fast moving, fast changing global economy—when the free flow of dollars and data are sources of economic and political strength, and whole new industries are born every day—governments must be lean, nimble, and creative or they will surely be left behind."

It is clear then, that there is substantial continuity in terms of neoliberal expansion. This is justified on the universalist grounds that a supposedly global free market promotes a level playing field, and so therefore, enhances the development potential of the poorer countries. This argument basically constitutes an endorsement of neo-classical interpretations of the theory of comparative advantage, in which countries specialize in those goods they can produce most cheaply and efficiently, and exchange their exports for the goods in which others have a comparative advantage. In this way, there is a mutual levelling up through the benefits of specialization (Bhagwati 2004; Wolf 2004). But this argument first ignores the selectivity of free trade promotion, and much has been made of the double standards of the Bush II Administration in promoting "free markets" abroad while protecting industry and agriculture at home. This is a fair point, but while it is true that Bush II was more explicitly protectionist than his predecessor, Clinton also employed protectionist policies, as did all postwar US Presidents. This was particularly true in agriculture but applied in other sectors, and Clinton also discussed the possibility of labor standards at the WTO talks in Seattle, a major reason for their collapse in late 1999. But there is a more important point to be made that has far wider implications, which is that even if they were consistently implemented, free trade policies would not necessarily lead to mutual advantage. This is not an argument against trade in itself, but more a recognition that "universal" free trade abstracts from the unequal basis on which countries trade. This is rooted in the unequal structures of production that ensure that established producers have competitive advantages over later developers. These advantages are reflected in more advanced technologies, Research and Development facilities, skills, productivity, infrastructures, marketing, and credit. All these serve to reinforce advantages for certain localities over others. The result for later developers is that free trade can undermine the long-term development of productive, competitive sectors. Free trade therefore benefits the most powerful at the expense of weaker, less competitive producers. Indeed, in most cases of successful capitalist development after Britain, this has occurred through selective protectionist policies (Chang 2002).

The multilateral turn in the 1990s can partly be seen in this light. The creation of the World Trade Organization in 1995 attempted to formalize the extension of free trade policies—precisely the kind of policies that were *not* practiced by the established producers (Wade 2003). This is why some critics have argued that the current free trade era is one that hinders rather than promotes "development" (Kiely 2005a: chs. 2, 4, and 5). The rapid growth rates in China and India are less the product of neoliberal policies and more a result of successful state intervention that includes continued selective protection, combined with capital friendly policies such as cheap and controlled labor. This is reinforced by continued controls on the movement of financial capital, which challenges the claims made for the opportunities presented by globalization. Before we return to the question of financial capital below, this discussion has enormous implications for understanding the limitations of multilateralism. In the case of the WTO, the principle of "one member one vote" is ineffective because it abstracts from the "market power" of the various nation-states that have signed to the WTO. Certainly, Bush II has been more critical of the WTO than Clinton, but this does not mean that Clinton represented benign multilateralism and Bush malign unilateralism, because the former is not necessarily a threat to US interests. WTO negotiations have never actually led to a vote on the principle of "one member one vote," but have involved less than open negotiations dominated by the most powerful states. Moreover, the basic sanction that the WTO can carry out—permission for a state that has faced discriminatory practices by another state to implement similar trade measures against the latter—similarly ignores the "market powers" involved in such transactions. Even if we leave aside the time and cost of such disputes, a decision in favor of a poor, trade dependent country against the US is unlikely to impact on the US, but if the decision works the other way than the result could be a catastrophe. This argument is made not to simply dismiss the WTO out of hand, where there are limited signs of a collective voice among poorer nations, but it is made to problematize the idea that multilateralism is as benign or independent of powerful nation-states as is sometimes implied.[2]

Indeed, this point can be extended to multilateralism in the 1990s. Rather than the 1990s providing an unambiguous opportunity for the extension of democratic global governance, as globalization theory contends, it was actually an era in which the most powerful nation-states saw an opportunity for liberal democratic and market expansion. Just as crucially, however, was the fact that given that there was no longer an alternative superpower, in this context weaker states actively courted alliance with the United States and its allies. This multilateralism was therefore, not only compromised by the selective approach of the most powerful states—the WTO but closed negotiations, the UN but used only when required—but also by the wider context in which these institutions operated. That such multilateralism was selective was hardly surprising, as similar debates had dominated discussion at the Bretton Woods conference of 1944, when US interests clearly won the day (Kiely 2005a: ch. 3). Similarly, the much heralded democratization of the 1990s was itself highly selective, amounting to limited political change, as the context of intensified inequality, lower growth and effective decision-making through the IMF and World Bank, tended to undermine or at least limit democratic advance.

In this section then, I have challenged the idea that there is a simple break between Clinton and Bush II, or between globalization and multilateralism on the one hand, and US self-interest and unilateralism on the other. This challenges the claims of *globalization* theory (although it does not necessarily challenge *theories of globalization*, as we will see). This has wider implications, which go to the heart of the problems of globalization theory. This is the conflation of two ways of understanding globalization: does it refer to a certain set of outcomes, or does it actually cause such outcomes? It is this conflation that lies at the heart of globalization theory; as Rosenberg (2000) has convincingly argued, the basic problem with this theory is that it replaces a social theory with one that excessively focuses on space. Thus, to return to the definitions cited at the start of this chapter, globalization theory tells us nothing about the character, the power relations, or the driving force of global interconnections. These are simply assumed to be inevitable and desirable, and (as with the Blair and Gore quotations above), something to which states must respond. The optimism is then derived from the multilateralism that is said to be the necessary result, but as we have seen, this ignores the non-institutional power that undermines genuine multilateralism. Moreover, it also downplays the neoliberal character of contemporary globalization. The likes of Scholte, Kaldor, Held and others are not complicit with neoliberal hegemony, but insofar as they critique neoliberalism, they do so by breaking with their claims regarding globalization. In Giddens' case, however, there is undoubtedly considerable continuity. In true third way fashion, he argues that globalization is a reality to which "new politics" must respond. Hay and Watson (1999: 422) draw out the general implications of this argument:

Like it or not, to accept the radical stance on globalisation as unquestioningly as Giddens does is to appeal to a set of ideas which have long been taken hostage by a distinctively neoliberal articulation of systemic economic "imperatives". Moreover, so long as this continues to be understood as just "how things are," the political space for democratising globalising tendencies and once more laying neoliberal "common-sense" open to question would appear to be strictly limited.

Put differently, globalization theory can all too easily accept the political parameters established by the victory of neoliberalism in the 1980s, which argued for the primacy of market forces, free trade, liberalized finance, and open competition. This neoliberal globalization is neither inevitable nor desirable. At best, globalization theory underestimates the neoliberal nature of the international order, and at worst, apologizes for it. Moreover, even in its more critical variants, this theory does not provide a convincing account of the nature of the contemporary international, or indeed global, order. The following section 3 attempts to provide the basis for an alternative account.

US HEGEMONY, IMPERIALISM AND GLOBALIZATION

An alternative approach to globalization theory is to emphasize the imperialist nature of the international order. The language of imperialism has returned with a vengeance since 2001, not least among those on the right (and some on the left) advocating form of benign, "liberal imperialism." It is not my intention to provide an assessment of these arguments here, and I have provided critiques elsewhere (Kiely 2005a: ch. 8; 2005b: ch. 3 and 5). Instead, here the focus will be on the utility of classical Marxist theories of imperialism. These are associated with Lenin, Bukharin, Hilferding and Luxemburg. The arguments of the first two have particularly been revived recently, and I want to briefly address them here.

After Marx's death, in the context of a new era of colonial expansion and the build up to the First World War, Marxists attempted to develop a theory of capitalist imperialism. These theories linked the rivalry between imperialist powers before 1914 to what they perceived to be a new stage of capitalism. Thus, Lenin (1975) argued that imperialism had five characteristics: concentration of capital which led to monopoly; the merger of bank and industrial capital (financial capital); the export of capital; the formation of trusts and cartels; and the territorial division of the world. Monopoly was for Lenin a key characteristic and this was linked to the concentration of production, seizure of raw materials, the rise of national banks, and colonial policy. This tendency towards monopoly did not mean the end of competition but rather its intensification. Bukharin (1972: 108–9) further developed this contention, arguing that the world-economy was dominated by competing blocs of nationally organized capital. Against Kautsky (2002), both Lenin and Bukharin argued that this intensified economic competition led to military conflict and the inevitability of war. Some theorists of the current new imperialism[3] argue that we are witnessing a repeat of the situation prior to the First World War. The war on terror and liberal humanitarianism are said to be merely ideological covers for the latest imperialist phase of capitalist expansion, and the conflicts that arise between the imperialist powers as a result. According to this theory, since the collapse of Communism we have returned to the situation of inter-imperialist rivalry that characterized the pre-Cold War era. This does not mean that the confrontations are necessarily direct—"(m)ore typically they involve, as they have done throughout the history of imperialism, minor powers— 'rogue states' in the modern parlance" (Rees 2001: 23). Thus, the 1991 Gulf War upheld US prestige against Germany and Japan, the 1999 conflict over Kosovo/ Serbia promoted US hegemony at the expense of the European Union, and the 2001 conflict in Afghanistan "hemmed in" Russia, Iran and Europe (Callinicos et al. 1994; Rees 2001). The 2003 conflict in Iraq was similarly a war exercised by the US for guaranteed long-term oil supplies, which involved the defeat of rivals like France and Germany, as well as potential long-term rivals such as Russia and China (Morgan 2003). Thus, for theorists of the new imperialism, Lenin and Bukharin's approach, which focuses on the international expansion of capitalism and inter-imperial rivalry, remains indispensable for understanding contemporary politics.

There are important reasons for questioning much of this approach. First, there were serious problems with these theories even in 1914. For example, there was little evidence of a close correlation between monopoly and the export of capital; accumulation within the exporting countries increased in this period, and much of the capital that was exported was actually to other "advanced" capitalist countries, and not to the colonies and semi-colonies (Olle and Schoeller 1982; Panitch and Gindin 2004). In terms of the theory's applicability to the current era, there are also a number of problems.

While the theory recognizes that some important changes have occurred, it is far from clear that it can deal with the full significance of these changes. Most obviously, colonialism is largely dead. Most nations have political independence, and many have developed strong indigenous classes—both exploiters and exploited—and states, with their own set of interests, which are not reducible to the imperialism of the big powers. The argument that the conflicts of the 1990s were simply arenas where imperialist rivalries were played ignores the local dynamics that led to these conflicts in the first place, and betrays a continued commitment to the methodology of underdevelopment theory. It may be true that the Gulf War of 1991 was in part about US imperialism, but it was also about the invasion of Kuwait by Saddam Hussein. The war that followed was primarily concerned with commercial and strategic interests, and reflected double standards, but it was far more than simply "functional" to the needs of imperialism. The small power imperialism of the Iraqi regime in 1991 is barely mentioned in these accounts, as "local" conflicts appear to be completely determined by global (big power) imperialist conflicts. The analysis, therefore, lacks a convincing account of processes of state formation and development, and primitive accumulation in the periphery.

Moreover, imperialist relations among the major powers have also changed substantially. The problems of classical theories notwithstanding (see above), the main trend before World War I was the concentration of capital on a national level, with colonial annexation facilitating market access, investment and raw materials (Hilferding 1981: 225). Today we have a far greater internationalization of capital, which flows mainly between First World countries. This scenario is not so different from the pre-1914 era, but what is novel is the rise of manufacturing in the periphery, and most crucially, the fact that the capital that is invested in developing countries does not originate from one nation. This does not mean that such capital is no longer tied to particular nation-states, but it does mean that the world cannot be divided into *exclusive* blocs. Economic competition has in many ways intensified, but in a free trade rather than colonial monopoly/territorial acquisition environment, power is exercised more by directly "economic" rather than "political" or military means (Green 2002: 58–59; Went 2002–3: 490). Moreover, although economic competition between major powers continues to exist, it does not *necessarily* lead to war. Indeed, given the overwhelming superiority of the US military, such a scenario is unthinkable.

The most convincing relevant Marxist account of imperialism is Kautsky's theory of ultra-imperialism that recognizes the possibility of cooperation between nation-states even as capitalist economic competition persists. Kautsky failed to adequately theorize the ways in which this cooperation could be led by a dominant state, and paid insufficient attention to the reality of uneven development in this ultra-imperialist order. Nevertheless, his theory is more relevant to understanding the current world order than those of either Lenin or Bukharin. What is equally clear is that, since 1945 at least, the US has not acted as a colonial power, but has attempted to secure its hegemony through allied sovereign states. Insofar as this relates to the "capitalist market," it is based on the recognition that sovereign states represent an important means of regulating capital. US hegemony is thus exercised through state sovereignty, a strategy that carries all sorts of risks as dominant political actors in the developing world may at times challenge "Americanism" within their own territories. These challenges have at times forced a variety of interventions based on the idea that what is good for the US state is also good for global capital, but which vary according to a number of political projects and policy proposals that cannot be reduced to the "logic of imperialism." Interventions have also taken place in contested areas of state formation where primitive accumulation has been particularly violent, factors which can be linked to the uneven development of capitalism and the relative marginalization of some areas of the globe that has intensified with neoliberalism. For all these reasons, post-1945 imperialism has been ultra-imperialist and led by the US state at one and the same time. Equally, the record of these military interventions—despite the rhetoric of promoting human rights and freedom—is poor.

The contemporary international order can thus be characterized as one based on an ultra-imperialist order, but led by a dominant state. In this order, US hegemony has changed its form, particularly since the 1970s and 1980s, and this is related to the rise of neoliberalism. The end of the gold–dollar link and of fixed exchange rates from 1971–73 was part of a strategy designed to recover competitiveness in industrial production. In particular, the US governments of Nixon, Ford, and (for a time) Carter pursued expansionary monetary policies and a relatively weak dollar, which were designed to increase production both at home and through cheaper exports abroad. However, the policy led to inflation and potentially undermined the international role of the dollar, and so a new tight monetary policy was adopted in 1979 under Carter, and especially under Ronald Reagan. In the early 1980s, the money supply came under tighter control, there were tax cuts for the wealthy, and increased deregulation of capital investment. From 1982 onwards, there was a big increase in military spending and a marked intensification of Cold War hostilities. The effect of these policies was a massive increase in the US' trade and budget deficits, and an increase in competition for capital investment to finance these deficits (Arrighi 1994; 2003). This involved an increase in interest rates to attract financial capital to the US, which, in turn led to a massive increase in interest payments for countries that had built up debt in the 1970s. The 1980s and 1990s, therefore, saw the promotion of continued US hegemony through the expansion of financial capital. US governments have therefore had some success in using the international role of the dollar to maintain hegemony since the 1980s, based on financing deficits through the selling of government debt securities (bonds), continued (but possibly declining) international demand for the dollar, and the promotion of liberalized financial markets, as in the East Asian financial crisis of 1997–98, which aims to maintain financial hegemony (Wade 2003). Moreover, its effective control of international financial institutions such as the IMF and World Bank, and the influence of the US Treasury and Federal Reserve Bank reinforces this hegemony (Peet 2003). Thus, for all the hype about the "new economy" boom of the 1990s, the United States became increasingly dependent on foreign purchase of debt securities, which itself helped to maintain a high value dollar in the absence of high interest rates, as well as low inflation due to cheap imports (Gowan 2001: 363).

The US now possesses an overwhelming military force in the world order, alongside the largest trade deficit in the world, and since the "election" of Bush, a massively increasing budget deficit. In 2001 and 2002, military spending grew by 6 percent and 10 percent a year, which amounted to around 65 percent and 80 percent of total increases in Federal government spending in those years (Brenner 2003: 21). Its military budget figures were already far higher than most of the combined spending of the next twelve or so powers, and at least twenty-six times greater than that of the seven main "axis of evil" countries. At the same time, since early 2000, the Federal budget deficit has grown from 1.8 percent of GDP to an estimated 3.7 percent in 2003 and 4.3 percent for 2004 (ibid). In 2001, the trade deficit was a record $435 billion, which increased to an unprecedented $489 billion by 2003 (*Monthly Review* 2003: 8). These deficits have been financed by foreigners speculating in the stock market, buying real estate, acquiring firms or setting up new sites, and buying US Treasury bonds. Equity purchases fell by 83 percent from 2000 to 2002 as share prices fell, and so there has been a sustained movement into buying government bonds. In 2001, 97 percent of the US current account deficit was financed by foreign purchases of these bonds. From 1992–2001, the foreign share of US national debt increased from 17 percent to 31 percent (ibid.: 10). None of this necessarily matters, so long as there is confidence in the US economy and the dollar, but there is a serious question mark as to whether a high trade deficits (5 percent of GDP in 2002) are sustainable—it is more sustainable for the US than for other countries because of the international role of the dollar, but ongoing deficits are likely to further erode this role. Continued US hegemony, therefore, rests on quite weak foundations, but it nevertheless remains a reality.

In terms of understanding globalization then, we have not seen a "hollowing out" of the nation-state. Indeed, in the postwar period we have seen the universalization of the nation-state system. But at the same time, what has changed is a generalized (but uneven) shift in nation-state policies, from an era of neo-Keynesian capitalism to one of neoliberal capitalism. This has impacted on the developed world through the end of full employment, the defeat of trade union protection for many workers, the resurgence of "flexible" labor markets, and the partial erosion of welfare states. In the developing world, it has led to an undermining of the space for states to promote developmental policies. As we saw above, pro-free trade arguments abstract from the market power of different traders, and in doing so they ignore the ways in which the "advanced" countries developed. The current era of neoliberal globalization can therefore be characterized as one based on the imperialism of free trade, in which established producers and nation-states effectively undermine the opportunities of others to develop. This leads to relative marginalization or unequal integration for many parts of the world, as free trade and liberal finance undermine the developmental prospects for much of the world. This intensifies political and social instability in the international order, which is combined with historical and social conflicts that further undermine stability. The international policing role of the United States should be seen in this context.

CONCLUSION

This chapter has examined two closely related issues: first, the extent to which the US state has broken from pro-globalization policies since 2001; and second, the broader question of what is globalization. My answer to these questions has focused on the similarities and differences between the "multilateral" 1990s and the "unilateral turn" after 2001, and I have shown that there are important differences. But equally, there are important similarities that relate to the expansion of neoliberalism and how, in the context of free trade and liberal finance, this is linked to the question of continued US hegemony. My discussion of these issues suggested that, while there are real differences between multilateralism and unilateralism (and by implication, institutions do matter), these may still be overstated. Certainly, the development of multilateral institutions does not necessarily lead to progress in terms of global democratic governance, nor indeed does it mean that US hegemony in a multilateral system is benign. The optimism of the "globalization talk" of the 1990s was thus misplaced, and this can be rooted in the weaknesses of globalization theory. As we saw, globalization theory made specific claims about "global society," and tended to be accompanied by a "cosmopolitan optimism." The problem in this approach was that just as globalization theory tended to ignore social relations, so cosmopolitanism tended to ignore the political form that such a philosophy could embrace. In both cases this could be linked to the fetishism of space, so that globalization focused on social relations beyond the territoriality of the nation-state, while cosmopolitanism focused on politics beyond the sovereignty of the nation state. Neither proposition was necessarily wrong, but both failed to specify the forms of social relations or politics beyond the state. Cosmopolitanism can thus be linked to the extension of "market forces" and global governance, or "humanitarian" military intervention; equally it could be tied to Marxist conceptions of international socialist revolution or anti-war politics. In the process of fetishizing spaces beyond nation-states, the specific content of politics can easily be lost.

The alternative account suggested in this essay, therefore focused on the continued centrality of a hierarchical nation-state system and the uneven outcomes of capitalist, neoliberal globalization. This suggests that the term imperialism retains some validity in the current international order, but it is an imperialism that differs sharply from the period 1880–1945. It is also one that can be differentiated from the postwar period, and it is one that sees a close relationship between US hegemony and neoliberalism. For all these reasons then, globalization theory remains unconvincing, but (in contrast to classical Marxist theories of imperialism) theories of globalization remain necessary. Finally, and by political implication, the reactionary nature of US foreign policy—and of many responses to this hegemony—does suggest that universalist, cosmopolitan alternatives are needed, but globalization theory has failed to convincingly specify what these may be.

Notes

1. A distinction should be made between globalization theory and theories of globalization. This will become clear in the argument that follows, but for now my focus is on the former, who suggest that globalization, rather than being the outcome of social processes, actually determines other factors. Not all globalization theorists are necessarily optimistic—Castells could be considered a pessimist for instance.

2. This begs the question of why states join the WTO in the first place. The simple answer is that it is better to be part of the formalized international trading order than not, and that of course trade can be beneficial, when at least compared to no trade. But this is not the same thing as arguing that because states choose to join the WTO, it must be fair and democratic. Such an argument betrays a hopeless optimism, assuming away the unequal social, political and economic context in which this institution operates, as well as the actual ways in which it operates.

3. My account of the "new imperialism" is specifically applied to those, like Callinicos, who call for a relatively straightforward "return to Lenin." The arguments above do however owe a debt to the essays in Panitch and Leys (2004).

References

Archibugi, D. 2000. Cosmopolitical Democracy. *New Left Review* 4: 137–50.
Arrighi, G. 1994. *The Long Twentieth Century*. London: Verso.
———. 2003. The Social and Political Economy of Global Turbulence. *New Left Review* 20: 5–71.
Bacevich, A. 2002. *American Empire*. Cambridge: Harvard University Press.
Barnett, T. 2003. The Pentagon's New Map. *Esquire*, March 1.
Bhagwati, J. 2004. *In Defence of Globalization*. Oxford: Oxford University Press.
Blair, T. 1999. *Doctrine of the International Community*. Speech to the Economic Club of Chicago. Available online at www.fco.gov.uk
Bobbit, P. 2002. *The Shield of Achilles*. New York: Knopf.
Brenner, R. 2003. Towards the Precipice. *London Review of Books* 25(3): 12–18.
Bukharin, N. 1972. *Imperialism and World-economy*. London: Merlin.
Callinicos, A., C. Harman, M. Gonzalez and J. Rees. 1994. *Marxism and the New Imperialism*. London: Bookmarks.
Castells, M. 1996. *The Rise of the Network Society*. Oxford: Blackwell.
Chang, H.J. 2002. *Kicking Away the Ladder*. London: Anthem.
Coates, D. and J. Krieger. 2004. *Blair's War*. Cambridge: Polity.
Cockburn, A. 2004. The Year of Surrendering Quietly. *New Left Review* 29: 5–25.
Doyle, M. 1983. Kant, Liberal Legacies and Foreign Affairs: Part One. *Philosophy and Public Affairs* 12(3): 205–35.
Giddens, A. 1999. *Runaway World*. Cambridge: Polity.
———. 2000. *The Third Way and its Critics*. Cambridge: Polity.
Gore, A. 1999. Remarks by Vice-President Al Gore. Available online at www.govinfo.library.unt.edu
Gowan, P. 2001. Explaining the American Boom: The Roles of "Globalisation" and US Global Power. *New Political Economy* 6(3): 359–74.
Green, P. 2002. "The Passage from Imperialism to Empire": A Commentary on *Empire* by Michael Hardt and Antonio Negri. *Historical Materialism* 10(1): 29–77.
Halper, S. and J. Clarke. 2004. *America Alone: The Neoconservatives and Global Order*. Cambridge: Cambridge University Press.
Hay, C. and M. Watson. 1999. Globalization: "Sceptical" Notes on the 1999 Reith Lectures. *Political Quarterly* 70(4): 418–25.
Held, D. 1996. *Democracy and the Global Order*. Cambridge: Polity.
———. 2003. Violence, Law and Justice in a Global Age, in D. Archibugi (ed.), *Debating Cosmopolitics*. London: Verso, pp. 184–202.
Held, D. and T. McGrew. 2002. *Globalization/Anti-Globalization*. Cambridge: Polity.
Held, D., T. McGrew, D. Goldblatt and J. Perraton. 1999. *Global Transformations*, Cambridge: Polity.
Hilferding, R. 1981. *Finance Capital*. London: Routledge and Kegan Paul.

Hulsman, J. 2004. The Coming Foreign Policy Civil Wars: Part Two—The Republicans. Available online at http://www.openDemocracy.com

Kagan, R. and W. Kristol. 2000. American Power—For What? *Commentary* (January) 30–32: 35–36.

Kaldor, M., H. Anheier and M. Glasius. 2003. Global Civil Society in an Age of Regressive Globalisation. In *Global Civil Society Yearbook*. 2003. Oxford: Oxford University Press, pp. 3–33.

Kaplan, L. and W. Kristol. 2003. *The War over Iraq: Saddam's Tyranny and America's Mission.* San Francisco: Encounter Books.

Kautsky, K. 2002. Ultra-Imperialism. *Workers Liberty* 2(3): 73–79.

Kiely, R. 2005a. *The Clash of Globalisations: Neoliberalism, the Third Way and Anti-Globalisation.* Leiden: Brill.

————. 2005b. *Global Myths, Imperial Realities.* London: Pluto.

Lake, A. 1993. From Containment to Enlargement. Available online at http://www.uiowa.edu

Lenin, V. 1975. *Imperialism: The Highest Stage of Capitalism.* Moscow: Progress.

Lieven, A. 2004. America Right or Wrong. Available online at http://www.openDemocracy.com

McGrew, A. 2000. A Second American Century? The United States and the New World Order? In A. McGrew (ed.), *Empire.* London: Hodder and Stoughton, pp. 211–50.

Mazarr, M. 2003. George W. Bush, Idealist. *International Affairs* 79(3): 503–22.

Monthly Review. 2003. Editorial: What Recovery?. 54(11): 1–14.

Morgan, P. 2003. Iraq, in F. Reza (ed.), *Anti-Imperialism.* London: Bookmarks, pp. 107–16.

National Security Strategy. 2002. *The National Security Strategy of the United States of America.* Available online at http://www.whitehouse.gov

Olle, W. and Schoeller. 1982. Direct Investment and Monopoly Theories of Imperialism'. *Capital and Class* 16: 41–60.

Panitch, L. and S. Gindin. 2004. Global Capitalism and American Empire. *The Socialist Register.* Available online at http://socialistregister.com

Panitch, L. and C. Leys (eds). 2004. The New Imperial Challenge. *The Socialist Register.* Available online at http://socialistregister.com

Peet, R. 2003. *Unholy Trinity: The IMF, World Bank and WTO.* London: Zed Books.

Pollin, R. 2003. *Contours of Descent.* London: Verso.

Project for the New American Century. 2000. *Rebuilding America's Defenses.* Available online at http://www.newamericancentury.org

Rees, J. 2001. Imperialism: Globalization, the State and War. *International Socialism* 93: 3–34.

Rosenberg, J. 2000. *The Follies of Globalisation Theory.* London: Verso.

Scholte, J.A. 2000. *Globalization: A Critical Introduction.* London: Palgrave.

Singer, P. 2004. *The President of Good and Evil.* London: Granta.

Wade, R. 2003. What Strategies are Viable for Developing Countries Today? The World Trade Organization and the Shrinking of "Development Space". *Review of International Political Economy* 10(4): 621–44.

Went, R. 2002–3. Globalization in the Perspective of Imperialism. *Science and Society* 66(4): 473–97.

Wolf, M. 2004. *Why Globalization Works.* New Haven: Yale University Press.

Wolfowitz, P. 2000. Remembering the Future. *The National Interest* 59. Available online at http://www.nationalinterest.org

4

THE FUTURE OF GLOBALIZATION

MANFRED B. STEGER

When President George W. Bush took office in January 2001, "globalization" was *the* buzzword of the dawning twenty-first century, pitting neoliberal free-market enthusiasts against skeptical anti-globalists. The former celebrated the rise of a new borderless world with seemingly no alternatives to "turbo-capitalism," while the latter bemoaned rising levels of social inequality, separating the rich countries of the Northern hemisphere from the impoverished and exploited global South. Regardless of whether one agreed or disagreed with the world view of globalists, one thing seemed to be certain: President Bush would have to focus on many of the same issues related to world trade, economic development, and political multilateralism that preoccupied his predecessor in the White House throughout the 1990s. In short, Bush the Younger would be the second American President in the era of globalization.

Then came the terrorist attacks of September 11, 2001. It sounds like a cliché to suggest that, on that day, "the world changed forever"—but even clichés can sometimes capture momentous historical shifts. Suddenly, the anticipated joys of an interdependent world turned into the dark fears of an interdependent world. A global network of Islamists opposed to the "Americanization" of the world gave an unexpected jolt to the *ideological* struggle over the meaning and the direction of globalization. Indeed, in his celebrated address to a joint session of Congress, nine days after the Al-Qaeda atrocities, President Bush made abundantly clear that the deep sources of the new conflict between what he called "the civilized world" and "terrorism" were to be found neither in religion nor culture, but in *ideology*. Referring to the global network of Al-Qaeda Islamists and governments that support them as "heirs of all the murderous ideologies of the twentieth century," Bush went on to describe the sinister ideological schemes of the terrorists: "By sacrificing human life to serve their radical visions, by abandoning every value except the will to power, they [the terrorists] follow the path of fascism, Nazism and totalitarianism."[1]

In the months that followed, heightened security and surveillance measures were applied to all aspects of social life, and many countries followed the US example of passing stringent "antiterrorist" laws that could easily be applied to a wide range of "enemies." Bush soon made public the controversial *National Security Strategy of the United States* (2002), which endorsed the dangerous idea of pre-emptive strikes. Finally, the American President and his Cabinet members reminded their audiences around the world that the War on Terror would be a lengthy conflict of global proportions.

By 2005, this struggle had expanded from the initial limited war against the Taliban regime in Afghanistan to the massive war in Iraq waged by an American-led "coalition of the willing" against Saddam Hussein's regime. The ensuing open-ended US occupation of the country has been plagued by frequent insurgency attacks on coalition troops, and a national election held in January 2005 was boycotted by a number of political groups, thus lacking legitimacy in the eyes of many Iraqis. In this new historical context, it is tempting to speculate on the future of globalization. Will the global War on Terror lead to more intensive forms of international cooperation and exchange, or will it fortify existing borders and divisions? Will the rise of the American empire be the harbinger of a benign global order, or will it breed furious resistance that might stop the powerful momentum of globalization?

After drawing necessary distinctions between often-conflated key terms involving the concept of "globalization," this chapter will discuss how the new political realities created by 9/11 and its aftermath have impacted what I previously identified as the three most likely future trajectories of globalization. Focusing on the ideological dimension of the phenomenon, I argue that in the years following the terrorist attacks on American soil, the dominant 1990s neoliberal version of globalization has been giving way to a more militaristic, neoconservative model supported by the current American government. Given the re-election of George W. Bush, I expect this trend to continue for at least four more years. In fact, I expect in the near future a further strengthening of this tendency towards an "imperial globalism" anchored in the unilateralist and militarist policies of the Bush Administration.

GLOBALIZATION: PROCESS, CONDITION, OR IDEOLOGY?

The term "globalization" denotes a range of processes nested under a rather hazy master concept. In part, its conceptual unwieldiness arises from the fact that global flows occur in different physical and mental dimensions, usefully divided by Arjun Appadurai into "ethnoscapes," "technoscapes," "mediascapes," "finanscapes," and "ideoscapes."[2] Moreover, as I have noted elsewhere, since its earliest appearance in the 1960s, "globalization" has been used in both popular and academic literature to describe a wide variety of phenomena, including a process, a condition, a system, a force, and an age.[3] Given the different meanings of these concepts, their indiscriminate usage invites confusion. A sloppy conflation of process and condition, for instance, encourages circular definitions that possess little explanatory power. For example, the often-repeated truism that globalization (the process) leads to more globalization (the condition) does not allow us to draw meaningful distinctions between causes and effects.

I use the term *globality* to signify a future *social condition*, characterized by thick economic, political, and cultural interconnections and global flows that make currently existing political borders and economic barriers irrelevant. Yet, it should not be assumed that "globality" refers to a determinate endpoint that precludes any further development. Rather, this concept points to a particular social condition destined to give way to new, qualitatively distinct, constellations. For example, it is conceivable that globality could eventually be transformed into something we might call "planetarity"—a new social condition brought about by the successful colonization of our solar system. Moreover, we could easily imagine different social manifestations of globality: one based primarily on values of individualism and competition, as well as on an economic system of private property; another embodying more communal and cooperative social arrangements, including less capitalistic economic relations. These future alternatives expose the fundamentally indeterminate character of globalization.

In my view, the term "globalization" should be confined to a set of complex, sometimes contradictory, *social processes* that are changing our current social condition based on the modern system of independent nation-states. Indeed, most scholars of globalization have defined their key concept along those lines as a multidimensional set of social processes that create, multiply, stretch, and intensify worldwide social interdependencies and exchanges, while at the same time fostering in people a growing awareness of deepening connections between the local and the distant.[4] At its core, then, globalization is about the unprecedented compression of time and space as a result of political, economic, and cultural change, as well as powerful technological innovations.[5]

The notion that "globalization is happening" implies that we are moving from the modern socio-political order of nation-states that gradually emerged in the seventeenth century, towards the "postmodern" condition of globality. Indeed, like "modernization" and other verbal nouns that end in the suffix "-ization," the term "globalization" suggests a dynamic best captured by the notion of "development" or "unfolding" along discernible patterns. Such unfolding may occur quickly or slowly, but it always corresponds to the idea of change, and, therefore, denotes the alteration of present conditions. This crucial focus on change explains why globalization scholars pay particular attention to shifting temporal modes and the reconfiguration of social and geographical space.

While "globalization" has, indeed, remained a rather unwieldy concept in the academic world, it was successfully popularized and ideologically decontested in public discourse during the late 1980s and 1990s.[6] With the collapse of communism in Eastern Europe, loosely affiliated power elites concentrated in the global North stepped up their ongoing efforts to sell their version of "globalization" to the public.[7] Seeking to make a persuasive case for a new global order based on their neoliberal beliefs and values, these "globalists" constructed and disseminated narratives and images that associated the concept of globalization with the virtues of inexorably expanding "free" markets. Their efforts at decontesting the master concept "globalization" went hand in hand with a rising political belief system I have referred to as *globalism*. This market ideology endows the buzzword "globalization" with norms and values that seek to cultivate consumerist and market-oriented identities in billions of people around the world.[8]

By the mid-1990s, large segments of the population in the both the global North and South had accepted globalism's core claims, thus internalizing large parts of an overarching neoliberal economic framework that advocated the deregulation of markets, the liberalization of trade, the privatization of state-owned enterprises, and the growing power of international economic institutions like the WTO and the IMF. Representing what Pierre Bourdieu and Zygmunt Bauman call a "strong discourse," globalism amounted to an economistic creed of market fundamentalism based on five core ideological claims.[9]

Embraced and propagated by the Clinton Administration throughout the 1990s, globalism proved to be difficult to resist because it relied on the tremendous power of corporate media to present globalist claims as "common sense," that is, the widespread belief that its prescriptive program ultimately derives from an objective description of the "real world." While not disavowing some of the coercive measures Joseph Nye has referred to as "hard power"—particularly the application of economic pressure through international lending institutions like the IMF and World Bank—this phalanx of neoliberal power elites led by the United States preferred enhancing the legitimacy of their world view by means of the "soft power," that is, the use of cultural and ideological appeals to effect their desired outcomes without directly commanding allegiance.[10]

Having drawn the necessary distinctions between our key terms in the context of the 1990s, we can now turn to a discussion of both the present situation and the future of globalization.

THREE FUTURE SCENARIOS

Shortly before 9/11, when an eclectic coalition of anti-globalist forces launched their most populous mass demonstration in the streets of Genoa, Italy, I identified what I considered to be the three most-likely future trajectories of the ongoing ideological confrontation between globalism and its challengers.[11] I called the first possible future scenario "globalism with a human face," perhaps best characterized by the slogan "rhetoric of reform, but business as usual." Having been confronted by their ideological challengers with a rather sophisticated and effective strategy of resistance that began on the streets of Seattle in 1999, globalist forces might pursue a less transparent road to their ultimate objective—the creation of a single, global, free market. Assuring people that they were willing to "manage globalization better," globalists would rely on their public relations efforts to sell their "human face" version of globalization to the global public. However, if implemented at all, their proposed "reforms" of the global economic architecture would likely remain largely symbolic. Without the implementation of actual social reforms on a global level, national and international disparities in wealth and well being would widen even further.

Designed to protect globalist business as usual, the rhetoric of reform has found ardent supporters not merely in conservative circles, but also among European social democrats and North American progressives. Invoking with gusto the trope of "globalization with a human face," European labor leaders took a page out of former President Bill Clinton's agenda to sell their constituency on a kinder and gentler version of globalism. For example, Prime Minister Tony Blair and Chancellor Gerhard Schröder issued a joint manifesto that calls for the replacement of "old social democratic dogmas" with more fashionable centrist views heralded as "The Third Way" in the United Kingdom and "*Die Neue Mitte*" in Germany. The much-publicized document starts with the globalist claim that the liberalization and global integration of markets provides the necessary content and unalterable context of globalization.[12] Likewise, a number of leading intellectuals on the political Left, like Anthony Giddens, fell in love with the idea that globalization with a human face would allow all sectors of society to benefit from the unleashing of market forces while also creating a compassionate world community that cares for those who have fallen behind.[13]

Referring to the second future scenario as the "global new deal," I argued that there existed the slim possibility for the rise of political forces that might create a "global civil society" committed to "globalization-from-below." New political and economic institutions of global governance would subject the global marketplace to greater democratic accountability by means of effective global regulatory policies. This scenario would require that most existing international political and economic institutions would have to undergo serious renovation and philosophical redirection, or perhaps be dismantled altogether. Advocates of this future scenario who formulated their vision in the 1990s hoped that the counter-systemic pressures generated by deteriorating social conditions would force market globalists to the bargaining table before the world descended into a social or environmental catastrophe beyond repair. In their view, the implementation of a significant reform agenda represented the only realistic change for reversing the steady rise of global inequality without surrendering to the parochial agenda of economic nationalists and other right-wing protectionists.

In short, attempts to build new global networks of solidarity lie at the very heart of the "global new deal" scenario.

Finally, I held out the possibility of a severe backlash against globalization caused by the geopolitical and cultural dynamics associated with the neoliberal economic dimension of globalization. I believed that such a cultural backlash had the potential to unleash reactionary forces that could dwarf even those responsible for the suffering of millions during the 1930s and 1940s. The theoretical argument underpinning this bleak trajectory is based upon the work of the late political economist Karl Polanyi, who located the origins of the social crises that gripped the world during the first half of the twentieth century in ill-conceived efforts to liberalize and globalize markets. Commercial interests came to dominate society by means of a ruthless market logic that effectively disconnected people's economic activities from their social relations. The principles of the free market destroyed complex social relations of mutual obligation and undermined communal values such as civic engagement, reciprocity, and redistribution. As large segments of the population found themselves without an adequate system of social security and communal support, they resorted to radical measures to protect themselves against market globalization.

Extending his analysis to the workings of modern capitalism in general, Polanyi extrapolated that all modern capitalist societies contained two organizing principles that were fundamentally opposed to each other:

One is the principle of economic liberalism, aiming at the establishment of a self-regulating market, relying on the support of the trading classes, and using largely *laissez-faire* and free trade as its method; the other is the principle of social protection, aiming at the conservation of man and nature as well as productive organizations, relying on the varying support of those most immediately affected by the deleterious actions of the market—primarily, but not exclusively, the working and the landed classes—and using protective legislation, restrictive associations, and instruments of intervention as its method.[14]

Referring to these tendencies as "double movement," Polanyi suggested that the stronger the liberal movement became, the more it would be able to dominate society by means of a market logic that effectively "disembedded" people's economic activity from their social relations. In other words, the principles of the free market tended to undermine communal values such as civic engagement, reciprocity, and redistribution, not to speak of human dignity and self-respect.[15] Hence, in their polished ideological formulation, the principles of economic liberalism provided a powerful justification for leaving large segments of the population to simply "fend for themselves." In a hypercapitalist world organized around the notion of individual liberty, understood primarily as unrestrained economic entrepreneurship, the market ideal of competition trumped old social conceptions of cooperation and solidarity.

Still, it is important to remember the other half of Polanyi's double movement: the rapid advance of free-market principles also strengthened the resolve of working people to resist the liberal paradigm and struggle against its social effects. Polanyi noted that European anti-globalist movements eventually gave birth to political parties that forced the passage of protective social legislation on the national level. After a prolonged period of severe economic dislocations following the end of the Great War, the particularist–protectionist impulse experienced its most extreme manifestations in Italian fascism and German National Socialism. In the end, the liberal–globalist dream of subordinating the whole world to the requirements of the free market had generated an equally extreme counter-movement that turned markets into mere appendices of totalitarian states.[16]

Needless to say, few people writing before 9/11 envisioned that the backlash scenario would materialize so quickly nor did they foresee the precise form it assumed. However, the applicability of Polanyi's analysis to our own age of global terror seems obvious. Like its nineteenth-century predecessor, the market globalism of the 1990s represented an experiment in unleashing the utopia of the self-regulating market on society. This time, however, the leading Anglo-American voices of neoliberalism were prepared to turn the entire world into their laboratory. Particularist forces of radical Islamism were the first to launch a massive counterstrike against what they considered to be a morally corrupt ideology of secular materialism that had "invaded" their region—most dramatically in the form of American troops permitted to establish military bases by the "corrupt" Saudi Arabian government. In response to the 9/11 attacks, the Bush Administration also radicalized its policies, switching from the soft power strategy that prevailed in the 1990s to the hard power model of imperial globalism.

THE RISE OF IMPERIAL GLOBALISM AND ITS FUTURE

In the volatile post-9/11 environment in the United States, neoconservative players in the Bush Administration drew on the existing climate of fear to promote their vision of a benign American Empire leading a coalition of "allies" in the open-ended War on Terror. President George W. Bush abandoned the mildly isolationist position he espoused during the 2000 election campaign, and instead adopted the bellicose views of inveterate hard-power advocates like Dick Cheney and Donald Rumsfeld. If the liberalization and global integration of markets was to continue as a viable project, many market globalists felt they had little choice but to enter into a shaky ideological compromise with the ascending neoconservative forces. A large number of neoliberal elites accepted that their core ideological claims had to be "hard-powered" to fit the neoconservative agenda, and, in turn, most neoconservatives continued to support a "free-market" discourse that also helped to soften their militarist posture in the public arena. Only few prominent neoliberals like George Soros or Joseph Stiglitz warned against striking any ideological compromises with neoconservatives, especially with their unilateralist and militarist approach to foreign policy and international law.

In this context, it is crucial to bear in mind that neoliberalism and neoconservativism in the United States are not ideological opposites. In fact, they represent variations on the same liberal theme, and their similarities often outweigh their differences. Contemporary American neoconservatives are far removed from classical British traditionalists who expressed a fondness for aristocratic virtues and bemoaned radical social change, disliked egalitarian principles, and distrusted progress and reason. Rather, American neoconservatives subscribe to a variant of liberalism that they relate to the world views espoused by Ronald Reagan, Theodore Roosevelt, Abraham Lincoln, and James Madison.

This uneasy and sometimes stormy marriage between the economic neoliberalism of the 1990s and the neoconservative security agenda of the 2000s marked the birth of imperial globalism with an "American face." While the hard-powering of market globalism led to a modification of some of globalism's economistic claims, it would be a mistake to assume that the neoliberal project came to an end with 9/11. The Bush Administration's adoption of free trade and market rhetoric despite its embrace of hard power has been amply documented and analyzed on the policy level in today's raging debates over the post-9/11 United States, and can accurately be described as the first global "empire" in human history—formal or informal.[17] Sociologist Jan Nederveen Pieterse neatly captures the ideological eclecticism of imperial globalism:

Neoliberal empire twins practices of empire with those of neoliberalism. The core of empire is the national security state and the military–industrial complex; neoliberalism is about business, financial operations, and marketing (including the marketing of neoliberalism itself). The IMF and World Bank continue business as usual, though with less salience and legitimacy than during the Clinton years; so imperial policies come in addition to and not instead of the framework of neoliberal globalization. Neoliberal empire is a marriage of convenience with neoliberalism, indicated by inconsistent use of neoliberal policies, and an attempt to merge America whose business is business with the America whose business is war, at a time when business is not doing great.[18]

Yet, the militarization of market globalism highlights an embarrassing secret at the heart of the neoliberal project: from its earliest inception in the Thatcher and Reagan years, the globalist enterprise required frequent and extensive use of state power in order to dismantle the old welfare structures and create new *laissez-faire* policies. As Karl Polanyi noted, "free markets" did not appear on the historical stage *ex nihilo*. Rather, they were the deliberate products of concerted political action coordinated by modern states that found themselves captured by liberal interests. Similarly, the creation, expansion, and protection of global free markets demands massive infusions of central state power. Hence, the resulting ideological contradiction: neoliberal social elites pushing for an ever-expanding mobility of capital must contend with the state's security logic that calls for inspection, surveillance, and other limitations on the free movement of people, goods, and information across national borders.

In the age of global terror, this embarrassing secret of neoliberalism is more easily exposed as the allegedly "invisible hand" of the market—claiming to operate best without interference from state power—but must openly call upon the iron fist of state to save itself. In short, the coercive power of the state apparatus has been bought at the cost of bowing to the empire. Thus, globalism's reliance on the forces of the old nation-state to battle its anti-globalist enemies has resulted in the dramatic disclosure of what, during most of the 1990s, remained hidden behind the ideological veil of the "self-regulating market": American Empire. With President Bush and his neoconservative inner circle setting American foreign policy for another four years, imperial globalism is bound to grow stronger.

What does the rise of imperial globalism mean for the future of globalization? On first thought, it seems highly implausible that even an expanding global War on Terror could stop, or even slow down, such a powerful set of social processes as globalization. Yet, there are already some early warning signs. More intense border controls and security measures at the world's major air and seaports have made travel and international trade more cumbersome. Policy initiatives for curtailing immigration and maintaining sharp cultural divisions can be seen more frequently in the global North than ever before. In addition, hyper-patriotic voices claiming to defend "us" from "them" are becoming more strident in many parts of the world.

A close look at modern history reveals that large-scale violent confrontations were capable of stopping, and even reversing previous globalization trends. As Karl Polanyi understood, the period from 1860 to 1914 constituted an earlier golden age of globalization, characterized by the unprecedented development of transportation and communication networks, the rapid growth of international trade, and a huge flow of capital. But globalization was capitalistic and openly imperialistic in character, involving the transfer of resources from the colonized global South in exchange for European manufactures. Great Britain, the world's sole superpower, had spread its political system and cultural values across the globe. These sustained efforts to engineer a single global market under the auspices of the British Empire resulted in a severe backlash against globalization that culminated in the outbreak of World War I. The anti-globalist forces of the twenty-first century—especially in their violent particularist manifestation—seem to be capable of attracting millions of disaffected "globalization losers" who are willing to employ violent means in order to achieve their political ends. Hence, it is quite conceivable that the Al-Qaeda attacks on the World Trade Center and the Pentagon were only the opening salvos of a widening global war waged by the US government and its dwindling allies against a growing list of terrorist organizations and their supporters around the world. Such a grim backlash scenario would surely put the brakes on globalization.

On the other hand, it is also possible that the ongoing efforts to contain these violent anti-globalist forces might actually increase international cooperation and encourage the forging of new global alliances. In order to eradicate the primary social causes of terrorism, the global North might be willing to replace the dominant version of globalization with a substantive reform agenda designed to reduce the existing disparities in global wealth and wellbeing. In that case, the "global new deal" scenario I outlined above might eventually become reality. However, there are currently few signs of such increased international cooperation towards such a global accord. In fact, the reverse seems to be true. American unilateralism is rampant and even voices of moderation from within the inner circles of power—like Secretary of State Colin Powell—have no longer a hand in the making of foreign policy in the second Bush Administration. Unwilling to involve itself in genuine multilateral efforts to combat global terrorism, the US government has acted as though it had all the right answers, demanding from its "allies" nothing less than unquestioning loyalty. Claiming that his country's responsibility to history was to "rid the world of evil," President George W. Bush famously put the world on notice that whoever was not with "us" was against America.[19] Bush's persistent Manichean portrayal of his country as the force of good battling the barbaric hordes of evil—combined with his administration's obvious disdain for the United Nations—fueled public perceptions around the world that America was an arrogant bully indifferent to what the rest of humanity thought.[20] Within months of the attacks, the thrilling prospect of a caring America leading a collective struggle for a better world had turned into the dark reality of a vengeful hyper-power unleashing its awesome military arsenal without much international consultation.

Countries that cooperate with the United States often do so for purely instrumental reasons, not because they want to emulate its example. The Bush Administration's switch from the soft power of attraction to the hard power of coercion carries a heavy price: the loss of legitimacy and authority as well as the increase of negative sentiments towards the United States. A series of global opinion polls has tracked the rising tide of anti-Americanism, particularly in the Muslim world. For example, a 2002 Pew Charitable Trust Poll found that 69 percent of Egyptians, 75 percent of Jordanians, 59 percent of Lebanese, 69 percent of Pakistanis, and 55 percent of Turks had unfavorable views of the United States.[21] Since then, these numbers have gone up even further. Surprised by the sharp increase of negative perceptions, the US government has remained nonetheless wedded to its militant unilateralism, doggedly pursuing its imperial vision for a "new American century."[22] Wrapped in its flag and donning the rhetorical cloak of waging a "just war on terror," the US escalated its military operations in the Middle East while at the same time seeking to convince skeptical audiences around the world that its real aim was to bring noble "American values" like "freedom" and "democracy" to the region.

No doubt, the terrorist attacks of September 11 and the ensuing global War on Terror have seriously impacted the future shape and direction of those social processes that go by the name of globalization. Humanity has reached yet another critical juncture. Lest we are willing to let global inequality climb to levels that virtually ensure new recruits for the violent forces of anti-globalist particularism, we must link the future course of globalization to a profoundly reformist agenda. Given its *de facto* status as a global empire, the United States carries a special responsibility to live up to those values it considers to be at the core of its very *raison d'être*. This means that Americans should stand behind a form of globalization that is not defined by economic and geopolitical self-interest alone, but one that is deeply infused with ethical concerns for humanity and our natural environment.

For the next few years, the world led by a militarily unchallengeable hyperpower faces the choice between strengthening imperial globalism or turning towards the promise of a global new deal, which, in the cosmopolitan vision of British economist George Monbiot, would be sustained by new global political and economic institutions such as a World Parliament, a Fair Trade Organization, and an International Clearing Union.[23] This struggle for the future is inextricably intertwined with matters of ideology: the kind of ideas, values, and beliefs about globalization that are circulating in the global public sphere. As former National Security Adviser Zbigniew Brzezinski emphasizes, the United States must be more sensitive to the significant risks of its increasing identification with an unjust version of globalization. Given that security depends not only on military power, the way America defines and pursues globalization will bear directly on its long-term security and that of the entire world.[24] If the second Bush Administration continues to rely on the dynamics of imperial globalism, the backlash scenario of a militaristic and increasingly authoritarian empire engaging in an endless war with global "terrorists" of all stripes might well become the permanent political context of the new century.

Notes

1. Bush, 2001a, p. 13.
2. Appadurai, 1996.
3. Steger, 2003, p. 7.
4. The literature on globalization is vast and rapidly growing. Some of the most influential definitions of globalization have been offered by Harvey, 1989; Giddens, 1990;

Robertson, 1992; Held, McGrew, Goldblatt and Perraton, 1999; Mittelman, 2000; and Scholte, 2000.

5. For a magisterial analysis of these changes, see Castells, 1996–98.

6. However, over the last few years, there have also been some emerging points of agreement among globalization scholars. For a discussion of these points, see Steger, 2004, pp. 1–4.

7. These power elites consist chiefly of corporate managers, executives of large transnational corporations, corporate lobbyists, high-level military officers, prominent journalists and public-relations specialists, intellectuals writing to a large public audience, state bureaucrats and influential politicians. It is questionable whether these social elites actually constitute a coherent "transnational capitalist class" (in a Marxist sense), as Leslie Sklair (2001) suggests. In my view, C. Wright Mills' (2000) notion of a "power elite" and Mark Rupert's (2000) concept of a "transnational historic bloc of internationally-oriented capitalists, liberal statesman, and their allies" seem to come closer to an accurate description of the loose, heterogeneous, and often disagreeing global alliance of political and economic elites that I have in mind.

8. Steger, 2005. Benjamin Barber (1996) famously referred to globalism as "McWorld."

9. See Bauman, 1999, pp. 28–29; and Pierre Bourdieu, 1998, p. 95.

10. While coined by Joseph S. Nye, the terms "hard power" and "soft power" have been described and analyzed in different terms by generations of political thinkers influenced by the writings of Antonio Gramsci. For the latest elaboration of Nye's perspective on power, see Joseph S. Nye, 2004.

11. Steger, 2002, ch. 6.

12. For a full text of the manifesto, including critical marginal notes by Joanne Barkan, see Blair and Schröder, 2000, pp. 51–65.

13. Giddens, 2000; and Hutton and Giddens, 2000, pp. 1–51.

14. Polanyi, 1957, p. 132.

15. For the concise explication of Polanyi's ethical theory, see Baum, 1996.

16. Polanyi, 1957, p. 237.

17. The post-9/11 literature on the power dynamics of "American Empire" is vast and rapidly growing. See, for example, David Harvey, 2003; Mann, 2003; Schmemann, 2003; Soros, 2003; Todd, 2003; Boggs, 2004; and Johnson, 2004.

18. Nederveen Pieterse, 2004, p. 45.

19. Bush, 2001a, 2001b.

20. For an excellent analysis of Bush's moral Manicheanism, see Singer, 2004.

21. See Nisbet et al., 2004, p. 14. This article also lists the results of other major opinion polls on the subject conducted in 2002–3. The latest in this series of polls is a comprehensive world opinion poll conducted between November 2003 and February 2004 in 19 countries. It found that 55 percent of respondents believed that the United States exerts a negative influence in the world. See World Public Opinion Poll published by The Program on International Policy Attitudes (PIPA), June 4, 2004. Available online at <www.pipa.org/OnlineReports/Global_Issues/globescan_press_06_04.pdf>.

22. For an enlightening discussion of the neoconservative "Project for a New American Century," see Barry and Lobe, 2003, pp. 39–49; and C. Ryn, 2003, pp. 383–97.

23. For a detailed blueprint of these new institutions and their functions, see Monbiot 2003.

24. Brzezinski, 2004, p. 228.

References

Appadurai, A. 1996. *Modernity at Large: Cultural Dimensions of Globalization.* Minneapolis: University of Minnesota Press.

Barber, B. 1996. *Jihad vs McWorld.* New York: Ballantine.

Barry, T. and J. Lobe. 2003. The People, in J. Feffer (ed.), *Power Trip: US Unilateralism and Global Strategy after September 11.* New York: Seven Story Press, pp. 39–49.

Baum, G. 1996. *Karl Polanyi on Ethics and Economics.* Montreal: McGill-Queen's University Press.

Bauman, Z. 1999. *In Search of Politics.* Stanford, CA: Stanford University Press.

Blair, T. and G. Schröder. 2000. The Third Way/*Die Neue Mitte. Dissent.* Spring.

Boggs, C. 2004. *The New Militarism: US Empire and Endless War.* Lanham, MD: Rowman & Littlefield Publishers.

Bourdieu, P. 1998. *Acts of Resistance: Against the Tyranny of the Market.* New York: The New Press.

Brzezinski, Z. 2004. *The Choice: Global Domination or Global Leadership.* New York: Basic Books.

Bush, G. 2001a. Address to Joint Session of Congress and Americans, September 20, 2001, in J.W. Edwards and Louis de Rose, *United We Stand.* Ann Arbor, MI: Mundus.

————. 2001b. Remarks in the National Cathedral, Washington D.C., September 14, 2001. Available online at http://www.whitehouse.gov/news/releases/2001/09.html

Castells, M. 1996–98. *The Information Age: Economy, Society and Culture* (3 vols.) Oxford: Blackwell.

Giddens, A. 1990. *The Consequences of Modernity.* London: Polity Press.

————. 2000. *The Third Way.* Cambridge: Polity.

Harvey, D. 1989. *The Condition of Postmodernity.* Oxford: Blackwell.

————. 2003. *The New Imperialism.* Oxford: Oxford University Press.

Held, D., A. McGrew, D. Goldblatt and J. Perraton. 1999. *Global Transformations.* Stanford, CA: Stanford University Press.

Hutton, W. and A. Giddens. 2000. *Global Capitalism.* New York: The New Press.

Johnson, C. 2004. *The Sorrows of Empire: Militarism, Secrecy, and the End of the Republic.* New York: Metropolitan Books.

Mann, M. 2003. *Incoherent Empire.* London: Verso.

Mills, C.W. 2000 (1956). *The Power Elite.* Oxford: Oxford University Press.

Mittelman, J. 2000. *The Globalization Syndrome.* Princeton, NJ: Princeton University Press.

Monbiot, G. 2003. *The Age Of Consent: A Manifesto for a New World Order.* London: Flamingo.

Nisbet, E., M.C. Nisbet, D.A. Scheufele and J.E. Shanahan. 2004. Public Diplomacy, Television News, and Muslim Opinion. *Harvard International Journal of Press/Politics,* 9(2): 11–37. Available online at http://www.pipa.org/OnlineReports/Global_Issues/globescan_press_06_04.pdf

Nye, J.S. 2004. *Soft Power: The Means to Success in World Politics.* New York: Public Affairs.

Pieterse, J.N. 2004. *Globalization or Empire?* New York: Routledge.

Polanyi, K. 1957. *The Great Transformation: The Political and Economic Origins of Our Time* (Reprint). Boston: Beacon Press.

Robertson, R. 1992. *Globalization.* London: Sage.

Rupert, M. 2000. *Ideologies of Globalization: Contending Visions of a New World Order.* London: Routledge.

Ryn, C. 2003. The Ideology of American Empire. *Orbis* (Summer): 383–97.

Schmemann, S. 2003. *America Unbound: The Bush Revolution in Foreign Policy*. Washington: Brookings Institution Press.

Scholte, J. 2000. *Globalization*. New York: St. Martin's Press.

Singer, P. 2004. *The President of Good and Evil: The Ethics of George W. Bush*. New York: Dutton.

Sklair, L. 2001. *The Transnational Capitalist Class*. Oxford, UK: Blackwell.

Soros, G. 2003. *The Bubble of American Supremacy: Correcting the Misuse of American Power*. New York: Public Affairs.

Steger, M.B. 2002. *Globalism: The New Market Ideology* (First Edition) Lanham, MD: Rowman & Littlefield Publishers.

————. 2003. *Globalization: A Very Short Introduction*. Oxford: Oxford University Press.

————. (ed.). 2004. *Rethinking Globalism*. Lanham, MD: Rowman & Littlefield Publishers.

————. 2005. *Globalism: Market Ideology Meets Terrorism*. (Second Edition). Lanham, MD: Rowman & Littlefield Publishers.

Todd, E. 2003. *After Empire: The Breakdown of the American Order*. New York: Columbia University Press.

5

GLOBALIZATION

Whose Benefit Anyway?

ABBAS MEHDI

WHAT IS GLOBALIZATION?

The romance with globalization meets its Waterloo as soon as you remember the possible erosion of cultural diversity, the facelessness of nations, and the overthrow of national identities. But as soon as free movement gets attached to free trade and market accessibility, the exchange of cultural values enters the stage, the drums can begin to beat again.

As if confirming the fears of the exploited of yesteryears who sense the translation of the operations of the multinational and transnational corporations into the global government of the few, Tabb does not forget to include them in the list of the beneficiaries of globalization. These corporations know the mentality of the political leaders of the developing countries very well—their weakness for soft money and in addition, in some cases, beautiful girls—and like the missionaries before them, know how to domesticate possible resistance and upheavals in those countries, all things being equal, this time around, with the huge financial resources at their disposal. In this case G8 is synonymous with an experiment with global government that lies hidden behind the veil of globalization. So, to the critics, globalization is history repeating itself, with children rewriting the stories of their grandfathers. And the fact that the term is coined in the West does not help the situation at all.

But what happens when globalization is not history of exploitation coming through the back door? What if it is a way of transforming the world into an open place for competition? And if open competition is the case, to what extent can a farmer in Egypt, an Arab African country compete with a farmer in Denmark, a European country? What if globalization sets out to break geographical boundaries and replace protectionism with openness? But what is globalization, which has become a buzzword, that is being bandied about to find lodging between the pendulum of free world and global control?

According to Jeffery (2002), as a word, globalization "existed since the 1960s, but the protests against this allegedly new process, which its opponents condemn as a way of ordering people's lives" brought it out of the financial and academic worlds where it has found currency. From this point, Jeffery points a rosy picture of globalization through the global market. For example, the modern communications make it possible for the British service sector to deal with its customers through a call in India, or for a sportswear manufacturer to design products in Europe, make them in south-east Asia and sell them in North America. The globe as a marketplace where geographical barriers become transparent paper walls is a strong defence for globalization.

Globalization seen from another prism gives a different picture:

Globalization, comprehensive term for the emergence of a global society in which economic, political, environmental, and cultural events in one part of the world quickly come to have significance for people in other parts of the world. Globalization is the result of advances in communication, transportation, and information technologies. It describes the growing economic, political, technological, and cultural linkages that connect individuals, communities, businesses, and governments around the world. Globalization also involves the growth of multinational corporations (businesses that have operations or investments in many countries) and transnational corporations (businesses that see themselves functioning in a global marketplace). The international institutions that oversee world trade and finance play an increasingly important role in this era of globalization. (Tabb 2002)

As if confirming the fears of the exploited of yesteryears, who sense the translation of the operations of the multinational and transnational corporations into the global government of the few, Tabb does not forget to include them in the list of beneficiaries of globalization. These corporations know the mentality of the political leaders of the developing countries very well—their weakness for soft money and in addition, in some cases, beautiful girls—and like the missionaries before them, know how to domesticate possible resistance and upheavals in those countries, all things being equal, this time around, with the huge financial resources at their disposal.

Perhaps globalization does not take that road to the world. Perhaps, as Jeffery says, it was born elsewhere only to be celebrated by the political class to boost national economies and improve the health of nations. Perhaps globalization is the product of the new telecommunication technologies. For example,

Advances in communications instantly unite people around the globe. For example, communications satellites allow global television broadcasts to bring news of faraway events, such as wars and national disasters as well as sports and other forms of entertainment. The Internet, the cell phone, and the fax machine permit instantaneous communication. The World Wide

Web and computers that store vast amounts of data allow instant access to information exceeding that of any library... (Tabb 2004)

Transforming the world into a global village, a candidate for globalization.

GLOBALIZATION AND THE ARAB WORLD

In the Arab world, globalization appears as a phenomenon on which there is a general consensus until the question of development arises. According to the author, "in the late twentieth century, 'globalization' replaced 'development' as the topic of discourse among political and corporate elites. *Although there was a consensus on the meaning of development*, each nation had its own version that responded to its own cultural and natural resources and political structures" (Mehdi 2003).

Here is where the rub comes in. Everybody knows what development is all about, even though in practice, the approach to it and the implementation of its terms of reference differ among the countries. Not so with globalization. There is no general consensus on the meaning of globalization. However, the Prime Minister of Egypt, Atef Ebeid, in his Address, *Egypt in a Globalizing World*, to the Fourth Annual Global Development Conference in Cairo, Egypt, with the theme *Globalization and Equity*, captures those features which, each time they come together, arrogate to themselves what could be understood as a working definition of globalization.

Industrial countries have maintained a hard line on reducing subsidies, opening up their markets for agricultural products from developing countries, liberalizing cross border labor movements, and allowing for concessionary terms for the South in the enforcement of intellectual property rights. I doubt that every aspect of these issues will be tackled at this meeting but you may well bring new ideas on how to compensate the losers from globalization under the aegis of corporate governance, public goods, global taxes or a review of the WTO rules themselves. (Ebeid 2003)

In this regard, globalization is a carrot to those who know the *rules of the game* (Ebeid 2003) and a stick to the developing countries.

Ebeid puts the matter succinctly. As a market driven process, says Ebeid, globalization

can hardly be equitable unless we introduce a dose of global intervention to regulate markets and ensure a fair distribution of the gains. Otherwise, the poor and the marginalized, both those outside the market system and those inside it, run the risk of exclusion. But the fact remains that whatever actions are taken, the heaviest burden of adapting to globalization is borne by the South countries, as they have less influence on the rules of the game.

In the same vein, Mehdi (2003) discloses the contents of the globalization package. Nations are driven by globalization towards liberalizing trade and capital markets, internationalizing of production and distribution strategies, and increasing technological change. Globalization encourages nations to rapidly dismantle barriers to international trade of goods and services and promote the mobility of capital. Also from Mehdi we know that unlike development on which everybody knows what is being talked about and could make prediction on the future, the mention of the word, "globalization" rakes up, on the side of the developing countries, the devastating effects of structural adjustment programs on their economies in which their currencies freewheeled to duds and crashed in the valley of devaluation. The notorious Structural Adjustment Program crippled and, in most cases, sent the economies of those that obeyed its conditionalities, crashing. "Some view [globalization] as a beneficial process—a key to the world of the future characterized by positive economic development. Others regard it with hostility, fearing that it increases inequality within and between nations, and that it threatens employment, living standards, and social progress" (Mehdi 2003).

In his *Globalization—Challenges and Responses in the Arab World*, Al-Hamad (2003) presents the two opposing sides of globalization without the sands of compromise between them. On the one hand, "Globalization basically means that people around the world are more connected to each other than ever before, information and money flow much faster than any time in human history; goods and services produced in any part of the world are available everywhere; international travel grows at a pace never perceived before; and international communications have become commonplace." While on the other, globalization is seen as investing the multinationals with growing power that threatens the sovereignty of small nations leading to social and political instability, exploitation of workers in developing countries, and the destruction of environment of small and poor nations that do not have the capacity to influence the policies of transnational corporations.

Al-Hamad tilts more to globalization, based on its meaning produced in the West—that is, globalization as free movement of goods—*you need money and reasons to do this*; a faster flow of information and money—*lack of technical facilities cripples the flow of information in most of the developing countries and there is not much money to flow around anyway*; availability of goods produced in one part of the world reaching the others everywhere—*most of the developing countries rely on agricultural produce for their export earnings but the goods that will benefit from globalization are technical products in the first place*—when he says, "We find ourselves today challenged by globalization in three basic domains." The first is *liberalization*. This should be political, institutional and cultural. This embodies free market and private initiative. The second is *modernization*. This represents an economic, technological and institutional change.

The third is *integration*. Al-Hamad speaks of "investment laws, foreign exchange regulations, trade barriers, unpredictable policies" as contributing "*to prevent Arab businesses from being partners in a global economic system.*"

STRUCTURAL ADJUSTMENT PROGRAM AND GLOBALIZATION

Apart from the devaluation of currency, the liberalization of the market to the relaxation of trade barriers, everything that is present in globalization could be found in structural adjustment program with a change of wording. Is globalization then another word for structural adjustment program on a global scale? But then, what is structural adjustment program?

Structural Adjustment Program, which was imposed by the World Bank and the IMF on most African countries in the early 1980s, was presumably to spur economic recovery and help the African (which include Egypt and some other Arab) governments pay for the debts that they had contracted during the previous decade in order to finance development projects. It is a conditionality package from IMF which prescribes land privatization (beginning with the abolition of communal land tenure), trade liberalization (the elimination of tariffs on imported goods), the deregulation of currency transactions, the downsizing of the public sector, the defunding of social services, and a system of controls that effectively transfers economic planning from the borrowing government to the World Bank and non-governmental organizations (NGOs), thus reducing the borrowing governments into spectators of what is happening to their countries.

This economic restructuring was presumably meant to boost productivity, eliminate inefficiency, and increase a borrower's "competitive edge" on the global market. Citing the African experience, Federici (2002) shows that the opposite has occurred. "More than a decade after its adoption, local economies have collapsed, foreign investment has not materialized, and the only productive activities…are mineral extraction and export-oriented agriculture."

Three features, which globalization demands of governments without the headmaster's cudgel of International Monetary Fund asking them to behave, are free market policies, trade liberalization, and the elimination of tariffs on imported goods. These features also belong to the conditionalities of IMF on Structural Adjustment Program.

Is structural adjustment program therefore a subset of globalization or is it the globalization of the conditionalities of IMF and the World Bank? Perhaps this question is premature since the developing countries that have experienced structural adjustments program to the collapse of most of their socioeconomic infrastructures need time to get adjusted to what globalization is all about. For now, one thing is certain: The removal of trade tariffs means an unprecedented influx of goods from everywhere into developing countries. And these goods are coming mostly from industrialized countries. The equation of the disadvantaged is easy to solve.

GLOBALIZATION—THE WINNERS

In the scramble for the rest that the earth can offer before it is completely liquidated at which point and before which point the scramble for the cosmos begins with the Heavens's cry and Nature's backlash as part of the inheritance by our grandchildren, the West which is ready to sew the earth into a garb in the search for or in defence of its so-called interest, is the primary winner of globalization. That may explain the intensity of its interest. Globalization in this sense is not an attempt by the West—the movement of critics of globalization, which is composed of some of the best minds of our times, most of them Western academics and intellectuals, would replace West with G8—to reduce the rest of the world into a footnote but to transform it into a huge marketplace, where profits fatten the purses of the multinational companies whose abode are in the West, of Western farmers that receive subsidies from their governments, and of producers who easily attract investors through connections even as the rest of the world wallow in skyrocketing trade deficits. In this case, the barometer of international trade doesn't look good for the developing countries of the world.

If globalization is what has been said so far it appears apocalyptic. Its advocates would quickly direct our lens at another possible scenario. Globalization would bring the developing countries into the spotlight of international trade.

Just as we were about to settle on what we got from Tabb, Bernard Cassen provided another perspective on globalization. In opening his speech, Cassen (2000) started with a line of demarcation between internationalization and globalization. "Globalization, to me, is the contrary of internationalization. Those people who are opposed to globalization...are not opposed to international trade or international exchanges. We are internationalists...we are not nationalists."

In his speech (Cassen 2000), globalization, according to what we got from IMF, OECD, WTO, the World Bank and European Commission means "that markets are efficient, that the state, or the states, are not necessary, that the poor and the rich have no conflicting interests, and finally that things turn out for the best if left alone. The role that remains for the state is to see to it that there is no inflation, the budget is balanced, and that law and order is guaranteed. That's about all."

In what follows, in showing globalization as a way of rectifying the injustices of the past, as a brave new world order that could liberate crawling economies from the misery of poverty by breaking boundaries, and opening doors of economic opportunities to the developing countries that is grossly inflated to the point of being a taint on the truth, Cassen presents examples that reveal the unwritten distortions in the above picture.

He gave examples of Russia, Brazil and India as three countries—which in tune with the conditionalities of the International Monetary Fund on loans to them such as taking measures to liberalize the economy, suppressing subsidies to basic products, these being some of the fundamental demands of all structural adjustment programs (SAP)—where instead of the IMF's official doctrine which says that with the demands of SAP met, there must be growth, and the more growth, the more redistribution, the less inequality, the contrary is the case.

From his conclusion, it is easy to deduce that the real winners of globalization are multinationals and financial markets whose objective is to bypass all political authorities as a result of the neutralization of national boundaries and obliteration of cultural identities.

However, Wolf (2002) in his own conclusion pitches two opposing camps on globalization, viz. "Globalization has dramatically increased inequality between and within nations" (Jay Mazur, "Labor's New Internationalism", *Foreign Affairs*, January/February 2000).

On the other hand, "So far, the current wave of globalization, which started around 1980, has actually promoted economic equality and reduced poverty" (David Dollar and Aart Kraay, *Foreign Affairs*, January/February 2002).

The question is *who is right?*

After presenting tables loaded with statistics, Wolf came to the following conclusions:

(i) Globalization is not guilty of causing growing poverty and inequality worldwide.

(ii) Overall, there has been declining inequality and poverty in the age of globalization. This breaks a trend that goes back almost two centuries.

(iii) But far too many countries have become less globalized and grown poorly.

(iv) This is the only sense in which globalization causes inequality: some seize opportunities and others do not.

(v) The challenge is to help the failures do better.

Of these conclusions, the fourth point, which is deduced from the third, could easily be seized upon by Jay Mazur to show that the soul of globalization is made of Darwinian natural selection of survival of the fittest. Some seize opportunities and others do not. The rich know how the market ticks and so could easily seize the opportunities it offers in a globalized context. There is something arrogantly dismissive about the concerns of the developing countries on globalization in this.

Nor did Wolf's, "The challenge is to help the failures do better" help the case he was trying to make for globalization, since the word "failures" gives the impression that those whose economies were damaged by harsh conditionalities of IMF, years of exploitation of their mineral resources by rich countries in the past, with the same exploitation still going on by the multinationals, and whose agricultural products, the mainstay of the economy in most of the developing countries, are reduced to worthlessness by subsidies to farmers in the rich countries and genetically produced agricultual products, are to blame for their estates.

It is only in one case that Wolf is right. *It is the fault of the developing countries if they cannot learn*! A case in point is Nigeria. Nigeria produces oil but the oil marketers would have overthrown the government with incessant increases in fuel prices were the Nigerians not fed up with military intervention in the affairs of state. The question is, "Who is behind the oil marketers that initiate increase in fuel price against the wishes of majority of Nigerians that has led to, and will continue to lead to nationwide strikes?" Globalization has the answer.

In conclusion, the winners of globalization, according to Jha (2003), "are the transnational corporations and a minuscule class of global professional managers. For them it has created hitherto undreamed of opportunities to work in and travel to far away places and earn vast sums of money."

GLOBALIZATION—THE LOSERS

In his "Globalization is creating only a handful of winners and a very large number of losers. A bit rich, really," Prem Shankar Jha (2003) while showing protesters lampooning G8 leaders at Cancun, points at the success story of Dubai which welcomes an open economy but the story turns gloomy as the tide of globalization ebbs the hope for meaningful growth and fans fear of the future. For Jha, the meaning of globalization seems clear, but from what he writes one could say he doesn't belong to the celebrants of globalization neither in policy nor practice. He cites the protesters against globalization as having a case and goes on to show how, for the developing countries, globalization is not a baby whose birth is worth a celebration.

While even the fiercest protesters have only a hazy idea of the reason why they oppose global economic integration, they share a dawning perception that their governments have not been entirely honest with them. For more than a decade, legions of economists, spokesmen of international organisations and heads of government of the rich nations have spared no effort to convince the world that Globalization, and the consequent removal of trade and investment barriers, increases efficiency and therefore raises income. It does this not only within a country but also across the globe. Witness the succession of "miracles" in East and Southeast Asia. Globalization, in short, creates only winners and no losers.

Even in that, the meaning of globalization doesn't come through. What we got is one of its corollaries, for example, in consequence to globalization, trade and investment barriers will be removed. But Jha tries harder to catch the mood of globalization, if not its meaning all the same. For example, what serves as harbinger of global economic integration—a candidate for globalization—in the industrialized countries in the 1990s are "centred on GDP growth rates, the need to keep inflation down, the exchange rate stable and the fiscal deficit at a minimum."

Even these didn't work out as expected. In this case one could say, globalization is a retarded concept because of lack of adequate incubation prior to its delivery.

GLOBALIZATION AS VICTIM

Whatever is wrong in the world today, from inequality to abuse of the rights of the women, the fate of workers in Dandenong—"The Heinz factory in Dandenong, Victoria has closed its doors to transfer production across the Tasman, and as Mark Simkin reports, it's all part of a process affecting companies around the world"—the dwindling population of fish and the decreasing income of fishers, what the United Nations should do but has not done or shouldn't have done, the workers at the cement industry, and you would add, to the crying of the baby at an unusual time, is laid at the doorsteps of globalization.

To some, globalization is the cause of whatever is wrong in and with the world. To the others, it is the cure of what went wrong somewhere along the line. In a way globalization, for as long as it is still being discussed without being decided, will continue to provide an escape from what matters, and that is, the need for the industrialized and developing countries to create a forum for serious exchange of ideas on how the world could justly be run.

What is happening now is the reverse. It is the bonding of the rich countries that is seen as divisive by the developing countries for it aims at controlling the world by using globalization as a palliative. This interpretation of intentions may be completely off the mark. And it looks like that as soon as one brings the meeting of NEPAD (New Partnership for Africa's Development) and the G8 (Italy, UK, France, Germany, Canada, USA, Japan, Russia) in Evian into the picture. For, at this meeting the G8 along with the African Heads of State representing NEPAD, launched the "Action Plan for Africa."

Speaking at the launch, the French President Jacques Chirac, in a tone that shows how much of a village the world has become, tells his colleagues and the African leaders who had gathered at Lake Leman: "Africa is going adrift. We either help it seriously or it will plummet, dragging down with it, in its collapse, all the other Continents, and first and foremost Europe." This is globalization as it is understood by its supporters—a world in which the destinies of nations are tied to one another as contained in the G8's Action Plan for Africa Implementation Report:

In 2001, a hope blossomed in Genoa. The Summit under the Italian Presidency welcomed the appeal made by a small group of African Heads of State and Government requesting that a real partnership of equals be established with donor Countries instead of the existing form of solidarity, which has proven to be barren through the NEPAD project (New Partnership for African Development).

The hopes raised at the Genoa conference of G8 were, however, marred by the death of an anti-globalization protester as the BBC reported:

An anti-capitalist protester in his 20s has been shot dead in clashes with police during the G8 summit in the Italian port city of Genoa.... Thousands of anti-Globalization demonstrators fought running battles with police for hours as the leaders of the world's richest countries and Russia—the Group of Eight (G8)—held their first day of talks.

The anti-globalization community, according to the BBC report, is also anti-capitalist. In that case, globalization is seen as letting go of the capital's horse to gallop around the world, carrying on its back, according to Jha, transnationals and managers and bringing them back home with bags loaded with profits.

However, when one juxtaposes the declaration of 2005 as Africa's Year—which includes Egypt and other Arab countries, viz. Libya, Tunisia, Morocco and Algeria—by the next president of G8, Tony Blair, and the vigor with which the British Labour government is at present pursuing a Marshall Plan for the continent, one would need to look at the terms of reference of globalization again. Together with Chirac's call and the launching of Action for Africa by G8, if this is globalization—or is it internationalization as we got from Cassen?—things look good for the continent. However, as soon as one remembers what the anti-globalization movement was calling for, and does not stop doing so, the romance with globalization becomes sour.

The question is, "If the G8 means good and the anti-globalization movement is right, where does misinterpretation of intentions come in then?" This brings us to the search for the true face of globalization.

GLOBALIZATION OR GLOBAL NATIONALIZATION?

There is something kaleidoscopic about globalization. At its first encounter, one comes off with the feeling, yes, here is the world coming together at last, like it used to be at the beginning. On reflection, one senses an attempt to carve a picture of two worlds, two ideologies with no sands of compromise between them. Yet on further reflection, this time more critical than the first, the cloud of fear of erosion of cultural diversity and the erasure of national identities is penetrated by the rays of a world where trade barriers are removed, and now we can all dance to the music of one world, one humanity that we are. But nor does this remove the cloud enveloping globalization either.

The central problem with globalization is its blurred meaning and the cloudiness of its implications. But we may agree on the common understanding, that the losers of the global economic game are the developing economies that hardly know the rules. Again, herein lies the problem. From all indications, it seems as if globalization is still an economic kite and a political weather gauge. It is being directed to an economic abode, and perhaps a political habitat by events in the world rather than driving them. It is by flying with the winds of the market that it gets its definition, which later becomes the pulse of the market.

What does all this mean? It means that there is a lack of consensus on what globalization really is, even if everything about who will benefit and are benefiting from it is clear. Is it the globalization of moral principles and the respect for our common humanity, in which, among other things, protectionism is replaced with free trade and fair terms or global nationalization, that is, management of the interests of developing economies by rich countries that hide under the veil of globalization? That it is difficult to know what globalization stands for is exemplified by divergent definitions and interpretations attached to it. Most of its nightmarish features are predicated on the fear of history repeating itself in the case of developing countries, while most of the glorious features are rooted in hope that the future could be the therapist of its past.

One thing is certain. Globalization is in search of identity; identity of meaning and its implication for international trade and relations. For, as long as there is no place for globalization to call a home, for that long shall the battle of the intellect continue between those who rock and cradle it on their laps for the benefits that the confusion of its meaning offers and those who would like to abort it rightaway to avoid, before it is too late, the birth of the monster of injustice and exploitation, once again, unto the world.

GLOBALIZATION—WHAT IS ITS FUTURE?

As in the affairs of the world, there is a tide in the life of a socio-political concept even when it is born with congratulatory messages from everywhere. These tides come in the form of cycles. A socio-political concept may be caught in an avalanche of events beyond its control, witness the setting of the sun on Communism and the end of red flag in the former East European bloc and so disappears in its eclipse. Or, it is caught in the wheel of lopsided logic bourne of diverse and conflicting interpretations of its promise while, as a result, its fears, feeding on confusion, explode to monstrous proportions. Globalization, where mass public education is not made to bear on its strengths and weaknesses, may face this tide in the near future. And so just when it should begin to boom, it might burst.

The problem is that not everybody welcomes globalization as they equate it with the erosion of national states that reduces national economic policies to footnotes in the books of multinational companies, NGOs, and economic blocs. In fact, to the anti-globalizers, come globalization in its full swing, developing economies shall be reduced to lilliputians even as the girth of industrial economies balloon to the belly size of a global elephant that consumes the hope of the struggling and crawling economies for a better future. The world shall become disappointingly unequal and grossly, sharply divided between the forever downtrodden and forever rising.

Paul Hirst and Grahame Thompson in their "The Future of Globalisation" encapsulate the threat to peace that globalization could pose if it is let loose to define itself. According to them,

If "globalization" is conceived as a process that promotes cross-border exchanges and transterritorial agencies at the expense of nation states then it would be deeply problematic. If all states, including the most powerful, were to cease to be the primary political actors across borders, being displaced by companies, NGOs, regional governments, networks, international agencies, etc., then one could anticipate a severe anti-globalization "backlash" as nationally-rooted publics experience a loss of the benefits of domestic governance and increased exposure to international pressures. If the majority of states cease to be effective actors, but the G7 still dominate in terms of economic governance and the USA alone dominates militarily, then Western and American dominance will be resented, resisted and challenged both nationally and trans-nationally in an increasingly unequal and conflictual world. This shows that there are inherent limits to globalization conceived as a process that leads to the decline of national economies and state power.

This means, for globalization to have a future, it needs a definite identity on which its terms of reference are anchored, and when this eventually comes, it should not include in its package the abrogation of the rights of nation-states to self-determination. This involves the right to conduct their economic policies without being reduced to appendages of multinational companies, even as the industrialized countries desist from practising protectionism while preaching open and free markets everywhere.

References

Al-Hamad, A.Y. 2003. *Globalization: Challenges and Responses in the Arab World*. Cairo, Egypt: Global Development Network, Arab Fund for Economic and Social Development.

Cassen, B. 2000. Who are the Winners, and Who are the Losers of Globalization? Speech delivered on June 17 at the Friends of *Le Monde Diplomatique* conference "Globalization: In Whose Interest?" Conway Hall, London.

Ebeid, A. 2003. *Egypt in a Globalizing World.* The Fourth Annual Global Development Conference on "Globalization And Equity". January 19–21, Cairo, Egypt.

Federici, S. 2002. War, Globalization and Reproduction. *Alternatives* (4). Available online at http://www.alternativesjournal.net

Hirst, P. and G. Thompson. 2002. The Future of Globalisation. *Cooperation and Conflict,* 37(3): 247–65.

Jha, P.S. 2003. Globalization is creating only a handful of winners and a very large number of losers. A bit rich, really. *The Hindustan Times,* September 6.

Mehdi, A. 2003. *Globalization, Labor Market, Social Policy, and the Arab World: A Sociological Perspective.* Cairo Conference on Globalization.

Simon, J. 2002. What is Globalization? The Origins and Meaning of the Now Ubiquitous Word. *The Guardian Unlimited.* Available online at http://www.guardian.co.uk

Tabb, W. 2004. *Globalization.* Microsoft Encarta Online Encyclopedia.

———. 2002. *Unequal Partners: A Primer on Globalization.* New York Press.

———. 2004. *Economic Governance in the Age of Globalization.* Columbia University Press.

The Challenge posed by the New G8–NEPAD Partnership. *Presidenza del Consiglio dei Ministri. The First Implementation Report of the G8 Africa Action Plan. The Italian contribution to the New Partnership for Africa's Development (NEPAD). G8 Africa Personal Representative* (The Prime Minister's Office).

Wolf, M. 2002. Is Globalization Causing World Poverty? *Financial Times,* February 25.

6

GLOBALIZATION AND ITS FUTURE SHOCK

SAMIR DASGUPTA

GLOBALIZATION DISCOURSE

Nowadays, globalization is the most widely used word. It is the buzzword in the speeches of intellectuals and academics, a catchword of the last decade of the twentieth century in research journals, magazines, and newspaper articles, in daily deliberations and discourses of specialists, journalists and traders, and in debates, seminars and symposia of academics. There have been attempts to define the theoretical identity and applied meaning of the word, and used to denote that the world is changing and shifting, that a new wave of economic, cultural, social, and political order is taking a new form and shape. Globalization panoramically refers to the extension and expansion of global linkages, the organization and institution of social living on a global parameter and the growth of a global consciousness, and hence to the consolidation of world society. This ecumenical definition is not enough to explore the real meaning of globalization. Human societies across the globe have established increasingly closer contacts. Modern technological devices and instant capital flows have made the world more interdependent than ever. Multinational corporations and consumerism have captured the world. Money, technology and raw materials move ever more promptly across national borders. Ideas, ideals and cultures circulate more freely. As a result, laws, economies, and social movements are forming at the international level. The intellectuals treat these trends as both inevitable and welcoming. A few days back, I was watching a news program in a television channel. An interesting story caught my eyes. A pious Hindu had invited some young Brahmins to a ritual lunch. Their age ranged from 14–17. They wore special clothes and the sacred thread. But they didn't like the traditional offerings such as sweets, fruits, and traditional *pooja* (Hindu ceremonial offering) dishes. They had accepted the invitation on the condition of having chicken burgers, rolls, pizzas and Coca-cola. The pious man, finding no other alternative, had to serve the fast food items to the young. This is the crisis of identity of tradition, values, and religious ethos and social sanction. For billions of people in the world, the recent trend of globalization means uprooting traditional ways of life, and threatening livelihoods, lifestyle patterns, social and moral values, and cultures.

The global social justice movement, itself a result of globalization, proposes an alternative path, one that is more responsive to public needs. Intense political disputes will continue over globalization's meaning and its future direction. Globalization is also a very powerful tool of capitalism, which comes dripping with blood and dirt from every pore, from head to foot, of ordinary people in the Third World. Nobody should be hurt if the unobtrusive and deadening condition of globalization is seen from the viewpoint of pessimism. The reality depicts that globalization is not necessarily one that reaches out and touches all parts of the globe. And the spatial and organizational dilemma creates a "globalization gloom." It is now both an exciting opportunity and a formidable threat. Besides its bright promises and potential, the globalization forces accentuate inequitable opportunities and benefits across present generations of the Third World countries and its future generations. Some say globalization is salvation of the present generation and some call it damnation. The global arena constitutes the individual self, the national society, the international system of societies and humanity (Robertson 1992), which results in social processes of globalization. In terms of its applied sense, the prescriptive version of globalization creates a strange interlude. If we assess globalization in terms of change in world-economy, world culture, world society and world polity, the progress of the rich appears alongside the misery of the poor. So in a one-world view of the globalizers, the strategy of liberalization becomes an economic, social, cultural, and human nightmare for the deprived majorities. Alan Greenspan argues that the expansion of efficient global financial markets is largely beneficial but also presents new risks. What are those risks? Is it disparity and dejection? Is it inequality? Is it cross-border terrorism and ethnic riots? Is it clash of culture or East–West confrontation and disequilibrium? Is it capitalistic implosion? If the answers to all of the questions are "yes," then we are on the verge of the "end of civilization." Capitalism develops by way of crisis. Capitalism had only just matured to become "capitalism-in-all," when it began to reveal its crisis-generating nature. And it was this forerunner of all subsequent crises that demonstrated for the entire world to see the main genetic feature of cyclical crises (Dadayan 1988). Is globalization a revised version of capitalism? The archetype classical cycle characterizing the growth of capitalism fits the paradigm of globalization (see Figure 6.1).

Capitalism destroyed the economic structure of the colonies and adjusted it to the requirements of growth of capital and its self-expansion. World trade had never developed as quickly as it did in the nineteenth century. In 1770, the ratio of the per capita product in the developed countries to that in the

Figure 6.1: Classical and Modern Cycles of Growth of Capitalism.

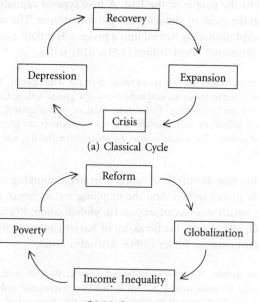

(a) Classical Cycle

(b) Modern Cycle

The deduction of the above two paradigms reveals the following propositions:

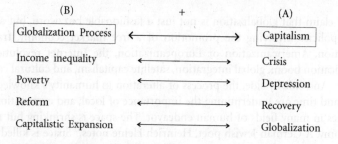

(B)	+	(A)
Globalization Process	⟷	Capitalism
Income inequality	⟷	Crisis
Poverty	⟷	Depression
Reform	⟷	Recovery
Capitalistic Expansion	⟷	Globalization

underdeveloped countries stood at about 1.2:1. By the start of World War I, the gap stood at 11.3:1 and by the year 2000 this gap was 14:1 (Dadayan 1988), and now it is steadily increasing. It is certainly for the appearance of capitalism. Dadayan (1988) notes, "The saturation of the domestic market, the exacerbation of the contradiction between production and accumulation, reflected the conflict between the limited purchasing power of the population and the tendency for capital to expand without any limits, caused capital, with its unquenchable thirst for surplus value, to set out in search of new markets" (1985: 108). Economic, social, political, and individual fragmentation has come about as a result of extreme commodification with the recent phase of capitalism.

The world was divided into the West and the East. The capitalism of the West was disposed to the people in the East. A new type of capitalism (flexible or managerial) in the guise of globalization got its entrepot. The word "globalization" as a concept ultimately turned into a process. Is it then a reality, or merely a knowledge-economy? Alvin Toffler (1993: 318) states,

Few words are more loosely thrown about today than the term "global." Ecology is said to be a "global" problem. The media are said to be creating a "global" village. Companies proudly announce that they are "globalizing." Economists speak of "global" growth or recession. And the politician, UN official, or media pundit does not exist who is not prepared to lecture us about the "global system." There is, of course, a global system. But it is not what most people imagine it to be.

It is undeniable that twenty-first century strategic thinking begins with the mapping of the global system. And the mapping system began with the end of the Cold War, which still has an impact on globalization. Primarily, the fall of the Berlin Wall, and second, the break-up of Soviet Union are the prime causes of such a system change. Toffler (1993: 319) also notes,

we are witnessing, instead, the sudden eruption of a new civilization on the planet, carrying with it a knowledge-intensive way of creating wealth that is trisecting and transforming the entire global system. Everything in that system is now mutating, from its basic components…to the way they interrelate…to the speed of their interactions…to the interest over which countries contend…to the kinds of wars that may result and which need to be prevented.

One may claim that globalization is not just a fashionable buzzword, but also a set of policies involving the promotion of a free market economy, trade liberalization, Americanization or Europeanization, the Internet revolution, communication boom, global integration, satellite capitalism, and cultural consumerism. And side by side, the process of alteration in humanity's knowledge of space and time are undermining the importance of local, and even national boundaries in many fields of human endeavor. The space is shrinking but not the economy. A German Jewish poet, Heinrich Heine notes, "Space is killed by the railways. I feel as if the mountains and forests of all countries were advancing on Paris. Even now, I can smell the German linden trees; the North Sea's breakers are rolling against my door." But on the contrary, I say, economy is not killed by equality and distributive social justice. I do not feel as if the globalizer's capital were advancing on India, Bangladesh, Argentina, Peru, Bolivia or Brazil. Even now, I can strongly smell the poverty; the waves of disparity, dejection, environmental catastrophe, war, hunger, and the cry of the deprived majorities are rolling against my door. I mean among critics of capitalism and global inequality, globalization now has a "pejorative ring." Beck (1992: 20) observes, "In the welfare state of the west a double process is taking place now. On the one hand, the struggle for one's 'daily bread' has lost its urgency as a cardinal problem overshadowing everything else, compared to material subsistence in the first half of this century, and to a third world menaced by hunger."

Practically, globalization catches aspects like compression of space using new and hyper-technology, communication and information technologies, abolition of distance, free trade, cultural consumerism, acceleration at all levels of human organization, extension of the scope of "virtual reality" (Heidegger 1971), and finally interconnectedness and dialog among civilizations. But the gap between winners and losers has intensified. The ethical version of globalization was something different. The speedy "globalizing and extraterritorial economy being freed from localization and political constraint is known to produce *the ever deepening wealth-and-income gaps between the better off and the worse off sections of the world population.*" (Bauman 2001: 114). In terms of the human face of globalization, only a few are winners and the great majorities are losers. This is because the Third World has not yet escaped from excessive population increase, missing institutions, lack of capital formation, ill entrepreneurship, debt burden, vicious cycle of poverty, infrastructure deficit and different endowment conditions. We are in the midst of an anti-democratic counter-revolution in which globalization and its imperatives are being used to weaken popular and elected authority in favor of a system of domination by super-citizens, the TNCs. This process sows the seeds of its own destruction, as it serves a small global minority, damages the majority, breeds financial instability, and exacerbates the environmental crisis. Its destructive tendencies are likely to produce an explosion if the process is not contained and democracy is not rehabilitated. History tells that integrated capitalists or the rulers of global economy and their industrial strength were continuously trying to exploit and destroy the economic bases of the Third World countries. This process affected economic, cultural, social, political and religious spheres of these countries. For example, in the cultural sphere, the Internet, video, and digital communication system have engulfed the tradition by what may be called "cultural imperialism." The day will come when the fetters of traditional cultural activities will completely lose its identity. Ferguson (1992) views that "Global Cultural Homogeneity" as a myth must presume a global cultural economy that completely ignores local, regional or national influences. Here lies a gap between global culture and local culture. Here there may arise a cultural upsurge, which take the shape of anti-globalization movement. Globalization principally benefits people who can play the capitalist game, but does little for the people who are resourceless, illiterate, and making a living through traditional and folk production activities. They are in the real sense under pressure for existence and identity crisis. Some globalization specialists talk about the different faces of the future and list few changes, such as nation-states to networks, traditions to options, export-led to consumer-driven, farms to super cities, labor intensive to high-tech, male dominance to emerging women, West to East. These are the world trends, and they are affecting Asia very much, especially the people of India. The social scientists also suggest certain challenges for the future. The challenges are education for the people, planning for better urbanization, fighting against anarchy and crime, removal of disparity between increasing wealth of the minorities and pennilessness of the majorities. For example, modern India has its stark contrasts and its own share of contradictions. With a vibrant democracy, India is emerging with its fascinating liberalization policies and market restructure, becoming a world leader in indigenous-built communications satellites and technologies. Yet, it is one of the poorest countries in the world, with a population boom, illiteracy, health hazard, environmental risks, political corruptions, caste and communal violence, religious bigotry, and know-how hazards. Many critics fear that globalization, in the sense of integration of a country into world society, will exacerbate gender inequality. It may harm women economically, through discrimination in favor of male workers, marginalization of women in unpaid or informal labor, exploitation of women in low-wage sweatshop settings, and/ or impoverishment through loss of traditional sources of income. Politically, it will affect through exclusion from the domestic political process and loss of control to global pressures; and culturally, through loss of identity and autonomy to a hegemonic global culture.

Many women's advocates recognize that globalization affects different groups of women in different ways, creates new standards for the treatment of women, and helps women's groups to mobilize. In situations where women have been historically repressed or discriminated under a patriarchal division of labor, some features of globalization may have liberating consequences. While in many countries women remain at a significant disadvantage, the precise role of globalization in causing or perpetuating that condition is in dispute. Globalization presents opportunities to some women but causes marginalization of many others; it advocates, "mainstreaming" as the way to achieve gender equality. Women play a distinct role in globalization, experience more harmful effects, and become a constituency for anti-systemic movements. The mission of rhetoric globalization was to promote gender inequality and the empowerment of women as effective ways to combat poverty, hunger, and disease, and to stimulate development that is truly sustainable, and also to combat all forms of violence and assault against women. But the recent trend shows a rather sordid picture of gender exploitation, and a nexus between the increase in workplace-based sexual harassment claims and the proliferation of work-based email and internet use is quite visible now. We can look at how email and internet technologies are implicated in sexual harassment and consider some of the reasons why these technologies have provoked harassment claims. This is, of course, the negative and other side of globalization, which is very dangerous for the identity of womanhood or motherhood in future. Many urban and rural women are forced into prostitution in the cities. Sex trafficking of women and children are increasing due to the wide network of multinational corporations in the industrial and rural areas. The facts and figures reveal that 98 percent of wealth on earth is in the hands of men, and only 2 percent belongs to women; the 225 richest "persons" in the world, who are men, own the same capital as the 2,500 million poorest people. Of these 2,500 million, 80 percent are women. While $780,000 million are spent on armaments worldwide, only $12,000 million are spent on women's reproductive health. In terms of child prostitution, 90 percent victims are girls and 100 percent of the beneficiaries are men.

Wars turn women into sexual slaves. Incidents of sexual assault, which I strongly consider, are the impact of digital globalization and deregulated cultural and moral freedom. The young generation is adversely affected and influenced by globalization of media, travels, fashions, McDonaldization, and economic changes. The values between older people and the young generation begin to clash. The shopping mall, the fast food centers, the cyber cafes are becoming the "Cathedral of cultural consumerism." The hallucination of globalization and the reality of poverty make them restive, which results in failure in socialization. The impact leads to corruption, crime, sexual vulgarism, civil and ethnic conflict leading to acts of violence, and denial of fundamental rights of humanity.

A THEORETICAL PUZZLE

Giddens' (1991) theory of reflexivity and time-space distanciation, Frank's (1971) dependency paradigm, Wallerstein's (1974) world-system theory, Lash and Urry's (1994) concept of "organized capitalism," Smart (1993) and Appadurai's (1990) concept of postmodernization–globalization linkage, Harvey's (1989) space time compression—all describe the dawn of globalization theory. Likely, a great number of theoretical puzzles have developed in the field of globalization. For some, globalization is the other name of global capitalism and imperialism, and is accordingly condemned as another form of the imposition of the logic of capital and the market on ever more regions of the world and spheres of life. For others, it is the continuation of modernization and representative of postmodernism, along with a sign of progress, wealth, freedom, democracy, and happiness. The theoretical spell produces a great number of concepts or nomenclature-puzzles, like "Creolization" (Hannerz 1992), "Hybridization" (Latour, cited in Schurmann 2001), "Second Modernity" (Beck, cited in Albrow 1990), "Glocalization" (Robertson 1995), "Grobalization" (Ritzer and Mike 2004), "Socio-scapes and Sociospheres" (Albrow 1997), "Globaloney" (Fukuyama 1992), "Civil Society" and "Good Governance," etc. The functionalists present globalization as beneficial, generating new economic opportunities, political democratization, cultural diversity, and the road to an enchanting new world. But the opponents view globalization as harmful, bringing about increased domination and control by the wealthier overdeveloped nations over the poor underdeveloped countries, thus increasing the hegemony of the *"haves"* over the *"have nots"* (Kellner). Most of the approaches are descriptive and rhetoric. So one may easily raise the question: Is globalization an ideology or a practice? Globalization is both a description and a prescription, and as such it serves as both an explanation—a poor one, it has to be said—and an ideology that currently dominates thinking, policymaking and policy practice.

As a description, "globalization" refers to the widening and deepening of the international flows of trade, capital, technology and information within a single integrated global market ... as a prescription, "globalization" involves the liberalization of national and global markets in the belief that free flows of trade, capital and information will produce the best outcome for growth and human welfare. (Petras and Veltmeyer 2001: 11)

The new age globalists view globalization either as a process of homogenization or new social movements. And ultimately the movements begin to identify the future of globalization. So the global advocates begin to rethink about new globalization in terms of some radical tunes like civil society, good governance, corruption removal projects, human values, and altruism. I have asked hundreds of people, including rickshaw pullers, cultivators, daily laborers, maid servants, factory workers and service holders: "Do you know what is globalization?" Very innocently they replied, "No." A few days back I was present as an invigilator in an examination hall. A large number of job seekers were writing essays on globalization. Most of them asked me, "Sir—do you know what is globalization?" The tragedy is this that they are not even familiar with the term. This is the globalization syndrome in most of the Third World countries. It rotates only among the circle of academics, political leaders, planners, traders, technocrats and bureaucrats. If this is the present reality, then we could easily imagine its future.

Perhaps so, a new discourse began to locate the future of globalization. Perhaps so, the deprived majorities of the world are facing globalization without inclusion and uniformity. Inequality is now coming into the fore and this rings the bell of global protest movements. The terrorist attack on the United States on September 11 and subsequent cross-border terrorisms across the world, and lastly, "the war on terror" declaration nakedly exposed the downsides of globalization.

The ways that global flows of technology, goods, information, ideologies, and people can have destructive as well as productive effects. The disclosure of powerful anti-Western terrorist networks shows that globalization divides the world as it unifies, that it produces enemies as it incorporates participants. The events disclose explosive contradictions and conflicts at the heart of globalization and that the technologies of information, communication, and transportation that facilitate globalization can also be used to undermine and attack it, and generate instruments of destruction as well as production. (Kellner)

He also views that the use of powerful technologies as weapons of destruction also discloses current asymmetries of power and emergent forms of terrorism and war, as the new millennium exploded into dangerous conflicts and interventions. As technologies of mass destruction become more available and dispersed, perilous instabilities have emerged that have elicited policing measures to stem the flow of movements of people and goods across borders and internally. Is our world waiting for a doomsday where killing, mass destruction and ferocity of wars would be our only identity? What will be the name of globalization in future? Will it be called fragmentization? Might be too. The events of September 11 also provide a test case to evaluate various theories of globalization and the contemporary era. In addition, they highlight some of the contradictions of globalization and the need to develop a highly complex and dialectical model to capture its conflicts, ambiguities, and contradictory effects (Kellner).

Capitalism with the authority to extend its power from metropolis to all satellites will dominate over the global village, where there will be no room for local, regional, and national democracy; or, democracy among the local community will exist and capitalism will perish. Some (dormant majorities) argue on globalization as a peril to world peace and humanity, and others (dominant minorities) argue that globalization will perish world crisis. This is a matter of heated controversy, which cannot predict the future of human society. The strange interlude of globalization with both sorrow and joy creates such a traumatic future. All the sorrows and pain of the depressed majorities have bursted into anger. Perhaps so the anti-globalization movement begins. "The West versus the East" dilemma is exerting tremendous pressure on globalizers. So the advocates claim, "If globalization is perceived as the domain of the powerful either by design or by default, it will not be conducive to international stability. Since globalization is not homogenization, imagined or real hegemonism is detrimental to the cultivation of a culture of world peace. The dialogue among civilizations is intended to reverse this unintended negative consequence of globalization" (Picco 2001: 63). If two sides can build enough trust to face each other with reciprocal respect, only then can a productive discourse begin. But how is it possible? The face of the king and that of the destitute cannot reciprocate each other.

One may raise a basic question: Is globalization an opportunity or threat? Some, of course, view it as a process that is beneficial—a key to future world economic development—and also inevitable and irreversible. Market economy, democratic polity, civil society and individual rights as characteristics of modernization have assumed global significance; at the same time, the strength of traditions in shaping the modern world compel us to move beyond the simple mentality of "either-or." They have just imagined the philosophy of global village as a virtual reality and indication of integration and harmony. Former

WTO Director-General Mike Moore (*WTO News*, June 16, 2000) argues in the context of assessing the "after-globalization,"

Few topics are as controversial as globalization. It is bringing distant markets and people across the world closer together, is a huge change that affects everyone, whether they are peasants in India, students in London or bankers in New York.... We need to reassure people that globalization in generally a force for good.... In the first half of the 20th century the globalization of the 19th century was rolled back. We cannot rely on people's grudging acceptance of the perceived inevitability of globalization. We must not shrink from making our case...when people say globalization lacks a human face, they may also mean that it does not benefit ordinary people. But this is simply not true.

It is fact that people in India talk on mobile phones, use Japanese cameras, drive cars, drink foreign scotch, eat American pizza, and communicate through the internet. It is also true that a great number of programers of Indian call centers sell their services to American companies. But they are very few in number. But what about the billion people who are totally faceless, who die in starvation, sell their blood for a day's meal, live in slum pockets, and become the victims of health hazard, environmental pollution, and illiteracy? To them, globalization lacks the human face.

It is true that general living standards in poor countries are not catching up with the richest ones. It is still a tragedy that 1.2 billion people—a quarter of the world's population—survive on less than a dollar a day and that a further 1.6 billion—another third of the world's population—make do with between one and two dollars a day (Moore 2004). It is obvious that the progress is not evenly dispersed. The gap between rich and poor countries, and the rich and poor people within countries has grown. The report of the IMF staff (2002) says, "The richest quarter of the world's population saw its per capita GDP increase nearly six-fold during the century, while the poorest quarter experienced less than a three-fold increase." Yes, it is the tragic present and gloomy future of globalization. UN Secretary-General Kofi Annan has spoken recently about how unevenly the bonanzas of globalization have been distributed. He has mentioned the existence of a *"digital divide"* in which only 5 percent of the world is connected to the World Wide Web—80 percent of which is published only in English. He has expressed in his deliberations that half of humanity has neither received nor made a simple telephone call. As for the distributive economic justice, he notes that almost half of humanity still lives on less than $2 a day, and that over a billion people earn less than $1 a day. Whether one looks at the availability of drinking water, sanitation, educational opportunities, other crucial facets of human development, one can see that globalization per se has offered no cure-all for humanity's welfare needs.

In the ambiguous global system, problems for the relatively poorer countries are not about empirical domination but sheer rejection and exclusion. The idea of a global world was predicated on the promises of a widespread prosperity, of economic globalization, and the further belief that this prosperity went hand in hand with delivering the fruits of liberal democracy. The betrayal of these promises, however, is evident in growing inequalities and increased poverty. It may now be argued that the globalization paradigm is no longer operative because its liberalizing potential was never realized. Some see the events of 9/11 as a symbol of the failure of globalization and the triumph of the local frustrations that it engendered. Indeed, the euphoric ideal of global freedom has been replaced by the very real threats posed by globally unbounded and unrestrained "others". The World Bank in its report could not justify the claims made in favor of globalization. It is undeniable that in the past twenty years the global economy has become increasingly integrated. International financial flows have grown. More people are on the move. And countries are exchanging more goods and services. In 2002, trade in goods and services as a share of world output reached 54 percent, up from 31 percent in 1980.

Still, there are many obstacles to global integration. National policies that protect home industries from competition or subsidize their output, distort patterns of trade and prevent developing countries from reaching their full potential. Risk and uncertainty also inhibit the flow of finance, while development assistance may be directed more by political considerations than by development opportunities. For example, by the beginning of the 1990s, most people in sub-Saharan Africa were poorer than they had been thirty years before. Of the population of about 500 million, nearly 300 million are living in absolute poverty (Kiely 1998). Not only that, the crisis in the Third World countries is severely aggravated by the heavy debt burden. It has increased enormously in the poor countries. It is evident from the report of World Bank that the debt of the developing countries increased by 8 percent to over $2 trillion in 1995. The Third World debt has grown from $9 billion in 1955 to $217 billion in 1996 (Gelinas 1998). As global capitalists view, the debt continues to increase not because of the inability to service it. It is mainly because of the degree and intensity of dependency caused by capitalist implosion, extension of power of the globalizers from metropolis to satellites, global–local confusion, and commercialization of aid-ethics. Humanity is certainly a global phenomenon. But integration and singularity of humanity in the age of economic inequality is rhetoric because "economy" dominates "humanity." Debt has been used as a stick by the international capitalist institutions of the IMF and the World Bank for over thirty years to force countries to introduce austerity packages that push up prices and devastate what few services exist. The production of goods for exports has been privileged over the production of what people need to survive. Often this has resulted in ecological degradation as monocultures of cash crops have replaced traditionally mixed agriculture. Poverty, disease and death have inevitably followed. A child dies in a dilapidated Third World country clinic.

Another suddenly drops out of school. The future of one suffered tremendous shock in infancy, the other's aspirations and dreams turned into nightmare before they could even begin to unfold. But they have something deeper in common—both are victims of the effects of the crushing debt burden facing the Third World. The debt burden is the only obstacle to development in the Third World, the most powerful tool that western nations use to keep whole countries in bondage. It is estimated that the Third World pays the developed North nine times more in debt repayments than they receive in aid. Africa alone spends four times more on repaying its debts than it spends on its health care. It is therefore, not surprising that most of the thirty-two debt-distressed countries in the world are in Africa (Moore 2004). The debt burden pervades and perverts the mission of so-called progressive globalization process and it dehumanizes human faces. It is undeniable that total globalization is a remote-controlled process and the remote lies in the hands of the capitalists, who can easily change the channels of development deals. The protagonists of course have not agreed to such black-hole games of the process. Meanwhile, the external debt zooms upward.

OLD WINE IN NEW BOTTLE

Neoliberalism is deeply rooted in the works of Adam Smith, David Ricardo and Herbert Spencer. Neoliberal ideas stepped into the applied world in the late 1970s, being supported by some prime factors of economic depression like inflation, high unemployment, etc. Making a strong ground for the return to free market policies of the past, the neoliberalists drew on the neoclassical *laissez-faire* economic theories. Some British advocates called it "Second-coming Capitalism" or "Turbo-capitalism" (Steger 2002). "By the late 1980s," Steger (2002: 11) notes, "British Prime Minister Margaret Thatcher and US President Ronald Reagan were both revered and reviled as the founding figures of a new market paradigm. Since then, their ideological heirs have marshaled their considerable resources to expand the neoliberal project into a full-blown globalist ideology." Market liberalization now creates "new-market ideology" that endows globalization as the new economic reform of the old capitalists. But the impact of neoliberalization on the Third World mostly appears as a gloomy mist. The ground was not ready to accept either time-space compression or free trade and market orientation. Also the Third World Country fails to delink its own development *modus operandi* from the world-economy and compels to be the part of imposed neoliberal economy of the West, which results in complete socioeconomic and socio-cultural stagnation. The globalization hegemony of the West might be real or rhetoric or abstract, but in some sense, very limited that fails to honor the importance of local, and thus intensifies the uneven

Table 6.1: Total External Debt

Country	Total Ext. Debt ($ million)		Long-term debt ($ million)		Public and publicly guaranteed debt ($ million)		Private misguaranteed debt ($ million)		Use of IMF Credit ($ million)	
	1990	2002	1990	2002	1990	2002	1990	2002	1990	2002
Afghanistan	–	–	–	–	–	–	–	–	–	–
Argentina	62,233	132,314	48,676	103,140	46,876	74,661	1,800	28,479	3,083	14,340
Australia	–	–	–	–	–	–	–	–	–	–
Brazil	119,964	227,932	94,427	183,710	87,756	96,565	6,671	87,145	1,821	20,827
Bangladesh	12,439	17,037	11,657	16,445	11,657	16,445	0	0	629	71
China	55,301	168,255	45,515	120,370	45,515	88,531	0	31,839	469	0
India	83,628	104,429	72,462	99,860	70,974	88,271	1,488	11,589	2,623	0
Iraq	–	–	–	–	–	–	–	–	–	–
Mexico	104,442	141,264	81,809	131,364	75,974	76,327	5,835	55,038	6,551	0
Pakistan	20,663	33,672	16,643	30,100	16,506	28,102	138	1,998	836	2,032
Peru	20,064	28,167	13,959	25,596	13,629	20,477	330	5,118	755	237
Poland	49,364	69,521	39,261	60,637	39,261	29,374	0	31,263	509	0
Russian Federation	–	147,541	–	124,738	–	96,223	–	28,514	–	6,481
Rwanda	712	1,435	664	1,305	664	1,305	0	0	0	85
Sri Lanka	5,863	9,611	5,049	8,805	4,947	8,455	102	351	410	310
Turkey	49,424	131,556	39,924	94,278	38,870	61,823	1,054	32,455	0	22,086
Vietnam	23,270	13,349	21,378	12,181	21,378	12,181	0	0	112	381

World	Total Ext. Debt ($ million)		Long-term debt ($ million)		Public and publicly guaranteed debt ($ million)		Private misguaranteed debt ($ million)		Use of IMF Credit ($ million)	
	1990	2002	1990	2002	1990	2002	1990	2002	1990	2002
Low Income	411,419	523,464	351,318	448,932	332,366	399,076	17,953	49,857	11,317	20,258
Middle Income	940,479	1,817,163	749,931	1,469,476	707,793	983,880	42,138	485,596	23,334	75,550
Lower Middle Income	583,682	1,149,118	477,625	925,294	453,753	651,767	23,872	273,527	7,811	59,160
Upper Middle Income	356,797	668,045	273,306	544,182	254,040	332,112	18,266	212,069	15,523	16,390
Low & Middle Income	1,351,898	2,340,627	1,101,250	1,918,408	1,041,159	1,382,955	60,091	535,453	34,651	95,809
East Asia and Pacific	234,092	499,133	194,633	388,064	172,998	272,783	21,635	115,281	2,085	11,618
Europe & Central Asia	217,224	545,842	176,378	434,625	171,457	276,350	4,921	158,275	1,305	34,245
Latin America and Carib	444,227	727,944	352,476	613,916	327,447	384,961	25,029	228,956	18,297	38,302
Middle East and N. Africa	155,134	189,010	120,603	148,851	119,101	142,396	1,502	6,455	1,815	2,219
South Asia	124,395	168,349	107,527	158,723	105,799	144,785	1,727	13,938	4,537	2,416
Sub-Saharan Africa	176,826	210,350	149,632	174,229	144,355	161,681	5,276	12,548	6,612	7,009

Source: 2004 World Development Report, World Bank, 242–44.

development. "And that, therefore, globalization, is differently and unequally experienced in the world today" (Kiely 1998: 17). Setting aside the good and altruistic words of, and about globalization, I say, and (majority) feel that the triumph of globalization today is the triumph of capitalism of a certain new kind with a certain human-tuned specific discourse. And it has been unmasked to the people with the naked exposure of the Third World crisis. Patnaik (1995) notes,

In a third world context, the correlation between the pursuit of liberal economic policies and the imposition of political authoritarianism is quite strong. The countries usually cited by the advocates of World Bank style "liberalization" as success stories to emulate, have all had authoritarian regimes or military dictatorship presiding over such "liberalization." But the very narrowing of the class base opens up the possibility of mobilizing broad section of the population against the imposition of World Bank style liberalization.

The neoliberal capitalism historically emerges through three successive stages of US power, i.e., industrial power, military power, and lastly hegemonic power. In the words of Wallerstein (2003),

In terms of the world class struggle, the weakening of the anti-systematic movements—old and new allowed establishment forces to launch a counter offensive of considerable magnitude that initially took the form of the neoliberal regimes in Britain and the US; the rise of the "Washington Consensus" which buried the ideal of developmentalism and replaced it with globalization; and the vigorous expansion of the role and activities of the IMF, World Bank and newly formed World Trade organization, all of which sought to curtail the ability of peripheral states to interfere with the free flow of goods and, above all, of capital.

This neoliberal capitalism thus compels the people in the Third World to being delocalized, detraditionalized, disempowered and helpless. The newly introduced "free market" gospel thus resists the ethics (imaginative or motivated!) of globalization, which deface common humanity. The protest movement thus begins from the dilemma of "revolutions of rising expectation" and "revolutions of rising frustrations." It is perhaps moving towards post-global arena because it exceeds the development era of multiculturalism and multilateralism, and replaces it with the concept of a unilateral dominant culture, which shatters the information-happy notion of a singular global village. So, post-global is not an end to globalization but the emergence of a different kind of engagement that is sharply at odds with the visions of liberal, multicultural globalization. Here, both religious fundamentalism and imperial hegemony begin to emerge as the new forms of global engagement. Ulrich Beck has called the attack on the World Trade Center "the Chernobyl of globalization," exposing "the false promise of neo liberalism." Joseph Stiglitz (2004) writes,

The war on terrorism and in Iraq has distracted much of the world's attention from the pressing issue of how globalization should be managed so that it benefits everyone. A new report, issued by the International Labor Organization's commission on the social dimensions of globalization, reminds us how far the Bush administration is out of line with the global consensus...this very heterogeneous group was able to crystallize the emerging consensus, that globalization—despite its positive potential—has not only failed to live up to that potential, but has actually contributed to social distress.

FUTURE OF FAIR GLOBALIZATION: WHAT DOES IT MEAN?

I took much time to write the beginning of this article. I was suffering very badly from acute ulceration in my eyes, which is the result of regular use of computer and internet. The doctor advised me to go back to the world of tradition where pen, ink, and paper are the safest ingredients. But it has become very difficult for me to return to our traditional roots. Globalization has swallowed my traditional identity. It is impossible to measure a nebulous concept like globalization precisely, but increasing interconnectedness is readily apparent in a host of economic, demographic, political, ethical, technological, and cultural changes. Alvin Toffler (1970), forecasts,

Today the whole world is a fast-breaking story.... In the three short decades between now and the twenty-first century, millions of ordinary, psychologically normal people will face an abrupt collision with the future. Citizens of the world's richest and most technologically advanced nations, many of them will find it increasingly painful to keep up with the incessant demand for change that characterizes our time.... This new disease can be called "future shock".... Future shock is the dizzying disorientation brought on by the premature arrival of the future. It may well be the most important disease of tomorrow.

Future Shock accurately foretold globalization and defined exactly how we would suffer from its effects. On the basis of such future paradigms we can say that globalization has really shadowed our lives, lifestyle, mindset, and our identity. And for billions of the world's people, capitalist globalization means uprooting old ways of life, and threatening traditional styles of living, livelihoods and cultures. The global social justice movement, itself a product of globalization, is moving to propose an alternative path, more responsive to the common man's needs. Intense political disputes will continue over globalization's meaning and its future direction. Here we can mention some of the prime threats of globalization, which may result in clouds of uncertainties and errors, hovering in the sky of future.

Over-Stress and Identity Crisis

In terms of our temperament, institutional behavior and self-identity, we are neither global nor local. Globalization has thus created an identity crisis, which is very dangerous for our mental and physical health. Man, overloaded with rapidly changing stimuli, starts reacting with his head instead of his heart to protect himself against the sweeping currents that would uproot him. As a consequence, he reacts less to emotional responses but responds more to the money economy and as a result money hollows out the core of individuality, devaluing the whole. The "don't care" attitude of children, commercial interaction among family members, the rise of individualism, breaking down of family ties, domination of individual identity and spatial disequilibrium are coming into the fore. The husband resides in India while the wife is in America or, the wife in India and husband in London. Family culture and neo-culture (that develops in fast food centers) clash, the older people feel frustrated and alienated. They are now the victims of a cursed loneliness. They suffer economic and mental insecurities. On the other hand, they have become potential burden to their sons who earn little. Not only that, the old age boom will be a global burden very soon. All are the results and consequences of globalization and consumerism. Globally people are running fast towards a goal where tradition, sense of localism, and community feelings have no room. The rat race of global civilization, the burden of money and minds create mental disorder and emotional dislocation. It is the real crisis in the era of globalization and such a crisis may cause identity fragmentation in future if the runway world runs so fast.

It is evident from the WHO report (2001),

Major depression is now the leading cause of disability globally and ranks fourth in the ten leading causes of the global burden of disease. If projections are correct, within the next 20 years, depression will have the dubious distinction of becoming the second cause of the global disease burden. Globally, 70 million people suffer from alcohol dependence. About 50 million have epilepsy; another 24 million have schizophrenia. A million people commit suicide every year. Between ten and 20 million people attempt it. Rare is the family that will be free from an encounter with mental disorders. One person in every four will be affected by a mental disorder at some stage of life.

The loss of mental and physical health—which is the result of high speed and velocity of globalization, communication technology, media flash, excessive and total dependence on computer and global networking mechanism, overuse of domestic and commercial technological gadgets, regular use of banned medicines, overuse of poisonous pesticides and fertilizers, and lastly the sorrow of the loser—project a vicious circle of globalization risk that results in the incidence of psychosomatic disease like depression, dementia, anxiety, chronic stress, bronchial spasm, heart problems, hypertension, neurotic expressions, psychosis, alienation, violence, alcoholism, schizophrenia and suicide. And thus the future of our global society, particularly the Third World countries is more horrible. The emotional disorders also affect 59 million people across the world and top the list of disabilities. The Harvard School of Public Health report predicts that in the coming couple of decades, 90 million Indians—more than the combined population of the four metros—will suffer from major clinical depression caused mostly by stress. Dr Gro Harlem Brundtland, Director-General, WHO, said in October 1999, "Today, as many as 300–400 million people worldwide are estimated to be suffering at any given time from some kind of neurological or psychological disorder, including behavioral and substance abuse disorders. The more technology advances towards a virtual world the more touch and emotional health becomes important. The lesson of history is that the more affluent we become, the more stressed and emotionally vulnerable we feel." George Kaplan, Director of the Center of Epidemology, says, "Stress, emotional responses, economic disadvantage and beleaguered neighborhoods are inter-related with health changes.... That's part of how social inequalities become health inequalities." In India, the breakdown of the joint family and the growth of consumerist culture, as the result of globalization, gives rise to aspirations that often cannot be met and create mental strain. Lacking the deep sense of belonging to a community, family or tradition, the individual will then begin to seek meaning in various pseudo-solidarities.

Global Burden of Disease

Health is no doubt a determinant of economic growth. It is evident from the study of the "Global Burden of Disease" that the burden will not change significantly from 1990 to 2020 in developed regions, developing regions, or as a whole. The study estimates the burden as a result of 107 diseases, accidents and their disabling sequels, disaggregated with respect to cause, sex, age, and geographical region. Does it have use in guiding future planning and preventive action? At a global level, exceeding ecological capacity primarily through relative overpopulation is likely to be the greatest threat to overall health, yet overpopulation is not considered a risk factor in itself. This reflects the understanding of health as an issue of the individual rather than the community as a whole. The western nations where corporations are based have, through colonialism and postwar global economics, fostered an environment that have led to further poverty and dependency of the poorer nations on the First World countries. Postwar policies from the IMF and World Bank have compelled the Third World countries to cut back on such social expenditures as health and education in the first place.

The impact of globalization on life-saving drugs depicts a very sordid picture. Multinational pharmaceutical companies bring not benefits to the humanity across the the world; their interest is to create more and more profits. The life-saving drugs of the tropical disease are not profitable to them because most people with such diseases are too poor to afford cures. In addressing the excessive quest for profits, poverty should be overlooked. This is really inhuman globalization where human lives, and the right to live is not included in their moral agenda. These pharmaceutical industries talk from capitalist corridors of power. Ken Silverstein (1999) says, "Millions for Viagra. Pennies for Diseases of the Poor." The multinational corporations sell viagra across the world mainly because they serve the people who are very much addicted to sexual pleasure. It gains more importance in the era of globalization because most people in the Third World countries have to depend on selling sex to satisfy the cravings of absolute hunger. Are we then getting to the root of promiscuity? This poses a basic question to the future society. As Noam Chomsky points out, "The World Trade Organization regime insists instead on product patents, so you can't figure out a smarter process. Notice that impedes growth, and development and is intended to. It's intended to cut back innovation, growth, and development and to maintain extremely high profits" (cited in Tempest, 2003). Jonathan Madeley (1999) is worth quoting in this context: "The global pharmaceutical corporations sell products in developing countries that are withdrawn in the West; sell their products by persuasive and misleading advertising and promotion; cause the poor to divert money away from essential items, such as foodstuffs, to paying for expensive, patented medicines, thereby adding to problems of malnutrition; sell products such as appetite stimulants which are totally inappropriate; promote antibiotics for relatively trivial illnesses; charge more for products in developing countries than they do in the West". A survey, in the *Annals of Internal Medicine* found that 62 percent of the pharmaceutical advertisements in medical journals "were either grossly misleading or downright inaccurate." This is certainly the violation of global human rights. And it senses the threat of globalization. It means the bleak future of humanity. Unless it is tackled by local community, the globalization implosion will grip the satellites. The upsurge of excessive media culture and consumerism that appear to the people as hallucination, not only damage mental health but also destroy the emotional mindset and social, moral, and ethical values which may cause severe humane crisis in future society, and certainly will divert people from social ideals and ideas that may ultimately enervate civil society. All these are the eruptions of profit-making and money-making motivations of TNCs and MNCs. "I would call it the extension of transnational corporate tyranny.... Their first interest is profit—but much broader than that it is to construct an audience of a particular type... addicted to a certain lifestyle with artificial wants, an audience atomized, separated from one another, fragmented enough," says Noam Chomsky.

Environmental Threat

Besides economic disorder, the ecological threat is also a major challenge. The high degree and intensity of environmental pollution, the degradation of eco-balance, deforestation caused by the growth of technology creates a risk society; we are slowly going back to the dark stage. It is unthinkable that we are each emitting about six tons of toxic gases in the world today. This century global temperatures could rise by six degrees, threatening the very survival of the human race (Layton 2004). He says, "We had the developed world fouling up the earth's atmosphere. There are only three choices: Stop developing; continue with the same carbon emissions or elope some fundamental principles that allow the developed world to develop while reducing emissions. Ideally, the developed world has to limit its own carbon production and provide clean technology for itself and other." It means that neoglobal order lags behind in developing clean development models. The introduction and transmission of neo-technologies and electronics create environmental hazards. The current debate on the environmental effects of globalization is particularly concerned with the question whether a worldwide liberalization of trade may provoke environmental collapse. "Three major environmental concerns related to trade are the domestic environmental effects caused by the use of imported products, the foreign environmental effects caused by the production of exported goods, and the environmental effects caused by transport movements needed for international trade." Globalization is also under tremendous pressure of environmental threat, which raises the question of future existence of spaces, habitat, and people. Resource depletion, overpopulation, excessive carbon emission, and loss of bio-diversity appear as major globalization crises, which may cause serious environmental injury in future. Anthony Giddens argues, "Are temperature shifts like this the result of human interference with the world's climate? We can't be sure, but we have to admit the possibility that they might be, together with the increased numbers of hurricanes, typhoons and storms that have been noted in recent years." Would it be unwise to comment that as the consequence of globalization, the world's environment may drastically change and can damage the habitat and economy of Third World countries? We are all bound up with risk and advancing towards a "risk society." "After all, haven't people always had to face their fair share of risks?" (Giddens 2000: 39). I do not agree with Giddens. If the mission of orthodox globalization, or neoglobalization or fair globalization is not to face fair share of risks, then why is the majority world victims of such a stratified globalization?

Estimating future emissions, the environmentalists argue, is difficult, because it depends on demographic, economic, technological, policy, and institutional developments. Several emissions scenarios have been developed based on differing projections of these underlying factors. It is reported by the environmentalists that by 2100, in the absence of emissions control policies, carbon dioxide concentrations are projected to be 30–150 percent higher than today's levels. Increasing concentrations of greenhouse gases are likely to accelerate the rate of climate change. Scientists expect that the average global surface temperature could rise 1–4.5°F (0.6–2.5°C) in the next fifty years, and 2.2–10°F (1.4–5.8°C) in the next century, with significant regional variation. Evaporation will increase as the climate warms, which will increase average global precipitation. Soil moisture is likely to decline in many regions, and intense rainstorms are likely to become more frequent. Sea level is likely to rise two feet along most of the US coast. Exposure to environmental health risks can be traced to historical and contemporary economic, spatial, ecological, and social situations of inequality that structure and determine where people reside, which groups have the political and economic power to construct and maintain secured and healthy environments, and which groups lack the power to influence the quality of their residential environment. The heightened health risks which people of ethnic disadvantaged groups and low-income people are subjected to, as a result of disproportionate exposure to toxins, and the lower aesthetic quality of their communities, are the result of economic and social arrangements of power and the inequitable distribution of resources in our society. It is our experience that the affected people of environmental hazards and natural disasters like tsunamis, Hurricanes Rita and Katrina, twisters, droughts, floods and pollution are the economically and politically marginalized groups who form the majorities. For example, the tsunami of December 26, 2004 left an estimated 8,010 dead and 3,432 injured in the southern Indian state of Tamil Nadu. The damage as a direct result of the waves, according to a United Nations–Asian Development Bank–World Bank Joint Assessment Mission is US$437.8 million, and the livelihood loss is estimated at US$377.2 million, amounting to a total of a stupendous US$815 million. Among the survivors, almost a million people (984,000) in twelve districts have become refugees in their own villages, and are still living in makeshift shelters. The report of Post-Tsunami Recovery Program: Preliminary Damage and Needs Assessment states: "that for every person directly employed in fisheries, four other persons were dependent on downstream employment (such as cleaning the fish, marketing it, boat repair, transport of ice, etc)." But the damage incurred by the fisheries sector stood at US$184.2 million out of a total of US$206.1 million.

The minorities, on the other hand, are also the winners and they keep themselves safe because of their residential and ecological choice of residence and, importantly, they can afford their choices. In theory, the emphasis on public participation is positive but in practice, poor and working-class communities are unable to participate on an equal level with industry, government, science, environment, or more affluent communities. Nor are they able to make recommendations, which might require extensive resources to eliminate the problem at its source. Disproportionate exposures to environmental health risks can only be eliminated through local efforts, which enhance the power of poor and dejected communities to shape their environment. Information and knowledge of local and regional environmental conditions must be made available to local community activists in an accessible form. There must be significant community representation at every discussion about environmental problems. Here globalization becomes insignificant and a trend of local community can be apprehended.

The merging global justice, anti-war movement and peace movements took to the streets with a plethora of creative slogans on their banners and placards. Globalization is linked inextricably to a military economy, and therefore any examination of the relationship between economic globalization and environmental destruction is more accurate when expanded to include militarism. According to Bandarage (cited in Eaton 2003), the global expansion of weapons production and military activities may be far more responsible for resource depletion and environmental destruction than other oft-cited reasons. Militarism was recognized as a major threat to the environment in *Our Common Future* (World Commission on Environment and Development, 1987). Militaries are the biggest threat to the global environment. Environmental destruction attributed to militarism includes not only the more obvious impacts of armed conflict (conventional war, weapons of mass destruction, and troop and tank activities), but also those created by the presence and wastes of military personnel and their bases, and the fuel consumption of the military vehicles, ships and planes, especially jet planes. Michael Rennerr (Eaton 2003) states that nearly one-quarter of all the jet fuel in the world, about 42 million tons per year, is used for military purposes. Bandarage (cited in Eaton 2003) records that the Pentagon is considered to be one of the biggest users of oil in the US, and perhaps, the world. For example, one B-52 bomber consumes 13,671 liters of fuel per hour, one F-15 at peak thrust consumes 908 liters of fuel per hour and a Carrier Battle group consumes over one and a half million liters per day. She also notes that although little work has been done to calculate the military contribution to global warming and ozone depletion, some sources estimate that total military-related carbon emissions could be as high as 10 percent of emissions worldwide. It becomes evident that the military industrial project of the present US administration and its allies, bent as it is on an empire, and linked as it is to the dominant neoliberal free market regime with its flawed logic and failed ethics, is leading the world down a path towards ecological catastrophe and global insecurity. The recent death toll in south-east Asia has mounted to an estimated more than 120,000, which adds a tragic dimension to the blueprint of "Asian Crisis" and indicates a severe global environmental warning. The earthquake that unleashed deadly tidal waves was so powerful (100 times more powerful than nuclear bombs) that it made the East wobble on its axis and permanently changed Asia's map (*The Times of India*, December 29, 2004).

It is said that earthquakes, volcanic eruptions, landslides, explosions, and the impact of meteorites cause tsunamis. Does this catastrophe signify the end of civilization? Will it be a lost world? What's the world coming to? Some abnormal climatic and environmental changes are occurring that ring the bell of destruction of the earth. And certainly, it is due to less of bio-diversity caused by the emissions of gases, explosion, continuous extraction of fuels, dumping of hazardous wastes (mainly nuclear wastes), and other technological hazards. And we are really going back to the "dark stage" (Chew 2004). But the time lapse between an earthquake and its mammoth waves slammed into the coastal areas. And time had lapsed because of the lack of monitoring and warning technology. Is this the bane of globalization? A US scientist laments, "we tried to do what we could.... We don't have contacts in our address book for anybody in that part of the world." Secondly, if we follow the ideal paradigm of globalization then we must accept the rationale that global warming is one of the major causes of such natural disaster, which is in fact the gift of technological advance. The global warming is thought to be accelerated by the emission of greenhouse gases. And it is rising steadily throughout the globe. The deadly sea waves caused by the tsunami has not only changed the climatic map but also damaged the eco-balance of south-east Asia. The deep core regions of the ocean, the scientists assume, might be displaced. The lagoons and the corals have been swept away, which not only damaged the sea's beauty but has also caused natural disequilibrium. Most of the beaches are now under the sea, causing an uncertainty of survival of sea creatures. The environmentalists are very worried to think ahead that eco-disbalances may cause future catastrophes that may be more severe and grimmer. The effect of natural disasters like earthquake, floods, droughts, mudslides, volcanic eruptions in countries may cause more poverty and economic and political instability. The notion of globalization on such countries may decrease at a greater scale and intensity. It is evident from past records that the world has as yet experienced with sharply increased and intensified natural disasters, i.e., a hundred environmental hazards per year by the early 2000s.

The disaster victims are mostly poor and belong to marginalized communities. They are deprived of the gifts of globalization. The disaster may not destroy the civilization, but it can worsen the prospects and development of a nation. Which is more important is that the tsunami of south-east Asia mostly damaged the prospects of the tourist economy, which has a great impact on national economic development. Second, the beach economy generates employment in a very large scale, which is now in severe crisis. It is now the right time for social scientists to take up the issue for assessing the consequences of "Dark Ages" characterized by severe environmental hazards and risks. The ten hottest years have occurred since 1990–98 and 2004 is the fourth warmest year. It has a great impact on eco-system and damages the eco-balance. So, globalization of environment is an impossible concept. It might be possible when the Noah with his Ark will return to a lost world to give mankind a fresh beginning. The technology of making fast food may be scientific but due to its preservation technique, which is very lengthy and its mode of distribution to the retailers (very unhygienic!), the people suffer badly from virus infections. This non-human engineering of local Mc foods also create health hazards. McDonaldization is also very alarming from an environmentalist's perspective; Douglas Kellner in his criticism states: "McDonald's products are environmentally degrading and contribute to depreciation of the soil, rain forests, and grain and other resources that are used to make its beef and dairy products. Practices are environmentally harmful." The ecological modernization as an offshoot of globalization threatens human species in the Third World. This is of course, another prime agenda of protest movement.

GLOBALIZATION AND POSTMODERN SHOCK

When you will dissect and cross-dissect the rhetoric body of globalization, something occurs in your mind. Is it just a buzzword or real? If it is real, then what are the realities? In the era of globalization some virtual images stand before us as perils that deface the concept of humanity. And perhaps so, an expected trauma is waiting for our doomsday when the cloud of uncertainty, economic insecurity and identity crisis will dominate over the world sky. Humans may be the replicants and will act like more human than human. The abstract identity of human existence will turn into simulacra-fashioned ecstasy. The impact of genetic engineering, a virtual innovation of postmodern science and technology introduces such a simulacra, which has overcome the boundary of time, space, and humanity. The dominance of information and communication technologies uproots the fetters of community feeling, family bondage, emotional interaction, and community closeness. It seems to dominate over real-life individuals. Alvin and Heidi Toffler's (2001) view after thirty years of Toffler's future prediction of society is more contextual. It is evident from the records that there are more than 3 million digital switches for every human being alive on the planet. There are nearly half a billion PCs over the world—one for every 13 human beings, if not more. The internet and cell phone are spreading at high speed. In the future these technologies will be ultra-modern. Is the hi-tech revolution virtual or real? Whatever it might be, it is certainly alarming for the comfortable growth of humanity, ethics, and human values that we possess and nurture, with the process of socialization and upbringing. Another important and alarming consequence of globalization is biological revolution—a product of interdisciplinary knowledge like chemistry, medicines, genetics, cloning, which are related to the "bio-digital convergence." "Biochips, which are on the horizon will give birth to bio-computers, bio-politics, bio-ethics, bio-wars, bio investing, and bio-everything before long. Economies will be revolutionized and human history changed forever." It is the postmodernity—an expression of globalization that will reshape and remake our future world. Lyon (2002) states,

"Postmodernism is a multi-layered concept that alerts us to a variety of major social and cultural changes taking place at the end of twentieth century within many advanced societies" (p. ix).

Rapid technological advance, involving communication networking, the cultural, political and economic shifts, are all implicated. A few days back an old rickshaw puller asked me, "Sir, have you seen a sparrow or vulture recently?" I was careless to his saying and responded in a low and ignoring tone, "No." But something was happening in my mind and after a brief silence I said, "You are right. The sparrows, vultures and a good number of traditional birds are not quite visible either in our courtyard or on the branches of trees or on the roofs of our houses. But why?" The old rickshaw puller replied very excitedly, "I am an illiterate man. But I do feel it is mainly because of the overuse of cell phones, its magnetic dimension and towers of accesses." Yes, the traditional poor fellow was 100 percent correct. The information technologies remove spatial distances, link time over space and help a lot to spread the vision of global capitalism but side by side, it has damaged not only the health and brains of individuals but also invited a future world without insects, birds and reptiles, which always keeps harmony with environmental equilibrium. This is perhaps the possibility of technological risk, which should remain outside the orbit of globalization, or it is itself the creation of globalization. This is the error of present day globalization that may give life to the globalization volcano in future. Globalization as a concept had developed in the 1990s following the birth of postmodernism in the 1980s. Globalization indicates the transitions of human society into the Third Millennium. Smart (1993) argues that globalization is far less controversial than postmodernism. But I believe that globalization is the shadow of post-modernism that creates post-capitalism. Time-space compression and creation of hyper-real social, cultural, economic and communication technologies invite a world of absence, of play of chance, of dispersal, of text and intertext, anti-form and surface, and lastly of anarchy (Ihab Hassan 1982). Any one observing us from outer space might experience a feeling of disgust and pity at the same time, concluding that the human race on a global scale has fallen victim to social and cultural insanity and economic inequality. This is very much true when we explain postmodernism and globalization. For example, communication technology performs a vital role in storing knowledge. The students nowadays do not demand or require classroom lessons or extensive written study materials, or books and journals. Learning is no longer intertwined with the training of minds by "Gurus." Knowledge now can easily be borrowed and stored from the websites. One, who is economically weak, can gain little knowledge from free versions like the abstract or the outline of the knowledge content. But he, who is economically capable, or has internet access, can store the amount of knowledge he requires. He has to merely purchase it. Here two points are very important: Knowledge selling, and knowledge quantity. In future, the storehouse of knowledge, I am afraid, will be the computer with website facility. A few days back I was in a doctor's chamber for a medical check-up. The nameplate was very interesting. It said: "My endeavour is to *Sign out* pain and *Sign in* happiness in your life." I thought that the nature of language now begins to suffer from globalization disease and consequently from postmodern vertigo. The language of "cure" and "recovery," which should be the right word, has been deconstructed and gains techno-digital codes like "*Sign out*" and "*Sign in*," which is unknown to the illiterate, the economically depressed, and the disadvantaged masses. This sort of *technological-language vertigo* in the Third World countries will create a dilemma between local and global language and knowledge nomenclature, which may create an off-world to the local people. The concept of knowledge as the emancipation of soul or asylum of ideas and the taste of the last generation will be converted into knowledge-commodity. Not only that, the transmission and storage of information will no longer depend on human beings but on computers. Information will be produced and sold. Nations and states will fight for information and zip it around the world at the speed of electricity, and people will also try to steal it. The role of the nation will grow weaker. Taking the place of states, huge multinational corporations will take over the world (Lyotard 1984). If this were the ideal type postmodernism, then future society would be in great identity trouble. What then was postmodernism? Ihab Habib (2001) explains it as: "What was postmodernism, and what is it still? I believe it is a revenant, the return of the irrepressible; every time we are rid of it, its ghost rises back. Like a ghost, it eludes definition. Certainly, I know less about postmodernism today than I did thirty years ago, when I began to write about it. This may be because postmodernism has changed, I have changed, the world has changed." But it is undeniable that postmodernism cult began with the process of globalization and accordingly, of capitalistic mechanism. Jameson (1991) argues that the ideological task of the concept remains that of coordinating new forms of practice, and social and mental habits, with the new forms of economic production and organization thrown up by the modification of capitalism. It is, in a word, the new face of capitalism and defacer of local and communitarian epoch. Barbaric capitalism has created a surface-oriented deconstructed social and cultural language called postmodernism. It is best understood as the reflex of yet another mutation of capitalism. Jameson (1991) sees postmodernism as an intensification and latest phase of a capitalist world-system where we witness the unrestricted growth of multinational corporations as the offshoot of neo-globalization. Here the chance of fragmented language, art and culture, high degree of alienation and frustration, shadow of virtual imagination and hallu-cination, consumerism, and technological repetitions is immense, which may create a society of the absurd; may create a virtual image that will express the majority's misery. Baudrillard (1968) argues that just like a young boy, who, nurtured by wolves behaves like a wolf; likely human beings in the era of postmodernism, growing up in a world of objects are to become more object-like. He states, "Though post modern society is based on the consumption of commodities—on buying and using things—this consumption can never make us happy." It was written in the Vedic Scriptures: "Truth is one—but the Sages call it by different names." Similarly we can say that capitalism is one but the Masters call it by different names: Economic liberalization, reform and recovery, globalization, postmodernism, neo-globalization, fair globalization, or civil society and good governance.

GLOBALIZATION: A PERIL TO WORLD SOLIDARITY?

It is impossible to measure the future of a nebulous concept like globalization. The increasing interconnectedness is readily apparent in a host of economic, demographic, technological, and cultural changes but side by side the failure of mainstream globalization appears as a sudden trauma to the global initiators. The ever-increasing economic gap between the West and the rest, the global–local cultural conflict, the upsurge of ethnic violence, the vibrant intensity of cross-border terrorism, fundamentalism, religious bigotry, and increasing in-equality within and between nations threatens the ethos and ethics of global-ization process. The crisis in the emerging markets has made it evident that globalization opportunities come with high risk. Hunger and poverty dominate over technology and communication. The "World Economic Outlook" in its report (2004) shows that the distribution of income among countries (forty-two countries representing 90 percent of world population) has become more unequal than at the beginning of the century. Pieterse notes, "we inhabit a global theatre of the absurd, a winner takes—all world in which the wealthiest billion-aires own as much as approximately half the world population" (2001: 165). So the neo-globalization initiators change the track and coined the words like "civil society," "good governance," uncorrupted privatization, government's transparency, etc. Joseph Stiglitz argues,

…I saw first hand, the devastating effect that globalization can have on developing countries, and especially the poor within those countries. I believe that globalization—the removal of barriers to free trade and the closer integration of national economies—can be a force for good and that it has the potential to enrich everyone in the world, particularly the poor. But I also believe that if this is to be the case, the way globalization has been managed, including the international trade agreements that have played such a large role in removing those barriers and the policies that have been imposed on developing countries in the process of globalization, need to be radically rethought. (2002: 9–10)

Stiglitz (2002) emphasizes on the issue of privatization with the motive of strong competition policies. He insists on "reinventing government," which would be responsive and efficient. The proposal is certainly good but, I do feel, is very much difficult in terms of globality. Because most of the governments of "the rest" are very much nationally tuned, regionally unique, and locally very traditional. The feature is also true in politics, which sometimes seems ethnic-oriented, caste-based and even religiously molded. Here, time-space compression or policies of global initiators, or Washington consensus cannot enter deeply into the political temperament of the local space.

Stiglitz (2002: 14–15) also argues that

the backlash against globalization draws its force not only from the perceived damage done to developing countries by policies driven by ideology but also from the inequities in the global trading system. Today, few apart from those with vested interests who benefit from keeping out the goods produced by the poor countries defend the hypocrisy of pretending to help developing countries by forcing them to open up their markets to the goods of the advanced industrial countries while keeping their own markets protected, policies that make the rich richer and the poor more impoverished—and increasingly angry.

It is the reality that if IMF, the World Bank, WTO and other associate global funding organizations could develop the models of development of local countries without improving direct authoritative intervention, the countries of "the East" could develop their own paradigms of development accordingly. But soil connection has been totally ignored by the global initiators. The global policies would be a misnomer if there were no room for the Third World to participate and to express. The gap between policymakers and policy-takers thus creates unfair globalization and indicates the sign of capitalistic game. This may be called oppressive globalization (Wiseman 2000), anarchic globalization (Wallerstein 2003), or bad globalization. And I call it capitalist globalization. When it has been unmasked (and it took a very lengthy time to perceive the downside of the rosy dawn of globalization), the initiators innovate another journey of implementing revised or neo-globalization. The challenge is to identify the link between actions at different levels of space and governance and "to think and act at a range of levels without losing our grounding in the particularity of our own home place" (Wiseman 2000: 214).

Theoretically speaking, the neo-globalization action follows the concept of "particularism" where "universalism" has no room. Does neo-globalism indicate the sense of localism? This is a new theoretical dilemma. This neo-globalization process stresses on the importance of global, national and local communities based on cooperation rather than consumerism, the creation of a neo-global market that will be democratically and ecologically sustainable in terms of economic relationship, intervention of new forms of transnational governance, development of transnational civil society, globalization from down to earth, democratization of local economic relationships, etc. (Wiseman 2000). But all this neo-globalization thinking remains rhetoric and the cry of the hungry people shatters such an imagination and economic romanticism.

ANTI-GLOBALIZATION MOVEMENT

A struggle already has begun to redivide the world. The epoch of capitalist globalization is about to collapse, and perhaps, is now mature enough to make way for a new type of socialism. This is the backdrop of the anti-globalization movement. Multinational corporations manufacture products in many countries and sell to consumers across the world. Money, technology and raw materials move swiftly. Along with trade and money, ideas and cultures circulate more freely. As a result, laws, economies and social movements are forming at the international level. But for billions of the world's people, trade globalization means uprooting traditional, communitarian and local ways of life, and threatening livelihoods patterns, style of living, and cultures. This is perhaps the backdrop of globalization protest movement. The global social justice movement, itself a product of globalization, proposes an alternative path, which is more responsive to public needs. Intense political disputes will continue over globalization's meaning and its future direction.

Some observers of the anti-globalization movement argue that it's not just an anti-poverty crusade. It's not just about debt relief, fair trade, economic deregulation, eradication of inequality, good governance, or environmentally sustainable development, though all these are a part of it. It is about protecting and building democracy, community, and identity. It's about changing a system that has been grossly unfair to the Third World, and has eroded individual and collective economic choices even in the developed world. Let me pronounce the words of great playwright Bertolt Brecht: "Those who take the meat from the table teach contentment/those for whom the taxes are destined demand sacrifice/those who eat their till speak to the hungry of wonderful times to come/those who lead the country into abyss call ruling too difficult for ordinary people." This hymn is very much true for the contemporary globalization process, which not only compresses the poor but also totally excluded them from the development scenario. All the sorrows and pains of the depressed majorities have bursted into anger.

And finally, the politics of resistance begins. We have experienced massive, sometimes silent and humble, and most times noisy and fierce movements at the grassroot levels around the world. Some call it anti-globalization movements, some say it is fighting against global anarchy, while most people believe in no globalization; either alternative globalization or another world is possible. But I say it is "neo-class struggle" in the age of neoliberal economic society. Two new contending forces, i.e., managerial capitalists and satellite poor are now in opposition to each other. Both the classes are neither "bourgeoisie" nor "proletariat," but they are the winners and the losers that emerge from the global anarchy. Then who are the protestors? Are they workers? Are they cultivators? No—they are totally absent from this anti-globalization scenario. Because they are completely ignorant and innocent. A number of political forums and social activists are on the frontline. They are the mouthpieces of common people. And resistance begins against the rhetoric idea of "the rising tide carries all boats." Wallerstein (2003) views that the global anarchy begins with the "post war apogee" of US hegemony from 1945 to 1967–73, "the late summer glow" stretching from 1967–73 until 2001 and the current time period i.e., from 2001 until 2025 or 2050: one of anarchy which the US cannot control. The frustrated majorities echo the philosophical saying: "Lord give me strength to change what I can change, give me patience to endure what I cannot change and give me wisdom to distinguish the first from the second". The ultimate expression of such rhetoric becomes real with the emergence of anti-globalization torment. With the motive of diluting protest movements, the globalization initiators called for dialog to develop new conceptual resources.

To those who may belittle and even ridicule us for trying to go beyond the world of "us" and "them," of governance through exclusion, of "enemy" as part of human nature, this young generation may wish to respond that such ridicule is simply the consequence of arrogance. This arrogance is to believe that what was achieved so far is the best that can be achieved. Well, we all know it is not. Is this not part of our human destiny: to explore, to discover, to strive, to reach, to achieve?

Picco notes, "We witnessed a spiral of tragedies linked to the fear of diversity and, indeed, to the perception that diversity is a threat. It was like an ill wind of misconceptions sweeping away the possibility for dialogue" (2001: 25, 35). Does this discourse indicate the uncertainty of globalization process? Yes— it does. "Globalization is now on trial…" (Naomi Klein 2002: 21). And a large number of anti-globalizers both in developed countries and the Third World countries turn to violence. The struggle is not like the class struggle— the struggle is about globalization that is in crisis—the struggle is for achieving local power within the system—it is to remove inequalities and asymmetries, to eliminate the neo-capitalistic policies that keep democracies in cage, to eliminate debt burden, to revive structural adjustment programs, and finally to be free from the curse of neoliberal globalization and hegemonic global social order that serves the interest of the big giants of MNCs. And the issue of de-globalized social order or otherwise locally fashioned global social order is the challenge of the new millennium. Suggesting a potential vision for the future is Klein's plaintive call for new directions: "What is now the anti-globalization movement must turn into thousands of local movements, fighting the way neo- liberal politics are playing out on the ground: homelessness, wage stagnation, rent escalation, police violence, prison explosion, criminalization of migrant workers, and on and on" (Naomi Klein 2001).

Why then does the anti-globalization movement only rise in the western world? Why have victims of corporate globalization not yet bursted into voices of protest? Is it then a "so-called" anti-globalization protest movement? (Kiely 2004). If the answer is "no" then the movement would be as local as anti-capitalist. Naomi Klein (2002) writes, "the irony of the media-imposed level 'anti-globalization' is that we in this movement have been turning globalization into a lived reality, perhaps more so than even the most multinational of corporate executives or the most restless of Jet-setters" (xv).

To resist the policies of globalization from above and to imagine a global order from below, the protest movements have emerged in different parts of the world with the protestors belong to left wings, social activists, NGO workers and trade minority, religious leaders, environmentalists, students and women rebels. They have demonstrated against the silver lining of globalization, a new-type capitalism. The movements have spread from Rio de Janeiro to Seattle (November 1999) and Washington (April 2000), Millace (June 30, 2000), Melbourne (September 11, 2000 against the World Economic Forum), Prague (against the IMF), Seoul (against the Asia–Europe Summit), Nice (against the European Union Summit), Quebec (2001, against the launching of FTAA), Gothenburg (against EU Summit). Those affected by globalization from above have converged and are brought together by common interests and purposes. It is the potential power of this confluence of capitalistic supremacy that holds its interests, not the threat of a few thousand protestors. Brecher, Costello and Smith (2000) note, "Participants in the movement for globalization from below have varied agendas, but the movement's unifying mission is to bring about sufficient democratic control over states, markets and corporations to insure a viable future for people and the planet." Will the protest movements' slogan "back to history" be a reality then? If it is the reality then one can easily claim that the anti-globalization movements echo the emergence of a new form of "class struggle." It is not by chance that movements have "migrated throughout the world." It is very much global. It's a global movement against globalization anarchy. But it is, as yet apparently, a de-politicized movement. It displays divergent orientation on the political levels i.e., radical orientation with an anti-capitalist vision, seeking dialogs with the supranational institutions with the motive of reformation and a protectionist orientation. When this pluralist movement will be globalized, then corporate neo-capital and hegemonic globalization will face another globalization, i.e., globalization of the poor, globalization of the anti-corporate masses, and lastly the globalization of the Third World.

And people are beginning to stir everywhere—from the factories and campuses of East Asia through the field of Zimbabwe and the Ghettos of South Africa to the farm lands of Brazil, the highland of Ecuador and the indigenous communities of Mexico. After a long period of sustained attacks by the imperialists in collusion with their own native governments of various stripes, the people of the Third World countries are beginning to fight back. (Jain 2001: 224–25)

The police atrocity on the protestors, the huge arrest and the death of Carlo Guilani in Genoa adds fuel to the global massive anti-globalization protest and according to Stiglitz (2002), "was just the beginning of what may be many more causalities in the war against globalization." The movement may be the result of an unprecedented reciprocity between globalization theorists and activity. In this particular conjunction, theory and practice, rhetoric and applied intellect bind together. Their tunes are different but they share the common conviction of forming "trans-border coalitions" capable of putting globalization from below.

The struggle now begins between global faces on the one hand and human faces on the other. The global faces being frightened are speaking about human-ity, moral values, ethics and ethos of love, compassion and altruism: "Dialogue is a proper instrument to achieve a new paradigm of global relations.... Dialogue begins from a common starting point, identifying common principles such as equity and the Golden Rule" (Picco 2001). But side-by-side, the uneven global-ization is making our globe culturally, economically, and ecologically deformed. So anti-globalization movement is getting stronger, as witnessed by the massive demonstrations against US attack on Afghanistan and Iraq. Globalization has an image of "twilight," which seems better to the beneficiaries, but the image of hybridization seems faded to the victims of deviant globalization because it doesn't say positively about what is going on. Because, it is insufficiently specific and thus insufficiently comforting (Appadurai 2002). He suggested that the terrorist clash is happening between two kinds of globalized world-systems, one cellular and one vertebrate. To eradicate such a clash, global initiators take the role of the radicalist and call for *tactical humanism*.

ANTI-GLOBALIZATION TO ANTI-WAR RESISTANCE

The anti-globalization movement is an effort to counter the perceived negative aspects of the actually existing process of globalization. Although adherents of the movement often work in concert, the movement itself is heterogeneous and includes diverse, sometimes opposing, understandings of this process, alterna-tive visions, strategies and tactics. The neoliberal capitalist administration has the wind in the sails with the conquests of Afghanistan and Iraq. By globalization we mean a better tomorrow not clashing of swords or firing explosives into masses and ploughshares. By globalization we mean ethically and morally governance-oriented industries, not the expansion of military industries. Toffler (1993: 1) notes, "we appear to be plunging in a new dark age...and wars multiplied by wars. How we deal with this threat of explosive violence will, to a considerable extent, determine how our children live or, perhaps, for that matter, die." Ideologies based on the extension of capitalism in the guise of perceiving diversity, space-time compression, free trade, altruistic aidocracy (aid industries!) humanism and singularity appear as a synonym of enmity and threat. The capitalist's regimentalism in recent Afghanistan and Iraq unmasked the anarchy of globalization. "Where innocents lost their lives because their only fault was to be different from their murderers, the large majority of humanity realized that no justification could be invented (Picco 2001: 35). The perpetrators of such attacks symbolize not the clash of civilizations but its end. Globalization has spawned multi-dimensional forms of uncertainty about ethnic identity, which create new kinds of ethnic and communal violence. In the large-scale ethnic wars of the 1980s and 1990s, cross-border movements of refugees, implosions of nationalist politics, fears of economic chaos, and rumors of tyrannical autochtonies have produced large-scale ethnic violence involving extreme forms of bodily brutality. Widely dispersed terrorist networks now present one of the most serious challenges to the capitalists. Douglas Kellner claims that the experience of September 11 points to the objective ambiguity of globalization, that positive and negative sides are interconnected, that the institutions of the open society unlock the possibilities of destruction and violence, as well as democracy, free trade, and cultural and social exchange. They attempt to use chemical, biological, radiological, and nuclear weapons, which are the products of technological advancement. The terrorist movements in the US, UK, Pakistan, Central Asia, south-east Asia, Africa, Gulf States. Afghanistan, Iraq, Libya, North Korea, Iran, China, Russia, and the potential regions for instability like Nigeria, Sudan, Brazil, Colombia, Costa Rica, Ecuador, Mexico, Nicaragua, Peru, and Venezuela, Columbia, Indonesia, Philippines—where the risk of escalation, the sources think, is very high—all signify the expressions of deviant globalization where the rich can be more richer and the poor poorer. In a word, the concept of "War on Terror" is just a buzzword to the depressed majorities and they are not thinking about the end of history or clash of civilization, rather they are afraid of economic and humane phobia. In the attack on the World Trade Center and in the continuing battering of the valleys, cities and caves of Afghanistan by the US-led alliance we see a state-led extension of these forms of vivisectional violence that the capitalists or global initiators call "diagnostic wars." A diagnostic war is a war in which major acts of violence are intended to both discover and decimate the enemy. In the name of identifying masks, they have done the brutal act of mass destruction. Is it for banishing terrorism, which is their creation, or to extend their touch of power to complete their unfinished project of globalization? The blueprint of American Internationalism mainly focuses on the expansion of economic development "which includes good governance, reduction of tariffs, removal of corruptions, proper utilization of capital and fair economic policies." The country, which fails to achieve these policies, will be referred to as "Rogue State." Is this the only reason to change regime in Afghanistan and Iraq? No, there was nothing to preach but only occupy with a view to material gain, i.e., oil. The Middle East is still viewed as the highest oil-producing countries in the world (i.e., 66 percent).

It can be assumed that the war on Afghanistan and Iraq is not just a war but a *war for oil*. Anti-globalization activists raised their heads against such a deadly war. The movement of anti-globalization across the world now transformed into an anti-war movement. Globalization on the one hand, and war on the other, are now the dual aspects of the same process of neo-capitalism and capitalistic expansion. A friendly alliance is established between multinational corporations and global initiators, which is termed as "Crony Capitalism"—a deadly friendship for the deprived majorities. The following table yields such a reality:

Table 6.2: Global Income of Some Multinational Corporations ($ US billion): 2001

Multinational corporations	Income	Capital	Wealth
1. Wallmart	220	7	83
2. Exon Mobil	192	15	143
3. General Motors	178	0.6	323
4. British Petroleum	174	8	141
5. Ford Motors	162	−5	277
6. Enron	139	NA	NA
7. Dailmer Critchler	137	−0.6	185
8. Royal Dutch	135	11	112
9. General Eleo	126	14	495
10. Toyota Motors	121	5	150
11. City Group	112	14	1,000
12. Mitsubishi	106	0.5	61
13. Mitsui	101	0.4	50
14. Shovran Texaco	100	3	76
15. Totalfina Elf	94	7	79

Source: *Fortune*, July 22, 2002.

Mandela (January 30, 2003) writes, "All that [Bush] wants is Iraq oil," when the policies and ethics of neo-globalization are echoing the message of equality, a new economic order, distributive social justice, and global anti-war sentiment, while the Third World is being driven "into" a nearly dead end. This is perhaps for the first time the protestors are raising their voices; "human of this world, unite" against war. This episode might be the gift of globalization. Serious observers of the anti-globalization movement know that it's not just an anti-poverty crusade. It's not just about debt relief, fair trade, reducing the gap between rich and poor, or environmentally sustainable development, though all these are a part of it. It is about protecting and building democracy, community, and identity. Sharon Burrow, President of the Australian Council of Trade Unions, recently said at the World Economic Forum in Melbourne:

"If companies continue to carve up the world and unchecked capital speculation makes the securities of communities increasingly volatile, then the tide of protest against globalization in its current form will grow."([1]80).

It's about changing a system that has been grossly unfair to the developing world, and has eroded individual and collective economic choices even in the industrialized world. The protest movement with its motive of viewing an alternative path of resisting capitalist implosion has spread like fire in the global arena (see Table 6.3).

Table 6.3: Anti-War Resistance in Major Cities of the World
(February 15, 2003)

Barcelona	1,300,000
Rome	1,000,000
London	750,000
Madrid	660,000
Berlin	500,000
Sydney	250,000†
Seville	200,000
Damascus	200,000
Montreal	150,000
San Francisco	150,000†
Melbourne	150,000†
Paris	100,000
New York	100,000
Oviedo	100,000
Dublin	100,000
Glasgow	80,000
Oslo	60,000
Brussels	50,000
Berne	40,000
Stockholm	35,000
Copenhagen	25,000
Vancouver	20,000
Helsinki	15,000
Vienna	15,000
Toronto	10,000
Amsterdam	10,000
Austin	10,000
Tokyo	5,000
Cape Town	5,000
Johannesburg	4,000
Quebec City	3,000
Dhaka	2,000
Ottawa	2,000
Kiev	2,000
Chicoutimi	1,500

Millions of protestors throughout the world gathered the voicing anger and hatred against capitalist expansionism. In fact, overall so little protested that few people even remember. The present-day protest movement against war perhaps indicates either the positive sign of fair globalization or it's an expression of fear psychosis for an uncertain and alien future. Of course, some activists in the movement are opposed to neoliberalism, and international institutions that promote neoliberalism, such as the World Bank (WB), the Organization for Economic Co-operation and Development (OECD), the World Trade Organization (WTO), International Monetary Fund (IMF), and the North American Free Trade Agreement (NAFTA), Free Trade Area of the Americas (FTAA), the Multilateral Agreement on Investments (MAI) and the General Agreement on Trade in Services (GATS), the World Economic Forum (WEF), the Trans Atlantic Business Dialogue (TABD) and the Asia–Pacific Economic Forum (APEC), as well as the governments which promote these agreements, institutions, and policies. Still others argue, if borders are opened to capital, borders should be similarly opened to allow free and legal circulation and choice of residence for migrants and refugees.

WHAT NEXT?

We stand at the threshold of an open door of global social order. The wave of globalization is rolling. The global initiators say, "The future is here." We have to settle how we will respond to such given movement? Will we struggle with the wave for an alternative? Or will we try to move ahead with the changing, ever-moving-ahead world? Marshall McLuhan says, "When faced with a totally new situation, we tend always to attach ourselves to the objects, to the flavor of the most recent past. We look at the present through a rear-view mirror. We march backwards into the future." One futurologist argues that the future is permanently discontinuous from the past. It is no longer predictable. It is hardly forecastable. While we can't predict the future, it is the outcome of the present episodes, and actually existing orders. The late American President John F. Kennedy, himself a man of great vision, said, "Some men see things as they are and ask, 'Why?' Others see them as they could be and ask, 'Why not?'" The vision of Kennedy was great and noble. But such a rhetoric symphony is not acceptable to the deprived majorities who die in starvation and toil under the boiling sun from morning till dusk for miserable rewards, and always face a very slow and agonizing death. They always want to be one of the "some" who see things as they are and ask "why?" Why such a disparity?

Wallerstein argues, "We move into the uncertain immediate future, and in moment of systemic anarchy such as the present, almost anything can happen." The tendencies, which Wallerstein foresees, are: commitment of US government to a unilateral, rather progressive foreign policy; European integration will proceed increasingly but with difficulty and there will be a distance between US and Europe; China, Korea and Japan will come more closer; nuclear proliferation in the South will continue and aggravate; The Port of Alegre will be more militant and solid. He claims that the democracy will be in a state of uncertainty and that human society in the future will be more egalitarian. The futurologists claim that six faces may spell the global future: *Fast*—economic instability, top speed decisions, virtual working, new technologies; *Urban*—mega cities, ageing population, feminization of society, increasing consumer expectations; *Tribal*—the greatest force in the world, corporate tribes, building tribes not teams; *Universal*—unstoppable forces, global citizens, global branding, mega-corporations; *Radical*—new political movements, gathering power of single issues such as the environment, altering the way we live; *Ethical*—how do we want to live in a fast, urban, tribal, universal and radical world? (Sylvia Caras 2002).

Fear and fear of fear is everywhere. The excluded are badly suffering from an alien fear psychosis. A deadly tsunami or earthquake or Katrina or volcanic eruption may anytime engulf their shelter, their architecture, their technology and lives. Coming after a century of unheard-of violence and social transformation, the incapacity to change free-market policies—even of governments born of popular disgust with neoliberalism—has profound roots in the ideologies and mentalities through which western societies have conceptualized nature, progress, and themselves since the Renaissance. Closely tied to such self-conceptualizations, the problems of impending ecological catastrophe and social–economic malaise loom before us as a double wall blocking the future, noxious waste products of the unsustainable productivity created by instrumental reason in the last century and a half (Mitzman 2003).

The health hazards and technological risks may anytime swallow the dejected majorities, the older people may be completely frustrated due to the social, economic, and moral sounds of silence, alienation, deadly loneliness and insecurity. The women may be the symbol of sex commodities and virtual images. The epidemics may anytime engulf any of the countries of the Third World. The unobtrusive and deadening poverty and hunger always warn them. The enchanting style of imaginary living is always being threatened by technological risks and hazards. The rejects are always working hard for the winners from morning till dusk for miserable rewards and premature deaths, not even knowing the reasons why. They are really at a puzzling crossroad. All these are the result of the fear of globalization. Are we then waiting for a doomsday? Beck (1992: 19) argues that we are living on the "volcano of civilization, the contours of the risk society." And in the context of modernity and globalization, he notes, "In advanced modernity the social production of wealth is systematically accompanied by the social production of risk." Setting aside the romantic and rhetoric discourse, can we manage the problems?

We are afraid that the liberal intellectuals and academics are taking over the anti-globalization movement as a rhetoric discourse. But reality tells us that the ultimate fate of such a struggle may be a discourse of confrontation between hegemony of the global initiators and hegemony of the anti-globalizers. W. Bello in a "Report on alternatives to corporate globalization" notes that two contradictory and opposite blueprints were opened to the post-Cold War visionaries, i.e., "Centralized socialism and Corporate capitalism."

But the emerging process of de-globalization with the notions of remaking of local economies "toward domestic markets," reorientation of income and land distribution, "policies de-emphasizing growth and maximizing equity and remaking of a policy that subordinates markets to Social Justice" are getting new entries in the arena of alternative globalization. When anti-globalizers are protesting against corporate capitalism, replacing its neoliberal principles and call for an alternative architecture, then the global initiators are speaking about "fair globalization" with the mission of "good governance." And the wave of such a discourse continues.

The sustainability challenge for the new millennium is whether global economic man can move out of the world view based on fear and scarcity, monocultures and monopolies, appropriation and dispossession and shift to a view based on abundance and sharing, diversity and decentralization, and respect and dignity for all beings. (Vandana Shiva 2002)

The people of the Third World feel de-trapped from economic globalization, because the ethics of globalization are undermining the ethics of justice and sustainability, of compassion, love, altruism, and sharing. The alternative way, some suggest, is to move from market totalitarianism to an earth democracy. Gandhiji states, "The Earth has enough for everyone's needs, but not for some people's greed."

It is but undeniable that people are the starter and end product of any movement. And the end product of such a conflict may be either total global dominance of capitalism and abolishment of socialism, or degeneration of capitalism and rebirth of neo-socialism. But as yet the future is unpredictable. What is the future of globalization then? What are the alternatives? Will if be only a few words, like cooperation and diversity, democratic and ecologically sustainable economic relationship, neo-transnational good governance and civil society, democratization of local economic relationship, local governance and globalization from below (Wiseman 2000)? What would be the future of neo-globalization? Will it fade away and will old capitalism appear with a new nomenclature, and will a reversed but a parallel globalization for the deprived majorities appear and will two contending forces be in conflict? I am afraid; we are going deep into an era, which will be only wars and anti-wars, globalization and anti-globalization. Are we going to plunge into a new dark age of hate, intolerance, violence, poverty, and global–local disorder? Will the postmodern simulacra engulf our identity of humanity? Will it be more human than human? I don't know. We can only say we are in transition and the nightmare of an alien future frightens us.

References

Albrow, M. 1990. Introduction, in M. Albrow and E. King (eds), *Globalisation, Knowledge and Society: Readings from International Sociology*. London: Sage.

————. 1997. Traveling Beyond Local Cultures: Socioscapes in a Global City, in J. Eade (ed.), *Living the Global City: Globalization as Local Process*. New York: Routledge, pp. 37–55.

Appadurai, A. 1990. Disjuncture and Differences in the Global Cultural Economy, in M. Featherstone (ed.), *Global Culture*. London: Sage.

————. 2002. Tactical Humanism. Available online at http://www.polis.sciencespobordeaux. fr/vo10ns/arti5. html

Baudrillard, J. 1968. *Revolutionary Messiahnisms of the Third World* (Translated by W.E. Mühlmann). Paris: Gallimard.

Bauman, Z. 2001. *The Individualized Society*. Cambridge: Polity Press.

Beck, U. 1992. *Risk Society*. London: Sage.

Bhagwati, J. 2004. *In Defense of Globalization*. New York: Oxford.

Brecher, J., T. Costello and B. Smith. 2000. Globalization from Below. *The Nation*. December.

Caras, S. 2002. *Shaping the Future of Global Health*. San Francisco: University of California.

Chakraborty, D. 2004. *When Baghdad is Burning* (Bengali version). Kolkata: NBA.

Chew, S. 2004. Globalization and Ecological Crisis, in Samir Dasgupta (ed.), *The Changing Face of Globalization*. New Delhi: Sage.

Cooper, M. 2002. From Protest to Politics. *The Nation*. March. Available online at http://www.thenation.com/doc/20020311/cooper/3

Dadayan, V. 1988. *The Orbits of the Global Economy*. Moscow: Progress Publishers.

Dasgupta, S. (ed.). 2004. *The Changing Face of Globalization*. New Delhi: Sage.

Eaton, J.M. 2003. Ecological Consequences of Globalization's Fist Militarism with Reference to Global Warming: Reflections from a Global Democracy and Anti-War Perspective. Available online at http://www.elements.nb.ca/theme/climate03/janet/eaton.html

Ferguson, M. 1992. The Mythology About Globalization. *European Journal of Communication* 7: 69–93.

Frank, A.G. 1971. *Capitalism and Underdevelopment in Latin America* (Revised Edition). Harmondsworth: Penguin.

Fortune, July 22, 2002.

Fukuyama, F. 1992. *The End of History and the Last Man*. New York: Free Press.

Giddens, A. 1991. *A Contemporary Critique of Historical Materialism*. London: Macmillan.

————. 2000. *Runway World*. New York: Routledge.

Hannerz, U. 1992. *Cultural Complexity: Studies in the Social Organization of Meaning*. New York: Columbia University Press.

Harvey, D. 1989. *The Conditions of Post Modernity*. Oxford, U.K.: Blackwell.

Hassan, I.H. 2001. From Postmodernism to Postmodernity: The Local/Global Context. *Philosophy and Literature* 25(1): 1–13.

Heidegger, M. 1971. The Thing. In *Poetry, Language, Thought*. New York: Harper & Row.

Huizer, G. 2003. *Globalization From Above and From Below: A Dialectical Process*.

Jain, N. 2001. *Globalisation or Recolonisation?* Pune, India: Elgar.

Jameson, F. 1991. *Postmodernism or, The Cultural Logic of Late Capitalism*. Durham, NC: Duke University Press.

Kellner, D. Theorizing Globalization. Available online at http://www.gseis.ucla.edu/faculty/kellner/kellner. html

Kiely, R. 1998. *Globalisation and the Third World*. London: Routledge.

—————. 2004. Neoliberal Globalisation Meets Global Resistance: The Significance of Anti-Globalization Protest, in Samir Dasgupta (ed.), *The Changing Face of Globalization*. New Delhi: Sage.

Klein, N. 2001. Reclaiming the Commons. *New Left Review* 9. Available online at http://www.newleftreview.org

—————. 2002. *Fences and Windows*. New Delhi: Left Word Books.

Lash, S. and J. Urry. 1994. *Economies of Signs and Space*. London: Sage.

Layton, C. 2004. Global Warning. *The Times of India*, November 1.

Lyon, D. 2002. *Postmodernity*. New Delhi: Viva Books Private Limited.

Lyotard, J.F. 1984. *The Postmodern Condition*. Minneapolis: University of Minnesota Press.

Madeley, J. 1999. *Big Business Poor Peoples; The Impact of Transnational Corporations on the World's Poor*. Zed Books.

Mandela, N. January 30. 2003. All Bush Wants Is Iraqi Oil. *Independent*. Available online at http://www.news.independent.co.uk

McBride, S. and J. Wiseman (eds). 2001. *Globalization and Its Discontents*. London: Macmillan Press Ltd.

McLuhan, M.H. and B. Powers. 1988. *The Global Village: Transformations in World Life and Media in the 21st Century*. Oxford: Oxford University Press.

Mitzman, A. 2003. We are sitting on a Volcano. *Counterpunch*. Available online at http://www.countercurrents.org/glo-mitzman170703.html

Moore, S. 2004. Scandal of Growing Third World Debt Burden. *Socialist Outlook*. Available online at http://www.labournet.org.uk/so/46debt.html

Patnaik, P. 1995. *Whatever Happened to Imperialism and other Essays*. New Delhi: Tulika.

Petras, J. and Veltmeyer. 2001. *Globalization Unmasked*. Delhi: Madhyam Books.

Picco, G. (ed.). 2001. *Crossing the Divide*. New Jersey: School of Diplomacy and International Relations.

Pieterse, J.N. 2001. *Development Theory*. New Delhi: Vistaar Publications.

Report of Mumbai Resistance. 2004. Available online at http://www.rwor.org

Ritzer, G. and R. Mike. 2004. Globalization of Nothing, in Samir Dasgupta (ed.), *The Changing Face of Globalization*. New Delhi: Sage.

Robertson, R. 1992. *Globalization*. London: Sage.

—————. 1995. Glocalization: Time-Space and Homogeneity–Heterogeneity, in M. Featherstone, S. Lash and R. Robertson (eds), *Global Modernities*. London: Sage.

Schuurman, F.J. 2001. *Globalization and Development Studies*. New Delhi: Vistaar Publications.

Shiva, V. 2002. Globalization and Poverty: Economic Globalization has become a War Against Nature and Poor. *Resurgence Issue* 202. Available online at http://www.resurgence.org

Silverstein, K. 1999. Millions for Viagra, Pennies for Diseases of the Poor. *The Nation*, July 19.

Smart, B. 1993. *Postmodernity*. London: Routledge.

Steger, M.B. 2002. *Globalism: The New Market Ideology*. Maryland, US: Rowman & Little-field Publishers, Inc.

Stiglitz, J. 2002. *Globalization and Its Discontents*. New Delhi: Penguin Books.

————. 2004. Consensus is Emerging On The Destructive Effects of Globalization. *The Guardian*, March 13.

Tempest, M. 2003. Noam Chomsky on the Anti-war Movement (An Interview). New York: Global Policy Forum. Voice 4 Change. February. Available online at http://www. gpf@globalpolicy.org

The Guardian, January 31, 2003.

The Times of India, December 27, 2004.

————. December 29, 2004.

The *World Economic Outlook* Report. 2004.

Toffler, A. 1993. *War and Antiwar*. London: Warner Books.

Toffler, A. and H. Toffler. 2001. *The Wall Street Journal*, March 29.

UNDP. 1992, 1994. *Reports of UNDP*.

Wallerstein, I. 1974. *The Modern World-system*. New York: Academic.

————. 2002. New Revolts Against The System. *New Left Review* 18, November–December. Available online at http://www.newleftreview.org

————. 2003. Entering Global Anarchy. *New Left Review* 22, July–August. Available online at http://www.newleftreview.org

Waters, M. 1995. *Globalization*. London: Routledge.

Wiseman, J. 2000. Alternatives to Oppressive Globalization, in S. McBride and J. Wiseman (eds), *Globalization and its Discontents*. London: Macmillan Press Ltd.

World Bank. 1998. *World Development Report*. Washington: World Bank.

————. 2004. *World Development Report*. Washington: World Bank.

World Commission on Environment and Development (WCED). 1987. *Our Common Future*, Oxford: Oxford University Press.

WHO. 2001. *The World Health Report*. Available online at http://www.who.int/whr/2001/en/

World Trade and Development Report. 2003. *Cancun and Beyond, 2003*. New Delhi: RIS & Academic Foundation.

WTO News, June 16, 2000. London.

Websites:

http://www.jubilee/2000/uk.org/debt.html

http://www.resurgence.gn.apc.org/issues/contents/202.html

http://www.labormet.org.uk/so/current.html

http://www.boloji.com

http://www.cyber.law.harvard.edu

7

GLOBAL ENVIRONMENTAL CRISIS AND ECOLOGICAL FUTURES

SING C. CHEW

PRELUDE

During the current era, the phrase "environmental crisis" comes quickly to the lips. As a result, whether it is deforestation or species extinction, there is an overwhelming concern of the dangers we face in the twenty-first century. Such fears are also married to the general view that the current environmental crisis is a new phenomenon, and that it is the result of the excesses of capitalism, and the associated economic and social changes that have occurred over the last century. This latter assumption, however, is historically myopic for it does not take into account the many phases of environmental crisis that have occurred throughout the course of world history for the last 5,000 years (Chew 2001). Furthermore, connected with these environmental crisis periods are also phases of socioeconomic and political crises. These latter crises are widely known and commonly understood as the Dark Ages of human history. They are periods when human progress was at a standstill. Over world history, there have been at least two or three occurrences (2200–1700 B.C.; 1200–700 B.C.; A.D. 400–A.D. 900) of these devolutionary phases or Dark Ages (Chew 2002, 2004a, 2004b, 2005). It is commonly understood that Dark Ages are times when human evolutionary transformations have been stymied, and the social, political and economic indicators of growth reflect signs of reversals. Ecologically, Dark Ages are moments of environmental stress, and given the reduced socioeconomic activities, moments of ecological restoration as well. Because Dark Ages are a recurring (not necessarily cyclical) phenomenon, they are interesting periods because they reveal the dynamics of the crisis of system reproduction. What results from these devolutionary periods are system reorganization and transformation. In spite of its devolutionary tendencies, from historical records Dark

Ages should also be seen as moments of opportunity for ecological restoration, societal learning, and power shifts.

Given the above, such a trajectory of historical occurrences provides us with the opportunity of using the past with the possibility of projecting possible futures. However, our historical myopia in social sciences has traditionally prevented us from considering the past with its patterns and structures in order to understand, project, and identify possible futures. This chapter is an attempt to overcome this historical myopia. In view of the state of globalization to date, and the global crisis we are facing, what follows is an attempt to map out some patterns of the past in order to project some possible ecological futures.

A THEORETICALLY GENERALIZED HISTORY OF DARK AGES[1]

Nature of Dark Ages

We need to abstract historically the several processes and factors that depict a Dark Age period in order to have a clearer understanding of the various factors that precipitate a system crisis and transformation. Such an abstraction starts by delineating the connections between the natural system and social system in the reproduction of the world (social) system.

Barriers to the reproduction of the world-system are formed when humans induced changes to the ecology and climate.[2] The degradative aspects of human activity are conditioned by social organizational factors (urbanization, accumulation, wars, technological innovations, and population) that impact on system reproduction. Natural disturbances such as earthquakes and volcanic eruptions also condition the reproduction and evolution of the world-system, and thus work independently. We need, therefore, to consider the degree of weight these factors have in precipitating a system crisis.

Through the course of human history, system crises have appeared in the "concrete" in the form of Dark Ages. Over world history, these historical phases are rare. Between 3000 B.C. and A.D. 1000, there have been indications of only two such identified phases, 2200 B.C.–1700 B.C. and 1200 B.C.–700 B.C. (considered as one phase in terms of the crisis of the Bronze Age), and A.D. 400– A.D. 800/900), occurring in the world-system from Northwestern India, West Asia, the Mediterranean, and Europe.[3] Several scholars such as Desborough (1972), Snodgrass (1971), and Braudel (2001) have discussed the conditions of life during past Dark Ages highlighting the economic, political and social disorder with population losses and deurbanization, etc. Furthermore, historical records and archeological evidence indicate a flattening of the social hierarchy, and devolution away from a complex form of socio-political organization and lifestyles that existed prior to the onset of Dark Ages. The trends and patterns of Dark Ages, therefore, show developmental reversals: fall in population levels, decline or loss in certain material skills, deurbanization and migration, decay in cultural aspects of life, fall in living standards, and thus wealth and trading contacts.

This symptomatic treatment of Dark Ages, however, misses the ecological and natural conditions during Dark Ages. Ecological deterioration, climate changes, volcanic eruptions, and earthquakes also depict this stressful period. Writing during the Roman period of third century A.D., Thascius Cyprianus's (cited in Toynbee 1939: 8) depiction underlines such conditions:

> This truth is proclaimed, even if we keep silence..., by the World itself, which testifies to its own decline by giving manifold concrete evidences of the process of decay. There is diminution in the winter rains that give nourishment to the seeds in the earth, and in the summer heats that ripen the harvests. The springs have less freshness and the autumns less fecundity. The mountains, disemboweled and worn out, yield a lower output of marble; the mines, exhausted, furnish a smaller stock of the precious metals: the veins are impoverished, and they shrink daily....

These conditions also extend to the periphery of the world-system as a consequence of core–periphery relations. Ecological shadows are cast over wide areas of the world-system. *What we have is ecological degradation on the world-scale depending on the extent the world-system has reached.*

The impacts of Dark Ages socioeconomically and ecologically *do not extend necessarily and evenly across geo-spatial boundaries of the world-system.* Depending on the systemic connections of the world-economy at a particular point in time, and the level of intensity of the social system and natural system connections experienced by a given region, the extent of the impact is uneven. The state of crisis and/or transition appears to have its greatest impact on the regions of the world-system that are considered the core(s) of the system at that specific point in time. No doubt, this is related to the fact that it is in the core region(s) where the social system and natural system relations are at its most heightened levels. It does not suggest that the periphery is void of any crisis conditions at all. The connections the core has with the periphery via several economic and political processes assure that at least some (if not all) crisis conditions are felt. The extent, of course, is based on how incorporated the periphery is in the productive processes of the core(s).

Besides these devastating ecological outcomes, climate changes are also associated with Dark Ages. Climate changes and natural calamities, when they occur during Dark Ages, generate further challenges to social system reproduction. Their occurrences and impacts on social systems have been noted during periods of the Dark Ages (see for example, Weiss 1993, Chew 1999, Keys 1999). Higher than normal temperatures can generate salinization problems for agricultural cultivation, especially in areas where irrigation is extensively used, and hence, lower harvest yields. It becomes a further issue if agricultural products are a major source of trade exports. The aridity that commonly occurs with high temperatures has often generated severe problems for pastoral herds that have led to nomadic migrations, thus causing further pressures on core centers.

If Dark Ages are prolonged ecological crisis periods, crisis provides opportunities. In other words, crisis conditions provide the opportunities for the resolution of contradictions that have developed to such a state that inhibits the reproduction of the world-system. It leads to pathways and processes that would mean system reorganization and transition. If reorganization does not occur, system collapse usually follows. This we have seen historically (see Kristiansen 1993, 1998; Chew 1997, 1998, 2001). If this is the case, ecological limits become also the limits of the socioeconomic processes of the world-system, and the interplay between ecological limits and the dynamics of the social system define the historical tendencies of the human enterprise (Kristiansen 1998; Chew 2001, 2002). To this extent, Dark Ages or system crises also offer opportunities for two parties in this overall equation: the natural system and the periphery. For the former, Dark Ages should be appreciated as periods for the restoration of the ecological balance that has been disrupted by centuries of intensive human exploitation of the natural system. The downscaling of socioeconomic processes during Dark Ages provides the opportunity for Nature to recover.

For the periphery, Dark Ages as system crises enables some peripheral areas to re-articulate themselves within the hierarchical matrix of the zonal production processes of the world-system. This opportunity is open only during system crisis periods, and has been exploited by some through the course of world history since 3000 B.C.

Duration of Dark Ages

Resolution of the ecological crisis moments along social time (i.e., for socioeconomic processes) has been varied. It takes at least 150 years in length (see for example, Wallerstein 1980; Frank 1993, Modelski and Thompson 1999). Utilizing pollen analysis of deforestation levels, ecological recovery seems to be much longer at the natural system level in comparison to the world-system level (Chew 2004a, 2005). Hence, ecological time of recovery during Dark Ages extend to between 500–900 years in length.[4] The lengthy duration (ecological time) provides the window of opportunity for the ecological balance to be restored so as to enable economic productive capacities to continue.

If the ecological balance or trade networks cannot be restored, new geographic areas of ecological assets have to be located, and/or replacement metals of much depleted natural resources are then adopted for production. Especially when there is resource depletion, the need arises for innovations in social organization and technology; take for example, the transition from bronze to iron production at the end of the Bronze Age. Along with all these changes, various social, political, and economic processes come into play as well during such crisis moments. They range from social upheavals (revolts, wars, etc.) and dislocations (such as migrations), to cultural/ideological shifts (rise of religious world views), along with social and political reorganizations.

LESSONS FROM THE PAST FOR THE FUTURE

From what we have delineated above, there are structural trends and tendencies that are ecological, socioeconomic, and political that distinguish Dark Age periods from other phases of incessant economic growth and expansion. Let us briefly examine them and provide the associated indicators and information to these trends and tendencies.

Deforestation

One of the enduring indicators of ecological stress is the level of deforestation. Wood has been a critical component of socioeconomic reproduction since the dawn of human civilizations. Deforestation thus provides a long-term window on the health and states of the ecological landscape and as well, the state and pace of socioeconomic transformation of the landscape. Long-range pollen analysis profiles indicate phases of deforestation and reforestation over the last 5,000 years, underlining the Dark Age periods we have identified in the previous pages.

From an empirical analysis of the trend lines of arboreal pollen, Table 7.1 presents forty arboreal pollen profiles of deforestation and reforestation starting from as early as 3854 B.C. These profiles cover four geographic regions of the world: Western Europe, Central and Eastern Europe including Russia, Northern Europe and the Mediterranean. If we examine Table 7.1, despite the lack of identification of a Dark Age period in the fourth millennium B.C. by historians and archeologists specializing on the Ancient World, it seems that twenty-nine of the pollen profiles indicate that there was a phase of deforestation during the fourth millennium B.C. Not only do the pollen profiles exhibit such a period of deforestation, they also reveal the widespread geographic coverage of the degradation of areas in Russia and the Ukraine through to Spain and Syria. In the course of world history, it should not be assumed that this was the first phase of deforestation as the available data are quite limiting. It might perhaps be the first phase of anthropogenically-induced deforestation with the advent of the Neolithic Revolution.

Table 7.1: Arboreal Deforestation Pollen Profiles and Plantago Growth Pollen Profiles

Area	Phase 1	Phase 2	Phase 3	Phase 4
Western Europe				
(1) Belgium (Moerzeke)				
Arboreal	3093 B.C.–2600 B.C.	2002 B.C.–1274 B.C.	A.D. 180–A.D. 544	
Plantago	3093 B.C.–2800 B.C.	2002 B.C.–1400 B.C.	A.D. 183–A.D. 362	
(2) Germany 1 (Lake Constance)				
Arboreal		2325 B.C.–270 B.C.	-A.D. 290–A.D. 1500	
(3) Germany 2 (Lake Steisslingen)				
Arboreal		2175 B.C.–144 B.C.	A.D. 348–A.D. 1594	
(4) Germany 3 (Ahlenmoor)				
Arboreal		2200 B.C.–1700 B.C.	A.D. 169–A.D. 664	
Plantago		1514 B.C.–722 B.C.	A.D. 128–A.D. 466	A.D. 763–A.D. 961
(5) Switzerland (Lonsigensee)				
Arboreal	3920 B.C.–2170 B.C.	1253 B.C.–A.D. 767		A.D. 1055–
Plantago	3920 B.C.–3200 B.C.	1253 B.C.–242 B.C.		A.D. 616–A.D. 1206
(6) France (Le Marais St. Boetien)				
Arboreal	3520 B.C.–585 B.C.	1897 B.C.–853 B.C.	A.D. 327–A.D. 936	
Plantago	4810 B.C.–3815 B.C.			A.D. 631–A.D. 1240
(7) Ireland (Arts Lough)				
Arboreal	3726 B.C.–1653 B.C.			
Plantago	4417 B.C.–3104 B.C.		A.D. 352–A.D. 1094	A.D. 681–A.D. 1176
Central and Eastern Europe, Russia				
(8) Bulgaria 1 (Besbog-2)				
Arboreal		1730 B.C.–A.D. 1160		A.D. 1500–A.D. 1832

(contd.)

Table 7.1 contd.

Area	Phase 1	Phase 2	Phase 3	Phase 4
(9) Bulgaria 2 (Mire Garvan)				
Arboreal	3901 B.C.–2123 B.C.	1235 B.C.–A.D. 882		A.D. 1162–A.D. 1628
Plantago	3605 B.C.–1827 B.C.			
(10) Hungary (Lake Balaton SW)				
Arboreal	4338 B.C.–2923 B.C.	2683 B.C.–816 B.C.	A.D. 381–A.D. 1296	A.D. 1296–A.D. 1824
Plantago		1274 B.C.–112 B.C.		
(11) Poland 1 (Bledowo Lake)				
Arboreal	3633 B.C.–2518 B.C.	724 B.C.–A.D. 967		A.D. 1533–
Plantago	3280 B.C.–1531 B.C.	257 B.C.–A.D. 967		A.D. 1533–
(12) Poland 2 (Puscizna Rekowianska)				
Arboreal	3638 B.C.–1331 B.C.	1331 B.C.–86 B.C.	A.D. 402–A.D. 881	A.D. 1349–A.D. 1800
Plantago	3638 B.C.–2604 B.C.			
(13) Poland 3 (Kluki)				
Arboreal	3803 B.C.–665 B.C.		A.D. 452–A.D. 884	A.D. 1000– A.D. 1573
Plantago	3082 B.C.–1277 B.C.		A.D. 597–A.D. 1703	
(14) Byelorussia 1 (Dolgoe)				
Arboreal	4800 B.C.–3850 B.C.	3400 B.C.–750 B.C.	A.D. 380–A.D. 1460	
Plantago	4030 B.C.–2500 B.C.	1150 B.C.–A.D. 380		
(15) Byelorussia 2 (Osvea)				
Arboreal	3600 B.C.–330 B.C.	1579 B.C.–A.D. 1100		A.D. 1334–A.D. 1778
Plantago	4277 B.C.–3153 B.C.			A.D. 1889–
(16) Ukraine 1 (Karsashinski Swamp)				
Arboreal	3673 B.C.–2170 B.C.	1338 B.C.–A.D. 300	A.D. 448–A.D. 1482	A.D. 1229–
Plantago	3316 B.C.–2170 B.C.			
(17) Ukraine 2 (Starniki)				
Arboreal		2600 B.C.–727 B.C.	A.D. 93–A.D. 1400	

(18) Ukraine 3 (Stoyanov 2)			
Arboreal	3900 B.C.–2020 B.C.	A.D. 300–A.D. 1660	
Plantago	2020 B.C.–600 B.C.		A.D. 863–A.D. 1528
(19) Ukraine 4 (Ivano-Frankovskoye)			
Arboreal	3937 B.C.–500 B.C.		
Plantago			
(20) Ukraine 5 (Dovjok Swamp)			
Arboreal	2062 B.C.–500 B.C.	A.D. 125–A.D. 1063	
Plantago	2700 B.C.–224 B.C.	A.D. 40–A.D. 800	A.D. 1200–A.D. 1700
	956 B.C.–122 B.C.	A.D. 395–A.D. 900	A.D. 1600–A.D. 1872
(21) Russia (Chabada Lake)			
Arboreal	3800 B.C.–1737 B.C.	1400 B.C.–306 B.C.	A.D. 1405–
Northern Europe			
(22) Sweden 1 (Agerods Mosse)			
Arboreal	3004 B.C.–256 B.C.	A.D. 435–A.D. 1682	
Plantago	3266 B.C.–2485 B.C.	A.D. 208–A.D. 1294	A.D. 1856–
(23) Sweden 2 (Kansjon)			
Arboreal	3752 B.C.–A.D. 978		A.D. 1647–
(24) Norway (Grasvatn)			
Arboreal	4064 B.C.–3032 B.C.	1612 B.C.–A.D. 323	A.D. 1097–A.D. 1700
(25) Latvia (Rudushskoe Lake)			
Arboreal	3955 B.C.–1700 B.C.	627 B.C.–A.D. 837	A.D. 1300–
(26) Greenland (Lake 31)			
Arboreal	2864 B.C.–2178 B.C.	1700 B.C.–121 B.C.	A.D. 1139–
(27) Finland 1 (Kirkkosaari)			
Arboreal	3030 B.C.–2656 B.C.	1898 B.C.–500 B.C.	A.D. 1065–A.D. 1213
Plantago	3022 B.C.–A.D. 1537		
(28) Finland 2 (Mukkavaara)			
Arboreal	3852 B.C.–87 B.C.		A.D. 1384–A.D. 1743
	3618 B.C.–A.D. 1757		

(contd.)

Table 7.1 contd.

Area	Phase 1	Phase 2	Phase 3	Phase 4
(29) Finland 3 (Hirvilampi)				
Arboreal	4283 B.C.–3540 B.C.	2611 B.C.–696 B.C.	A.D. 389–A.D. 1040	
Plantago	3726 B.C.–2797 B.C.		696 B.C.–A.D. 400	A.D. 823–
Mediterranean				
(30) Greece (Edessa)				
Arboreal	3998 B.C.–2852 B.C.	1941 B.C.–292 B.C.		A.D. 1026–A.D. 1800
Plantago	3500 B.C.–2852 B.C.		739 B.C.–292 B.C.	A.D. 1595–
(31) Greece 2 (Khimaditis 1B)				
Arboreal		1641 B.C.–A.D. 1700		
Plantago			A.D. 400–A.D. 1639	
(32) Italy(Selle di Carnino)				
Arboreal	4539 B.C.–3000 B.C.		A.D. 436–A.D. 1220	A.D. 1529–A.D. 1634
Plantago	3774 B.C.–2626 B.C.		A.D. 1070–A.D. 1270	A.D. 1581–
(33) Spain 1 (Saldropo)				
Arboreal	3630 B.C.–1431 B.C.	2202 B.C.–774 B.C.	A.D. 300–A.D. 948	A.D. 1266–
Plantago			3 B.C.–A.D. 684	
(34) Spain 2 (Sanabria Marsh)				
Arboreal	3500 B.C.–1700 B.C.	2192 B.C.–110 B.C.		
Plantago				A.D. 856–A.D. 1850
(35) Spain 3 (Lago d Ajo)				
Arboreal	4963 B.C.–2059 B.C.	1884 B.C.–552 B.C.		
Plantago		768 B.C.–A.D. 94	A.D. 309–A.D. 1170	A.D. 1600–A.D. 1900
(36) Spain 4 (Puerto de Los Tornos)				
Arboreal	4200 B.C.–A.D. 395			A.D. 1200–A.D. 1750
Plantago	3965 B.C.–756 B.C.			A.D. 1101–A.D. 1767

(37) Spain 5 (Laguna de la Roya)			
Arboreal	4500 B.C.–2728 B.C.	968 B.C.–A.D. 848	A.D. 1600–
Plantago	4431 B.C.–2728 B.C.	1594 B.C.–A.D. 700	A.D. 1762–
(38) Syria (Ghab)			
Arboreal	3592 B.C.–1505 B.C.	983 B.C.–A.D. 500	
Plantago	4636 B.C.–4000 B.C.	1505 B.C.–1000 B.C.	A.D. 269–A.D. 1000
(39) Turkey 1 (K'ycegiz G¹)			
Arboreal	2306 B.C.–616 B.C.	180 B.C.–A.D. 916	A.D. 1700–A.D. 1941
Plantago	3694 B.C.–2990 B.C.	1278 B.C.–419 B.C.	A.D. 1223–1852
(40) Turkey 2 (Beysehir G¹)			
Arboreal	3500 B.C.–2527 B.C.	243 B.C.–A.D. 1100	A.D. 1100
Plantago	4451 B.C.–3489 B.C.	1556 B.C.–724 B.C.	A.D. 1560–

Source: Based on data from (van Zeist, W. et al. 1980; Rankama, T. and Vuorela, I. 1988; Bottema, S. 1974; Eronen, M. and Hyvrinen, H. 1982; Lazarova, M. 1995; Stefanova, I. 1995; Verbruggen, C. et al. 1997; Bezusko, L.G. 1987; Ammann, B. 1985; Watts, W.A. et al. 1996; Penalba, M.C. 1994; Binka, K. et al. 1988; Khomutova, V. et al. 1994; Bradshaw, R.H. et al. 1988; Eisner, W.R. et al. 1995; Behre, K.E. and Kucan, D. 1986).

Following this first phase of deforestation from 3854 B.C.–2400 B.C., there were three/four subsequent phases of deforestation followed by reforestation that occurred towards the latter period of the course of a Dark Age. Table 7.2 exhibits the phase periods based on the mean of the dating periods for the forty arboreal pollen trend lines. If Dark Age Phase 1 started around 3854 B.C., Dark Age Phase 2 started around approximately 2400 B.C. This is the start of the Bronze Age crisis—the early phase of the Dark Ages during the Bronze Age. This dating also corresponds with Barbara Bell's (1971) identification of the first Dark Age of the Ancient World. In Western Europe, arboreal pollen from areas in Belgium, Germany, and France exhibit the deforestation period starting around 2200/2000 B.C. In Central and Eastern Europe, trend lines of arboreal pollen show deforestation levels in areas of Hungary and Ukraine. In Northern Europe, the trend line of arboreal pollen in an area in Finland also supports this deforestation pattern. Finally, in the Mediterranean, we find areas of Greece, Spain, and Turkey exhibiting such trends. It should be noted that nestled within this Phase 2 Dark Age, there was another Phase 2A that began around 1200 B.C.—the commonly accepted time period for the start of the crisis that witnessed the final demise of the Bronze Age world-system. Dark Age phase 2A was followed by Dark Age Phase 3 at around A.D. 300, and Dark Age Phase 4 at A.D. 1300.

The above deforestation levels and phasing is anthropogenic in nature and this is confirmed by the rise in the number of *plantago lanceolata* pollen. The rise in the pollen record of indicator plants and ground weeds such as *plantago lanceolata* suggest fragmentation and deforestation as a consequence of agriculture and anthropogenic actions (Behre 1990: 224; Williams, 2003:12–25). Table 7.1 provides time phases of the *rise* in the number of *plantago lanceolata* pollen when there was a *decline* in the number of arboreal pollen. The identification of arboreal pollen phases in Table 7.1 does not imply that deforestation follows a cycle. Rather, I am suggesting that there is a length of time when the ecological threshold is reached as a consequence of natural system and social system connections that require a time period (ecological time) for ecological recovery, and/or social system adaptation (such as reorganization, learning processes, technological adaptation, etc.) to take place. This necessitates a time period. For ecological recovery, time-wise, it is ecological time that is the underlying basis. For social system adaptation, social time is the case. In this sense, the duration

Table 7.2: Periodization of Dark Ages*

Phase 1	Phase 2	Phase 2A	Phase 3	Phase 4
3854 B.C.– 2400 B.C.	2402 B.C.– 594 B.C.	1188 B.C.– A.D. 689	A.D. 296– A.D. 1171	A.D. 1311– A.D. 1733

* Mean of 40 Pollen Profiles of Deforestation Phases.

is of different lengths. We assume that ecological recovery will take a much longer time period measured on a social time scale since Nature has its own intrinsic rhythm driven by factors such as generation time, disturbance frequencies, and age of reproduction, and other spatial scales like topography, interaction lengths, etc. (Redman and Kinzig 2003).

Similarly, social system adaptation and recovery has its own rhythm as well as is dependent on the internal intrinsics of the social organizations and social institutions. From what we have been able to surmise from Tables 7.1 and 7.2 and the periodization of Dark Ages by historians, archeologists, and anthropologists, the period of social adaptation, i.e., the duration of a Dark Age based on social distress and recovery is nestled within the long duration of ecological time. The latter suggests that deforestation phases (or ecological recovery) are/ is naturally longer and that ecological scars continue despite the fact that social adaptation and recovery have been completed.

What needs to be noted, however, is that the advent of each deforestation phase dovetails with the concentration/urbanization process that Modelski (1999a: 390) and Modelski and Thompson (1999: 182) have identified in world history from 3400 B.C. to 1200 B.C. According to them, there were three periods of concentration/urbanization starting around 4000 B.C.–3400 B.C., 1200 B.C., and A.D. 930. These time points fall within Phases 1, 2, 2A, and 3 of deforestation phases as outlined in Table 7.1. Phase 4 of deforestation began around A.D. 1300 and ended around A.D. 1700. In social time, this time period was also the crisis of the "long" fourteenth century in Europe, and the prelude to the later expansion of the world-economy. These identified periods of Dark Ages of human history exhibit deforestation and then recovery (reforestation), with the slowdown in socioeconomic activity or a drop in human population, enabling for the ecology to recover. In the long run, however, with the exception of certain geographic areas and during certain time periods, forest loss has outpaced reforestation. From Neolithic times to the present day we have lost between seven and eight million kilometers of closed forest, and two to three million kilometers of open woodland and scrubland (World Commission on Forests and Sustainable Development 1999). Thus, deforestation has a long history (Chew 2001).

With deforestation there are also other consequences such as soil erosion, etc. The lack of vegetative cover increases the amount of erosion. The amount of erosion is about fifty times higher on a landscape devoid of cover than one that is under a well-developed forest (Redman 1999). Besides this, the rate of rainfall run-off is five times higher on a landscape that is bare. Soil erosion generates significant issues for social systems dependent on irrigation-fed agriculture. The loss of moisture means that with climate changes, such as an increase in temperature and shifts in wind patterns carrying rain, there are heightened distressed conditions.

There is ample evidence even as early as 2200 B.C., during Dark Age Phase 2 (2200 B.C.–1700 B.C.), in Mesopotamia, Harappa, and Egypt that soil erosion resulting from deforestation had tremendous consequences for the agricultural economies of these early civilizations (Chew 2001; Butzer 1976). It led to severe economic stress on these social systems and, coupled with climatological changes and natural disturbances, led to crises in the social and natural systems (Chew 1997, 2001, Redman 1999). Soil erosion was also a condition experienced by Minoan Crete and Mycenaean Greece during the Dark Age period 1200 B.C.– 700 B.C. The occurrence of soil erosion during the period of decline of the Roman Empire, prior to the onset of the Dark Age period A.D. 300–A.D. 900, underlines the recurring nature of widespread soil erosion punctuating Dark Age periods.

Climate Changes and Tectonic Shifts

Considerations of climate changes, natural disturbances, and catastrophes impacting on the reproduction of the social (world) system have not warranted much attention in the social and historical sciences in comparison to capital accumulation issues, class and elite dynamics, technological adaptation, and ideological/cultural processes. This line of thinking is followed closely in explanations that have been provided for the widespread collapse of cities and civilizations in the later phase of the crisis of the Bronze Age (see for example, Friedman 2003; Drews 1993; Yoffee 1988). Such adherence to anthropogenic induced explanations for political-economic declines, and even collapse of social systems is limiting, for there are some indications linking climate changes and tectonic shifts affecting social (world) system reproduction during the Bronze Age crisis. Throughout world history, socioeconomic and political changes (such as trade collapses and political changes), and including large-scale migrations, have occurred during periods of climate change, proving this relationship is quite clear. What needs to be brought up is the clustering of these climate changes, natural disturbances, and the occurrence of catastrophes during phases of Dark Ages.

Climate-wise, there is evidence of temperature changes (higher temperatures) and increasing drought-like conditions persisting in the Eastern Mediterranean, Egypt, West Asia, Mesopotamia, north-western India, Central Asia, Africa, and parts of the New World starting from 2200 B.C. onwards during the onset of the Dark Age of the third millennium (Neumann and Parpola 1987; Chew 2001; Weiss and Bradley 2001; Bentaleb et al. 1997; Enzel et al. 1999; Ratnagar 1981; Fagan 2004; Issar 1998). The start of this warming phase was by no means a phase that followed the mini Ice Age of 6200 B.C. to 5800 B.C. An earlier phase began around 3800 B.C. and lasted for over 1,000 years (commensurate with our

Phase 1 of deforestation or Dark Age Phase 1, see Table 7.1) when the climate began to be drier, affecting south-western Asia and the eastern Mediterranean. By 3500 B.C. the drought intensified, engendering a climatic crisis (Fagan 2004). This crisis deepened further between 3200 and 3000 B.C. Following this, the climatic cycle changed and swung back to conditions prior to 3800 B.C.

Eight hundred years later, again, we witnessed the start of another warming trend around 2200 B.C. According to Fagan (2004), who has argued on the impact of climate change on civilizations, this repetition of a warm trend was a global event. Affected areas covered Egypt, northern Africa, Greece, Indus, the Fertile Crescent, Crete, Russia, West Asia, and Palestine (Bell 1971; Bottema 1997; Hassan 1997; Hole 1997; Krementski 1997; Issar 1998; Chew 2001; Weiss and Bradley 2001; Fagan 2004). For social systems with agricultural practices that are reliant on irrigation waters or annual floods, this loss of moisture would place tremendous stress on the agricultural systems and hence, the economy and social-political stability (Neumann and Parpola 1987).[5] Such was the case for the core centers of Mesopotamia, Egypt, and the Harappan civilization. Each responded differently to such stressed conditions, depending on what they were facing.

Later in the period, a warm spell prevailed over the ancient Near East between 1200 B.C. and 900 B.C. (Neumann and Parpola 1987). Such a warming trend had an impact on the stream flow of the Tigris and Euphrates where there was a maximum peak between 1350 B.C. and 1250 B.C., followed by a sharp drop reaching a minimum at around 1150 B.C. (Kay and Johnson 1981). Recovery of moisture only returned around 950 B.C. Textual evidence also indicates a number of severe droughts experienced in Assyria and Babylon. Around 1090 B.C., a severe drought occurred, and a period of drought years extended from 1050 B.C.–1007 B.C. (Neumann and Parpola 1987: 176). Drought conditions also prevailed for Greece and the Eastern Mediterranean from 1200 B.C.–850 B.C. (Carpenter 1968; Weiss 1982). Bryson et al. (1974: 49) have also reported of drought conditions and increases in land temperature for the Anatolian plateau. Precipitation rate was 20–40 percent below normal, and the temperatures were 2.5–4 degrees centigrade above normal. Circumstances were also similar for Libya where precipitation was 50 percent below normal, and the temperature was 1.5 degrees centigrade above normal.

Climatic changes in the form of temperature increases and rising aridity have severe implications for already ecologically stressed social systems crippled by deforestation and soil erosion. The impacts are translated to lower harvest yields, and at times, crop failures along with loss of animal pasture. It has been estimated that a mere one degree centigrade rise in winter temperature may reduce rainfall by as much as 30 mm. For the Ancient Near East where 200 mm of annual rainfall is a threshold for rain-fed agriculture and any level below is dependent on irrigation, such a decrease would spell crisis for the region

(Neumann and Parpola 1987: 173). In eastern Mediterranean, social systems such as Crete that relied on agricultural products as cash crops, and thus reliant on bountiful harvests to offset its imports of needed natural resources, such as metals and wood, faced extreme stress during the late Bronze Age when the climate started to change. For Egypt, the temperature increases led to droughts, and this impacted on agriculture even as far south as Nubia after 1260 B.C. (Butzer 1983, 1997; Hassan 1997). Famines extended even as far as Libya that led to attacks on Egypt. Reduced flow in Nile because of lowered volumes in the lake levels in the Ethiopian Highlands from about 1260 B.C. onwards further intensified the drought conditions that were being experienced (Butzer 1983). Lowered flood levels from the Nile started around the reign of Ramses III from 1182 B.C. onwards. The aridity and drought conditions led to dust storms being reported and continued encroachment of desert sand on the urban environment. At Aksha, sand dunes spread over the flood plain, and the lack of flooding led to the build up of salt in the flood plain (Butzer 1983).

Beyond the temperature changes and drought, natural disturbances in the form of volcanic activity and earthquakes have been attributed to exacerbate the already precarious ecological landscape. Crete, for example, lies on the Aegean plate (Manning 1994). For this period, the volcanic eruption on Thera (Santorini) is one that has been widely examined as a factor in the demise of Minoan Crete (Marinatos 1939; Chadwick 1976; Hammer et al. 1980; Warren 1985; Pang 1991; Baillie 1994, 1995, 1998, 1999; Driessen and MacDonald 2000). Initially, the date of the Thera eruption was identified between 1400 B.C. and 1390 B.C. (Marinatos 1939; Hammer et al. 1980). This date has been revised by a new ice-core boring, and it is now determined to be around the calibrated age of 1630–1530 B.C. or around conventional Carbon-14 dating of 1376 B.C.–1342 B.C. (Hammer et al. 1987). Examining acidity peaks, the determination of the eruption date is around calibrated 1645 B.C. or 1390 B.C. (C-14 dated) (Hammer et al. 1987).

In terms of impact to the socioeconomic reproduction of the region, such as Crete, such a volcanic eruption was far-reaching. The spread of the plume of tephra, dust, and gases was across most part of the eastern portion of the Mediterranean east of Thera, impacting on crops, livestock, buildings, and water supplies. The eruption column reached a height of almost 29 kilometers and penetrated well into the stratosphere. Prior to this eruption (2–5 years), there was a serious earthquake perhaps triggering the eruption. Archeological excavations have indicated of site abandonments on the island of Crete. There has been also evidence of tsunamis occurring via discoveries in archeological excavations of 15 centimeters of silt layer suggesting a water event, and of tsunami deposits being overlaid by tephra on the coasts of Asia Minor. The tsunamis also destroyed ships in Cretan harbors that faced north, such as Poros, Amnisos, and Nirou Chani, and salinated the northern coastal areas, turning them unfit for agriculture. Following the eruption, a massive ash fall of more than 15 centimeters covered the eastern portion of the island, and parts of Asia Minor. Such devastation covered plant and animal life and as Driessen and MacDonald (2000: 85) have suggested: "Olive trees, vines and other crops may have suffered, a situation aggravated by any ash fall, which would also have been extremely dangerous for animals as it would have abraded their teeth and clogged their digestive system."

The volcanic tremors would have also shaken buildings causing migrations out of urban complexes. What resulted would be a reduction of occupied space, absence/decrease of new constructions, erection of protective structures, abandonment of old wells and the digging of new ones, hoarding of precious metals and objects, and political fragmentation. All the Cretan settlements showed signs of the lack of new construction and settlement contraction, such as in Vathypero, Galatas, Petras, Zakros, Kammos, and Palaikastro where the plume of ash fell and covered. Hoarding was quite evident, with daggers hidden beneath pithoi and copper ingots in storage spaces of the palaces at Malia and Zakros and in houses at Mochlos and Palaikastro.

Excavations have also noted political and economic fragmentation and decentralization with the rise of local economic and administrative systems and the failure of palatial administrations. Furthermore, the eruption from the generated tsunamis and ash fallout destroyed the Minoan naval fleet (Chadwick 1976). This loss undermined Cretan Naval supremacy that for a long period provided Minoan Crete the power to exercise its dominant position in this region of Bronze Age world-system. Besides the volcanic eruption at Thera that impacted on Crete, Evans (1921) has also remarked of the destruction of Knossos from an earthquake around 1400 B.C. According to Evans, the earthquake disrupted lamps and open fires and fanned by the wind, the blaze destroyed the urban community and the palace. This destruction thesis by volcanic eruption has, however, been challenged by some archeologists (see Drews 1993).

With volcanic eruptions, climate changes would also follow, such as a "volcanic winter" with the volcanic aerosols influencing the radiation balance, thus impacting on the economy and agriculture (Hammer et al 1980; Driessen and MacDonald 2000). Besides those parts of the eastern Mediterranean that were impacted by the volcanic eruption, it has been suggested as well that the environment of Egypt at this point in time was affected by a major dust veil with a reduction in rainfall (Baillie 1999).

In the other parts of the systems such as mainland Greece, there have also been indications of earthquakes leading to urban damage. Excavations at Tiryns on the Plain of Argos, showed tectonic shift damages in the lower citadel of the city (Zanggar 1993). This occurred around the LH (Late Helladic Period) IIIB period (1335/25 B.C.–1190 B.C.), with another round of tectonic activity impacting during LH IIIC (1190 B.C.–1050 B.C.). There were also signs of flash flooding with evidence of alluvium being deposited. Whether the earthquakes engendered flash flooding resulting in urban damages, or that the flash floodings were a result from the eruption of Hekla 3 in Iceland on 1159 B.C. is difficult to delineate. For clearly in the latter's case, climate changes would follow from such volcanic activity, with perhaps unusually heavy rainfall that could have generated flash flooding (Zanggar 1993). Either way, in terms of causal relationship, the socioeconomic life would have been affected. Other parts of mainland Greece that suffered from earthquakes were Midea and Mycenae. Iakovides (1977) attributed the destruction of Mycenae during the late LH IIIB period to earthquake fires, and so did Åstrom (1985) for Midea.

In Asia Minor and Syria, Schaeffer (1968) has indicated that cities were ruined by earthquakes around 1200 B.C. Ugarit, the trading center for the Hittites, was one of those that was impacted. So were Alalakh, Hattusas, Alishar, Alaca Hoyuk and others that were shaken by the natural disaster. Troy also suffered from a catastrophic earthquake with fires ensuing from the tremors around 1275 B.C. (Blegen et al. 1950).

Similar conditions occurred also during the 2200 B.C. Dark Age period in northwestern India. Tectonic shifts occurred that diverted water courses. In turn, these diversions transformed some rivers into dry riverbeds, thus further exacerbating the aridity, and thereby impacting on socioeconomic life. The drying up of the Sarasvati River had major implications for Harappan urban complexes located on its banks (Possehl 2001). Agrawal and Sood (1982) have noted tectonic shifts that diverted the course of the Satluz and the eastern rivers away from the Ghaggar, which over time became a lake-like depression during this period. Thus, in northern and western Rajasthan, unstable river systems impacted on socioeconomic life. Furthermore, tectonic disturbances also cut off Lothal from its feeder river and eventually the port's access to the sea, impacting on the trade of the Harappans.

In all, climatic changes and natural disturbances as factors impacting on the reproduction of these ancient economies and societies further exacerbated the already precarious nature of the world-system and the entities that form it. Similar climatic changes also occurred during the Dark Age between A.D. 300 and A.D. 900. Temperature increases occurred in Europe, West Asia, China, and parts of the Americas (Bryson and Padoch 1980; DeMenocal 2001; Weiss and Bradley 2001; Broecker 2001). In fact, Broecker (2001) has suggested that this warming trend was a global phenomenon and lasted until A.D. 1200. Analysis of tree rings in Sweden also suggests such climatological shifts.[6] Tree ring evidence from Western Europe, Britain, and North America also reveals drought-like conditions and slow growth (Keys 1999). This warming trend resulted in drought-like conditions being felt in the above mentioned geographic areas, leading to widespread famine, for example, in northern China and Korea during A.D. 530s. Besides the socioeconomic tragedies experienced such as trade route disruption, diseases, etc., there were also political collapses such as the decline of the Roman Empire, the classic Mayan culture, and the Moche civilization of northern Peru. Some scholars have suggested that climate changes might also be a contributing factor besides those of overpopulation, deforestation, soil erosion, social warfare, etc. (Davis and Shaw 2001; Weiss and Bradley 2001).

Socioeconomic and Political Changes: Deurbanization, Population, Regime Changes and Innovations

Deurbanization, Population and Migration

The spectrum of changes in this dimension is generally better known, though not necessarily better documented. Some recent attempts by Modelski (2003) and Thompson (2004) on urbanization and economic expansion have provided us with the broad contours on these processes. As we have stated previously, all trends show reversals in terms of their trajectories. Urbanization is one such trend. If we trace the urbanization process in one of the first places where urbanization started i.e., southern Mesopotamia, we find by 2200 B.C., the start of Dark Age Phase 2, the total population of Mesopotamia had been reduced to 210,000 during the Akkadian period. From 210,000 during the Akkadian period (2200 B.C.), the population in Mesopotamian cities was reduced to 190,000 by the Isin-Larsa period (1900 B.C.). This was a loss of 10 percent. The population level was reduced further to 70,000 by the Old Babylonian Period (1600 B.C.). Overall therefore, between the start of Dark Age Phase 2 (Akkadian Period) to its end around 1700 B.C. (Isin-Larsa and Old Babylonian periods) we see a loss of over 66 percent of the urban population in Mesopotamia.

This shift is also reflected in the proportion of declining urban settlement sizes (see Table 7.3). During the Early Dynastic Period II/III (2800 B.C.–2300 B.C.) the percentage of urban settlements with more than 40 hectares was about 78.4 percent, by the Akkadian Period (2200 B.C.) it was reduced to 63.5 percent. Further deurbanization continued that by Ur III and Isin-Larsa periods (2100 B.C.–1900 B.C.), the percentage has dropped further to 55.1 percent. This

Table 7.3: Urban and Non-urban Settlements in Mesopotamia, 2800 B.C.–1600 B.C.

Period	Percentage Non-urban (10 ha or less)	Percentage Urban (more than 40 ha)
Early Dynastic II/III (2800 B.C.–2300 B.C.)	10.0	78.4
Akkadian (2200 B.C.)	18.4	63.5
Ur III-Isin-Larsa (2100 B.C.–1900 B.C.)	25.0	55.1
Old Babylonian (1600 B.C.)	29.6	50.2
Kassite (1400 B.C.)	56.8	30.4

Source: From Adams 1981: 138.

slippage continued into the Old Babylonian Period reducing further to 50.2 percent (1600 B.C.). Conversely, non-urban settlement sizes (less than 10 hectares or less) increased. During the early Dynastic II/III period it was about 10 percent, and almost doubled by the Akkadian Period. With the arrival of the Ur III and Isin-Larsa periods, the percentage has risen to 25 percent, and almost tripled to about 29.6 percent by the Old Babylonian Period in comparison to the Early Dynastic period.

Deurbanization and population losses were also repeated in north-western India. According to Possehl (2001), by the late third millennium B.C., there was evidence of abandonment of important buildings in the highly urbanized settings such as Mohenjo-daro. Concurrently, the Sindh region and the Baluchi Highlands also witnessed depletion and deterioration. By the early second millennium B.C., Baluchistan was uninhabited. Cholistan, in north-western India, experienced a drop in size in terms of settled areas from an average of 6.5 hectares in 3800 B.C.–3200 B.C. to 5.1 hectares by 1900 B.C.–1700 B.C., and finally to almost 50 percent less (2.6 hectares) by 1000 B.C. (Possehl 2001; Chew 2004b). In the Sarasvati region, the shifting and drying up of the river system saw the abandonment of settlements in the inland delta of Fort Derawar. In northwestern India, migrations from the urban complexes were also of the same order. Mohenjo-daro and Harappa saw population disappearances, so were the settlements of the Harappans in Sindh. With the drying up of the Sarasvati, the eastern region saw an increase in settlements indicating the relocation of the population in areas where the drainage system had disappeared. Similar migratory movements also occurred in West Asia and central Eurasia.

Elsewhere for the time period of 2200 B.C., similar signs of deteriorating conditions were also encountered in Anatolia, with abandonment of urban centers such as Troy II to Troy III-IV (Wilkinson 1990, Mellink 1986:139–52). Sedentary population settlements on the Anatolian plateau were also abandoned. To the west of Anatolia, Palestine also suffered such crisis conditions (Butzer 1997). Walled towns were replaced by unwalled villages. There were signs of cave occupation and migratory movements. In some areas, settlements completely disappeared, and remaining settlement sites were reduced by more than half of what existed before 2200 B.C. (Harrison 1997: 1–38). Across the Mediterranean from Palestine, the Aegean experienced distress, though to a lesser extent. Between 2300 B.C. and 1900 B.C. there was a loss of sedentary population. Such losses were experienced both on mainland Greece and even Crete (Jameson et al. 1994; Watrous 1994).

Similar stress conditions also prevailed in central Eurasia. The changed ecological landscape led to migration of the sedentary population from river valleys over time, and exploitation of the steppes for animal feed. Denucleation occurred with the establishment of smaller communities near oases. This spread occurred in Central Asia at Korezm (south of the Aral Sea) and Margiana (Murghab Delta) in Turkmenistan, Bactria, and western China. This process, prompted by ecological degradation and environmental changes, also occurred in Syria and Jordan. It resulted in migration out of urban centers located on the coast to the interior, and the establishment of smaller village type-settlements. (McGovern 1987: 267–73).

Loss of population through migration has been noted in several locations such as West Asia, Mesopotamia, northwestern India, and central Eurasia (Weiss 1993; Algaze 1993a; Harrison 1997; Possehl 2001; Hiebert 2000; Fagan 2004). With climate changes between 2200 B.C. and 1900 B.C., there was desertion of the Habur Plains in northern Mesopotamia, followed with population reduction in the northern settlements such as Tell Leilan, Tell Brak, and Mohamed Diyab. Population losses for Tell Leilan was estimated to be about 14,000–28,000 persons. In Sumer, where 80 percent of the population was living in urban centers by 2800 B.C., by 2000 B.C., this number had declined to under 50 percent (Fagan 2004). For centuries, Amorite pastoral peoples had populated the open country surrounding the Euphrates. With the climate changes discussed above, they started to encroach on the urban settlements. With their movements down the Euphrates and Tigris they forced the ruler of Ur to erect a wall—Repeller of the Amorites Wall—to prevent further migration. This wall was 180 kilometers and in spite of its length it failed in its task (Fagan 2004; Weiss 2000). The Hurrians and the Gutians to the north were also displaced.

Colin and Sarah McEvedy (1972) have also reported slow population growth for the second Dark Age period starting around A.D. 300–A.D. 900 when growth of the global population was only about 15 percent in comparison to the prior period when it was about 100 percent. Biraben (1980:5), however, has noted that world population at A.D. 1 was 255 million and at A.D. 200 was 256 million; this total was reduced to 206 million by A.D. 400 and continued at this level until A.D. 700. Most of the losses were in Europe, the former Soviet Union, and Africa. Table 7.1 details the global population losses during the Dark Ages 1200 B.C.–500 B.C. and A.D. 400–A.D. 900.

For the Dark Age that occurred between A.D. 300–A.D. 900, besides the population decreases indicated above, we find social, economic and political reversals, for example, for the Roman Empire, similar to what Greece experienced in the earlier Dark Age between 1200 B.C. and 700 B.C. We witness these reversals by the fourth century A.D. For centuries prior to the onset of the Dark Ages, the Roman Empire was expanding, and in the course of this expansion it developed increasingly into a complex system of taxation and administration. By the fourth century A.D., it was feeling the strain of this infrastructure of support. Furthermore, by the late fourth century, the tribal groups could no longer be kept out of the Roman Empire. Incursions were the order of the day. Hinterland invasions into the core have been documented that were precipitated by deteriorating environmental conditions and climatological changes for these warring activities (Brown 1995, 2001; Modelski and Thompson 1999). The "barbarian" invasions were into Roman territory in Western Europe and North Africa.

In the area of urban complexes, we find that cities were beginning to reduce in size. For example, in the western part of the Roman Empire such as Gaul, the cities shrank in size. For example, Lyon was reduced from 160 hectares to 20 hectares and Vienne shrank from 200 hectares to 20 hectares (Hodgett 1972; Randsborg 1991). As the Dark Age progressed, towns became sparsely populated in Gaul, and there was a lack of evidence in terms of continuity. Deurbanization seems to be the trend in the western part of the Roman Empire. The city of Rome itself was depopulating. At A.D. 367, it had a million persons, but by A.D. 452, the population was reduced to about 400,000. The latter number was further reduced to 30,000 by the tenth century A.D., which is the end of the Dark Ages. Urban decay, disintegration, illiteracy, and depopulation were the characteristic features depicting the urban landscape. Along with the urban deterioration, the Roman social hierarchy and bureaucracy were reduced and flattened with local administrators taking over. In the end, the western part of the Roman Empire no longer could sustain itself and collapse followed. The eastern part of the Empire continued though Dark Age conditions predominated. In Byzantium, there was little education and literature was non-existent. Cities across Anatolia went through a deurbanization process, and contracted to fort-like enclosures located on hills (Haldon 1990; Treadgold 1988, 1997).

Political Reorganizations and Innovations

If we examine Dark Age Phase 2 (2200 B.C.–1700 B.C.), political instability is one feature that highlights the political economic events. Climate changes as identified above led to famines that in turn generated political upheavals. In Egypt, drought conditions and lowered Nile flooding impacted the farmers' ability to pay taxes because of lower harvest yields. This resulted in local administrators and governors, who collected taxes, having to delay their transfers to the Royal House. In turn, the king's revenues plummeted, and thus impaired his ability to pay for an army or to deal effectively with drought and famine. As a result, the stability of the political regime was affected. The sum effects of this in terms of political stability, as Bell (1971) has concluded, were short reigns. Hassan (1997), covering a slightly different period, 2180 B.C.– 2134 B.C., reported that eighteen pharaohs reigned during this short time span.

Besides political instability in Egypt during the third millennium Dark Age of 2200 B.C., other reversals also occurred, such as artistic degeneration and the downsizing of monumental buildings as a result of diminishing resources. The size and elaborateness of the pharaonic tombs were reduced; by this time, the tombs of kings were one-chambered affairs with less ambitious layouts (Bovarski

1998: 316–19). To deal with the famine and droughts, temporary dams were built at the edges of the alluvial flats to retain as much of the annual flood waters of the Nile on the agricultural fields. Grain was stored and distributed to the famine areas to show the pharaoh's largesse. Boundaries of provinces were also closed to prevent mass migration out of famine-stricken areas. Similarly, in Palestine, there was a structural simplification (devolution) of socio-political institutions (Esse 1991). There was a reduction in social complexity whereby the urban society in place with a stratified system had transformed to a less urban system determined by a clan/tribe structure, and very slowly even changing to hamlets. This was a transformation that is a reversal of structures, as even by the late Chalcolithic Period the social–political structures in Palestine had evolved to a stratified system, and the economic institutions by the Early Bronze Age had shifted from raw materials manufacturing to agricultural surplus production with market exchange. With Egypt in close proximity, the socio-political structures and economic institutions were also transformed as a consequence of trading and bilateral exchanges.

Later for this period starting around 1300 B.C., we find further political upheavals, invasions and migrations. Starting with Egypt that remained a significant power in the eastern Mediterranean littoral under Pharaoh Ramesses II (1304 B.C.–1237 B.C.), rivalry with the Hittites under Muwatallish saw Syria coming under Hittite control, though the Egyptians maintained control over Palestine. With the death of Rameses II, Egyptian power was significantly challenged by invading forces of Libyan and sea people around 1232 B.C. that Pharaoh Merneptah decisively repelled. The constant military and political challenges continued with Pharaoh Rameses III fending off another invasion by the sea people from 1194 B.C. onwards when they attacked the fertile lands of Syria, Palestine, and the Delta, and ending by 1188 B.C. with the final victory for Rameses III. With the death of Rameses III, domestic and political turmoil ensued. Climate changes that forced the sea people to leave their abodes have been attributed for their migratory invasions of lands that were under Egyptian control (Weiss 1982; Hassan 1997; Bryce 1998; Braudel 2001). In a wider context and over a longer historical period, Modelski and Thompson (1999) have documented this migratory pattern of incursions that coincided with the socioeconomic pulsations of the world-system.

To the northeast of Egypt in western Anatolia, the Hittite kingdom experienced widespread economic and political chaos as well. From documents excavated at Ugarit, the collapse of the Hittites took place between the end of the thirteenth century B.C. and the beginning of the twelfth century B.C. Political challenges were posed by neighboring vassal rulers and the migratory sea peoples (Braudel 2001, Bryce 1998).

The reasons for all these conflicts and military excursions are not clearly known from the archeological discoveries to date. Friedman (2003) has suggested that political violence and conflicts were outcomes of the development initiative of the world-system where the accumulation of surplus and the search for natural resources were political-economic activities undertaken by the kingdoms of the late Bronze Age in the eastern Mediterranean. Though important, such a rationale addresses only one aspect of world history during this conjuncture. Again, other considerations that are ecologically conduced need to be inserted, such as a continuous drought and famine condition.

When the final end came for the kingdom of Hittites, Hattusa the capital, according to Bryce (1999), was consumed in "a great conflagration" and its associated satellite vassals also followed suit. Site abandonment seemed to be the prevailing motif, thus underlining the process of deurbanization that is a predominant feature of the Dark Ages that we have pinpointed in the previous sections. The slide into less than complex lifestyles can be seen from the pottery recovered from this period. There was a falling off of the ceramic design, and the color of pottery tends to be monochrome and ranges from brown to reddish-brown to red, and of poor quality (Macqueen 1986). Could this drop in quality and lack of vitality be a result of the diminishing natural resources required for making this pottery? There has been no attempt to hypothesize this set of changes. In other parts of Anatolia, such as the eastern region, there was not even any evidence of ceramics at all. The argument for this total absence is that this region had retrogressed into nomadism (Macqueen 1986).

Across the Mediterranean from Anatolia, similar socioeconomic and political changes were also occurring. Greece encountered a decline in socioeconomic life from 1200 B.C. till 700 B.C.: decline or loss of certain material skills, decay in cultural aspects of life, a fall in living standard and thus wealth, deurbanization, population losses, and loss of trading contacts within and without Greece (see for example, Childe 1942; Snodgrass 1971, 1980; Desborough 1972; Whitley 1991; Ward and Joukovsky 1992; Deger-Jalkotzy 1998; Harrison and Spencer 1998; Morris 2000; Chew 2001). The archeological evidence unearthed suggests socioeconomic patterns that are distinctively different from the style and level of socio-cultural life prevailing prior to the onset of the Dark Age. Population decreases occurred between 1250 B.C. and 1100 B.C. Morris (2000) has estimated losses of about 75 percent followed with emigration from the core areas of the Mycenaean civilization; this trend continued for central Greece as well by 1100 B.C. Pottery and other objects recovered from excavated sites along with the architecture and design of dwellings reflect ecological stress and scarcity of natural resources. Architectural standards were lowered and there were very few signs of good stone-built construction. Small stone construction was prevalent, and we also increasingly see signs of mud-brick construction. Mud brick structures predominated in the building structures between the eleventh and tenth centuries. The emergence of a class of hand-made burnished pottery, "Barbarian Ware," had few obvious links to Mycenaean styles. Furthermore, pottery styles of the period in Greece became austere, unlike the decadent style of the previous era.

Starting with the Submycenaean style of pottery (1125 B.C.–1100 B.C.), the austerity of the design can be noted. As Desborough (1972) has put it, the standards deteriorated sharply not only in the making of the pottery but also in the painting and decoration. It was as Desborough (1972: 293) put it, "a depressed and debased style of pottery" reflecting the conditions of the period. There was also reduction in variety of styles in terms of vase shapes of this type of pottery. Rutter (1989) has also suggested that luxury vases and other pottery items were quickly abandoned as unnecessary frills when hard times hit. There was less variety of material goods, the artifactual correlate of a less complex social order. The emergence of the Protogeometric style (900 B.C.) continued to reflect the austerity of the period (Snodgrass 1971). This latter style was supposed to have originated in Athens and then copied by all the other regions of Greece, whereas the Submycenaean was deemed to have originated in Western Attica (Desborough 1972; Snodgrass 1971). Desborough (1972) has pointed out that the decorative motives for the Protogeometric style was, as a rule, confined to a small area of the pottery and decoration was used sparingly. Snodgrass (1971) has also alerted us to the appearance of hand-made pottery during the Dark Ages. The reversion to hand-made pottery when the pottery wheel had been adopted in prior times suggests to us the decay of manufacturing production, or even perhaps the loss of manufacturing skills. It could also mean that with social decay and collapse, there was a revival of the utilization of indigenous materials in view of the disruption in trade routes. From Protogeometric style we have the transformation to Early Geometric by 860 B.C./840 B.C., and Middle Geometric 770/760 B.C., and finally the Geometric pattern by 710/700 B.C.

In terms of decoration and finishing, the bulk of the pot or vase was usually left plain in the natural color of the clay while the decorations covered a third of the surface area at most (Desborough 1972). The lack of intense firing also suggests to us dwindling energy supplies. The compass and the multiple brush were used for decorating the pottery. As recovery proceeds and the balance of nature is restored, we find the plain, rectilinear or curvilinear patterns in pottery design giving way to images depicting animals and humans. In the later Protogeometric style period, we already saw the introduction of silhouette figures of a horse or a human in the designs. If we consider the decay of cultural life and the loss of the art of writing, and view pottery design as a way the potter as an artist could depict socio-cultural life, then, the motifs that we find in these pottery designs would summarize life in Dark Age Greece. The range of representational media in which representational art occurred during the Dark Age was also reduced (Rutter 1989). Whereas prior to the Dark Age period, during the exuberant Mycenaean times, painters produced lively colored frescoes of stylized patterns, humans, animals, and creatures from the sea (Desborough 1972). With such shifts in decorating motifs, it suggests the return of biodiversity to the environment and the loss of biodiversity at the onset of the Dark Ages. By the late Geometric style period, we find scenes of organized groups of men in uniforms, the portrayal of warfare and chariots depicting social life when the Dark Age was receding.

Beyond pottery styles, other objects recovered indicate a scarcity of natural resources, especially metals, or, that the supply sources had dried up. The use of obsidian, stone, and bones for blades and weapons underscores such scarcity, and also suggests that trading routes and centers for sourcing the metals might have disappeared or were disrupted. Other primitive materials reappear as apparent substitutes, such as bone spacer-beads for amber in jewellery, and stones that were used to replace lead in sling bullets. Objects buried with the deceased increasingly were made out of iron, such as iron pins and fibulae and even weapons, which all in the past were bronze. Bronze wares returned only towards the end of the Dark Age period (Snodgrass 1980). Where bronze was used, it was found on the bulb of pins thus revealing the scarcity of bronze (Snodgrass 1971; Desborough 1972). In all, as Snodgrass (1971) has commented, poverty was abounding, and the fondness for heirlooms revealed signs of deprivation. Fine jewelry was no longer made and whatever were found in the excavated tombs were heirlooms passed down that were manufactured prior to the onset of the Dark Age.

Ecological scarcity required a downscaling of material and cultural lifestyles. Such changes are reflected in burial practices that exhibited a reorganization of life along modest lines. The design of clothing and shoes was of the plainest kind (Snodgrass 1971). A one-piece woolen garment that required no cutting or sewing gained popularity among the female population in Submycenaean Athens and became the predominant dress design in the Protogeometric period. Pins for dresses were scarcely used. The downscaling process is exhibited further in the formation of decentralized communities and associated population losses. The collapse of the palace-driven economies with centralized monarchies was replaced by smaller political organizations dominated by an aristocrat and his family. Whether this lifestyle is one that was actively sought as a consequence of ecological scarcity or occurred as an outcome of the depressive conditions of the Dark Age is difficult to gauge. It is clear however, that there was a shift from the Mycenaean way of reproducing life for they longer provided practical models. The loss of sophistication is clearly seen and as Morris (2000: 207) has stated, "in their funerals people seem more concerned with showing what they were *not* than with what they were." What we are sure of is that as recovery proceeded—we begin to witness this by the mid-half of the tenth century B.C.— trading networks were re-established and communities revived. Such an upswing was characterized by exuberance, materialistic consumption and accumulation. As the social system recovered, we see the rise of the Bronze industry, increasing quantity of pottery buried in the tombs, the quantity of gold deposited in the burials, and signs of social-cultural recovery.

What the Dark Age of this period represented for the Mediterranean region is one where extreme degradation of the ecological landscape precipitated socioeconomic and organizational changes to meet the scarcity of resources, so as to reproduce some semblance of cultural and economic life of prior times. As a consequence, systemic reorganization occurred at various levels, from the way commodities were produced to clothing fashions and designs. Hierarchical social structures disappeared during the Dark Age, as evident by burial practices, and were restored when recovery proceeded (Whitley 1991). To Whitley (1991: 20), burial practices "may be seen as an expression both of social relations and ideology…" During the Dark Ages, there was a shift from multiple tombs burial to single burials, which reflected the change from an emphasis on heredity signifying a stratified order within ruling classes to one that reflected no expectations of descendants and little regard for extravagance (Snodgrass 1971; Desborough 1972). The single tombs lack monumental significance and architectural quality. In the excavated graves of the Protogeometric Period (900 B.C.) there are no indications of disparities in wealth and social distinction, as exemplified in the Athenian graves. Distinction was based on age and sex rather than other social dimensions (Whitley 1991:115). This was to change by the Early Geometric Period (860/840 B.C.) where there is an amplification of status of the buried person. Social and sexual identities of the person interred became more evident. Thus, we find the return of a hierarchical pattern and a departure from the more egalitarian structure of the Protogeometric Period. Such hierarchization continued into the Middle to Late Geometric Periods (770 B.C.– 700 B.C.).[7] By this period, however, there was also a breakdown of the aristocratic order with the arrival of early state formation, though social hierarchical differentiation remained in place.

With the Dark Ages as we have stated in the previous pages, not only was there a loss of population, but deurbanization was also underway. The latter process continued to give rise to small communities with lower population levels (Jameson 1994; Watrous 1994). Seen from an ecological point of view, this downscaling provided the necessary timing for Nature to restore its balance, and for socioeconomic life to start afresh when recovery returned. The collapse of the palace economies enabled the ecological landscape to restore itself that in the past were intensively exploited by the palace-driven economies. In the Argolid and Messenia, according to Deger-Jalkotzy (1998: 123–24), the land recovered and the tree population increased. Furthermore, with the loss of centralized control from the various palaces, there occurred not only deurbanization but decentralization too. Each region thus had the opportunity to search for new mechanisms and ways to administer and reproduce socioeconomic life in general. New trends emerge following the collapse of the palaces as a consequence of the unexpected liberty that resulted from the collapse, and each region/community began to make contacts with others outside Greece towards the end of the Dark Age.

From these small communities, in the case of Greece, the preconditions for the rise of the Greek *polis* (cluster of villages) were put into play, and what followed was a flourish of political and economic life as soon as the social system recovered (Snodgrass 1971, 1980). Muhly (1989: 20) has put this in a succinct fashion: "the importance of the Dark Age, then, must be that it created the conditions that made possible the growth of this distinctly Greek political organization." To this extent, the stressed ecological conditions that engendered deurbanization and the formation of small isolated communities precipitated the rise of the *polis* and the Greek city-states. We need to realize, therefore, that perhaps scarcity of resources can also have productive outcomes that otherwise under bountiful conditions might not have occurred. Stanislawski (1973: 18) has suggested that instead of seeing the Greek Dark Ages as a period of darkness, it should be seen as one of enlightenment with contributions such as: the first use of stone-walled agricultural terraces, the use of chicken eggs in domestic diet, the beginning of the spread of alphabetic writing, the spread of iron, the general use of olive as food, and the first use of waterproof plaster.

Systemic reorganization occurred, and the lengthy duration of the Dark Age is one that we need to note. The fact that it is of such a long duration underscores the length of time required for ecological recovery to take place, and the immensity of the degradation that occurred. What followed in the recovery phase, however, was a Dark Age-conditioned social–cultural and political lifestyle that formed the basis of Western civilization as we know it today.

ECOLOGICAL FUTURES

The recurring nature of these Dark Ages over world history does suggest certain tendencies that we need to consider in light of our present globalized political–economic circumstances, along with the widespread perceptions and agreements that we face a global environmental crisis in the near future, *if we are not in it already*. Warnings of the environmental crisis trends have been announced at various global meetings organized by the United Nations from Rio de Janeiro to Johannesburg. Studies have been published sounding global environmental alerts from the World Commission on Forests and Sustainable Development (1999) and the Intergovernmental Panel on Climate Change and the United Nations Environment Programme (2002) to selected publications to name a few, such as Paul and Anne Ehrlich's *One with Nineveh*, James Speth's *Red Sky At Morning*, Edward Wilson's *The Future of Life*, and Meadows et al., *Limits to Growth* (*The 30-Year Update*).

The prognosis is dire regardless of which study one examines. Global warming, species extinction, soil erosion, pollution, fresh water scarcity, and deforestation are the major signs and tendencies that the current globalized world faces. These trends and tendencies are hardly new as the previous pages on the characteristics of Dark Ages have outlined. They are repetitions of the past, albeit in the past they might not be as intense, and as widespread and globally encompassing.

What are the possible ecological futures that we can anticipate? Let us use the patterns and tendencies of the past to be our guide to project possible ecological futures. We know from our discussion in the previous pages that Dark Age tendencies operate in phases, though not necessarily periodic in nature. Hence, we cannot pinpoint a possible beginning of the crisis nor the end, as the latter timing is dependent on the state of degradation of the environment (if the reproduction of material life is dependent on natural resources), and the opportunities for recovery either through natural renewal or through the incorporation of new territories. If the deforestation phases as outlined in Table 7.1 are used as a guide, Dark Age Phase 4 started around A.D. 1300. When does the next Dark Age (Phase 5) start? If Table 7.2, which provides the average durations of each Dark Age phase, reflects the past, it is hard to pinpoint that there does not seem to be any periodicity. What we can project is to look for similar ecological and socioeconomic trends and tendencies of past Dark Ages and our present conditions. If we hypothesize along this line, we can begin to see such parallels of present conditions with the past (Chew 2002).

Unlike past Dark Ages, the options today are limited in terms of the various paths for recovery. In the past, there was the opportunity for the incorporation of new virgin areas into the world-system that provided geographic room for expansion, and for new natural resources to be made available for further accumulation and population consumption. This recovery path is no longer an option as the world-system is now globalized and connected unless we consider outer space planetary conquest as an opportunity for expanding the limits of the world-system. Even if this option is considered, the path is fraught with difficulties in view of the current state of the global environment, the extent of globalization processes such as accumulation and urbanization, the size of the world's population, and the political foresight to pursue anthropocentric progress beyond the limits of the current planet. Terra forming has been broached in some circles but this has not been declared the official policies of any legitimate core nation-state.

The only choice thus left for recovery, if social progress and development are the goals, would be to instead of extensifying the geo-spatial boundaries of the world-system following the practices of the past, intensify the socioeconomic processes of the world-system to meet the conditions of incessant accumulation, urbanization and population growth, or to totally reorganize the manner human societies have organized the reproduction of material life. However, before this can happen and if we follow the trends of the Dark Ages, we can anticipate first reversals in socioeconomic growth, and disruptions and instability of political regimes along with climate changes and natural disturbances in view of the current environmental crisis. These are the characteristics and possible conditions we face as we slide further into a devolutionary phase (Dark Age) of world-system development. The similar conditions of the late twentieth and early twenty-first centuries to the previous Dark Ages have been described in an earlier study (Chew 2002), and the present conditions have also been identified at least for the late twentieth and early twenty-first centuries by Ehrlich and Ehrlich (2004), Speth (2002), Wilson (2002), and Meadows et al. (2004). All indications suggest that the degradation of the environment will increasingly accelerate with the current economic globalizing forces all over the planet, and the ecologically impactful rapid industrialization and advanced technological developmental strategies of the People's Republic of China and India in the short to medium terms. Besides the incessant consumption of nation-states in the core zone, People's Republic of China and India pose major challenges for our planet's natural resource availability in view of their population sizes, and their potential mega pollution sources. If the past is any indication, the Dark Age conditions will fortify and deepen in the short to medium terms.

Like previous Dark Ages, we will continue to see social, political, and economic turmoil, much like the Bronze Age crisis that occurred almost 4,000 years ago. During those times, natural resource trade disruption and shortages led to adoption of a new base metal, and economic scarcities and social constraints such as population losses and deurbanization led to the development of new political governance and political formation such as the Greek *polis,* while other political entities such as Assyria, Babylonia, and Egypt continued their traditional political monarchical systems. Where socio-political changes occurred, traditional elites lost their economic and political dominance. In short, major socioeconomic and political restructuring took place then that led to a new path of political experimentation and different ideas of human governance and equality, i.e., the promotion of authority being vested in the community and the sanctioning of individual human rights. All these occurred within an environment of natural resource constraints and ecological stress whereby these conditions induced the rethinking of normal practices of governance of the past based on empire and kingship, and the adoption and experimentation with different formulations, for example, the Greek *polis.*

In the late twentieth and twenty-first centuries we are also witnessing numerous political unions, political instabilities and collapses in Africa, Asia, Latin America, and Europe. The formation of regional unions such as the European Community, the Association of South-east Asian Nations, Economic Commission of West African States (ECOWAS), and the African Union, for example, are political attempts to redefine political sovereignty and political rights. The collapse of the former Soviet Union and various other countries in Africa along socioeconomic lines are cases in point. By no means are these latter occurrences over, for as the Dark Age crisis proceeds and deepens, more instability will appear.

The present levels of natural resources availability reflect similar tendencies to conditions over 4,000 years ago during the Bronze Age crisis. It is clear we are seeing the increasing scarcity of fossil fuel availability, and some have anticipated that there is about 50–80 years of resource life expectancy left for oil, and 160–310 years left for natural gas (Meadows et al. 2004: 90). The condition is critical especially when most of the world's industries and reproduction of social life is dependent on oil. Replacement base materials for commodity production will need to be determined and adopted. The trend is towards carbon composites and silicon-based materials. The production of these base materials requires not only energy but also fresh water in abundant quantities. It is clear that these natural resources will increasingly be limited in terms of known sources and replacement sources or alternate forms of energy will be needed. It is not clear that the solution will be there. Some, like Rifkin (2002) have suggested a hydrogen-based economy, while others are stating and hoping that new technologies will save the human population or at least those in the core zone of the world-system.

Beyond ecological devastation and dwindling supply of natural resources for global consumption, we anticipate climate changes and natural disturbances as we have experienced in previous Dark Ages over world history, as documented in previous discussions. Climate warming has been declared by the Inter-governmental Panel on Climate Change and the United Nations Environment Programme (2002), and its associated effects identified. For example, in a recent study on the impact of climate change on the state of California, which has the fifth largest economy in the world-system, the magnitude of the effects antici-pated appears to be catastrophic (Hayhoe et al. 2004). It is projected under one scenario that by the end of the century for California, heat waves and extreme heat will quadruple in frequency with heat-related mortality, increased by two to three times, along with alpine and subalpine forests reduced by 50–75 percent, and the Sierra snow packs being reduced by 30–70 percent. Another scenario with more elevated climate changes will further exacerbate the condi-tions delineated. The decrease in the Sierra snow packs will mean cascading impacts on reduced run-offs and stream flows, which will impact on agricultural production in the Central valley of California—a major agricultural production zone for the United States and the rest of the world.

Increasingly evidence of tectonic shifts and El Niño have pervaded the latter half of the twentieth century, and most recently, the tsunami-related devastation in late December 2004 in South-east Asia and South Indian region are comparable to the tsunami event that impacted on Crete and the Eastern

Mediterranean during the late Bronze Age. The World Disasters Reports by the International Federation of Red Cross and Red Crescent document the costs to economies and political systems. It has been suggested that global warming and climate change may have been responsible for the harsher natural disasters and flooding that we have been experiencing. Droughts caused by El Niño have caused huge forest fires in Brazil and Peru in the late twentieth century. In 1998 for example, typhoons and floods killed 500 and affected five million in the Philippines; floods killed 4,150 and affected 180 million people in China; killed 400 and affected 200,000 in Korea; killed 1,000 and affected 25,000 in Pakistan; killed 1,400 and affected almost 340,000 in India. Two hurricanes killed a total of 14,000 people and affected seven million people in the Caribbean and Central America. Economic costs alone are staggering. For 1998, losses were $16 billion in Central America and the Caribbean, $2.5 billion in Argentina, $868 million in Korea, $223 million in Bangladesh, and $150 million in Romania. The recent tsunami event in South Asia, Thailand, Indonesia, and Malaysia has devastating economic costs and loss of lives. These costs in terms of economies and human lives have not been finalized.

Climate changes, landscape degradation, neocolonial exploitation via trans-national operations, and indigenous elite domination have dislocated rural populations that have led to large-scale migrations within and between nation-states. These migrations have occurred since the sixteenth century and will continue through the twenty-first century and beyond. Much like previous Dark Ages where we witnessed movements across vast expanse of land masses, we also see large-scale legal and illegal migrations on all continents of the world-system today. The much discussed illegal Mexican/Latin American migration into the southern United States is not a unique situation. Illegal and legal migrations have occurred everywhere in this globalized world now and since the sixteenth century. What is clear is that the movement has been from the periphery and semi-periphery to the core areas, and on occasions, from the core to the periphery during periods of expansion to extensify the boundaries of the world-system. Unlike the previous Dark Ages we have not witnessed the extensive deurbanization and population losses. In the case of deurbanization, this development has not manifested itself. Perhaps the environmental crisis has not deepened enough to the extent that shortages have arisen that will hinder urban living; since urban living is the most intensive in terms of natural resource consumption for everything has to be transported to an urbanized landscape to reproduce socioeconomic and political life (Chew 2001). Deurbanization will occur should energy shortages start to appear and climate warming begin. For the latter, current architectural designs and infrastructures do not afford the opportunity to conform to temperature increases nor are they geared for living for long periods under conditions of energy shortages and high tempera-tures. Definitely, those living in the enclaves in the core zone will experience tremendous daily living challenges. Preliminary circumstances of this nature have occurred in West Africa in the 1980s though it is not in the core zone and in Europe during the summer of 2003.

Population losses have also yet to appear. It is anticipated that the global population will peak at 2035 to about 7.5 billion people and then retreat to 7.4 billion by 2050 based on a low projection by the United Nations (Ehrlich and Ehrlich 2004). If a medium projection is used, the numbers come up higher, reaching 8.9 billion by 2050; and if a high projection is used, the total by 2050 would be 10.6 billion. The latter would mean a doubling of numbers in just 25 years! There is no reason to believe that previous trends of population losses during prior Dark Ages will not be repeated. It is too early to suggest that population declines will not occur. Climatic changes impacting on crop harvest will generate famines, natural catastrophes such as earthquakes, El Niño and tsunamis will take lives, and so will diseases and conflicts as a result of natural resource scarcity. We have already seen a glimpse of the effects of a tsunami in South Asia and South-east Asia where over 200,000 lives were lost. Diseases such as AIDS have reduced populations as well. The United Nations has estimated that by 2050 world population will be reduced by 200 million due to AIDS; and seven countries in Southern Africa will have little or no population growth (Ehrlich and Ehrlich 2004).

The above tendencies are likely to occur in the medium to long-term, and perhaps in the short term, if short is equivalent to within this century. What is clear is that the global threats are the warming of the planet, the rapid defor- estation of the world's forests, the loss of arable land and clean water, all that form the basic material conditions for the reproduction of material human lives. Besides all the above trends and tendencies, Dark Ages are also supposed to be system transformative. What can we expect in terms of structural socioeco- nomic and political changes? Let us use what happened during the late Bronze Age as a guide for us to anticipate possible tendencies.

SYSTEMS TRANSFORMATION

Given that Dark Ages in world history are significant moments signaling system crisis and system reorganization; the final phase of the Bronze Age crisis led to ecological recovery, certain political–economic realignments and reorganiza- tion, and the transition to a new working metal: iron. The Dark Age crisis was *system transformative* for it led to fundamental social system changes, evolving a set of new patterns (Sheratt and Sheratt 1993; Chew 2002).

The adoption of iron brought to an end centuries of bronze use that was in the control of palace economies and elites. Gordon Childe (1942) has sug- gested that cheap iron with its wide availability provided the opportunities for agriculture, industry, and even warfare by adopting it as the base metal. With trade route disruption and copper scarcity, the adoption of iron spread further, especially among the communities in Greece which were isolated as a consequent of Dark Age conditions, for iron was now available locally. It led to the development of local iron producing industries (Snodgrass 1971). The low cost of iron because of its local availability facilitated its widespread use in agriculture and industry (Childe 1942; McNeill and McNeill 2003).

All over Europe, the Mediterranean, and the Near East, cultivation was made easier with iron ploughshares in heavy clay soils. This enabled the rural communities to participate further in the economy beyond subsistence, and in maintaining a class of miners, smelters, and metalsmiths fabricating the iron implements to reproduce material life. Such an explanation is also supported by Heichelheim (1968) and Polanyi (1977), who have suggested that the widespread adoption of iron was the result of the opportunity for rural communities in South Russia, Italy, North Africa, Spain, Gaul, Germany, and Eurasia to work the heavy soils with iron implements, thus increasing their production levels. Production increases can be seen by the fluctuations in grain prices according to Heichelheim (1968). The consequence of such transformation is that the urban elites in the Near East, who in the past controlled the grain and other commodities trade, suffered losses as a consequent of changing prices, and the falling demand in the copper, tin and bronze trade, which they also controlled. As a result of this, the social structures were transformed with the formation of different regional centers in the periphery and in the Mediterranean. The opportunity for farmers to farm in heavy clay soils utilizing cheap iron implements also provided the conditions for economic and system expansion following the end of the Dark Age, where in the past these areas were not as productive. It enabled economic expansion and the move into newer areas for agriculture as by this time some of the older settled areas were ecologically degraded and overworked.

At the social system level as well, the Dark Age crisis thus usher forth the dissociation of high value commodities away from the control of the palace/state, for by the end of the Dark Age, the command palace economies that were in the eastern Mediterranean were dissolved. What emerged was the continued differentiation of commercial /economic structures from the political structures (Polanyi 1977). Instead of bureaucratic palace-centered trade, we see the development of mercantile city-states where merchant enterprise replaced the palace-controlled exchange. With this transformation, new forms of political powers and structures emerged. We have the emergence of a new political structure, the city-state (*polis*) in the Aegean, and the continuation of empire-type political structures where the rule was via direct political and military control.

The new political structure, the *polis*, as a social organization and political concept emerged in eighth century Greece (Morris 1987, 1988). It was as Morris

(1988: 752) has stated, unique among ancient states for "its citizen body was actually the state." The rise of such a state form was a consequence of the collapse of the aristocratic society during the Greek Dark Ages. Other factors also precipitated its formation. Deurbanization and the loss of population in the urban areas resulting in the development of isolated communities during the Dark Age engendered the structural conditions for the development of the *polis*. In addition, with the scarcity of resources and the abundance of poverty leading to less hierarchical social structures, the groundwork for the development of the polis was also put into place. The *polis* thus was one where all authority was divested to the community, unlike previous political forms in Mycenaean Greece. Force, therefore was located in the citizen body as a whole, and thus, there was little need for a standing military. Individual natural rights were not sanctioned by a higher power and the highest authority was the *polis*, i.e., the community. Such a political structure found expression in the Aegean. However, in other parts of the Near East, divine kingship was maintained with some minor modifications. According to Childe (1942), Assyria, Babylonia, and Egypt continued as Bronze Age states.

The above has revealed what occurred in the past; there is no reason to consider that what happened will be repeated in similar fashion. The adoption of a new base metal during the late Bronze Age was system transformative for it reduced the monopolization of bronze manufacturing of the palace based monarchical systems, and thus opened the opportunity for other communities to fabricate iron. According to Childe (1942), the manufacture of iron was made possible by traveling metalsmiths where they were paid for their services, and their knowledge was transmitted. It has been stated that the shift to iron democratized the world-system in terms of giving political entities room for expansion, and thus jeopardized the traditional Bronze Age monarchical systems. Will we see this pattern of resolution of natural resource scarcity for the current world-system as it evolves into the future? That is hard to predict. What is clear is that we are heading towards an ecological crisis of scarcity and degraded landscapes. If this is the case, perhaps we will witness different political and economic trajectories for the world-system. There will be a continuation of the current economic and political systems for some political entities as a trajectory, just like what happened during the late Bronze Age. That continuation, we project, will be based on how much impact each entity will experience during the height of the Dark Age crisis. Those that continue with the same socioeconomic and political organizations and systems that they have prior to the crisis will be those that were impacted the least. They will have the least pressure to rethink and restructure. However, if history can be our guide, they will not persist in the very long-term, for their systems will be less innovative than those that proceed on other possible trajectory/ies that are not resource intensive in terms of material production.

Let us perhaps discuss another possible trajectory, and there are possibly others as well; as human history is always an open process. Assuming that there is tremendous scarcity of resources, deurbanization, population losses, and *isolation* because there is no energy available for transportation, etc.; the current established political–economic systems based on a centralized and federalized configuration of command and control will be non-functional as far as the isolated communities are concerned. In this context, a different type of political and economic structure will have to be developed. It will be one that relies on the immediate landscape for the reproduction of socioeconomic life. This type of set-up can be in the form of a bio-region whereby artificial human political boundaries are replaced by boundaries of nature, i.e., the watersheds and the mountains, as limits of human community living (Dodge 1981; Sale 1991; Devall 2001). Such a shift requires a total rethinking of social, economic, and political structures and processes that reorient the human enterprise away from an anthropocentric orientation to one that is ecocentric. For by this time, there should be the realization of living in an interconnected natural/social world. This reorientation is prompted not by a voluntaristic human agency shift but by the structural conditions these communities face in terms of ecological and natural resource scarcities as a consequence of Dark Age conditions, just like what the Greeks faced during the Bronze Age as we have discussed earlier. In terms of specifics about socioeconomic choices and lifestyles for this world, Devall (2001) has outlined such options, and so has Naess (1993).

It is difficult to project which political systems in the current configuration of the world-system will propel along which trajectory/ies. It is all dependent on the extent of their reliance on the ecosystem and the level of impact they sustain from Dark Age conditions. What is clear is that with the level of globalization that we are witnessing today, almost all will be impacted tremendously. Such is the human nightmare we will face in the future, and also a hope in a hopeless condition of a globalized totalitarian world. That hope is our transition to bio-regional communities not by choice but by circumstances!

Notes

1. This endeavor is to move away from a history understood and interpreted within a geo-spatial dependent and time contingent framework. The aim is to abstract a theoretically generalizable account of the dynamics and structures of the evolution of world-system from historical events.
2. Some like Fernand Braudel (1972, 1981, 1982, 1984, 1989) have couched the social, political, and economic factors in concert with the natural environment and climatological patterns as determinants of long-term and large-scale transformations. For a fuller explication of Braudel's analytical levels of long-term social change, see Chew (1997).

3. There is some evidence of an earlier Dark Age around 3800/3400 B.C. but it has not been widely documented. Arboreal pollen profiles that we have analyzed provide some indications (see Table 7.1), and in addition, analysis of economic conditions suggests a period of economic stress (Thompson 2001).

4. Ecological time is discussed more in depth in Chew (2005).

5. For example, it has been estimated that a mere 1-degree centigrade rise in temperature may reduce annual rainfall by 30 millimeters in the Near East.

6. Dendroclimate charts were provided by Professor Bjorn Berglund, Department of Quaternary Geology, Lund University, Lund, Sweden.

7. Morris (2000) however has argued that the shift from egalitarianism to stratification might not be the case. Rather, the grave burials reflecting an upper class strata, the *agathoi,* prompting some to conclude of a shift to stratified society by the eighth century did not represent the total spectrum of Athenian society, and that the lower order people were disposed of (or buried) in a different way that have not been excavated by the archeologists.

References

Abu-Lughod, J. 1989. *Before European Hegemony.* New York: Oxford University Press.

Adams, R. McC. 1981. *Heartland of the Cities.* Chicago: University of Chicago Press.

Agrawal, D.P. and R.K. Sood. 1982. Ecological Factors and the Harappan Civilization, in G. Possehl (ed.), *Harappan Civilization: Contemporary Perspective.* New Delhi: Oxford University Press, pp. 223–31.

Algaze, G. 1993. *The Uruk World-system.* Chicago: University of Chicago Press.

Ammann, B. 1985. Lobsingensee-Late Glacial and Holocene Environments of a Lake on the Central Swiss Plateau. *Diss. Bot* 87, 127–34.

Ästrom, P. 1985. The Sea Peoples in the Light of New Excavations. *Centre d'etudes chypriotes,* 3: 3–17.

Baillie, M. 1994. Dendrochronology Raises Questions about the Nature of A.D. 536 Dust-Veil Event. *The Holocene* 4(2): 212–17.

———. 1995. *A Slice Through Time.* London: Routledge.

———. 1998. Hints that Cometary Debris Played Some Role in Several Tree-Ring Dated Environmental Downturns in the Bronze Age. *Cambridge BAR International Series* 728: 109–16.

———. 1999. A View from Outside: Recognizing the Big Picture. *Quaternary Proceedings* 7: 625–35.

Bar-Mathews, M. and A. Avalon. 1997. Late Quaternary Paleoclimate in the Eastern Mediterranean Region from Stable Isotope Analysis of Speleothems at Soreq Cave, Israel. *Quaternary Research* 47, 155–68.

Bar-Mathews, M., A. Avalon and A. Kaufman. 1998. A Middle to Late Holocene Paleoclimate in the Eastern Mediterranean Region, in A.S. Issar and N. Brown (eds), *Water, Environment and Society in Times of Climate Change.* Amsterdam: Kluwer, pp. 203–14.

Bar-Mathews, M., A. Avalon, A. Kaufman and G. Wasserburg. 1999. The Eastern Mediterranean Paleoclimate as a Reflection of Regional Events; Soreq Cave, Israel. *Earth and Planetary Science Letters* 166: 85–95.

Barry, R. and R. Chorley. 1992. *Atmosphere, Weather, and Climate*. New York: Routledge.

Behre, K.E. and D. Kucan. 1986. Die Reflektion archaologisch bekannter in Pollendiagrammen verschiedener Entfernung, in K.E. Behre (ed.), *Anthropogenic Indicators in Pollen Diagrams*. Rotterdam: Belkema, pp. 95–114.

Behre, K.E. 1990. Some Reflections on Anthropogenic Indicators and the Record of Prehistoric Occupation Phases in Pollen Diagrams, in S. Bottema, G. Entjesbieburg and W. Van Zeist (eds), *Man's Role in the Shaping of the Eastern Mediterranean Landscape*. Balkema: Rotterdam/Brookfield, pp. 219–30.

Bell, B. 1971. The Dark Ages in Ancient History I: The First Dark Age in Egypt. *American Journal of Archaeology* 75: 1–20.

————. 1975. Climate and History of Egypt. *American Journal of Archaeology*, 79: 223–79.

Bentaleb, I., C. Caratim, M. Fontugne, M. Morzadec-Kerfourn, J. Pascal and C. Tissor. 1997. A Monsoon Regime: Variations During the Late Holocene in Southwestern India, in H. Dalfes and G. Kukla (eds), *In Third Millennium B.C. Climate Change and Collapse*. Berlin: Springer Verlag, pp. 193–244.

Bezusko, L.G. 1985. Paleobotanical and Radiological Studies of Deposit from Bog Starniki. *Ukr. Botan. Zhurn* 42: 27–30.

————. 1987. The Oak Forest of Maloye Polessie in the Late Post Glacial Period. *Ukr. Botan. Zhurn* 71: 4–8.

Binka, K., T. Madeyska, B. Marciniak, K. Szeroczynska and K. Wieckowski. 1988. Bledowo Lake: History of Vegetation and Lake Development During the Last 12 Kyr. *Bulletin Acad. Polon. Sci.* 36(2): 147–58.

Bintliff, J. 1982. A Climate Change, Archaeology and Quaternary Science in the Eastern Mediterranean Region, in A.F. Harding (ed.), *Climate Change in Later Prehistory*. Edinburgh: Edinburgh University Press, pp. 143–61.

Biraben. 1980. Essai sur l'evolution du nombre des hommes. *Population* 1: 13–25.

Blegen, C. 1950. *Troy*, Vols 1–4. Princeton: Princeton University Press.

Bosworth, A. 1995. World Cities and World Economic Cycles, in Stephen Sanderson (ed.), *Civilizations and World-systems*. Walnut Creek, Cal.: AltaMira Press, pp. 206–28.

Bottema, S. 1974. Late Quaternary Vegetation History of Northwestern Greece. Ph.D. Dissertation. Groningen University, Netherlands.

————. 1997. A Third Millennium Climate in the Near East Based Upon Pollen Evidence, in H. Dalfes, G. Kukla and H. Weiss (eds), *Third Millennium BC Climate Change and Old World Collapse*. Heidelberg: Springer Verlag, pp. 488–515.

Bovarski, E. 1998. A First Intermediate Period Private Tombs, in K. Bard (ed.), *Encyclopedia of Ancient Egypt*. New York: Routledge, pp. 316–19.

Bradshaw, R.H.W., T. Young and K. McNeil. 1988. The Extent and Time Course of Mountain Blanket Peat Erosion in Ireland. *New Phytologist* 108: 219–24.

Braudel, F. 1972. *The Mediterranean and the Mediterranean World in the Age of Philip II*, Vol. 1. London: Fontana.

————. 1980. *On History*. Chicago: University of Chicago Press.

————. 1981. *The Structure of Everyday Life*, Vol. 1. New York: Harper and Row.

————. 1982. *The Wheels of Commerce*, Vol. 2. New York: Harper and Row.

————. 1984. *The Perspective of the World*, Vol. 3. New York: Harper and Row.

————. 1989. *The Perspective of France*, Vols. 1–2. New York: Harper and Row.

————. 2001. *Memory and the Mediterranean*. New York: Alfred Knopf.

Broecker, W.S. 2001. Was the Medieval Warm Period Global. *Science* 291: 1497–99, February 23.

Brown, N. 1995. *The Impact of Climate Change: Some Indications from History A.D. 250–1250*. Oxford Centre for the Environment, Ethics and Society Research Papers.

—————. 2001. *History and Climate Change: A Eurocentric Perspective*. London: Routledge.

Bryce, T. 1999. *The Kingdom of the Hittites*. Oxford: Oxford University Press.

Bryson, R.A., H.H. Lamb and D.L. Donley. 1974. Drought and the Decline of Mycenae, *Antiquity* Vol. XLVIII (189): 46–50.

Bryson, R.A. and C. Padoch. 1980. On the Climates of History. *Journal of Interdisciplinary History* 10(4): 583–97.

Bryson, R. and T. Swain. 1981. Holocene Variations of Monsoon Rainfall in Rajasthan. *Quaternary Research* 16: 135–45.

Bryson, R. and R. Bryson. 1998. An Application of a Global Volcanicity Time Series on High Resolution Paleoclimatic Modeling of the Eastern Mediterranean, in A. Issar and N. Brown (eds), *Water, Environment and Society in Times of Change*. The Netherlands: Dordrecht, pp. 1–19.

Burgess, C. 1989. Volcanoes, Catastrophe, and Global Crisis of the Late 2nd Millennium BC. *Current Anthropology* X(10): 325–29.

Butzer, K.W. 1976. *Early Hydraulic Civilization in Egypt*. Chicago: University of Chicago Press.

—————. 1983. A Long-term Nile Flood Variation and Political Discontinuities in Pharaonic Egypt, in J.D. Clark and S. Brandt (eds), *From Hunters to Farmers*. Berkeley: University of California Press, pp. 102–12.

—————. 1997. A Socio Political Discontinuity in the Near East c. 2200 B.C.E. Scenarios from Palestine and Egypt, in H. Dalfes and G. Kukla (eds), *Third Millennium BC Climate Change and Old World Collapse*. Heidelberg, Berlin: Springer Verlag, pp. 245–96.

Carpenter, R. 1968. *Discontinuity in Greek Civilization*. Cambridge: Cambridge University Press.

Chadwick, J. 1972. Life in Mycenaean Greece. *Scientific American* 227(4): 36–44.

—————. 1976. *The Mycenaean World*. New York: Cambridge University Press.

Chase-Dunn, C. and T. Hall. 1997. *Rise and Demise: Comparing World-Systems*. Boulder: Westview Press.

Chew, Sing C. 1997. Accumulation, Deforestation, and World Ecological Degradation 2500 B.C. to A.D. 1990. *Advances in Human Ecology, Vol 6*. Westport CT: JAI Press.

—————. 1998. Ecological Relations and the Decline of 2500 B.C.–1700 B.C. Civilizations in the Bronze-Age World-system: Mesopotamia and Harappa, in W. Goldfrank, David Goodman and A. Szasz (eds), *Environment and the World-system*. Greenwich CT: Greenwood Press.

—————. 1999. Ecological Relations and the Decline of Civilizations in the Bronze Age World-system: Mesopotamia and Harappa 2500 B.C.–1700 B.C., in W. Goldfrank, David Goodman and Andrew Szasz. *Ecology and the World-system*. Greenwich CT: Greenwood Press.

—————. 2001. *World Ecological Degradation: Accumulation, Urbanization, and Deforestation*. Lanham, MD: AltaMira Press/Rowman and Littlefield Publishers.

—————. 2002. Globalization, Dark Ages, and Ecological Degradation. *Global Society* 16(4): 333–56.

Chew, Singh C. and D. Knottnerus (eds). 2003. *Structure, Culture, and History*. Lanham, MD: Rowman and Littlefield Publishers.

—————. 2004a. Ecology in Command, in Sing C. Chew and J. David Knottnerus (eds), *Structure, Culture, and History. Recent Issues in Social Theory*. Lanham, Maryland: Rowman and Littlefield Publishers, pp. 217–30.

Chew, Sing C. 2004b. From Mycenae to Mesopotamia and Egypt to Mycenae: Dark Ages, Political Economic Declines, and Environmental/Climatic Changes 2200 B.C.–700 B.C., in Christopher Chase-Dunn and E.N. Anderson (eds), *The Historical Evolution of World-Systems*. Pp. 52–74. London: Palgrave MacMillan.

—————. 2005. Dark Ages over World History: Ecological Crisis and System Changes, International Symposium on Environment and Society in Chinese History, Nankai University, Tianjin, People's Republic of China, August 17–19, 2005.

Childe, G. 1942. *What Happened in History*. Harmondsworth: Penguin.

—————. 1950. The Urban Revolution. *Town Planning Review* 21: 3–17.

Dales, G.F. 1977. Shifting Trade Patterns between Iranian Plateau and the Indus Valley, in J. Deshayes (ed.), *Le Plateau Iranien et l'Asie Centrale*. Paris: CNRS, pp. 67–78.

—————. 1979. The Decline of the Harappans, in G. Possehl (ed.), *Ancient Cities of the Indus*. New Delhi: Vikas, pp. 307–12.

Davis, M. and R. Shaw. 2001. Range Shifts and Adaptive Responses to Quaternary Climate Change. *Science* 292: 667–73, April 27.

Deger-Jalkotzy, S. 1998. The Last Mycenaean and their Successors Updated, in G. Seymour, M. Mazhar and E. Stern (eds), *Mediterranean Peoples in Transition*. Jerusalem: Israel Exploration Society, pp. 114–28.

DeMenocal, P.B. 2001. Cultural Response to Climate Change During the Late Holocene. *Science* 292: 667–72, April 27.

Denemark, R., J. Friedman, Barry Gills and George Modelski (eds). 2000. *World-system History: The Social Science of Long-Term Change*. London: Routledge.

Desborough, V.R. 1972. *The Greek Dark Ages*. London: Ernest Benn.

—————. 1975. The End of Mycenaean Civilization and the Dark Age, in I.E.S. Edwards C.I. Gadd and N.G.L. Hammond (eds), *Cambridge Ancient History*. Cambridge: Cambridge University Press, pp. 658–77.

Devall, B. 2001. The Deep, Long-Range Ecology Movement: 1960–2000. *Ethics and the Environment* 6(1): 18–41.

Dodge, J. 1981. Living by Life: Some Bioregional Theory and Practice. *CoEvolution Quarterly* Winter: 6–12.

Drews, R. 1993. *The End of the Bronze Age*. Princeton: Princeton University Press.

Driessen, J. and C. MacDonald. 2000. The Eruption of the Santorini Volcano and its Effects on Minoan Crete, in W.J. McGuire, D.R. Griffiths and P.L. Hancock (eds), *The Archae-ology of Geological Catastrophe*. London: Geological Society, pp. 81–93.

Ehrlich, P. and Anne Ehrlich. 2004. *One With Nineveh*. Washington DC: Island Press.

Eisner, W.R., T.E. Tornquist, E.A. Foster, O. Bennike and J.F.N. Van Lecuwen. 1995. Paleoecological Studies of a Holocene Lacustine Record from the Kangerlussnaq. *Quaternary Research* 43: 55–66.

Enzel, Y., L.L. Ely, S. Mishra, R. Ramesh, R. Amit, B. Lazar, S.N. Rajaguru, V.R. Baver and A. Sandler. 1999. High Resolution Holocene Environmental Changes in the Thar Desert, Northwestern India. *Science* 284: 125–28.

Eronen, M. and H. Hyvrinen. 1982. Subfossil Dates and Pollen Diagrams from Northern Fennoscandia. *Geologis Frem* 103: 437–55.

Esse, D. 1991. *Subsistence, Trade, and Social Change in Early Bronze Age Palestine*. Chicago: University of Chicago Press.

Evans, A. 1921. *The Palace of Minos*. London: Macmillan.

Fagan, B. 1999. *Floods, Famines, and Emperors: El Nino and the Fate of Civilizations*. New York: Basic Books.

Fagan, B. 2004 . *The Long Summer*. New York: Basic Books.

Fairbridge, R., O. Erol, M. Karaca and Y. Yilmaz. 1997. A Background to Mid-Holocene Climate Change in Anatolia and Adjacent Regions, in N. Dalfes, G. Kukla and H. Weiss (eds), *Third Millennium BC Climate Change and Old World Collapse*. Heidelberg: Springer Verlag, pp. 240–75.

Fairservis, W. 1979a. The Harappan Civilization: New Evidence and More Theory, in G. Possehl (ed.) *Ancient Cities of the Indus*. New Delhi: Vikas, pp. 50–65.

————. 1979b. The Origin, Character, and Decline of an Early Civilization, in G. Possehl (ed.) *Ancient Cities of the Indus*. New Delhi: Vikas, pp. 66–89.

Frank, A.G. and B.K. Gills. 1992. World-system Cycles, Crises, and Hegemonial Shifts. *Review* 15(4): 621–88.

————. 1993. Bronze Age World-system Cycles. *Current Anthropology* 34(4): 383–429.

Friedman, K. 2003. *Structure, Dynamics, and the Final Collapse of Bronze Age Civilizations in the Second Millennium*. Unpublished MS.

Gasse, F. 2000. Hydrological Changes in the African Tropics Since the Last Glacial Maximum. *Quaternary Science Review* 19: 189–212.

Gelb, I.J. 1973. Prisoners of War in Early Mesopotamia. *Journal of Near Eastern Studies* 32: 70–98.

Gibson, McGuire. 1970. Violation of Fallow and Engineered Disaster in Mesopotamian Civilization, in T. Downing and M. Gibson (eds), *Irrigation's Impact on Society*. Tucson: University of Arizona Press, pp. 45–67.

————. 1973. A Population Shift and the Rise of Mesopotamian Civilization, in Colin Renfrew (ed.), *The Explanation of Culture Change: Models in Prehistory*. London: Duckworth, pp. 447–63.

Goldstone, J. 1991. *Revolution and Rebellion in the Early Modern World*. Berkeley: University of California Press.

Haldon, J.F. 1990. *Byzantium in the 7th Century*. Cambridge: Cambridge University Press.

Hammer, C.H., H.B. Clausen and W. Dansgaard. 1980. Greenland Ice Sheet Evidence of Post Glacial Volcanism and its Climatic Impact. *Nature* 288: 230–35.

Harding, A. (ed.). 1982. *Climatic Change in Later Prehistory*. Edinburgh: Edinburgh University Press.

Harrison, A.B. and N. Spencer. 1998. After the Palace: The Early History of Messinia, in Jack Davis (ed.), *Sandy Pylos*. Austin: University of Texas Press, pp. 147–66.

Harrison, T. 1997. Shifting Patterns of Settlement in the Highlands of Central Jordan During the Early Bronze Age. *Bulletin of the American School Oriental Research* 306: 1–38.

Hassan, F. 1986. Holocene Lakes and Prehistoric Settlements of the Western Fayum. *Journal of Archaeological Science* 13: 483–501.

————. 1997. A Nile Floods and Political Disorder in Early Egypt, in N. Dalfes, G. Kukla and H. Weiss (eds), *Third Millennium BC Climate Change and Old World Collapse*. Heidelberg: Springer Verlag, pp. 1–23.

Hayhoe, K., D. Cayan, C.B. Field, P.C. Frumhoff, E.P. Maurer and N.L. Miller. 2004. Emissions Pathways, Climate Change and Impacts on California. *Proceedings of National Academy of Sciences* 101(34): 12422–27, August 24.

Heichelheim, F.M. 1968. *An Ancient Economic History Vol. 1*. Leyden: A.W. Sijthoff.

Hiebert, F. 2000. A Bronze Age Central Eurasian Cultures in their Steppe and Desert Environments, in G. Bawden and R. Reycraft (eds), *Environmental Disaster and the Archeology of Human Response*. Albuquerque: University of New Mexico Press, pp. 51–62.

Hodgett, G. 1972. *A Social and Economic History of Medieval Europe*. London: Methuen.

Hole, F. 1997. Evidence for Mid-Holocene Environmental Change in the Western Khabur Drainage, Northeastern Syria, in N. Dalfes, G. Kukla and H. Weiss (eds), *Third Millennium BC Climate Change*. Berlin: Springer-Verlag, pp. 41–65.

Hooker, J.T. 1976. *Mycenaean Greece*. London: Routledge.

Hughes, D. 1994. *Pan's Travail*. Baltimore: Johns Hopkins University Press.

————. 2001. *Environmental History of the World*. London: Routledge.

Iakovides, S. 1977. The Present State of Research at the Citadel of Mycenae. *Bulletin of the Institute of Archaeology* 14: 99–141.

Issar, A. 1998. Climate Change and History during the Holocene in the Eastern Mediterranean Region, in A. Issar and N. Brown (eds), *Water, Environment, and society in Times of Climatic Change*. Hague: Kluwer, pp. 113–28.

Jacobsen, T. and R.M. Adams. 1958. Salt and Silt in Ancient Mesopotamian Agriculture. *Science* 128: 1251–58.

Jameson, M.H., C.N. Runnels and T.V. Andel (eds). 1994. *A Greek Countryside: The Southern Argolid from Prehistory to the Present Day*. Stanford: Stanford University Press.

Kantor, H. 1992. The Relative Chronology of Egypt and its Foreign Correlations Before the First Intermediate Period, in Robert W. Ehrlich (ed.), *Chronologies in Old World Archaeology* Vol. 1. Chicago: University of Chicago Press, pp. 56–75.

Kay, P.A. and D.L. Johnson. 1981. Estimation of Tigris-Euphrates Stream Flow from Regional Paleoenvironmental Proxy Data. *Climate Change* 3: 251–63.

Keys, D. 1999. *Catastrophe*. New York: Ballantyne Books.

Khomutova, V., K. Pushenko and L. Harrison. 1994. Lake Status Records from the Former Soviet Union and Mongolian Database. *Paleoclimatology Publication Report* 2: 86–88.

Knapp, B.A. 1993. Thalassocracies in the Bronze Age Eastern Mediterranean Trade: Making and Breaking a Myth World. *Archaeology* 24(3): 332–47.

Krementski, C. 1997. The Late Holocene Environmental and Climate Shift in Russia and Surrounding Lands, in N. Dalfes, G. Kukla and H. Weiss (eds), *Third Millennium BC Climate Change*. Berlin: Springer-Verlag, pp. 351–70.

Kristiansen, K. 1993. The Emergence of the European World-system in the Bronze Age: Divergence, Convergence, and Social Evolution during the First and Second Millennia B.C. in Europe. *Sheffield Archaeological Monographs* no. 6.

————. 1998. *Europe Before History*. Cambridge: Cambridge University Press.

Ladurie, L. 1971. *Times of Feast and Times of Famines*. New York: Doubleday.

Lamb, H. 1967. R. Carpenter's Discontinuity In Greek Civilization. *Antiquity* 41: 233–34.

Lambrick, H.T. 1967. The Indus Flood Plain and the "Indus" Civilization. *The Geographical Journal* 133(4): 483–89.

Lazarova, M. 1995. Human Impact on the Natural Vegetation in the region of Lake Srebarna and Mire Girvan, in T. Bozilova (ed.), *Advances in Holocene Paleoecology in Bulgaria*. Sofia: Pensoft Publication, pp. 47–67.

Lemcke, G. and M. Sturm. 1997. d20 and Trace Element Measurement as Proxy of the Reconstruction of Climatic Changes at Lake Van, in N. Dalfes, G. Kukla and H. Weiss (eds), *Third Millennium BC Climate Change*. Berlin: Springer-Verlag, pp. 653–78.

MacQueen, J.G. 1986. *The Hittites and their Contemporaries in Asia Minor*. London: Thames and Hudson.

Mann, M. 1986. *The Sources of Social Power Vol. 1*. Cambridge: Cambridge University Press.

Manning, S.W. 1994. The Emergence of Divergence: Development and Decline in Bronze Age Crete and the Cyclades, in C. Mathers and S. Stoddatm (eds), *Development and Decline in the Mediterranean Bronze Age*. Sheffield: J.R. Collins, pp. 221–70.

Marinatos, S. 1939. The Volcanic Eruption of Minoan Crete. *Antiquity* 13: 425–39.

McEvedy, C. and S. McEvedy. 1972. *Dark Ages*. London: Macmillan.

McGovern, P. 1987. Central TransJordan in Late Bronze Age and Early Iron Ages: An Alternative Hypothesis of SocioEconomic Collapse, in A. Hadidi (ed.), *Studies in the History and Archaeology of Jordan 3*. London: Routledge and Kegan Paul, pp. 267–73.

McNeill, J.R. 2000. *Something New Under the Sun*. New York: W.W. Norton.

McNeill, J. and W. McNeill. 2003. *The Human Web*. New York: Norton.

Meadows, D., J. Randers, D. Meadows. 2004. *Limits to Growth: The 30-Year Update*. White River Junction, VT: Chelsea Green.

Mellink, M. 1986. The Early Bronze Age in Western Anatolia: Aegean and Asiatic Correlations, in G. Cadogan (ed.), *End of the Early Bronze Age in the Aegean*. Leiden: Brill, pp. 139–52.

Modelski, G. 1999a. Ancient World Cities 4000–1000 B.C.: Center/Hinterland in the World-system. *Global Society* 13(4): 383–92.

————. 1999b. Classical World Cities: 1200 B.C. to A.D. 1000, in K. Watt (ed.), *Human Ecology*, pp. 46–67.

————. 2001. Evolutionary Pulsations in the World-system in Sing Chew and David Knottnerus (eds), *Structure, Culture, and History*. Lanham, MD: Rowman and Littlefield.

Modelski, G. 2003. *World Cities*. Washington, DC: Faros.

Modelski, G. and W. Thompson. 1999. The Evolutionary Pulse of the World-system: Hinterland Incursion and Migrations, 4000 B.C. to A.D. 1500, in N. Kardulias (ed.), *World-system Theory in Practice*. Lanham, MD: Rowman and Littlefield, pp. 241–74.

Moorey, P.R.S. 1987. On Tracking Cultural Transfers in Prehistory: The Case of Egypt and Lower Mesopotamia in the 4th Millennium B.C., in M. Rowlands, K. Kristiansen and M. Larsen (eds), *Centre and Periphery in the Ancient World*. Cambridge: Cambridge University Press, pp. 36–46.

Morris, I. 1987. *Burial and Ancient Society: The Rise of the Greek City-State*. Cambridge: Cambridge University Press.

————. 1988. Changing Perceptions of the Past: The Bronze Age—A Case Study, in J. Bintliff (ed.), *Extracting Meaning from the Past*. Oxford: Oxbow Books, pp. 213–33.

————. 2000. *Archaeology as Cultural History: Words and Things in Iron Age Greece*. Malden, MA: Blackwell.

Muhly, J.D. 1989. The Organization of the Copper Industry in Late Bronze Age Cyprus, in E.J. Peltenburg (ed.). *Early Society in Cyprus*. Edinburgh: Edinburgh University.

Mylonas, G. 1966. *Mycenae and the Mycenaean Age*. Princeton: Princeton University Press.

Naess, A. 1993. *Ecology, Community, and Lifestyle*. Cambridge: Cambridge University Press.

Neumann, J. and R. Sigrist. 1978. Harvest Dates in Ancient Mesopotamia as Possible Indicators of Climatic Variations. *Climate Change* 1: 239–52.

Neumann, J. and S. Parpola. 1987. Climatic Change and 11–10th Century Eclipse of Assyria and Babylonia. *Journal of Near Eastern Studies* 46: 161–82.

O'Connor, D. 1983. New Kingdom and the Third Intermediate Period, 1552–664 B.C., in B.G. Trigger, J.D. Faye and R. Oliver (eds), *Ancient Egypt: A Social History*. Cambridge: Cambridge University Press, pp. 135–57.

Pang, K.D. 1991. The Legacies of Eruption. *The Sciences* 31(1): 30–33.

Penalba, M.C. 1994. The History of the Holocene Vegetation in Northern Spain from Pollen Analysis. *Journal of Ecology* 82: 815–32.

Perlin, J. 1989. *A Forest Journey*. Cambridge: Harvard University Press.

Polanyi, K. 1977. *The Livelihood of Man*. New York: Academic Press.

Ponting, C. 1991. *A Green History of the World*. London: Penguin.

Possehl, G. 2001. The Drying Up of the Sarasvati, in G. Bawden and R. Reycraft (eds), *Environmental Disaster and the Archaeology of Human Response*. Albuquerque: University of New Mexico Press, pp. 63–74.

Raikes, R. 1964. The End of the Ancient Cities of the Indus. *American Anthropologist* 66(2): 284–99.

————. 1984. *Water, Weather, and Prehistory*. Atlantic Highlands: Humanities Press.

Raikes, R. and R. Dyson. 1961. The Prehistoric Climate of Baluchistan and the Indus Valley. *American Anthropologist* 63(2): 265–81.

Raikes, R. and G.F. Dales. 1977. The Mohenjo-Daro Floods Reconsidered. *Journal of the Palaeontological Society of India* 20: 251–60.

Randsborg, K. 1991. *The First Millennium AD in Europe and the Mediterranean*. Cambridge: Cambridge University Press.

Rankama, T. and I. Vuorela. 1988. Memo. Soc. Fauna Flora. *Fennica* 64: 25–34.

Ratnagar, S. 1981. *Encounters: The Westerly Trade of the Harappan Civilization*. New Delhi: Oxford University Press.

Redman, C.L. 1999. *Human Impact on Ancient Environments*. Tucson: University of Arizona Press.

Redman, C.L. and A.P. Kinzig. 2003. Resilience of Past Landscapes Resilience Theory, Society, and the Longue Durée. *Conservation Ecology* 7: 14–17.

Renfrew, C. 1972. *The Emergence of Civilization*. London: Collins.

————. 1979. Systems Collapse as Social Transformation: Catastrophe and Anastrophe in Early State Society, in C. Renfrew and K.L. Cooke (eds), *Transformations: Mathematical Approaches to Cultural Change*. New York: Academic Press, pp. 481–506.

Rifkin, J. 2002. *The Hydrogen Economy*. New York: Putnam.

Rutter, J. 1989. Cultural Novelties in the Post Palatial Aegean World: Indices of Vitality or Decline, in W. Ward and M. Joukowsky (eds), *The Crisis Years: The 12th Century BC*. Dubuque: Kendall Hunt, pp. 61–78.

Sale, K. 1991. *Dwellers in the Land*. Philadelphia, PA: New Society Publishers.

Schaeffer, C.F.A. 1948. Stratigraphie comparee et chronologie, de l'Asie occidentale (III et II millenaire). *Economics and Social History of the Orient* 5: 279–308.

————. 1968. Commentaires sur les letters et documents trouvés dans les bibliothèques privées d'Ugarit. *Ugaritica* 5: 607–768.

Sheratt, S. and A. Sheratt. 1993. The Growth of the Mediterranean Economy in the Early First Millennium BC. *World Archaeology* 24(3): 361–78.

Snodgrass, A.M. 1971. *The Dark Age of Greece*. Edinburgh: University Press.

————. 1980. *Archaic Greece*. London: Macmillan.

Speth, J. 2002. *Red Sky At Morning*. New Haven: Yale University Press.

Stanislawski, D. 1973. Dark Age Contributions to the Mediterranean Way of Life. *Annals of the Association of American Geographers* 63(4): 397–410.

Thompson, W.R. 2000. *C-Waves, Center-Hinterland Contact and Regime Change in the Ancient Near East: Early Impacts of Globalization*. Paper presented at the International Studies Association Annual Conference in Los Angeles, USA.

————. 2001. *Trade Pulsations, Collapse, and Reorientation in the Ancient World*. Paper presented at the International Studies Association Annual Meetings, Chicago, US.

————. 2004. *Complexity, Diminishing Marginal Return and Serial Mesopotamia Fragmentation*. Santa Fe Institute, Santa Fe, New Mexico.

Toynbee, A.J. 1939. *A Study of History IV and V.* Oxford: Oxford University Press.

Treadgold, W. 1988. *The Byzantine Revival 780–842.* Stanford: Stanford University Press.

—————. 1997. *A History of the Byzantine State and Society.* Stanford: Stanford University Press.

Tucker, R. 2000. *Insatiable Appetite: The United States and the Ecological Degradation of the Tropical World.* Berkeley: University of California Press.

Van Zeist, W., M.R. vander Spel-Walvins. 1980. A Palynological Study of the Late Glacial and the Post Glacial in the Paris Basin. *Paleohistoria* 22: 67–109.

Verbruggen, C., G. Hammer and P. Mol. 1997. Paleoecological Events in Belgium During the Last 13,000 Years, in C. Verbruggen (ed.), *Paleoecological Events in Europe During the Last 15,000 Years: Patterns, Process, and Problems.* Chichester, UK J. Wiley, pp. 145–67.

Wallerstein, I. 1974–80. *The Modern World-System, Vols. 1–3.* New York: Academic Press.

—————. 1979. Kondratieff Up or Down. *Review* II(4): 663–73.

Ward, W.A. and M.S. Joukovsky. 1992. *The Crisis Years: The 12th Century BC From Beyond the Danube to the Tigris.* Dubuque: Kendall Hunt.

Warren, P.M. 1985. Minoan Palaces. *Scientific American* 253(1): 94–103.

Watrous, L. Vance. 1994. Review of Aegean Prehistory III: Crete from earliest Prehistory Through the Protopalatial Period. *American Journal of Archaeology* 98: 695–753.

Watts, W.A., J.R.M. Allen and B. Huntley. 1996. The Vegetation and Climate of Northwest Iberia over the Last 14,000 Years. *Journal of Quaternary Science* 11: 125–47.

Weiss, H. 1982. The Decline of Late Bronze Age Civilization as a Possible Response to Climate Change. *Climate Change* 4: 173–98.

—————. 2000. Beyond the Younger Drayas, in G. Bawden and R. Reycraft (eds), *Environmental Disaster and the Archaeology of Human Response.* Albuquerque: University of New Mexico Press, pp. 75–98.

Weiss, H. and M.A. Courty. 1993. The Genesis and Collapse of Third Millennium Northern Mesopotamian Civilization. *Science* 261: 995–1004, August 20.

Weiss, H. and R. Bradley. 2001 Archaeology: What Drives Societal Collapse. *Science* 291: 609–10, January 26.

Whitley, J. 1991. *Style and Society in Dark Age Greece: The Changing Face of a Pre-Literate Society 1100–700 B.C.* Cambridge: Cambridge University Press.

Wilkinson, T. J. 1990. *Town and Country in South-eastern Anatolia.* Chicago: Oriental Institute.

Williams, M. 2003. Dark Ages and Dark Areas: Global Deforestation in the Deep Past. *Journal of Historical Geography* 26(1): 28–46.

Wilson, E.O. 2002. *The Future of Life.* New York: Alfred Knopf.

Wolf, Eric. 1982. *Europe and the People without History.* Berkeley: University of California Press.

World Commission on Forests and Sustainable Development. 1999. *Our Forests Our Future.* Cambridge: Cambridge University Press.

Wright, H.E. 1968. Climate Change in Mycenaen Greece. *Antiquity* 42: 123–27.

Yoffee, N. 1988. The Collapse of Ancient Mesopotamian States and Civilization, in N. Yoffee and G. Cowgill (eds), *The Collapse of Ancient States and Civilizations.* Tucson: University of Arizona Press, pp. 44–68.

Zanggar, E. 1993. Neolithic to Present Soil Erosion in Greece, in M. Bell and J. Boardman (eds), *Past and Present Soil Erosion.* Oxford: Oxford University Press, pp. 56–75.

8

ART, McDONALDIZATION AND THE GLOBALIZATION OF NOTHING

GEORGE RITZER

If anything would seem to be immune, at least to a large extent, from the processes of McDonaldization[1] and the globalization of nothing,[2] it would be art. In fact, as we will see, art would simply not be art if was McDonaldized to any great extent and if was to have the basic characteristics of nothing. While there is certainly much that passes for art that is McDonaldized, at least to some extent, and has many of the characteristics of nothing, most of us would have a difficult time thinking of such work as art, at least in any ideal, or pure sense of the term.

The objective here is to examine art from the perspectives of McDonaldization and nothing-ness, and their proliferation, even globalization. This will allow us to reflect on both the nature of art as well as its place in a society increasingly McDonaldized and characterized by nothing.

While the idea of McDonaldization is unknown in the art world, at least as far as I know,[3] interestingly, and perhaps not surprisingly, nothing is a significant issue in that world. It has been the subject of a number of exhibitions (and publications), including the recent (May 1–August 1, 2004) "The Big Nothing" at the Institute of Contemporary Art at the University of Pennsylvania in Philadelphia (as well as associated events in other venues throughout the city).[4] In fact, this was one of many museum exhibitions and gallery shows devoted to this topic. Many schools of art (e.g., dadaism, minimalism, abstract impressionism) and particular artists (especially Andy Warhol) are associated with the production of nothing, or at least something approximating it. However, the problem with discussing nothing in art is the same one that I encountered in researching the topic more generally—there is far from any consensus on the meaning of nothing in art. Among the meanings of nothing is art that is abstract, monochromatic, invisible, closed, silent, obfuscating, destructive, alienated, alienating, ephemeral, cipher-like, superficial, banal, mundane, of everyday life (the quotidian), mortal, virtual, and so on.

Close to what I mean by nothing is the description of the work of Gareth James who closed his studio, but invited critics and artists to come even though *no works* would be displayed or sold. He was described as responding to "the homogenization of contemporary art—an interjection of reflexivity amidst the art industry's over-production of marketable experience."[5] An interesting concept in this context is the "culturepreneur," a new position in the art world, described as "equal parts organizer and mouthpiece, who gladly parlayed the traditional, and real, flexibility of the artist into a kind of networking savvy or wheel-grease for new private-public collaboration."[6] Among others, the culturepreneur is seen as diminishing the "image of the artist as an autonomous, thinking figure resistant to society's uses."[7] It is this marketing of the artist and his/her work, this turning of art into a homogeneous, saleable commodity, that is the focus of this discussion of nothing in the art world.

An excellent example of this is art.com.[8] At the moment this successful website with 5 million visitors a month employs about 200 people in its warehouse in Raleigh, North Carolina. It currently specializes in spitting out "custom-framed posters and prints on an assembly-line modeled after the mass-customization computer line created by Dell".[9] However, what makes it even more relevant to our concern here is that it has recently begun offering original paintings and photographs for sale on its website. For a small fee artists can display their wares on the site and if they sell, the artists keep the revenue.

The latter seems innocent enough, but it has two interesting aspects from the point of this essay. First, the owners of the site are seeking to transform the process of purchasing art more into nothing not only by controlling it, but by simplifying it and reducing it to a relatively small number of simple, repeatable steps. Second, they want to transform art itself into nothing by, for example, selling artists "advanced services, such as preparing their images for limited edition reprints".[10] Of course, the ultimate step here would involve the actual employment of artists in the Raleigh warehouse where they can turn out original art in an assembly line fashion.

However, the major example of what will concern us throughout this essay is the artist Thomas Kinkade (the "painter of light"—a registered trademark!) and the various enterprises that he has created, or have grown up around his work, especially Thomas Kinkade Company/Media Arts Group, Inc.[11] This corporation, devoted to the sale of Kinkade's work, is listed on the Nasdaq, and in 1999 had $126 million in revenue producing an astounding (given the revenues) $84 million in profits. In addition, there are over 300 independently owned stores—Signature Thomas Kinkade Galleries—devoted to the sale of work associated with him and his associates. Kinkade does paint, but his paintings (and other work) are created with the development of a "multitude of multiples"[12] in mind so that they can be sold through a wide range of outlets to what he claims are the one in twenty American homes that own his art. In addition, his work appears on or influences such things as La-Z-Boy Furniture, placemats, Hallmark stationery, Avon gifts,[13] a Kinkade screen saver, and even a series of homes in Vallejo, California. Thus, Kinkade has created a highly commercialized operation with links to a variety of other well-known businesses.

Kinkade is clearly far more successful and commercially oriented than most other artists, but he is nonetheless an artist, although his work is not taken seriously, and is more usually derided by art experts. Whatever the artistic merits of his work, Kinkade (another is Wyland and his marine art[14]) represents a useful example of both McDonaldization and nothing, as they apply to the art world.

McDONALDIZATION

The essence of McDonaldization involves its proliferation from its roots in the fast food industry to many other settings, and from its source in the United States to many other parts of the world. More specifically, what is involved is the spread of its underlying principles—efficiency, predictability, calculability, control through non-human technology, as well as the irrationality of rationality. Let us look at art, especially the work of Thomas Kinkade, from the perspective of each of these characteristics.

Efficiency involves the search for the best possible means to an objective, whatever it may be. The emphasis is clearly on the means far more than the end, indeed the means often become ends in themselves. Thus, the goal becomes to operate efficiently with little attention to the ultimate goal, especially the qualitative characteristics of that goal. As in much else about McDonaldization, quality, in this case of the end-product, takes a back stage to the efficiency of the process by which it is produced or attained. In the fast food restaurant, the emphasis is on the efficiency with which a Chicken McNugget can be produced, cooked, served and eaten, rather than quality of the chicken and of the McNugget in which it is entombed.

It would be hard, to put it mildly, to think of art that is produced efficiently, let alone art that is produced—and consumed—as efficiently as a Chicken McNugget. After all, in art the ultimate goal is the quality—and the qualities— of the end-product and not the maximization of the efficiency with which it is produced. Theoretically, the artist cares little about the efficiency of the production process, but mainly about producing a high-quality, and qualitatively unique end-result, no matter what it takes to achieve such goals. Similarly, artistic creations that have the character of Chicken McNuggets—mass-produced and virtually identical to every other one—would be thought of by few, if any, as art. In spite of this, one finds much emphasis on efficiency in the artistic productions of Thomas Kinkade. For example, each of his lithographs is highlighted, by hand, to give the appearance of an original. However, it would be inefficient, probably physically impossible, for Kinkade to highlight each himself. Thus, there are "highlighters" employed to do the work, although the most coveted, and presumably most expensive, works are those highlighted by Kinkade himself.

Calculability is an emphasis on quantity rather than quality, on that which can be counted. Thus, at McDonald's the emphasis is on the size of products—the Big Mac, for example—and the numbers sold—"billions served"—than on the quality of those products. This often has an adverse effect on their quality. Big Macs are large in size, but few would think of them as being high in quality. The mere fact that billions of them have been sold does not mean that they are high in quality. Indeed, such popularity is usually associated with that which is quite modest in quality, if not downright mediocre.

Art, of course, is defined by qualitative characteristics. On the one hand, great art is distinguished from the mundane by its high quality. On the other, the work of one important artist is distinguished from that of another by its distinctive, even idiosyncratic qualities. A work of art is not notable because it is large, or was produced quickly, or a lot of them were produced. As we know, a work of art often has the opposite characteristics, indeed it would more likely be a work of art if it was produced slowly and there was only one of them. Artists who turn out similar pieces of work in an assembly-line manner rarely, if ever, achieve notoriety as great artists, although they may receive another, far less desirable form of notoriety. Of course, Kinkade does turn out art in assembly-line fashion. He is attuned to quantitative factors in various ways, most notably the profitability of his work. He seems proud of the number of people (one in twenty families) that own his work. And, he is willing to adapt the physical size of what he offers to the needs of the buyer and the size of the buyer's room. Few other painters offer their work in sizes to fit any need. Indeed, most art is produced with little regard to such mundane concerns as the size of the room in which it might hang.

Predictability involves the production and consumption of essentially the same, or a very similar, product or service from one time or place to another. Thus, a Burger King Whopper is pretty much the same today as it was yesterday, and as it will be tomorrow. Similarly, is looks and tastes very much the same in New York, London or Tokyo.

Predictability, of course, is just about a death sentence for a work of art. If one's art is just like someone else's, especially one who is better known, then one is unlikely to achieve much notoriety. Copying someone else's work, or even style, is not likely to lead to fame in art. Similarly, if all of one's work is pretty much the same, if one repeats one's self endlessly, one is apt to be regarded as a hack. Of course, an artist could produce an early work that is regarded as true art and earn a lifelong reputation for it. However, that reputation is likely to erode if all succeeding works are but pale imitations of the original. To the degree that an artist's work becomes predictable in these and other ways, is the degree to which it is not likely to be considered significant art.

On the surface, style would seem to represent a problem in that having a style appears to imply doing something consistently, or predictably. Yet, developing a distinctive style does not mean doing the same thing over and over. Indeed, great artists are more likely to bring their distinctive style to bear on diverse subjects in very different ways. Of course changes in, and diversities of, style are also highly valued, as reflected in the various periods represented in Picasso's *oeuvre*. Kinkade's work does have a style. He generally paints quaint scenes ("cozy cottages", "quaint arched bridges") that are suffused with a warm light that seems to spill over into the homes and workplaces of the owners. However, in his case, this does seem to mean doing pretty much the same thing over and over. His work is highly predictable. This predictability is greatly amplified by the fact that what he creates is produced in multiples with each succeeding iteration much like every other one.

Finally, McDonaldization is characterized by control over various unpredictabilities, especially the *use of non-human technology to control the unpredictabilities* caused by human beings.[15] This often involves a deskilling whereby skills are extracted from humans and built into technologies that then exercise control over them. Thus, in the fast food restaurant, automatic French fry machines now determine when the fries are done, automatically lift them out of the hot oil, and sound an alarm alerting the worker that the fries are done.

Clearly, artists, at least those who hope to be considered significant artists, cannot afford to be deskilled or controlled by non-human technologies. Great art is associated with great skill, especially great technical skill, and if technologies are used, they are to be controlled by, rather than controlling, the artist. Artists are supposed to be creative and creativity is greatly reduced, if not totally eliminated, if there is external control, especially by non-human technologies that, by definition, lack creativity. Non-human technology dominates Kinkade's work, at least in the production of the endless multiples that are derived from it. There is great control over his "highlighters," whether or not they are trained by him, who are permitted to add only limited "highlighting" to an already finished work of art.

Among the *irrationalities of rationality* spawned by McDonaldization are dehumanization and disenchantment. McDonaldized systems are not conducive to human capabilities and human relationships, whether they involve those who work in such systems and/or those who are served by them. Thus, they can be said to be alienated from their human potential as workers, consumers, and ultimately as human beings. The high rate of employee turnover in the fast food industry is a reflection of worker alienation, and customers are treated in a variety of non-human ways such as being dealt with in a highly scripted manner by generally disinterested employees. It is likely that the work of the highlighters employed by Kinkade is dehumanized and alienating.

McDonaldized systems are also by definition disenchanted systems since the latter is simply another way of saying that they are rationalized (a synonym for being McDonaldized). There is no magic, mystery, enchantment associated with highly McDonaldized systems. Indeed, McDonaldized systems systematically root out all lingering elements of enchantment. Thus, for example, there is no mystery about what you are going to get in a fast food restaurant and how it has been prepared. Although fans and owners of Kinkade's work often describe it as enchanted, it is highly unlikely that there is much magic involved in its creation, especially the endless repetition of multiples or in the repetitive work of highlighting.

Art would simply not be art if the human element was removed and/or it was lacking in enchantment. For example, Mona Lisa is clearly the product of Leonardo Da Vinci; it certainly could not have produced by a non-human technology and almost certainly by no other human being. And there is great magic and enchantment associated with that painting, indeed virtually all great art, not the least of which is the mysterious, enigmatic quality of Mona Lisa's famous smile. Thus, it is very difficult, to put it mildly, to associate art and a high degree of McDonaldization in general, as well as a high degree of efficiency, predictability, calculability, and the control exerted by non-human technologies, as well as the irrationalities of rationality such as dehumanization and disenchantment. However, that is not to say that art has been unaffected by the process of McDonaldization and that is well-illustrated in the case of the work of Thomas Kinkade. Indeed, it is difficult to think of any sector of society that has been unaffected by this ubiquitous process.

Of course, a major force in the McDonaldization of art is commercialization, especially the desire of artists to be global commercial successes (and few rival Kinkade in this regard). To be successful commercially, art must have each of the dimensions of McDonaldization, at least to some extent. Art can never be as McDonaldized as, say, fast food, but it certainly can be McDonaldized to some extent. First, an artist who wants to be a commercial success would need to be able to produce work in a comparatively efficient manner since the more art that is produced, the greater the likely profits. If an artist is able to attract a large, global audience, there would need to be a measure of predictability about his/her work so that a buyer anywhere in the world will be able to know who produced it, and perhaps even what it means. Calculability enters at various points including how long a given work should take and how much income it is likely to produce. Non-human technologies may be employed to do at least part of the work and increase the speed with which art can be produced. Such work is likely to have at least some irrationalities of rationality, including some measure of dehumanization and disenchantment. Of course, all of the above are true of Thomas Kinkade's work, at least to some degree.

Naturally, such art is not likely to be highly esteemed in the art community, is apt to be reviled by experts and critics, and may not even be considered to be art by most observers. And, all of these things are true of Kinkade's work.

Virtually any level of McDonaldization is a threat to art as we usually conceive of it, but a high degree of McDonaldization would be the death knell of art and there are those who think that Kinkade is sounding that death knell.

ART AND THE GLOBALIZATION OF NOTHING

If globalization itself is something of a threat to art, then the globalization of nothing would seem to be totally destructive of it. We need a few definitions before we can proceed further. Nothing is defined as a *social form that is generally centrally conceived, controlled and comparatively devoid of distinctive substantive content.* This leads to a definition of something as *a social form that is generally indigenously conceived, controlled and comparatively rich in distinctive substantive content.* This makes it clear that neither nothing nor something exists independently of the other, *each makes sense only when paired with, and contrasted to, the other.* While presented as a dichotomy, this implies a *continuum* from something to nothing and that is precisely the way the concepts will be employed here—as the two poles of that continuum. Thus, while we often refer to some phenomena as nothing or something, the fact is that all phenomena manifest degrees of nothing-ness and something-ness.

One thing to clarify immediately is that nothing–something should not be equated with bad–good. That is, that which is nothing (e.g., a meal at a fast food restaurant) is not necessarily bad and that which is something (a meal at a local café) is not necessarily good.

Art, at least in its ideal sense, would be something. Certainly, we think of all great—or even merely good art—as something. But, as pointed out above, even bad art would be something because it is indigenously conceived, controlled, and rich in distinctive content. The artist, embedded in a local context, conceives of the work, controls every step in its creation, and whatever its artistic merits, the end-product has distinctive content—no one else could ever produce exactly the same piece of work. In this context, the problem for art is the pull toward the nothing end of the continuum and clearly a central force pulling art in that direction today is commercialization. By the way, this is not the first such force pulling art in this direction. The medieval guild system exerted even greater and more direct control over artists through its creation and enforcement of standards, its power over apprentices to induce conformity, its control over tools and raw materials, and its limitations on output.[16]

Whether or not it is more productive of nothing than the guild system, there are pressures today in art in that direction, especially from commercialization. Agents and agencies, companies that commission and purchase art, museums, and most generally the art market all pull in the direction of nothing. This is certainly clear in the sense that all would involve some measure of centralized control over art. Centralized conception would exist to the degree that outside forces are dictating various things about the nature of the art project, or the content of the art. And, of course, pressures such as the latter would lead to art that is lacking in distinctive content. That is, centralized forces and their demands might lead to greater uniformity in art that seeks to accede to such demands. Again, it is important to emphasize that art that does accede to such pressures could be quite good, but it will still be nothing as that term is discussed here.

Thomas Kinkade's work would obviously fall towards the nothing end of the continuum. It is certainly centrally conceived and controlled from Kinkade's studios and perhaps ultimately from Media Arts Group, Inc. The issue of distinctive content is more complex. On the one hand, Kinkade's original paintings, whatever their quality, do have distinctive content. No one else could have painted exactly the same picture. However, it becomes nothing when it is reproduced endlessly with each iteration being a copy of what came before it, and of the original. One sees this in the Thomas Kinkade Collectors' Society (over 20,000 members) where those who participate buy, trade and collect the various iterations of Kinkade's work. Such societies encourage the "limited" production of a large number of identical works that members are encouraged to buy and add to their personal collections. Such collections and societies are much more likely to be associated with kitsch than art, and when they exist in the world of art (as they do in the case of Kinkade's work), they tend to transform art into kitsch.

In fact, it is the concern about dangers of nothingness that lies, at least implicitly, behind the highlighting of Kinkade's work. It is the particular nature of the highlighting that distinguishes one iteration from all the others. Thus, the buyers of highlighted works feel that they are getting something that does have distinctive content. Furthermore, that which is highlighted by a "master highlighter" trained by Kinkade himself is valued more highly, and seen as more distinctive, than one highlighted by less elite highlighters. The ultimate, however, is that work that has been highlighted by Kinkade personally. As if this isn't enough, greater distinctiveness can be added by the buyer at an opening who is permitted to highlight his/her own lithograph, naturally at extra cost.

Art, in its various forms, is in many ways the paradigmatic form of something. That is one of the reasons why it is so important that art retain its status as something. If art were to move increasingly in the direction of nothing, what would be safe from this general process? Certainly, there is much evidence that much else in the world, especially in the commercial world, is moving in the direction of nothing. If art were to move increasingly toward the nothing end of the continuum, there would be little, or nothing, to stand in the way of what already is a flood of nothing-ness. Furthermore, the erosion of this quintessential form of something-ness would leave more and more people without a sense and a standard of that which is something. Without a sense of something, the ability even to recognize the tidal wave of nothingness would disappear. Eventually we would cease to know what we have lost—that is, something.

If the art work of Thomas Kinkade is a paradigmatic form of nothing, then out of a wealth of examples, we could focus on that of Skip Schuckmann as an example of something.[17] Schuckmann does environmental art. He adapts what he creates to *both* the nature of the surroundings (dirt, brush, trees, water, and so on) and the desires and dispositions of the client. In fact, Schuckmann works with only one client at a time and one day at a time. After each day, artist and client decide if and when the work is to continue. What Schuckmann creates (say, a subterranean pit house or an "embankment of dry-stacked fieldstone"[18]) is truly locally conceived and controlled out of the interaction of artist, client and nature. And what emerges is rich in distinctive content. He produces his work one at a time and each is one of a kind (compare this to the multiples of Kinkade). A work produced by the artist on a different day, let alone with a different client and in a different physical setting, would have content, that while also being very distinctive, would be quite different. Thus, Schuckmann's work, like that of many other artists, meets the three elements of the definition of something.

In *The Globalization of Nothing*, I argued that the fundamental problem was not the proliferation of nothing per se, but what I called *loss amidst monumental abundance*. That is, there is a sense of the loss of something within the increasingly monumental abundance of nothing. Thus, the isolated and limited number of creations by an artist like Schuckmann tend to be completely lost in the avalanche of copies produced by Kinkade, Inc. However, a sense of loss depends on the continued existence of something, at least to some minimal degree in some specific areas of life (such as art). Thus, works like those of Schuckmann play a very important role in the contemporary world. However, if nothing continues to proliferate, even in the world of art, then it will be increasingly difficult to realize and understand that there has been a loss—of something.

In addition to a general sense of nothing and something, a variety of continua are necessary to distinguish better between them, and more specifically, art from non-art (Table 8.1).

Table 8.1: The Something–Nothing Continuum and Its Five Sub-Continua

Something	*Nothing*
Unique (One-of-a-Kind)	Generic (Interchangeable)
Local Geographic Ties	Lack of Local Ties
Specific to the Times	Time-less
Humanized	Dehumanized
Enchanted	Disenchanted

First, the *unique, one-of-a-kind–generic, interchangeable* sub-continuum is premised on the idea that that which is unique is highly likely to be indigenously created and controlled and rich in distinctive substance while that which is generic is likely to be centrally created and controlled and lacking in much, or even any, distinctive substance. Thus, art that is something tends to be unique and one of a kind (Schuckmann's works), while non-art is generic and interchangeable (Kinkade's multiples).

The second sub-continuum, *local geographic ties–lack of local ties*, is based on the view that phenomena with local ties are more likely to internalize the rich complexity and the distinctive substance of the local environment while those without such ties are likely to be lacking in such complexity and distinctive substance. Art that is something tends to reflect and be tied to a specific geographic area (for example, the art of Rembrandt and Hals as a reflection of the Netherlands of the seventeenth century in which they lived). This is particularly true of Schuckmann's work, who literally works with the geographic realities that he encounters at a given site where he is working. Non-art tends to lack such relationships to the local (Kinkade's art is not tied to any specific locale).

However, non-art is often not totally without local ties. Over time, McDonald's has had to adapt to the local environment to some degree both in cuisine and architecture. However, these have always been in the form of minor additions to the basic menu (a pseudo-local item or two) and structure (a few minor architectural embellishments that reflect the local culture), and not in fundamental changes in either. However, there are cases in which greater adaptation to the local is mandated. In the fast food industry this is more likely to occur among the weaker chains that do not have the visibility and power to lead locals to adapt to their fundamental character. For example, a few years ago I was in Bangkok, Thailand and ran into a Big Boy restaurant that had adapted so much to the local environment both in cuisine and architectural structure that it was almost impossible to recognize it as part of that chain. However, this sort of thing is unlikely to happen to a powerful chain like McDonald's, as well as other major cathedrals of consumption, that can get by with minor modifications as nods to the local culture.

More importantly, there are examples of art—"true art"—that lack local ties. For example, modern abstract art (e.g., Jackson Pollack's later work where he poured, dripped, and flung paint on canvas—earlier, Pollock's work had a strong sense of local ties, including the rural Long Island locale in which he lived for a time) shows few, if any, discernible ties to any locale. However, in using the five continua developed here, it is not necessary that all have the same, or even similar, rank on every continuum. It is the overall analysis, based on all the continua, that gives us a sense of where any phenomenon stands on the something–nothing continuum. In fact, the next one to be discussed does a good job of showing why abstract art can be something even though it may lack local ties.

The *specific to the times–relatively time-less* sub-continuum posits that what is specific to a time period would tend to have distinctive content (and more likely to be something), while that which is more time-less would tend to lack such distinctiveness (and more likely to be nothing). Thus, art that reflects the time in which it was created, and/or the period in the history of art during which it was created, would be something. The works of Rembrandt and Hals would represent both a period in Dutch and world history, as well as a period in the history of art. While Pollock's later work may not show much of the impact of world history, it certainly powerfully reflects a particular point in the history of art. Not only does Pollock's work reflect various strands that had come before, but it also constitutes the beginning of a new stage in the history of art. Non-art would have no ties to either time period; it would be time-less in both world and art history. Non-art might be tied to many different time periods; it might offer a pastiche of styles from many different time periods. Or, it might reflect little or nothing of the history of the world or of art.

Returning to our two paradigms, Kinkade's work lacks ties to any specific time period (although it usually feels pre-industrial), including any specific time period in the history of art. Schuckmann's work is very much tied to the immediate time period in which he is working. Indeed, his work will change from one moment to the next with climatic changes (wind, rain and so on will alter the environment and materials with which he works). In terms of the history of art, he is reacting against the dominance of museums and the creation of permanent creations for display in them.

For purposes of the *humanized–dehumanized* sub-continuum, those things that are enmeshed in strong human relations are likely to manifest a great deal that is substantively distinctive about such relationships (e.g., the detailed interpersonal histories associated with them) while dehumanized phenomena are far less likely to reflect any personal relationships among those involved. Thus, art that is something often tells us much about the person who created it. For example, the piece ("Orange Head") painted by Pollock in the late 1930s and early 1940 reflected his own awareness—stemming from a mental breakdown and Jungian psychoanalysis—of his mental problems. Non-art is likely not to reflect much of the person creating it. Furthermore, in the era of great commercialization, art might come to be dictated to by corporate policies and directives and be more likely to be produced by committee and/or computer. The people involved in such art are apt to be following well-established, tried-and-true blueprints for such art. Schuckmann's creations are highly humanized, involving not only his input but that of his client. On the other hand, those of Kinkade, especially the multiples and the creations to be employed by corporations (e.g., Hallmark), are highly dehumanized.

Finally, the *enchanted–disenchanted* sub-continuum is based on the idea that that which is something tends to have an enchanted, magical quality, while that which is nothing is more likely to be disenchanted, lacks mystery or magic. This seems to be the key factor in distinguishing art from non-art. That is, art seems to be enchanted, while non-art seems to lack such a magical quality. There is much magic in the interaction between Schuckmann, his clients and the physical environment, while the work of Kinkade's highlighters seems highly disenchanted.

However, a problem in thinking in these terms would be art that is highly geometric; that is created on the basis of fundamental mathematical principles and is therefore highly rationalized, which means it is *dis*enchanted. Again, we are back to the point that while any one of these continua may fail to differentiate adequately art from non-art, it is in combination with one another that they work best, although even in that case they may not work perfectly.

GLOBALIZATION: GLOCALIZATION AND GROBALIZATION

Globalization encompasses a number of transnational processes that, while they all can be seen as global in reach, are separable from each other. It is beyond the scope of this essay to deal with the full range of globalization processes, but two broad and important types—glocalization and grobalization—will be of interest here. The concept of glocalization gets to the heart of what most contemporary analysts associated with globalization theory think about the nature of transnational processes. Glocalization can be defined as *the interpenetration of the global and the local resulting in unique outcomes in different geographic areas*. The concept of grobalization, coined for the first time in my recent book as a much-needed companion to the notion of glocalization, focuses on *the imperialistic ambitions of nations, corporations, organizations, and the like and their desire, indeed need, to impose themselves on various geographic areas*. Their main interest is in seeing their power, influence, and in many cases, profits *grow* (hence the term *grobalization*) throughout the world. No necessary value judgment is implied here; there can be negatives associated with the glocal (lack of openness to some useful grobal inputs) and positives tied to the grobal (the delivery of new medications and medical technologies throughout the world).

It is argued that grobalization tends to be associated with the proliferation of nothing (e.g., the fast food restaurant) while glocalization tends to be tied more to something (e.g., a Provencal meal) and therefore stands opposed, at least partially (and along with the local itself, to the degree that it can be said to still exist in the face of the pervasive process of globalization that rarely, if ever, leaves the local untouched), to the spread of nothing. It is the fact that these two processes co-exist under the broad heading of globalization, and because they are, at least to some degree, in conflict in terms of their implications for the spread of nothingness around the world, that globalization as a whole does *not* have a unidirectional effect on the spread of nothingness. That is, in some of its aspects (those involved in grobalization), globalization favors the spread of nothing, but in others (those related to glocalization), it tends towards the dissemination of something.

Those who emphasize glocalization tend to see it as militating against the globalization of nothing and, in fact, view it as leading to the creation of a wide array of new, "glocal" forms of something. In contrast, those who emphasize grobalization see it as a powerful contributor to the spread of nothingness throughout the world. This being said, it must be noted that there are important similarities and differences between glocalization and grobalization.

Notes

1. See George Ritzer, *The McDonaldization of Society*. Revised New Century Edition. Thousand Oaks, CA: Pine Forge Press, 2004.
2. See George Ritzer, *The Globalization of Nothing*. Thousand Oaks, CA: Pine Forge Press, 2004.
3. Although the ideas and issues associated with it are certainly of concern.
4. See Ingrid Schaffner, Bennett Simpson and Tanya Leighton, *The Big Nothing*. Philadelphia: University of Pennsylvania, Institute of Contemporary Art, 2004.
5. Ingrid Schaffner, Bennett Simpson and Tanya Leighton, *The Big Nothing*. Philadelphia: University of Pennsylvania, Institute of Contemporary Art, 2004: 41.
6. Ingrid Schaffner, Bennett Simpson and Tanya Leighton, 2004: 44.
7. Ingrid Schaffner, Bennett Simpson and Tanya Leighton, 2004: 44.
8. See Leslie Walker, "A New Mart for Original Art," *Washington Post-Business*, July 8, 2005: E1. E6.
9. Leslie Walker, 2005: E1.
10. Leslie Walker, "A New Mart for Original Art," *Washington Post-Business*, July 8, 2005: E1.
11. See Linda Weintraub, *In the Making: Creative Options for Contemporary Art*. NY: DAP, 2003: 18–23; http://flakmag.com/misc/kinkade.html.
12. Linda Weintraub, 2003: 18.
13. For a full list of brands with which Kinkade is associated, see http://www.mediaarts.com/coprofile/our_partners.html.
14. See John Seed, "McDonalds-ized Art?," http://artsiteguide.com/mcd.html.
15. This may relate to one of the reasons for Andy Warhol's dubious reputation as an artist. The setting in which he did his best known work was known as the "factory" (it was literally housed in old factory) and a factory is, of course, linked intimately to non-creative production reliant heavily on non-human technologies.
16. See Linda Weintraub, *In the Making: Creative Options for Contemporary Art*. NY: DAP, 2003: 9.
17. Linda Weintraub, 2003: 34–42.
18. Linda Weintraub, 2003: 38.

9

THE IMPACT OF GLOBALIZATION ON LOCAL COMMUNITIES

ROBYN BATEMAN DRISKELL

"Globalization" is most commonly applied to the economy of international markets and the various impacts it has on social and cultural life. The process of globalization usually describes the changes in the overall society or nation, but rarely addresses the impacts on the local community. This chapter will examine the factors of globalization, characteristics of *Gemeinschaft*, and the loss of community due to globalization. Many critiques of globalization often include the loss of community. Community sociologists debate whether the quality of the community is reduced as globalization occurs.

Most theories of globalization assess the changes in the economy, political system, and sometimes cultural and technological advances. The basis of globalization is the emergence of a single social system, characterized by a worldwide network of economic, political, and social relationships (Dasgupta 2004). The global economies are linked across the globe with multinational corporations creating a flow of global investments. In a political economy, globalization is best described as the final stages of capitalism, where all parts of the globe are inhabited and used for the expansion of the marketplace. The idea of globalization is a future world with a single economy based on the capitalist market principles, and ultimately beneficial to all consumers and workers.

The world-systems theory conceives of globalization as the extension of capitalism, yet everyone does not ultimately benefit. According to Immanuel Wallerstein (1974), the global system is a hierarchy of power in the international system: core, periphery, and semi-periphery. The system of hierarchy is based on inequalities between the rich and poor nations.

Regardless, one of the most important impacts of globalization has been on the human habitat—the community. The globalization perspective has important implications for the study of community. The influences on community and local development are often derived from the global level. Important economic and political powers can come from the local community, creating a change. As the globalization of the economy and changes in communication and transportation technology reach their local extreme, city and hinterland will become one: the globe. That is, with routine and instantaneous communication about market-relevant information, the geographic space in which individuals live and act is everywhere at the same time. In effect, all points of the globe are localized, at least with respect to certain strategic decision-making dimensions of economic existence (Flanagan 2002: 65).

THE POLITICAL ECONOMY APPROACH

In assessing the impacts of globalization on the community, the political economy approach aids the understanding of the globalization process and highlights the community and urban structure. The political economy paradigm assesses the changing nature of the global economy and the impacts on the community (Kleniewski 1997). The viewpoint draws from the works of Karl Marx, Manuel Castells and David Harvey, arguing that urban changes are best understood in the global framework of economic and political forces (Macionis and Parrillo 2004). The political economy paradigm examines the growth of suburbs, the closing of industrial facilities in the urban center, the relocation of the companies to the suburban areas, and the decline in industrial jobs and inner urban residents that often follow. The characteristics of global political economy are described by Nancy Kleniewski (1997: 37–39):

1. Cities are part of the political, economic, and social arrangements of their times rather than products of natural processes.
2. Competition and conflicts over the distribution of resources help shape urban patterns and urban social life.
3. Government is an important institution influencing urban patterns.
4. Economic restructuring, or a pattern of widespread shifts in the economy, is one of the most important factors affecting local communities.

One key focus is the role of global economic development in shaping cities. In addition, the political economy approach examines conflicts between races, classes, industries, and economic institutions as influencing the characteristics of the city. The urban political economy paradigm is often criticized for its overemphasis on uniformity of the cities and ignoring local political and economic variations (Kleniewski 1997). As with the other Marxist and conflict approaches, the micro level analysis of individual actors are often overlooked in the context of the capitalistic urban area.

Continuing in the political economy perspective, David Harvey (1988) illustrates how global capitalism changes urban spatial patterns in an attempt to save itself from its own excesses. In order to maximize profits, individual capitalists produce more than can be consumed, leading to glutted markets, falling prices, and rising unemployment. This problem can be temporarily solved by switching investment from "primary circuits" (production) to "secondary circuits" (warehouses, offices). By reinvesting in their capital, they are able to temporarily reduce production, and at the same time, of course, they are remaking the urban environment through expansion and construction. Eventually, however, production is increased to even higher levels. The recurring problems of market glut are now exacerbated by the demolition of structurally sound buildings for new, but now largely vacant, blocks of offices. Thus, the physical patterns of urban structure and growth reflect the exploitation, development, and contradictions of capitalism.

Harvey's (1988) analysis is better suited to pointing out the injustices and inefficiencies of global capitalist cities than to projecting the changes necessary to create a more just city. Harvey thus ends *Social Justice and the City:*

An urbanism founded upon exploitation is a legacy of history. A genuinely humanizing urbanism has yet to be brought into being. It remains for revolutionary theory to chart the path from an urbanism based in exploitation to an urbanism appropriate for the human species. And it remains for revolutionary practice to accomplish such a transformation. (1988: 314)

The exploitive nature and process of globalization and capitalism is further discussed in Harvey's case study of Baltimore in *The Urbanization of Capital* (1985b), the case study of Paris in *Consciousness and the Urban Experience* (1985a), and the historical view of capitalism in *The Urban Experience* (1989). Harvey demonstrates that globalization and urban development is not a single growth process, but a boom, recession or uneven growth, and is basic to the cycles of urbanism within a capitalist system. Thus, Harvey sees territories as continually being reorganized, redefined, and changed by a world dominated by global capitalism (Ritzer and Goodman 2004). Finally, in true Marxist tradition, Harvey describes the future utopian space and offers hope for the oppressive spaces of today.

More recently, Manuel Castells offers a modern and global perspective of our new technological and computerized world in his triology (1996, 1997, 1998) with the overarching title *The Information Age*. Castells is concerned with the growth of *The Informational City* (1991) and the development of the network society. According to Castells, the flow of computerized information has allowed the transformation of our cities and created problems in the process (Ritzer and Goodman 2004). The new technologies have fundamentally reshaped the regional structure and the dynamics of the city (Castells 1985). The restructuring of capitalism with the technological revolution has impacted spatial dynamics and created a global info-capitalism (Castells 2000) and the rise of the dual city in regards to production and manufacturing (Castells 1991). In *The Informational City*, he interprets the impacts of information technologies on the restructuring of the city. However, with his concepts on information technology, the network society and global capitalism, the local community is merely a place where national or international economic forces determine events. The neo-Marxist analysis and global capitalism approach does not focus on local community change and development as much as the global economic forces of society. Another dimension of globalization includes the rise of mass society and its impact on community.

THE RISE OF THE MASS SOCIETY

A mass society is a standardized, homogeneous society devoid of major ethnic and class divisions and, most importantly for the community, devoid of substantial regional and local variation. Because of mass media, standardized public education, and residential mobility, the intercommunity variation in norms, values, and behavior has been reduced to a remarkable degree. The territorial community, then, is of little scientific importance in a mass society. Residents of New York, New Haven, New Orleans, and New Deal, Texas will be much more alike than they are different. They watch the same TV shows and movies, read the same magazines and syndicated columnists, study the same textbooks in the same grades, and travel from one city to the next with ease. Under such circumstances, the logical site of scientific inquiry is the national society, not the local community.

In the late 1950s and 1960s, theories about the structure and dynamics of *societies* became common. Similar theories about *communities* were no longer in vogue. Research based on national samples replaced studies of single communities. Decisions reached in corporate headquarters and state and national capitals far beyond the local community precluded the relevance of community power. In short, the rise of interest in the mass society was matched by the concomitant decline in analysis of the community.

The issue of universalism and cultural homogenization model is connected with globalization. The first evidence of a major movement from community to mass society came from the early holistic community studies. In a book aptly titled *The Eclipse of Community*, Maurice Stein (1960) showed how the classic studies of Middletown, Yankee City, and Chicago could be combined to trace the transformation of America into a society much nearer the *mass society* end of the continuum. Stein used the Chicago studies of Robert Park et al. to illustrate the effects of urbanization on our lifestyles, the two Middletown volumes of Robert and Helen Lynd to document the effects of industrialization, and the five volumes reporting W. Lloyd Warner's study of Yankee City to describe the growing impact of bureaucratization. These three processes (urbanization, industrialization and bureaucratization), Stein concludes, combined to produce a mass society that eliminated many of the *Gemeinschaft*-like relationships associated with community:

All of these studies during the 1920s and 1930s, then, show increasing standardization of community patterns throughout the country with agencies of nationwide diffusion and control acting as centers of innovation. Intimate life patterns become susceptible to standardized change as the mass media begin to inform each age group about new fashions and styles. Thus, the conditions for the formation of a mass society were found in these previously examined social processes, even though more advanced forms had not yet appeared. (1960: 108)

Other holistic studies such as Vidich and Bensman's *Small Town in Mass Society* (1958) illustrate the "more advanced forms" of mass society referred to by Stein. We find in Vidich and Bensman's study of Springdale, a small village in upstate New York, a community that has become politically impotent, economically dependent, and culturally subservient when compared to the larger, more powerful, national society. They conclude that "[a] central fact of rural life then, is its dependence on the institutions and dynamics of the urban and mass society" (Vidich and Bensman 1958: 101). Thus, in addition to the psychological alienation described by Tönnies and Simmel, another important consequence of the growing influence of the global mass society is the diminishing importance of the territorial community.

George Ritzer further addresses the issues of mass society in *The McDonaldization of Society* (2000). McDonaldization is the process of global homogenization of culture through five basic principles: efficiency, calculability, control, the substitution of non-human for human technology, and the irrationality of rationality. Most reviews of McDonaldization focus on the dehumanizing effects of the process, thus the loss of human interaction, and thus the loss of community. As with the McDonaldization of food service, the proximate cause of McDonaldization is often the rapid expansion of an economic sector. The planned community or suburban development mass produced with cookie-cutter housing designs is the mark of McDonaldization on our communities.

Macrosystem Dominance and the "Great Change"

Roland L. Warren continues with the theme of mass society in his description of the dominating impact of a national society on a local community. Warren has made significant contributions to community theory, most of it within the framework of systems theory. The basis for Warren's analysis is the macrosystem dominance of community subsystems that result in what Warren calls "the great change."

The great change, Warren (1978: 52) explains, "includes the increasing orientation of local community units toward extracommunity systems of which they are a part, with a corresponding decline in community cohesion and autonomy." In an extensive and insightful extension of Tönnies's *Gemeinschaft* and *Gesellschaft*, Warren traces the "great change" through seven developments in society–community relations: (1) the increasing division of labor and the breakdown of mechanical solidarity á la Durkheim; (2) growing differentiation of interests and associations; (3) increasing systemic relationships to the larger society via Durkheim's organic solidarity; (4) more bureaucratization and impersonalization á la Weber; (5) the transfer of functions to profit enterprise and government, functions traditionally allocated to families and local ad hoc groupings; (6) urbanization and subsequent suburbanization; and (7) changing values, such as the gradual acceptance of governmental activity in traditionally private concerns, the shift from moral to causal interpretations of human behavior, and a change in emphasis from the "Protestant Ethic" of work and production to enjoyment and consumption. The cumulative effect of these seven changes is to create a new kind of community almost totally dependent on the larger mass society.

In macrosystem dominance, the community becomes a reflection of the larger society, or in Warren's terms, "a node of the macro system." Thus, one finds similar land use, values, and behaviors in all communities:

To be sure, there are differences among communities in values, norms, dominant interests, styles, and other cultural aspects. But again, if one is to watch the *public behavior* of people on a busy street corner, or at the supermarket, or in their homes, or at athletic events, one would be hard put to it to know that one is in Pittsburgh rather than St. Louis, in Bridgeport rather than in Rockland, in Atlanta rather than in Denver. Surely, the thought systems, the ideational and behavioral patterns indigenous to the locality are important, but an observer from Mars would be struck by their overwhelming similarity as one moves across the country, indicating once more that they may best be considered local enactments or implementations of thought and behavior systems of the national culture. (1978: 429)

There are two inferences that can be drawn from the dominance of the macrosystem. One is that a research focus on the community is clearly misplaced. For example, Brian Taylor (1975: 282) argues that community studies that analyze local systems typically miss the prime cause of the social problems they encounter:

To begin with, so far as problems have been examined at all, the use of a *locality framework* has tended to restrict attention to problems within the settlement-area, and thus either to miss some problems altogether or to ignore their true locations, which in many cases are in social systems which extend beyond the village, parish, slum, suburb or town itself, in the context of the wider society.

The causes of crime, poverty, pollution, and other community problems lie not so much with the characteristics of the local subsystem as with the society's macrosystem. The state of the national economy, for example, will be reflected in local unemployment rates. In terms similar to those used for the mass society, the macrosystem is the prime mover. Causes and cures for social problems will be found at the national, not the local, level. Thus, one implication of macrosystem dominance is that community studies are no longer justified.

Warren, however, reaches a different conclusion about macrosystem dominance and the role of community studies:

There must be some broad area of middle ground for investigation between the incurably romantic conception of community as a focal point of virtually all meaningful social activity and the equally remote conception of a territorially undifferentiated mass society in which people's relation to the macrosystem is utterly independent of their geographic location. For in this admittedly difficult theoretical area lie numerous questions not only of theory, ideology, and social policy but also of focal issues around which people are increasingly involved. Many people want locality to be made more, not less, relevant to the administration of the police, to the operation of the schools, to the ownership and operation of business enterprise, to the operation of the sanitation department, the health department, the social agencies, the location of highways, transit systems, and on and on through some of the most hotly contested issues of the day. Like Mark Twain's comment about the fallacious report of his own death, the death of the community has been highly exaggerated. Transformed, si'— muerto, no!

The theoretical task, and also the practical one, is to determine with greater depth of analysis those areas—many of the critical issues of our time—where the local organization of social life is an integral component of the social problem. (1978: 442)

According to theories of globalization, mass society and the great change, communities have been transformed. Although, there is some speculation that the community transformation have moved beyond globalization and mass society, creating a third type of society.

THE THIRD TYPE: POST-GLOBALIZATION SOCIETIES

There is a still emerging theoretical position stating that modern industrial societies have moved beyond the elements of globalization and mass society and are entering an entirely new basis for social relationships. Various names for this new stage have been offered: "The Third Wave" (Toffler 1980), "The Informational City" (Castells 1991), "The Global City" (Sassen 1991), "Edge City" (Garreau 1992), "Cyberspace Communities" (Rheingold 1993), "Postmodern Urbanism" (Ellin 1996), and "Edgeless Cities" (Lang 2003). The claims of distinctiveness for this new type are often quite extensive. Alvin Toffler (1980: 10) saw us entering

a genuinely new way of life based on diversified, renewable energy sources; on methods of production that make most factory assembly lines obsolete; on new, non-nuclear families;

on a novel institution that might be called the "electronic cottage"; and on radically changed schools and corporations of the future. The emergent civilization writes a new code of behavior for us and carries us beyond standardization, synchronization, and centralization, beyond the concentration of energy, money, and power.

Still, the most pertinent question for those who argue for a post-globalization typology is precisely what Toffler takes as given: Are we already entering into a new social order based on relationships *fundamentally* different from the *Gesellschaft* condition described by Tönnies less than 100 years ago? Perhaps the best way to explore this question is to compare the three "polar" (if it is possible to have *three* poles) types. Anthony Richmond (1969) has contrasted the three types in order to show the distinctiveness of the new type. The degree to which each of Richmond's post-*Gesellschaft* characteristics has or will become predominate is debatable, but for students of community at least, the key debate centers on interaction. If electronic communication via e-mail, the Internet, and text messaging replaces the written word, that would not, in itself, constitute a new "wave," "stage," or "type." Rather, we would want to know if this new form of communication significantly changed social interactions. Will a computer- linked social network replace the associations that replaced informal neighboring? Will people begin to view one another, their communities, or their societies in substantially different ways? Between *Gemeinschaft* and *Gesellschaft* (global/mass society), the answer is reasonably clear and affirmative. Between *Gesellschaft* and post-globalization a clear consensus opinion has not formed.

Table 9.1: Characteristics of the Continuum Type of Societies

	Gemeinschaft	*Globalization/ Mass Society*	*Post- Globalization*
Typical way of interaction	Communities	Associations	Social networks
Principal mode of production	Agricultural	Mechanical	Automated
System of stratification	Quasi-feudal	Class	Meritocracy
Main means of communication	Oral	Written	Electronic
Main means of transport	Horse and sail	Rural–urban	International

For now, we would do well to remember that much *Gemeinschaft*-like community remains even in our global, industrialized, mass society. Thus, even if a third "wave" is upon us, we would expect considerable *Gesellschaft* to remain in a post-globalization society. The transformation into this third type may not be as sweeping as its proponents claim, yet it is evident that the community reminiscent of *Gemeinschaft* is lost.

LOSING COMMUNITY IN GLOBAL SOCIETY

Critiques of modern global societies often include the loss of community, due to weak connections with local places and changing modes of social interactions. The idea that societies lose community as they modernize and globalization occurs has been an ongoing theme in sociology since Tönnies' *Gemeinschaft und Gesellschaft*. Tönnies, Simmel, Wirth, and to a lesser degree, Durkheim, Marx and Weber, all concluded that, on balance, the quantity and quality of community is reduced when a society becomes more global, more urban, more industrial, more *Gesellschaft*-like. Simmel's (1936) famous observation that "one nowhere feels as lonely and lost as in the metropolitan crowd" illustrates a common theme of alienation and lost community in classic social theory. More recently, analysts such as Nisbet (1953), Bellah (1996), and Putnam (2000) traced this theme, concluding that community is indeed diminished. Often then, assessments of modern and even postmodern societies include the "eclipse of," "decline in," or "loss of" community. While the nature of community decline remains debatable, there is nonetheless a wide acceptance of this decline and numerous searches for the lost community.

While only a few attempts have been made to measure the decline of *Gemeinschaft*-like relations in Western societies, there is nonetheless a wide acceptance of this decline and numerous prescriptions for appropriate remedies to restore the lost community. First, we will look at the research tracing the decline in *Gemeinschaft*-like relations, and then we will examine attempts to guide our quest toward re-establishing them.

The Loss of the Territorial Community

Although few terms can match "community" in definitional imprecision (Hillery 1955; Sutton and Munson 1976), most sociologists could accept a working definition of community that included a specific geographic area, an identification by the residents with that area, and social interaction among the residents. The lost community thesis often argues that what was lost was a village or small town, a local place where one was born, raised, and died—a local place with inherently intimate, holistic relationships. Tönnies stresses the importance of place in his original description of the *Gemeinschaft*-like community: "A common relation to the soil tends to associate people who may be kinsfolk or believe themselves to be such. Neighborhood, the fact that they live together, is the basis of their union...this type is the rural village community" ([1887] 1957: 257).

In order to assess the necessity for an identification with place for community, it is important to note that when sociologists speak of the "loss" of community, there are at least two distinct meanings (Bernard 1973; Bateman and Lyon 2000). The psychological meaning focuses on the social interaction dimension of the community and analyzes the alienation that can come from the loss of community (Bellah 1996; Putnam 2000). The territorial meaning focuses more on the specific area and the diminishing identification with place (Gans 1962; Greer 1962; Kasarda and Janowitz 1974; Hunter 1975; Ahlbrandt 1984; Wellman and Wortley 1990). Both meanings share the same primary source for the loss of community—the global, industrial mass society—and both describe similar problems—excessive individualism, alienation, and a resultant lower quality of life.

Although the two types of community that are "lost" can be conceptually distinct and are treated as separate phenomena in most literature, they are, nonetheless, closely related. Robert Nisbet, in the preface to the more recent printings of his famous treatise on individual alienation in the mass society, *The Quest for Community* (originally published in 1953), relates the decline in identification with the place and property of the territorial community to the more psychological alienation from close, personal interaction.

Similarly, I think alienation from place and property turns out to be, at bottom estrangement from those personal ties, which give lasting identity to each. Native health is hardly distinguishable from the human relationships within which landscape and animals and things become cherished and deeply implanted in one's soul. (Nisbet 1976: xii)

While some research argues that the territorial community still matters (Morgan and Clark 1973; Hunter 1975; Guest, Lee and Staeheli 1982; Ahlbrandt 1984; Chaskin 1997), some document a decline in the importance of territorial community. The decline in the relevance of and identification with the territorial community is related to the decline in *Gemeinschaft*-like interpersonal relations; both reinforce one another, and both are seen as symptoms of a global society.

The original concept of community was an ideal type that emphasized local place, common ties, and social interaction that is intimate, holistic, and all-encompassing. Tönnies contrasted the types of relationships appearing typically in extended families or rural villages (*Gemeinschaft*) with those found in modern, capitalist states (*Gesellschaft*). *Gemeinschaft*-like relationships are based on sentiment, tradition, and common bonds. The basis for these relationships is in either the family or the "soil" (i.e., living and working in a local place). *Gemeinschaft* is characterized by a strong identification with the community, emotionalism, traditionalism, and holistic conceptions of other members of the community (i.e., viewing another as a total person rather than only as a segment of his status or viewing a person as significant in her own right rather than as a means to an end). Since *Gemeinschaft* is an ideal type, there is no place where one can find total *Gemeinschaft* or, for that matter, complete *Gesellschaft*. Rather, they are hypothetical, extreme constructs, existing solely for the purpose of comparison with the real world. This "gold standard" community where residents identify with the local place, where common ties bind them together, and where all interactions are completely holistic, has never existed. Instead, human organizations and relationships fall somewhere in between *Gemeinschaft* and *Gesellschaft*.

The Loss of Psychological Community

In contrast to the body of research supporting a decline in territorial community, little direct evidence supports the claims of isolation, alienation, and individualism that are supposed to accompany the loss of psychological community. Although distinguished sociologists from Tönnies to Parsons to Bellah have described various social pathologies associated with the move from *Gemeinschaft* to *Gesellschaft*, the preponderance of research shows that psychologically significant neighboring (Gans 1962; Greer 1962; Kasarda and Janowitz 1974; Hunter 1975; Ahlbrandt 1984; Wellman and Wortley 1990) continues to exist. Other research (Lystad 1969; MacDonald and Throop 1971; Seeman, Bishop and Grigsby 1971; Fischer 1973; Putnam 1995) have failed to find the higher levels of isolation thought to be associated with more global (and therefore more *Gesellschaft*-like) populations. The observation that isolating, alienating individualism is replacing community typically receives broad popular acceptance and little empirical support. A few prominent examples will illustrate this phenomenon in more detail.

Bellah's Habits of the Heart

Robert Bellah describes the excesses of individualism that can lead to isolation and alienation in his work, *Habits of the Heart* (1985), and to a lesser degree in *The Good Society* (1992). According to Bellah, many of the ills of today's society result from too great an emphasis on individualism and too weak a commitment to the community. As individualism, selfishness, and greed (in America) have grown, our civic commitment and our sense of responsibility to society have declined. Bellah believes that it is our moral duty to deny our obsession for material accumulation and consumerism and restore the traditions of civic concern and responsibility that have been eroded by individualism. Participation in the community will reduce alienation and "enable people to belong and contribute to the larger society" (Bellah 1996: xxxiii). Bellah's call for the renewal of civic membership is often based on Christian ideologies, biblical accounts, and the beloved community of yesterday. Finally, Bellah contends that while increased individualism is not proven, it is certainly probable (Bellah 1996). As we shall see in the Putnam example that follows, these issues remain unresolved.

Putnam's Bowling Alone

A decade later, Robert Putnam (1995: 70) sides with Bellah and ominously notes that we are "bowling alone" in that "more Americans are bowling today than ever before, but bowling in organized leagues has plummeted in the last decade or so." Putnam claims a decline in the traditions of civic engagement weakening our society and sense of community, and unlike Bellah, he backs up his claim with empirical data. Putnam documents the noticeable absence of the average American's involvement in voluntary associations and the reduced patterns of political participation. The trend is disengagement from membership in fraternal organizations, religious affiliations, labor unions, and voluntary associations, such as women's societies, school-service groups. Thus, Putnam (1995: 75) concludes that due to (1) women's participation in the labor force; (2) social mobility; (3) current demographic trends in marriage and family size; and (4) privatizing leisure time with recent technological advances such as television, Americans are less trusting and the social capital of society is eroding.

Other scholars and critics are suspicious of the documentation supporting the decline of civic engagement and the decreased membership of voluntary associations. Everett Carll Ladd debates Putnam's position in *The Ladd Report* (1999). Ladd challenges Putnam regarding diminishing group membership and the lack of communal ties. While Putnam refers to "striking evidence" of the decline in membership, Ladd assesses empirical records of American trends in civic engagement, finds no such decline, and concludes that

…if the country's civic life isn't declining, but rather churning, transforming itself to meet modern conditions without losing positive energy, we should acknowledge it and get on with the task of building upon the new. An insipid nostalgia, which looks to a past that never was and laments the absence of a perfect present which can never be, can only detract from constructive effort. (Ladd 1999: 4)

Robert Wuthnow's Loose Connections

Robert Wuthnow (1998) provides a more nuanced version of Putnam's thesis in his book *Loose Connections*. Wuthnow states that community-mindedness is eroding and civic involvement is indeed declining, and "loose connections" now tend to suit residents. We are still connected to some extent, but in different ways. Organizational membership is not necessarily decreasing,[1] but rather shifting from traditional voluntary organizations to new types of groups. A rise in support groups and specialized hobby groups demonstrate they have become a rather poor substitute for tradition communities[2] and our loose connections that define them.

The social contract binding members together asserts only the weakest of obligations. Come if you have time. Talk if you feel like it. Respect everyone's opinion. Never criticize. Leave quietly if you become dissatisfied…. We can imagine that these small groups really substitute for families, neighborhoods, and broader community attachments that may demand lifelong commitments, when, in fact, they do not. (Wuthnow 1994: 3–6)

In short, while there are extremely powerful theories associating various psychological problems with global mass society, the analysts who promote these theories have produced much more popular support for their positions than they have provided empirical research support. It may well be that the effects of the global mass society and individualism have been overestimated, and the same may be said for the loss of community. It is a qualitative decline rather than a total loss, and therefore most quests for community proceed accordingly.

FINDING COMMUNITY IN GLOBAL SOCIETY

In this section, we search for and find the community through various avenues. Attempts to find territorial community in the neighborhood are examined. Then the aspects of the psychological community as it is found through voluntary associations and in cyberspace are explored. A relatively new and especially appropriate method to search for territorial and psychological community is network analysis.

Additional evidence for *Gemeinschaft*-like relationships has now emerged from a more objective type of community research. With the advances in survey research and the development of powerful, computer-supported tools for the statistical analysis of social networks, the quantity and quality of social interactions can be empirically assessed.

Barry Wellman (1979) was among the first to demonstrate the applications of network analysis by positing three possibilities to the community question. The possible answers include: (1) community lost, in which communal ties have disintegrated with the rise of industrial bureaucratic nations; (2) community saved, in which the territorial neighborhood remains an important means of support; and (3) community liberated, in which the social interactions have expanded well beyond the neighborhood and are no longer tied to the community. Based on the networks of social interaction reported in his surveys in East York (a working-class neighborhood in Toronto), Wellman concluded that community is definitely not lost, partially saved, and clearly liberated. While significant social interaction occurs, some of it is within the neighborhood, but much of it is outside East York. According to Wellman and Leighton (1979), psychological community (i.e., liberated) appears stronger than the territorial community (i.e., saved).

Claude Fischer (1982) extended Wellman's analysis by surveying a larger and broader sample that included residents with substantial variation in social class, family status, and residence (urban San Francisco, suburbs, small towns, and rural North California). Fischer found social class to be extremely important in defining the nature of social interactions, with what Wellman called the "community liberated" arrangement being especially common among higher-class respondents. They have the means and inclination to move beyond their neighborhoods and establish broad, metropolitan social networks. Fischer found significant rural/urban differences in social interaction exist beyond those associated with social class and family status. Studies also show that in most cases, territorial locality still matters for interactions in rural communities (Goudy 1990; Beggs, Haines and Hurlbert 1996) and it is to the territorial community that we now turn.

Finding Community in the Territorial Neighborhood

Wellman's (1979) "community saved" argument maintains that neighborhoods have survived despite globalization, urbanization, industrialization, and technological advances. Residents still have a sense of local ties for social support and sociability. The local neighborhood serves various functions for its residents providing primary relationships, social support, organizations, local pride, and numerous facilities and services near their place of residence (Ahlbrandt 1984; Williams 1985). According to Wellman (1979), the thesis of the saved community includes heavy involvement of residents in a single neighborhood; strong network ties; extensive networks that are densely knit; solidarity of activities and sentiments; and the mobilization of assistance.

New emphasis is being given to geographically-located, neighborhood-based interactions influenced by issues of spatially defined empowerment, social organizations, and sustainability efforts to weave the fabric of the community. Research shows that communities still exist in which residents identify with an area, known as the neighborhood, and personal interactions may still be examined within the boundaries of the neighborhood (Chaskin 1997). Although individuals may define the boundaries of the neighborhood differently, residents who define the neighborhood in terms of network interactions and personal relationships tend to identify with the geographic unit compared with those considering the neighborhood in terms of the institutions and facilities. The neighborhood community provides the residents a way to deal with large-scale, urban institutions. Saved ideologies stress the importance of preserving existing neighborhoods against the destructive growth of the urban machine. Neighborhood dwellers committed to combating the ills of urban society have been forming local groups at what may be an unprecedented rate (Williams 1985). Neighborhood improvement associations seek to protect the quality of life in the local environment. Membership and participation in these neighborhood associations develop social solidarity among the residents and attachment to the community (Oropesa 1992).

Previous research finds that neighborhood sentiment is often dependent on the social integration of the residents and in turn, the social integration has a significant impact on the attachment to the neighborhood (Austin and Baba 1990). Many factors, such as statuses and personal network characteristics, will influence the level of involvement and attachment to the neighborhood (Campbell and Lee 1992), but it is usually argued that whenever social integration can be enhanced, it is beneficial to the resident as well as the neighborhood. In sum, neighborhoods remain the spatial focus of meaningful social interaction, important political organization, and significant psychological attachment.

Finding Community in Glocalization

Glocalization refers to the combination of globalization (global connectivity) and the local community (local activity). The idea of glocalization can be traced back to Marshall McLuhan's (1962) phrase, "the global village," defined prior to the Internet and the perception that people can use technology to maintain active network ties (both long-distance and local) and use the mass media to stay connected to worldwide events. In 1995, Roland Robertson used "glocalization" to explain the relationship between the homogeneous factors of globalization and the heterogeneous factors of local communities (Robertson 1995).

The determining factors of glocalization include advance development in communication, technology, and transportation. With affordable means of transportation and telephone service, more people are able to easily maintain long-distance ties. The Internet is the most recent technology that has been identified as a destroyer of community (discussed later in this article), yet through the glocalization perspective, the Internet has provided increased capacities to maintain communication and ties outside of the local community (Wellman 2001). While ideas of glocalization are often discussed and referred in globalization and sociological research, few empirical studies measuring the level of, the impact of, or the existence of glocalization have been conducted. For glocalization to occur, a hybrid balance must exist between global society and the local community (Ritzer 2004). Rather than our interactions being solely face-to-face in the neighborhood or anonymous in cyberspace, glocalization of our social networks is a complex series of interactions in-person, online, through scheduled meetings, on the telephone or cell phone, through emails, and in chat rooms or discussion groups. The complete shift from *Gemeinschaft* to *Gesellschaft* weakens community ties, but the glocalization of society combine the local community of *Gemeinschaft* and the global context of *Gesellschaft*.

Finding Community in Voluntary Associations

Much of the literature provides evidence for communities without propinquity (Webber 1963), communities of limited liability (Suttles 1968), or liberated communities (Wellman 1979) that transcend the geographic boundaries of the neighborhood. The idea is that we have experienced an eclipse of territorial community (Stein 1960) and that community interactions now occur outside the neighborhood.

Some argue that community had not really been lost since common ties and social interaction can exist without the local place. They can exist in a more generic, non-residential shared space, such as a school, workplace, church, or social club. The common tie could be to a company or a religion; the social interactions could be of an intimate and holistic nature. Therefore, some analysts argue that voluntary associations, the workplace, or other meeting places can meet the same psychological needs that we assumed small towns and neighborhoods once met (Webber 1963; Rubin 1969; Zablocki 1979; Fischer 1982; Oldenburg 1989).

Urban planner Melvin Webber was among the first analysts to suggest that the concern for the lost local community is unnecessary and that attempts to revive the territorial community are misplaced. In an article, subtitled "Community without Propinquity", he argued that the concerns of analysts such as Nisbet over the standardization and centralization of the mass society are unfounded because "rather than a 'mass culture' in a 'mass society' the long-term prospect is for a maze of subcultures within an amazingly diverse society" (Webber 1963: 29). However, the basis for this subcultural variation is not the territorial community. Rather, "Americans are becoming more closely tied to various interest communities than to place communities" (ibid.). A similar observation is made by Israel Rubin (1969: 116):

The romantic theme that modern man has "lost" his community is fed by the common observation that the neighborhoods, towns, and cities have ceased to serve as significant foci of identification for the mobile man of industrial society. However, from our vantage point we see no reason for saddling the concept with the territorial element.

Rubin, like Webber, argued that the territorial, local place community is becoming irrelevant. Still, the idea of community requiring a local place is a powerful one with remarkable staying power. Thirty years after Rubin's observations, we find that network analysts like Barry Wellman (Wellman and Gulia 1999: 169) still feel obligated to "educate traditional, place-oriented, community sociologists that community can stretch well beyond the neighborhood." Research has established a widespread connectivity in cities. In the shared space, the community ties are often long-distance relationships extending far beyond the neighborhood (Gans 1962; Greer 1962; Wellman 1979; Fischer 1982; Hampton and Wellman 2001).

The idea that community can exist without territory commands considerable support. The foundations of globalization include a worldwide network of economic, political, and social relationships. Recent technological advances and the wide use of the Internet allow for the possibilities of a single world network. Organizational ties and networks found in shared space serve as a predecessor to the types of relationships found in cyberspace. The search for community continues outside the territorial local place and outside the confines of an organization meeting in a shared space to the virtual environment of non-spatial cyberspace. A highly technological and highly publicized example of the quest for non-territorial community is found through Internet searches for virtual community in cyberspace.

Finding Community in Cyberspace

The most recent extension of the idea that community can exist without local place is the concept of a virtual community existing in cyberspace. Now the argument is pushed further: Not only is local place not necessary,[3] neither is shared space of voluntary associations. This means that face-to-face contact is not necessary for the common ties and social interaction associated with community (Driskell and Lyon 2002).

Barry Wellman has long argued that communities can be liberated from traditional spatially compact, densely-knit neighborhoods to a person-to-person community that is completely independent of local place or shared space (e.g., connectivity through wireless cell phones where one interacts with another regardless of location). Wellman (2001: 228) defines community "as networks of interpersonal ties that provide sociability, support, information, a sense of belonging and social identity...not limited to neighbourhoods and villages." According to Wellman, communities function as networks, not local groups. These networks of family, neighbors, friends and co-workers are partial communities that are loosely connected and fragmented (Wellman and Leighton 1979; Wellman 2001). From this perspective, the community networks can exist in local places, shared spaces, and cyberspace. People effectively use the technology of the Internet to create networks and sustain community ties in cyberspace, thus forming relationships that are both meaningful and supportive (Wellman 2001). If Wellman is correct, then virtual communities in cyberspace can provide the same quality of common ties and social interactions that can be found in shared spaces and even local places.

What is the nature of virtual communities? According to much current analysis, the explosion of Internet use provides either a new medium for an expanded, enhanced community (Wellman and Gulia 1999) or a refuge for social isolates avoiding real world relationships (Kraut et al. 1998; Kraut et al. 2002; Nie 1999; Nie and Erbring 2000). What many believe to be the most profound interpretations of communications revolution since Gutenberg, these arguments seem both extreme and mutually exclusive. However, both positions may be correct, depending on how we conceptualize community and what aspects of the Internet who choose to emphasize. We will begin by briefly sketching what is known about the nature of the Internet and then see what that means for community.

Significant, much less definitive, research on how the Internet affects community is rare. A few non-random surveys are the best of what is available, and anecdotes are the more common and less reliable information about Internet use. Further, as Internet use expands and Internet technology evolves, what may be true now could be quite different in the near future. Still, based on preliminary studies of an extremely dynamic phenomenon, it would appear that communities in cyberspace are qualitatively different from the *Gemeinschaft*-like communities typically associated with a particular place. Three differences are especially important for our discussion: (1) Most online relationships are narrowly focused on information processing (Kling 1996). Internet relationships are highly segmented and usually based on interest rather than the more holistic relationships based on family, neighborhood, or work relationships. Your parent, your spouse, your neighbor, even your co-worker may be interested in what you had for dinner, what you think about the local football team, and how late your teenager stayed out last night; members of your Star Trek chat room will not. (2) Virtual communities tend to be more heterogeneous in social characteristics such as race, region, or income, but more homogenous in interest (Hiltz and Turoff 1993). While you are likely to resemble your family, neighbors and co-workers in racial and social background, you may have quite different tastes in music or movies. The online Trekers, conversely, may be of any racial category, educational level, political party, or income, but they will all know and care about the Borg's battles with the Federation. (3) The ties binding Internet relationships are typically weak, reflecting a marketplace approach to community much like that described in the recent analysis of Wuthnow (1998). It is not easy to leave your family, your neighborhood, or your workplace, but a new e-mail address, chat room, website, or Usenet is only a click away. If the cyber relationship is unsatisfying, it is much easier to replace it with another than it is to try and work out differences.

The inherent qualities of cyberspace suggest that the virtual community members will be liberated from geographic and social boundaries, develop ramified social connections, become topically fused in their interests, and yet remain psychologically detached, with only a limited liability toward other residents. In this sense, if we understand the elements of community to include the close, emotional, holistic ties of *Gemeinschaft*, then cyberspace does not contain these elements and, therefore, the environment of cyberspace is less likely to support true community than the environments of local place and shared space. That does not necessarily mean, however, that the cyberspace relationships are the antithesis of true community relationships or even that they are merely weak, unfulfilling substitutes for holistic community relationships (Driskell and Lyon 2002).

The Internet is better conceived not as a substitute for community, but as a new enhanced means of communication with effects on community similar to that of the telephone (Pool 1983; Fischer 1992, 1997). For example, an e-mail relationship may enhance community, just as a telephone conversation could, by leading to more holistic, more personal, face-to-face interactions. The phone, and now the Internet, can be the first limited contact toward developing closer levels of community (e.g., when asking for a date), and they can provide important substitutes when face-to-face encounters are impossible (e.g., when families are physically separated). Most of the interaction that occurs on the Internet is relatively narrow communication of specific information. Although communication is necessary for community, communication alone cannot create community.

Thus as we search for community, the Internet may: (1) *reduce community* with hours devoted to impersonal searches of websites for information leading to social isolation and the absence of community, by any definition of community; (2) *create a weak community replacement* by including significant amounts of e-mail correspondence and chat room conversations, leading not to a *Gemeinschaft*-like community, but to a virtual community of specialized ties with a weak set of secondary relationships; or (3) *reinforce community* by providing the initial or supplemental connections that lead to the *Gemeinschaft*-like community (Driskell and Lyon 2002). All three connections to community currently exist in cyberspace, and if the telephone is a reasonable analogy, our growing use of the Internet will continue to simultaneously reduce, replace, and reinforce community.

The quest for community continues in cyberspace. However, after the first few years of this search, the proposition that non-spatial virtual communities can replace the local place and shared space community as the primary basis for the psychological feelings of community remains questionable. For now, at least, Internet relationships can compliment the community found in the local place and in voluntary associations, but they are poor replacements for the *Gemeinschaft*-type relationships found in the place called *The Community*. Communities still exist most readily, most naturally, and most often when people identify with place—the neighborhood, the school, the church, or the workplace—and personal, face-to-face interactions are still important within the boundaries of a geographic area.

The Final Quest for Community in Global Society

The idea that community is lost with the process of globalization, urbanization, modernization, and industrialization has been part of sociology since the early writings of Tönnies, Simmel and Wirth. Indeed, it is one of the seminal themes in sociology. While they are somewhat similar and often combined, analysis of the "quest for community" research is sharpened by framing the search in the context of globalization and distinguishing between the "territorial" and "non-territorial" (cyberspace) community. The decline (but not the loss) of the territorial community is supported by qualitative evidence from holistic studies. The loss of the psychological community is supported by the works of Bellah, Putnam and Wuthnow.

Network analysis allows a search for social linkages regardless of territorial boundaries by examining the community as a set of interpersonal relations. Quests for territorial community were found in the role of the neighborhood. Communities still exist in which residents identify with the territorial area, often known as the neighborhood, and personal interactions are still important within the boundaries of the neighborhood. While the progress of globalization continues at an unprecedented rate, the importance of the local communities and their local identities have experienced a resurgence. The cultural homogenization model of globalization does not fit many communities.

The search for psychological community in our global society continues through voluntary associations and in cyberspace. The thesis that non-territorial voluntary associations and cyberspace relationships can replace the territorial community as the primary basis for the psychological feelings of community is questionable. Voluntary associations and cyberspace relationships can compliment the territorial community, but it is hard to accept that they can completely replace the *Gemeinschaft*-type relationships found in the community. Overall, the community has been impacted by globalization and both the territorial and psychological versions of community are still relevant and still matter. Community continues to evolve as the traditional memberships in voluntary associations shift and the Internet expands, yet the territorial community continues to provide the basis for much psychological community in our global society.

Notes

1. Christopher Jencks (1987) has published data showing that individual volunteering for charity and service activities has increased during the past three decades.
2. See Skocpol and Fiorina (1999) for a strong critique of voluntary associations' inadequacies for addressing larger community issues. More generally, *Freda Skocpol* in *Civic Engagement in American Democracy* (1999) contends that community development efforts and civic engagement are enhanced by and prosper with an active government and inclusive democratic politics, producing a *Gemeinschaft*-like community.
3. Ironically, references to space and spatial metaphors abound in the electronic environment. Internet users often refer to navigating through cyberspace, traveling the information highway, and visiting different virtual communities around the Net (Hiltz and Turoff 1993; Howard 1997). Further, high technology facilities that could be located anywhere in the new global economy tend to be spatially congregated in high-tech centers such as Silicon Valley (Webster 2001).

References

Ahlbrandt, R.S., Jr. 1984. *Neighborhoods, People, and Community*. New York: Plenum Press.

Austin, D.M. and Y. Baba. 1990. Social Determinants of Neighborhood Attachment. *Sociological Spectrum* 10(1): 59–78.

Bateman, R.L. and L. Lyon. 2000. Losing and Finding Community: The Quest for Territorial and Psychological Community from the Neighborhood to Cyberspace, in Dan A. Chekki. (ed.), *Research in Community Sociology* Vol. 10. Connecticut: JAI Press, Inc., pp. 59–78.

Beggs, J. J., V. A. Haines and J. S. Hurlbert. 1996. Revisiting the Rural–Urban Contrast: Personal Networks in Non-metropolitan and Metropolitan Settings. *Rural Sociology* 61(2): 306–25.

Bellah, R. 1992. *The Good Society*. New York: Vintage Books.

————. [1985] 1996. *Habits of the Heart: Individualism and Commitment in American Life*. Berkeley: University of California Press.

Bernard, J. 1973. *The Sociology of Community*. Glenview, IL: Scott, Foresman.

Campbell, K.E. and B.A. Lee. 1992. Sources of Personal Neighbor Networks: Social Integration, Need or Time? *Social Forces* 70(4): 1077–1100.

Castells, M. (ed.). 1985. *High Technology, Space, and Society*. Beverly Hills, CA: Sage Publications.

————. 1991. *The Informational City: Information Technology, Economic Restructuring and the Urban–Regional Process*. Oxford: Blackwell Publishing.

————. 1996. *The Rise of the Network Society*. Malden, Mass.: Blackwell Publishing.

————. 1997. *The Power of Identity*. Malden, Mass.: Blackwell Publishing.

————. 1998. *End of Millennium*. Malden, Mass.: Blackwell Publishing.

————. 2000. Information Technology and Global Capitalism, in W. Hutton and A. Giddens (eds), *Global Capitalism*. New York: The New York Press, pp. 52–74.

Chaskin, R.J. 1997. Perspectives on Neighborhood and Community: A Review of the Literature. *Social Service Review* 71(4): 521–45.

Dasgupta, S. 2004. *The Changing Face of Globalization*. New Delhi: Sage.

Driskell, R.B. and L. Lyon. 2002. Are Virtual Communities True Communities? Environments and Characteristics of Communities. *City and Community* 1(4): 373–90.

Ellin, N. 1996. *Postmodern Urbanism*. Oxford: Blackwell.

Fischer, C.S. 1973. On Urban Alienations and Anomie: Powerlessness and Social Isolation. *American Sociological Review* 38(3): 311–26.

————. 1982. *To Dwell Among Friends: Personal Networks in Town and City*. Chicago: University of Chicago Press.

————. 1992. *America Calling: A Social History of the Telephone to 1940*. Berkeley, CA: University of California Press.

————. 1997. Technology and Community: Historical Complexities. *Sociological Inquiry* 67(1): 113–18.

Flanagan, W.G. 2002. *Urban Sociology: Images and Structure* (Fourth Edition). Boston: Allyn and Bacon.

Gans, H. 1962. *The Urban Villagers*. New York: Free Press.

Garreau, J. 1992. *Edge City: Life on the New Frontier*. New York: Anchor Books.

Goudy, W.J. 1990. Community Attachment in a Rural Region. *Rural Sociology* 55(2): 178–98.

Greer, S. 1962. *The Emerging City*. New York: The Free Press.

Guest, A.M., B.A. Lee and L. Staeheli. 1982. Changing Locality Identification in the Metropolis. *American Sociological Review* 47(4): 543–49.

Hampton, K. and B. Wellman. 2001. Long Distance Community in the Network Society. *American Behavioral Scientist* 45(3): 476–95.

Harvey, D. 1985a. *Consciousness and the Urban Experience*. Baltimore: The Johns Hopkins University Press.

—————. 1985b. *The Urbanization of Capital*. Baltimore: The Johns Hopkins University Press.

—————. 1988. *Social Justice and The City* (Second Edition). Oxford: Blackwell Publishers.

—————. 1989. *The Urban Experience*. Baltimore: The Johns Hopkins University Press.

Hillery, G. A., Jr. 1955. Definitions of Community: Areas of Agreement. *Rural Sociology* 20(4): 779–91.

Hiltz, S.R. and M. Turoff. 1993. *The Network Nation* (Second Edition). Cambridge, MA: MIT Press.

Howard, T.W. 1997. *A Rhetoric of Electronic Communities*. Greenwich, Connecticut: Ablex Publishing Corporation.

Hunter, A. 1975. The Loss of Community. *American Sociological Review* 40(5): 537–52.

Jencks, C. 1987. Who Gives to What?, in W.W. Powell (ed.), *The Nonprofit Sector: A Research Handbook*. New Haven: Yale University Press, pp. 321–39.

Kasarda, J.D. and M. Janowitz. 1974. Community Attachment in Mass Society. *American Sociological Review* 39(3): 328–39.

Kleniewski, N. 1997. *Cities, Change, and Conflict: A Political Economy of Urban Life*. Belmont, CA: Wadsworth Publishing.

Kling, R. 1996. Social Relationships in Electronic Forums: Hangouts, Salons, Workplaces and Communities, in R. Kling (ed.), *Computerization and Controversy: Value Conflicts and Social Choices* (Second Edition). San Diego, CA: Academic Press, pp. 426–54.

Kraut, R., M. Patterson, V. Lundmark, S. Kiesler, T. Mukopadhyay and W. Scherlis. 1998. Internet Paradox: A Social Technology That Reduces Social Involvement and Psychological Well-Being? *The American Psychologist* 52(9): 1017–32.

Kraut, R., S. Kiesler, B. Boneva, J. Cummings, V. Helgeson and A. Crawford. 2002. Internet Paradox Revisited. *Journal of Social Issues* 58(1): 49–74.

Ladd, E.C. 1999. *The Ladd Report*. New York: Free Press.

Lang, R. 2003. *Edgeless Cities: Exploring the Elusive Metropolis*. Washington, D.C.: Brookings Institution Press.

Lystad, M.H. 1969. *Social Aspects of Alienation*. Washington, D.C.: US Government Printing Office.

MacDonald, A.P., Jr. and W.F. Throop. 1971. Internal Locus of Control. *Psychological Reports*, Supplement, I–V28.

Macionis, J.J. and V.N. Parrillo. 2004. *Cities and Urban Life* (Third Edition). Upper Saddle River, New Jersey: Prentice Hall.

McLuhan, M. 1962. *The Gutenberg Galaxy: The Making of Typographic Man*. Toronto: University of Toronto Press.

Morgan, W. and T. Clark. 1973. The Causes of Racial Disorders. *American Sociological Review* 38(5): 611–24.

Nie, N. 1999. ZEITGEIST—Telecommuting and the Future of the Social Sphere. *American Demographics* 21(7): 50–80.

Nie, N.H. 2001. Sociability, Interpersonal Relations, and the Internet: Reconciling Conflicting Findings. *American Behavioral Scientist* 45(3): 420–35.

Nie, N. and L. Erbring. 2000. *Internet and Society: A Preliminary Report*. Stanford, CA: Stanford Institute for the Quantitative Study of Society.

Nisbet, R. [1953] 1976. *The Quest for Community*. New York: The Free Press.

Oldenburg, R. 1989. *The Great Good Place: Cafes, coffee shops, community centers, beauty parlors, general stores, bars, hangouts and How they get you through the day*. New York: Paragon House.

Oropesa, R.S. 1992. Social Structure, Social Solidarity and Involvement in Neighborhood Improvement Associations. *Sociological Inquiry* 62(1): 108–17.

Pool, Ithiel de Sola. 1983. *Forecasting the Telephone: A Retrospective Technology Assessment of Telephone*. Norwood, NJ: Ablex Publishing.

Putnam, R.D. 1995. Bowling Alone: America's Declining Social Capital. *Journal of Democracy* 6(1): 65–78.

—————. 2000. *Bowling Alone: The Collapse and Revival of American Community*. New York: Simon and Schuster.

Rheingold, H. 1993. *The Virtual Community*. New York: Addison-Wesley.

Richmond, A. 1969. Migration in Industrial Societies, in J.A. Jackson (ed.), *Migration*. London: Cambridge University Press, pp. 238–81.

Ritzer, G. 2000. *The McDonaldization of Society*. Thousand Oaks, CA: Pine Forge Press.

—————. 2004. *The Globalization of Nothing*. Thousand Oaks, CA: Pine Forge Press.

Ritzer, G. and D.J. Goodman. 2004. *Sociological Theory* (Sixth Edition). Boston: McGraw-Hill Publishers.

Robertson, R. 1995. Glocalization: Time-space and homogeneity–heterogeneity, in M. Featherstone, S. Lash and R. Robertson (eds), *Global Modernities*. London: Sage, pp. 25–44.

Rubin, I. 1969. Function and Structure of Community: Conceptual and Theoretical Analysis. *International Review of Community Development* 111–22: December 21–22.

Sassen, S. 1991. *The Global City: New York, London, Tokyo*. Princeton, New Jersey: Princeton University Press.

Seeman, M., J.M. Bishop and J.E. Grigsby. 1971. Community and Control in a Metropolitan Setting, in P. Orleans and R. Ellis (eds), *Race, Change, and Urban Society. Urban Affairs Annual Review* Vol. 5. Los Angeles: Russell Sage Foundation, pp. 423–50.

Simmel, G. [1936] 1950. The Metropolis in Mental Life, in Kurt H.W. (ed. and translated), *The Sociology of Georg Simmel*. New York: The Free Press, pp. 17–25.

Skocpol, F. and M.P. Fiorina (eds). 1999. *Civic Engagement in American Democracy*. Washington, D.C.: Brookings Institution Press.

Stein, M.R. 1960. *The Eclipse of Community*. Princeton, NJ: Princeton University Press.

Suttles, G.D. 1968. *The Social Order of the Slum*. Chicago: University of Chicago Press.

Sutton, W., Jr and M. Thomas. 1976. *Definitions of Community: 1954 through 1973*. Paper presented to the American Sociological Association. New York, August 30.

Taylor, B. 1975. The Absence of a Sociological and Structural Problem Focus in Community Studies. *Archives Europeens de Sociologie* 16(2): 282–84.

Toffler, A. 1980. *The Third Wave*. New York: Bantam Books.

Tönnies, F. [1887] 1957. *Community and Society*. Translated and edited by Charles P. Loomis. East Lansing, MI: Michigan State University Press.

Vidich, A. and J. Bensman. 1958. *Small Town in Mass Society*. Princeton, NJ: Princeton University Press.

Wallerstein, I. 1974. *The Modern World-system*. New York: Academic Press.

Warren, R.L. 1978. *The Community in America*. Chicago: Rand McNally and Company.

Webber, M. 1963. Order in Diversity: Community without Propinquity, in L. Wingo, Jr. (ed.), *Cities and Space: The Future Use of Urban Land*. Baltimore: John Hopkins University Press, pp. 23–56.

Webster, F. 2001. Re-Inventing Place: Birmingham As An Information City? *City* 5(1): 27–46.

Wellman, B. 1979. The Community Question: The Intimate Network of East Yorkers. *American Journal of Sociology* 84: 1201–31, March.

———. 2001. Physical Place and Cyberplace: The Rise of Personalized Networking. *International Journal of Urban and Regional Research* 22(2): 227–52.

Wellman, B. and B. Leighton. 1979. Networks, Neighborhoods, and Communities: Approaches to the Study of the Community Question. *Urban Affairs Quarterly* 14(3): 363–90.

Wellman, B. and S. Wortley. 1990. Different Strokes from Different Folks: Community Ties and Social Support. *American Journal of Sociology* 96(3): 558–88.

Wellman, B. and M. Gulia. 1999. Virtual Communities as Communities: Net Surfers Don't Ride Alone, in M.A. Smith and P. Kollock (eds), *Communities in Cyberspace*. New York: Routledge, pp. 167–94.

Williams, M.R. 1985. *Neighborhood Organizations: Seed of a New Urban Life*. Westport: Greenwood Press.

Wuthnow, R. 1994. *Sharing the Journey: Support Groups and America's New Quest for Community*. New York: The Free Press.

———. 1998. *Loose Connections: Joining Together in America's Fragmented Communities*. Cambridge: Harvard University Press.

Zablocki, B. 1979. Communes, Encounter Groups, and the Search for Community, in Kurt Black (ed.), *Search for Community*. Boulder, CO: Westview Press.

———. 1980. *Alienation and Charisma: A Study of Contemporary American Communes*. New York: The Free Press.

10

GLOBALIZATION AND AFTER?

Continuity and Change in the Politics of Securitization and Responsibility

JARROD WIENER AND JESSICA YOUNG

Whether something else comes "after globalization"—the title of this volume—is an interesting question. The question assumes, of course, that globalization can end, which means that it can be periodized as belonging to a particular historical epoch, and not to another one. The appropriate historical terms of reference to adopt for such a periodization is an even more interesting question: should "globalization" be seen as a process of the *longue durée*,[1] or as a short-term phenomenon of post-Cold War triumphalism? The implications of the choice are great. For, if the most contemporary manifestation of "globalization" is the culmination of 5,000 years of social processes,[2] then the magnitude of globalization's end is nothing short of a fundamental transformation of the overlapping political, cultural, economic, religious, and social forces that propel civilisation itself.[3] This is especially true since "globalization" entered into the contemporary lexicon in the late 1980s, at the earliest, and reached its zenith in the late 1990s.[4] The idea that a few short years after that *might* witness the abrupt ending of the sources of social power[5] that gave rise to "globalization" is a disturbingly profound one, on the order of the proclamation that history *can* end, abruptly.[6]

Yet, there are good reasons to believe that there is continuity in the processes that gave rise to the very rapid intensification of transnational relations that we call "globalization". We therefore do not begin on the premise of the civilizational equivalent of the earth grinding to a halt on its axes. Thankfully, there are good reasons to believe that globalization was simply a phenomenon of post-Cold War exhilaration; in other words, a fad. That being the case does not make any less interesting the idea that "globalization" may have ended; but it does increase the possibility that it *can* end, and at the same time makes its ending much less profound. "After globalization" would be less a product of fundamental social forces at work, and more a result of exhaustion. And, if globalization is seen as a post-Cold War fad, its ending is also much less surprising: one expects a fad, by its nature, to wear off.

Instinctively, the title of this book could be entirely appropriate in the post-September 11, 2001 world-system characterized by the "war on terror." The discourse on "globalization" *itself* arose at the same time as a profound shift in the international security environment. If one accepts the premise that this is not simply coincidental, and that the new security environment caused a change in public consciousness with respect to "globalization," then there is good reason to expect that another change in the security environment could impact on the discourse. In particular, while the end of the Cold War entailed the retrenchment of the state, the "war on terror" entails its marked reassertion. We are not the first to suggest that globalization might be overtaken by concern for terrorism: just a month after the terrorist attacks in the United States on September 11, 2001, Mary Kaldor was among the first to call for a sober focus on the continuities of global politics, lest they be overtaken by the new security environment.[7]

Indeed, there have been clearly identifiable trends in the way in which the conceptualization of "globalization" has evolved over time in public and academic discourses.[8] As we outline below, the debate began on a very fashionable note, touting the global spread of liberalism after the demise of the last viable ideological challenger, and the consequential empowerment of private economic actors leading to the "death of the state"—and along with that, the inability of public authority to assume responsibility for the effects of an amorphous structure of the economy that operates according to its own "natural laws." The fashion in the academic literature has come around recently to a much more nuanced set of questions about the transformation of governance, as we explore in more detail. Our point here is not necessarily that the content of the trends is indicative of a "fad," but the very fact that there are observable trends in its treatment.

Does this mean that it is appropriate to talk about what comes "after" globalization? As we show in our first section, "objective" analysis of global trends of inter-nationalization, trans-nationalization, and liberalization, which might be taken as synonyms for "globalization" show that for the most part these processes are continuing apace. The discourse on globalization—as evidenced by the appearances of key terms in major newspapers and political speeches—has also continued apace. If there is a change, it is a change in the content of that discourse, and it is a change in the perception of the dangers posed by globalization. What we are saying is that "globalization" has not ended, in either an objective or subjective sense. The "war on terror" has not replaced "globalization".

Obviously, we do not suggest that the fact that people talk about something means it is necessarily real in an objective sense, much less that because there is more talk about something it must be more real. There need not be an objective reality at all to "globalization," or for that matter, the "war on terror": they are both discursive constructions. And, we argue, these discourses share fundamental *political* aspects, since they are both discourses on the "securitization"[9] of social relationships, though in very different ways. However, within that they are both political statements about the extent of the state's *responsibility to safeguard society.*

In particular, we argue that the discourse on globalization is one of avoiding responsibility, while the discourse on the "war on terror" is one of a state actively assuming responsibility. Both are *political.* Yet, the discourse on globalization is characterized by priority of the economy over society, the objectification of economic "laws" separate from politics to which politics is seen to adjust, the loss of agency within the structure foreclosing alternative policies, an acceptance of structural risk (as opposed to threat), the structural diffusion of "risk," and within that a politically constructed discourse of helplessness of being at the "mercy" of the forces of globalization that absolves public authority of responsibility. By contrast, the "war on terror" is everything that the discourse on globalization is not. It is the creation of one's destiny over fate. It is the prioritization of security and, in particular, societal security over global systems, the assertion of the state by virtue of an idea that the application of political power is necessary, desirable, possible, and can affect change. It is about replacing a discourse of risk that is at best *manageable*, with a language of threat in a way that makes the threat *eradicable.*

We understand that this began as a specifically American discourse. As such, it has many features of American political ideology that are not new, or peculiar to current events. The change in attitude from one of passivity over globalization to activism over the "war on terror" can be seen as a mere reflection of deeper political trends in the *politics of freedom.* If the history of American political discourse can be characterized as an oscillation between "freedom from" the state and "freedom by" the state, then "globalization" can be characterized as belonging to the former, while the "war on terror" is clearly a paternalist construct about active responsibility. Indeed, the "war on terror" combines a rhetoric of fear with the classic American notion of a "shining city on a hill" that warrants an activist state to protect it.[10] As such, interestingly, this so-called "new" rhetoric that somehow is seen to "replace" the discourse of globalization is actually *not* new at all. While terrorism is new to America, the discourse about how to deal with it is not: it is embedded deeply in the symbols and concepts of American political culture.

DEFINING GLOBALIZATION: FAD, FANTASY, OR FIELD?[11]

Having said that "globalization" might have dropped like a lead balloon in the wake of the "war on terror," it is incumbent on us to define what we mean by "globalization". Obviously, this raises several questions. If it is a *fad*, then is it just that the buzzword has seen its time and is now being phased out? Or, relatedly, could the concept be dying, because it always has been a *fantasy*—essentially a political construction, a rhetorical device—and as such it has been overtaken by a new rhetoric? Finally, and more fundamentally, do we mean that globalization as an objective force might have ended—perhaps because of the reassertion of the state?

Addressing these questions is no less difficult than much else in the study of "globalization"—it is predicated on the assumption that we can define exactly what we mean by it. This always has been difficult, since "globalization" remains an essentially contested term in International Relations.[12] Consistent with the well-known definitions of essential contestability, the concept is not only ambiguous and disputable, but it is deployed regularly both aggressively and defensively.[13] It always has been more correct to say that "globalization" has been a *debate*—often a heated one—about its very nature, rather than a settled concept.[14] It is an ontological debate first: is it a process or a condition? Is it novel or ancient? Is it really global in its scope? And, is it even happening? Then, those fundamental questions are overlain with epistemological and methodological problems: what is the appropriate unit and level of analysis? What are the appropriate criteria for selection? And, what is the proper means for evaluation?

A lack of definitional rigor is a major problem for any social concept, and possibly more so for one that can portend to take the entire "globe" as its unit of analysis, in name at least. The laxity of the concept is amplified by the fact that much writing uses "globalization" as short-hand for a mixture of other processes—notably internationalization, liberalization, and privatization—and as is the nature of short-hands, it often lacks the precision of the proximate concept.[15] It also does not help that it is a concept claimed by a number of different academic disciplines, where it can mean very different things. Finally, it is also part of a discourse of praxis in which journalists, policymakers, and civil society contribute their own understandings. Predictably, we think there is an emerging consensus in the literature on this point: "globalization" has not been very helpful in suggesting a generalized research program.

Globalization as a "Field" of Study

This is not to say that the concept cannot be operationalized in *specific* research programs as an objective concept. And on some measures, especially that of internationalization, the extent of "globalization" is growing.

This makes sense: a lot has happened since "globalization" entered mainstream discourse in the late 1980s, but not everything has changed and many of the factors that led to the surge in globalization as a discourse are still alive and well. Among them are the principles of free trade and liberal capitalism, advancing technology, and international interdependence, both economically and politically, through international institutions and multinational corporations. Companies are still, at heart, profit-seeking private entities looking for global opportunities to increase their profit potential. The "new international economic environment", though no longer new, is not fading away. More than ever, companies are international, and concern continues about outsourcing and mergers.[16] Global trade volume is ever increasing and shows no signs of stopping.[17] There is continuity in this aspect of the global economic system, a continuity that is further evidenced by the popular discourses that centered on the American election. In these debates, outsourcing and the "dangers of globalization" featured as strongly as they did in the late 1980s. The buzzword in this most recent electoral battle was "outsourcing", but the worry was the same: American jobs and American market control lost to foreigners because of the open international market system.[18] The potential for gaining benefits from economies of scale is not going to disappear; larger markets are available for the company that goes "international"; larger markets tend to translate into larger profits. Therefore, there is a case for continuity.

Another element entrenched in "globalization" that speaks to continuity is technology. In the last fifteen years, technology has improved immensely. In 1990, 22 percent of Americans owned personal computers, by 2002 that number had grown to 66 percent.[19] In that same vein, less than a percent of people in the United States had Internet access in 1990, but by 2002 over 55 percent of the US population had access.[20] This drastic increase in computer and Internet usage opened new doors for businesses. Through simple websites, once local, businesses could sell their products to any consumer with an Internet connection, regardless of their location. Furthermore, advances in shipping and communication technology are providing new ways for companies to take advantage of the global market. For example, radio frequency identification technology (RFID) built into shipping containers, in conjunction with automated identification systems (AIS), allows both companies and customs officials to track and log shipments of goods, streamlining the transport system.[21] Technology is improving and will continue to do so. Other things being equal, businesses will continue to take advantage of these improvements, and so, there is yet another reason to believe that there is, and will continue to be a continuity to "globalization" as praxis.

However, globalization is not simply about businesses and commerce taking advantage of international opportunities, thereby creating a smaller more interconnected world; it is also about the interconnectivity of peoples and cultures. As technology advances and the Internet becomes more widely used, cultural items and norms are also crossing borders. For example, Hollywood is making movies that are seen all over the world, and television shows, like "Law and Order" can be seen in over seventy countries around the globe.[22] There is no reason to believe that this is ending. On the contrary, it is more likely that it will increase. Internet radio, streaming video, and chat services mean that someone can sit in an Internet café in Japan while listening to French radio, and watching a Hungarian news program. Not only do individuals have greater access to other cultures' products, but they can get at them instantaneously. However, individuals are not only accessing other cultures from the comfort of their own country, but more and more people are traveling and taking in these cultural products first-hand. Data taken from sixty-two countries over the five years between 1998 and 2002 indicate that overall tourism is growing steadily. Travel volume in the United States fell following the events of September 11, 2001, but the growth reflected in the data from the other sixty-one countries more than compensated, revealing an overall increase in tourism for the year.[23] Availability of phone service and the volume of international calls are increasing as well.[24] People are more interconnected than ever; at least in this respect, the world is getting smaller. Technology and time is bound to improve the speed and availability of these services, making the case for continuity in globalization.

Another argument for continuity in globalization is found in the tenets of neoliberal institutionalism, which argues that states' cooperation in international organizations can mitigate the effects of the fundamentally anarchic structure of the global political system.[25] The popular globalization discourse minimizes the role of the state as the world becomes ever more interconnected, and international institutions are a huge source of this interconnectivity. The United Nations, the International Monetary Fund, the World Bank, the World Health Organization, the World Trade Organization, all of these limit governments' ability to act in different ways, but at the same time they connect the various states and enable them to act together. Through their systems of protocol and procedure, they create a global framework that perpetuates itself. Globalization has continuity in part because of this system. Membership in such institutions is increasing. Of sixty-two countries surveyed over the years 1998 to 2002, not a single country cut down its membership in international organizations. In fact, all of the sixty-two countries in the data pool were members of at least one more international organization in 2002 than they were in 1998.[26] Treaty ratification followed a similar trend: each of the nations in the data pool ratified more treaties in 2002 than they did in 1998.[27] Though state power is not fading away, as some originally feared, the globalization process in the form of international institutions is increasing and creating ties that are difficult to break.

Therefore, if one is content to accept "globalization" as an objective phenomenon, then there clearly is an observable set of social and economic data that can provide the foundation for a research program—and it does. Moreover, it is clear that these aspects of "globalization" are not only continuing, they are increasing in magnitude. On the basis of objective criteria, therefore, it is inappropriate to speak of "after globalization."

Globalization as "Fad" and "Fantasy"?

However, there are other ways to conceptualize "globalization"—as a "fad" or even a "fantasy." If globalization is merely a fad, objective criteria mean little: fads are subjective, and socially constructed. They begin with discourse and end when the discourse stops—irrespective of an objective reality to which they may, or may not, relate. Thus, as a *fad*, globalization might be just a buzzword, and in that case, it is entirely possible that it has seen its time and is now being phased out. Relatedly, the concept could be dying, because it always has been a *fantasy*— essentially a political construction, a rhetorical device—and as such it has been overtaken by a new rhetoric, that of the "war on terror."

We might expect the prolific rhetoric on the "war on terror" since September 11, 2001, significantly to overshadow talk about "globalization." We find that it has. However—taking the *New York Times* as an indicator of political mood— it is interesting to note that these discourses are not competing. Interestingly, there is a relative increase in talk about *both* "globalization" and "war on terror" since September 11, 2001. "Globalization" appears eighty-nine times between January 1, 1995 and September 11, 2001. That increases to 449 appearances in full-text *after* September 11. On the other hand, the "war on terror" yields 770 full-text citations post-September 11. Before September 11, there are 11 hits to a full-text search.[28] Similarly, a search of the *Daily Telegraph* reveals 192 hits for "globalization" in the five years before 2001, and 307 hits in the last three years. By contrast, the "war on terror" yields 27 mentions for the five years before 2001, and 331 for the last three years.

Thus, in absolute terms, the discourse on globalization has continued apace, showing a marked increase in the number of occurrences in major newspapers since September 11, 2001. Were "globalization" really a fad, it would be as easily discarded as not the "in thing." As a political construction, it would be overtaken much more easily by a new rhetoric. If "globalization" really were ending, one would expect the number of mentions to decrease rather than increase. Furthermore, the increase in hits is almost a doubling. At least in popular discourse, it is fair to say that "globalization" is far from dead.

CONTINUITY AND CHANGE IN
SCHOLARSHIP ON GLOBALIZATION

There also have been broad trends in the evolution of research and scholarship in the area of "globalization"—and again, we are not the first to have identified these.[29] The debate began with overstatements, often in a frenzied tone, about the "death of the state." Indeed, the term "globalization" first appeared in the *New York Times* on August 28, 1988. The article, which was entitled, "The Dark Side of Globalization," outlines the dangers of the supposedly seamless international market.[30] The article expresses concern for American companies and American jobs vulnerable to takeover by firms from other nations. It outlines the need for public policy intervention, as it screams of the dangers of this "new international economic environment."[31] Basically, it frets that the world was becoming too small too fast.

That and many other arguments centered around the erosion of effective state capacity: faced with ever-increasing speed and volume of transnational relationships, it was thought that the state was losing its traditional role as a "gatekeeper"—of goods, money, and ideas. As a consequence of this, it was felt that the state no longer was able to govern effectively—the thesis on "diminished state capacity." The possibility of regulatory arbitrage among transnationally-mobile, and powerful economic actors, made fiscal policy at the mercy of capital movements, currency values determined by traders, and corporate taxes driven down by footloose corporations. Thus, there was felt to be a serious loss of national autonomy, and the erosion of difference to an homogenizing force, essentially enveloped within a uni-causal and structuralist account of economic determinism.[32] This strong thesis argued that structural power had shifted from territorially-bounded states to transnationally-mobile economic actors, who by virtue of their transnational mobility, could force the adoption of policies favorable to themselves. At stake was nothing short of the continued viability of the Westphalian model of social organization: the diminishing of the state within the troika of state–market–society complex left the society exposed to the market. It was not only the end of the state as we knew it, but it was the end of social and societal security as well—at least from the International Political Economy perspective.

In International Relations, thinking followed more or less the same lines, but more profound than these *regulatory* issues, the state was felt no longer to be the legitimate unit for the traditional *political and social* roles that it had evolved. Clearly, the "de-linking" of the economy from territorial frames of reference was a part of this, but so, importantly, was the inability of public authority to "localise" politics onto a well-defined territorial space—the very foundation of the Westphalian system. Here, identity politics is the central issue. Without a national identity from which flows the interests and relative values of the nation, what purpose is the state? While International Political Economy conceived of different models of statehood, such as the "competition state,"[33] in International Relations the focus was on the emergence of an "international civil society." This was thought to have become a space of political inter-mediation between the state and the economy—defined not in terms of territory or relative national values, but in terms of a cosmopolitan "global society."[34]

The *politics of people*, therefore, had become internationalized. They had become aware of the events in the four corners of the globe through a twenty-four hour global media, and the ever-decreasing costs of air travel meant that they could also be transnationally mobile: "go there, and do something about it" became the mantra of the exploding number of non-governmental organizations—some of which laid the groundwork for interstate agreements, and which became recognized with the award of global peace prizes for their humanitarian work.[35] Whereas the globe was a very large place even in the early 1960s when most people still crossed the Atlantic Ocean by boat, it suddenly had become quite small.[36] Partly as a result of this awareness—and partly because of the development of liberal cosmopolitan norms that sustained, legitimated, and expressed "cosmopolitics"—individuals (at least in the advanced liberal democracies) came to have a global *identification*.[37] Clearly, those groups—discussed at greater length by other contributors to this volume—who began with high degrees of coordination in different parts of the world to mobilize, to make their views heard on such issues as nuclear testing, conditionality of the international financial institutions, and then most visibly, at the Seattle Ministerial Meeting of the World Trade Organization in 1999, felt they had a legitimate cosmopolitan right to do so. Thus, the emerging global system recognized individuals as international actors for the first time—and indeed international law began to debate the question of whether individuals would remain objects of international law or whether they also could become its subjects. Concrete manifestations of this ethic began to touch ground, in the form of the European Court of Justice, the various war crimes tribunals for post-conflict justice, the International Criminal Court, and most especially the evolving norm of "humanitarian intervention". Cosmopolitan norms were no longer fanciful ideas in the sole preserve of philosophers: armies were quite materially removing state leaders from power and prosecuting them. The meaning and purpose of the state as the final arbiter of social conflict therefore changed to one where there was indeed a higher authority, and even the Secretary-General of the United Nations—that organization whose very existence depends on the continuation of the sovereignty of its membership, and to the politics of accommodating moral relativism—began to suggest that sovereignty no longer should be an obstacle to the effective enforcement of cosmopolitan human rights.[38]

As the recognition of the reality of a plurality of actors engaged in politics took hold in the academy, so too did the trend in scholarship about "globalization" take hold. There were those who denied outright the process of globalization[39] and who took issue with the structuralism of neoliberalism, and disputed the notion of "un-governability" of the economy.[40] Others in the same genre point to continuing divergence in national perspectives on "appropriate" economic and social strategies, even among advanced capitalist states.[41] That debate likely will continue to rage, possibly because it remains unclear how many examples of policy divergence it takes to kill the theory.

The fact remains, there was a distinct "climb down" from the initial exuberance of the "death of the state" thesis, to a more subtle and nuanced recognition that patterns of authority had evolved and changed—but this did not necessarily mean that they had gone away. That understanding was later modified by a "transformationalist"[42] account. This recognized the continuance of the state as a social fact, although the mechanisms of governance of the state were required to change in the context of new realities. Granted, it is often the case that when a target moves rapidly, it takes some time to re-adjust the sights. Once re-adjusted, it became apparent that transnational global processes did not necessarily hail the death knell of the state as an authoritative actor. Rather— in what has been called the "second wave" of theorizing about globalization— there was a consensus point on the idea that the state cooperated to a much greater extent with private actors in the function of governance. That cooperative governance was recognized as operating at many different levels of global society: (1) international, among states in international institutions, and especially cooperation *between* international institutions; (2) cooperation between states and non-state actor; (3) and *inter-mestic* governance, in which domestic networks of governance spill over into domestic arrangements in other states.[43]

Internationally, two phenomena were important. The first is that the institutions of global governance depended to a far greater degree on cooperation with non-governmental groups. This was for two crucial purposes. One was for the input of grassroots level expertise into the design of policies.[44] In that regard, a great deal of work began to be undertaken on the ways in which NGOs could be accredited, involving the ways in which their own transparency, accountability, and internal organization could be ascertained on a set of criteria.[45] The second aspect to this is the actual implementation of aid on the ground, through, for instance, sub-contracting from the international institutions to the non-governmental organizations—with the interesting effect that these different international actors are evolving specialized social functions in the governance of global society. The former have become coordinating centers and finance gathering authorities, while the latter are the foot-soldiers.[46] Theoretically, the implications here are profound. Not only is there evolution in international institutional forms, but such evolution seems to be taking place on the basis of social and institutional learning, leading to functional adaptation, and to specialization.[47]

The second important phenomenon with respect to the change in global governance was the recognition that international institutions needed to cooperate with each other. This had come to the fore in the case of complex emergencies, in which there were simultaneous needs for military action, civil policing, and humanitarian relief. The North Atlantic Treaty Organization (NATO) coined the term "interlocking institutions" when referring to the need for cooperation among the specialized functions of European security institutions.[48] Indeed, the coordination of different specialized agencies became a key feature of the evolution of global governance. Environmental issues, for instance, cut across a range of social systems from the causes of pollution to sustainable development, migration, and human settlements. The management of "complex emergencies," similarly, requires the fast mobilization of a host of specialized functions. A most recent example is the coordination effort for the relief of the December 2004 Tsunami in south and south-east Asia. Simply put, "global" problems mandate "global" solutions, not simply in the sense of their geographic scope, but in the sense of the systems of social governance that are potentially involved, and are increasingly necessary.[49]

This is also the case, possibly to a more marked degree, in the international political economy. While it never has been the case that the systems of the international economy were self-supporting, the legacy of Keynesian protective fire-walls between finance, trade, and development had rendered the institutions of the General Agreement on Tariffs and Trade (GATT), the International Monetary Fund (IMF), and the International Bank for Reconstruction and Development (World Bank) more or less self-contained from their early years until the turbulence of the 1970s–80s. There were references to one another in their Charters, for instance, the exception to trade concessions in the case of IMF-mandated balance of payments exceptions. However, the overall philosophy was that these aspects of the economy were sufficiently discrete in their own terms that coordination among them in the development of their agendas and work programs was thought not to be necessary. That changed in the mid-1990s when these institutions began seriously to have regular consultative discussions with each other. Indeed, the Agreement establishing the World Trade Organization (WTO) called explicitly for greater coordination with the Bretton Woods "sister" institutions to better promote sustainable development.

In addition, a greater range of informal consultative bodies, such as the Organization for Economic Cooperation and Development (OECD), and the G-8 provide forums for discussion of issues, building consensus, and of course, research and knowledge formation that is required to underwrite epistemic communities as new issues of global governance are brought onto the international agenda—such as "trade in services" and "intellectual property rights" that found their way into the WTO, not many people understanding what these were or how they could be traded before the epistemic centers of the international political economy got busy on them.[50] Positions evolve, adapt, and interim consensus points are reached, sometimes long before discussion in the WTO. Indeed, it is often the case that powerful states are able to "forum shop" among institutions: when the US and EU grew frustrated with the weak enforcement mechanisms of the World Intellectual Property Organization (WIPO), they moved the issue of intellectual property to the GATT/WTO. Similarly, when they were unsatisfied with the Trade-Related Aspects of Investment Measures (TRIMS) agreement in the Uruguay round, they launched the process of the Multilateral Agreement on Investment in the OECD. The same might be said of regional agreements, in particular the North American Free Trade Agreement (NAFTA) (whose dispute settlement structure influenced the WTO) and the European Union (EU) (and here the number of illustrations is great indeed).

The point here is that all of this hardly confirms the hyperglobalization thesis of the "terminal state." It illustrates that sovereign states remain important "global managers," especially in agenda setting, in shaping the international institutional and regulatory environment that both constitutes and supports the processes of "globalization" (especially liberalization and internationalization), and in using the prime instruments of global governance—international institutions—to further those agendas.

There is also a bigger agenda of what *is* "international" to begin with. What is being recognized as a "legitimate" issue on the international agenda for discussion, agreement, and eventual scrutiny has both widened and deepened considerably. A good example is the expansion and deepening of the international trade agenda. Trade concerns increasingly "market access" issues rather than simply "border measures" like tariffs and quotas. And, market access can put on the table a host of national regulatory issues that heretofore had been thought to be discretely within the realm of the domestic politics—ranging from service industries to issues of biotechnology. Normative coordination has become imperative—taking the issue of biotechnology, it is clear that the issue of "cultural sovereignty" is an operative norm in the Cartagena protocol including as it does the precautionary principle (favored by Europe) and on the other hand, the WTO agenda is one that seems to favor trade rights on a more restrictive understanding of scientific evidence (promoted by the United States). The issue of forum shopping among international institutions is becoming as great an impetus to coming to terms with some form of coordination as the issue of complex emergencies seems to be in the security and humanitarian fields. In any event, there is a very great and urgent need for scholarship in International Relations and in International Political Economy to come to terms with the economic equivalent of NATO's "interlocking institutions."

There has been such scholarship in the third important aspect of governance, that which we have called *intermestic* governance that we define as domestic networks of governance that spill over into domestic arrangements in other states. What this means is that in the management of the domestic economy, there has been a development of privatized or semi public–private mixed systems of governance—ranging from education to health care to the regulation of securities and exchanges commissions.[51] Such diffuse policy networks often at times cannot perform a domestic regulatory role, for instance, in the banking and exchanges issue areas, unless domestic governance involves a plurality of domestic actors, and also becomes itself transnationalized.[52]

Thus, there is now a much more nuanced appreciation of the location of the state and *society* within global processes. The most important aspect of that nuance is the appreciation that domestic politics, societies, and economies are *constitutive* of global processes. What was perhaps the most interesting, yet silly thing about the strong thesis of the terminal state was the way in which it objectified "the global" as a structural force apart from the state—almost as a kind of "superstructure" to which states were merely responsive and mostly at the mercy. Holding the state as an ahistorical artefact with a high degree of constancy, and setting it within a sea change of power in the international economic systems was to assume an *a priori* naturalness to the state as an entity that was both apart from global processes and unchanging—or at least, normatively, the assumption was that it was a *bad* thing for it to have to change. Thus, the "state is dead" thesis for the most part took place on curious frames of reference—just how much effective sovereignty had the state lost, without really questioning what it takes to make sovereignty *effective*.

What perhaps really killed the hype of globalization was the rediscovery of a paradox (put forth in 1978) in liberal political economy: that the more open a state is to the international economy, the larger the involvement of the state in the domestic economy. That positive correlation between the size of the national public economy and the openness of the state was attributed to the need for the state to manage social risk. Simply put, the more open the state to transnational economic processes, the more demands for the state to retain its legitimacy by acting as a mediator between the destabilizing vagaries of the international market and national stability, and the more responsive the state became to such demands. This argument that began in the trade system was later extended, with similar positive results, to both capital markets and to portfolio investment.[53] As a result of these empirical studies, a debate that began as overstatements about the wholesale transformation of the territorial state has become a much more grounded set of propositions that actually shows the extent and role of the state *increasing* the more social risk there is for it to manage.

While managing risk is perhaps less sexy party conversation than the end of the world as we know it, it is nevertheless more serious, from the perspective of social science, to be able credibly to ask answerable questions. The point is that a new consensus has emerged that centers the analysis back on the question of *what it takes* to govern effectively, rather than posing the question of *whether* the state is capable of governing—both internationally and domestically—while not prejudicing the outcome by assuming the "death" of an unchanging social concept, "state".[54] Therefore, what comes "after globalization"—in the academy—is social science.

DISCOURSE ON "GLOBALIZATION" AND
THE POLITICS OF SECURITIZATION

But since when is politics grounded on reality? Having said all of this, it perhaps misses the point of what "globalization" is all about. Such objective accounts of positive social science mean little to people who are rioting on the streets of Seattle out of a sense of powerless desperation, fretting about the loss of their culture to the onslaught of Hollywood films, worrying about the ending of a social model of capitalism under which they had grown up expecting to have a pension, or being thrown off the family farm because a faceless institution in Geneva made a new treaty. This is obviously not to say that "globalization" is some all-encompassing force responsible for all the evil in the world, but it is to say that this is often believed to be the case. *Belief* matters—especially *belief about the legitimacy of the state*, belief about the nature of social risk, and beliefs about the efficacy and efficiency of the societal defence mechanisms, paramount among which is the state. Belief about the ability and extent of the state to provide societal security are what matter, and this was the whole point of why the issue of the "death of the state" and effective state capacity to ensure national autonomy was important. In fact, it does not matter if globalization is an objective phenomenon at all; what matters is that it is believed to be. And as a dominant discourse, the essential theme of globalization has been that of *enforced social change*.

Clearly, there have been anti-foundationalist accounts of globalization, and "critical" approaches always have constituted an important aspect of scholarship on globalization in the discipline of International Relations.[55] They are beneficial in a number of respects, in particular in demonstrating how social concepts evolve and change over time as discursive practices for the purpose of advancing particular interests. What such accounts have not been very good at is locating the agency that engineers the world to its own purposes through that discourse—agency remains rather amorphous.

However, that is changing. If there is a "new direction" to the study of globalization it is precisely in appreciating the socially constructed and discursively created idea of globalization, along with greater degree of precision in the location of agency.[56] Distinct language games can therefore be identified within the *rhetoric* and *persuasion* of globalization—as forms of *activist* social engineering—which is quite correctly distinguished from a generalized *discourse* on globalization. Maria Laura Pardo has examined the political persuasion effect of globalization discourse in Argentina.[57] Colin Hay and Ben Rosamond noted recently in their study of European states' use of the term that there are both "positive" and "negative" language games associated with globalization. As a positive rhetorical construct, it is used to motivate and enfranchise a political constituency behind a policy preference; as a negative construct, it is used to "blame" unpopular policies on the necessity of responding to "globalization".[58] Forthcoming work by Michael Veseth, similarly, demonstrates how globalization is constructed through speech acts in a range of issue areas.[59]

Therefore, "Globalization" is a social concept with essential contestability. The meaning of globalization remains ambiguous, yet the concept nevertheless assumes a political function as a rhetorical device capable of motivating behavior—either to encourage an actor to take measures that will permit the "embrace" of globalization, or to assume a defensive posture to "meet the challenges" of globalization. A concept need not be precise and unambiguous for it to have a political function. Indeed, rhetorical devices—including the familiar "national interest," "security," and indeed "nation" itself—derive power to motivate behavior from the very fact that they are *not* precise.[60]

State Responsibility—from "Risk" to "Threat"

It is perfectly reasonable, on the understanding that globalization is a discursive construction, to have expected the discourse on globalization to give way to a new dominant discourse—the discourse on the "war on terror" in the United States. This is for several reasons, mostly because the war on terror can be understood, on the surface, as a conservative reaction—an almost reactionary anti-globalization—to the very liberal atmosphere that enabled globalization.[61]

Globalization was about the *porosity of borders*, and the ability of people, money, goods, and ideas to move freely across them. Porous borders and a relaxed attitude to foreign travelers not only enabled the hijackers of September 11 to cross into the United States, but it enabled them to do so under the cover of the background noise of hundreds of thousands of other travelers. It was after all, literally from the "open skies" that the terrorists struck. The globalization of finance and the large-scale flows of capital across borders have made it exceedingly difficult to track the particular transactions from terrorist paymasters to a particular cell that might need finance for an attack.[62] The ever-increasing shipments of goods across borders also provides the cover of scale that makes finding one shipment of arms—or weapons including potentially the materials needed for a dirty bomb—similar to the proverbial needle in a haystack. Finally, with the Internet, websites, and email agnostic to the effects of political borders, physical goods need not actually move across borders—if ideas and knowledge of how to construct weapons of mass destruction can move across borders, they can be manufactured locally.

Al-Qaeda itself is a private, non-governmental organization that presumably does not even exist in terms of a head office or physical location. It is for all intents and purposes a "truly globalized" non-territorial network—one that, lacking a territorial base on which to amass a power-base of its own, uses the open society and its own technology against itself. The imagery is thus of a changing landscape of geopolitics to one that has no landscape at all: terrorists are loose fraternities, possibly non-hierarchical in terms of their organization, fluidly joining for specific attacks and disbanding into the ether to hide. This clearly blurs the traditional distinction between the "inside" and the "outside" of a state, since the terrorist cells could be as easily hiding in the Tora Bora mountains in Afghanistan as they could be members of a sleeper-cell who have been next-door neighbors for several years. It is this very blurring of boundaries that is constitutive of the discourse on globalization. Indeed, the imagery is that of terrorist networks being spiders that effectively hide within the webs of interconnectedness brought about by processes of globalization. In fact, it is an image in which the terrorists are constituted as global networks that use globalization to their advantage. Thus, the first difficulty encountered by a state—as an obviously territorial form of social organization—in engaging a global network was, after "surprise," one of "knowledge" and "definition." It is not surprising that the "war on terror"—like "globalization"—is a big, imprecise, and purposely undefined concept. The "war on terror" was defined as the first war of the twenty-first century, "a new kind of war" unlike other wars, and without being susceptible to the application of criteria for success like other wars.[63] It would be both international—taking the fight to the terrorists—as well as domestic. It would be military, but also financial, economic, and intelligence based. It would use the hard resources of the state—as well as softer resources to win hearts and minds. Finally, it would have clear successes that could be touted, and it also would have successes that never would come to light. In short, it is everything, like globalization.[64]

"Globalization" and the "war on terror" have in common the fact that they are discourses on security, and on state responsibility. The clear difference is that in the wake of the attacks on September 11, 2001, the last thing the Bush Administration could permit was for the discourse on securitization of "terrorism" to remain as it had been under "globalization": the thesis of the "terminal state" and "diminished state capacity" were precisely the discursive constructions that would have eroded the legitimacy of the state. Certainly, this is in the sense of the American state, meaning its political system, its institutions, and its capacity to adapt to the changed environment. But it perhaps also meant the legitimacy of *the state*, as a form of human social organization: the Westphalian state already had been battered, scarred, and left diminished by the transnational forces of economic globalization; would it finally succumb as a viable unit in the face of transnational forces with weapons? It was this context of the essential legitimacy of both the *American state*, and *stateness* itself, that needed to be reasserted by projecting a very capable state, capable of providing not only societal security but also the physical security that is the very raison d'être of the Westphalian model.[65]

Internationally, there was a similar reassertion of the state. The response to the attacks on September 11, 2001 were not against an international ideology, a transnational religion, or a de-territorialized civilization: they were firmly against two states, Afghanistan and Iraq. The question became one of geopolitics over transcendental identities. The language of the "war on terror"— notwithstanding pretence to the "novelty" of this kind of war—had the effect of bringing the response to terrorism within the domain of legitimate state tools. "War" is, and always has been, a set of legal arrangements that are exclusive to states. The "war" on terror therefore brought the response into the *language of states*. Similarly, the announcement "We will make no distinction between the terrorists who committed these acts and those who harbor them" was a clear statement of state responsibility.[66]

But domestically, the anti-globalization aspects of the "war on terror" are precisely about the reassertion of the *national state*, with a vengeance in a very literal sense, such that the state determines the pace and extent of social adaptation—to the point that it may never be the same again.[67] An immediate reaction to 9/11 was a crack-down in the form of a man-hunt for individuals who had immigration violations.[68] The state has increased its domestic surveillance to a point that offends libertarians who worry about the trade-off between security and liberty. Borders are not sealed, but the movement of people has been curtailed, certainly among foreign students. Domestic policing was increased, new laws enacted, in particular search and seizure laws, phone-tapping, and a whole host of technologies were deployed in the service of the state to locate individuals in time and space.

Most interesting was the manner in which the language of *state adaptation* was deployed to demonstrate that the institutions of the state both *could* and *would* be changed to meet the new security challenges.[69] That an act of political will could remodel the institutions of domestic governance—first through the creation of the Department of Homeland Security, and then the creation of an overarching intelligence "tzar" in the Cabinet to coordinate different agencies— was telling for a whole host of reasons.[70] Most obviously, unlike the discourse on globalization that perceived an ontologically *a priori*, structural determined loss of state power—about which, on the strong reading, the state *could not* do anything effectively to change, let alone reverse—here was the state asserting *agency* in the process of remodeling itself better to cope with the new environmental realities in which it found itself. Obviously, there is an aspect of structural adaptation here, but the notion that agency is possible is clearly against the ontology of globalization that relegated public authority to a position of passivity. Within that agential process was a reassertion of "political science" in its most rationalist sense: the approach to terrorism is exactly as the approach to medicine extricating disease from the body—that one can extricate terrorism from the body politic by mobilizing individuals to become the immune system;

all they need is the proper formula, the proper mode of organization and the proper technologies of governance in order to deliver health to the body politic.[71]

Importantly, the continued legitimacy of the state policies rested on the belief in a single, united, and indivisible nation, united by forces of common heritage and values that could be summoned as a powerful rallying point for all of the members of American society.[72] Indeed, nationalism is a powerful force, as demonstrated most markedly when people donated more blood than was required in the days following 9/11, and newspapers began printing flags on their back pages as supermarkets had sold out. Whatever rhetoric there had been of individual loyalties to iconic brands, or of individuals identifying with a cosmopolitan political community, and "de-bordering" the practice of politics in the spirit of pluralist non-state activism very quickly shrank into a miniscule, and quite politically incorrect, set of fanciful statements were set alongside the power of the spirit of the territorial nation. Within this, the Bush Administration did try to re-engineer—with a certain degree of success—what certain essential concepts of the political culture meant—including the discourse on "homeland," "the heart and soul of America," "righteousness," "goodness," and the very meaning of "American" as opposed to "un-American."[73]

Finally, and this is crucial, *the state itself assumed the discourse on the politics of fear*, and in doing so it assumed ownership over the meaning, terms, and nature of societal risks. The culture of "globalization" was a culture of fear to perceived but undefinable "risks"—as opposed to "threats."[74] The nature of risk had become not knowing whether an unseen force would destabilize a currency, commit a corporate fraud and imperil the future of pensions, or act in ways that would cause harm to people or to the natural environment absent a centralized international oversight authority. This amorphous, undefined, set of economic and social risks had replaced the notion of identifiable threat that had been the very heart of the Cold War. During the balance of terror with the Soviets there was a massive insecurity, but at least there was a certainty that there was an identifiable enemy, which had a territorial address, and it was well known that it was pointing a large number of nuclear missiles at identifiable targets. Threat therefore had become risk,[75] and it was the discourse of that *risk* that could not be permitted to continue with respect to the harder form of life and death insecurity that emanated from the risk of terrorism. In short, the stealthy risk of terrorism had been replaced by the threat of weapons of mass destruction.

Arguably, the ownership over the politics of fear had characterized the 2004 American Presidential elections. First, and tellingly, there was the dominance of the issue of security over the issue of the economy. Globalization had been principally about economics—and recalling the 1992 elections here is instructive, particularly the famous pronouncement by Bill Clinton that "It's the economy, stupid".[76] The puzzle that emerged in the election is instructive on this point: the economy did not figure as highly in the rankings of voter preferences as was expected. Only one in five voters ranked the economy as the issue with the highest priority—an issue thought to favor the challenger John Kerry. This is indeed paradoxical, given that the trade and budget deficits were ballooning, and employment was recovering much more slowly than expected. On the basis of objective criteria the American economy was not doing badly overall, but the so-called "misery index" nevertheless showed that voters perceived the economy to be in poor shape. What is more, those voters actually cast ballots against their perceived economic interests, rendering the "misery index" an unreliable indicator of voting behavior. It seems that the electorate voted against their economic self-interest, and the Republicans managed to capture the middle-class, including blue-collar workers.[77] Rather, a major issue in the election was terrorism—by a margin of 4 to 1 (and on this point voters trusted Bush more than Kerry).[78]

CONCLUSION

"Globalization" has not ended, either as an objective feature of the internationalizing landscape, or as a discourse. It has not been replaced by the newest rhetoric of the "war on terror." This is interesting, because one could reasonably expect for the new discourse of terrorism, and a very nationalist, state-based response to overwhelm public sentiment. We have shown this not to be the case, as in fact popular media show that if anything the mentions of "globalization" have increased (sometimes more than doubled) since September 11, 2001. One might also have expected the limitations imposed by the reassertion of state control over society and international transactions in the name of "security" to have interrupted the processes of internationalization. Again, quite to the contrary, objective data sets continue to demonstrate that the world is becoming more open, more interconnected, and in short more "global." It is therefore inappropriate to speak of "after globalization."

In the process of our analysis we argued that globalization and the war on terror are opposing ideas in many ways. Globalization is about the dominance of structure, whereas the war on terror prioritizes agency. The logic of globalization impels state authorities to implement policy decisions on the basis of perceived constraints created by market forces. In contrast, the state's emphasis on security allows it to make policy decisions that is purposefully decided to effect the domestic and global environment. Globalization sets the society as subordinate to the economy, and its "natural laws." The war on terror prioritizes societal security over anything else. It is not at the mercy of the environment, where insecurities emanate from the global system. Rather, through the war on terror, the state assumes ownership over the politics of fear, believing it can change the course of history. The reason lies in its understanding of the dangers within the system. Globalization sees the role of the state as managing risk that is ever present. The war on terror, by contrast, identifies threats that it can locate and destroy.

What these have in common is that they are both political discourses. Yet, what is most interesting is that the political agenda of reclaiming ownership of one's destiny by assuming responsibility in political and social relationships began before the attacks of September 11, 2001. Even before September 11, the Bush Administration was pushing a discourse in the traditional "city on a hill" model. Behind "faith-based initiatives," privatized social security initiatives, and "no child left behind" was a notion of personal responsibility. In his remarks at the President's Dinner of June 28, 2001, President Bush outlined his desire for this "cultural shift" back to personal responsibility and the "city on a hill":

And we can also change America, for those of us fortunate enough to hold positions of responsibility, by setting good examples, by working hard to usher in a period of personal responsibility. We must reject the old cultures which said, if it feels good, just go ahead and do it; and if you've got a problem, blame somebody else. Ours is a group of citizens caring about America who want to work together to usher in a period of personal responsibility. A period where the moms and dads of America understand our most important job will be to love our children with all our hearts and all our souls. A period when each of us must turn to a neighbor in need and say, what can we do to help. A period of time when those of us who have been elected to office understand the high responsibilities of the offices to which we have been elected.

I welcome a cultural shift in America. I'm going to work hard to call all those who care about our nation to join me in changing the culture, and join me in ushering in a period of personal responsibility. And I want you to know that assuming the responsibility of President is a high honor, an honor I hold dearly, an honor I hold sacred, and an honor I will not abrogate to the American people.[79]

The desirability and necessity of political power is re-awakened by the politicization of responsibility, and this is more a function of a particular American political culture than anything else. In the tradition of Leo Strauss, an external threat facilitates the reconstruction of a moral society.[80] September 11 was such an event, as arguably, was the war in Iraq.

However—and more contentiously—more profound still than the neo-conservative agenda is a deeply embedded American political ideology that harkens back to the beginnings of the nation itself. The original American discourse was "the city on a hill," blessed by God. Americans had a responsibility to be an example to the world, a shining beacon of light.[81] First articulated by Governor John Winthrop of the Massachusetts Bay Colony in 1630, this phrase and this idea have been repeated by American presidents for generation after generation. John F. Kennedy, in a speech to the Massachusetts legislator, quoted Governor Winthrop in saying,

"We must always consider," [Winthrop] said, "that we shall be as a city upon a hill—the eyes of all people are upon us." Today the eyes of all people are truly upon us—and our governments, in every branch, at every level, national, State, and local, must be as a city upon a hill—constructed and inhabited by men aware of their grave trust and their great responsibilities.[82]

Ronald Reagan also borrowed from Governor Winthrop. In his farewell address he says, "...she still stands strong and true on the granite ridge, and her glow has held steady no matter what storm. And she's still a beacon, still a magnet for all who must have freedom, for all the pilgrims from all the lost places who are hurtling through the darkness, toward home."[83]

When George W. Bush borrowed the rhetoric—on the very day of the attacks—he was drawing upon a very long lineage in the representation of the responsibility of political authority towards society—yet, with a twist that alludes to the ways in which the "war on terror" would require an active responsibility, increasing the need for and legitimacy of the reassertion of political power. He said: "America was targeted for attack because we're the *brightest beacon for freedom* and opportunity in the world. And no one will keep that light from shining...we go forward to defend freedom and all that is good and just in our world. (emphasis added)"[84] This discourse was always one of responsibility: Governor Winthrop's quote ends with a warning of the loss of God's favor if the puritans were to fail in their mission to be that "shining city on a hill." President Bush gives it a new spin: by re-appropriating the politics of fear, political agency reasserts itself over the construction of a *threat* for which we cannot just sit back and idly wait. Instead, President Bush emphasized pre-emptive action to seek out and destroy the frightening threat: "By promoting freedom and hope in other lands, we remove direct threats to the American people...increas[ing] our safety for years to come."[85] However, America was exporting not only freedom, but the mission itself, asserting that the world must act: "This is not, however, just America's fight, and what is at stake is not just America's freedom. This is the world's fight. This is civilization's fight. This is the fight of all who believe in progress and pluralism, tolerance and freedom."[86]

In so doing, the reformulated discourse adds the politics of fear to the general rhetoric of responsibility to make it the discourse of the "war on terror." In the week immediately following September 11, President Bush spoke frequently of the attacks and he spoke of America's character. Certain themes prevailed. One was the strength of America and its brave, honorable, democracy-loving citizenry of amazing spirit and faith. Another was uncertainty for the future, a heightened level of alert for impending threats, and sacrifice. Finally, there was the theme of justice, of hunting down the cowardly attackers, doing whatever was necessary and taking down anyone and anything standing in the way of that goal. His words created a powerful discourse that can be summed in a quotation taken from his remarks to the nation at the National Day of Prayer and Remembrance Service of September 14, 2001: "But our responsibility to history is already clear: To answer these attacks and rid the world of evil."[87]

These themes take the classic responsibility of Winthrop, that of a passive good example for the world to emulate, and reformat it for the world of globalization and the global threats that go along with it. The war on terror discourse is an *active responsibility*: actively seeking out threats, actively "destroying" them with every resource the state has available. This is a very different discourse than the abnegation of responsibility of "globalization," but the reality is firmly embedded within an ever-globalizing system.

Notes

1. Fernand Braudel, "Histoire et Sciences Sociales: La Longue Durée", *Annales E.S.C.*, No. 4, 1958, pp. 725–53.
2. As suggested by André Gunder Frank and Barry Gills, *The World-system: Five Hundred Years or Five Thousand*, Routledge, London, 1996.
3. Arnold Toynbee, *A Study of History*, Oxford University Press, London, 1995.
4. A Lexis-Nexis search of the *New York Times* shows the first occurrence of "globalization" in August 1988.
5. In the sense used by Michael Mann, *The Sources of Social Power*, Cambridge University Press, Cambridge, 1986.
6. Francis Fukuyama, *The End of History and the Last Man*, Hamish Hamilton, London, 1992.
7. It is also incumbent on us to say that we are not the first to have suggested that this might be the case. See Mary Kaldor, "Wanted: Global Politics", *The Nation*, October 18, 2001. Available: http://www.thenation.com/doc.mhtml%3Fi=20011105&s=kaldor.
8. Ben Rosamond, "Babylon and On? Globalization and International Political Economy", *Review of International Political Economy*, Vol. 10, No. 4, November 2003, pp. 661–71. This also was the topic of a conversation at the Brussels School of International Studies with Jan Aart Scholte in January 2005, to whom we are grateful for sharing his ideas.
9. We use this in the sense meant by Barry Buzan, Ole Waever, and Jaap de Wilde, *Security: A New Framework for Analysis*, Boulder, Co., 1998.
10. George W. Bush. "Address Before a Joint Session of the Congress on the United States Response to the Terrorist Attacks of September 11", *Weekly Compilation of Presidential Documents*, Vol. 37, No. 37. September 20, 2001, pp. 1319–55.

    "It is natural to wonder if America's future is one of fear. Some speak of an age of terror. I know there are struggles ahead and dangers to face. But this country will define our times, not be defined by them. As long as the United States of America is determined and strong, this will not be an age of terror; this will be an age of liberty, here and across the world great harm has been done to us. We have suffered great loss. And in our grief and anger, we have found our mission and our moment. Freedom and fear are at war. The advance of human freedom, the great achievement of our time and the great hope of every time, now depends on us."
11. We borrow this conceptual categorization from James Rosenau, "Comparative Foreign Policy—Fad, Fantasy, or Field?", *International Studies Quarterly* Vol. 12, No. 3, 1968, pp. 296–329.

12. While the concept clearly is inter-disciplinary, we confine ourselves to the literature that touches upon the central problematique in our discipline International Relations, which is the transformation of the state's effective capacity to govern social relations that take place on the Westphalian model of tying authority structures to a well-defined territorial space.

13. Christine Swanton, "On the 'Essential Contestedness' of Political Concepts", *Ethics*, Vol. 95, No. 4, 1985, p. 813. See also W.B. Gallie, "Essentially Contested Concepts", *Proceedings of the Aristotelian Society*, Vol. 56, 1955–56, p. 189.

14. Leslie Sklair, "Competing Conceptions of Globalization", *Journal of World-systems Research*, Vol. 5, No. 2, 1999, pp. 143–63; Jan Aart Scholte, "What is Globalization: The Definitional Issue Again", CSGR Working Paper No. 109/02, University of Warwick, Coventry, UK, 2002.

15. Jan Aart Scholte, "Global Capitalism and the State", *International Affairs*, Vol. 73, No. 3, 1997, pp. 427–52, esp. pp. 429–31.

16. "Trade Disputes." *The Economist*, September 16, 2004. Available online at http://www. economist.com

17. WTO. *International Trade Statistics 2004*, November 2004. [Available online at http:// www.wto.org/english/res_e/statis_e/its2004_e/its2004_e.pdf].

18. "Grappling with Globalisation." *The Economist*, October 7, 2004. Available online at http://www.economist. com

19. UN. *Millennium Indicators Database*, Statistics Division. [Available online at http:// www.millenniumindicators.un.org/unsd/mi/mi_series_results.asp?rowID=607&fID= r15&cgID=514].

20. Ibid.

21. Peter A. Buxbaum, "SST extending supply chain security program to Africa", *Homeland Security and Defense*, January 12, 2005. Lexis Nexis. [Available online at http://www. web.lexisnexis.com.chain.kent.ac.uk/executive/].

22. "Exporting the American Dream," *BBC News World Edition*, February 23, 2004. [Available online at http://www.news.bbc.co.uk/2/hi/americas/3512897.stm].

23. "Total International Tourism and Arrivals", *Globalisation Index Data*. Foreignpolicy. com.

24. "Total International Telephone Traffic", *Globalisation Index Data*. Foreignpolicy.com.

25. See Joseph M. Grieco, "Anarchy and the Limits of Cooperation: A Realist Critique of the Newest Liberal Internationalism", *International Organization*, Vol. 42, Summer 1988, pp. 585–607; and Robert Powell, "The Neorealist-Neoliberal Debate", *International Organization*, Vol. 48, Spring 1994, pp. 313–44.

26. "Membership in International Institutions", *Globalisation Index Data*. Foreignpolicy.com.

27. "Numbers of Treaties Ratified", *Globalisation Index Data*. Foreignpolicy.com.

28. Interestingly, three of them deal with Uganda, one is about France and Algeria, and one of them is the use of "war on terror" by former United States President Bill Clinton.

29. See Rosamond, *op. cit.*

30. Robert L. Dilenschneider. "The Dark Side of Globalization", *The New York Times*, August 28, 1988, Late City Final Ed., sec. 3:2.

31. Ibid.

32. See Richard O'Brien, *Global Financial Deregulation: The End of Geography,* Pinter, London, 1990; Kenichi Ohmae, *The Borderless World: Power and Strategy in the Interlinked Economy,* Fontana, London, 1990; Malcolm Waters, *Globalisation,* Routledge, London, 1995; Susan Strange, *The Retreat of the State,* Cambridge University Press, Cambridge,

1996; Thomas L. Friedman, *The Lexus and the Olive Tree*, Farrar, Straus, Giroux, New York, 1999.

33. Phil Cerny, "Paradoxes of the Competition State: The Dynamics of Political Globalization", *Government and Opposition*, Vol. 32, No. 2, 1997, pp. 251–74.

34. Martin Shaw, *Global Society and International Relations, Sociological Concepts and Political Perspectives*, Polity Press, Cambridge, 1994; Mervyn Frost, *Constituting Human Right: Global Civil Society and the Society of Democratic States*, Routledge, London, 2002.

35. For instance, the award in 1997 of the Nobel Peace Prize to the International Campaign to Ban Landmines.

36. Marshall McLuhan, *The Gutenberg Galaxy*, Routledge and Keegan Paul, London, 1962; McLuhan, *The Global Village: Transformations in World Life and Media in the 21st Century*, New York, 2001; Manuel Castells, *The Rise of the Network Society*, Blackwells, London, 2000.

37. Andrew Linklater, *The Transformation of Political Community: Towards a Post-Westphalian Era*, University of South Carolina Press, Columbia, 1998.

38. *The Responsibility to Protect: Report of the International Commission on Intervention and State Sovereignty*, December 2001. Available: http://www.iciss.ca/pdf/Commission-Report.pdf. See also the *Report of the High Level Panel on Threats, Challenges, and Change*, December 2004.

39. Paul Hirst and Grahame Thompson, *Globalization in Question: The International Economy and the Possibilities of Governance*, Polity Press, Cambridge, 1996; Linda Weiss, *The Myth of the Powerless State: Governing the Economy in a Global Era*, Polity Press, Cambridge, 1998; Kenneth Waltz, "Globalization and Governance", *PS: Political Science and Politics*, December 1999, available: http://www.apsanet.org/PS/dec99/waltz.cfm.

40. Paul Hirst, "The Global Economy: Myths and Realities", *International Affairs*, Vol. 73, No. 3, 1997, pp. 409–25.

41. S. Berger and R. Dorè (ed.), *National Diversity and Global Capitalism*, Cornell University Press, New York, 1996; Colin Crouch and Wolfgang Streek, *Political Economy of Modern Capitalism*, Sage, London, 1997; Hollingsworth, Schmitter and Streek (ed.), *Governing Capitalist Economies*, Oxford University Press, Oxford, 1994; Jagdish Bhagwati and Robert Hudec, *Fair Trade and Harmonization: Prerequisites for Free Trade?*, MIT Press, Ann Arbor, 1996.

42. David Held, Anthony McGrew, David Goldblatt and Jonathan Perraton, *Global Transformations: Politics, Economics and Culture*, Polity, London, 1999. See also Jan Aart Scholte, *Globalization: A Critical Introduction*, Macmillan, London, 2000.

43. This term is meant to depict the international relationship between domestic systems. It is little used in International Relations, surprisingly. Coined by the Pluralist, John Burton, it denotes a system of social organization that does not respect the impact of borders, and as such is a convenient descriptor for the many social relationships that scholarship in "globalisation" discusses. See John Burton, *World Society*, Cambridge University Press, Cambridge, 1972.

44. Robert O'Brien, Anne Marie Goetz, Jan Aart Scholte and Marc Williams, *Contesting Global Governance: Multilateral Economic Institutions and Global Social Movements*, Cambridge University Press, Cambridge, 2000; Alison van Rooy (ed.), *Civil Society and the Aid Industry*, Earthscan, London, 1998.

45. See Jan Aart Scholte, "Civil Society and Democratically Accountable Global Governance", *Government and Opposition*, Vol. 39, No. 2, 2004, pp. 211–33.

46. Thomas G. Weiss and Leon Gordenker, *NGOs, the UN, and Global Governance*, Lynne Reinner, Boulder, 1996; Thomas G Weiss, *Beyond UN Subcontracting: Task-Sharing With*

Regional Security Arrangements and Service-Providing NGOs, Macmillan, Basingstoke, 1998.

47. The possibility to revisit this idea through a structural-functionalist approach to the evolution of structures of governance in global society is probably one of the cutting edges for future research.

48. NATO, Rome Declaration on Peace and Cooperation, NATO Summit Meeting, November 1991.

49. See Aseem Prakash and Jeffrey A. Hart (eds), *Globalization and Governance,* Routledge, London, 1999; James Rosenau, "Governance in the Twenty-First Century", *Global Governance: Review of Multilateral and International Organization,* Vol. 1, No. 1, 1995, pp. 13–43; Martin Hewson and Timothy Sinclair (eds.), *Approaches to Global Governance Theory,* State University of New York Press, Albany, 1999; and Raimo Vayrynen (ed.), *Globalization and Global Governance,* Rowman and Littlefield, Oxford, 1999.

50. Obviously the knowledge structures are more diffuse than this, but space militates against a fuller exposition. See William J. Drake and Kalypso Nicolaïdis, "Ideas, Interests, and Institutionalization: 'Trade in Services' and the Uruguay Round", *International Organization,* Vol. 46, No. 1, 1992, pp. 37–100; Christopher May and Roger Tooze, *Authority and Markets: Susan Strange's Writings on International Political Economy,* Palgrave, London, 2002.

51. See R.A.W. Rhodes, *Understanding Governance: Policy Networks, Governance, Reflexivity and Accountability,* Open University Press, London, 1997; John Shields and Mitchell Evans, *Shrinking the State: Globalization and Public Administration "Reform",* Fernwood Publishing, Halifax, 1998; Jarrod Wiener, *Globalization and the Harmonization of Law,* Pinter, London, 1999; M.R. King and T.J. Sinclair, "Private Actors and Public Policy: A Requiem for the New Basel Capital Accord", *International Political Science Review,* Vol. 24, No. 3, July 2003, pp. 345–62.

52. Geoffrey R.D. Underhill, "States, Markets, and Governance for Emerging Market Economies: Private Interest, the Public Good, and the Legitimacy of the Development Process", *International Affairs,* Vol. 79, No. 4, July 2003.

53. David Cameron, "The Expansion of the Public Economy: A Comparative Analysis", *The American Political Science Review,* Vol. 72, No. 4, December 1978, pp. 1243–61; Dani Rodrik, "Why Do More Open Economies Have Bigger Governments?", *The Journal of Political Economy,* Vol. 106, No. 5, October 1998, pp. 997–1032; Thomas Bernauer and Christoph Achini, "From 'Real' to 'Virtual' States? Integration of the World-economy and its Effects on Government Activity", *European Journal of International Relations,* Vol. 6, No. 2, 2000, pp. 223–76; Brian Burgoon, "Globalization and Welfare Compensation: Disentangling the Ties That Bind", *International Organization,* Vol. 53, No. 3, Summer 2001, pp. 509–51; Alicia Adsera and Carles Boix, "Trade, Democracy, and the Size of the Public Sector: The Political Underpinnings of Openness", *International Organization,* Vol. 56, No. 2, Spring 2002, pp. 229–62.

54. See Linda Weiss, *The Myth of the Powerless State: Governing the Economy in the Global Era,* Polity Pess, London, 1998; Theda Skocpol, *Bringing the State Back In,* Cambridge University Press, Cambridge, 1985.

55. Stephen Gill, "Globalisation, Market Civilisation, and Disciplinary Neoliberalism", *Millennium: Journal of International Studies,* Vol. 24, No. 3, 1995, p. 399; Eleonore Kofman and Gillian Youngs, *Globalization Theory and Practice,* Pinter, London, 1996; and the engaging Ian Robert Douglas, *The Myth of Globali[z]ation: A Genealogy of Speed and Reflexivity,* Doctoral Thesis, University of Bristol, 1998.

56. Michael Veseth, *Selling Globalization: The Myth of the Global Economy*, Lynne Reinner, Boulder, Co., 1998; Jarrod Wiener, "Globalisation: The Political Function of Ambiguity" in Bart Deschutter and Johan Pas (eds), *About Globalisation: Views on the Trajectory of "Mondialisation"*, VUB Press, Brussels, 2003, pp. 19–49.

57. Maria Laura Pardo, "Linguistic Persuasion as an Essential Political Factor in Current Democracies: Critical Analysis of the Globalization Discourse in Argentina at the Turn and at the end of the Century", *Discourse and Society*, Vol. 12, No. 1, 2001, pp. 91–117.

58. Colin Hay and Ben Rosamond, "Globalization, European Integration, and the Discursive Construction of Economic Imperatives", *Journal of European Public Policy*, Vol. 9, No. 2, 2002, pp. 147–67.

59. Michael Veseth, *Globalization and Globalony*, Rowman & Littlefield, 2005.

60. See Joseph Frankel, *National Interest*, Pall Mall Press, London, 1970.

61. In this section, we undertake a discourse analysis of major policy speeches of the Bush Administration in the two weeks following September 11, 2001. There is a number of aspects to the policy response not mentioned here. For details, the reader is referred to John Gershman, "A Secure America in a Secure World", FPIF Task Force on Terrorism, 2004. Available online at http://www.fpif.org.

62. "Teams Set Up to Block Terrorist Funds", *The Financial Times*, September 16, 2001.

63. George W. Bush. "Remarks in a Telephone Conversation With New York City Mayor Rudolph Giuliani and New York Governor George Pataki and an Exchange With Reporters." *Weekly Compilation of Presidential Documents*, Vol. 37, No. 37. September 13, 2001, pp. 1291–1317. [Available online at http://www.gpoaccess.gov/wcomp/index.html]. "But make no mistake about it, my resolve is steady and strong about winning this war that has been declared on America. It's a new kind of war. And I understand it's a new kind of war. And this Government will adjust. And this Government will call others to join us, to make sure this act, these acts, the people who conducted these acts, and those who harbor them are held accountable for their actions. Make no mistake."

64. George W. Bush. "Address to the Nation on the Terrorist Attacks". *Weekly Compilation of Presidential Documents*, Vol. 37, No. 37, September 11, 2001, pp. 1291–1317.

"Americans should not expect one battle but a lengthy campaign, unlike any other we have ever seen. It may include dramatic strikes, visible on TV, and covert operations, secret even in success. We will starve terrorists of funding, turn them one against another, drive them from place to place, until there is no refuge or no rest. And we will pursue nations that provide aid or safe haven to terrorism. Every nation, in every region, now has a decision to make. Either you are with us, or you are with the terrorists. From this day forward, any nation that continues to harbor or support terrorism will be regarded by the United States as a hostile regime." And from Bush's address to the joint session of Congress, September 20, 2001: "Americans are asking, how will we fight and win this war? We will direct every resource at our command, every means of diplomacy, every tool of intelligence, every instrument of law enforcement, every financial influence, and every necessary weapon of war, to the disruption and to the defeat of the global terror network."

65. George W. Bush. "Remarks at the National Day of Prayer and Remembrance Service." *Weekly Compilation of Presidential Documents*, Vol. 37, No. 37, September 14, 2001, pp. 1291–1317.

"But our *responsibility to history* is already clear: To answer these attacks and rid the world of evil. War has been waged against us by stealth and deceit and murder. This Nation is peaceful, but fierce when stirred to anger. This conflict was begun on the timing and terms of others. It will end in a way, and at an hour, of our choosing." (emphasis added)

66. George W. Bush. "Address to the Nation on the Terrorist Attacks" *Weekly Compilation of Presidential Documents*, Vol. 37, No. 37, September 11, 2001, pp. 1291–1317.

"The search is underway for those who are behind these evil acts. I've directed the full resources of our intelligence and law enforcement communities to find those responsible and to bring them to justice. We will make no distinction between the terrorists who committed these acts and those who harbor them."

67. George W. Bush. "Address Before a Joint Session of the Congress on the United States Response to the Terrorist Attacks of September 11." *Weekly Compilation of Presidential Documents*, Vol. 37, No. 37, September 20, 2001, pp. 1319–55.

"Our Nation—this generation—will lift a dark threat of violence from our people and our future. We will rally the world to this cause by our efforts, by our courage. We will not tire; we will not falter; and we will not fail. It is my hope that in the months and years ahead, life will return *almost* to normal." (emphasis added)

68. George W. Bush. "Address to the Nation on Homeland Security From Atlanta." *Weekly Compilation of Presidential Documents*, November 9, 2001, pp. 1599–1630.

"We've passed a new antiterrorism law which gives our law enforcement officers the necessary tools to track terrorists before they harm Americans. A new terrorism task force is tightening immigration controls to make sure no one enters or stays in our country who would harm us. We are a welcoming country. We will always value freedom. Yet we will not allow those who plot against our country to abuse our freedoms and our protections."

69. This was an extremely serious concern in the light of the March 2001 commission on national security, chaired by former Senators Gary Hart and Warren Rudman, that had warned of a "catastrophic attack against American citizens on American soil is likely over the next quarter century. The risk is not only death and destruction but also a demoralisation that could undermine US global leadership. In the face of this threat, *our nation has no coherent or integrated government structures*". See "The New Enemy", *The Economist*, September 15, 2001, p. 16. http://www.economist.com.

70. George W. Bush. "Address Before a Joint Session of the Congress on the United States Response to the Terrorist Attacks of September 11." *Weekly Compilation of Presidential Documents*, Vol. 37, No. 37, September 20, 2001, pp. 1319–55.

"So tonight I announce the creation of a Cabinet-level position reporting directly to me, the Office of Homeland Security. And tonight I also announce a distinguished American to lead this effort to strengthen American security, a military veteran, an effective Governor, a true patriot, a trusted friend, Pennsylvania's Tom Ridge."

71. We are thankful to Dr Peter Mandaville for sharing this idea while attending a symposium on "Globalization and Governance" at the new Center for Global Studies at George Mason University in September 2004.

72. Ibid. "Americans are asking, why do they hate us? They hate what we see right here in this Chamber, a democratically elected government. Their leaders are self-appointed. They hate our freedoms—our freedom of religion, our freedom of speech, our freedom to vote and assemble and disagree with each other."

73. Europeans find totally bizarre this notion that American Civic nationalism makes possible the identification of people through the discursive redefinition of unstable norms. Indeed, the very idea that it is possible to say that someone is "*Un*-American" in how they act or what they believe is *a distinct* part of the continual redefinition

of "Americanism," in a way that it would be unthinkable to say that a Frenchman is "Un-French." And therein to our minds lies the source of a good deal of transatlantic misunderstanding. See *Transatlantic Trends 2004*, A Project of the German Marshall Fund of the United States and the Compagnia Di Son Paolo, Washington D.C., 2004.

74. George W. Bush. "Address Before a Joint Session of the Congress on the United States Response to the Terrorist Attacks of September 11."
    "I know many citizens have fears tonight, and I ask you to be calm and resolute, even in the face of a *continuing threat*. I ask you to uphold the *values of America* and remember why so many have come here. We are in a fight for our principles, and our first *responsibility* is to live by them." (emphasis added)

75. See Ulrich Beck, *Risk Society: Towards a New Modernity*, Sage Publications, London, 1992; Barbara Adam, Ulrich Beck and Joost Van Loon, *The Risk Society and Beyond: Critical Issues for Social Theory*, Sage Publications, London, 2000.

76. William Clinton. "Remarks at Cooper Union for the Advancement of Science and Art in New York City." *Weekly Compilation of Presidential Documents*, Vol. 29, No. 19, May 12, 1993, pp. 791–869.

77. The headlines are indicative of this, for instance, Thomas Frank, "Democrats Forgot the Common Folk", *International Herald Tribune*, November 6–7, 2004, p. 7.

78. That is in itself extremely interesting, since from a policy perspective, terrorism was off the agenda as the war in Iraq took over, which leads to the very important issue of how the Bush Administration seized the policy agenda to engineer the Iraq war as part of the War on Terror, but that is a separate matter.

79. George W. Bush. "Remarks by the President at the President's Dinner." *Weekly Compilation of Presidential Documents*, Vol. 37, No. 26, June 27, 2001, pp. 963–97.

80. See Stefan Halper and Jonathan Clarke, *America Alone: The Rise of the Neo-Conservatives*, Cambridge University Press, Cambridge, 2004.

81. "Winthrop, John" *The Concise Oxford Dictionary of Quotations*. Ed. Elizabeth Knowles, Oxford University Press, 2003, *Oxford Reference Online*, Oxford University Press. Kent University. January 25, 2005.

82. United States. *Congressional Record*, January 10, 1961, Vol. 107, Appendix, p. A169.

83. Ronald Reagan. "Farewell Address", *Miller Center of Public Affairs: Scripps Library and Multimedia Archive*. January 11, 1989. [Available online at http://www.millercenter.virginia.edu/scripps/diglibrary/prezspeeches/reagan/rwr_1989_0111.html].

84. George W. Bush. "Address to the Nation on the Terrorist Attacks." *Weekly Compilation of Presidential Documents*, Vol. 37, No. 37, September 11, 2001, pp. 1291–1317.

85. George W. Bush. "The President's Radio Address." *Weekly Compilation of Presidential Documents*, Vol. 39, No. 42, October 11, 2003, pp. 1371–1412.

86. George W. Bush. "Remarks Before a Joint Session of Congress on the United States Response to the Terrorist Attacks of September 11." *Weekly Compilation of Presidential Documents*, Vol. 37, No. 37, September 20, 2001, pp. 1319–55.

87. George W. Bush. "Remarks at the National Day of Prayer and Remembrance Service." *Weekly Compilation of Presidential Document*, Vol. 37, No. 37, September 14, 2001, pp. 1291–1317.

11

CAPITALIST GLOBALIZATION AND THE ANTI-GLOBALIZATION MOVEMENT

LESLIE SKLAIR

While the events of September 11, 2001 have understandably dominated the media and politics in many parts of the world, the period from 1995 to the beginning of the twenty-first century was a turning point for capitalist globalization, and perhaps it will be seen some day as a turning point for humanity. In 1995 the World Trade Organization opened its doors for business (the ambiguity is intended) and the OECD began, with very little publicity, to plan for a Multilateral Agreement on Investment (MAI). Both these institutional movements signaled the intent of those who promote capitalist globalization, those who own and control the transnational corporations and their allies in state, international and transnational politics and bureaucracies, the professions, and consumerist elites.[1]

Those who were running the WTO and planning the MAI paid little attention to genuinely democratic procedures. The WTO had emerged from the GATT negotiations and the initiative for the MAI came from a little known committee of the OECD. Global trade matters are normally decided by what I have termed "the transnational capitalist class" (Sklair 2001), a combination of corporate executives, globalizing bureaucrats, politicians, professionals, and consumerist elites. In the late 1990s, the scope and level of organization and the ferocity of opposition on the streets in sites of resistance all over the world to various manifestations of capitalist globalization caught the pundits by surprise. To explain the defeat of the MAI and the significance of the battle of Seattle and subsequent battles against capitalist globalization, it is necessary to consider what led up to these two defining moments, namely the counter-movements that began in the 1960s against the status quo, against a multitude of ills of modern society, and the gradual emergence of movements against capitalist globalization. It makes sense to combine analysis of campaigns, networks, and movements and not to make too fine a distinction between them here.

The concept of social movement can be usefully understood in a very general sense as well as in a more precise, technical sense. Here social movements against the status quo are to be understood in general terms to include campaigns, networks, counter-movements of various types with varying degrees of organizational capacity and with varying, sometimes competing, goals. There is emerging a coherent movement against globalization that is beginning to focus on the target of capitalist globalization. However, the strong and mostly positive influence of the counter-movements from before 1995 has led to some confusion over strategy and tactics in the anti-globalization movement. While none of these counter-movements mounted a coherent challenge to capitalist globalization, they all contributed to what is now, undeniably, a variety of anti-globalization movements with the potential to become a serious movement offering a serious alternative to capitalism (Singer 1999). The struggle to resist globalization from above through globalization from below has begun (Falk 1999). The three counter-movements are protectionism (an important source for the localizing challenge to globalization); the New Social Movements that became an important source for identity-based challenges to the status quo; and Green movements (explaining and politicizing the ecological crisis). The radical wings of these movements have campaigned against what I have elsewhere identified as the crises of class polarization and ecological unsustainability (Sklair 2002: ch. 3).

PROTECTIONISM

Protectionism is, of course, not a new phenomenon. Indeed, the most potent argument against it may be that we know only too well how protectionism contributed to the great worldwide depression of the 1930s. Nevertheless, as the World Bank and other august proponents of the perpetual increase of global trade never tired of reminding us throughout the 1980s, many First World governments began to step up protectionist measures in that decade and continue to do so when it serves the interests of big capital. The free entry of goods (particularly consumer goods) from abroad is frequently a contentious feature of global trade. Restrictive measures have been directed at Third World manufacturers whose electronic and electrical products, garments, shoes, toys, sporting, and household goods were said to be unfairly flooding vulnerable First World markets. The interesting twist to this issue is that it was Japan, clearly now a First World country and undoubtedly the most dynamic economic power in the world between 1970 and 1990, that was often identified in the United States and in Europe as the worst offender, with the four East Asian Newly Industrializing Countries (NICs) not far behind. The Asian Tigers, ironically, all prospered from protected markets in the USA as did, to some extent, the economies of Third World countries in the British Commonwealth and the French overseas empire, from various forms of trade preference.

There are two main varieties of protectionism. The first comes from within the capitalist mode of production, conceptualized and popularized in terms of the special interests of local business groups as opposed to the systemic interests of capital as a whole. This form is I label selective protectionism. The second form is what Lang and Hines (1993) call the new protectionism. Hines (2000) has developed this into a more fully localized alternative. A parallel thesis, labeled the subsistence perspective (Mies and Bennholdt-Thomsen 1999), is a more direct alternative to the culture–ideology of consumerism, and thus to capitalist globalization. These will be discussed as part of the anti-globalization movement later.

The tendency to selective protectionism is increased by the belief that a substantial part of Trans National Corporation (TNC) manufacturing industry is footloose, i.e., liable to move around the globe to maximize its profits with scant regard for the welfare of the workers in abandoned factories and their communities. This is quite ironic, as selective protectionism was often used by governments in the Third World to entice TNC investment with the guarantee of protected markets. Import substitution industrialization, for example, frequently relied on what Evans (1979) labeled the triple alliance between the state, local capital and multinational corporations. As transnational corporations tend increasingly to integrate their production and trading processes into globally organized networks (Dicken 1998), the barriers to footloose corporations are reduced. Offshore plants tend to be financially controlled from abroad, they are often rented rather than owned, and their managers tend to have cosmopolitan rather than local perspectives. And, of course, much TNC "foreign investment" is actually subcontracting to local, often largely unregulated sweatshops. All of these factors weaken the ties that such businesses have with the communities in which they are located and make it less difficult for them to close down and/or relocate if and when business conditions deteriorate in one site relative to other sites. This happens all over the world, though workers and communities in the Third World tend to enjoy fewer legal protections against redundancy than those in the First World. A related and complex issue is that of child labor and the struggles it has provoked, overlaid by issues of "Western morality" and underpinned by issues of "economic survival" for very poor communities. A recent example is the study of the garment industry in Bangladesh by Brooks (in Bandy and Smith 2004: ch. 6). The mobility of the TNCs, the job losses that usually follow, and the comparison of cheap imports with goods previously produced at home, increase protectionist pressures among labor and small local capitalists alike. Many local struggles are inspired by this selective form of protectionism.

Selective protectionism is not a wholesale challenge to the status quo though the threat of it is ever present as a reminder that the orderly progress of global trade in the interests of capitalist globalization is from time to time disturbed by voracious TNCs and local capitalists in collusion with government agencies and organized labor. This works both ways. Genuine free traders argue that if Third World markets are to be open to goods and services from the rest of the world, then those markets should also be open to them. The protectionist policies towards domestic agriculture in the USA and Japan, and the Common Agricultural Policy of the EU, linger on as good examples of how powerful local interests can resist the general globalizing trend (Bonanno et al. 1994). With the creation of the WTO, the pressures for free trade and open borders increased dramatically for governments all over the world. And as we shall see below, opposition to this version of "free trade" has become one of the central pillars of the anti-globalization movement.

Protectionism is frequently conceptualized by members of the transnational capitalist class as archaic, and its ideology is identified with corrupt traditional practices. All parties realize this, and so selective protectionism acts as a bargaining counter for the rich, and a bluff for the poor, and mainly comes to life in its use as a rhetorical device to satisfy local constituencies. For example, desperate politicians tend to fall back on it to appease working-class voters all over the world. As Aaronson (2001) convincingly argues, it is emotive issues like food safety, the environment and labor standards that bring people out on to the streets against so-called free trade. Many protests and some social movements contain strong elements of selective protectionism.

NEW SOCIAL MOVEMENTS

Social movements, under a variety of labels, have always been of interest to social scientists. It is significant that social movement research, previously rather marginal, has been gradually drawn into the center of social theory, particularly under the rubric of new social movements (Scott 1990). The argument that even when they are not apparently interested in seizing state power, new social movements (NSM) can still be as interesting as revolutionary movements, has in some ways liberated the study of them.[2]

Globalization is often seen in terms of impersonal forces wreaking havoc on the lives of ordinary and defenseless people and communities. It is not coincidental that interest in globalization since the 1960s has been accompanied by an upsurge in NSM research (Smith 2004). NSM theorists, despite their differences, agree that traditional labor movements based on class politics have won substantial gains for workers (especially in the First World) but have generally failed to transform capitalist societies. A new form of analysis based on identity politics (notably of gender, sexuality, ethnicity, age, sub-cultures, community, and belief systems of a bewildering variety) has developed to document and explain the movements dedicated to effective resistance against sexism, racism, environmental damage, warmongering, capitalist exploitation, and other forms of injustice.

Of all the social movements, the Green (environmental) movements present the greatest contemporary challenge to capitalist globalization. This is paradoxically confirmed by the fact that capitalists, politicians and ideologues (and some scientists) have all tried to jump on to the Green bandwagon and to appropriate their policies for themselves (see McCormick 1992; McManus 1996; Sklair 2001: ch. 7). This is not surprising because green movements are largely based on a straightforward conception of planet earth and what needs to be done at the local and global levels to sustain human life on it.[3] The challenges that green movements posed to capitalist globalization (and state socialism) concerned the consumption of non-renewable resources and the impacts of industrialization. While green movements operate on the belief that the resources of the planet are finite and have to be carefully tended, capitalist globalization is predicated on the belief that the resources of the planet are virtually infinite, due to the scientific and technological ingenuity released by the capitalist system. This belief system argues that there is unlimited potential for replacement or substitution of resources as they are used up and that we will always find ways of coping with our waste and repairing the planet. This, of course, underpins the culture–ideology of consumerism.

We can hypothesize that the transnational capitalist class has helped create a global environmental elite that has been more or less incorporated into the transnational capitalist class and thus is becoming further and further distanced from anti-capitalist deep greens. These deep greens (short-hand for a range of radical ecological views) are diametrically opposed to the business proponents of sustainable development led by TNC reformists. The mission of the sustainable development historical bloc that these TNC reformists have created is to ensure that development (almost entirely defined in terms of economic growth) and sustainability (heavily conditioned by the technical capacities of capitalist globalization) are inextricably linked. All that is possible is done to distance global capitalism from the sources of environmental problems and, in particular, to insulate the culture–ideology of consumerism from such criticism. The relative success of the transnational capitalist class in this endeavor is the reason why it is analytically more useful to conceptualize green movements in the plural, rather than as a movement in the singular and to see the movement–movements relationship as dialectical, not static. Not all green movements have thrown in their lot with the sustainable development historical bloc, though most of the major green movements and many of the smaller local ones have some relations with it. There is a good deal of funding for green groups that play the capitalist game and there can be a good deal of trouble for those that do not (see Rowell 1996).

The arguments between corporations and their critics on the environmental impact of capitalist globalization were supposed to have been brought out into the open by the United Nations Conference on Environment and Development, the Earth Summit in Rio in 1992 (see Panjabi 1997). Problems were identified particularly in the spheres of production and trade. However, what actually happened in the opinion of many radical environmentalists was the corporate capture of the Earth Summit by the TNCs, led by the Business Council for Sustainable Development under the dynamic leadership of Stephan Schmidheiny with the active support of Maurice Strong, the secretary-general of the conference. This coalition blocked any major threat to the interests of global capitalism at Rio. Environmental discourse is a powerful weapon for all sides in disputes over green issues and the corporations used it to good advantage, particularly in the elaboration of the sustainable development historical bloc (Sklair 2001: ch. 7). It is certainly remarkable how quickly so many corporate executives and other members of the transnational capitalist class actively sought green credentials (Robbins 2001; Bruno and Karliner 2002). We can divide these into at least two groups, the critical optimists and the cynical optimists. The critical optimists, like Schmidheiny himself, have done an excellent job of working out what is necessary, individually and collectively, to ensure that the planet will continue to be habitable at ever-improving standards of living. The cynical optimists, on the other hand, see sustainable development as a series of good business opportunities. In the shameless words of an executive from Loblaw, Canada's major food distributor, to an environment summit sponsored by Advertising Age: "If we made a lot of money destroying this planet, we sure can make money cleaning it up" (quoted in Vandervoort 1991: 14). Waste management is one of the fastest growing industries of the current period.

THE ANTI-GLOBALIZATION MOVEMENT

The focus of most contemporary social movements has been on either polarization issues (primarily class, ethnic and gender polarization) or ecological issues, but the greatest challenge remains to make viable connections between them. Many of the successes of the anti-globalization movement, in the short time since its emergence, have been due to its capacity to make these connections.

The globalization of social movements involved the establishment of transnational networks of people with similar interests and, to some extent, converging identities outside the control of international, state and local authorities. There is a substantial volume of research and documentation on such developments (see, for example, Smith et al. 1997; Keck and Sikkink 1998; Cohen and Rai 2000). Some of these new movements were established as a result of and/or in direct response to state and inter-state initiatives. For example, UN conferences such as UNCED in Rio in 1992 and the Women's Conference in Beijing in 1995, spawned thousands of official and alternative organizations and movements (Vig and Axelrod 1999: Part III; O'Brien et al. 2000). Such movements flourished outside the UN system too. The Zapatista movement that rose up in Chiapas, Mexico, is a prime example of how identity-based collective action in even a remote community can successfully connect polarization and ecological crises in a way that attracts significant transnational support (see Nash 2001), and other movements have built on this (see, for example, Wood, in Bandy and Smith eds. 2004: ch. 5).

The challenges to capitalist globalization can be usefully distinguished in terms of the economic, political and culture–ideology spheres. Concretely, these are challenges to the TNCs, to the state and inter-state fractions of the transnational capitalist class, and to the culture–ideology of consumerism. Challenges to the TNCs usually involve disrupting their capacity to accumulate private profits at the expense of their workforces, their consumers, and the communities that are affected by their activities. An important part of economic globalization today is the increasing dispersal of the manufacturing process into many discrete phases carried out in many different places (global commodity chains). Being no longer so dependent on the production of one factory and one workforce gives capital a distinct advantage, particularly against the strike weapon that once gave tremendous negative power to the working-class. Global production chains can be disrupted by strategically planned stoppages, but this generally acts more as an inconvenience than as a decisive weapon of labor against capital. The global division of labor builds flexibility into the system so that capital can migrate anywhere in the world to find the cheapest reliable, efficient sources of labor. Few workforces can any longer decisively hold capital to ransom by withdrawing their labor. At the level of the production process, globalizing capital has all but (though not quite) defeated labor.

Capitalist globalization, if we are to believe its own propaganda, is continuously beset by opposition, boycott, legal challenge, and moral outrage from the consumers of their products, and occasionally by disruptions from their workers. There have been some notable economic successes for labor movements in many countries in achieving relatively high standards of living for their members and political successes in establishing genuinely democratic practices. The emergence of new transnational networks of workers, through established unions and by other means, has been happening quietly. For example, Murray (2000) describes how transnational labor movement organizations (the ILO and the ICFTU [International Confederation of Free Trade Unions]) have begun to use the Internet for organizational, educational, and campaigning purposes through the interactive Organized Labour 2000 conference, what Shostak (1999) terms CyberUnion. New technologies also bring new resources for peasant organizations (Edelman 1998). Initiatives like these have led some researchers to argue that the prospects for labor to play a more important role in the struggle against capitalist globalization may be improving (see, for example, Munck and Waterman 1999; Walker 1999). On the basis of research on European Works Councils, Wills (1999) concludes that TNC-driven economic globalization may actually improve the prospects for transnational labor organization (compare Leisink 1999).

Nevertheless: "Nationalization—the use of national political and regulatory resources to constrain the boundaries of markets to overlap with actual national geographical frontiers—leaves labor deeply committed to the nation as its home, however. This is the nub of labor's problems today" (Ross 2000: 89). Apart from a rather hopeful nod towards labor legislation in the EU, Ross gives no clear idea of how these problems can be resolved, though there are signs that labor movements, notably in the US and Europe, are beginning to grapple with these issues. For example, a study to evaluate the place of globalization and international solidarity in ten leading worker education programs in the USA usefully distinguished transformatory education from accommodatory education (Salt et al. 2000). This highlights the contradiction between those who chose to work within and for the system for their own benefit and those who attempt to globalize labor resistance to capitalism. While a viable alternative to capitalist globalization is unlikely to come primarily from the labor movement in the near future, the active practice of transformatory education (on the shopfloor and in the office as well as in the classroom) is necessary for this ever to take place. It is clear that no viable alternative to capitalist globalization can be created without the active participation of a significant part of the labor movement, globally. This moves us on from challenges to the TNCs to challenges to the state and inter-state fractions of the transnational capitalist class.

The issue of democracy is central to the advance of the forces of globalization and the practices and prospects of movements that oppose them, local and global. The rule of law, freedom of association and expression, freely contested elections, as minimum conditions and however imperfectly sustained, are as necessary in the long run for mass market-based global consumerist capitalism as they are for alternative social systems.[4] In order to work this out it is necessary to problematize the globalization of human rights (see Sklair 2002: ch. 11), but here I focus on the analytically (though not necessarily temporally) prior issue of democratization as a channel for movements that challenge the state and inter-state fractions of the transnational capitalist class. A significant analytic feature of these movements (and the new theoretical frameworks being developed to research them) is the critique of state-centrism. For example, the collection edited by Smith et al. (1997) is subtitled *Solidarity Beyond the State*. The idea of solidarity beyond the state, so difficult for traditional political scientists, sociologists, and International Relations theorists to comprehend, connects at many points with the critique of state-centrism that lies at the heart of genuine theories of globalization.

Working along similar lines, Cohen and Rai (2000: 8–10) highlight six factors that make movements go global. The first and most powerful is that a global age requires global responses; this is facilitated by cheap communications that permit a transnational level of organization; governments have to adapt to the increasing powers of other actors, notably TNCs and social movements; these movements (particularly environmental) have been forced to adopt a global logic for the reason that environmental problems respect no state frontiers; in movements focused on human rights there is an implied universal logic by virtue of human qualities; and there is some convergence on values (notably democratization). This last factor is, in my view, the fundamental link between transnational movements and the anti-globalization movement.[5]

Not all movements need to, want to, or actually do become transnational to achieve their aims. What Smith et al., Cohen and Rai, and many others are really getting at is that more and more social movements need to, want to, and actually do become transnational (or global) for good reason. Precisely because capitalist globalization works mainly though transnational practices, in order to challenge these practices politically, the movements that challenge them have to work transnationally too, confronting officials and politicians at all levels in towns and cities, in the countryside, and in sites of symbolic significance for the state and inter-state system. For example, opposition to what are seen as unnecessary, ecologically unsustainable and class polarizing mega-dam projects in India (Dwivedi 1998), China (L. Sullivan, in Vig and Axelrod 1999: ch. 14) and elsewhere (*New Internationalist*, 2001) has involved struggles with local officials, state agencies, and international financial and other institutions. By making transnational connections, movements against local injustices can become part of an anti-globalization movement, and if the correct diagnosis of the problems is made, part of a movement offering an alternative to capitalist globalization. This refers back to the dialectical relationship between movements in the plural and a movement in the singular.

A notable example of the process of connecting movements and a movement and, at the same time, the local and the global, was Global View 2001. This was a campaign of twenty-four well-known NGOs working in the UK and worldwide for all-party action during the 2001 general election in the UK. The platform of the campaign was extremely wide, covering aid, health and education, HIV/AIDS, debt and poverty reduction, reform of the IMF/World Bank/WTO, investment, labor standards, corporate responsibility, capital flows, climate change, GMOs, conflict prevention and resolution, arms, and asylum seekers. While most of the NGOs supporting the campaign were specialized in only one or two of these issues as separate movements, they could all work together within a movement for a specific political purpose.

Tarrow (1998: ch. 5) provides a useful framework within which to analyze the ways in which campaigns, organizations, and movements can lead to substantive changes. From the study of the emergence of the politics of contention in the former Soviet Union, he demonstrates the importance of political opportunities in transforming mobilization into action. He highlights the following dimensions: (1) opening of access to participation for new actors; (2) evidence of political realignment within the polity; (3) emerging splits within the elite and the appearance of influential allies (Tarrow treats these separately); and (4) decline in the state's capacity or will to repress dissent.

Let us examine each of these in turn with respect to the emergence of an anti-globalization movement and struggles against capitalist globalization.

(1) Increasing access: Tarrow suggests that the easiest way to open up access to participation for new actors is through elections, and historically this is certainly true. As we shall see in the explanation of the defeat of the MAI later, the threat that they would lose votes and find it more difficult to be re-elected was crucial in the decisions of the governments that abandoned the MAI. The role of the Internet, and to some extent increasing access to the mass media, means that different publics can make their voices heard, both to other publics with whom they share interests and to political leaders and gatekeepers of public opinion (Walch 1999).

(2) Shifting alignments: In his study of the short-lived alliance between greens and organized labor in the USA from 1948 to 1970, Dewey (1998) demonstrates the potency of this alignment and the importance that the transnational capitalist class (TCC) attached to destroying it. My argument is that the alliance between greens and labor is crucial for the success of the anti-globalization movement.[6] In many (perhaps most) places around the world the labor unions and the green movements have more members and are better organized and funded than any other movements. The networks and alliances that sprung up around the anti-globalization movement in the 1990s brought many activists involved in the new social movements based on identity politics into close contact with labor and green activists (some activists are members of multiple organizations, of course). While not wishing to minimize the significance of the destructive sectarian splits that have undermined the effectiveness of many radical movements throughout history, an anti-globalization movement built on these alliances will help to focus opposition to capitalist globalization more clearly than has been possible in the past. This has certainly been the case with support networks around the Zapatistas in Mexico and many other indigenous groups (Starr 2000: ch. 3), and the global coalitions against the MAI and the WTO, etc.

(3) Divided elites and influential allies: If one factor is to be singled out as the most important spur to the creation of an anti-globalization movement since 1995, it is surely the divisions that appeared to be growing in the transnational

capitalist class. Splits have emerged within the corporate elite (particularly over climate change and sweatshops), and within the globalizing bureaucracies of the World Bank and other parts of the international financial establishment (particularly over the Asian financial crisis). While the modest Tobin tax proposal (Tobin 2000; Wachtel 2000) to recoup a little of the enormous profits of global financial transactions for social ends has not yet proved acceptable to those who own and control private finance, discussion of it has had a certain shaming effect.[7]

Globalizing and more skeptical members of the OECD and the G-7 have also disagreed over globalization, and the UN system has seen some important internal struggles over closer links with corporate partners. At Davos, and even in the articulation of various Third Ways, the capitalist triumphalism that greeted the collapse of communism in eastern Europe and the Soviet Union has diminished. Prominent individual members of the transnational capitalist class have broken ranks, even if only temporarily, to deplore the negative consequences of capitalist globalization. For example, Bill Gates is on record as a critic of the digital divide, George Soros has criticized the globalization of finance, Sir John Browne (the chief executive of BP) has defended the environment. Ravi Kanbur of Cornell University resigned as author of a World Bank report on poverty and Joseph Stiglitz departed as chief economist at the World Bank, all contributing to the ever-growing critique of the so-called Washington Consensus (see Makinson 2000) from within the capitalist system. WTO produced a defensive website item on ten common misunderstandings, declaring: "Is it a dictatorial tool of the rich and powerful? Does it destroy jobs? Does it ignore the concerns of health, the environment and development? Emphatically no. Criticisms of the WTO are often based on profound misunderstandings of the way the WTO works". A rather bemused feature in *Business Week* expressed the mood well:

It's hard to figure how a term that once connoted so much good for the world has fallen into such disrepute. In the past decade, globalization—meaning the rise of market capitalism around the world—has undeniably contributed to America's New Economy boom. It has created millions of jobs from Malaysia to Mexico and a cornucopia of affordable goods for Western consumers. It has brought phone service to some 300 million households in developing nations and a transfer of nearly $2 trillion from rich countries to poor through equity, bond investments, and commercial loans. It's helped topple dictators by making information available in once sheltered societies. And now the Internet is poised to narrow the gulf that separates rich nations from poor even further in the decade to come. (November 6, 2000: 41).[8]

Sophisticated social scientists as well as political activists may be forgiven for a touch of skepticism on the severity of these splits and the extent to which these people and institutions can be considered as useful allies.[9] This is not the point. The significance of these public demonstrations of divisions over globalization is that they send messages of confusion to the public at large, and the anti-globalization movement can use them to great advantage. Ashwin (2000: 110) argued that "governments and the international financial institutions are in the midst of a mini-crisis of confidence regarding the potential negative effects of liberalization [meaning capitalist globalization]". Despite the "war on terrorism" the mini-crisis has been escalating ever since, particularly in light of fears of a global recession combined with revelations about state-sponsored brutality against peaceful protesters against the many forms of capitalist globalization.

There are at least two ways to read this evidence. The first is the cynical view of co-option and selling-out. Certainly, my thesis of the creation of the sustainable development historical bloc might err on the side of cynicism. Members of the transnational capitalist class who appear to take sustainable development seriously and who appear to acknowledge ecological crisis (like Sir John Browne and those other CEOs who took their companies out of the anti-Kyoto Global Climate Coalition), may simply be playing at gesture politics. The second view is the thesis of organizational learning. This means that movements might actually convert some influential members of the transnational capitalist class to their views on important issues. In his critique of what he terms predatory globalization, for example, Falk (1999) argues that neoliberals have undermined the social contract between state and society. In his view, a global civil society based on normative ideas of sustainable development, human rights, and cosmopolitan democracy (not to be confused with what he calls "closet Marxism") can replace globalization from above.[10]

This analysis suggests that not all victories and defeats are matters of crude power struggles but that ideals matter. In their discussion of the role of NGOs in the human rights field, Steiner and Alston (2000) argue that these organizations have had some real successes, notably the 1997 Ottowa Landmine Treaty, the 1998 Rome Statute on the International Criminal Court, and (less convincingly) the 1999 Seattle WTO meeting. Another significant issue is the blurring of the distinction between the insiders and the outsiders as NGO representatives have become part of governmental delegations. They have also increasingly become key partners in the delivery of humanitarian and other forms of development assistance, partners with government in performing a variety of functions such as human rights education, the monitoring of voluntary codes of conduct and even the delivery of basic social services, and even partners with business and labor unions in various areas. While it seems unlikely to me, it is certainly possible that as many members of the transnational capitalist class are influenced by the anti-globalization movement as vice versa. Time will tell!

(4) Tarrow's final dimension is repression and facilitation: In a striking and rather frightening forecast of what capitalist globalization could become, Jones argues:

There is some reason to believe that the globalization process (and the modernization project) will be less integrative in the future than in the past, thereby leaving space for cultural integrity in the many backwaters of what I term Blade Runner [after the dystopian Ridley Scott film] capitalism. This is primarily due to the fact that the organizational drivers of the international economy and the globalization process, are impelled by a strict and simple logic: to improve their cost and revenue structures. If a site has nothing to offer these firms, they will bypass it. Many lesser developed countries and indigenous cultures fit this profile. (1998: 288)

In Blade Runner capitalism the techno-economy of the formal sector needs the grunge economy of the informal sector. Here I focus on the violence and polarization implicit in the Blade Runner scenario rather than on Jones' confidence that it has potential for saving indigenous cultures.[11] The vision of Los Angeles, where the film is set, is not too far distant from many cities of the present: sharp high-tech corporate and official architecture interspersed with piles of discarded people and garbage, policed and menaced by ruthless killers operating under no recognizable rule of law. It would be an exaggeration to characterize the sites of resistance since 1995 in these terms. However, one of the enduring symbols of the anti-globalization movement is the picture of heavily-armoured militia protecting Niketown in Seattle, an image straight out of Blade Runner.

In democracies, even the flawed democracies of the First World, the costs of repression for the authorities (official or, on occasion, corporate) should not be underestimated. There is no doubt that the costs of the repression of protests against the Vietnam War in the 1960s and 1970s were an important factor in persuading the US government and their allies to disengage. The same can be said about the anti-Poll Tax protests in Britain, anti-World Bank and IMF food riots in the Third World, and many other movements. To these we can add the costs to transnational corporations and local officials of repressing protests against dams and involuntary relocation of large numbers of people (in India and China, for example), industrial pollution hazards (all over the world), controversial power stations (Enron in India), and threats to the habitats of indigenous peoples (in Nigeria, for example). The great transformation that occurred in the 1990s was the speed and scale of communications making almost instantaneous information available through what Langman and his colleagues (2002) have termed cyberactivism. As all these social movements and protests become transnationalized, as they become parts of many interlocking global networks and, simply, as they spread the word about the real nature of how the transnational capitalist class reacts when challenged, the potential for a movement against capitalist globalization increases. The section on the battle of Seattle below examines some possible consequences of the violent repression of protesters as members of the various fractions of the transnational capitalist class (mostly peace-loving men and women in their own spheres) were besieged in cities all over the world.

Tarrow argues that any decline in the state's capacity or will to repress (though it is not only the state that can repress) will lead to more political opportunities for contentious social movements to exploit. The first decade of the twenty-first century will probably be decisive in at least one respect, namely the extent to which political leaders in each state are prepared to ignore the rule of law in order to discourage protests against globalization. If the rule of law prevails then this will undoubtedly facilitate the movement for the globalization of human rights. However, the principle of the rule of law absolutely depends on an ongoing critical dialog with actually existing legal codes especially, as Rajagopal (2003) so powerfully argues, existing codes of international law. The evidence does suggest that we are entering a new transnational cycle of contention.[12] However, the question of exactly what these movements are trying to achieve needs to be addressed. For this we must move on to studies of anti-corporate movements. The key issue, according to the analysis of programs of social movements derived from their websites by Starr (2000), is the unaccountability of global institutions, particularly globalizing corporations.[13] However, anti-corporate, for critics of globalization, does not necessarily mean anti-capitalist. Starr argues that the foundational logic of the dominant global system is not necessarily capitalist, but involves a complex of factors including economic growth; enclosure of the commons and the increasing concentration of economic power in the hands of bigger and bigger corporations; dependency; colonialism; and anti-democratic tendencies (as consumerism replaces the rights of citizenship). This is a very mixed bag but certainly all these and more are to be found within anti-globalization movements.

It is easy to draw the conclusion from all this that it is not capitalism that is the enemy, but big business, whether private or state. Economic globalization driven by major corporations (or faceless bureaucracies) is an easy target, made even easier by the fact that the ownership class has been transformed. Small capitalists are gradually being squeezed out of the system, families are being replaced by unrelated blocks of stockholders, and human corporate owners are being replaced by non-human computer programs that move investments funds around according to abstruse formulas, enriching the few while destroying lives and communities.

Starr's analysis covers a bewildering variety of anti-corporate movements and protests, from those involved in the struggles against structural adjustment, for peace and human rights (for example, the Permanent People's Tribunal on TNC violations of human rights), and for land reform. The US Greenbelt Alliance asks: "Imagine your metropolitan area if you had to get all your food and take all your vacations within a fifty mile radius" (ibid.: 63). The cyberpunk hackers, crackers, phreakers, cyphers, and cyberchic not only expose corporate crimes and misdemeanors, they also penetrate corporate and governmental computer systems and cause occasional havoc (73–78). But generally these groups do not articulate an alternative vision.

Through delinking and relocalization, the refusal of distant authority can become a reality, the first step in creating an alternative to globalization. Pacione

(1997) shows how Local Exchange Trading Systems (LETS) are already beginning to do this. Anarchism, while it has failed to discard its bad but not totally fair reputation for chaos and violence, has created movements that focus on small-scale local autonomy against socialist and capitalist statism that have inspired many others. Movements for local sustainable development (for example permaculture), groups organized around the "small is beautiful" approach, bioregionalism, urban agriculture, farmers' markets, sustainable cuisine from the Chefs' Collaborative, small business groups growing out of anti-WalMart campaigns, local barter economies (Ithica HOURS, LETS, Grain de Sel in France, for example) and sovereignty movements of indigenous peoples and even religious nationalists, all offer alternatives in their own spheres to a corporate world (Starr 2000: ch. 4).[14] However, capitalist globalization could accommodate and subvert most of these initiatives and turn them into variations on the consumerist theme.[15]

Starr not unreasonably concludes that the only viable alternative is some kind of post-corporate relocalized economy, but the politics of the transition to this are, as yet, difficult to discern. The modern capitalist state obviously could not lead humanity to this destination, even if most of us wanted to go there.[16] Localism, therefore, appears the more convincing strategy, for example, shortening food links would be one way to undermine globalization of agriculture, retailing, and trade. Starr commends the principle of site here to sell here (Lang and Hines 1993). This new protectionism is a challenging set of ideas that presents, in theory at least, a viable alternative to globalization, though not to capitalism.

Hines has developed this thesis under the somewhat playful title *Localization: A Global Manifesto* (2000). He defines globalization narrowly as: "the process by which governments sign away the rights of their citizens in favour of speculative investors and transnational corporations" (Hines 2000: 4) and argues that it leads to the erosion of wages, welfare, and environmental protection. His alternative is localization. Globalization, therefore, is delocalization. Actually, most studies of globalization, including my own work on globalizing corporations and the transnational capitalist class, suggest that exploiting local workforces, resources, environments, symbols, and cultures is the basis of corporate profits. This exploitation is not new though the scale of it is, and it does not necessarily destroy the local, which changes anyway. Localization for Hines does not mean overpowering state control, "merely that governments provide the policy framework which allows people and businesses to rediversify their own local economies" (Hines 2000: 29). There is one important question that needs to be asked here. Why are governments not doing all this now? (Most would claim they were.) Hines proposes ten criteria of a sustainable community: basically good facilities accessible to all; good education, work and local economy; ecology; lifestyles, information, culture, participation, and ongoing improvements. Against this is the triple threat of globalization: more international competitiveness and less public expenditure and community activity; opening of government procurement to international competition that disadvantages local providers; and competitive agribusiness that undermines agriculture to feed people locally (ch. 5). How are all these admirable goals to be achieved? Hines argues that single issue groups will never achieve much unless they challenge the need to be internationally competitive in the interests of regional and national self-reliance. International development requires that the WTO be revised to become a General Agreement for Sustainable Trade (not an easy task when companies have to site here to sell here).[17] While the critique of international competitiveness is a very significant part of the alternative to capitalist globalization, it is not exactly a rallying cry that is likely to mobilize the population and, as Hines conceptualizes it, the implications for workers and farmers in the Third World are far from clear. So, it is not surprising that such views are usually seen as variations on the old imperialist protectionism rather than a genuinely new version.

The same can be said for the subsistence perspective of Mies and Bennholdt-Thomsen (1999). The title of the original German edition was *A Cow for Hillary*, referring to the deprived condition of the wife of the then US President when she met some women in Bangladesh. Poor Hillary, no cow, no income of her own, and only one daughter! This true story teaches us five lessons:

(*i*)   the importance of the view from below;

(*ii*) the importance of people's control over their means of subsistence;

(*iii*) the fact that such control gives women pride, dignity, courage, and a sense of equality (the Bangladeshi women felt no inferiority to Hillary);

(*iv*) the positive mindset of the women in Bangladesh (and, potentially, people everywhere); and

(*v*)   the need to abandon First World/Third World schizophrenia. We know that it exists, they say, but we need not accept it. (ibid.: 4).

The subsistence perspective (SP) explicitly rejects the developmental model of catching up. Rather than poor people being brought to the destructive and unsustainable standards of living of the rich, everyone should be encouraged to live a subsistence existence. Mies and Bennholdt-Thomsen are realistic about this apparently absurd thesis. They describe a Women and Ecology congress in Cologne in 1986 where speaker after speaker brought up objections to the SP. It was criticized for being unfriendly to women (who would be the first to make sacrifices); for being too moralistic (economics, after all, is about interests); for being good for the rich in the First World who can afford to buy ethically (but not for the poor); that it sounded like a fascist blood and soil ideology; it was Luddite; it might work for small groups, but cannot destroy capitalism; and, the final barb, it is apolitical, a "patchwork quilt of a thousand subsistence communes or eco-villages" (q. in ibid.: 15). The authors naturally argue energetically against all these objections. The central analytical thrust in the SP is the critique of the concepts of need and sufficiency and this leads to a critique of the culture–ideology of consumerism (though not in these terms). Chapters on subsistence and agriculture, the market, the city, the commons, wage labor, women's liberation, and politics, while not totally convincing are no less so than most rather more sensible alternatives to capitalist globalization. Both the localization and the subsistence perspectives have added vital components to the intellectual armory of the movement against capitalist globalization.

THE BATTLE OF SEATTLE AND AFTER

Walden Bello was not alone when he stated in 2001: "The last year will probably go down as one of those defining moments in the history of the world-economy, like 1929" (Bello 2001: 71). The year in question began in December 1999 with a WTO summit meeting in Seattle. Despite many differences among the protesters, Bello claims that "most of them were united by one thing: their opposition to the expansion of a system that promoted corporate-led globalization at the expense of social goals like justice, community, national sovereignty, cultural diversity and ecological sustainability" (Bell 2001: 72). In other words, the many anti-globalization movements that had been fermenting over the last decades of the twentieth century were transforming themselves into a singular movement against capitalist globalization.[18]

The WTO was born with a reputation for lack of transparency, undemocratic procedures, and an inbuilt susceptibility to corporate lobbying (Barker and Mander 2000). Its meeting in Seattle was well-publicized and it was evident that those promoting capitalist globalization saw it as a good opportunity for positive media coverage, after all, the mission of the WTO was to make us all prosperous (Dunkley 2000; O'Brien et al. 2000: ch. 3). The organization of the protest against the WTO in Seattle has now passed into activist folklore, and with the help of the capitalist-controlled mass media, into the collective memories of people all over the world. The presence of hundreds of thousands of protesters confronting large numbers of heavily armored police forced the WTO to abandon the meeting and beat a hasty retreat. Some violence occurred, mostly to property, and groups of protesters attacked global brand stores, such as McDonald's and Nike.[19] This demonstration of opposition to capitalist globalization was rapidly followed in the first half of 2000 by tens of thousands of people protesting at the World Bank/IMF headquarters in Washington D.C., and by about 2,000 protesters who asked the leaders of the Asian Development Bank to leave Chiang Mai in Thailand. The Bank belatedly established an NGO Task Force to deal with the issue. Bello observes that poor Thai farmers had joined with middle class youth in Chiang Mai and that this was one link in the worldwide chain of protest against globalization. By September, the focus had shifted to Melbourne, site of the World Economic Forum Asia-Pacific Summit. This attracted around 5,000 protesters, and street battles erupted that forced delegates to be moved around the city by helicopter. Later in September, 10,000 people demonstrated in Prague, where World Bank leaders were besieged and their meeting abandoned. In Prague, as in many other places, the struggle against imperialism was identified with opposition to McDonald's franchises. Czech Republic President Vaclav Havel hosted a consultation between leaders of the World Bank and the IMF, financier George Soros, and representatives of various NGOs (the voice of civil society), but nothing came of it.

The leaders of the World Economic Forum in Davos in January 2001, one of the loudest voices of capitalist triumphalism in the early 1990s, visibly shaken, put reform of the global system at the top of its agenda. But this agenda was discussed behind a high fence and massive police presence to shut out thousands of protesters. A platform was given at Davos to anti-globalization activists and many fine words were exchanged between them and members of the transnational capitalist class, but little action followed. An alternative Davos met at the same time with an impressive array of anti-globalization organizations discussing resistance and struggles all over the world (see Fisher and Ponniah 2003). The G-7 plan to lessen the burden of debt servicing of the 41 poorest countries, a key demand of the protesters, had delivered only one billion dollars of relief between 1996 and 2000 (3 percent of the total).[20] Despite trying to sound conciliatory, the World Bank, the IMF and the WTO all dug in their heels, dismaying prominent World Bank and other reformers. Much of the focus of protests was on the abuse of power by TNCs (many of whom were named by well-informed campaigning groups).

New and more ominous elements were to emerge in 2001. In June a large protest took place in Gothenburg and a protester died. And in July, during even larger demonstrations during the G-8 summit in Genoa a protester, Carlo Giuliano, was killed by a military conscript (he was then run over by a police vehicle as he lay dying, the driver pleaded panic). Later that night, hundreds were beaten as they slept in a school in the city that was being used by the Genoa Social Forum, a peaceful group well-known to the authorities. Some protesters were later tortured by police and militia units. Disturbing and incontrovertible evidence quickly came to light that the authorities had ignored self-styled anarchist groups with public policies of violence who had already demonstrated violently. Instead, they attacked peaceful protesters. This appeared to be a deliberate tactic of terrorizing innocent people in order to scare off protesters in the future. The political opportunity for this tactic to succeed, of course, was the original pre-publicized violence of a tiny minority of the protesters. This permitted leaders such as Tony Blair to continue to condemn the entire anti-globalization movement as violent and irrelevant and to remain silent about the state-sponsored violence that had occurred in Genoa (and elsewhere).[21]

The catalog of protest from Seattle to Genoa (and beyond, without any doubt) is difficult to fit into a neat analytical framework. It is clearly a real movement against globalization. Its most widespread popular manifestation is certainly the World Social Forum (WSF) movement that began in Porto Alegre, Brazil, in January 2001. WSF was established directly as a progressive anti-capitalist response to Davos and has subsequently expanded both geographically and ideologically (see Fisher and Ponniah 2003). The work of Starr illuminates both the variety of anti-corporate and anti-globalization movements, and the most potent themes that inspire them and could focus their opposition to appropriate targets. What appears to be happening is that these movements and protests are becoming more and more clearly focused on the four fractions of the transnational capitalist class. The movement against major corporations is clear for all to see. As documented elsewhere (see Sklair 2001), and frequently reported even in mainstream mass media, the practices of companies like Exxon, McDonald's, Nike, The Gap, BP, Shell, Nestle, Monsanto, Philip Morris, BAT, Mitsubishi, and many others are closely monitored all over the world and their wrongdoings exposed. Globalizing bureaucrats like those who run the WTO, World Bank, IMF, OECD, and so on are clearly targets, as are the globalizing politicians who lead the governments of G-7 and other countries. Globalizing professionals are more difficult to identify, though the neoliberal think tanks and the scientists that provide them with evidence for GM crops and evidence against the existence of global warming certainly qualify. So do the legions of professional lobbyists, consultants, and PR people who are often the mouthpieces of TNCs, states and inter-state bodies. Finally, and significantly, the movement has focused specifically on consumerist elites (merchants and media) in many sites of resistance, targeting many global brand names, despised symbols of capitalist globalization, and places where they are sold.

Those sympathetic to global capitalism and respectful of their governments and inter-state institutions will quite properly observe that this is a one-sided picture of Seattle and after. For these people, and there are very many of them, the most important single fact about anti-globalization protests is their violence against global leaders, those whose duty it is to maintain law and order, and their destruction of public and private property. The violence gives the transnational capitalist class and those who speak for them the perfect excuse for marginalizing, sometimes avoiding entirely, most of the issues that the anti-globalization movement is raising. Corporate executives, globalizing bureaucrats, politicians, professionals, and consumer elites are all appalled by acts of violence and random destruction that they can attribute to protesters, but have been notably silent about similar corporate and state-sponsored acts, precisely the type of hypocritical behavior that many of the protesters are campaigning against.

What the twentieth century taught us is that revolutionary social change brought about principally by violent means is unlikely to produce democratic outcomes, although some violent overthrows of dictatorships have brought improvements to the lives of ordinary people. Nevertheless, non-violence is the only long-term strategy for the construction of any viable alternatives to capitalist globalization.[22]

THE NON-VIOLENT ALTERNATIVE TO CAPITALIST GLOBALIZATION

"In the twentieth century, non-violence became more of a deliberate tool for social change, moving from being largely an ad hoc strategy growing naturally out of religious or ethical principles to a reflective, and in many ways institutionalized, method of struggle" (Zunes et al. 1999: 1). These tactics include strikes, boycotts, mass demonstrations, popular contestations of public space, tax refusal, destruction of symbols of government authority (like official identification cards), and more positively creations of alternative institutions. The power of non-violent social movements is based on non-cooperation with the authorities, to undermine their legitimacy.

There is a good deal of research and opinion poll evidence that shows a declining level of support in societies with democratic institutions for the aims of protesters who are identified with violent tactics, and an increasing level of support for those who are not (Porta Della and Diani 1999: 182; see also Tarrow 1998: 95–96). Therefore, it is obviously to the advantage of the targets of movements and protests to label protesters as violent. And just as obviously, it is to the advantage of movements and protesters who wish to win mass support to avoid violence. In two cases related to the movement against capitalist globalization that have been discussed above, opposition to the Enron project in India in the 1990s and the protest against the G8 summit in Genoa in 2001, the issue of violence loomed large. In both cases there is at least prima facie evidence of the use of provocation and intimidation by the authorities, and this is a very alarming prospect for parliamentary democracies. The case for non-violence in the movement and protests against capitalist globalization is overwhelming.

Organized non-violence was a twentieth century innovation. Most scholars agree that this was largely due to Gandhi who was responsible for the transition from informal and unorganized to formal and organized non-violence as a political strategy. One development of this is defensive defense, i.e., disarming behavior without threat to the threatener (in Zunes et al. 1999: ch. 1). In a textbook from the 1970s, Gene Sharp identified three tactical categories: non-violent protest and persuasion (petitioning, picketing, demonstrating, and lobbying); non-violent non-cooperation (boycotts, strikes, tax resistance); and non-violent intervention (physical obstruction, blockades, civil disobedience, sit-ins). In all, Sharp lists 198 tactics.[23]

History is replete with convincing and inspiring examples of the successes, usually under-reported, of non-violent social movements. Perhaps the most publicized case in which a non-violent movement defeated an authoritarian leader and paved the way for the transfer of state power was the people's movement in the Philippines in 1986 (Zunes et al. 1999: ch. 7). What the media dubbed "77 hours that toppled Marcos" have been analyzed by many, but Zunes demonstrates that the decades of non-violent education and movement-building that made it possible have been largely ignored. He utilizes the frame-work of Lakey to analyze five theoretical stages of non-violent revolution. The categories would be similar everywhere, but the details of course differ from place to place. The first stage is cultural preparation (in the Philippines this involved the Catholic Church and various left-wing and student organizations). Second, organization building (this must be accomplished across sectors, and deep into the grassroots, "vast networks of decentralized popular organization"). Third is the propaganda of the deed (massive public demonstrations, people's strikes that were organized by 500 and more grassroots organizations claiming 1.5 million members, and crossing class and ethnic lines). The fourth stage is massive non-cooperation that makes it difficult for the authorities to govern (for example, disrupting government-controlled banking services, and delaying payment for public utility charges). Last, and decisive if a real revolution is to occur, is the establishment of parallel institutions (what Gramsci called counter-hegemony). In the Philippines, a network of rural cooperatives, alternative educational institutions, and an alternative election commission partly fulfilled this role.

The spark that ignited this organizational and ideological tinder was the assas-sination of the popular reformer, Benigno Aquino, by agents of the state. This brought middle class non-violent opponents of the regime into the struggle in greater numbers. However, Zunes argues, "it is highly unlikely that most of them [opponents of Marcos] considered themselves pacifist in orientation. It appears, then, that most of the non-violent activists favored non-violence on largely pragmatic grounds". The Tagalog expression for non-violence is *alaydangal*, meaning to offer dignity, contrasting Gandhian active non-violence to Christian passive non-violence, turning the other cheek. All commentators are agreed that the very high level of non-violent discipline meant that the US government and military, up until then largely uncritical backers of the regime, found it impossible to support Marcos in the face of popular opposition. The courage of the people on the streets and their level of non-violent organization were the key factors.[24]

Zunes asks: why did this strategy succeed in the Philippines while it failed or was not even attempted elsewhere? He cites the importance of a relatively free press and freedom of movement, nominally democratic institutions, and the power of the Church. All these (plus, of course, the unwillingness of the US government even under the hawkish Reagan Administration, to intervene) made continued repression unworkable. This reasoning, which is not wholly convincing, does highlight one factor of particular relevance for the study of capitalist globalization and the struggle against it, namely that free markets and neoliberal political doctrine do entail a minimal level of state intervention, in theory if not always in practice. This is historically associated with the processes of democratization and re-democratization that have occurred all over the Third World and postcommunist Europe while capitalist globalization has been gathering pace there. Parliamentary democracies, for all their failings, tend to be less violent than authoritarian states. Though armed intervention in the affairs of sovereign states still goes on, it is not these cases but that of the Philippines that will most likely provide the model for the future of intervention. Non-violence, therefore, gives social movements much more prospect of spreading their message, if not achieving their ends, without repressive outside intervention.

The movement against capitalist globalization appears to present a dilemma for this analysis, as intervention is hardly likely to come from outside the planet. However, this dilemma is more apparent than real. The movement is global, but its activities are always local, always in one or more sites of resistance. Certainly, many members of the state militia in Seattle and Genoa were from outside the city (as were many of the demonstrators). It is a commonplace that civil disturbances are best repressed by forces from outside the locality. Determined active non-violence will always be an effective challenge to parliamentary democracies because most politicians want to be re-elected and we must assume that they would want to avoid excessive state violence against ordinary people protesting peaceably on their streets. As long as the movement against capitalist globalization can be convincingly characterized as violent and chaotic, the authorities need not worry very much about their repressive violence.

The membership of the anti-globalization movement is at present split between small violent minorities (some of whom correctly see violence as an attention-getting tactic, some of whom indulge in violence for cathartic reasons as well) and a huge non-violent majority. As with most large gatherings, there are usually hangers-on whose presence at demonstrations has little to do with the movement.[25] At all the major protests, groups specializing in non-violence have attempted to teach their tactics and inculcate their ideology as far and as wide as possible. In Seattle and Prague they achieved a good measure of success.

Slowly, labor, environmental and other movements are being drawn into the non-violent fold.[26] Just as militarism and corporate capitalism have become global, so must non-violent movements. The future success of the movement against capitalist globalization and the viability of an alternative to it ultimately depend on the victory of non-violence as a universal principle. The growing influence of the globalization of human rights in movements against global capitalism is a positive contribution to these ends.

Notes

1. This paper is a revised and updated version of material first published in Sklair (2002: chapters 10–11).
2. For current research on social movements see Porta Della and Diani (1999), Hamel et al. (2000), Smith et al. (1997), Bandy and Smith (2004), Cohen and Rai (2000) and Zunes et al. (1999), an important study of non-violent social movements.
3. On green movements see Redclift and Woodgate (1995), Peet and Watts (1996), and Faber (in Bandy and Smith 2004: ch. 3).
4. I say in the long run. In the short-term, authoritarian regimes can ignore demands for democratization and push forward consumerist market reforms. It is by no means obvious that everyone in the world prefers democracy to economic prosperity, if that is the choice they are persuaded to accept.
5. However, many social movements advocating democracy often lack much democracy in their own organizations. Fennema and Tillie have a point when they argue with respect to political participation in Amsterdam: "To have undemocratic ethnic organisations is better for the democratic process than to have no organisations at all" (1999: 723, italicized in the original).
6. Reisner (2001) shows the potential for such mobilization against genetic engineering.
7. The growing transnational network of the Association for Taxation of Financial Transaction to Aid Citizens (ATTAC) promises to make this issue more visible than it is at present.
8. It had previously run a powerful cover story arguing that: "The [anti-globalization] protesters have tapped into growing fears that US policies benefit big companies instead of average citizens—of America or any other country" (Bernstein 2000: 50). *Fortune, The Economist*, and others also joined in.
9. Higgot and Phillips (2000) make a strong argument that these splits have long-term significance for the future of capitalist globalization. We shall see!
10. Risse et al. (1999) show how "international human rights norms" can promote domestic change. For the convoluted history of human rights, see Ishay (2004).
11. Jones makes the unusual argument that this is less of a threat to indigenous cultures than either Fordism or state socialism. "The threat globalization poses to indigenous cultures is thus overrated—in fact it seems (in retrospect) that the modernist obsession with developing the Third World reached its peak in the 1970s and has been receding ever since (except in a relative handful of NICs)" (1998: 293). This, he suggests, opens the way for recombinant local cultures as hybrids upon which consumer capitalism can be overlaid. The research of McGuckin (1997) on the Tibetan refugee carpet industry is a challenging test of this thesis.
12. For some case studies see Petras and Harding (2000), Bandy and Smith (2004).
13. One example indicates the tone: "Monsanto should not have to vouchsafe the safety of biotech food. Our interest is in selling as much of it as possible. Assuring its safety is the FDA's [US Federal Food and Drug Agency] job" (Director of Corporate Communications, q. in Starr 2000: 9). See also, Lappe and Bailey (1999), Sklair (2001: esp. 224–27).
14. Enthusiasm is infectious, but for a sobering assessment of thirty comprehensive community plans for sustainable development in the USA, see Berke and Conroy (2000).
15. Raynolds (2000) shows how major food TNCs (Dole for example) are already moving into organic production and ethical trading. Barrientos (2000) calls ethical trade a "paradox of globalization."

16. Starr, of course, is not the only writer who finds this difficult. Held et al. (1999: Table C.1) in their apparently more sophisticated model of three political projects for globalization—liberal-internationalism, radical republicanism, and cosmopolitan democracy (their preference)—list many factors but fare no better. For my own preference (socialist globalization of human rights) see Sklair (2002: ch. 11).

17. For a sharp critique of WTO neglect of human rights and how it can be reformed (less convincing) see Petersmann (2000).

18. There is a particularly rich variety of websites on the topic (notably indymedia.org). While the mass media focus is usually on one place at a time, the protests are often in many places simultaneously. However, as Fox and Brown (1998: 30) argue in their collection on NGOs and the World Bank, many networks are "fragile fax-and-cyberspace skeletons." On Seattle, see Smith (2001) and Langman et al. (2002), and the special issue of *Monthly Review* (July/August 2000).

19. This had already happened in other cities, see Klein (2000: ch. 13) on the "Reclaim the Streets" movement in London in the 1990s. See also Hamel et al. (2000) on urban social movements.

20. The Jubilee 2000 Campaign had campaigned in over 40 countries since 1996 for debt forgiveness. See also Dent and Peters (1999).

21. The Italian government carried out a rapid inquiry into these events. Predictably, this found no evidence of official wrongdoing.

22. The suicidal destruction in New York and Washington in September 2001 and the military campaigns that followed only deepens my conviction that this is true, though I have no easy solutions.

23. See McAllister (in Zunes et al. 1999: 22–23), who highlights the centrality of women in the history of non-violence but their relative invisibility in textbooks about it.

24. The presence of brave foreign NGO personnel has provided some degree of safety for local activists in many other non-violent struggles, for example, with the Zapatistas in Chiapas (Nash 2001: ch. 4), Peace Brigades International in Sri Lanka (Coy, in Smith et al. 1997: ch. 5), and SERPAJ in Latin America, (Pagnucco in ibid.: ch. 7).

25. See Smith (2001) and a multitude of evidence from websites.

26. The thesis of Bayat (2000) that global restructuring transforms the urban poor in the South from dangerous classes into quiet rebels deserves more empirical research.

References

Aaronson, S. 2001. *Taking Trade to the Streets: The Lost History of Public Efforts to Shape Globalization*. Ann Arbor: University of Michigan Press.

Ashwin, S. 2000. International Labour Solidarity after the Cold War, in R. Cohen and S. Rai (eds), *Global Social Movements*. London: Athlone Press, pp. 101–16.

Bandy, J. and J. Smith (eds). 2004. *Coalitions Across Borders: Transnational Protest and the Neoliberal Order*. Lanham MD: Rowman and Littlefield.

Barker, C. and J. Mander. 2000. *Invisible Government: The World Trade Organization*. San Francisco: International Forum on Globalization.

Barrientos, S. 2000. Globalization and Ethical Trade. *Journal of International Development* 12: 559–70.

Bayat, A. 2000. From "Dangerous Classes" to "Quiet Rebels": Politics of the Urban Subaltern in the Global South, *International Sociology* 15(3): 533–57.

Bello, W. 2001. 2000: The Year of Global Protest. *International Socialism* 90: 71–76.

Berke, P. and M.M. Conroy. 2000. Are We Planning for Sustainable Development? *Journal of the American Planning Association* 66(1): 21–33.

Bernstein, A. 2000. Backlash: Behind the Anxiety Over Globalization. *Business Week*, April 24.

Bonanno, A., L. Busch, W. Friedland, L. Gouveia and E. Mingione (eds). 1994. *From Columbus to ConAgra: The Globalization of Agriculture and Food*. Lawrence: University Press of Kansas.

Bruno, K. and J. Karliner. 2002. *EARTH SUMMIT BIZ.: The Corporate Takeover of Sustainable Development*. Oakland, CA: Food First.

Brysk, A. and G. Shafir (eds). 2004. *People out of Place: Globalization, Human Rights, and the Citizenship Gap*. London: Routledge.

Cohen, R. and S.M. Rai (eds). 2000. *Global Social Movements*. London: Athlone Press.

Della Porta, D. and M. Diani. 1999. *Social Movements: An Introduction*. Oxford: Blackwell.

Dent, M. and B. Peters. 1999. *The Crisis of Poverty and Debt in the Third World*. Aldershot: Ashgate.

Dewey, S. 1998. Working for the Environment: Organised Labor and the Origins of Environmentalism in the United States, 1948–1970. *Environmental History* 3: 45–63.

Dicken, P. 1998. *Global Shift: Transforming the World-economy* (Third Edition). London: Paul Chapman.

Dunkley, G. 2000. *The Free Trade Adventure: The WTO, the Uruguay Round and Globalism, A Critique*. London: Zed Books.

Dwivedi, R. 1998. Resisting Dams and 'Development': Contemporary Significance of the Campaign against the Narmada Projects in India. *European Journal of Development Research* 10(2): 135–83.

Edelman, M. 1998. Transnational Peasant Politics in Central America. *Latin American Research Review* 33(3): 49–86.

Evans, P. 1979. *Dependent Development: The Alliance of Multinational, State and Local Capital in Brazil*. Princeton: Princeton University Press.

Falk, R. 1999. *Predatory Globalisation: A Critique*. Cambridge: Polity Press.

Fennema, M. and J. Tillie. 1999. Political Participation and Political Trust in Amsterdam: Civic Communities and Ethnic Networks. *Journal of Ethnic and Migration Studies* 25(4): 703–26.

Fisher, W. and T. Ponniah (eds). 2003. *Another World is Possible: Popular Alternatives to Globalization at the World Social Forum*. London: Zed Books.

Fox, J. and L.D. Brown (eds). 1998. *The Struggle for Accountability: The World Bank, NGOs, and Grassroots Movements*. Cambridge MA: MIT Press.

Hamel, P., H. Lustiger-Thaler and M. Mayer (eds). 2000. *Urban Movements in a Globalising World*. London: Routledge.

Held, D., A. McGrew, D. Goldblatt and J. Perraton. 1999. *Global Transformations: Politics, Economics and Culture*. Cambridge: Polity Press.

Higgot, R. and N. Phillips. 2000. Challenging Triumphalism and Convergence: The Limits of Global Liberalization in Asia and Latin America. *Review of International Studies* 26: 359–79.

Hines, C. 2000. *Localization: A Global Manifesto*. London: Earthscan.

Ishay, M. 2004. *The History of Human Rights*. Berkeley and Los Angeles: University of California Press.

Jones, M. 1998. Blade Runner Capitalism, the Transnational Corporation, and Commodification: Implications for Cultural Integrity. *Cultural Dynamics* 10(3): 287–306.

Keck, E. and K. Sikkink. 1998. *Activists Beyond Borders: Advocacy Networks in International Relations*. Ithaca, NY: Cornell University Press.

Klein, N. 2000. *No Logo*. London: Flamingo.

Lang, T. and C. Hines. 1993. *The New Protectionism: Protecting the Future Against Free Trade*. London: Earthscan.

Langman, L., D. Morris and C. Davidson. 2002. Globalization and National Identity Rituals in Brazil and the USA: The Politics of Pleasure or Protest?, in Paul Kennedy (ed.), *Globalization and National Identities*. London: Macmillan.

Lappe, M. and B. Bailey. 1999. *Against the Grain: The Genetic Transformation of Global Agriculture*. London: Earthscan.

Leisink, P. (ed.). 1999. *Globalization and Labour Relations*. Cheltenham: Edward Elgar.

Makinson, D. 2000. Editorial. The Development Debate: Beyond the Washington Consensus. *International Social Science Journal* 166: 439–40.

McCormick, J. 1992. *The Global Environment Movement: Reclaiming Paradise*. London: Belhaven.

McGuckin, E. 1997. Tibetan Carpets: From Folk Art to Global Commodity. *Journal of Material Culture* 2(3): 291–310.

McManus, P. 1996. Contested Terrains: Politics, Stories and Discourses of Sustainability. *Environmental Politics* 5: 48–53.

Mies, M. and V. Bennholdt-Thomsen. 1999. *The Subsistence Perspective: Beyond the Globalised Economy*. London: Zed Books.

Munck, R. and P. Waterman (eds). 1999. *Labour Worldwide in the Era of Globalization*. Basingstoke: Macmillan.

Murray, J. 2000. Labour Faces the Future: The Online Conference on Organised Labour in the 21st Century. *The International Journal of Comparative Labour Law and Industrial Relations* 16(1): 103–7.

Nash, J. 2001. *Mayan Visions: The Quest for Autonomy in an Age of Globalization*. London: Routledge.

O'Brien, R., A.M. Goetz, J.A. Scholte and M. Williams. 2000. *Contesting Global Governance: Multilateral Economic Institutions and Global Social Movements*. Cambridge: Cambridge University Press.

Pacione, M. 1997. Local Exchange Trading Systems as a Response to the Globalization of Capitalism. *Urban Studies* 34(8): 1179–99.

Panjabi, R. 1997. *The Earth Summit at Rio: Politics, Economics, and the Environment*. Boston: Northeastern University Press.

Peet, R. and M. Watts (eds). 1996. *Liberation Ecologies: Environment, Development, Social Movement*. New York: Routledge.

Petersmann, E.U. 2000. The WTO Constitution and Human Rights. *Journal of International Economic Law* 3: 19–25.

Petras, J. and T. Harding. 2000. Introduction: The Radical Left Response to Global Impoverishment. *Latin American Perspectives* 27(5): 3–10.

Rajagopal, B. 2003. *International Law from Below: Development, Social Movements and Third World Resistance*. Cambridge: Cambridge University Press.

Raynolds, L. 2000. Re-embedding Global Agriculture: The International Organic and Fair Trade Movements. *Agriculture and Human Values* 17: 297–309.

Redclift, M. and G. Woodgate (eds). 1995. *The Sociology of the Environment*. Aldershot: Edward Elgar.

Reisner, A.E. 2001. Social Movement Organizations' Reactions to Genetic Engineering in Agriculture. *American Behavioural Scientist* 44(8): 1389–1404.

Risse, T., S.C. Ropp and K. Sikkink (eds). 1999. *The Power of Human Rights: International Norms and Domestic Change.* Cambridge: Cambridge University Press.

Robbins, P. 2001. *Greening the Corporations: Management Strategy and the Environmental Challenge.* Sterling, VA: Earthscan Publications.

Ross, G. 2000. Labor Versus Globalization. *Annals of the American Academy of Political and Social Science* 570: 78–91, July.

Rowell, A. 1996. *Green Backlash: Global Subversion of the Environmental Movement.* London: Routledge.

Salt, B., R. Cervero and A. Herad. 2000. Workers' Education and Neoliberal Globalization: An adequate response to transnational corporations? *Adult Education Quarterly* 51(1): 9–31.

Scott, A. 1990. *Ideology and the New Social Movements.* London: Unwin Hyman.

Shostak, A. (ed.). 1999. *Cyber Union: Empowering Labor Through Computer Technology.* Armonk: M.E. Sharpe.

Singer, D. 1999. *Whose Millennium? Theirs or Ours?* New York: Monthly Review Press.

Sklair, L. 2001. *The Transnational Capitalist Class.* Oxford: Blackwell.

—————. 2002. *Globalization: Capitalism and Its Alternatives.* Oxford: Oxford University Press.

Smith, J. 2004. Globalizing Resistance: The Battle of Seattle and the Future of Social Movements. *Mobilization* 6(1): 1–19.

Smith, J., C. Chatfield and R. Pagnucco (eds). 1997. *Transnational Social Movements and Global Politics: Solidarity Beyond the State.* Syracuse: Syracuse University Press.

Smith, M.P. 2001. *Transnational Urbanism: Locating Globalization.* Oxford: Blackwell.

Starr, A. 2000. *Naming the Enemy: Anti-corporate Movements Confront Globalization.* London: Zed Books.

Steiner, H. and P. Alston (eds). 2000. *International Human Rights: Law, Politics, Morals.* Oxford: Oxford University Press.

Tarrow, S. 1998. *Power in Movements: Social Movements and Contentious Politics.* Cambridge: Cambridge University Press.

Tobin, J. 2000. Financial Globalization. *World Development* 28(6): 1101–4.

Vandervoort, S. 1991. Big "Green Brother" is Watching. *Public Relations Journal:* 14–26, April.

Vig, N.J. and R.S. Axelrod. 1999. *The Global Environment: Institutions, Law, and Policy.* London: Earthscan.

Wachtel, H. 2000. Tobin and Other Global Taxes. *Review of International Political Economy* 7(2): 335–52.

Walch, J. 1999. *In the Net: An Internet Guide for Activists.* London: Zed Books.

Walker, R. 1999. Putting Capital in its Place: Globalization and the Prospects for Labor. *Geoforum* 30: 263–84.

Wills, J. 1999. Taking on the CosmoCorps? Experiments in Transnational Labor Organization. *Economic Geography* 75: 111–30.

Zunes, S., L. Kurtz and S.B. Asher (eds). 1999. *Nonviolent Social Movements: A Geographical Perspective.* Oxford: Blackwell.

12

SOCIAL MOVEMENTS IN A GLOBALIZED WORLD

ELVIRA DEL POZO AVIÑÓ

By the mysterious forces of destiny mankind is confronted with a stern dilemma: either to continue its predatory policies of individual and tribal selfishness that lead to its inevitable doom, or to embark upon the policies of universal solidarity that brings humanity to the aspired for heaven on earth. It is up to every one of us which of the two roads we prefer to choose.[1]

Pitirim A. Sorokin, 1954.

Sorokin presents us with a serious challenge: which path do we choose for our future? Should we choose to act individually for our own benefit, or collectively for the benefit of the whole? While this may often be interpreted on a micro level of individuals and small groups, it also applies to larger structures such as nation-states and international non-governmental organizations (NGOs). Indeed, Sorokin's debate is alive today, and is one of the most compelling issues as we confront increasing globalization. Should nation-states act alone or through building alliances? Can NGOs or other international organizations and social movements provide a means to achieve what Sorokin termed "the policies of universal solidarity"? This is the real-life test for our current world where new challenges, confrontations, and coalitions are in flux. The purpose of this chapter is to systematically discuss the meaning of globalization from the perspective of those who have chosen the path of solidarity.

GLOBALIZATION AND SOCIAL MOVEMENTS

The concept of globalization is not new for its origins began back in the late nineteenth and early twentieth centuries, with the work of intellectuals such as Karl Marx and Saint-Simon. They noticed that modernity was taking over the entire world (Held & McGrew 2003: 13). But the term globalization was first defined (and popularized) in 1962 by Marshall McLuhan as the way of life towards which humanity was heading: a "global village." In the 1970s it was also related to the concept of imperialism and Wallerstein's concept of the "world-system" or the "world-economy" (Beltrán 2002). It is the process throughout which sovereign nation-states mingle with transnational actors (Beck 1998). Most scholars agree that it is a process that began with capitalism in the fifteenth century, and that it has been shaped throughout the years to what could now be called "the new capitalism."

The idea that we are in an era of *new* social movements, originated with the emergence of new styles of political action at the beginning of the 1970s. What distinguished these *new* actions was citizen's direct participation—rather than indirect, traditional political representation—in the affairs that affect their lives (Dalton et al. 1992). Such argument has been further reinforced by the rise of distinct social movements (in defense of human rights, the environment and the like) in advanced industrial societies of the past two decades.

Since the 1980s, there has been much literature on globalization, or the pervasive effects of the "neoliberal globalization" on humanity.[2] Since the 1990s, there has been a growing amount of literature discussing the emergence of *new* social movements. Additionally, at the beginning of the twenty-first century, both in academic and non-academic circles, there emerges literature linking these two areas of study. In real life, the clearest expression of this dynamic is the growing strength of neoliberal globalization resistance movements and their massive presence at the World Social Forums (WSFs). The January 2004 WSF meeting at Mumbai highlighted that discourses on the future of globalization are now (more than ever before) being focused on action, and on its connection to theory or ideology. I believe that these types of discourses might change the course of action for both activists and social scientists and need to be interpreted.

In light of recent discussions surrounding globalization and social movements in the social sciences, these pages raise some of the following questions: What are the main challenges under discussion? What can social movements do to confront the challenges brought about by globalization? Are there proposals for action? Why has literature on these topics increased dramatically in the past few years? Are the effects of globalization more pervasive today, or are social scientists more aware of the consequences? Are social movements more influential today than they were previously? What is the impact of the WSFs?

This chapter is divided into three sections and a conclusion. The first three parts address some of the dominant perspectives on social movements stemming from the disciplines of sociology and political science, as well as some commentaries from some social movements' activists.[3] These pages do not focus on each movement's themes.[4] Rather, they analyze discussions held with regard to three aspects: (1) the challenge of globalization; (2) the response to social movements; and (3) suggestions for future action. In other words, globalization and its challenges are viewed from a social movement perspective.

The questions raised are geared towards answering a larger question, addressing the possibility of the existence of a perspective change that emerged around the time of the 2003/2004 WSFs, and especially in 2004. This perspective gives a growing importance to the connection between theory and action, or between social movements' activism and collective action studies. The last two sections of this chapter reflect on the causes and consequences of that perspective. The possibility of a perspective change alone merits attention as it can have important implications towards larger societal transformations. The "Thomas Theorem" can serve to illustrate this point for he said that "if men define situations as real, they are real in their consequences" (Merton 1995).

What follows is a basic summary on the impingement of social movements in a globalized world. It contains relevant commentaries from notable social scientist and activists. The main objective of this reflection is to better understand where we are and where we are heading. Alternatively, the aim is to measure the sociological impact of social movements on current debates.

THE IMPACT OF GLOBALIZATION

The Sociology of Globalization: Theoretical Framework

Back in 1983, the British cultural theorist Raymond Williams analyzed the powerful influence of the modern international capitalist system for society and the economy. He explained that this system consists of extending and accelerating the economic fluxes that go across national frontiers with no regard for the wellbeing of the environment and humanity. He told the following story: you might have a field of strawberries that is fruitful and ready to crop. But one day you find that some businessmen decide that it is beneficial for them to import other strawberries at a lower cost allowing your product to rot. By the way, these businessmen could very well be your own neighbors. In Williams' view, this is what happens with globalization. People penetrate and destroy other people's economies to benefit their own (or other multinational companies) economy. They act without respect towards national frontiers. And all that the victims can do is reduce the cost of their product and/or improve it, or go bankrupt and join the real world.

But the term globalization is not well understood by many. It comprises the following dimensions: the technological (the global network); the ecological (a *sustainable development*); the economic (the unregulated transnational monetary fluxes); the labor organizational (the reallocation of workers); the cultural (the sharing of music, art, and cooking internationally); and others.

Globalization is a perception of the loss of national frontiers in one's life, constructed around the economy, media, environment, transcultural conflicts, and civil society. It modifies our entire lives while forcing us to adapt and respond to the changes. Basically, it is the immersion in a transnational way of life, which is often neither desired nor comprehended (Beck 1998).

According to Beck (1998), the sociology of globalization has been dominated by the "container theory of society." It is a theory on which most of the sociology of the first age of modernity is based upon. It means that societies—and all social phenomena—are contained in national states. Thus, in the European paradigm of the "First Age of Modernity" of the late nineteenth century and early twentieth century, globalization was interpreted within the territorial frontiers of state and politics, society and culture, and it involved interconnectedness. But this theory is fading away. Now, we are on the "Second Age of Modernity," and this means that we live in a world in which national sovereignty is no longer the dominating institution. Thus, the debate around globalization in the social sciences has now been replaced by the study of unities of analysis that substitute the nation-state. Research is now focused on migrating to *transnational social spheres*; on the capitalist system of the world-economy; on the political relationships between the nation-states and transnational organizations; on risks societies; on cultural studies integrating both the global and the local; and on a global civil society (Beck 1998).

According to Beck (1998), a transnational civil society should consider the processes, experiences, conflicts and identities oriented towards creating a "world model" comprised of transnational social movements. That is, a globalization "from below" or a new cosmopolitism. In essence, this is like a world with no world-state, or a society not organized politically. In such organizations, Beck (2004) finds that there are new opportunities for action and power for transnational actors. Although these actors have not been democratically legitimized, he argues that they are not illegal.

The idea that sociologists should abandon the concept of the nation-state as a unit of analysis is not new. Both Wilbert Moore and Wallerstein maintain that in order to comprehend social change in a civilized way, the "world society," or the "world-system" is the only social system to be used as a unit of analysis (García Ferrando 2004). The argument is the following. According to Manuel García Ferrando, sociology was born under the influence of intellectuals such as Auguste Comte and Marx with the interest of studying all cultures and societies. And although around the 1930s sociologists began having a difficult time studying societies outside of the industrial western world, this changed with the Second World War. A new distribution of the international social order gave protagonism to other new nation-states outside of Europe. And at European and American universities, scholars began studying non-Western societies, which also helped the development of sociology in other countries. Once sociologists from both developing and developed countries began studying social change, scholars realized that the model of the industrial development that originated at the end of the eighteenth century in Europe (and extended to the United States) was not applicable to most non-Western countries. Similarly, sociological studies from these countries also emphasized that the diversity of societies makes it very difficult to speak of a country in general terms, or to compare between nation-states. Sociologists should therefore study global issues from a global perspective.

If we choose to follow the historical assessments of Sorokin, Williams, and Wallerstein (among others), one concludes that the consequences of globalization are chaotic for humanity. And also, that the current chaos requires people to be morally and politically responsible. But this is no easy task, for criticisms on the current state of affairs are multiple, and often times, found to be in confrontation with one another. So, we must begin this task with the knowledge that reaching some sort of consensus or middle ground is a challenge in and of itself. However, I believe that collective action studies can suggest a way to approach that common ground.[5]

For Held and McGrew (2003), there are *globalists* and *skeptics*. For *skeptics*, globalization is simply synonymous with Americanization, Westernization or Internationalization. The discourse contributes to justifying the neoliberal political project, that is, the creation of a free global market and the consolidation of Anglo-American Capitalism. For *globalists*, it is a real and transforming process. For them, *skeptics'* discourse might serve the interests of the Western economic and political forces, but globalization is also the expression of a deeper structural change in the scale of modern social organization. The profound transformation is manifested, among other things, in the growth of multinational corporations, of world financial markets, of the rapid diffusion popular culture and on the importance of global environmental degradation. The three aspects emphasized by this perspective are: the transformation of the traditional socioeconomic organization (the emergence of networks); the territory (national becomes global) and; power (the definition of politics and nation-states). With respect to the latter, Held and McGrew discuss that the modern state's regional and global interconnected network is being (more than ever before) dominated by supranational, intergovernmental and transnational forces. This causes the erosion of the state's capacity to determine its own future. The nation-state can no longer provide to its citizens the goods and services it once did without international cooperation. And international cooperation sometimes escapes the control of political regulations.

One way to assess globalization from a social movements' perspective is to follow Roland Roth's (2003) suggestion that a global organization should address the relationship between NGOs and transnational politics from three different ideologies or perspectives: the "realists," the "liberal or reformists," and the "radicals." Realists protest that NGOs are illegitimate actors in international politics, and that the nation-states are the only ones who can legitimately integrate their opinions in international programs. Liberals (or reformists) consider NGOs as creative actors of a *global governance,* who can contribute to the process of globalization and control the abuses committed by nations or transnational corporations. Finally, radicals are anti-global and question the dominating path of globalization, named neoliberal or the "Washington agreement." Radicals include NGOs, transnational movements, and protest mobilizations.

Given the different ideologies, Beck's suggestion of creating a "world model" comprised of transnational social movements presents itself as quite an ideological challenge to civil society. This chapter discusses such a challenge, departing from the perspective of the so-called "liberals," "reformists" or "radicals."

Globalization: An Ideological Challenge

Globalization is a threat to social movements. However, not everyone agrees on how to face its challenges. Among globalists or liberals (reformists), there are two trends. On one side, people indicate that it is still too early to predict the consequences of globalization, and/or that it is too early for social movements to confront globalization. Thus, more scientific knowledge is needed. On the other side, activists and some social scientists object we are ready to confront globalization challenges. Therefore, more action (instead of more theory) is needed as we already have the tools necessary to plan and implement it. The following paragraphs offer the main arguments of those who believe that the effects of globalization are pervasive for humanity. First, I offer Bauman's interpretation of globalization. Then, I discuss the causes and consequences. And finally, I conclude with how globalization should be addressed according to activists.

Everyone uses the concept of globalization; everyone knows that it is process that affects us all, and that it affects the human condition. "It is a new and disturbing perception that things are getting out of control," that we are facing a "new global disorder" (Bauman 2003: 80). It is a concept that replaced the concept of *universalization,* which constituted the term used to refer to modern global issues, but which is no longer in use. Universalization transmitted hope and a desire to change and create a better world. It was about the creation of a universal order, the creation of similar life chances for everyone, everywhere; even the creation of equality. But globalization as it has been used in today's discourses does not convey these same ideas. Up to now, globalization has primarily referred to what happens to all of us, to the global effects, with the idea that these are undesirable and unpredictable. The concept has not been overly related to what we hope to do, to our initiatives and actions. This might be due to the fact we have not scientifically known how to obtain the means to plan and implement actions. For Bauman, it is still too early to predict the consequences of an accelerated globalization, and we still need to learn about the social skills that are necessary to control and confront those (*El País* 2003).

As to the causes of globalization, Salinas (2001) argues that globalization is the result of national governments' failures. That is, globalization is the *excuse* that some governments give to hide some of their national political errors. For him, the concept does not necessarily indicate a confrontation between anti-globalization and globalization followers. The confrontation is rather about the alternatives to regulate and govern the world markets. Also, it is about the way to define the role of national democratic states, and regional and international financial, commercial, and political institutions in a new context.

The consequences of globalization are thought to be political and organizational by activists and social scientists like Held, Roy, Roth, and Romero. The result of globalization is the growth of NGOs, international organizations and agencies (transnational corporations), and social movements.

Globalization has influenced the institutional and political structures of modern economic systems (Held and McGrew 2003). People speak of a *global governance* to signify the growing interconnection between conventional political systems and new, multiple, and complex ways of governing. It appears that there is a plurality of political identities represented both by the elites of the global order (transnational corporations), social movements, unions, and some politicians and intellectuals (Held and McGrew 2003: 139–40).

The consequences of neoliberalism are devastating (Roy 2004).[6] One of the effects is that NGOs keep growing as these consequences become more pervasive. Roy supports the following argument: In India, non-autonomously financed NGOs have been increasing since the late 1980s, and during the 1990s. This coincides with the time when India opened its markets to neoliberalism. That is, when the government stopped financing some of the more traditional areas (rural development, agriculture, energy, transportation, and public health), NGOs began working in those areas. NGOs have a great social impact and even "give the impression that they are filling the emptiness left by the State who is leaving" (Roy 2004).

Roth (2003) also analyzes NGOs and international politics. For him, NGOs are a rapidly growing phenomenon that feeds and is fed by globalization. We know from the result of research that there is a clear relationship between the growth of international organizations and agencies (such as transnational corporations) and the growth of NGOs.[7] As nation-state systems and the world-economy have expanded, NGOs have been globalized. This development needs to be analyzed for it influences the structure of those who make decisions in world politics. For instance, there are now new ways of establishing multi-lateral and multinational politics that involve the participation of many actors:

governments, international governmental organizations, transnational pressure groups, and international NGOs.[8] But the future is uncertain. And, as Roth notes, we still do not know what the political system institutional structure will be, or the role that NGOs will play within that structure.

For Romero, globalization has exacerbated the control of the market economy over all social relations, and extended it universally. The political consequence is a crisis of the representativeness of institutions and political parties, particularly at the international level (Romero 2003). The most fundamental decisions affecting people's lives are taken internationally, but that is also where there is a great lack of resources for citizens to participate. Thus, it appears that the "anti-globalization movement" is born as a response to both crises: the social and the political. The movement manifests as a confluence of organizations, forums, campaigns, and initiatives seeking to rebuild the public sphere, questioning traditional ways of political representation and judging the institutions that rule globalization. The process is very young but very rapid. What will come out of this is not predictable, but what is predictable is that that is where the new ideas, programs, and organizations that will build the alternatives to a neoliberal globalization will be (or are already being) born.

However, globalization should also be addressed from the perspective of people who are in a position to plan and implement actions that help us create a better world. They believe in the powerful impact of the phenomenon of social movements, and other collectively oriented behavior.[9] Susan George, Vice-President of the Association for Taxation of Financial Transaction to Aid Citizens (ATTAC France) states that "another world is possible" and defines globalization as:

…no more than the integration of some regions of the world by the financial and industrial transnational corporations. It is simply, the twenty-first century Capitalism. Globalization feeds itself by eating the planet, benefits the rich, creates more inequality, rejects democracy and excludes millions of people. (George 2003)

In sum, the sociology of globalization notes that there is disagreement regarding the effects of globalization with regard to the role social movements should play as transnational social actors. Whereas some people contend civil society is a legitimate actor of a global governance, others do not. But regardless of who is right or wrong, in practice, the dynamics between civil society and government are changing. There are new challenges associated with the structure of the nation-state. Thus, the relationship between nation-states and social movements needs to be reorganized. And the resulting institutional structure should give a more inclusive consideration to social movements. But how can such a proposal be articulated? First of all, people need to agree: (1) on whether we scientifically know enough to predict the (negative) consequences of globalization; and (2) on whether we are in a position to plan and implement actions. The response to the first statement was discussed in this section: globalists and liberals (and reformists and radicals) agree that globalization must be either controlled or opposed. And a segment of them think we know enough to propose actions and plans. The response to the second statement will be discussed in the following sections.

The following paragraphs discuss what Manuel Castells (1997: 94) describes as "the other face of earth," the place of "humanity." That is, the place "where the dreams of the past and the nightmares of the future inhabit in a chaotic world made out of passion, generosity, prejudice, fear, fantasy, violence, failed strategies and lucky strikes."[10]

SOCIAL MOVEMENTS

There are diverse opinions regarding what social movements can do to confront the challenges brought about by globalization. First, I present a brief introduction to literature on social movements. Then, I present discussions on how social movements can address globalization, which I divide into two separate sections. The first section gathers discussions centered on the perspective of the WSF and the second section collects reflections on other non-WSF related perspectives.

Social Movements: Theoretical Framework

The most common definitions associated with globalization and social movements are social movements, the WSF (or other forums), anti-globalization movements, alternative globalization movements, and "counter-summits."

An historical study of *Antisystemic Movements* by Arrighi, Hopkins and Wallerstein (1999) reflects on collective social movements that have confronted the dominating structures of the capitalist system. This study discusses the 1848, 1917, 1968 and 1989 historical periods. With regard to the most recent antisystemic or antagonistic experiences, the authors emphasize that the traditional nation-states' jurisdictional capacity to develop the means of production of the capitalist *world-economy* is declining. The state's authority (and its law) is seen as corroded by transnational networks, secessionists' interests, corporation and consumer interests, religious fundamentalisms, and other tendencies. With respect to civil society, it is a structural and not a juncture problem that affects *new antisystemic movements* and the way they must operate. It is therefore a new scenery for new social movements, different from the scenery in which old social movements appeared. This new scenery presents itself as "polymorphus, wider, and more challenging to understand theoretically and to transform in practice" (Arrighi et al. 1999: 113).

For Beck (2004) social movements might be "multiple, uncoordinated, and contradicting" (2004: 314), but they have "weapons" within which they can attack the nation-states. The "weapons" are: (1) that they are organized, and (2) that they are informed through networks that allow them to attack from every part of the entire world. The attacks help "counterbalance the transnational power of their consortiums" (Beck 2004: 315). In other words, they have the "power of public opinion," because they can produce informed public opinion in a legitimate way. However, they do not have any real political or economic power, for they cannot make any legally binding collective decisions. For Beck,

The power of actors in the world of public opinion and of the strategies of public opinion does not stem, or at least not fully, from themselves, but essentially, from the legal emptiness in which global decisions are taken, which are also "collectively" binding at the beginning of the Second Modernity. (2004: 317)[11]

A social movement can be defined as an interactive network of individual people, groups, and organizations that have demands towards civil society and the authorities. They participate (with some continuity) in the process of social change, mainly through non-conventional ways (Casquette 1998).

Current research of social movements in Europe (but not elsewhere) is centered on *new* social movements (human rights, feminist, environmental and others). Some studies conclude that most social movements originate as an expression of a political identity. The identity derives from post-industrial and post-material social conflicts, and it emphasizes a desire to participate in civil society in non-traditional ways (Inglehart 1992).

A recent debate also associates collective action and volunteering with *new* social movements (Zubero 2003). The concept of volunteering appears to be substituting the concept of social movements of the 1970s and 1980s. There are diverse opinions as to why that might be the case. Whereas some people feel that it could be a simple conceptual substitution, others think that it could be because of the emergence of a new social phenomenon (different from classical social movements). For example, for Zubero, "what characterizes volunteering is the weakening of the potential that classical social movements once had for transforming polity." However, as Zubero notes, citing Francisco Fernández Buey (2003: 47), the difference also rests on the fact that while social movements stem, primarily, from the direct socioeconomic interests of the disadvantaged, the origins of NGOs are born out of people's ethics regarding what one should do (altruism and generosity). Thus, the latter are not the directly excluded but they identify with them.

For Richard Flacks (1994: 463–64), the crisis of the citizens' participation in classical political parties suggests that we make an effort to combine the collective action of volunteering and other actions from organizations and social movements. He suggests that:

If a movements' coalition intends to create a viable polity, it needs to be founded on a vision that goes beyond the welfare state. We are living in a time where the economy has been globalized and society decentralized. I suggest that the essence of this conception is found on the logic shared by all great movements, whether *new* or *old*. This has been scarcely articulated up to now. What movements share is precisely the requirement that society is structured in such a way that people can decide with respect to their own lives.[12]

Both Casquette (1998) and Tejerían (2003) have extensively compiled literature from research studies on social movements. Casquette suggests that further studies on social movements address the following dimensions: the symbolic (Alberto Melucci's theories on *new* social movements), the structural, and the process (McAdam, Tarrow and Tilly's resource mobilization theories). Additionally, Tejerían (2003: 341) suggests that future analyses also address activists as agents of social change. Such studies should address the behavior of activists and the resulting transformative processes or "interacting structures." That is, the "different levels and changing contexts of mobilized action": activists' interpersonal relationships; the construction of a collective identity; the interaction among organizations and groups; the interaction among social movements and political agents; and the processes of political transformation resulting from social mobilization.

Other social movements' definitions have been especially linked by the media to the WSF. The most common classifications are: "anti-globalization movements," "alternative globalization movements," and "movements for a global justice." Uses of different concepts can lead to confusion but what lies behind them are theoretical battles. These concepts are similar to the ideologies mentioned above (globalists, liberals and radicals). For some analysts, "anti-globalization movements" are different from "alternative globalization movements" and for others, they are synonymous. In general, "anti-globalization movements" reject globalization as such: they reject capitalism or international markets. And "alternative globalization movements" object not to capitalism per se but rather, to the negative consequences of unregulated globalization. They oppose globalization abuse, an interpretation of globalization as neoliberalism, or the fact that international institutions, such as the World Bank (WB), the International Monetary Fund (IMF), or the World Trade Organization (WTO), promote neoliberalism with no regard to ethical standards. The latter are viewed as movements that accept another type of globalization, or who are "pro-globalization."[13]

The humanitarian crisis created by the neoliberal globalization led to the WSF, and to the so-called "anti-globalization movements" (Díaz-Salazar 2003). The WSF was created as an international movement integrating the search and construction of alternatives to the neoliberal globalization of capitalism and for a new social order. It is an open space for reflecting, for sharing experiences, and articulating actions. The movements that are now emerging, at the beginning of the twenty-first century, are *social movements for a global justice*. When they were first born, they were resistant social groups, however, they are now much more than that; they have suggestions for building a global justice (ibid.).

The forum has unfortunately also attracted people fighting for other causes, and there have emerged "violent" segments. The "anti-globalization" term was therefore born out of the experience of the WSF. The protests began in November 1999 in Seattle, against the World Trade Organization (WTO) meeting. They were aimed to challenge the financial international institution, and are typically labeled "counter-summits." The following protests continued in 2001, in Qatar, again against the WTO. Then, it was in Washington, Prague, Gotembourg, Barcelona, Geneva, Porto Alegre and Mumbai. But the protests are a minority within the alternative movement. Indeed, the majority of the movement does not agree with actions that seek physical confrontation with the police (Romero 2003). The term is unfortunate because although the movement rejects violent behavior, it has created negative stereotypes.

Throughout these years, local organizations have become international thanks to networks such as ATTAC and People's Global Action. They help coordinate activists and the flux of information around the world. In summits, demonstrations, "counter-summits," and annual meetings, people rehearse new ways of making politics and participating towards building up a better world (Victor Hugo 2002).

Finally, "anti-globalization" movements are labeled as different from "social movements" in general because they act sporadically, hold explicit objectives, elaborated projects, identifiable interventions, and homogeneous practices (Romero 2003). They have been labeled as a "mosquito cloud," to emphasize a type of movement that does not have a leader or a representative democratic base. Rather, it is a network, such as the Internet, that links many movements (Klein 2002).

Social Movements as Actors

Is Another World Possible? The Experience of the World Social Forum

The impact that the WSF has on the international community forces it to be the main topic of discussion for most critics. The relationship between NGOs and globalization began in 1992 in the *Earth Summit* and *Global Forum* celebrated in Rio de Janeiro and has continued to develop throughout the years.[14] The last WSF was celebrated in January 2004, in Mumbai (India). Some people refer to the WSF as a "movement of movements". In the next few paragraphs, I discuss on the one hand, the experience of the WSF as viewed by participants in the 2001–03 WSFs (George, Ramonet, and Díaz-Salazar), and on the other hand, the views of participants in the 2004 WSF (Wallerstein, De Sousa Santos, and Esther Vivas).

For George (2003), participants in the worldwide forums are a key element to help fight neoliberal globalization. ATTAC's slogan, "Another World is Possible" was actually adopted as the movement slogan. George contends that a world that fights to end North–South inequalities, obscene wealth gaps, environmental destruction or the inordinate power remaining in the hands of a small minority is possible *if* we work together (see next section).

The WSF is an open discussion forum for social movements, NGOs, unions, and other civil society organizations. In 2003, Ramonet said that the WSF has experienced two stages, and it is now in its third. The first stage began in the mid-1990s and it represented the study and comprehension stage of the phenomenon of globalization. The second stage represented the protest and street demonstrations (Seattle, Prague, Barcelona, Quebec, and Genoa). And a third stage started with the 2001 Porto Alegre Social Forum, symbolizing the beginning of a more human globalization, with the contribution of actors that propose alternatives, and programs towards change. Since 2001, participants offer two types of discourses; one is a complaint of the damages caused by neoliberal globalization in different areas such as women, indigenous people, workers, and others. The other type of discourse concerns the alternatives that each social movement suggests to reduce the damages caused by "an external debt, businesses allocations, the destruction of the environment, financial manipulation, media manipulation, the exploitation of women or children, the lack of medicine for the ill, the lack of lands for peasants, the lack of drinking water." For Ramonet, the WSF is like a "World Organization for Social Movements" (Ramonet 2003: 11–13).

Díaz-Salazar also documents the multiple events that have led to today's *social movements for a global justice* or an international civil society. He explores a series of emancipatory events that start with the First International in 1864, and continue with today's movements which began in the 1990s with the great social forums (in 1992, Rio de Janeiro). What has emerged since then is a multitude of world meetings, civil society forums, "counter-meetings," international networks, great international social movements, NGOs, and more, that critique globalization, expose alternatives, and focus on strategies for action.

What characterizes this latter phase of internationalism is that it is based on a type of social action that celebrates demonstrations, massive protests in large cities, and international campaigns. In addition, concentrations are celebrated along conferences, workshops, seminars, and more. It has become the most important network of international movements ever, for it is a representation of each continent's social movements, NGOs, unions, and alternatives research institutes and centers. On the one hand, the WSF is the "maximum expression of the emergence of an internationalist citizenship for there had never been so many people linking the global with the local" (Díaz-Salazar 2003: 32). For instance, in southern countries, many social movements have been increasingly created to replace the failing representation of the government and political parties of the last decades of the twentieth century. On the other hand, the WSF gathers, for the first time, a spectacular diversity of people and causes offering a mixture of cultures, politics, religions, projects and identities. They aim at a common goal: "a world social project centered on the human being rather than on the attainment of more and more benefits" (ibid.).

In conclusion, social movements for a global justice are a real threat to globalization as they go beyond traditional NGO collective behavior—which focus on development projects and limited political pressure programs, and combine other non-violent strategies: direct action, civil disobedience, boycotts, and new ways of pressuring the government and media with real alternatives.

Wallerstein (2004a) evaluates the WSF after its fourth meeting (Mumbai, 2004) and concludes that it has become an important actor in the past five years. For him, a first stage in its development began with the anti-system movements (the 1999 Seattle protests against the WTO world reunion and the 2000 "Anti-Davos" reunion to fight neoliberalism); a second stage was constituted by the three Porto Alegre social movements with the slogan of "Another World is Possible"; and a third stage begins with the first WSF to be implemented outside of Porto Alegre: the Mumbai Social Forum in India.

The main difference between the 2004 social forum and the previous ones is that at Mumbai, participants discussed, for the first time, whether the WSF should continue to be an "open" forum or a movement. The WSF was born in 2001, as an "open" forum. This means, among other things, that individual people or social movements can take stances and propose alternatives to capitalism, but "WSF events are non-deliberative for the WSF as a body forum". That is, the forum:

"...does not constitute a locus of power to be disputed by the participants in its meetings" and no one will be "authorized, on behalf of...the Forum, to express positions claiming to be those of all its participants." Nonetheless, "organizations or groups of organizations that participate in the Forums meetings are assured the right...to deliberate on declarations or actions they may decide on" (WSF).

It also means that the forum is not anti-party, but that the direct participation of political parties and military organizations is excluded. That is:

"...party representations or military organizations shall not participate in the Forum." This does not mean, "that government leaders and parliamentarians who abide by this Charter cannot be invited to participate, in a personal capacity" (WSF).

Up to now, Porto Alegre "was a process and not an organization" (Wallerstein 2004a). From now on, the WSF will continue to be an open forum, but it might try to find ways to include and institutionalize groups that aim to participate in common actions. For example, the *Movements Assembly* already creates resolutions and proposes concrete actions.

In addition, Mumbai was another great success in the consolidation of the WSF process. Essentially, it showed how the WSF is a universal aspiration that can be recreated in other countries. According to De Sousa Santos "Mumbai is the living symbol of the contradictions of capitalism in our time" (de Sousa 2004). The following issues were at the forefront of the WSF debates: the economic, sexual and ethnic inequalities (caste inequalities); religious fundamentalism; and the Social Movements Assembly against the war.

Further, there are other international forums (African, Asian, and European forums) apart from the WSF that are increasingly growing. The WSF has been encouraging the implementation of local, national, regional (in different continents), and thematic forums (dedicated to specific issues such as education). These forums are important in that they generate and bind the local with the global. Also, they enable the diversity of social groups to discuss their own specific struggles. The joint work of the bases and international networks allows for decentralization and a larger participation of local groups (Esther Vivas 2004).

The 2004 WSF signals a change in the course of the WSF events. Social movements have moved a step forward. They have gone from each social movement's discussions, and proposals for action, to specific requirements from all social movements regarding the forum as a movement organization itself. These referred to the identity of the forum, the places where it should be celebrated, and the themes it should cover.

Other Social Movements' Contexts

Other authors have emphasized the analysis of aspects not directly related to the WSF. Some address structural problems such as world inequalities (Bauman and Beltrán); others focus on the culture of organizations, such as the relationship between globalization and organizations or NGOs (Rucht, Romero, Roth and Roy), and identity processes (Castells).

With regard to the importance of a global civil society or to the emergence of *new* social movements, Bauman (*El País* 2003) admits that although we still do not know enough about these emerging social processes, solutions to global problems are not found locally but globally. Also, massive movements, such as the recent protests against the war are important not only because they work towards creating a feeling of a shared humanity,[15] but that they are weak. The weakness lies in that their objective is to confront just one problem (the war), so the action becomes spontaneous, diffused, creates weak social ties, and disappears as soon as the object of concerned is not on the social agenda. A bigger problem is that world inequality, which is at the heart of the lack of trust, prejudice and enmity, still remains alive after the protests. Thus, for Bauman, the only way to advance in the creation of civil society is to openly confront inequality, by making serious and shared efforts to mitigate it.

Miguel Beltrán (2002) agrees with Bauman in that both the nation-states and social movements must challenge globalization by questioning the dynamics of the new capitalism, and the autonomy of their financial elite. The time has come when it is imperative to oppose the growth of inequality, injustice, and the social exclusion caused by globalization. This might be achieved by the inclusion of the nation-states in supranational organisms such as the European Union, which is an institution that could develop common policies by assuming part of the national sovereignty of the member states in wider political areas.

With regard to the culture of organizations, experts point out the importance of an organization's political opportunities, professionalism, and its member's identity processes.

An organization's political opportunities are key aspects to its success. For example, with the concept of the "protest cycle," Tarrow was able to analyze collective action movements in the Western world since the eighteenth century (Romero 2003).[16] As a result, Romero integrated Tarrow's theory in a study of the cycles of protests that has characterized "anti-globalization movements" since the 1994 Zapatista uprising to the 2002 WSF of Porto Alegre. The conclusion to this study was that up to 1994, an international resistance movement to neoliberalism had been created, but this type of social action had far too general proposals and objectives, and no "political opportunities" to directly influence the course of international events. However, since 1992, several events[17] allow us to determine that the movement is in good health (Romero 2003: 223).

Roth also agrees that political opportunities are essential elements to the success of an organization. From an analysis of NGOs' institutional contexts, Roth evaluates that their presence in the international public sphere has indeed augmented considerably during the 1990s.[18] Before then, NGOs had little presence in the United Nations system, but since then, they participate in world conferences, and are accepted in most UN network institutions. Based on these results, he concludes that NGOs are in a position to influence a new global policy.[19] The consequences of the greater presence of NGOs in the international sphere are two-fold. On the one hand, NGOs are considered to be "the professional part of global social movements" even though international conference agreements are rarely taken into consideration by the nation-states. On the other hand, NGOs have become a challenge to the politics of social movements as they are able to act outside of national contexts and also rely on highly competitive workers. Thus, in the international community, NGOs are cautiously valued for what they do. This leads Roth to say that there is not enough knowledge on the future impact of NGOs on global democracy, for more research that uses uniform criteria on NGOs is needed.

In Rucht's (2001) analysis of *transnational mobilization of social movements* (*TMSM*), he also accentuates that the most creative variant of social movements is the various organizations of professional protests (such as Greenpeace). He considers them to be similar to corporations. However, he also believes that the link between globalization and TMSM is weak, and that although TMSM has been growing, they are not that new or creative in comparison to older social movements.

The focus on the importance of the professional aspect of NGOs is also stressed by Roy (2004) who thinks that non-autonomously financed NGOs (usually financed by governments, development agencies, the World Bank, the United Nations, and multinational corporations) have a big influence on alternative politics. NGOs work with budgets that employ paid workers. Most of those workers are local people, who identify with the goals of NGOs and support them in a legitimate way. If they were not employed, they would probably act as politically resistant groups towards the advancement of a social movement. This is where the strength of NGOs lie. They can serve as vehicles between the governments and the citizens and this is something that the political resistance organizations cannot do.

Finally, for Castells (1997) recent social movements are not a response to identity processes related to the old civil society but to current resistances. They are processes of resistance identities (such as the protests against the dominating capitalist system) and project identities (such as the proposals to transform society). They come from the subjects of the information age and their collective actions "whether a victory or a failure, transform values and societal institutions."

The role social movements can play is rich in content. Literature suggests that the WSFs are a powerful contribution to social change. Additionally, other perspectives not directly focused on the forums are quite enriching for they underline many relevant aspects. For instance, social movements should address some of the following dimensions: the structural, the organizational, and finally, the social–psychological. What all of these approaches have in common is a desire to participate in a global social transformation. But how can this be articulated? The next section addresses the specific proposals for action.

FUTURE ACTION

Williams (1984) reasoned that to think about the future is a type of activity exercised by people that are not only serious and concerned, but are also progressive and advanced in their thinking. In 1984, Williams tried explaining the mentality of the new politics, and how this could be opposed. He said that new politics are based on "Plan X." This is a way of thinking about the future with the idea that it is pervasive and dangerous. But above all, that it is predict-able. Proponents of this plan could not think about the possibility of political opportunities to make things better, but they could act to protect themselves. That is, they always thought and prepared to have a temporary competitive advantage on their side, a part of their plan that would give them a margin to play the game when the time came. For Williams, this was essentially the rational ideology of the future of capitalism.

For Williams, Plan X mentality was dangerous because it did not trust the possibility of a new order or a transformed society. For their proponents, there was no hope for the better. Thus, according to Williams, the only alternative to confront that kind of political conspiracy is to be just as rational and informed in politics as proponents of Plan X. For Williams, the alternative is ethically stronger in its concern for the common wellbeing, especially because it is more rational and better informed. Williams thought that we could find resources that have the potential to create extremely new political activities. For example, he pointed out that the resources available to oppose the perspective of capitalists were campaign movements (peace and environmental). In fact, he thought it was tempting to want to substitute the existing political and social ways of organizing and institutionalizing the social order with these growing human movements.

These following sections collect different proposals for action that have been made both at the ideological or intellectual level, and at the organizational or strategical. The first part gathers suggestions that were made prior to the 2004 WSF at Mumbai, and the second part collects those that were made after the forum.

Before Mumbai

Up to the 2004 WSF, suggestions for future actions gradually shifted from debates about the need for each movement to work towards establishing a decentralized structure, to discussions about political projects such as a *civil governance*, a *global governance*, or a new *International*.

First of all, Naomi Klein (2002) and Samir Amin (2003) expressed that what social movements really need to acquire is perhaps not a political party or some sort of centralization, but rather, a real decentralization. They argue for a better coordination among social movements and organizations. For Klein, the chal-lenges social movements face are based on structural problems. That is, some activists uphold direct democracy, self-management and transparency while many NGOs organize themselves according to traditional hierarchies, with charismatic leaders and executive committees. Samir Amin (2003) also reflects on an alternative to globalization based on building up a convergence of the totality of the diversity of social movements. The idea is that diversity must be respected in order for change to take place. For Amin, the real challenge lies in that there are different degrees of regulating capitalism or of being against imperialism. Some stances are more radical than others. Some movements vindicate only small regulations (reformists) and some others are more political (revolutionaries). But if movements get closer to one another, we will all benefit. After all, it is impossible for the victims of capitalism to achieve their immediate and limited goals in solitude.

Second, starting with sociologist Pierre Bourdieu (1930–2002), social scientists began suggesting the need to focus on how to build up a political democracy. Pierre Bourdieu's (2001) legacy reminds us of the importance of analyzing the consequences of globalization from the perspective of the dominating power of the neoliberal political agenda. For Bourdieu, to confront today's political globalization, what is needed is a group of independent intellectuals (artists, writers and researchers) that are linked to social movements. Especially the latter, *independent* or *committed scholars,* can commit to a sociological strategy that challenges the ideological construction of the neoliberal project. Scholars can go beyond national frontiers and discuss international problems. Also, they can go beyond the academic divide between scholarship and commitment and do both: "scholarship with commitment" (Bourdieu 2001: 109).

According to Roth (2003: 279–81), the possibility that NGOs create a "civil governance" is a vision of a global political democracy that integrates NGOs as the critical observers of the neoliberal globalization and civil society. It is a "globalization from below," in which NGOs are the "alternative" agents of transnational politics. For this to be achieved, more research and further actions on both the local and global must be considered. Further studies on NGOs and the international political system are needed on the following areas: (1) analyzing national and local social movements; and (2) analyzing the international political system, which includes a cooperative multilateral culture between the "world states," "world societies and economies," and a greater number of public and private associations. For instance, many local NGOs were created "from above," by transnational programs, international organizations and international NGOs.

After research is performed, actions towards a "global governance" should involve the professional participation of NGOs (and institutional recognition) in international politics, in two areas: (1) within the United Nations, NGOs need to achieve Habermas' proposal, Galtung's or the Lisbon Group's regarding a Second Assembly, and an official statute (in addition to the ECOSOC [Economic and Social Council]one); and (2) within the world community, NGOs need to create new transnational institutions (such as a world environmental organization), that solve some of the most serious problems, for example, strengthening NGOs transnational statutes, or achieving greater rights to information and transparency in international organizations and politics (Roth 2003).

For Romero, the success of the "anti-globalization movement" begins with a long-lasting "protest cycle" that establishes: (1) political projects such as those suggested in the large international forums;[20] (2) an egalitarian network of people that can communicate on an equal ground, such as Pierre Bourdieu's proposal of a "European Social Movement"; and (3) the integration of all social actors into a common program that finds ways to improve trust towards political international organizations (Romero 2003).

Third, experts and activists, such as Susan George and Díaz-Salazar, discuss more holistic projects. Although they also have "political" proposals for the future of social movements and globalization, their programs for action are more comprehensive. They encompass both structural and ideological aspects. For George (2003), the first steps that must be taken to achieve a "democratic, fair, and ecologic globalization" are ideological, for people must learn that there is an alternative to the neoliberal globalization.[21] It is certainly not an unavoidable phenomenon, and capitalism cannot rule our entire lives. Thus, some of the following concepts need to be redefined: "globalization," "privatization," and "anti-globalization movements." Also, people need to learn to be critical of the politics of the World Bank (WB), the International Monetary Fund (IMF), and the WTO.

George asserts we must follow certain strategies: First, we must find creative ways (through art for instance) to perform public demonstrations in both regional and international contexts, in addition to participating at the WSFs. Second, we must continue to define ourselves as non-violent and isolate groups that are violent; to have ideas, propositions for action[22] (for example, people's and businesses' international capital must be taxed). Third, we must aspire to the maximum of our goals. Fourth, we must propose limitations to the neoliberal program, and impose substituting the existing capitalist system by one that is more cooperative and even allows markets to have a place. Fifth, we must work towards achieving the wellbeing of all human beings. And finally, we must base our fights on national coalitions that reunite peasants, unions, women, workers, the unemployed, immigrants, human rights activists, and other forces. In sum, we must first build strong national bases, and then add the regional, and finally international (George 2003: 355).

Díaz-Salazar believes in the creation of a new International. He claims that *movements for a global justice* should go beyond the WSF, and the confluence of alternatives, campaigns, and mobilizations. They have a *resistance identity* and a *project identity*. They protest the international system of capitalist domination, and also have specific alternative proposals to build a different type of globalization. The difficulty lies in that there are many disagreements among movements with relation to concepts, strategies and priorities for action. Therefore, there should be unity in the proposals for action. The creation of a new International would be completely different in nature from the past ones. It would be an International of movements and not political parties. This would not substitute the WSF but complement it. The WSF should continue to be a non-political open space for all movements to participate, but movements should get more organized and their efforts systematized elsewhere.

A world priority and action list on basic themes needs to be elaborated. An International with a new organizational system could be created if we preserve the movements' identity as a reference connecting unity and diversity. The tools necessary for this type of work are the following:

(1) A permanent ideological debate about the objectives, diagnosis, proposals, and strategies;
(2) The creation of an international policy program for a global justice by a network of research centers, research institutes for action, and social movements;
(3) A working place that plans and coordinates international political pressure campaigns and mobilizations adapted to the needs of each region;
(4) A network of media professionals creating public opinion and influencing the mass media;
(5) An international evaluation and follow-up group;
(6) A stable and permanent International Council (Díaz-Salazar 2003: 82–83).

After Mumbai

The main challenges and proposals for future action debated at the forum centered on the WSF as an entity that encompasses all social movements participating at the forums. The following themes were the most popular: the forum as an open space or a movement; its organizational structure; the relationship between political parties and movements; and the debate between activists and intellectuals.

The January 2004 WSF in Mumbai, India, set a different political stage for the future of globalization and social movements. As Wallerstein (2004a) has noted, this year's forum altered the way social forums will continue to develop. The first theme was that the forum is an "open" space for movements to discuss alternatives to neoliberal globalization. It will continue to be. But since this year's 2004 forum, participants have agreed to step forward, and move from discussions to propositions for action. The *Movements Assembly* is an example of this, for they have issued calls for action at the end of each European Social Forum (ESF) and WSF.

For some experts, the concept of an "open" forum as a place to discuss and not make decisions made great sense in the initial stages of the forum for it probably helped reunite very different forces. The strength of the forums lies in its interplays (at seminars and workshops) and the calls for action. Thus, "we should be looking for ways that promote this interplay while maintaining unity" (Callinicos 2004: WSF). However, for activist Vandana Shiva (2004), the forum should not be institutionalized or centralized. Instead it should have a platform that embraces the diversity of tendencies, cultures, and movements. For Shiva, "Bigness is the strength of power, the vulnerability of people. Smallness and diversity, in contrast, are the strength of people, the vulnerability of power" (Shiva 2004: 90).

The second most discussed theme by participants at the 2004 WSF was the importance of redefining the role of the internal structure of the WSF, relegated to the International Council. The process to integrate new members needs to be more democratic as people are dissatisfied with the approval of norms by the consensus of the majority and not by all members (Vivas 2004). People claim a more open structure, allowing greater activists' participation in the decision-making processes that affect all, such as the places where assemblies are to be celebrated, the key speakers, the exclusions for participating, and others.

Next, participants claimed that the debate between political parties and social movements needs to be further redefined. The WSF Charter of Principles limits the participation of political parties. But the reality is that many do participate (Vivas 2004). For instance, according to Callinicos (2004), the WSF could not have taken place in India without the support of at least the large communist parties. Their presence in the Indian mobilizing committee—along with other independent activists and intellectuals—was discreet but important.

Finally, according to De Sousa (2004), at Mumbai, two things became obvious: first, that we now have much knowledge regarding organizations and movements, the world we live in, and proposals for change. Second, that we also have more of a need to develop plans for collective action. Plans should relate mainly to the strategies of the WSF—with regard to other international actors such as the WB and the IMF, and World Economic Forums—rather than to its effectiveness (now measured not by global actions but rather by local and national actions). For example, a proposal for a Popular University of Social Movements was presented this year.

The two-fold need to evaluate the knowledge we now have and to develop collective action plans, led to discussions about the relationship between social scientists and activists. This also led to a debate, which is at the center of public sociology:

the relationship between expertise and engagement; from critique to plans for action; the reliability of the knowledge underlying social struggles and its critique; the impact on social scientists of their engagement with lay or popular knowledge; activists as producers of knowledge. (De Sousa 2004)

Social movements have more answers to the effects of globalization than ever before. Debates center on volunteers, NGOs, transnational organizations, and WSFs. The WSFs are the highlight of the impact of social movements in the global community as they gather the attention of the media, thus, of the entire world. The media attention is necessary for it depicts the colorful and spectacular events representing the world community. However, besides the WSF debates, we should also consider other experts' suggestions, both intellectual and organizational, to plan for future actions.

THEORY AND APPLIED SOCIOLOGY

De Sousa's idea of combining different kinds of knowledge at WSF events, the theoretical and the practical, might sound like a novelty to activists participating in Social Forums. But it is not a new idea to sociologists and especially, applied sociologists. As noted by Jay Weinstein:

Applied (or practicing) sociologists tend to embrace an essentially pragmatic philosophy of science in which the ultimate test of theory is the extent to which it can produce knowledge that "works". (2000)

In 1984, Williams already noticed that social movements had a great potential for influencing the global social order. However, he was afraid that the groups were weakly linked to useful scientific research. He pointed out that the most notable trade of these movements was their relative success of combining scientific information with direct action. While he said that it was not an easy or stable combination, the degree of its success in several countries indicated that it is a political factor. Additionally, he also maintained that the relationships between the initiatives and the potential of small groups and the dominating system are the reason why these groups are not more successful.

Bourdieu (2001) also appealed to an "interdisciplinary and international collective intellect" necessary for creating an action program (ibid.: 219). For Bourdieu, two urgent tasks are needed. One is to convince competent researchers to join their efforts towards collective research that discusses, elaborates and imposes progressive propositions for action (so far, this type of work is marginal and diffused). Another task is to "coordinate (that is, integrate) the critical activities, theoretical and practical, of all researchers and activists...and to invent a new way of doing politics" (Bourdieu 2001: 220).

Social movements at the WSF organize in horizontal, networking ways. This is said to be, in part, a result of the need for practical, non-traditional ways of sharing knowledge (Wainwright 2004). If networking is necessary for social movements to oppose globalization, then discussions between activists and social scientists will benefit both groups. The latter can offer the theoretical and research tools that will complement activists' knowledge. And alternatively, the former will be able to share the wisdom acquired from the (physical) experience of participating in the events that represent them. Both can be equally powerful tools.

For one, activists need social scientists in order to influence public policy. As Weinstein notes (2000), "the soundest sociological theories" and the "most conscientious research possible" should inform public policy. If it does not, then "less carefully construed formulas will simply take their place." Additionally, social scientists need to learn from activists for knowledge embedded in practice cannot always be codified and documented (De Sousa 2004). Social scientists (and sociologists in particular) who are interested and involved in the dynamics of social movements need to learn the intricacies of the diversity of organizations, and their relationship to their specific governments, among other issues.

The WSF should indeed incorporate plans for action that combine the efforts of both academic and non-academic experts. If the objective of all participating in the WSF (and other pro-democracy events) is the creation of a better world, then an absolutely necessary step towards achieving that goal is to maximize the skills (intellectual and experiential) that are available. And at the WSF, these can be easily reached as both scientists and activists participate in the yearly events.

CONCLUSIONS

This chapter began with the assumption that literature (and discourses) on globalization and social movements has increased dramatically in the past few years. I asked the following questions: Why is it? Are the effects of globalization more pervasive today? Are social scientists now more aware of the negative consequences of globalization? Are social movements more influential today than they were previously? To respond to those questions, I analyzed three main aspects: (1) globalization's main challenges from a social movement's perspective; (2) social movements' responses to globalization; and (3) proposals for future action.

Looking at the responses to those questions, it appears that the increase of literature in the past ten years is taking place in both academic and non-academic circles. Globalization has been discussed especially since the 1980s, and *new* social movements since the 1990s. But the connection between globalization and social movements' literature has intensified in the past five years, coinciding with the beginning of the Word Social Forums in 2001. Thus, the increase of literature seems to be a result of the combination of knowledge and action. Social scientists are more informed today of the pervasive consequences of globalization for humanity. And social movements are also more influential (than they ever were before) on a global scale.

The sociology of globalization indicates that the role social movements play as transnational social actors requires further clarification. Some scholars argue civil society is an illegitimate actor of a global governance. But others assert that "the participation of human beings that think and act occupies a higher and growing position in the entire world" (Beck 2004: 314). The latter group addresses the importance of structural, organizational, and identity processes. All in all, the consensus lies upon the need to acquire a new and global definition of the political relationships between nation-states and transnational organizations. The structural and cultural reorganization of a global order suffers from a cultural lag. Globalization is a rapidly changing phenomenon, and the influence of social movements is also rapidly advancing. However, the structure of the relationship between social movements and the world community was last framed in 1992, by the United Nations inclusion of NGOs forums. Thus, it needs to be updated, and in light of recent social transformations, it needs to be more inclusive of social movements. But for such a redefinition of roles to be established, a preliminary step is needed. People first have to acknowledge that we have enough knowledge and expertise (from research and experience) to confront globalization. A preliminary analysis of the literature on globalization and social movements indicates that these two aspects are being acknowledged. On the one hand, globalists, liberals (or reformists), and radicals agree that globalization must be controlled and/or opposed. On the other hand, activists and other social scientists have concrete propositions for actions in the context of both WSFs and beyond, at local and national institutional levels.

What is taking place at the WSF is much more than a convergence of movements, networks, NGOs and the like. Participants at the WSF believe they can improve the world and based on that knowledge, they make suggestions for action. Proposals started with suggestions about the convergence of movements, and the ways to create new political programs. However, since 2004, debates have shifted to discuss the WSF as an organization itself. Participants are ready to create a "movement of movements." For that reason, at the 2004 WSF in Mumbai, the debates emphasized the identity of the forum, its structure, the extent to which it can have deliberative actions, and the interplay between theory and action, or expertise and intellect.

It is important that we have already arrived here, especially, that activists and social scientists are discussing the possibility of a "movement of movements." Indeed, proposals for action should be sound and well articulated. Both social scientists and activists should continue to dialog towards creating a new way of organizing social justice. They can combine their efforts, the theoretical and the practical, and integrate the particular with the universal. Activists can create new alliances. And applied sociology is essential to this task.

To conclude these pages, I raise and leave for discussion a larger question, addressing the possibility of a perspective change in the study of social movements, giving a growing importance to the connection between theory and action. That is, activists and social scientists are finally exchanging information. I argue that the growing importance of the WSF has at last offered the opportunity for these groups to work together. It is not that social movements are not powerful in and of themselves, for they are founded on strong local and national alliances. However, the open and diverse character of the WSFs has served as a catalyst for these two groups to finally concur and attract the attention of the media internationally. This will affect the way social movements continue to influence the global social order.

The possibility of a perspective change bonding theory and action in academic and non-academic circles (the political, the media, and public opinion) is a powerful way to continue advancing towards the creation of a more human social order, and a more human globalization. However, for this perspective change to go beyond the scope of social scientists and activists, and really extend itself universally, it needs the support of the larger legitimizing institutions (such as the United Nations) working to represent many parts of the world community. After all, the United Nations is much more than a peacekeeper and forum for conflict resolution. "Often without attracting attention, the United Nations and its family of agencies are engaged in a vast array of work that touches every aspect of people's lives around the world" (United Nations 2004).

Notes

1. Sorokin, P.A. 1954. *The Ways and Power of Love*. Beacon Press.
2. See Susan George (1999) for the social implications of neoliberalism, defined as the global power exercised by international corporations and business organizations in the international political system.
3. Although I have focused on sociological literature (national and international) published in Spanish, the voices represented here cross borders with other countries and disciplines. Almost all of the literature presented in the reference section has been published in both the English and the Spanish languages.
4. See the following studies providing essays on each movement's main complaints or propositions: Houtart and Polet (2001); Galdon (2002); Díaz-Salazar (2003); and Foro Social Mundial (2004).
5. See Wallerstein's analysis of how historical political struggles have shaped the creation of *universalisms* and *particularisms*. These ideological divisions have limited the ability of social scientists to agree on the values and truths that must be prioritized to arrive to some sort of consensus, or a *middle-run* that helps eliminate inequality (Wallerstein 2004b).
6. Arundhati Roy, "La resistencia al peligro de la ONGeización", en *Le Monde Diplomatique*, nº 108. October 2004.
7. See Boli's study on the development of NGOs from 1875 to 1973, and its relationship to the process of globalization (Roth 2003: 258).

8. See Roth (2003: 265–66), for a more in-depth explanation of how global transformations within the past two decades have offered opportunities to the development of transnational NGOs.
9. Unless otherwise indicated, this chapter will consider social movements and non-governmental organizations (NGOs) as similarly related concepts.
10. English translation by Elvira del Pozo.
11. English translation by Elvira del Pozo.
12. English translation by Elvira del Pozo.
13. George (2003: 349) contends that she is not anti-globalization. Rather, she is in favor of sharing friendship, culture, cooking, solidarity, wealth, and resources, thus she should be labeled "pro-democracy" or "pro-planet."
14. The UN Conference on Environment and Development, the "Earth Summit," was held in Rio de Janeiro. Attended by leaders from over 100 countries, it was the largest intergovernmental gathering in history, resulting in Agenda 21, a plan of action for sustainable development (UN).
15. See the work of political psychologist Kristen Monroe (1996) with regard to the importance of developing a concept of a shared humanity, or a *common humanity*, in understanding the meaning of altruism.
16. See Romero (2003) for an explanation of how Tarrow's concept of a "cycle protest" can be a useful methodology in interpreting today's "anti-globalization movements." The characteristics of these movements are organized around four poles: the confrontation repertoires, the collective action frameworks, the movement structures, and the political opportunity structures.
17. Some of these events are the following: the United Nations creation since 1992 of "NGO's Forums"; the 1998 protest against Multilateral Agreement on Investments (MAI); the 1999 Seattle protests; the 2001 Social Forum in Geneva; and the 2002 World Social Forum of Porto Alegre.
18. Roth summarizes research on the growing presence and contributions of NGOs in his article "NGOs and International Politics".
19. For some theorists, such as Roth, NGOs are equivalent to social movements (and especially, to new social movements), and for others, NGOs are an element (among others) of international social movements or specific organizations within a movement, such as the human rights movement. In either case, the study of transnational mobilizations is recently connecting these two areas of study more tightly (Roth 2003: 252, 261).
20. See George's "Planetary Contract", Petrella's "World Welfare" or Mary Kaldor and David Held's "Global Agreement for Justice and Peace".
21. See sociologist Ricardo Petrella's (2003) main suggestions for the ideological pillars that are necessary to build another world.
22. See George (2003: 353–55) for the rules that should be recognized as legitimate by the international community.

References

Amin, S. 2003. Convergencia en la Diversidad de los Movimientos Sociales, in R. Díaz-Salazar (ed.), *Justicia Global. Las Alternativas de los Movimientos del Foro de Porto Alegre*. Barcelona: Icaria, pp. 343–46.

Arrighi, G., T.K. Hopkins and I. Wallerstein. 1999. *Movimientos Antisistémicos*. Madrid: Ediciones Akal.

Bauman, Z. 2003. *La Globalización. Consecuencias Humanas*. México: Fondo de Cultura Económica.

Beck, U. 1998. *Qué es la globalización?: Falacias del Globalismo, Respuestas a la Globalización*. Barcelona: Ediciones Paidós Ibérica.

————. 2004. *Poder y Contrapoder en la Era Global. La Nueva Economía Política Mundial*. Barcelona: Ediciones Paidós Ibérica.

Beltrán, M. 2002. Globalización, in Antonio Ariño (ed.), *Diccionario de la Solidaridad*. Valencia: Tirant lo Blanch, pp. 257–73.

Bourdieu, P. 2001. *El Campo Político*. Bolivia: Plural Editores.

Callinicos, A. 2004. Mumbai: un Festival de los Oprimidos, in *Mumbai (Foro Social Mundial, 2004): Balance y Perspectivas de un Movimiento de Movimientos*. Barcelona: Icaria, pp. 27–32.

Casquette, J. 1998. *Política, Cultura, y Movimientos Sociales*. Bilbao: Bakeaz. Centro Documentación Estudios para la Paz.

Castells, M. 1997. *El Poder de la Identidad*. Madrid: Alianza Editorial.

Dalton, R.J. and M. Kuechler. 1992. *Los Nuevos Movimientos Sociales*. Valencia: Institución Alfonso el Magnánimo.

De Sousa Santos, Boaventura. 2004. Mumbai and the Future. *Footnotes Newsletter* 32(3). Available online at http://www.2.asianet.org/footnotes/mar04

Díaz-Salazar, Rafael (ed.). 2003. *Justicia Global. Las Alternativas de los Movimientos del Foro de Porto Alegre*. Barcelona: Icaria.

El País, "Zygmunt Bauman", May 10, 2003.

Flacks, Richard. 1994. The Party Is Over; Qué hacer ante la crisis de los partidos políticos? in E. Laraña and J. Gusfield (eds), *Los Nuevos Movimientos Sociales. De la Identidad a la Ideología*. Madrid: Centro de Investigaciones Sociológicas.

Foro Social Mundial. 2004. *Mumbai (Foro Social Mundial, 2004): Balance y Perspectivas de un Movimiento de Movimientos*. Barcelona: Icaria.

Galdón, G. (ed.). 2002. *Mundo, S.A.: Voces Contra la Globalización*. Barcelona: Ediciones de la tempestad.

García Ferrando, M. 2004. *Globalización y Choque de Civilizaciones. Pensando Nuestra Sociedad Global*. Valencia: Universidad de Valencia.

George, S. 1999. *A Short History of Neoliberalism. Twenty Years of Elite Economics and Emerging Opportunities for Structural Change*. Conference on "Economic Sovereignty in a Globalizing World". Bangkok, March, 24–26.

————. 2003. Qué hacer ahora? in R. Díaz-Salazar (ed.), *Justicia Global. Las Alternativas de los Movimientos del Foro de Porto Alegre*. Barcelona: Icaria, pp. 347–56.

Held, D. and A. McGrew. 2003. *Globalización/Anti-globalización: Sobre la Reconstrucción del Orden Mundial*. Barcelona: Ediciones Paidós Ibérica.

Houtart, François and François Polet. 2001. *El otro Davos. Globalización de Resistencias y de Luchas*. Madrid: Editorial Popular.

Hugo, V. 2002. Introducción. Otro Mundo es Posible, in G. Galdón (ed.), *Mundo, S.A.: Voces Contra la Globalización*. Barcelona: Ediciones de la tempestad.

Inglehart, R. 1992. Valores, Ideología y Movilización Cognitiva, in J.D. Russell and M. Kuechler (eds), *Los Nuevos Movimientos Sociales*. Valencia: Institución Alfonso el Magnánimo, pp. 71–100.

Klein, N. 2002. Como una Nube de Mosquitos, in G. Galdón (ed.), *Mundo, S.A.: Voces Contra la Globalización*. Barcelona: Ediciones de la tempestad.

Laraña, E. and J. Gusfield. 1994. *Los Nuevos Movimientos Sociales: de la Ideología a la Identidad*. Madrid: Centro de Investigaciones Sociológicas.

Merton, R.K. 1995. The Thomas theorem and the Matthew effect. *Social Forces* 74(2): 379–424.

Monroe, K.R. 1996. *The Heart of Altruism: Perceptions of a Common Humanity*. Princeton, NJ: Princeton University Press.

Petrella, R. 2003. Los Pilares Prioritarios para la Construcción de Otro Mundo, in J.M. Vidal Villa (ed.), *Un mundo para todos. Otra globalización es posible*. Barcelona: Icaria.

Ramonet, I. 2003. Cambiar el Mundo, in R. Díaz-Salazar (ed.), *Justicia Global. Las Alternativas de los Movimientos del Foro de Porto Alegre*. Barcelona: Icaria, pp. 11–14.

Romero, M. 2003. El Futuro de la Sociedad Civil, in V. Beneyto (ed.), *Hacia una Sociedad Civil y Global*. Madrid: Taurus Ediciones. Grupo Santillana.

Roth, R. 2003. Las ONG y las Políticas Internacionales, in V. Beneyto (ed.), *Hacia una Sociedad Civil y Global*. Madrid: Taurus Ediciones. Grupo Santillana, pp. 245–87.

Rucht, D. 2001. Transnacionalización y Globalización de los Movimientos Sociales, in R. Máiz (ed.), *Construcción de Europa, Democracia y Globalización*. Santiago de Compostela: Universidad de Santiago de Compostela, pp. 341–60.

Salinas. 2001. Presentación, in *Documentación Social* 125: 7–13.

Shiva, V. 2004. La Lucha Epica contra el Capital. *Mumbai (Foro Social Mundial, 2004): Balance y Perspectivas de un Movimiento de Movimientos*. Barcelona: Icaria.

Tejerían, B. 2003. Movimientos Sociales, in A. Ariño (ed.), *Diccionario de la Solidaridad*. Valencia: Tirant lo Blanch.

United Nations. 2004. Major Achievements of the United Nations. Retrieved November 23. Available online at http://www.un.org/english/.

Vivas, E. 2004. De Porto Alegre a Mumbai, *Mumbai (Foro Social Mundial, 2004): Balance y Perspectivas de un Movimiento de Movimientos*. Barcelona: Icaria.

Wainwright, H. 2004. From Mumbai with Hope. *Red Pepper*, March. Available online at http://www. redpepper.org.uk.

Wallerstein, I. 2004a. La Fuerza Creciente del Foro Social Mundial. *La Jornada sin fronteras*, February.

————. 2004b. Cultures in Conflict: Who are We? Who are the Others, in S. Dasgupta (ed.), *The Changing Face of Globalization*. India: Sage, pp. 79–97.

Weinstein, J. 2000. The Place of Theory in Applied Sociology: A Reflection. *Theory & Science*: 1(1). Available online at http://www.theoryandscience.icaap.org/content/vol001.001/01weinstein_revised. html

Williams, R. 1984. *Hacia el Año 2000*. Barcelona: Editorial Crítica.

World Social Forum. 2004. Available online at http://www.forumsocialmundial.org.br/home.asp

Zubero, I. 2003. Voluntariado y acción colectiva, in T. Montagut (ed.), *Voluntariado: la lógica de la ciudadanía*. Barcelona: Editorial Ariel, pp. 33–50.

13

THE EFFECTS OF GLOBAL ECONOMIC EXPANSION ON ORGANIZED RESISTANCE

ERNEST M. DE ZOLT

Acts of organized resistance are traditional responses to the inherent exploitation that accompanies global economic expansion. Global economic expansion efforts often set as rivals the will of law against the wishes of individuals. Middle European history offers two examples of the role of law promoting feudal and mercantile interests over the welfare of serf labor. During the fourteenth century, English vagrancy laws mandated serf labor back to the estate system that formerly employed it. The reason given for the passage of vagrancy laws was to prevent the encouragement and transfer of serf labor to other regions because of labor shortages due to the cholera epidemic and the lure by distant merchants. In this example, the will of law is seen to protect the feudal economy against the advances of mercantilism. By the early eighteenth century, with mercantilism the accepted proxy to feudalism, a law was written supplanting serf rights to share in the advantages of common land in exchange for the exclusive rights of elites to convert this land to private property. The will of law in this example was seen to protect the interests of mercantilism through the creation of an economic structure that encouraged the ownership of private property for profit. This shift in economy forever changed the relational aspects of labor between owners and workers (Chambliss 1964).

In both examples, economic expansion laid claim to legal favor but not without considerable resistance. Though resistance to global economic expansion lasted for hundreds of years, with the onset of industrial society much of its organized sustainability was lost. With acts of organized resistance weakened, core nations turned their primary attention away from economic dominance and towards the erosion of sovereignty and the national identity of semi-peripheral and peripheral nations. Max Weber (1958) foreshadowed this understanding in *The Protestant Work Ethic and the Spirit of Capitalism* when he wrote:

The desire for wealth has existed in most times and places, and has in itself nothing to do with capitalistic action, which involves a regular orientation to the achievement of profit through normally peaceful economic exchange. (1958: Introduction)

Wallerstein (1984), Rahman (2004), and Sciulli (1999), like Weber (1958) before them, have concerns that economic expansion unavoidably leads to world dominance. This concern is based on the promise to semi-peripheral and peripheral nations of greater global economic participation in exchange for their labor and resources. It is through the encouragement of this false promise that core nations have successfully weakened organized resistance.

Although the facts surrounding the political and economic *causes* of global economic expansion and the exploitation *effects* on semi-peripheral and peripheral nations are not seriously challenged, this chapter questions whether global economic expansion has reached a threshold that has the latent effect of reviving organized resistance. Everything from the Kyoto Protocol, which is not discussed in this work to the Iraq War, which is discussed, seems to indicate a renewed relational interdependence between global economic expansion and organized resistance.

In an attempt to address the global economic expansion/organized resistance relationship, this paper will examine: (1) the underlying theoretical assumptions of global economic expansion; (2) the role of legal legitimation; (3) the role of the mass media; and (4) the reasons for organized resistance. Because the methodology here utilizes an archival review of organized resistance, this chapter provides a description of grassroots organizations and their participation in organized resistance. What this methodology does not provide is an *objective* assessment of the structural and psychological factors of organized resistance.

In an attempt to compensate for the limitations of this methodology, this chapter develops a number of theoretical assumptions that *subjectively* link global economic expansion with acts of organized resistance. The first six of these assumptions analyze the ways and reasons behind global economic expansion. The remaining two assumptions analyze the content and form of organized resistance.

THE ROLE OF LEGITIMATION AND GLOBAL ECONOMIC EXPANSION

While organized resistance to global economic expansion has been on the increase since 1994, this resistance has had no appreciable effect on the state management of economic life. The state management of economic life for core nations is essentially predicated on the application of national and international laws, the receptivity of home and foreign governments, and an unquestioning mass media. These structural institutional links to global economic expansion are founded on an ideology that espouses legitimation. To the extent that these structural institutional links remain unchallenged, semi-peripheral and peripheral nations are likely to remain dominated as core nations manage the "transnational encouragement of the hyper-mobility of capital, the unending search for cheap labor, and the immobility of domestic labor" (Chirayath and De Zolt 2004: 151–52).

Yet to be determined, even after ten years of unprecedented organized resistance, is whether local and international resistance organizations will have an impact on the state management of economic life. To be successful, these organizations must extend beyond traditional strategies of resistance (the mass demonstrations against the Vietnam War and the 1968 Democratic National Convention are illustrative here). In particular, future organized resistance must convince individuals of the inherent inequities found in the ideology of global economic expansion that expresses the values of achievement, self-reliance, equality of opportunity, and meritocracy. To the extent that organized resistance does not successfully challenge this ideology, core nations will be able to lower the consciousness of world nations by convincing them that an ideology comprised of these values is important to the democratization of the world, with inherent advantage to all (Marger 2005).

Assuming a successful challenge by organized resistance to core nation ideology, there is no guarantee that core nations will oblige with a willingness to alter the norms of global economic expansion. World history is clear on the unwillingness of core nations to abandon their quest for cheap labor and investment capital for the concerns of distributive justice. If the current practices by core nations remains as is, serious challenges to global economic expansion is unlikely.

Perhaps the success for organized resistance lies not in its ability to halt the spread of global capitalism (its form) but to take issue with the unquestioned legitimacy of economic expansion (its content). The content of economic expansion may very well be vulnerable to organized resistance efforts. If the form of economic expansion is suggested to rest on its perceived legitimate authority over global resources and labor, then protestors will be able to position their organized resistance in terms of challenges to core nation colonization of foreign resources and labor. Through a suggested change in the fundamental values of core nations, organized resistance can develop a new paradigm for global economic expansion that would successfully limit the inequities to semi-peripheral and peripheral nations (Mannheim 1936; Kuhn 1970).

THE ROLE OF LAW AND GLOBAL ECONOMIC EXPANSION

The role of law in global economic expansion is mentioned in the beginning of this chapter. As indicated, the conflict over public and private legal advantage, then as now, features a competition based on the contractual relation to social value. At issue here is the balance struck between the maximization of social value for its own sake versus the maximization of social value for competitive corporate advantage (Schiller 1989). If conflicts of interest between public and private advantage are not complicated enough in their negotiation, the fact that there is no precedent for the maximization of social value on its own merits makes this conflict even more precarious to regulate. According to Allen (1992), the consequence of not having a universal value standard renders schizophrenic the law-making process governing global economic expansion.

The likelihood that the law will reverse its position on limiting public good for private gain is slight (Domhoff 2002). If organized resistance is to be more effective in the future, two goals must be accomplished: (1) organized resistance must gain influence over the law; and (2) organized resistance must expose global economic expansion as in violation of civil society (Enron's failed promise to develop an energy grid for Dhabhol India is illustrative here).

THE ROLE OF THE MASS MEDIA AND GLOBAL ECONOMIC EXPANSION

While a system of legitimation and legal intervention establish the context for global economic expansion, the mass media provides its reference point of meaning. The Great American Public, as Mills (1956) called it, is the stage upon which world dominance is performed. The question is whether an international public is able to discern legitimacy from propaganda when considering the agenda of global economic expansion.

Unlike the classic eighteenth century version of public where a competition of ideas existed between people over reason and interest, today's public is hindered by the inability of individuals to compete against core nation control over the marketplace of ideas (Habermas 1984). As Mills (1956) notes, "[i]n the mass society of media markets, competition, if any, goes on between the manipulators with their mass media on the one hand, and the people receiving their propaganda on the other" (105).

If, as Mills believes, mass media propaganda is legitimized, then economic world dominance is likely to worsen in coming decades (Lippmann 1922). The question for organized resistance is how to both inform and invigorate protest in a manner that maximizes world public opinion.

CONTEMPORARY ORGANIZED RESISTANCE

Contemporary organized resistance is at a significant disadvantage in successfully overcoming ideological, legislative, and media influences on global economic expansion due to the challenges of corrupt national leaders, the diversity of opportunity for resistance actions, and a disproportionately young, student, and local resistance base (O'Neill 2004). Notwithstanding these problems, Green and Griffith (2002) believe that organized resistance has established itself over the past ten years as an authentic "anti-globalization movement." The principal challenge to organized resistance comes from a need to more effectively monitor marginalized resistance groups like the "Black Bloc" who employ destructive tactics for their own purposes and to the detriment of legitimate resistance concerns. The failure to attend to inter-group and intra-group conflicts will undermine the ability of organized resistance to be viewed as a viable partner in future "global economic governance."

METHODOLOGY

The methodology for this paper reviews ten archived cases of organized resistance from 1994 to 2003. The ten selected cases are: the (1994) Zapatista Movement; the (1997) United Parcel Post Strike; the (1999) "Battle of Seattle"; the (1999) National Autonomous University of Mexico Student Strike; the (2000) World Bank Summit; the (2000) Porto Alegre Summit; the (2000) Okinawa Summit; the (2000) Bolivia "Water War"; the (2001) G-8 Genoa Summit; and the current Iraq War (see Table 13.1). The reason for the selection of these ten cases is because of their routine citing in the literatures that inform sociology, political science, international relations, and economics (Seoane and Taddei 2002).

Table 13.1: Cases of Organized Resistance by Structural Attributes

---

(1994) Zapatista Movement

Location of Resistance: Mountains of Southwestern Mexico.

Specific Act of Global Domination: The development of the Multilateral Investment Agreement which protects foreign investment from the regulatory powers of semi-peripheral and peripheral nations.

Nation Where Global Core Domination Occurred: Mexico.

Structure of Organized Resistance: Social Movement of 3,000 people from forty countries led against the ills of neoliberal globalization. An initiative entitled: "Second Declaration of Reality."

Impact of Resistance: Successful in obtaining an international treaty designed to protect foreign investments to the detriment of semi and peripheral nations.

(1997) United Parcel Post Strike (UPPS)

Location of Resistance: Headquarters of Private Mail Company.

Specific Act of Global Domination: Two-week strike against company's labor policies.

(contd.)

Table 13.1 contd.

Nation Where Global Core Domination Occurred: United States.

Structure of Organized Resistance: Teamsters and AFL-CIO trade unionism.

Impact of Resistance: Successful in reversing prior erosion of worker gains.

(1999) "Battle of Seattle"

Location of Resistance: Seattle, Washington.

Specific Act of Global Domination: The development and exploitation of the World Trade Organization.

Nation Where Global Core Domination Occurred: International focus.

Structure of Organized Resistance: Protesters from seventy different nations converged onto the streets of Seattle.

Impact of Resistance: Successful in bringing about the most important demonstration since the Vietnam War protests.

(1999) University of Mexico Student Strike

Location of Resistance: National Autonomous University, Mexico.

Specific Act of Global Domination: IMF pressure on the Mexican government to reduce expenditures for public higher education.

Nation Where Global Core Domination Occurred: Mexico.

Structure of Organized Resistance: Student insurgency and take-over of the University.

Impact of Resistance: Successful in bringing attention to the corporatist insurgency of universities.

(2000) World Bank Summit

Location of Resistance: Prague, Czech Republic.

Specific Act of Global Domination: International Monetary Fund (IMF) Abuses.

Nation Where Global Core Domination Occurred: International focus.

Structure of Organized Resistance: 15,000 demonstrators protested the role of the IMF for the increase of poverty in the region.

Impact of Resistance: Successful in forcing the IMF to adjourn early and presenting to IMF members a document denouncing the increase in poverty as a result of their practices.

(2000) Porto Alegre

Location of Resistance: Classrooms at the Catholic University of Rio Grande do Sul and the streets of Porto Alegre.

Specific Act of Global Domination: Hosted a World Social Forum on the struggle against neoliberal globalization.

Nation Where Global Core Domination Occurred: Brazil.

(contd.)

Table 13.1 contd.

Structure of Organized Resistance: 4,700 individuals from labor unions, peasant organizations, women's movements, and the military protested globalization.

Impact of Resistance: Successful in developing international "movement" against anti-globalization.

(2000) Okinawa Summit

Location of Resistance: Okinawa, Japan.

Specific Act of Global Domination: Establishment of foreign debt and the creation of military bases.

Nation Where Global Core Domination Occurred: International focus—primarily in poor countries.

Structure of Organized Resistance: Demonstrations urging debt forgiveness by core nations of semi- and peripheral nations and also the removal of military bases.

Impact of Resistance: Unknown.

(2000) "Water War"

Location of Resistance: Cochabamba, Bolivia.

Specific Act of Global Domination: The privatization of the water supply to Bolivians.

Nation Where Global Core Domination Occurred: Bolivia.

Structure of Organized Resistance: Week-long violent protest that began with resistance to the privatization of water but extended to additional government corruption.

Impact of Resistance: Successful in forcing the government into concessions in several areas.

(2001) Genoa G-8 Summit

Location of Resistance: Genoa, Italy.

Specific Act of Global Domination: World Trade Organization and International Monetary Fund involvement in the spread of global neoliberalism.

Nation Where Global Core Domination Occurred: International focus.

Structure of Organized Resistance: Violent street demonstrations and police reactions that ended in the death of one protester.

Impact of Resistance: Considered as one of the most influential acts of resistance, along with the "Battle of Seattle" and the World Summit in Prague.

(2002–2003) Iraq War

Location of Resistance: Worldwide demonstrations.

Specific Act of Global Domination: US involvement in deposing a nation's president and establishing non-bid contracts to Halliburton and Bechtel Corporations.

Nation Where Global Core Domination Occurred: Iraq.

Structure of Organized Resistance: Worldwide demonstrations supported by seven million protesters.

Impact of Resistance: Unsuccessful in stopping the war, the awarding of non-bid contracts, and US involvement in nation-building.

As a means of qualitatively assessing these cases, this chapter originates a template to analyze: (1) the location of the organized resistance; (2) the specific act of global domination; (3) the nation where the global domination occurred; (4) the structure of the organized resistance; and (5) the immediate influence of the resistance on global economic expansion. In addition, each case is examined against the eight theoretical assumptions that inform this work in order to analyze whether there is any correlational agreement between them and the cited acts of organized resistance (see Table 13.2).

Capitalism is an economic system predicated on the unrestrained global expansion of markets. Core nations, through their utilization of capitalism, exploit the labor and resources of peripheral and semi-peripheral nations. Global economic expansion is increasing due to the role of multinational corporations and the corrupt governments that host them. Global economic expansion leads to the submission of political and economic self-determination by peripheral, and semi-peripheral nations to core nations. Loss of political and economic self-determination for peripheral and semi-peripheral nations establishes an exchange of indigenous production for cash crop exportation.

As organized resistance increases, the governments of core, semi-peripheral and peripheral nations will adhere to harsh sanctions to restore global economic expansion. Organized resistance is a protest against both the content and the form of global economic expansion. Anti-neoliberal sentiments against core nations and the multinational corporations that do their bidding are the social glue that holds together acts of organized resistance.

A SUMMARY OF ORGANIZED RESISTANCE

Though rich in a tradition centuries old, organized resistance has established a recent historical pattern of effective struggle against global economic expansion.

Table 13.2: Cases of Organized Resistance by Theoretical Assumptions

Assumptions	1	2	3	4	5	6	7	8
Cases								
(1994) Zapatista Movement	+	+	+	+	+	–	+	+
(1997) UPPS Strike	–	–	–	–	–	–	+	–
(1999) "Battle of Seattle"	+	+	+	+	+	–	+	+
(1999) Student Strike	–	+	+	+	+	+	+	+
(2000) World Bank Summit	+	+	+	+	+	–	+	+
(2000) Porto Alegre	+	+	+	–	+	+	+	+
(2000) Okinawa Summit	+	–	+	+	+	–	+	+
(2000) Bolivia "Water War"	–	–	–	–	+	+	+	+
(2001) Genoa G-8 Summit	+	+	+	+	+	–	+	+
(2002–2003) Iraq War	+	+	+	+	+	–	+	+

+ Indicates case adherence to theoretical assumption based on the known facts of each case.

A review of the cases of organized resistance indicates a nationalizing and, in some examples, an internationalizing of resistance. This has produced impacts ranging from successful insurgencies to demands that semi-peripheral and peripheral governments reverse prior erosions of standards and ways of living. Though the advantages of these recent struggles against global economic expansion outweigh the disadvantages, it is not until organized resistance gains influence over governing laws that its sustainability will be secured.

The ten cases in this chapter deal with organized resistance against the questionable motives and practices of core nations in their pursuit of global economic expansion. While case adherence to the theoretical assumptions is mixed, the (1997) United Parcel Post Strike and the (2000) Bolivian "Water War" appear to represent the weakest association to the motives and practices of core nations as stated in the eight assumptions. This is not meant to suggest that these cases of organized dissent remain totally apart from core nation influence but only that a review of the facts in these cases does not link them theoretically to the ill effects of global economic expansion. The remaining cases indicate a structural link to at least six of the eight theoretical assumptions.

IMPLICATIONS AND APPLICATIONS
OF ORGANIZED RESISTANCE

The lasting effects of organized resistance on global economic expansion are indeterminate. Given the past instrumental behavior of core nations, it is possible for the future of economic expansion to entertain with equal merit the extremes of avariciousness and open-handedness. Without the insights of ethnographic data applied to the efforts of both organized resistance and economic expansion, there is no way of discerning whether and how organized resistance can contribute to a value change to the current ideology of core nation dominance.

A review of the cases in this chapter suggests that there is a growing internationalism to formerly local grassroots organizations and their acts of resistance. If this proves to be more than a transient development, organized resistance may hold the key to limiting the future frequency and versatility of applied global economic expansion. Though a reduction in the frequency and versatility of global economic expansion is not predicted, there may be significant gains available in structuring a less destructive way for global economic expansion to occur.

To the extent that global economic expansion refuses the suggestions or demands of organized resistance, a new pattern of global struggle may arise with indigenous people demanding resource entitlement over their lands. This would cause problems not only for core nations but the semi-peripheral and peripheral governments that host them. Together with this entitlement claim may come a revolutionary reaction to corruption. If this reaction were to intensify, we may see a significant decline in economic dominance by core nations.

One final consideration regarding the future success of organized resistance revolves around the mobilization of resources. All successful twentieth century social movements possessed the ability to enlist labor and technological resources in the struggle over their causes. In the case of contemporary resistance, instant global access through the Internet may prove a potential ally. Access to dot-com organizations and websites provide local protesters with proximity to a wider international community of organized resistance. Save for a "pay-to-use" Internet tax or a denial of access on the basis of national security, grassroots organizations should be able to extend their net of influence to the construction of what Seoane and Taddei (2002) refer to as a "social arc of organizations."

If organized resistance can overcome the internal and external challenges associated with it, the global economic influence of core nations over semi-peripheral and peripheral nations should begin to erode along with the myth of a global economic village (Rhoads 2003). As core nations proceed onward, they may be underestimating the influence of organized resistance to accomplish what was previously theorized in utopian terms—proletariat solidarity and resistance against global economic expansion and the system of capitalism that promotes it.

References

Allen, (Chancellor) W.T. 1992. Our Schizophrenic Conception of the Business Corporation. *Cardozo Law Review* 14: 261–81.

Chambliss, W.J. 1964. A Sociological Analysis of the Law of Vagrancy. *Social Problems* 12: 45–69.

Chirayath, V. and Ernest M. De Zolt. 2004. Globalization, Multinational Corporations, and White-Collar Crime: Cases and Consequences for Transitional Economies, in S. Dasgupta (ed.), *The Changing Face of Globalization*. New Delhi: Sage Publications, pp. 151–65.

Domhoff, G.W. 2002. *Who Rules America? Power and Politics* (Fourth Edition). Boston: McGraw-Hill.

Green, D. and M. Griffith. 2002. Globalization and Its Discontents. *International Affairs* 78(1): 49–68.

Habermas, J. 1984. *Reason and the Rationalization of Society*. Boston: Beacon Press.

Kuhn, T.S. 1970. *The Structure of Scientific Revolutions* (Second Edition). Chicago: University of Chicago Press.

Lippmann, W. 1922. *Public Opinion*. New York: Macmillan.

Mannheim, K. 1936. *Ideology and Utopia*. New York: Harcourt, Brace, and World, Inc.

Marger, M. 2005. *Social Inequality: Patterns and Processes* (Third Edition). Boston, MA: McGraw-Hill.

Mills, C.W. 1956. *The Power Elite* (First Edition). London: Oxford University Press.

O'Neill, K. 2004. Transnational Protest: States, Circuses, and Conflict at the Frontline of Global Politics. *International Studies Review* 6: 233–51.

Raham, A. 2004. Globalization: The Emerging Ideology in the Popular Protests and Grassroots Action Research. *Action Research* 2(1): 9–23.

Rhoads, R.A. 2003. Globalization and Resistance in the United States and Mexico: The Global Potemkin Village. *Higher Education* 45: 223–50.

Schiller, H.I. 1989. *Culture Inc.: The Corporate Takeover of Public Expression.* New York: Oxford University Press.

Sciulli, D. 1999. *Corporations versus the Court: Private Power, Public Interests.* London: Lynne Rienner Publishers.

Seoane, J. and E. Taddei. 2002. From Seattle to Porto Alegre: The Anti-Neoliberal Globalization Movement. *Current Sociology* 50(1): 99–122.

Wallerstein, I. 1984. *The Politics of a World-economy: The State, The Movements and the Civilizations.* New York: Cambridge University Press.

Weber, M. 1958. *The Protestant Work Ethic and the Spirit of Capitalism* (Translated by T. Parsons). New York: Charles Scribner's Sons.

14

DIVISION AND DISSENT IN THE ANTI-GLOBALIZATION MOVEMENT

TOMÁS MAC SHEOIN AND NICOLA YEATES

That social and political conflict is integral to processes of "globalization" is widely accepted. Not only has the world become more integrated since 1945 but it has also become more turbulent, at least in part due to that growing global interdependence (Rosenau 1990). Rather than the prophesized end of history, the 1990s have been characterized by an increase in contentious political activity: with the processes and effects of globalization spreading throughout the world, a range of social movement organizations and NGOs are increasingly cooperating and coordinating at national and transnational levels, most often in the sharing of information and debate and also in their actions. Over the same period, the academic literature on transnational social movements and activism has proliferated[1] and a range of concepts has been elaborated to explain these developments: "transnational advocacy networks" (Keck and Sikkink 1998); "transnational social movement organizations" (Smith et al. 1997); "global social movements" (Cohen and Rai 2000) and "global civil society" (Anheier et al. 2001). These analyses have in common an attempt to explain what are considered to be "new" politics occurring on a scale "above" and "beyond" the national, whether this involves supra-territoriality or de-territorialization, and involving non-traditional political actors, organizing methods and tactics. Whether the focus is an empirical one or a theoretical/conceptual one, a common theme within this literature is that social movement organization has moved from the national level to transnational level, with new targets (transnational governmental institutions) and a concomitant reduction in the importance and occurrence of national contention. Thus, for example, Passy (1999) argues that "the emergence of new political opportunities on the international level brings about a radical change in the nature of protest, which tends to globalise, as well as in the structure of social movement organisations, which become transnational in scope" (152). More cautiously, Cohen and Rai (2000: 16) conclude "without a transnational framework—a global social space or forum—the possibilities of opposition and protest are seriously weakened. We need to think of the possible emergence of an alternative global society."

The anti-globalization movement (AGM) has been widely used to illustrate this "new" politics, combining as it does the varying scalar and spatial dimensions held to be key to these developments. To begin with, the AGM opposes nothing less than a world-system; thus the target is truly transnational. In addition, the AGM is a global social movement *par excellence*, uniting as it does all the other major global social movements. Furthermore, it is organizationally new in its use of social and technological networks, such as the Internet, and its use of consensus methods of decision-making and lack of hierarchy in organizational structures, many of which are temporary.

While many analysts of the AGM have stressed its novelty, we contend that the AGM has much in common with previous social movements, whether "old" or "new." There are two aspects to our argument. First, an overemphasis on the transnational elements of the AGM ignores the importance of its local and national bases. We correct this by stressing the national character of major AGM actions and by highlighting, even within the transnational aspects such as solidarity demonstrations, the national character of these actions in terms of their composition and choice of target. In doing so, we situate our analysis within a body of work challenging the popularization of claims that anti-globalization campaigns and networks are forging new modes of collective political action and constructing a new "global" political community, a "global citizenship" (Keck and Sikkink 1998; Anheier et al. 2001; Laxer and Halperin 2003). As Tarrow (2001) argued, too many observers have made a hasty analytical leap from protests against globalization to transnational social movements to global civil society. Indeed, it is not hard to see these leaps as the working out in social movement studies of the strong theory of globalization that overemphasizes the degree of economic and political de-territorialization that has actually occurred (Yeates 2001).

Second, we emphasize the continuation of "old" forms of politics in the AGM by exploring the conflict between "old" and "new" forms of politics over demonstration tactics and the new social spaces created by the AGM, notably the World Social Forum (WSF). In doing so, we extend previous analyses of contemporary transnational politics that have highlighted the centrality of "traditional axes of discrimination and disadvantage: patriarchal gender relations, racial hierarchies, class inequalities and differential access to the means of production, distribution, exchange and communication" (Cohen and Rai 2000: 14; summarizing Guarnizo and Smith 1998). In particular, we argue that the AGM displays the most traditional division of all in social movements—that between reformists and radicals/revolutionaries. This division between the "verticals"—hierarchical national and international NGOs and political parties—on the one hand and the "horizontals"—looser affinity groups, anarchists and direct actionists—on the other hand is summarized in Table 14.1.

Table 14.1: Reformist and Revolutionary Wings of the AGM

	Reformist	Revolutionary
Exemplar AGM group	ATTAC	PGA
Exemplar AGM institution	World Social Forum	Indymedia
Position on globalization	Globalization with a "human face"	Anti-globalization
Organizational format	Centralized hierarchy	De-centralized network
	Permanent administrative apparatus	Temporary administrative apparatus
	Directed organization	Self-organization
Democracy	Representative	Direct
	Non-transparent	Transparent
	Closed participation	Open participation
Tactics	Lobbying, alternative policy formation	Confrontational
Strategy	Reform system	Overthrow system
	Statist	Anti-statist

In this chapter we examine these contradictions through a focus on the three main manifestations of the movement, namely street protests, social fora and new media of communication, and the expression of the tensions between the reformist and revolutionary wings of the AGM. The discussion is organized into three main sections. It begins with a general introduction to the AGM in which we review the problems of definition and terminology and outline the various characteristics of the movement. In section two, the discussion proceeds through a comparison of the approaches of two contrasting organizations within the movement—PGA and ATTAC. In section three we examine the two principal "institutions" that the movement has created—the Social Forum and Indymedia—as a means of further illustrating issues of coalition and conflict in the movement.

THE AGM: DEFINITIONS AND CHARACTERISTICS

Definitions

While not as contested as "globalisation" itself (Yeates 2001), the term "anti-globalization movement" is the subject of some controversy, in terms of identifying both the movement's constituent elements and its aims and objectives. Having come to the attention of the western mass media following the "Battle of Seattle" in 1999, the movement has mainly been portrayed as being constituted by the large mobilizations in opposition to official summits organized by international governmental organizations (IGOs) and in the accompanying opposition policy fora. (See Table 14.2 for an overview of the main mobilizations.) Others define the AGM as one that opposes neoliberalism, wherever and however it is manifested, and include the movements in opposition to structural adjustment programs and other IMF/World Bank programs implemented in "peripheral" countries.

Some commentators condemn the "anti-globalization" tag as too negative and a variety of more positive appellations have been applied, such as the globalization movement, the global justice movement, the critical globalization movement, grassroots globalization and the alterglobalization (from "alternative globalization") movement (this latter by continental European scholars).[2] These differences in naming have political implications. There is an obvious chasm between those who reject the AGM label as "too negative" and those who explicitly describe the movement as anti-capitalist. Similarly, the term anti-corporate globalization seems to imply that the movement is opposed only to the internationalization strategies of commercial corporations (e.g., McDonalds, Union Carbide) and industry sectors (e.g., genetically-modified organisms, dams). In fact, a variety of targets have been identified. Some groups target finance capital and oppose the IMF/World Bank; they oppose the economic restructuring after the Asian Financial Crisis as well as organize anti-city demonstrations. Yet the movement has opposed economic summits more generally (e.g., G8, EU) as well as political summits. A further problem arises in that, just as "globalization" is a movable label applied to whatever social phenomenon the user wants to call globalization, so the only thing required for a local or national struggle to be "anti-globalization" is for an analyst to declare it to be so.

There are various versions of the AGM's history.

- North American-focused, abbreviated, ahistorical version. The AGM appeared in an act of immaculate conception at Seattle.
- A longer-term version, which traces the beginning of the movement to the impetus given by the EZLN revolt against NAFTA and the Encunetros, and which includes the development of the critique of free trade around

Table 14.2: Number of Cities Staging Protest Actions Across the World

	Africa	Asia	Aus/NZ	EU	Latin America	US
May 1998	–	5	4	21	2	9
June 1999	2	3	3	27	4	14
Nov 1999	–	20	2	41	–	34
Sept 2000	3	14	2	26	11	32
Nov 2001	2	15	5	95	10	25

Source: Wood (2004).

which the Seattle protestors united and the development of the methods of direct action that they practiced.[3]

- Similar to the above but also includes the European movement's history. One version traces the movement back to the Berlin demonstrations in 1988. Thus, Gerhards and Rucht (1992) examine the Berlin demonstration against WB/IMF that found feminists, ecologists and third world solidarity organizations taking to the streets together along with autonomen (Katsiaficas 1997).

- The movement that dare not speak its name: anti-globalization = anti-neoliberalism. This strand extends the history of the movement back into the anti-IMF/structural adjustment food riots of the 1970s and 1980s and includes the movement in peripheral countries (Seddon and Dwyer 2002).[4]

Diversity and Division

The most striking characteristic of the AGM is its diversity. In terms of composition, it involves the convergence of many global social movements, both "old" social movements—labor, peace—and "new" social movements—environment, women, human rights and development. It is, in fact, a coalition of coalitions, comprised of citizens' initiatives, advocacy organizations and representative organizations. This was evident in the Seattle demonstrations, which included "anti-corporate globalisation groups; joint anti-corporate globalisation/environmental organisations; farm, sustainable agriculture and anti-genetically modified organisms (GMO) groups; organised labour; consumer groups; development activist/world hunger groups; animal rights groups; religious organisations and the governments (as well as NGOs and activists) of many countries of the south" (Buttel and Gould 2004: 48). In terms of organisation, the AGM employs "a rich and growing panoply of organisational forms and instruments—affinity groups, spokescouncils, facilitation tools, break-outs, fish-bowls, blocking concerns, vibes-watchers and so on" (Graeber 2001: 14). This is closely mirrored by innovative tactics—ranging from street theatre to a "revolutionary knitting action" led by the World March of Women in Calgary, Canada, to teddy bear catapults (also in Canada) to radical cheerleading and other methods of tactical frivolity (Prague). However, while most of the AGM's publicity comes from the summit protests, these protests are only part of a much wider range of anti-globalization campaigns waged in more or less traditional ways: lobbying legislators, letter-writing campaigns; exposing illegal activities; class action suits through the courts; pickets, strikes and riots; consumer boycotts and physical attacks on products, centers of consumption and infrastructure. These campaigns are the base from which the AGM mobilizes. Finally, the AGM operates on a variety of geographical scales: at the global level in opposition to institutions of global governance, be they IFIs (IMF/WB) or other multilateral economic coordination groupings (G8/OECD); at the regional level in opposition to regional and trans-regional trade agreements and economic coordination (NAFTA, FTAA, APEC, ASEM); at the national level in opposition to SAPs and other neoliberal economic policies; at the local level in opposition to privatization of local government services and local branches of TNCs. The AGM also operates at the virtual level through its use of new information and communication technologies (ICTs), notably the Internet.

Divisions are a central characteristic of this diversity. At one level this manifests itself as a division of labor. Thus, some groups, often large NGOs, undertake research, arrange conferences, publish critical papers and briefing documents, providing intellectual legitimacy for and framing of the AGM. Other groups specialize in news and PR (e.g., Indymedia). Other groups deal with the organization of individual protests or provide coordination functions (PGA or Peoples' Global Action), while others specialize in street demonstrations (e.g., Reclaim the Streets [RTS]). At another level, these divisions relate to the territorial scale on which groups operate: some exclusively on a national basis, others transnationally as well as nationally or sub-nationally, or a combination of all of the above.

While the AGM's shared ideology is opposition to neoliberalism, there is no strategic agreement on how opposition to neoliberalism can best be advanced. The primary tension here exists between those who want to reform the international financial and economic system and those who want to abolish it and replace it with some alternative. This is the key division we have posited, between the reformist and revolutionary wings of the AGM. On one side are mainly NGOs and traditional political parties and their fronts (various socialist, Trotskyist, ex-communist, and social democrats) that are hierarchical in nature and organization, and believe that IFIs can be reformed. On the other has been the direct action contingent, with strong anarchist representation and influence,[5] using direct democracy and confrontational tactics up to and including violence, and with a political position that the IFIs are unreformable, and organized in loose affinity groups without hierarchical organization. This characterization is based on ideal types and organizations/groups may be differently located along this spectrum. Thus, there are radical reformists, left reformists, centrist reformists, all with a different version of "globalization with a human face." On the activist side, there are also strong divisions between those who accept or reject violent tactics, between autonomists and anti-civilization anarchists.

As Juris (2004) notes, these tensions between grassroots network-based movements and their more traditional organizational counterpoints are integral to the AGM rather than a recently-emerged phenomenon. In fact, there are two main parallel processes of organization in the AGM. The first is radical, anarchic, confrontational, prefigurative in its politics, decentralized, non-hierarchical, anti-capitalist, and anti-statist. Its place is in the streets and its exemplar is the Black Bloc. The second is reformist, hierarchical and more centralized and involves civil society/NGOs and more traditional political groups. Its place is in the Social Forum and its exemplar is the self-appointed Organizing Committee (OC) of the World Social Forum.

These tensions have surfaced in the demonstrations themselves. Much was made of the temporary alliance between labor and social movements in the Seattle protests, exemplified in the phrase "Teamsters and Turtles," but this was strictly limited, with union bureaucrats doing their best to ensure their members remained under their control.[6] While many praised the alliance between labor and new social movements in anti-globalization demonstrations, it is essential to stress that labor has consistently maintained its separate space in AGM demonstrations and, at times forcefully, maintained separation between its members and AGM militants. Similarly, in Europe trade union marches have been kept separate from social movement/general marches. Furthermore, one practice of the AGM has been to reclaim Mayday from the official trade union movement.

The issue of the tactical use of violence at mass demonstrations is another major dividing line in the AGM: as well as providing a handy marker as to whether fractions of the movement are reformist or revolutionary and drawing mass media attention and condemnation, it is also the axis on which the state has tried to split the AGM, calling for the respectable NGOs to denounce the "hooligan violence" of some protesters. Lori Wallach of Global Trade Watch described her view of the McDonalds' trashing at Seattle:

And these anarchist folks marched in there and started smashing things. And our people actually picked up the anarchists. Because we had with us steelworkers and longshoremen who, by sheer bulk, were three or four times larger. So we had them literally just sort of, a teamster on either side, just pick up an anarchist. We'd walk him over to the cops and say this boy just broke a window. He doesn't belong to us. We hate the WTO, so does he, maybe, but we don't break things. Please arrest him. (Wallach 2000)

This was not confined to one specific NGO: "Some protest leaders from DAN [Direct Action Network] and large NGOs, like Sierra Club and Global Exchange, immediately condemned the property destruction, characterising it as violent and vandalistic. More controversially, they called for the arrest of the people smashing windows and, in some cases, reportedly pointed offenders out to the police" (Conway 2003: 514).

To a neutral observer, the emphasis on violence seems excessive. Much of the "violence" was symbolic in nature, rather than actual as shown by the low level of casualties. Indeed what is startling about the AGM is how non-violent it has actually been: "After two years of increasingly militant direct action, it is still impossible to produce a single example of anyone to whom a US activist has caused physical injury" (Graeber 2002: 61). Similarly, "there has not been a single case of weapons preparation or use by anti-globalization protestors in North America" (Starr 2003: violence3.htm, p.15). More generally, to quote a Marxist observer of some note,

what precisely characterises this generation and this movement in contrast with earlier ones on the European and North American left is the explicit eschewal, even among its most militant elements, of either armed revolutionary struggle or terrorism...as a means of effecting change in the advanced capitalist countries. (Panitch 2002)

Despite these tensions, the AGM has been able to maintain its unity through inclusiveness: the response of the AGM to the debate over violence has created "an evolving framework of 'diversity of tactics,' in which there have been attempts to isolate (geographically and/or temporally) within a protest day actions involving different levels of 'risk,' while also maintaining a united front of solidarity among activists and organisations with divergent beliefs about tactics" (Starr 2003: violence3.htm, p.19). As one example of this, at Prague there were three separate axes of action exemplified in the Yellow march (Tutti Bianchi/ Ya Basta!—symbolic opposition, oriented to communication and mediation), the Blue march (anarchists and autonomen—direct and confrontational) and the Silver/Pink march (Earth First/Reclaim the Streets—playful and carnivalesque protest) (Chesters and Welsh 2001). Similarly in Genoa, the march by marginals, which would have included many illegal aliens liable to deportation if arrested, was agreed to be totally non-confrontational. The attempt to apply the methods of Prague through operating white, pink and black columns (rather than blocs) fell apart with the police attack on all columns.

Bringing the National Back In

While the existence of either transnationally mobile demonstrators or transnational elements in anti-globalization mobilizations is undeniable, registers and surveys of attendance at the various global and regional social fora and demonstrations repeatedly make obvious the markedly "national" composition of anti-globalization manifestations. While many of the analyses of the Seattle protest have focused on the number of NGOs from other countries involved, the vast majority of demonstrators were North American: of the 50,000 protesters at Seattle, at most 3,000 came from outside Canada and the US. Data assembled by Fisher et al. (2003) from four AGM protests confirms the paucity of transnational participation in protest mobilizations at summits in North America. At the February 2002 WEF protests in New York, just 3.2 percent of the sample were international; at the A20 WB demo in Washington

0 percent; at G8 in Calgary in June 2002, 2.3 percent and at the WB in Washington in September 2002 only 2.2 percent of the sample were international.

Similarly, an analysis of EU summit demonstrators at Brussels on December 14, 2001 found that 62 percent of demonstrators were Belgian and 31 percent were from the four nearest EU countries (the Netherlands, France, Germany and England) with the remaining 7 percent of demonstrators arriving from "elsewhere" (Bedoyan et al. 2003: 15). Concluding that practicalities like time, distance and money remain barriers to transnational mobilization, Bedoyan et al. surmise that "It is not at all sure that Western democracies will witness the transformation from movement society to transnational movement society in the near future" (p. 15). While Prague has been described as the most international of the European summit protests, "the total number of those detained is more than 400: of these, about 100 are foreigners, and the rest Czechs" (Kagarlitsky 2003: 266). These results confirm previous research on the Europeanisation of protest action: Imig and Tarrow's (2001) study of the 1984–97 period shows that "of all contentious action within the EU... only a tiny 0.85 percent of all actions were truly transnational European actions directly or indirectly targeting the EU and involving protestors from different EU member states" (cited in Bedoyan et al. 2003: 3).

The overwhelmingly "national" composition of anti-globalization protests is further borne in the social fora. Ninety percent of the delegates at the first ESF (European Social Forum) in Florence, Italy, were Italian (Farrer 2003: 175). The Profile of Participants at the WSF in Porto Alegre, Brazil, coordinated by the WSF International Secretariat, found nearly 86 percent of the 170,000 officially registered participants at the first three WSFs were Brazilian; the largest foreign delegations were from Latin American countries, especially those that neighbor Brazil. Similarly, the Asian SF was a pan-Asian meeting only in a very restricted sense with only a few hundred out of the total 20,000 participants coming from other parts of Asia (Sen 2003: 297).

If the main summit protests are not where the transnational element is located, we must look to the accompanying solidarity protests. The Prague demonstrations were accompanied, for example, by eighty-two protests in cities in seventeen different countries outside the Czech Republic, while the anti-FTAA protest in Quebec in April 2001was accompanied by solidarity protests in at least 50 cities outside Canada. For Seattle, 306 anti-WTO protests in Seattle, the US and globally, occurred between November 15 and December 14, 1999, some 48–60 percent of which were reported for the opening day of the WTO on November 30 (Almeida and Lichbach 2003). Table 14.3 shows the global spread of five anti-globalization days of action.

If the national nature of many of the manifestations has been underplayed, possibly due to the desire to emphasize the novel transnational aspects of the events, a related problem is that many of these analyses attempt to force

Table 14.3: Evolution of PGA 1996–2001

Date	Place	Event	Numbers of people attending	Numbers of countries represented
July–August 1996	Chiapas, Mexico	First International Encounter	3,000	43
July–August 1997	Spain	Second International Encounter	Thousands	50
February 1998	Geneva, Switzerland	PGA founding conference	300	71
August 1999	Bangalore, India	PGA second conference	100	25
September 2001	Cochabamba, Bolivia	PGA third conference	250	23

sections of the movement from different countries and continents into the same framework, thereby obscuring major national or continental political histories that are useful in explaining differences within the AGM. Amory Starr, for instance, reports "One distinct difference between US and European actions is the US emphasis on dignified protests, in contrast with the European use of the theatre of the absurd" (Starr 2003: 10). Wood (2004), in a study of 467 protest events in sixty-nine countries on the five global days of action between 1998 and the end of 2001, reports that "protests target neoliberalism differently on each continent" (77), adding that "in order to understand the variation between continents in terms of target choice, one must consider pre-existing political repertoires, social movement networks, and the diffusion processes that spread innovations to new sites" (69).

Political ideology more generally is an important predictor of opposition methods. Wood has observed the difference in targeting between reformist and revolutionary groups, with demonstrations linked to ATTAC, ICFTU and Jubilee 2000 targeting WTO, G8, IMF and/or WB, while those associated with PGA and RTS were more likely to select a local target (Wood 2004).[7] For targets, MNCs were most popular, with 27 percent of actions aimed at their local branches or headquarters, with MNCs the choice of target in Canada, Australia, New Zealand, Europe and the US—countries without an already existing anti-neoliberal repertoire (Wood 2004: 79). The next most popular target was national governments, with 19 percent of the protests aimed at them, with African and Asian protests most likely to target national governments (ibid.: 81). The third most popular target (15 percent of the sample) were banks and/or stock exchanges, with Latin America being the region most likely to target them (ibid.: 81). As regards the division between the "core"/"periphery," the majority of demonstrations (69 percent) took place in Europe and North America, while the largest events took place in Asia and South America (ibid.: 75).

Overall, then, diversity is the AGM's essence and there is no one unitary AGM to be described. Instead, the AGM is highly diverse in composition, organizational features, targets and tactics; it expresses itself at local, national, regional, and global levels in very different ways. In the following sections we examine the political ideologies and methods used by contrasting groups and institutions (see Table 14.1). In section two we contrast the modes of organization by looking at one organization from each wing of the AGM: PGA and ATTAC. In section three we focus on two contrasting institutions founded by the AGM: the World Social Forum and Indymedia.

TRANSNATIONAL ORGANIZATIONS

People's Global Action

For those who consider the AGM to be a struggle against neoliberalism, finally appearing in the "core" a decade after it appeared in the "periphery", the most important channel of diffusion is People's Global Action (PGA). Founded in Geneva in 1998, the original impetus for the PGA stems from the International Encounters Against Neoliberalism and for Humanity called by the Zapatistas. PGA is a new kind of International, significantly allying the Zapatistas and other peripheral country peasant organizations with radical "core" country groups like RTS and Ya Basta! Although there is a wide diversity of groups and interests allied with the PGA,[8] the PGA describes itself as having neither membership nor a juridical character. No organization or person represents the PGA, nor does PGA represent any organization or person. The PGA is a transnational network comprised of a loose coalition of ninety-four "core" organizations from forty-three countries which facilitates communication, information sharing, solidarity, coordination and resource mobilization. Its operations are mainly conducted through its website and various e-mailing lists. The PGA has been key to issuing AGM calls to action[9] and a total of more than 1,500 organizations attended its regional fora, three international conferences and/or participated in five "global days of action" between 1998 and 2001 (De Marcellus 2000; Wood 2002; Routledge 2004: 7).

What is notable in PGA is a coalition between mass-based (primarily peasant and indigenous) organizations in "peripheral" countries and activists in "core" countries who are unaffiliated to any mass-based organization. What the two groups share in common is a commitment to direct democracy and new forms of organization. As Petras (2001) notes, "Today, the most promising and dynamic movements—the unemployed workers' movement in Argentina, the MST in

Brazil, the Cocaleros of Bolivia, the Zapatistas in Mexico—are based on popular assemblies and consultation, direct democracy" (3). This ideological commitment to new forms of organization has allowed PGA to successfully organize highly diverse organizations transnationally.

This success is not, however, unqualified. There is the issue of "core" country dominance due to differential access to resources, with activists from core countries better able to bear the costs of international travel and having better Internet access. The importance of European-based Support Groups of activists in propelling PGA activities has reinforced this "core/periphery" division. One issue here is language: "e-mail communication within PGA Asia that form part of its networking strategies are in English—a language that is neither spoken nor understood by the majority of peasant farmers who comprise the mass base of movements who participate in the movement. Moreover, the proceedings of PGA international conferences are also conducted in Spanish and English" (Routledge 2004:12). Another issue is the dominance of the core countries/ groups' perspectives within the PGA. As Routledge reports, "in the PGA conference in Cochabamba, many Latin American delegates felt that meetings were controlled from a 'European' perspective, which was obsessed with particular forms of 'process' and 'consensus'" (2004: 13). This also manifests itself through the different alternatives to neoliberal globalization posed by "core" and "peripheral" fractions of the PGA:

Northern activists articulate alternatives that are conditioned by their embeddedness within—and alienation from—an already industrialised capitalist society. The fundamental concerns of Southern activists are with the defence of livelihoods and of communal access to resources threatened by commodification, state take-overs and private appropriation (e.g., by national and transnational corporations). Their alternatives are rooted, in part, in some of the local practices being undermined by neoliberal globalisation. (Routledge 2004: 11)

The PGA has tried to address the issue of core group domination of transnational networks by stressing the importance of diversity and difference, including local development of alternatives to neoliberalism and by limiting participation by groups from "core" countries in its conferences (for example, the Cochabamba conference limited it to 30 percent of delegates).

ATTAC

Whereas the PGA is comprised of local groups operating as a transnational network, ATTAC's mode of organization is essentially national and hierarchical. ATTAC was founded in 1998 following enthusiastic and voluminous response to an article published in *Le Monde Diplomatique* after the Asian Financial Crisis. It is a radical reformist group, characterized by its supporters as a "'triple movement'—a popular education movement with a goal of action, a protest movement and one that 'wishes to be present where real decisions are made not after the fact or 50 kilometres away'" (Susan George cited in Birchfield 2004: 8). From the beginning, ATTAC France enjoyed strong trade union and other institutional support.[10] Six months after it was founded, the international movement was launched at a meeting in Paris in December 1998, attended by representatives from Africa, Asia, Europe and Latin America; by summer of the following year it held its first major international conference in Paris (Birchfield 2004: 14). ATTAC has no global organizational structure (Birchfield 2004); it is essentially an international network of national organizations. As of 2003, it has local branches in forty-eight countries and a web presence in thirty-three countries. This global presence, however, has firmest roots in Western Europe and Latin America; it has less of a presence in North America while in Africa it is only present in five former French colonies. It is absent from Asia-Pacific and the Middle East (Cammaerts and Van Audenhove 2003). Variations are noticeable in the national formations of ATTAC. Whereas ATTAC France was a group with extensive membership and support, ATTAC Germany is "above all one thing: a product for and of the media" (Kolb 2003: 19) while ATTAC Denmark emerged primarily as a marketing and political project by a newspaper (Christenden 2002: 1). Organizationally, there are also variations with some national organizations, such as ATTAC Sweden, lacking a chairperson and an official spokesperson.

Unlike the PGA, ATTAC France exhibits a markedly hierarchical structure, with over 200 committees spread throughout France (*Red Pepper* July 26–27, 2001), a central secretariat, a chairperson and spokespeople. Decision-making takes place at its General Assembly at least annually, where members "hold a simple majority vote on most decisions to be made" (ibid.: 5) thus deviating from the use of consensus in most of the AGM. It attaches a high degree of importance to the non-elected members of the "college des fondateurs," leaving relatively little room for influence from members and local groups (Uggla 2004: 8–9). This adherence to a traditional political model is exemplified in a feat of almost Orwellian doublespeak with Bernard Cassen (2003) proudly explaining:

I proposed national statutes that on first sight might appear undemocratic, but in my view are by no means so. There are 30 members of the national executive, of whom 18 are elected by the 70 founders of Attac, and 12 by the 30,000 membership at large.

Cassen further explained this structure as an attempt to defeat possible entryism: thus, to prevent undemocratic manipulation of the national structure, the national structure was made undemocratic. The juxtaposition of a formal commitment to local autonomy alongside an undemocratic central administrative and political leadership structure is a source of internal tension (Birchfield 2004).

ATTAC France showed its predominantly national character by allowing the demand for a Tobin tax to evaporate after the French National Assembly voted in November 2001 for the introduction of the tax (Uggla 2004). If the demands are increasingly national, so are the institutions on which the demands are made: in France (and Sweden) "national institutions (parliament, government) absolutely dominate as primary targets for the groups' actions, and amount to around half of those. In contrast, global institutions are only rarely targeted" (ibid.: 12). As one French chapter representative explained to Uggla "I think that fundamentally the answers are [to be found] at the local and national levels…I don't think you can do anything at the international level" (p. 18). In any case, both the Swedish and French versions have been found wanting as an example of the new transnational politics, with Uggla noting that "Attac also maintains quite conventional aspects in terms of demands, action repertoires and targets" (2004: 1).

This section has focused on two organizational models that co-exist within the AGM. The PGA is an exemplar of the new global politics, a non- or virtual organization which is manifest on its website, through its conferences and its global coordination of days of action. However, despite this global organizational form, the constituents of PGA are locally and nationally-based groups whose main activity is local or national organizing, as shown through their target selection. By comparison, ATTAC appears decidedly French in its nature. Explicitly set up as a nationally-based reformist organization, the transnational ramifications (outside the WSF process examined in the next section) were unexpected. ATTAC is an exemplar of the "old" politics, with strong trade union support and more than a whiff of "democratic centralism" to its mode of organization. In the following section we further explore these tensions through an examination of the two major global spaces created by the AGM—the social fora and Indymedia. Again, these spaces exemplify the dichotomy in organizing methods we have identified. The social fora are an initiative of the reformist wing of the AGM involving the reappearance of the decidedly "old" politics with the French organization ATTAC playing a central role, while the "new" global politics is exemplified by the new virtual spaces of Indymedia. We pay extended attention to the former since it is there that the tension between both wings of the movement is most explicit and where there is most need for continuation of inclusive politics if the movement is to retain its diversity.

TRANSNATIONAL SPACES

Counter-summits and Social Fora

Counter-summits and social fora are a major manifestation of the movement's existence. Dating to the International Encounter Against Neoliberalism and to the alternative summits of the 1980s,[11] these events have proliferated over the last twenty years.[12] Half of the sixty-one parallel summits were located in

Europe, one-quarter were based in the US, while the rest of the globe accounted for the remaining quarter (Pianta 2001). These counter-summits always include a conference, mostly include street protests, and sometimes include a "media event" and "grassroots" meetings. They are usually well-attended though only one-third of organizers of these events consider mass participation to be a significant indicator of the success of the event (ibid.).

In what follows we focus in the main on the World Social Forum, founded by eight Brazilian organizations (which form the Brazilian Organizing Committee, also known as the Brazilian OC) in alliance with ATTAC.[13] An international council of 150 members was formed in 2001, by cooptation rather than election (Wallerstein 2004), whose activities are funded by WSF entry fees.[14] The WSF does not depict itself as an organization or a united front platform, but rather

an open meeting place for reflective thinking, democratic debate of ideas, formulation of proposals, free exchange of experiences, and inter-linking for effective action, by groups and movements of civil society that are opposed to neoliberalism and to domination of the world by capital and any form of imperialism, and are committed to building a planetary society centred on the human person. (WSF Charter of Principles)

The WSF has been presented as prefigurative of future forms of political organization, a new way of doing politics, a process rather than an institution. At the level of attendance, there is no doubt about the WSF's success. Attendance at the first Forum in Porto Alegre, Brazil, in January 2001 involved 20,000 participants and 4,000 delegates,[15] increasing to 60,000 participants and 12,000 delegates the following year. By WSF 3 in 2003, participants reached 100,000 and delegates 20,000, while WSF 2004 at Mumbai involved 135,000 participants and 75,000 delegates. On closer inspection, however, it suffers from exceedingly old forms of political organization and the WSF is not as democratic, open and accountable as it is sometimes presented.

First, the organization of, and range of discussion in the WSF have been strongly controlled by NGOs and political parties (the latter of which are supposedly excluded from participating in the WSF). From the outset, this exclusion was undermined by the involvement of the PT (Brazilian Workers' Party) in Porto Alegre. Indeed, the first three WSF meetings (like all European Social Fora) benefited from political parties who were in power in the cities where the fora were held. The most obvious problem raised by the return of the social democrats is that of democracy. In Porto Alegre, Mumbai and London, control by political party cadres led to allegations of lack of accountability, democracy and transparency, along with problems of exclusion of groups and movements as well as tight control over fora sessions. Jai Sen (2003) notes "the actually existing Forum is not the 'open space' that it is said to be, but is instead highly structured and, in several dimensions, exclusive" (210) and observes "the tendency of the organisers, both in Brazil and India, to *control* things: by making closed-door decisions about key organisational issues, by reserving 'sensitive' roles to its own members (such as who takes part in roundtable discussions with political parties), and tending to act as a vanguard and a politburo" (Sen 2003: 214, emphasis in original).[16]

Secondly, the WSF suffered from confusion over the issue of violence. The WSF Charter denies access to groups "that seek to take people's lives as a method of political action." On this basis the Brazilian Organizing Committee excluded various groups, such as those sympathetic to the Maoist People's War Group, Basque organizations and the Zapatistas (Sen 2003: 217). However, this critical attitude to violence was not applied to politicians. As King (2002) critically noted "a wide range of WSF panels were (sic) composed of European politicians, legislators and NGO representatives, including Ministers from France, Belgium and Portugal who had only recently voted to support the attacks on Afghanistan and the present 'War on Terror.'"

Thirdly, the WSF is dominated by a particular section of civil society. As one member of the Organizing Committee noted, "we are an elite of citizen activism. The larger, more excluded sectors, although organised in social movements and networks, do not participate in a meaningful way in the Forum, whether because they lack the economic means to do so or because the Forum, because of its dynamic, does not draw them in." (Gryzbowski 2004). As Petras (2002) echoed,

Many of the European and US NGOs present are paper organisations and the majority of Third World NGOers [sic] are members of small groups of professionals with few, if any, organised supporters and possess little power of convocation. On the other hand, there were a small number of representatives from mass movements in Africa, particularly South Africa, and Asia who represent hundreds of thousands of grassroots activists. Yet it was the well-known intellectual notables from the NGOs which crowded the platforms and informed the public about the movements in their regions.

This domination is further illustrated by the social composition of participants: "the Forum is an initiative that still belongs mostly to the middle class, middle and upper castes, and male leadership of the 'civil,' 'present' world" (Sen 2003: 218). According to the WSF participants' profile, 73.4 percent of those attending WSF 2003 had attended university (though not all had graduated) and 9.7 percent had done some post-graduate coursework. Of the delegates, 18 percent had graduate degrees and/or had studied on post-graduate programs. Sixty-three percent of those attending were under 34 years of age, but since most of these were non-delegate participants they lacked a means of expression in the debates (Gryzbowski 2004).

Fourth, despite the ready availability and power of feminist critiques of neoliberalism and global economic restructuring, the WSF, like the AGM, has failed to adequately take on board issues such as reproductive rights and male violence or the critique of patriarchy and capitalism developed by second-wave socialist-feminists (Rebick 2002; NextGENDERation 2004). As the Mercosur Feminist Articulation noted:

In the first year of the [World Social Forum], there was little representation of women on panels or in the leadership of the process. This led to a spontaneous street protest during the Forum. In 2002, women gained greater presence on key panels, but in general, a gender analysis was still absent from debates on neoliberal globalisation and its alternatives. In the Third Forum...Articulation Feminista Marcosur and the World March of Women coordinated two of the five themes, making selections of panel speakers.[17]

Again here Gryzbowski located the problem within "civil society" itself:

In the WSF I'm learning something fundamental...Women are a "minority" created by ourselves within civil society. With respect to that, there is no point in blaming capitalism, neoliberalism, globalisation, exclusionary states, etc. This is a major problem that is engendered, developed and maintained in the culture of civil society itself. (cited in AWID 2004)

All of these problems were manifested in the organization of WSF Mumbai. As Sen noted, "the norms most commonly practiced in the WSF India Secretariat during 2002 were ad hoc decision-making, lack of accountability and a lack of respect for collective process by leadership" leading to "a culture of nepotism and opportunism" (2003: 302). He reports the failure of the WSF India Organizing Committee to arrange an open mobilizing process, so that the aim became merely to organize an event rather than starting a process only one of the results of which would be the event. Here the blame lies squarely with the Left groups, political parties (especially CPI[M]), and their front organisations that controlled the mobilizing process. Sen expresses the contradiction basic to the WSF process (and not just its Indian manifestation): "organisation with *old* vocabularies of politics, and old ways of organising and relating to others, are leading the process of forging what are said by some to be *new* politics" (Sen 2003: 300).

This contradiction was illuminated, once again, by the fact that the political party most centrally involved in organizing the WSF in India was also tainted by its acceptance of neoliberalism in the state government it leads in West Bengal. Here we might also note another contradiction in the Communist Party of India (Marxist) (CPI[M]) involvement in the WSF due to the party's position in a major Indian controversy over local NGOs accepting foreign funds: "The CPI(M), in particular, has denounced foreign-funded voluntary organisations as being 'lackeys of imperialism.' The CPI(M)-led state government in West Bengal, in power for the past twenty-six years, has periodically victimised such organisations and their work" (Sen 2003: 304). When international funding was accepted for parts of the WSF process, the charges of hypocrisy (and not only from ML critics of the CPI[M]) were understandable. The total budget of the Mumbai WSF was estimated at US$1.8 million, of which approximately 60 percent came from overseas organizations (from Switzerland, US, Britain, Sweden, Canada, France, Germany, and the Netherlands) with the remainder contributed by the Indian General Council, consisting of some 200 Indian organizations.

With the ESF in London in October 2004, the contradiction reached breaking point. By all accounts, except, understandably, those of the organizers, the London "bid" to hold the ESF was secretly produced and implemented by a small coalition of Ken Livingstone's Greater London Authority (GLA) and the Socialist Workers' Party, "all relevant administrative decisions were made at closed meetings among GLA advisers" (Nunes 2004) and much of the organizing work was contracted out to commercial companies, leading Chesters to describe it as "an ideologically homogenous trade fair".[18] Instead of prefiguring their desired society, as the autonomous spaces did by using activist kitchens such as Food Not Bombs to provide food, at the ESF "the food was all provided by catering companies employing low-wage work, plastic packages and corporate brands everywhere" (Nunes 2004). This commercialization was reflected in the high cost of attendance: unemployed people were charged £20 (€29, US$36) for entry and employed £30 if paid in advance, rising respectively to £30 and £40 if paid on the door (by comparison entrance fees in Paris ESF were €3 to €50 depending on income). Total costs of London ESF were £1 million, nearly half of which was met by GLA.

Overall, the WSF and ESF in their organization seemed to deny the democracy that was deemed to be defining characteristic of the AGM. Indeed, there is a strong fear that they are being used by a minority of individuals to parachute themselves as leaders onto a movement that developed without their participation in the first place. In some ways it seems hard not to interpret the WSF (and other Social Fora) as attempts by the traditional left—social democratic, radical reformist and ex-communist (in particular ATTAC and PT)—to obtain hegemony over the AGM. Although it is only fair to say that some members of the Social Fora recognize the problematic treatment of social movements as object rather than subject and the issue of how representative the Fora are, because of their exclusionary organization and capture by political parties, the social fora generated their own organized opposition, inside, outside, and close to the official fora themselves, through the establishment of parallel summits by groups excluded from the official fora. In most of these, the opposition was anarchist, but in Mumbai it was Maoist. The Mumbai WSF saw previously articulated critiques of the WSF expressed strongly by Marxist–Leninist (ML) elements and mass-based organizations, which organized their own counter-summit, *Mumbai Resistance* 2004 (MR).[19] MR took over WSF's rhetoric, with one Organizing Committee member telling *Frontline*, "While MR was a process, WSF was an event" (Bavadam 2004). Certainly there were class differences between MR and WSF Mumbai, with Bavadam (2004) noting "The majority of MR participants were peasant farmers and field-based activists. The disproportionately high number of police personnel at the MR venue bore testimony to this." MLs were not the only group to organize autonomous spaces. According to De Marcellus (2000),

not only the major Indian movements didn't unite [sic] to win an adequate space within WSF, they also ended by organising several parallel spaces outside rather like (though on a much larger scale) the parallel spaces outside the ESF events. All these divisions led to others, since networks that spanned them, like Via Campesina or PGA were obliged to find neutral meeting spaces outside all the others.

In the London ESF, the more vibrant and direct action fraction of the English AGM, including the WOMBLES, acting in cooperation with sympathetic transnationals, organized their own parallel fora, *Beyond ESF*, the Indymedia Centre and the *Laboratory of Insurrectionary Imagination*, among others. The most satisfactory response to the London ESF came from Jeff Juris:

Our movements are too diverse, even contradictory, to be contained within a single space, however open it may be. This does not mean abandoning the process, but rather building on the London experience to recast the forum as a network of interconnected, yet autonomous spaces converging across a single urban terrain at a particular point in time...Moreover there will necessarily be contradiction and struggle, even within and between our networks. Such conflict should not be feared, but rather recognized as an integral part of the forum itself. In places like Prague and Genoa urban space was divided among diverse forms of direct action. In London we finally began to incorporate a similar logic on our own terms, without reacting to an enemy. (Juris 2004)

This position is also shared by some members of the Brazilian OC who stress that the self-organized workshops/seminars are more important than the "official" WSF program, with Gryzbowski (2004) noting "the enormous contradiction between the major events within the Forum and the numerous free activities, self-organised, that the participating delegates carry out."

Indymedia (IMC)

The use of ICTs, especially the Internet and the development of both protest-specific websites and the IMCs (Independent Media Centers), have been crucial to the development of the AGM. Those groups that organized the Carnivals Against Capitalism and the anti-MAI, -WTO and -IMF campaigns did so to a large extent over the Internet. Indeed, "in conflict after conflict, e-mail and web pages have been cited by protagonists on both sides as playing key roles" (Cleaver 1999: 10), while Hoechsmann notes that "as a communications tool for activists located in far-flung corners of the world but united in the struggle for social justice in the brave new global economy, the Internet is a powerful new technology" (1996: 34). The movement's use of new ICTs makes global communication, information exchange and dialog easier and cheaper for highly disparate and isolated groups, many of whom cannot afford international travel.

If the WSF embodies a mode of transnational communication and mobilization directed by a central group, Indymedia represents an alternative mode linking together autonomous and locally-based self-organized groups in a virtual network. Founded in 1999 to cover AGM demonstrations from within the protest, rather than from the police side or from some notionally neutral position outside the demonstrations, they have been crucial to challenging mainstream media coverage that focused on violence, delegitimized the protests, and encouraged repressive state responses (Brooten 2004). Indymedia is a result of a coalition: the Seattle IMC brought together "three sets of commoners from earlier struggles over the cyber and terrestrial commons: techies from the Open Source movement, activist media producers, and social activists from the global justice coalition" (Kidd 2003: 231). While the first IMCs were set up to cover international summit mobilizations, as IMCs multiplied so their coverage expanded to the myriad of local, national and international campaigns associated with members of the AGM coalition. Indymedia not only represents a model of alternative media work based on collective production but, through its network form, embodies an alternative mode of political organization based on direct democracy and open access at all levels of the network.[20] In this respect, it is an exemplar of the form of political organization operating through autonomous networks characteristic of the "new" politics attributed to the AGM.

Most comment on the IMC emphasizes the novelty of the use of the Internet, its liberatory potential, and the "new" knowledge workers that developed and utilized it (Kidd 2003), but less frequently remarked on how Indymedia also uses other, older means of expression and distribution. This juxtaposition of "old" and "new" is shown in Seattle where

the convergence of new and old technologies and platforms allowed for a variety of distribution strategies. The Internet site was supplemented with a daily printed news sheet, live coverage from a downtown micro-radio transmitter, a daily national Radio Project programme distributed via satellite, and conventional mail to community radio stations throughout North America. (Kidd 2003: 231)

Of course there have been problems with Indymedia. The first is its concentration in core countries, embodying what has come to be described as the "digital divide." This divide not only exists between core and peripheral countries,[21] but also runs along class, gender and ethnic divides in both core and peripheral countries. If the Internet facilitates the transnational spread of the AGM, lack of access to the Internet also limits its spread: "Countries, regions and groups that have little access to the internet or transnational activist organisations will less likely hold anti-[multilateral economic institutions] protest events" (Almeida and Lichbach 2003: 253). The utilization of a variety of methods have therefore also been used by IMCs in peripheral countries where Internet access is a luxury, in an attempt by the "new" movement to respond to the "old" divisions noted by scholars of transnational social movements. As Kidd notes,

In Brazil, they also mix old and new media. In Rio de Janeiro, the IMC has taken video documentaries from favela to university to foster discussion of the upcoming FTAA agreement. In Porto Alegre, they use the Internet to gather and circulate news, which is then sent to a network of free and community radio stations. In Sao Paulo, the IMC set up a free Internet centre to enable poor people to access it. They also take the video documentaries of demonstrations and land occupations to the neighbourhoods, setting up monitors for everyone to watch. Almost all of the IMC centres also distribute printed news-sheets that are photocopied and posted on walls all over the city, because of lack of funds for printed copies. (Kidd 2003: 235)

Another traditional axis of discrimination—patriarchal gender relations—within the AGM is also of relevance to Indymedia. The core voluntary labor on which the IMCs depend tends to be young, white, middle-class males from Europe and North America (Kidd 2003: 234). Moreover, "despite the rhetoric to the contrary appearing in official IMC documents, much of the IMC's mediated text still operated through the perpetuation of patriarchal and ethnocentric images" (Brooten 2004: 2). A women-only listserv[22] for the IMC has discussed "the perceived maleness of (and overemphasis on) technical work within the IMC, the silencing of women during meetings, a lack of social support for women within individual collectives, and outright harassment in some cases" (ibid.: 19). This has led to discussion of sexism in the IMC in the network and the beginning of various attempts to deal with the problem.

Our examination of two institutions set up by the AGM—WSF and the IMCs—has shown the same division between "old" and "new" politics as the previous section on PGA and ATTAC did. Despite the rhetoric of "open space" and "new politics," the organization of WSF (and ESF) has shown the continued existence in the AGM of "old" forms of politics masquerading as the "new", leading to conflict between both wings of the movement. By comparison, Indymedia, while suffering from problems relating to the digital divide and gender relations, embodies the "new" forms of organizing in the AGM, being based on voluntary labor, allowing open access to all, and networking transnationally various autonomous local and national IMCs.

CONCLUSIONS

Much emphasis has been placed on the novelty of AGM politics both in its transnational/global scope, scale, and its constituent actors, but this chapter has shown that this emphasis needs to be tempered with caution. Not all the actors involved are new: indeed, the example of the "new public space" we examined most closely in this chapter, the WSF and ESF, contains some political groups and practices that are definitely a hangover of the "old" politics. While the AGM is indeed a "new" global movement, it is also decidedly locally or nationally based. Here the point has been made that the AGM demonstrations have been markedly national in composition, while the accompanying solidarity demonstrations have shown strong national characteristics. Furthermore, in general the AGM is not only exemplary of new politics but shows evidence of decidedly old politics. The achievement of the AGM has been to unite these two contrasting and often contradictory modes of organizing in a coalition, the basis for which is respect for the movement's diversity, whether in accepting of diversity of tactics in street demonstrations, or in including in social fora organizing spaces of both wings of the movement.

Notes

1. See, for instance, bibliographies by Gupta, Tarrow and Acostavalle (2001), John H. Henning Center (n.d.), and Waterman (2003).
2. For the continental European literature see the website for Colloque Les Mobilisations Alter-Mondialistes (Available online at www.afsp.msh.paris.fr/activites/groupe/germm) and the bibliography by S. Postel-Vinay and J.C. Mouret posted there.
3. On the years of debate and struggle over the meaning of opposition to neoliberalism which preceded Seattle, see Ayres (2001, 2004) and Conway (2003). See Shepherd and Hayduk (2002) on the movements and micro-movements that came together in disputed unity at Seattle.
4. In the first phase, from the mid-1970s to the late 1980s, Structural Adjustment Program (SAPs) were met by more or less spontaneous popular protest, whose primary expression was the food riot. The second phase, from the late 1980s to the late 1990s, where, while food riots continued, opposition became more organized and mobilized through formal structures (political parties, trade unions, etc). Phase three witnessed the explicit politicization of anti-globalization protest and resistance "with an unprecedented degree of coherence and self-consciousness and a potential for trans-national, regional, if not actually global coordination and orchestration" (2). If the main revolts against SAPs in the peripheral countries were urban, the 1990s saw the rural areas move into revolt. It is not insignificant that the Zapatistas, who provided both a beginning and an impetus to the AGM, were a peasant, indigenous army. Indeed the fate of indigenous peoples has been a main theme in the AGM in both "peripheral" and "core" countries.
5. As the Canadian Security Intelligence Service has noted, "Like the internet itself, the anti-globalist movement is a body that manages to survive and even thrive without a head ... One of the most impressive innovations has been the method of organizing, arranging and directing the operational and administrative activities associated with the demonstrations, accomplished effectively without the obvious influence of central authority, command and control. In many ways, the system is very similar to that advocated by anarchists of the libertarian socialist philosophy" (CSIS 2000: 8).

6. As Conway notes, in Seattle the AFL-CIO march "bypassed the downtown intersections that were occupied by direct action protesters, thus avoiding conflict with the police and withholding the protection and legitimacy of their numbers from the blockaders. Some participants in the march proceeded on their own to join the ranks of the direct action activists in the downtown core, but most were dissuaded by the parade marshals from participating in the blockade" (513), while in Quebec a similar distance between official marchers and the direct action milieu was observed: "in an uncanny replay of Seattle, organizers of the official march led tens of thousands of people away from the wall to a park far from the confrontation. According to some reports, parade marshals from the Quebec Federation of Labour aggressively prevented people from diverging from the official route" (Conway 2003: 522).

7. As Wood notes, "226 of the 467 demos made claims against a concrete target other than the transnational institutions explicitly under protest" (Wood 2004: 79).

8. "Teachers hunger-striking against privatisation in Argentina met women organizing against quasi-slavery in the maquila factories of Mexico, Bangladesh, Salvador and Nicaragua; women's rights activists; farmers struggling against globalization in India, the Philippines, Brazil, Estonia, Norway, Honduras, France, Spain, Switzerland, Bangladesh, Senegal, Mozambique, Togo, Peru, Bolivia, Columbia and many other countries; Ogoni, Maori, Maya, Aymara, U'wa and other indigenous peoples fighting for their cultural rights and physical survival; students struggling against nuclear power or the repression of striking workers in Ukraine and South Korea; postal workers from Canada resisting privatization, militants against 'unfree' trade from the United States, environmentalists, the unemployed, fisherfolk, anti-racists, peace mobilisers, animal rights activists..." (De Marcellus 2000: 94)

9. Wood's (2002) dataset shows that 53 percent of the demonstrations were organized by groups identified as parts of the PGA (through inclusion on the PGA webpage).

10. The European Industrial Relations Observatory cites ATTAC-affiliated trade unions representing members in banking, finance, infrastructure and transport, education, the judiciary, the public service and posts and telecommunications. http://www.eiro. eurofound.eu.int/2002/03/feature/fr0203106f.html. Over 20 percent of French parliamentary delegates from 1997 to 2002 were members of ATTAC, while even the right-wing French government sent ministers to attend WSF 2003 (Birchfield 2004).

11. These fora first saw the light of day in 1984 in Britain when The Other Economic Summit (TOES) was set up as a people's response to the G7 summit being held in London that year. Since then each year a TOES has been held in response to G7/G8 meetings, while other TOESs have also occurred. The Alternative Economic Summit held in 1989 by TOES/France had 1,000 participants, while the first US-based TOES, held in Houston, Texas in 1990, had over 1,000 participants from over forty countries.

12. A chronology of regional, thematic and national social fora from December 2001 to July 2004 listed 73 events, 26 in Latin America, 21 in Europe, 15 in Africa, 7 in North America, 3 in Asia and 1 in Oceania. Available online at http://www.transform.it/newsletter/892004530007.php). In some countries the forum phenomenon has spread widely: "The Italian social movement is characterized by the local social forums (sic) that developed after the events of Genoa–more than 200 have been formed since last summer" (Available online at http://www.cpgb.org.uk/worker/447/agnoletto.html).

13. On the origins of the WSF see Fisher and Ponniah (2003).

14. WSF charge $50/25 participation fee per delegate. In 2002 this amounted to $385,000, which is used to run the Secretariat until the next WSF.

15. Participants are non-affiliated individuals attending, while delegates are representatives of social movements or NGOs that are registered to partake in the WSF official program.
16. This is echoed by others. According to Jason Adams (2002) "For two years now, the ruling Workers Party (PT)…has jealously controlled the organizing committee of the WSF."
17. Available online at http://www.wicej.addr.com/wsf03/note1.html
18. Available online at http://www.indymedia.org.uk/en/2004/10/299962.html
19. For an attack on the reformism of the Indian organizers of the WSF, NGOs and the Indian parliamentary communist parties, and a partial defense of the MR, see Giri (2003). For excellent coverage of MR see Bavadam (2004). For a stinging attack on MR see Nigam (2004).
20. IMCs allow—indeed encourage—direct access to the means of expression in its forum. Its "open publishing" software allows anyone with web access to upload material to an IMC site without editorial filtering. However, some IMCs drop or hide posts that are explicitly racist/sexist/etc.
21. In 1999 there was one IMC; as of October 2004, IMC had fifty-three websites in US cities and eighty-nine websites in six continents (forty in Europe, twelve in Canada, four in Africa, sixteen in Latin America, ten in Oceania and seven in Asia) (Almeida and Lichbach 2003; Brooten 2004).
22. Listserv is a mailing list program for communicating with other people who subscribe to the same email list.

References

Adams, J. 2002. *Hopes for a True International.* Available online at http://www.zmag.org/content/visionstrategy/AdamsWSF.cfm

Almeida, P. and M. Lichbach. 2003. To the Internet, from the Internet: Comparative media coverage of Transnational protests. *Mobilization* 8(3): 249–72.

Anheier, H., M. Glasius and M. Kaldor. 2001. *Global Civil Society 2001.* Oxford: Oxford University Press.

AWID. 2004. *How can the Feminists and Women's Movement Learn from the Third World Social Forum?* Association for Women's Rights in Development, February 24.

Ayres, J. 2001. Transnational Political Processes and Contention Against the Global Economy. *Mobilization* 6(1): 55–68.

————. 2004. Framing Collective Action Against Neoliberalism: The Case of the "Anti-globalization" Movement. *Journal of World-system Research* X(I): 11–34.

Bavadam, L. 2004. A Militant Platform. *Frontline* 21(3), January 31. Available online at http://www.flonnet.com/fl/2103/stories/20030131008401600.htm

Bedoyan, I., P. van Aeist and S. Walgrave. 2003. Limitations and Possibilities of Transnational Mobilization: The Case of the EU Summit Protestors in Brussels, 2001. Paper to Colloque "Les mobilizations altermondialistes", Association Francaise de Science Politique, Paris, December 3–5.

Birchfield, V. 2004. *Institutionalised Power and Anti-establishment Politics in France: The Case of ATTAC.* Paper to conference "Interest Groups in 21st Century France and Europe", September 24–25, IEP/CEVIPOF, Paris, France. Available online at http://www.cevipof.msh-paris.fr

Brooten, L. 2004. Gender and the IMC: How alternative is this alternative? Paper to International Association of Media and Communication Researchers 2004 Congress, July 25–30, Porto Alegre, Brazil. Available online at http://www.pucrs.br/famecos/iamcr/textos/brooten.pdf

Buttel, F. and K. Gould. 2004. Global Social Movement(s) at the Crossroads: Some Observations on the Trajectory of the Anti-corporate Globalization Movement. *Journal of World-Systems Research* 10(1): 37–66. Available online at http://www.jwsr.ucr.edu

Cammaerts, B. and L. Van Audenhove. 2003. *ICT-usage's [sic] of Transnational Social Movements in the Networked Society: To organize, to mediate and to influence. ASCoR* (Amsterdam School of Communications Research), Amsterdam Free University, Amsterdam. Available online at http://www.users.pandora.be/bart.cammaerts/docs/EMTEL_KD_final.pdf

Canadian Security Intelligence Service. 2000. Anti-Globalization: A Spreading Phenomenon. Report no. 8. Available online at http://www.csis-scrs.gc.ca/eng/misdocs/200008e.html

Cassen, B. 2003. On the Attack. *New Left Review* 19: 41–63.

Chesters, G. and I. Welsh. 2001. *The Rebel Colours of S26.* Working Paper no. 18, Department of Social Science, Cardiff University, Wales. Available online at http://www.edgehill.ac.uk/research/smg/GrahamChesters/htm

Christenden, B.M. 2002. *Constructing a Social Movement. The Case of ATTAC: A Case of Constructive Journalism.* Paper to conference, "Making Social Movements" Edgehill College, Omskirk, England, June 26–28. Available online at http://www.modinet.dk/pdf/no1_constructing_a_ social_movement.pdf

Cleaver, H. 1999. *Computer-linked Social Movements and the Global Threat to Capitalism.* Available online at http://www.eco.utexas.edu/Homepages/Faculty/Cleaver/polnet.html

Cohen, R. and S. Rai. 2000. Global Social Movements: Towards a Cosmopolitan Politics, in R. Cohen and S. Rai (eds), *Global Social Movements.* London: Athlone, pp. 1–17.

Conway, J. 2003. Civil Resistance and the "Diversity of Tactics" in the AGM: Problems of violence, silence and solidarity in activist politics. *Osgoode Hall Law Journal* 41(2/3): 505–29.

De Marcellus, O. 2000. People's Global Action: A Brief History. *Race and Class* 41(4): 92–99.

Farrer, L. 2003. World Forum Movement: Abandon or Contaminate, in J. Sen, A. Anand, A. Escobar and P. Waterman (eds), *The WSF: Challenging Empires.* New Delhi: The Viveka Foundation, pp. 168–77.

Fisher, D., K. Stanley, D. Berman and G. Neff. 2003. *Do Organizations Matter?: Mobilization and Support for Participants at Five Globalization Protests.* Paper to the American Sociological Association, Atlanta, Georgia.

Fisher, W. and T. Ponniah (eds). 2003. *Another World is Possible: Popular Alternatives to Globalisation at the World Social Forum.* London: Zed.

Gerhards, J. and D. Rucht. 1992. Mesomobilization: Organizing and Framing in Two Protest Campaigns in West Germany. *American Journal of Sociology* 98(3): 555–95.

Giri, S. 2003. *Mumbai Resistance and the World Social Forum.* Available online at http://www.info.interactivist.net

Graeber, D. 2001. The Globalisation Movement: Some Points of Clarification. *Items* 2(3–4): 12–14.

————. 2002. The New Anarchists. *New Left Review* 13: 61–73. January–February. Available online at http://www.newleftreview.com

Grubacic, A. 2003. *Life After Social Forums.* Available online at http://www.zmag.org/content/showarticle.cfm? SectionID=41&ItemID=3010

Gryzbowski, C. 2004. *Challenges, Limits and Possibilities of the WSF*. Available online at http://www.ipsnewsnet/focus/tv_mumbai/newstory.asp?idn=244

Guarnizo, L. and M.P. Smith. 1998. The Locations of Transnationalism, in M.P. Smith and L.E. Guarnizo (eds), *Transnationalism from Below*. New Brunswick, NJ: Transaction Publishers, pp. 3–31.

Gupta, D., S. Tarrow and M. Acostavalle. 2001. *Transnational Politics: A Bibliographic Guide to Recent Research on Transnational Movements and Advocacy Groups*. Available online at http://www.falcon.arts.cornell.edu/sgtz/contention/TransnationalBibliography.htm

Hoechsmann, M. 1996. Revolution Goes Global: Zapatistas on the Net. *Convergence: Journal of Research into New Media Technologies* 2(1): 30–35.

Imig, D. and S. Tarrow. 2001. Political Contention in a Europeanising Polity, in K. Goetz and S. Hix (eds), *Europeanised Politics? European Integration and National Political Systems*. London: Frank Cass.

John. H. Henning Center for International Labour Relations. n.d. *Bibliography*. Available online at http://www.henningcenter.berkeley.edu/projects/abstracts-html)

Juris, J. 2004. *The London ESF and the Politics of Autonomous Space*. Available online at http://www.zmag.org/content/print_article.cfm?itemID=6552&sectionID=1

Kagarlitsky, B. 2003. Prague 2000: The People's Battle, in E. Yuen, G. Katsiaficas and D.B. Rose (eds), *The Battle of Seattle*. NY: Soft Skull Press, pp. 253–67.

Katsiaficas, G. 1997. *The Subversion of Politics*. New Jersey: Humanities Press.

Keck, M. and K. Sikkink. 1998. *Activists Beyond Borders: Transnational Advocacy Networks in International Politics*. Ithaca: Cornell University Press.

Kidd, D. 2003. Become the Media: The Global IMC Network, in A. Opel and D. Pompper (eds), *Representing Resistance*. New York: Praeger, pp. 224–40.

King, J. 2002. *The ESF: Sovereign and Multitude*. Available online at http://www.makeworlds.org/book/print/27

Kolb, F. 2003. *The Impact of Transnational Protest on Social Movement Organizations: Mass Media and the Making of ATTAC Germany*. Paper presented at the conference on, "Transnational Politics and Social Movements". Bellagio, Italy, July. Available online at http://www.falcon.arts. cornell.edu/sgt2/working_paper.htm

Laxer, G. and S. Halperin. (eds). 2003. *Global Civil Society and Its Limits*. Basingstoke: Palgrave Macmillan.

NextGENDERation Network. 2004. Refusing to be the Women's Question—Embodied Practices of Feminist Intervention at the ESF 2003. *Feminist Review* 77: 141–51. Available online at http://www.nextgenderation.net/projects/esf2003/femrearticle.htm

Nigam, A. 2004. *The Old Left in a New World: The Mumbai Resistance*. Available online at http://www.info.interactivist.net

Nunes, R. 2004. *Territory and Deterritory: Inside and Outside the ESF, New Movement Subjectivities*. Interactivist Information Exchange. Available online at http://www.info.interactivist.net/print. pl?=04/10/29/1410226

Panitch, L. 2002. Violence as a Tool of Order and Change. *Monthly Review* 54(2): 12–32. Available online at http://www.monthlyreview.org/0602panitch.htm

Passy, F. 1999. Supranational Political Opportunities as a Channel of Globalisation of Political Conflicts: The Case of the Rights of Indigenous Peoples, in D. della Porta, H. Vricsi and D. Rucht (eds), *Social Movements in a Globalising World*. London: Macmillan.

Petras, J. 2001. *NGOs in a Conjuncture of Conflict and War Psychosis*. Available online at http://www.rebelion.org/petras/english/ngo170102.htm

Petras, J. 2002. Porto Alegre 2002: A Tale of Two Forums. Available online at http://www.rebelion.org/petras/english/twoforums170202.htm

Pianta, M. 2001. Parallel Summits of Global Civil Society, in H. Anheier, M. Glasius and M. Kaldor (eds), *Global Civil Society 2001*. Oxford: OUP, pp. 169–94.

Rebick, J. 2002. Lip Service: The Anti-globalization Movement on Gender Politics. *Horizons* 16(2): 24.

Rosenau, J. 1990. *Turbulence in World Politics*. London: Harvester.

Routledge, P. 2004. *Convergence of Commons: Process Geographies of People's Global Action*. Available online at http://www.commoner.org.uk/08routledge.pdf

Seddon, D. and P. Dwyer. 2002. *Food Riots, Past and Present: Globalisation and Contemporary Popular Protest*. Paper to conference "Making social movements. Edgehill College, Omskirk, England, June 26–28. Available online at http://www.edgehill.ac.uk/research/smg/pdf%20-%20conference/

Sen, J. 2003. The Long March to Another World, in J. Sen, A. Anand, A. Escobar and P. Waterman (eds), *The WSF: Challenging Empires*. New Delhi: The Viveka Foundation, pp. 293–311.

Shepherd, B. and R. Hayduk. 2002. *From ACT UP to the WTO*. New York: Verso.

Smith, J. 1997. Characteristics of the Modern Transnational Social Movement Sector, in J. Smith, C. Chatfield and R. Pagnucco (eds.), *Transnational Social Movements and Global Politics: Solidarity Beyond the State*. New York: Syracuse University Press, pp. 42–58.

Smith, J., R. Pagnucco and C. Chatfield. 1997. Social Movements and World Politics: A Theoretical Framework, in J. Smith, C. Chatfield and R. Pagnucco (eds), *Transnational Social Movements and Global Politics: Solidarity Beyond the State*. New York: Syracuse University Press, pp. 59–80.

Starr, A. 2003. "... *Excepting barricades erected to prevent us from peacefully assembling*": *So-called 'Violence' in the First World Anti-globalization Movement*. Available online at http://www.1.chapman. edu/~starr/streetviolence3.htm

Tarrow, S. 2001. Transnational Politics: Contention and Institutions in International Politics. *Annual Review of Political Science* 1: 1–20.

Uggla, F. 2004. *A Movement of Popular Education Oriented towards Action? Attac in France and Sweden*. Paper to European Consortium of Political Research Workshop "Emerging Repertoires of Political Action". Uppsala, Sweden, April 14–18.

Wallach, L. 2000. Lori's War. *Foreign Policy* 118: 28–55, Spring.

Wallerstein, I. 2004. *The Rising Strength of the WSF*. Available online at http://www.cadtm.org

Waterman, P. 2003. *The WSF and a Global Justice and Solidarity Movement: A Rough Guide to Print and Web Publications*. Available online at http://www.labournet.info/wsfbooks2004/guide.doc/view

Wood, L. 2002. *Bridging the Divide: The Case of People's Global Action*. Available online at http://www.riseup.net/pga/ljwood.html

———. 2004. Breaking the Bank and Taking to the Street: How Protestors Target Neoliberalism. *Journal of World-Systems Research* X(1): 69–89. Available online at http://www.jwsr.ucr.edu

Yeates, N. 2001. *Globalisation and Social Policy*. London: Sage.

———. 2002. The "Anti-globalisation" Movement and Its Implications for Social Policy, in R. Sykes, C. Bochel and N. Ellison (eds), *Social Policy Review: Developments and Debates, 2001–2002*. Bristol: The Policy Press, pp. 127–50.

Appendix: "Anti-globalization" demonstrations by International Organization and Date

Date	Location	Numbers		Comments
		Demonstrators	Security forces	
		GATT/World Trade Organisation		
December, 1990	Brussels, Belgium	10,000 (farmers)	3,500 (police)	
December, 1992	Strasbourg, France	40,000 (farmers)		
March, 1993	New Delhi, India	10,000 (farmers)		
December, 1993	Geneva, Switzerland	Several thousand farmers		
April, 1994	New Delhi, India	150,000		80 injured including police.
May, 1998	Hyderabad, India	200,000		
May, 1998	Geneva, Switzerland	10,000		First mass protest at WTO headquarters, 450 arrests.
September, 1998	New Delhi, India	100,000		
November, 1999	Seattle, USA	50,000–70,000		450 arrests.
November 9, 2001	Doha, Qatar	100		Agreement in advance not to make any arrests.
November 10, 2001	New Delhi, India	25,000		
		International Monetary Fund/World Bank		
September, 1988	Berlin, Germany	80,000		Several hurt, 936 arrests.
September, 1990	Washington DC, USA	80		
April, 2000	Washington DC, USA	20,000		1,000 arrests.
September 26, 2000	Prague, Czech Republic	15,000	11,000	30 demonstrators injured, 20 police injured; 20 arrests. Meeting ended a day early.
June, 2001	Barcelona, Spain	Several thousand		33 injured, 22 arrests. Conference cancelled.
September 30, 2001 ('S30')	Washington DC, USA			Cancelled due to September 11 attack.
November 16–17, 2001	Ottawa, Canada	2,000		Police attack demonstrators.

(contd.)

Appendix contd.

Date	Location	Numbers		Comments
		Demonstrators	Security forces	
		GATT/World Trade Organisation		
April, 2002	Washington DC, USA	Over 3,000	3,800 police	
June, 2002	Oslo, Norway	10,000		
April, 2004	Washington DC, USA	3,000		
		G8/G7		
May, 1985	Bonn, Germany	25,000	5,000	Some demonstrators seriously injured, 11 police slightly injured; 60 arrests.
July, 1991	Munich, Germany	17,000		500 arrests.
May 5, 1998	Birmingham, England	10,000		First Global Street Party organized in 30 countries.
June, 1999	Cologne, Germany	35,000		
June 18, 1999	London, England	5,000		Carnival Against Capital; 50 stock exchanges worldwide targeted.
July, 2000	Okinawa, Japan	27,000	22,000	
July, 2001	Genoa, Italy	200,000		1 dead, 240 injured; 200 arrests; allegations of police torture; 2,000 demonstrators refused entry to city.
June, 2002	Kananaskis, Canada	2,500 at Calgary		20 arrests at Halifax.
June, 2003	Evian, France	5,000 at Lausanne, 800 at Geneva		2 serious injuries, mass arrests, heavy use of tear gas, rubber bullets, concussion grenades.
June, 2004	Sea Island, Georgia	Hundreds	20,000 security personnel	50 law enforcement agencies involved in summit security.

World Economic Forum

Date	Location	Demonstrators	Police/Army	Notes
January, 2000	Davos, Switzerland	Thousands	Hundreds of police, 70 army	100 arrests.
January, 2001	Davos, Switzerland	Hundreds		Police attack demonstrators.
February, 2001	Cancun, Mexico	1,500	7,000	13 arrests.
July, 2001	Salzburg, Austria	2,000		
January, 2004	Chur, Switzerland	9,000		2 demonstrators injured.
June, 2004	Seoul, South Korea			

European Union

Date	Location	Demonstrators	Police/Army	Notes
December, 1994	Essen, Germany	50,000	8,000	Demonstration banned. 918 arrests.
June, 1997	Amsterdam, The Netherlands			Several hundred demonstrators arrested.
December, 2000	Nice, France	100,000	11,000	Trade union march.
June, 2001	Gothenburg, Sweden	30,000	2,000	77 injured, including 20 police. 3 demonstrators shot by police. 900 arrests. Hundreds expelled from Sweden.
December 13–15, 2001 ('D13'; 'D14'; 'D15')	Brussels, Belgium	80,000–100,000 on 'D13' trade union march. 25,000 on 'D14' march. 4,000 on 'D15' march.		Legal team members and 150 demonstrators arrested. Demonstrators attacked by police using water cannon, tear gas and plastic bullets. 3,000 police on German–Belgian border.
March, 2002	Barcelona, Spain	250,000		100 arrests, 9 hospitalized.
May, 2004	Dublin, Ireland	3,000		Banned march takes place, 10 arrested.

(contd.)

Appendix contd.

Date	Location	Numbers		Comments
		Demonstrators	Security forces	
		Free Trade Area of the Americas		
June, 2000	Windsor, Canada	3,000	2,200	
April, 2001	Quebec, Canada	30,000 on general demonstration; 50,000 on trade union march	6,000	46 police and 57 demonstrators injured. 400 arrests.
April, 2001	Sao Paulo, Brazil	1,000		
November, 2003	Miami, USA	Thousands		US$8.5 million spent on repression, 100 protesters injured, 250 arrests.
January, 2004	Monterey, Mexico	200	4,200	
		Asian-Development Bank		
May, 2000	Chang Mai, Thailand	1,500		
May, 2001	Hawaii, USA	1,500		
		Asia-Pacific Economic Summit		
September, 2000	Melbourne, Australia	Several thousand	2,000	
		Association of South-East Asian Nations		
November, 1999	Manila, Philippines			Thousands broke through security cordon. Workers and students.
October 20, 2000	Seoul, South Korea	20,000		

Date	Location	Protesters	Police	Outcome
Asia Europe Meeting				
October, 2000	Seoul, South Korea	15,000	29,000	
Asia-Pacific Economic Cooperation (Forum)				
November, 1996	Manila, Philippines	130,000		
October, 2003	Bangkok, Thailand	1,000		
November, 2004	Santiago, Chile	50,000	4,000 police	17 police injured, 180 arrests.
European Economic Forum				
April, 2004	Warsaw, Poland	3,000		
Organization for Economic Cooperation and Development				
June, 2000	Bologna, Italy	6,000	Thousands	
EU-Latin American Summit				
May, 2004	Guadalajara, Mexico	4,000		20 demonstrators injured, 90 arrested. Alleged torture of arrestees including sexual abuse.

Adapted from Yeates (2002) and extended by the authors.
Sources: Derived from various "anti-globalization" and independent media websites and webcast news reports (e.g. http://www.indymedia.org; http://www.protest.net; http://www.flora.org; http://www.nadir.org/nadir/initiativ/agp).

15

NEW LABOR PROTEST MOVEMENTS IN HONG KONG

The Experience of the Student–Worker Mutual Aid Campaign

KAXTON YU-KWAN SIU

The "game" played from the 1950s to the 1970s was called "developmentalism" (Wallerstein 2003), the game played from the 1980s has changed to "globalization"; the rule of the game of developmentalism among national states was to achieve by some kind of control over the economy (Wallerstein 2003), the rule to the globalization game has changed to deregulation, liberalization and deterritorialization. Neoliberals proclaim loudly that they are the only competitive players in the globalization game; neoliberals also declare that they are the faithful followers of the rule of deregulation, liberalization and de-territorialization through advocating: (1) the changing regulatory framework to facilitate labor market flexibility and mobility within national economic space (deregulation); (2) the liberalization and deregulation of foreign exchange movements with the effect of internalizing and accelerating capital flows; and (3) modifying institutional frameworks in order to promote international trade and foreign direct investment as well as to promote appropriate conditions for global spread of national and regional capitalism—de-territorialization (Jessop 2002: 138; cited by Chiu and So 2004).

By means of deregulation, liberalization and deterritorialization, globalization has changed industrial relations, labor market formation and class politics, as well as given rise to the flexible accumulation regime by the late 1980s (Harvey 1989). One form of the change of industrial relations and class politics under flexible accumulation regimes is the increasing practicing of flexible employment in different local economies. The focus of this chapter is to identify the new pattern of labor insurgencies in the context of flexible employment in Hong Kong.

Flexible employment has four features in comparison to the traditional type of employment. First, in terms of employment patterns, traditionally, workers labor as full-time and regular workers. Full-time and regular workers usually enjoy many fringe benefits, such as housing allowances, medical insurances, spouses' educational allowances, long-term services payments, bonus, etc. However, under flexible employment conditions, large amount of full-time and regular workers disappear from the labor market. Instead, new employment patterns appear in form of part-time workers, casual labor, outsourcing workers, contract workers, subcontracting workers, short-term workers, etc (Reilly 2001). These new employment patterns have step by step displaced traditional form of employment patterns and become dominant in labor markets worldwide (Harvey 1989). Second, in terms of gender distribution, traditionally, the labor market is male dominant; yet, under the age of flexible employment, large number of females have entered labor markets. These female workers usually labor in services sector, such as cleaning services food catering services and the like (Sassen 1991). Third, flexible employment also means the alternative work arrangement to standard work arrangement (Polivka 1996). In terms of work arrangement, traditionally, workers labor under standard work arrangement in a large factory or in a single office with fixed work location and within fixed work time period ("from nine to five" was the catch phrase to describe this situation); however, under flexible employment, employers can assign employees to labor at different work locations and request employees to work on several shifts a day. In this sense, the change is evident in shifting from fixed work location and work time period to multiple work locations and unstable working time (Chiu and So 2004). Last but not the least, in terms of employment relationship, traditionally, the employer–employee relationship forms the majority in most workplace contexts. However, nowadays, such employer–employee relationship blurs and other actors may be involved indirectly in the industrial relations. For example, in an outsourcing work environment, workers engage in a network of relations among employers, outsourcers, subcontractors, stakeholders and managements of the worksites (for example, residents of a public housing estate). From labor control's perspective, this diverse network of relations widens the scope of members in monitoring workers' labor process. In some sense, these actors altogether form a coalition to monitor workers.

All the above features of flexible employment are suppressive to workers and labor movement practitioners. To workers, the change from full-time and regular work to non-traditional type of work means not only the loss of their fringe benefits but also their job and income securities (Withagen and Tros 2003). The loss of job and income securities contributes to the great fear of layoff and further implies the unwillingness to participate in collective labor resistances towards their employers in the workplaces.

To labor movement practitioners, the increasing trend of non-standard work arrangement poses difficulties in labor organizing. For example, provided trade unionists want to organize a company's workers to challenge their employer, but their target mobilizing workers need to change their work locations several times once a month or need to take several shifts daily, the trade unionists will find it very difficult to group a large amount of workers together for holding necessary strategy-formulating meetings or concrete collective actions such as the protest and strike. On the other hand, the blurring of employer–employee relationship also gives difficulties to local labor movement organizers. Under such a diverse network of relationship, movement organizers usually find hard to identify the appropriate antagonist to challenge. In the situation where multilayered subcontracting system exists, management of a worksite shifts responsibilities (such as workers being injured during work time, earning extremely low salary, and laboring exceptionally long working hours) to the top tier subcontractor, and then top tier subcontractor similarly shifts responsibilities to the lower tier subcontractors. Sometimes, the blurring of employee–employer relations may hinder labor insurgency because workers find hard to identify the boss against whom to struggle as they are often hidden behind layers of subcontractors (Chiu and So 2004).

This chapter has one objective. It purposes to examine new patterns of labor insurgency under globalization in Hong Kong. In particular, we highlight the differences between old and new patterns of labor insurgencies from organization and resources perspectives. Instead of resorting to pessimism, this chapter argues that local labor organizations learn, equip, and transform their mobilizing strategies and tactics to cope with globalization. In the end, we will go back to reflect on the nature of flexible employment.

By using the "Student–Worker Mutual Aid Campaign" (SWMA) as the empirical case, we are informed that: under the support of transnational nongovernmental organization or TNGO, local labor organizations form new connective networks and formal hierarchical organizations through specific campaigns. These new networks and organizations can widen the scope of participants in the movement to participate in labor protests.[1] Secondly, local labor organizations also get new resources under their organizational transformation; these resources range from manpower, mass media attention, financial aid, to administrative supports.

This chapter is divided into three parts: in the first part we will show how globalization nested with neoliberal ideology and led to a neoliberal project in Hong Kong, unpinning the outsourcing initiatives in Hong Kong universities. Afterwards, we will detail the SWMA campaign to see one local trade union (Hong Kong Confederations of Trade Union, or HKCTU) under the support of Oxfam (one of the TNGO concerning human right issues) to hold a series of protest movement for rank-and-file workers at local universities in Hong

Kong. In the third part, we will pinpoint several characteristics of SWMA so as to compare the difference between traditional and new patterns of labor insurgencies. In conclusion, I will end this chapter by rethinking the nature of flexible employment by exposing its inherent rigidity, uncertainty, and dilemma, which is engendered when flexible employment is put into practice.

GLOBALIZATION AND NEOLIBERAL IDEOLOGY IN HONG KONG

Hong Kong presents quite a good example of two distinctive periods of globalization. Each of the period confirms different patterns of flexible employment. During the 1960s to the 1980s, Hong Kong's manufacturing industry has already exercized certain level of flexible employment practices. At that moment, Hong Kong labor engaged in small and medium firms under the system of global subcontracting network (Chiu and So 2004). In responding to the ever changing global market and the tight competition with neighboring cities, such as Taiwan, Singapore and South Korea, the kind of flexible employment and the flexible production in general contributed Hong Kong a great degree of competitive edge in global markets by seizing opportunities to get effective supply of materials and orders, acquisition of market information, and connections with foreign buyers provided by the global commercial networks at that time (Lee 1997: 162–79).

The global production conditions and international political environment also ensured Hong Kong firms to get enough supply of orders from overseas. The major growth of global subcontracting was due to: (1) the tremendous increase of demand for labor intensive consumer goods in the advanced capitalist countries propelled capital to mass production; (2) the increasing competition from Japan and West Germany in the mid-1960s urged American transnational capital to meet this challenge by means of global subcontracting. This in turn forced Japan and West Germany into similar strategy (Landsberg 1982).

From the 1960s to 1980s, the profit generated through flexible production constituted to a rise in wages and living standard of the working class, social stability, as well as low unemployment rate. However, despite that Hong Kong's economy has taken off, there was not much development in trade unionism in Hong Kong. The reason for the underdevelopment of Hong Kong's trade unionism was political. As Chiu and So (2004) stress, one of the reasons of Hong Kong's weak trade unionism is that trade unions in Hong Kong concentrated more on Chinese national affairs in comparison to local economic issues. This was explicated in two major trade unions' (Federation of Trade Unions and Hong Kong and Kowloon Trade Union Council) clear political inclinations towards Mainland Beijing regime and Taipei regime, respectively, in Hong Kong during the 1960s and 1980s.

In the 1980s everything changed. Since the mid-1980s, after years of economic take-off, Hong Kong has stepped into its structural transformation period. Due to rising land rent, protectionism, and keen competition from neighboring Asian countries, Hong Kong's manufacturing industry has started to relocate across the border to Pearl River Delta to seek for a large pool of docile and cheap labor (Chiu and So 2004). The number of Hong Kong manufacturing workers dropped drastically from 892,140 in 1980 to 275,766 in 1995 (So, forthcoming). On the other hand, the number of service workers increased from 789,454 in 1980s to 2,648,600 in 1999 (Yeung 1997: 251). These figures inform us that by the mid-1990s the hollowing out of Hong Kong's manufacturing industry was followed by a rapid expansion of service sector. Ironically, it was Hong Kong's manufacturing industry displaced from the center of global economy that signals that Hong Kong has become *less* globalized. The fear of being further displaced from the global triggered changes in local political landscape. The question of how to transform Hong Kong in order to meet the new requirements of the new global economy puzzled its business and political leaders. The eagerness of getting global could be seen in the way that numerous projects aimed at making Hong Kong more attractive to investors, visitors and tourists have funded away from public services to corporate subsidies (Lopez 2000). The projects ranged from the grand tourist projects of construction of Disneyland in Lantau Island and West Kowloon cultural development district to other scientific and technological projects, such as Cyberport and Herbal port; these have been justified with reference to the necessity of making Hong Kong a more attractive location for global investment.

The trend of government expenditure being funded away from public services could be seen in how government subsidies have been pumped out from higher education expenditure. Since the Asian Financial Crisis in late 1997, under the reason of unfavorable fiscal environment and the budget stringency, as well as the imperative of efficiency maximization, the government has gradually reduced its expenditure on education since the financial year of 1997–98, despite the short-lived increase in 1998–99. Table 15.1, adopted from government statistics, shows the decreasing trend of government approved recurrent grants in Hong Kong's higher education between 1997–98 and 2003–04 while Table 15.2 shows similar trend in government expenditure as percentage on education from 1997–98 to 2003–04.

Hong Kong Government also deployed neoliberal ideas about the superiority of private markets over public administration. Local government funded universities also experienced heavy neoliberal ideological pressure from the Audit Commission of the Government to urge all institutions to seek outsourcing as cost-efficiency measure in services that ranged from campus cleaning, security,

Table 15.1: Approved Recurrent Grants for UGC-funded
Institutions (1997–98 to 2003–04)

Financial Year	Approved Recurrent Grants (in $m)
1997–98	11,618
1998–99	12,623
1999–2000	12,040
2000–01	11,965
2001–02	11,676
2002–03	11,633
2003–04	11,566

Source: UGC statistics, 1997–98 to 2003–04.

Table 15.2: Approved Grants As Percentage of Total
Government Expenditure on Education

Financial Year	Percentage of Approved Government Grants
1997–98	27.7%
1998–99	29.2%
1999–2000	28.8%
2000–01	28.4%
2001–02	26.5%
2002–03	25.8%
2003–04	23.6%

Source: UGC statistics, 1997–98 to 2003–04.

lifeguard, landscaping to repair and management, etc. In March 31, 2003, the Audit Commission released its report (Audit Commission 2003) criticizing some institutions which still retained a large number of in-house staff responsible for various estate management services. In particular, the report commented that if all institutions outsourced all the campus cleaning and security services, potential savings could be amount to HK$31 million a year. Here, we see how the necessity of competing for global investment seems to make public service expenditure unsustainable, too expensive, and non-competitive; while on the other hand, the ideology of market efficiency provides "solutions" and plans for eliminating public service provisions. However, with the holly grail of "being global," the neoliberal argument has been unquestioned for the threat of disinvestment and capital flights looms over everything (Lopez 2000). As we will see, these complex relationships between discourses about globalization and neoliberal ideology is not without its local challengers. In the case of SWMA campaign, we will see how HKCTU mounted challenges to the neoliberal ideology and flexible employment through transforming their mobilization structure and getting new resources.

THE STUDENT–WORKER MUTUAL AID CAMPAIGN (SWMA CAMPAIGN)

The SWMA Campaign was a student–worker cooperative campaign launched officially in Hong Kong in August 2003 which aimed to mount efficient collective actions at universities so as to: on the one hand raise students' concerns on various labor issues, such as the worsening working conditions of campus outsourced workers; while on the other, push a series of salary raising movement at university campuses.

The evolution of the SWMA campaign could be divided into three stages. They were: the preparation stage, consolidation stage, and mobilization stage.

The Preparation Stage: The Student Volunteer Workshop

Before detailing how HKCTU prepared the campaign from its outset, we have to understand how the idea of "student–worker cooperation" came into the mind of HKCTU trade unionists.

The origin of the idea had great relationship with the nature of HKCTU trade unionists themselves. In fact, HKCTU usually recruited fresh graduate students who were active in different local universities, such as those having experience of being core members in student organizations or being student activists in concerning social (especially labor) issues, as their trade unionists. As such, large number of HKCTU trade unionists had rather tight connections with their former serving student organizations and student activist groups inside the universities. Hence, when HKCTU started its concern on the salary issue of outsourced workers laboring in local universities, the first thing these HKCTU trade unionists did was to contact the student organizations and student activist groups inside local universities. And the first action was an establishment of "student volunteer workshop."

In fact, the triggering of HKCTU's concern on salary issue of outsourced workers at Hong Kong's universities was based on HKCTU's observation of increasing outsourcing found in Hong Kong's university campuses. The government's policy to cut its expenditure on university education has led local universities to outsource many of the non-academic and administrative works. The cleaning service was one of these outsourced kinds.

The student volunteer workshop began by concerning the outsourcing workers at local universities. The workshop was formed in May 2003. Major participants of the workshop were those student activists from established student organizations and social issue concern groups. Others, such as students in related disciplines like social work and sociology also participated. The major work done in the workshop was both educational and action oriented. In the workshops,

HKCTU trade unionists tried to let the volunteers understand the hardship of Hong Kong workers by showing a large amount of statistical data (such as Gini coefficient, salary inequality, low salary statistics of outsourced cleaning workers laboring at public funded agencies, such as Hospital Authority, Housing Authority, and local universities). On the other hand, the workshop also requested volunteers to collect most updated data concerning outsourcing workers' working conditions (such as salary rate, working hours, work arrangement) by interviewing workers at their own universities. In addition, HKCTU also mobilized these student volunteers to protest at local universities. For example, in June 2003, the workshop mobilized their student volunteers to protest at Hong Kong Polytechnic University (POLYU) at the president's office to request a raise of outsourcing cleaning workers' salary rate (*Apple Daily*, June 11, 2003).

However, although HKCTU had launched the student volunteer workshop, HKCTU still encountered great difficulty in intervening into universities or holding activities inside campuses. To account for this difficulty, simply put: HKCTU had no legitimate status to hold activities inside these university campuses. The lack of legitimate status further limited HKCTU's options to hold appropriate activities. For example, they could not set counters or post posters inside university campuses to recruit members to join their volunteer workshop. This made the volunteer workshop confined to a small circle activity. However, as we will quickly see, these difficulties were solved after HKCTU built a two-tier hierarchical organization through the SWMA campaign in the consolidation and mobilization stages.

The Consolidation Stage: The Forming of a Two-Tier Hierarchical Organization

Having two months of experience of student volunteer workshop, HKCTU found that the composition of volunteer workshop had sufficient enough to serve as the building block of a more formal organization. Hence, they then decided to make further consolidation. As such, HKCTU sought help from Oxfam.

On August 2003, HKCTU submitted a proposal to Oxfam to apply for funding for subsidizing the establishment of various formal grassroots labor concern groups at four local universities, Hong Kong University, Chinese University of Hong Kong, Hong Kong University of Science and Technology (HKU, CUHK, HKUST) and POLYU, under the name of SWMA campaign. In the proposal, HKCTU stated that they have tried to build coalitions between university students and grassroots workers by establishing separate grassroots labor concern groups at the four local universities. HKCTU also stated that they would hire one university student (in name of liaison person) at each university for the recruitment of students into concern groups, for formulating actions, for activating discussions and activities inside campuses, for holding meetings, workshops and seminars with students, as well as for leading students to conduct interviews with campus rank-and-file workers. The liaison person was paid a maximum sum of HK$2,000 (US$256) monthly as student helper. The major purpose of establishing concern groups was to let HKCTU set up legitimate bases at different university campuses. The liaison person served as the bridge between HKCTU and students.

Having received HKCTU's proposal, Oxfam was immediately hooked by the innovative idea of forming a coalition between students and workers. During the meeting before endorsing subsidies to the SWMA campaign, Oxfam met with HKCTU trade unionists and students for further clarification of details of the campaign. HKCTU trade unionists detailed their former experiences of student volunteer workshop and the students detailed their intentions to try the scheme. In turn, Oxfam shared their foreign experience with HKCTU trade unionists and students. One of the foreign experience cited by Oxfam, the "United Students Against Sweatshop" campaign or USAS campaign launched at Harvard University, which had great similarities in terms of purpose and movement strategies with HKCTU's proposal of campaign.

Oxfam also suggested HKCTU should form a two-tier hierarchical organization to facilitate and monitor the campaign. For the upper tier, it was the management board, which was composed of two HKCTU trade unionists, four university students elected from members of four labor concern groups, one person from any occupation who worked in Hong Kong. The management board met regularly once a month. The main function of the management board was to ensure the continuous functioning of each concern group and discussed cross-university action plans mounted at different universities. For the lower tier, it was composed of the four labor concern groups. In each labor concern group, there consisted of an elected student liaison person, an elected person at management board, and other members of the concern group. Each labor concern group had autonomy to decide what kind of activities and actions to hold; the management board would not intervene into the administration of each labor concern group.

Having such a formal two-tier hierarchical organization, the difficulties posed in the preparation stage were resolved easily. When HKCTU wanted to recruit more students to participate in the SWMA campaign, they just did it through those student unions' already established networks and broadcasting channels, to join their affiliated labor concern groups based at each university. On the other hand, the legitimate status problem was also solved as well. After forming the two-tier hierarchical organization, whenever SWMA campaign wanted to hold activities or do mobilization inside the university campus, the campaign could hold the activities and mobilization in name of a trinity, Student—Oxfam—HKCTU, rather than just in the name of HKCTU. As students had legitimate status, identity, and rights to hold activities that concerned labor issue, the SWMA campaign was advantageous in lowering university administration's hostility towards their held activities.

The Mobilization Stage: Confrontation

In August 2003, Oxfam officially endorsed HKCTU's proposal on SWMA campaign and started to subsidize and support the SWMA campaign. On getting financial support from Oxfam, HKCTU quickly invited one of the already established labor concern group at CUHK as part of their lower tier organizations and invited other students' unions at HKUST, HKU and POLYU to nominate their executive committee members to collectively build three similar concern groups at HKUST, HKU and POLYU.

One should note that, except the concern group at HKUST, the other three concern groups had overlapping membership with the executive committee of students' unions at these three universities. The executive committee of these university students' unions contained many student activists interested in concerning social and political issues, and received high recognitions from the university administrations. For the concern group at HKUST, the members who participated were mostly ex-members of the executive committee of the students' union, as well as post-graduate students from the division of social sciences.

In late August 2003, after having a certain level of organization, the management board of the SWMA campaign suggested holding their first collective action at one of the local universities as a kick-off of their salary raising protest movement for outsourcing workers inside local universities. And they finally decided to protest at the annual congregation at HKUST.

Protest at HKUST Annual Congregation Ceremony

The decision made to confront HKUST administration was not by choice. There was a long story behind that made members in the management board (HKCTU unionists and students from four concern groups) hate the HKUST administration so much.

The critical issue identified that led to the subsequent protest at HKUST was the issue of contract renewal of the cleaning service contractor—Wai Hong. In September 2002, HKCTU knew that Wai Hong's cleaning service contract with HKUST would end in August 2003. HKCTU thought the renewal a golden opportunity to request the raise of salary of these outsourced cleaning workers from HK$4030 to HK$6800. They decided to request HKUST administration to raise outsourced cleaning workers' salary through negotiation. However, what HKCTU received from the HKUST administration was either "no reply" or excuses such as responsible officers being on leave. From December 2002 to June 2003, HKCTU tried a dozen times to issue invitation letters, petitions, warning letters or make phone calls requesting a meeting for discussion on outsourced cleaning workers' salary matters. Yet, HKCTU received no response from the administration throughout the whole period. In June 2003, knowing HKUST administration's unwillingness to negotiate with them, HKCTU issued a "final warning" to them by stating that "if HKUST does not meet with us, we will escalate our action to a more violent level." Despite, having received such final warning, HKUST administration played new tricks. HKUST administration scheduled the meeting with HKCTU trade unionists in mid-August, which was the date *after* the contract renewal process with Wai-Hong (and no salary rate of outsourced workers had changed). And in mid-August 2003, during the meeting with HKCTU trade unionists, HKUST administration just dismissed HKCTU's request by reason of "the contract renewal process has ended. We will consider the raising of outsourcing cleaning workers' salary in next contract renewal—three years later."

After HKCTU found that they were cheated, they were very angry toward HKUST administration. As such, HKCTU at the management board meeting of the SWMA campaign suggested holding a protest at the university's annual congregation ceremony so as to embarrass HKUST administration to the greatest extent. The protest was taken on November 7, 2003, the last day of HKUST's eleventh congregation ceremony. For wider publicity, twenty members of the SWMA campaign (students from four different concern groups, HKCTU trade unionists) decided to hold the protest on the last day of ceremony, for many news media would come to cover all honorable degrees to be conferred and medal presentations that were to be held.

Members of SWMA campaign formulated a two-battle-front strategy. First, they allocated twelve to fourteen participants to protest overtly at the entrance piazza of the campus. They distributed leaflets to the people attending the congregation, on which were printed the HKCTU public statements opposing the low salary of outsourced workers in HKUST. At the entrance, they also displayed a large banner declaring "HKUST exploits workers" and some billboards with slogans. They also made use of their loudspeakers to voice slogans. However, the public protest at the entrance was just a strategy of sidetracking the security guards. There was another "sudden attack" planned. Four of the protest participants smuggled secretly to the first floor where there was a terrace facing directly the ceremony stage. They stayed hidden there, occupying an eye-catching place, and waited. When the president of HKUST began his speech, the four participants suddenly bought a large square red banner, which printed "Please pay outsourcing workers reasonable salary" and suspended it from the terrace. The banner could almost be seen in front of all audiences' eyeballs. The senior officer called three to four security guards just to observe the protesters as they had no right to arrest them, but they feared that the protest may lead to violence. He also called a photographer to spot all protesters. Later, HKUST administration called the police for help. However, the coming of police force made not much intervention to the protest. What the police merely did was to forbid protesters to use loudspeakers to voice their slogans. The protesters ignored the warning from police; they went on voicing their slogans on loudspeakers. Embarrassed as the president of HKUST was, whenever he spoke, he was interrupted by the protesters' loud voices and slogans. Indeed, the day after, about three to four major local newspapers reported the protest. The protest received wide publicity and forced the president of HKUST to confront squarely with the question of exploitation inside HKUST raised by the news reporters (*Ming Pao*, November 8, 2003). The HKUST administration could only respond by appeal to language of market price to justify the low amount of salary earned by outsourced workers. President of HKUST said, "HKUST's outsourcing cleaning workers do not receive the lowest wage among local universities. We are just in the middle in the market." (ibid.). However, the "market" the president of HKUST referred to was not the private market in the cleaning industry. The private market value of monthly salary of an outsourced cleaning worker was about HK$6,000; yet the outsourced cleaning workers received in HKUST was just the one lower HK$5,000. Actually, the "market" the president of HKUST referred to was the internal market among local public funded universities. However, the president of HKUST's justification could not sustain long. In May 2004, about half a year after the protest, Hong Kong Government enforced an internal guideline for all government departments stating that the minimum wage an individual outsourced janitorial worker received monthly could not be lower than a salary of HK$5,060. Although the scope of guideline did not include public funded universities in Hong Kong, HKUST still voluntarily increased each outsourced cleaning worker's monthly salary from HK$4,030 to HK$5,060 through HKUST's direct subsidization extracted from the university's reserve fund.

NEW PATTERNS OF LABOR INSURGENCY
UNDER FLEXIBLE EMPLOYMENT

Having detailed the case of SWMA campaign and one of the protest movements at HKUST, we now turn to discuss the difference between traditional and new patterns of labor insurgencies from organization and resource perspectives.

In traditional patterns of labor insurgency, first, the membership of a trade union was limited only to workers while other social groups such as students were excluded. Even though workers could build alliance with other actors during labor struggles, the kind of alliance was mostly temporary and did not codify into any formal hierarchical organizational structure. Second, the stewardship in traditional patterns of labor insurgency was directed either by trade unionists or workers. Third, in terms of resources, financial supports were confined either in form of donation or in form of union membership fee, and manpower were limited to how many trade unionists and worker activists did the trade union have.

However, in new patterns of labor insurgency under flexible employment, changes have taken. First, from organization perspective, HKCTU through the SWMA campaign formed a new connective network and organization structure. As we could see, after building the two-tier hierarchical organization, the SWMA campaign tightened their existing networks; for example, by hiring student volunteers involved in student volunteer workshop as liaison persons in each labor concern group, the volunteers became obliged to participate and to devote themselves to the campaign, rather than just come when interested and go when passions fade away (However, even so, one should be warned not to view these student volunteers' participation to be too instrumental—for the mere purpose of earning that monthly HK$2,000. In the SWMA campaign, some committed student volunteers, after being hired as liaison persons, did not receive their salaries which they re-donated back into campaign for other administrative expenses. These committed students were crucial actors in maintaining the continual functioning of labor concern groups and in sustaining prolonged and tight relationships with other student members who participated in the campaign, through day-to-day contacts inside the university campuses.)

In addition, HKCTU also extended their network to other established student groups to participate in their campaign. The extension of network does not simply mean the increase in number of participants in the campaign. It also means continuously adding pressure on the university administration's burden. With more and more students in the university community taking up the concern of the workers' laboring conditions in their own campus, the university administration is forced to face the labor issue squarely as an internal affair and student concerning affair, rather than just a simple industrial dispute between contractor and outsourced workers or trade unions by shifting all responsibility to the contractor.

On top of the extension of network, the two-tier hierarchical organization also facilitated a new form of stewardship in labor insurgency. Under flexible employment, workers lack job and income security. This makes them very unwilling to join labor actions in their workplace, not to mention being labor activists or stewards in collective actions. However, under the two-tier hierarchical organization, the stewardship role shifted to university students. Each liaison person at individual labor concern groups exactly functioned as a steward in contacting workers and students as well as mounting collective actions inside the university campuses. There is one great advantage here: as students inside their own campus are free to hold any activities without being sanctioned, they could go to chat with the rank-and-file workers to collect information on these workers' labor conditions and to invite workers to join any activities inside the campus. The university administration is also reluctant to intervene in student activities for fear of being accused by students of suppressing their freedom of right to hold assembly and organize activities. Even at the workplace where labor control is paramount, (for example, outsourced cleaning workers are warned by their supervisors that once they were found participating in protests, they would be fired immediately), students and trade unionists could represent workers to protest against university administration. This makes possible for resistances to emerge in the workplace even with extremely tight control.

Second, from the resource point of view, in the SWMA campaign HKCTU received resources directly and indirectly from Oxfam. There are two kinds of direct resources provided by Oxfam. The first kind of direct resources is financial support. Under Oxfam's financial aid, HKCTU launched the SWMA campaign by hiring liaison persons for each individual labor concern group, the coverage of daily expenses, and funding for necessary equipment for mounting collective actions, such as protest banners, billboards, etc. The second kind of direct resources is foreign movement experience. For example, when HKCTU and student volunteers submitted their proposal to Oxfam, Oxfam in turn shared the USAS campaign held at Harvard University and advised what sort of organization structure HKCTU should take up in their campaign. These contributed immensely to the later development of the SWMA campaign.

On top of direct resources provided by Oxfam, indeed, it also facilitated many indirect resources to the SWMA campaign. First, because the SWMA campaign held their activities and protests in name of the trinity, Student–Oxfam–HKCTU, it attracted mass media's attention to report their actions. For mass media, industrial disputes between trade unionists and employers may not be very news worthy, unless there is any violation of labor ordination or human right matters; however, university students' eagerness to concern and even participate in labor action inside their university campus can have much news worthiness. The mass media's coverage in turn translates into one form of bargaining power when trade unionists negotiate with public funded agencies, such as public funded universities that treasure their public image and reputation fondly. These agencies would try to avoid any destruction of their reputation. Seizing on these agencies' weakness, the degree of success in achieving their demands will be considerably higher.

Second, since Oxfam is a recognized TNGO concerning human right issues, this, on the one hand, helped attract students who respect Oxfam to join in the SWMA campaign. On the other hand, as the SWMA campaign was framed as an educational program to let students explore social issues presented in front of them, it provided students justifiable grounds to concern and participate in the disputes in industrial relations. Then, as more and more students participated in the campaign, gradually, these students in turn contributed their free time to take on responsibilities of some administrative matters in the campaign as well. This then softened HKCTU's administrative burden to a great extent.

Third, as HKCTU also had limited manpower, they could not go frequently to these university campuses to observe whether the working conditions of outsourced workers had worsened. However, with the participation of university students, HKCTU could get the data of changing working conditions at these campuses by requesting participating students to interview the outsourced workers on a weekly basis. In addition, students also provide valuable information for trade unionists to formulate their action strategies. In the protest at HKUST congregation, the students studying at HKUST provided the information about the geographic layout of the campus. Armed with the information, HKCTU knew where they should hide their protest participants for the sudden attack and where to uphold their large banners so as to receive the greatest media and public attention.

DISCUSSIONS AND CONCLUSION

Having discussed the new patterns of labor insurgency under flexible employment, we revert to discuss the nature of flexible employment. First, from the HKUST protest and HKUST administration's voluntary action to raise outsourced cleaning workers' monthly salary rate, we can see that the forces of globalization are far from all encompassing and powerful. We see different loopholes of flexible employment that provide new ground for labor resistance to appropriate. The neoliberal imperative to push public sector agencies, such as public funded universities, to obtain efficiency from private market by measures of outsourcing and privatization in turn exposes the weakness of these public sector agencies. These agencies are impotent to protect their image and reputation in front of news media and the public when they are accused of being immoral. For example, when university administration is accused by trade unionists that exploitations take place inside its campus, to defend its reputation, it will usually concede to fulfill the trade union's demand.

Second, far from the argument that flexible employment is the ready-made "solution" for solving management's rigidity and enhancing flexibility in various forms (Reilly 2001), flexible employment just covers its inherent rigidity, uncertainty, and dilemma that it confronts in practice, in the guise of flexibility.

Again, the contract renewal issue taken up at public funded universities in Hong Kong is instructive here. Theoretically speaking, the purpose of seeking outsourcing to provide campus cleaning service can save costs in sustaining a large team of in-house cleaning staff, and provide university quality services and the right to change service providers when contract renewals get over. However, this argument masks the complex process of the whole contract renewal process and the dilemma confronted by the university administration. In practice, it is very hard for university administration to determine how long the contract with the service provider should be. If the period is too short, the university administration needs to take care of other costs to deal with frequent contract renewal procedures. In addition, for the short contract period, many small-size service providers will be scared off for such service providers usually cannot achieve a break-even within the contract period, and this in turn limits university administration's possible choices for the appropriate service provider. Even worst, it should be noted that a new service provider after receiving a new contract from the university also needs time to train its workers to familiarize with the servicing site. Given the short contract period, where the service provider and its employed workers lack experience and familiarization at the servicing site, the service quality provided is hard to sustain.

On the other hand, provided the contract period is too long where political uncertainties are not taken seriously into account so as to establish appropriate regulatory mechanisms to cope with, the university administration will confront a certain extent of rigidity. For instance, within the contract period, if there is any sudden change in government policy (such as the minimum wage guideline enforced by Hong Kong Government in our case), university administration will be trapped. For university administration cannot force their service provider to increase outsourced workers' salary rate; university administration can either breach the contract with existing provider so as to find a new one who promises to provide its employed workers as per the government's policy (but this will incur the cost in university administration's unilateral action of breaching the contract), or, as what HKUST administration did in our case, directly subsidize outsourced workers by using university's own reserve funding. Taken as a whole, both actions will incur new costs.

In sum, this chapter identifies the new patterns of labor insurgency in the context of flexible employment. The new patterns of labor insurgency engender new organizations in form of student–worker coalition by undergoing specific funded campaigns and providing new resources for practitioners to challenge flexible employment. This chapter also unveils the mask of flexibility discourse by exposing the rigidity, dilemma, and uncertainty encountered by management of public sector agencies when advocating flexible employment.

Hong Kong's SWMA campaign is certainly not alone. Similar patterns of labor insurgencies are burgeoning as well. For example, students from 160 colleges and universities in United States and Canada joined the league of USAS and have launched a "National Campus Living Wage Campaign" by organizing and mobilizing students across United States and Canada to fight for living wages on their campuses.[2] So long as the globalization game is still the fashionable game to play at the advent of the twenty-first century, we look forward to new rules and new players, and not just those arrogant neoliberals!

Notes

1. Empirical data provided in this chapter is collected through participant observation by involving in the SWMA campaign from February 2003 to August 2004. During my participation, I firstly positioned as a student volunteer during the preparation stage of SWMA campaign to one of the members of the labor concern group, to participate in their protests, meetings and activities. On top of data collected through participant observation, I also conducted interviews with participating students, trade unionists and workers in the campaign as well as analyzed documents such as trade union's published newsletters, promotion materials, minutes of meeting, campaign proposals, etc.
2. The history and current campaign of USAS is available online at http://www. studentsagainstsweatshops.org/about/history.php (accessed January 8, 2005).

References

Apple Daily. 2003. June 11.

Audit Commission. 2003. Report of the Director Audit (Report No. 40) on the results of value for money audits University Grant Committee Funded Institutions—General Administrative Services. Government Printing Department, Hong Kong.

Chiu, S.W.K. and A.Y. So. 2004. Flexible Production and Industrial Restructuring in Hong Kong: From Boom to Bust? in G.G. Gonzalez (ed.), *Labor Versus Empire: Race, Gender, and Migration*. New York: Routledge.

Harvey, D. 1989. *The Condition of Postmodernity: An Inquiry into the Origins of Cultural Change*. Cambridge, MA: Blackwell.

Jessop, B. 2002. *The Future of Capitalist State*. Cambridge, UK: Polity Press.

Landsberg, M. 1982. Export-led Industrialization in the Third World: Manufacturing Imperialism. *The Review of Radical Political Economics* 11(4): 57.

Lee, K.M. 1997. Flexible Manufacturing in a Colonial Economy, in T. Ngo (ed.), *Hong Kong's History: State and Society under Colonial Rule*. Hong Kong: Oxford University Press, pp. 162–79.

Lopez, S.H. 2000. Contesting the Global City: Pittsburgh's Public Service Unions Confront a Neoliberal Agenda, in M. Burawoy (ed.), *Global Ethnography: Forces, Connections, and Imaginations in a Postmodern World*. Berkeley and Los Angeles, California: University of California Press.

Ming Pao. 2003. Hkust Cleaning Workers' Protest. *The Daily News* (Toronto), November 8.

Polivka, A.E. 1996. Contingent and Alternative Work Arrangements Defined. *Monthly Labor Review*, 119: 3–9.

Reilly, P. 2001. Types and Incidence of Flexibility, in P. Reilly (ed.), *Flexibility at Work: Balancing the Interests of Employer and Employee*. Hampshire: Gower Publisher Limited, pp. 28–36.

Sassen, S. 1991. *The Global City: New York, London, Tokyo*. Princeton, N.J.: Princeton University Press.

So, A.Y. (forthcoming). Hong Kong's Pathways to Global City: A Regional Analysis, in J. Gugler (ed.), *World City in Poor Countries*. Cambridge: Cambridge University Press.

Wallerstein, I. 2003. US Weakness and the Struggle for Hegemony. *Monthly Review* 35(3): 23–29.

Withagen, T. and F. Tros. 2003. *Dealing with the "Flexibility–Security–Nexus": Institutions, Strategies, Opportunities and Barriers*. Working Paper 9. Amsterdam Institute for Advanced Labour Studies.

Yeung, Yue-Man. 1997. Planning for Pearl City: Hong Kong's Future, 1997 and Beyond. *Cities* 14(5): 249–56.

16

GLOBALIZATION AND NEW SOCIAL MOVEMENTS

Lessons from South Asia

PONNA WIGNARAJA

THE EMERGING DEVELOPMENT CHALLENGE IN SOUTH ASIA

The response to the wider development challenge being faced in South Asia, as the region moves into the new Millennium, is inextricably linked to the inadequacy of the mainstream development thinking and action to deal simultaneously with problems of globalization, as well as, poverty, youth employment and violence, resulting from sharpening contradictions in the polity. The manner in which globalization reality is impacting on the political economies of South Asia after liberalization raises new implications for governance in all these countries.

This probing did not take the form of a mere critique of global and national policies and recommending of marginal reformist policies. South Asian Perspectives Network Association (SAPNA) through a holistic interdisciplinary action research process, began drawing lessons from the ground in South Asia and attempted to identify undogmatic critical elements, which could be a basis for an alternative paradigm, for a value-led culturally rooted pattern of development and democracy in South Asia. There was no a priori theorizing. Instead the social science methodology used also involved social praxis for management of a transition, in a given time frame. The results of this three decade pioneering intellectual quest was reflected in seven published studies, with one more forthcoming in 2005 (See Annex.).

THE INTELLECTUAL QUEST:
PREPARING TO MEET THE CHALLENGE

The first of these studies, *Towards a Theory of Rural Development* attempted to analyze the problem of rural mass poverty, with a view to identifying critical elements in a conceptual framework for an alternative approach to rural development and the operational guidelines that went with it. This was a pioneering study by a team of South Asians, where the analysis is still relevant. The conclusions provide a response to the sharpening contradictions that have emerged.

The critical elements in this approach were derived initially from the actual macro-micro experience of several Asian countries (India, Bangladesh, Sri Lanka, China, and South Korea). The broad construct of the theory that emerged, albeit rudimentary, sought to explain the long-run direction and goals of a holistic development effort and the social mobilization process involved, with the poor as subjects in the process. A new social movement called "Bhoomi Sena" in the State of Maharashtra in India provided the material basis to refine the theory. Bhoomi Sena, which means land army, is the name of the movement for liberation from feudal and elite oppression and the establishment of countervailing power by the poor and marginalized in rural areas for greater self-reliant development.

The methodology used by the team was based on "collective creativity." The interdisciplinary group of researchers and the Bhoomi Sena cadres engaged in a constant interplay between theory and practice. In other words, the reality was investigated together. Every resulting hypothesis was tested in the field and the result was fed back into reflection to enrich the theory, *i.e., the methodology of praxis*. This underlies what is now called the methodology of participatory action research (PAR).[1] A new departure in relevant social science methodology, which SAPNA uses.

The study was able to highlight emerging dangers such as: (*i*) polarization between the rich and poor; (*ii*) the resource waste and environmental degradation; (*iii*) youth alienation and the dead end, which would result, even in the short term, if the development strategies of the past were uncritically followed. This study showed that redistributive justice, based on a two-sector growth model, "trickle down" or "top down" or "delivery of services" to the poor and a conventional accumulation process was not a sustainable option for the large numbers of poor.

In the second study entitled *The Challenge in South Asia: Development, Democracy and Regional Cooperation*, in the midst of a deepening crisis that threatened not only some of the existing state structures but the very fabric of society. The three other interrelated dimensions of the crisis:

(*i*) The growing polarization of society along ethnic, linguistic or religious lines. Associated with this, the undermining of fundamental social values, through which diverse communities had lived together in tolerance and accommodation in a pluralistic society.

(*ii*) The perceived failure of highly centralized structures of political power (private and public) to give effective political representation to all strata of society and the growing militarization associated with the use of coercive state power to quell resurgent sub-nationalism.

(*iii*) The inadequacy of the approach to capital-intensive development adopted in the post-colonial period in South Asia. The growth and accumulation process associated with this approach, based on capital, the factor in short supply, has generated endemic poverty, growing interpersonal and interregional disparities, erosion of the ecological environment and finally, growing dependence on foreign aid in the case of a number of countries in South Asia.

The alternative framework reinforced in this study pointed towards the potential to reconstruct both the consciousness and political/economic institutions, through which stable supportive state structures and viable regional cooperation based on "Unity In Diversity" could be achieved for the benefit of all the people of South Asia, in a win-win game.

This study also went on to analyze the new reality of globalization. As state structures in a number of South Asian countries were threatened by internal upheavals, in a number of cases their elites were forming alliances with super-powers and economic forces outside the region as a means of acquiring political and economic support for elite and regime survival. As a consequence, they were incorporated into an iniquitous global system and supplied with economic aid, arms, and the technology and tactics of crowd control and counter-insurgency from powerful countries outside the region. It was clear as the superpowers got drawn into the national crisis with over-internationalization, it accentuated the momentum of violence and fragmentation within, creating "soft" societies and "failed" states. The ruling regimes, unable to find a fundamentally different solution to the problem of poverty and inequality, unable to provide a political framework and a value-based intellectual vision, within which the diversities of culture, language, and religion can enrich rather than undermine society, tended to show a knee-jerk reaction to the crisis and emerging challenge.

The book concludes, no South Asian country can solve these problems by itself; hence the need for regional cooperation. Sustainable regional cooperation must be based on a restructuring of the ideological, political, and economic systems in each of the countries of South Asia. At the level of ideology, the deep-rooted civilizational consciousness of tolerance, humanism, and freedom of belief must be tapped. At the level of politics, what is needed is decentralization and devolution of power and the emergence of local institutions, through which the individual and groups, whatever their social status, can participate in the decisions that affect their immediate economic, cultural, and ecological environment.[2] The study clearly stated at the level of economics, a wider holistic development strategy and accumulation process, which combines self-reliance, equity, and a balance between people, nature and growth, is required.

The third study entitled, *Women, Poverty and Resources*, identified another dimension, i.e., the issue of eradication of women's poverty. Poor women had a double burden of being poor and female. Even in the global discourse at that time, the gender equity issue was not addressed in depth. Lessons from case studies showed that the solutions to this double burden can only come from actions by women's groups and by the better organization of poor women. Individuals cannot address the problem of their powerlessness; this can only be done through collective action. The organization of women around issues of common concern is a prerequisite for effective and sustainable economic and social development. Mere provision of credit in the absence of this organization is not developmental. The study highlighted that credit alone results in deepening the debt trap, and further erodes self-respect and dignity.

The fourth study, *Participatory Development: Learning from South Asia*, probed further the decade of the 1980s in South Asia which had been a "lost decade" for development, following upon the golden years of the 1950s and 1960s and the illusionary debt-led growth of the 1970s. For many poor countries development has gone into reverse (with some exceptions where the Keynesian welfare system had worked temporarily). Conventional development thinking then moved away from the Keynesian consensus to an even more sharply monetarist and Neo-classical approach.

Given the present crisis of development, increasing doubts are being felt about the validity of this dominant neo-classical paradigm. Important segments of the global academic community and parts of the UN System have added their voices to the critique. While this critique began to place emphasis on human and social basis for sustainable development and broader based growth and the importance of participation, their action was still "marginal tinkering."

Lessons from this study, while further highlighting the multifaceted crises, not only in economic terms but also in political and human terms also pointed to the need for new forms of accumulation, and indicated through case studies that participatory development at the micro-level reflects a new approach to resource mobilization, resource use, and growth. A third growth sector at the base of the political economy can also be an economically viable and a cost-effective approach to poverty eradication, as well as, help political stability. A development strategy focused on the strengths of the poor can help reverse much of the past imbalances and contradictions created by the conventional development pathway and marginal tinkering with it. By elaborating on the methodology of participatory development, the study made a deeper contribution to an understanding of the new approach and the key instrumentalities, where the poor themselves were not the problem and can be part of the solution.

In its fifth study, *New Social Movements in the South: Empowering the People,* new element was introduced, i.e., how to multiply and sustain successful experiments and "seeds of change." It also highlighted the dangers of an overcentralized state even with a welfare orientation. The study also made a distinction between the new social movements such as the ecological movements, the women's movements, and the older social movements such as the trade union movement and peasant movements. The former reflected collective strategic efforts to bring about transformative social change, while the latter were more systems maintaining. There were several lessons from these new social movements to reinforce an emerging School of Thought:

First, the social transformative movements and experiments are in effect part of a peoples response to the reality of the contemporary global crisis. There was a time when all social movements in countries of the South were engaged in common struggle, namely the anti-colonial fight. Therefore, the myriads of new social movements do not fight to assume state power. They constitute in this sense an integral part of the present crisis and response and aim at building countervailing power.

Secondly, the social movements are looked at as new actors, performing multiple functions—political, economic, social and cultural. These new actors, while fighting to counter state power, not because they do not know what to do with state power, but rather because they represent a new breed of actors, interested not narrowly in state power but rather in creating a free space from where a democratic society can emerge.

Thirdly, in these social movements, there are "seeds" preparing a future desirable society. The role of these new social movements thus transcends not only state power, but also wants to go beyond the existing fragmented NGOs in civil society, with their built-in inequality and unauthenticity, hidden behind the window-dressing of "democracy" or "development" (Report of the Independent South Asian Commission on Poverty Alleviation).

The analysis concludes on the lost historical opportunity that the national liberation movements represented, leaving an unfinished agenda. The social movements are the carriers of this message of alternative modernity, which projects more endogenous, more participatory, and more authentic processes. This thinking and practices can also be the basis of a new Social Contract yet to be forged, for which the material basis has emerged on the ground.

The sixth study, *Readings on Pro Poor Planning Through Social Mobilisation in South Asia: Strategic Options for Poverty Eradication,* knits together its thinking to date. South Asia, with more than 1.1 billion people, accounts for more than one-fifth of the world population. In terms of numbers, it has the highest concentration in the world of poverty, hunger, malnutrition, child mortality, and illiteracy. In this regard, two aspects of the recent development experience of the South Asian countries are further analyzed.

First, as elsewhere, South Asia is also liberalizing these reforms that comprise trade and foreign exchange liberalization, reduction of government budgetary deficits, lifting of administrative controls on domestic economic activity, and encouragement of foreign investment resulting in a greater role for markets and the private sector in the economy. If fully implemented, the reforms could contribute to a significant acceleration in the growth rate in the medium term. But as experience indicates, they are also likely to result in an accentuation of economic inequalities. Furthermore, unless the process of economic expansion is broad-based, there is no inherent reason to believe that it will necessarily lead to reduction in poverty and sustainable human development.

The second distinctive aspect of South Asian experience relates to the origins and process by which social movements and grassroots and micro initiatives themselves emerged either spontaneously, or through catalytic action. Of all the developing regions of the world, South Asia has recently generated the most impressive and diverse range of new social movements. Many of them have been recognized to be extremely effective in poverty reduction and promotion of human development. The key to their success is the building up of participatory organizations of homogeneous groups, and they're strengthening through awareness raising, education, learning by doing, and capacity building.

Finally, this study emphasized two important issues concerning the pace and pattern of development in the region in the coming years. Taken together, while the contribution of the new social movements has been significant, their impact has fallen short of the needs.

In the seventh study, *Pro Poor Growth and Governance in South Asia— Decentralisation and Participatory Development*, the pursuit of good governance was accepted as a widely shared goal among various development actors since the early 1990s. However, in the intellectual discourse for some, good governance is a means of ensuring effective macro-economic management through downsizing of the state and reduced scope for bureaucratic interference. Others emphasize the opportunities presented for increasing participation in decision-making and resource allocations, especially for the poor. There is yet no consensus or synthesis.

Apart from this, two other agendas have also become increasingly important in recent years, namely those of poverty reduction and decentralization, though not always in tandem with good governance. Poverty reduction is rightly considered as the primary purpose of development and the UN Millennium Declaration for 2015 represent a clear commitment from among governments and donors to this end. Decentralization is another focal point for donor policy and many governments around the world are making efforts to devolve powers and resources to lower tiers.

Despite their high visibility and scope for complementarity, these three agendas centering on governance, poverty reduction, and devolution are rarely brought together in a coherent framework of thinking and action. This is where SAPNA makes its particular contribution, in recognizing that the governance agenda, with an emphasis on participatory development, can be combined with systematic devolution of power and resources to the grassroots, in order to lay the basis for sustained poverty reduction. The key to this process is community mobilization through social movements that can catalyze change through partnerships with sensitive state organizations, and by advocating for deeper reforms in governance that bring about systemic changes in the conditions of the poor. When combined with decentralization and devolution, there are opportunities for poverty reduction. But decentralization without social mobilization and empowerment creates scope for vested local interests to monopolize power and resources to their advantage.

The case studies confirm that neither poverty reduction nor filling the democratic deficit results automatically from decentralization reforms alone. The case studies in this South Asian Perspectives Network Association volume, document the various experiments taking place in Bangladesh, India, Nepal, Pakistan, and Sri Lanka and illustrate how social movements and local organizations are mobilizing the poor to take advantage of the decentralization reforms to mobilize resources and influence to bring about pro-poor development, starting from the base of political economies of South Asia. These successful pro-poor efforts hinge on other, complementary reforms in governance that foster participation, accountability, and transparency, without which decentralization can simply concentrate power and resources in the hands of the few at the local level. What is critical is the capacity of the organizations of the poor in the new social movements to mobilize, conscientize and organize the poor to articulate their rights as citizens and elected representatives in local governments, channel the creative potential of democratic decentralization, and initiate sustainable development in a manner that empowers and enhances pro-poor growth.

This process, which also results in new partnerships, can reinforce civil society protest movements and provide a complementary strategic thrust to the more conventional financial sector and administrative reforms.

The eighth study, currently in a draft manuscript form, deals with the "Role" and "How" facilitators/animators are to be sensitized and trained in order to catalyze and generate a massive transformative process and complete the unfinished agenda of decolonization in South Asia, on the assumption that a "spontaneous process" is insufficient to cope with the magnitude and challenges. A major social mobilization process is called for.

REVISIONING SOUTH ASIAN REGIONAL COOPERATION: FROM CONSTRUCTIVE DISSENT TO MAINSTREAMING NEW THINKING AND PRACTICE

It was not until 1990 that the South Asian Perspectives Network Association constructive dissent and coherent macro and micro policy options for an alternative modernity, greater self-reliant, pro-poor growth in development, and a participatory democratic approach could be brought squarely into the mainstream of policy and debate/dialog on governance and development. No individual SAARC country could initiate the social transformation and social mobilization process by itself. A collective regional effort was required.

In 1990, the Heads of States of SAARC at their Maldives Summit had themselves begun to sense the sharpening contradictions and polarization between rich and poor in South Asia, the link between poverty and violence, and inadequacy of conventional thinking and action to respond to the realities within one outside the region. By then the multifaceted crisis was increasingly visible and the compulsions for a shift in strategic thinking was strong.

In 1984, the South Asian Association for Regional Cooperation (SAARC) started with a vision but moved cautiously through a series of purely inter-governmental activities, based on fragmented, ad hoc and sectoral issues, many of them already on the global inter-governmental agenda. They were perceived as an Integrated Programme of Action (IPA). The IPA and the annual, mostly ceremonial, Heads of State Summits dominated much of the official SAARC attention in the first six years. There was insufficient attention given to emerging national, regional, or global changes and realities, with a view to evolving a rigorous and comprehensive strategic response to them. The intellectual under-pinnings for vigorous South Asian Regional Cooperation were weak.

At their Male Summit in 1990, however, the Heads of State took two impor-tant decisions recognizing that SAARC, as it was evolving, was unprepared for the globalization scenario, to the new challenges posed by "Europe 1992" and other regional groupings, and the emerging multifaceted crisis of governance and development in South Asia itself, which could no longer be ignored.

The first decision was that SAARC should focus on core areas of economic cooperation. Second, it was also decided that scholars, professionals, NGOs and the media should help reinforce the official SAARC process in moving into these core areas. The second decision, regarding the need for a new partnership between the official SAARC process and independent actors, reflected concern amongst the Heads of State that SAARC could not move forward purely as an official inter-governmental process. Both these decisions reflected the political awareness that there was a potential for a South Asian Economic Community, but it required an intellectual stimulus, a real process of learning from the ground, and translating the lessons into a coherent agenda for action had to be initiated to achieve this.

SAARC Moving into Core Areas of Regional Cooperation: Unity in Diversity

In 1991, a group of South Asian scholars, professionals, and policymakers in their personal capacity, under the auspices of South Asian Perspectives Network

Association, was one of the first to respond systematically to this challenge of an innovative dialog and partnership, which could help identify Core Areas of Cooperation within the framework of "Unity in Diversity."

Reports of the SAARC Secretariat also provided background material for their analysis. The Independent Group on South Asian Cooperation (IGSAC) Report of 1991 provided three powerful messages for the SAARC Heads of State, in addition to an agenda for immediate action.

The Messages
South Asia has a common history, common eco-system, and shared fundamental values, which could provide a vision of a South Asian Community based on unity in diversity. The unity came from an indivisible eco-system, common history and culture, subordination and fragmentation of the economies, and the common ordeal of decolonization. These could be the building blocs for a common future. Today, South Asia is facing a multifaceted crisis of poverty, slow economic growth, uneven development, population pressure, natural resource erosion, high defense expenditure and an internal arms race, social polarization, religious fundamentalism, youth alienation, ethnic and other conflicts. These conflicts and problems are becoming unmanageable. Together with external trends, they are pushing South Asia further and further to the margins of both the world-economy and the international political arena.

A more complex, sustainable politico development strategy, than hitherto adopted, which includes greater decentralization, social mobilization, and empowerment of the poor, could provide a transitional response to the region's immediate need. It could mediate the sharp contradictions that had arisen in the political economy of South Asia.

The Recommendation
The IGSAC Report stated that SAARC had come to stay, but the compulsions for closer economic and political cooperation were strong and left no choice for South Asia. The report concluded that no South Asian country could solve the multifaceted crisis individually and collective regional cooperation must be vigorously pursued for the region's collective benefit, by creating a vibrant value-led culturally rooted Economic Community of South Asia (ECSA).

The Agenda for Immediate Action recommended was:

- The establishment of a High Level Independent Commission on Poverty Alleviation in South Asia.
- The establishment of a Food Security System, with the Right to Food for the Poor in South Asia.
- The establishment of a South Asian Free Trade Area (SAFTA).
- The establishment of a South Asian Payments Union to be managed by the Central Banks of the region.

- The establishment of a South Asian Development Fund initiated by SAARC countries, initially with their own contributions.

The five core areas—poverty eradication, food security, trade cooperation, payments union, and external resource mobilization—are not only closely interrelated, but also necessary prerequisites for achieving the vision of a South Asian Economic Community with sustainable human development, real democratic political formations, good governance, and poverty eradication. Without the eradication of the worst forms of poverty, however, SAARC could not establish the one-billion-strong South Asian mass market. Food security is the other side of the poverty coin in a region, which has a food surplus and further potential for food production and food for work programs in the transition. Poverty eradication and the right to food go hand-in-hand and could be combined with the right to work by the poor. For trade cooperation, payment arrangements are essential. In Europe, the Payments Union preceded economic cooperation. The mobilization of external resources is necessary both for poverty eradication as well as for industrialization and building South Asia's technological capabilities. Trade cooperation was not supposed to end with the signing of a framework agreement. The recommendation was for SAFTA, not a bureaucratic and unworkable South Asian Preferential Trade Agreement (SAPTA). The report urged that since the opening up of regional trade will help expand production and employment in all countries, bring down costs of living, and help reap the benefits of a larger mass market, there should be reductions across the board of tariff and non-tariff barriers within five years. An appropriate strategy of decentralized labor-intensive industrialization could then follow in all SAARC countries, leading to a real reduction in unemployment and improvement in the quality of life with a better balance between work, social responsibility, and leisure. The South Asian Development Fund would be for cutting edge policies, reflected by current convergence of IMF, World Bank strategies. This fund could then organize a major mobilization of global surpluses for South Asia's industrialization, the implementation of a poverty eradication strategy, and for trade and balance of payments support. Additionally, it will provide finance for multi-country development projects. Such a South Asian Development Fund would enhance the region's capacity to take full advantage of the surpluses generated in other regions of the world for development in the widest sense, poverty reduction, and structural adjustment.

In 1994, a follow-up enquiry was initiated by SAPNA to look deeper into the monetary and financial aspects of trade cooperation, decentralized industrialization, food security, and of moving towards a South Asian Economic Community. Representatives of Central Banks of the region and some leading South Asian economists collaborated in this enquiry. This complementary report to the IGSAC entitled *Towards a Regional Monetary and Financial System in South*

Asia urged that the SAARC look at a coherent vision for Trade, Payments, Monetary and Financial Cooperation and, then proceed to implement the strategy in a step-by-step well-researched manner. This report made clear that financial cooperation and payment arrangements did not require anything like a common currency. However, it required going much further than the pure book-keeping arrangements of the Asian Clearing Union. This report too was widely disseminated to the official SAARC process.

Unity in Diversity: Entering through the Poverty Contradiction

Of the five interrelated core areas for action, it was the establishment of the Independent South Asian Commission for Poverty Alleviation in 1991 that provided a common ground for stimulating regional cooperation on the basis of "Unity in Diversity". In effect, it was a Commission on Governance and Development to sort out the contradictions between the reality and conventional development thinking and action, and provide practical solutions that they could implement politically in a given time frame.

The Independent South Asian Commission on Poverty Alleviation (ISACPA) was an innovative collaborative partnership between SAARC governments and an independent group of southern scholars and civil society activists. The inclusion of several SAPNA members in the Commission and in its advisory group provided SAPNA with the ability to make a coherent intellectual contribution, from its three-decade intellectual quest. The Report of the Commission, which emerged from an enquiry and wide-ranging dialogs with a range of stakeholders over an eight-month period in 1992, explored the complementarities between measures of economic reform and participatory development by the poor themselves. It helped to mainstream ideas that were at the margins and reinforce the debate/dialog towards practice of decentralized participatory democracy and development in general, and to macro–micro policy options and institution building for cost-effective sustainable eradication of the worst forms of poverty in a given time frame. The terms of reference required the Commission to clearly diagnose what went wrong with past attempts at poverty alleviation, draw positive lessons from the ground, where the poor have been mobilized successfully to contribute to growth and human development and, finally, to identify the critical elements in a coherent but practical overall strategy of development for poverty alleviation in South Asia. These terms of reference also reflected an underlying realization that without poverty eradication, liberalization and the one-billion-strong mass market in South Asia could not come into its own.

The report that emerged was a unanimous one. It was not merely a report on poverty in a narrow sense. It conveyed some sharp political messages, an overall development perspective and practical recommendations to the SAARC Heads of State on a coherent transitional development framework and agenda for responding to the globalization reality, and eradication of the worst forms of poverty in a given time frame. The innovativeness of this transitional strategy was that at the micro level it was based on the factor in surplus in South Asia, *i.e., the creativity and efficiency of the poor and culturally rooted knowledge system, the factors in surplus, could be an asset, and not capital, the scarce factor, as in conventional development theory.* It also required a net macro level transfer of resources to this efficient sector.

The report took the form of three coherent messages and one composite but multidimensional strategic recommendation.[3]

Message No.1:

The number of people living in poverty in the region, in 1991, based on the conventional "poverty line" estimates would be 440 million. The structural adjustment policies, which accompany the open-economy industrialisation strategy currently being adopted by most SAARC countries, are likely to put further strains on the poor, particularly in the shorter term. The conclusion was inescapable that the magnitude and complexity of the problem of poverty in South Asian countries, not only puts democracy at risk, but also poses a threat to the very fabric of South Asian societies.

Message No. 2:

The conventional development interventions with its faith in "trickle down" and administrative redistribution to the poor, over the past 50 years, are inadequate. The role of the State had to change from that of a highly centralised doer to that of an enabler and supporter of growth in a three-sector growth model.

Message No. 3:

The eradication of poverty in South Asia would require a major political rather than a techno-cratic approach in which social mobilisation and empowerment of the poor play a critical role. Where the poor participate as subjects and not as objects of the development process, it is possible for them also to generate additional growth. In this pattern of growth human development and greater equity, are not mutually exclusive trade-offs, but are complementary elements in the same process.

Recommendation:

There should be a Pro Poor development strategy based on a three-sector growth oriented approach, which is un-ambiguously reflected in a coherent plan for the poor. This Pro Poor Plan has to ensure a net transfer of resources to the poor. The new premise for action is an overall pattern of development, which in a transitional time frame moves on two fronts:
A cautious open-economy industrialisation front with pro poor reforms; and the pro poor poverty eradication front with rigorous social mobilisation and participation.
These two parallel strategic thrusts, having long and short-term time frames, can be harmonised as the two processes evolve to provide a transitional response to both the poverty and global problematique. The recommendation elaborated how the Pro Poor Plan can generate pro poor

growth, with a lower capital output ratio, food security and increased work for the poor. Growth in the formal public and private sectors of 6% to 7% will be complemented by 2% to 3% generated by organisations of the poor to reach a growth rate of approximately 9 percent, through the three complementary sectors and the accompanying new accumulation process, with increased savings.

(Quote from SAARC Poverty Commission Recommendation)

At the Seventh SAARC Summit in Dhaka, in April 1993, the Heads of State unanimously endorsed the 1992 Poverty Commission recommendations and reiterated this in the SAARC Summits of 1995 and 1997.

This consensus of the Heads of State of SAARC constituted at that time a major coherent response in an era of inequalities and globalization and to critical elements in the multifaceted crisis in South Asia, as well as, reflected the strong compulsions to bring poverty to the centrestage of national and regional concern with innovative action.

A critical mass of South Asian policymakers, scholars, and even civil society leaders have yet to have fully internalize the contents of the report and the coherent macro–micro options available. They are continuing to underestimate the magnitude and complexity of the problem and continuing with marginal reforms to centralized decision-making processes, mesmerized by generalities on human development and equating it with poverty eradication, and continuing to provide reformist options in terms of two-sector growth models and fragmented safety nets, welfare and charity, with a view to tranquilizing the poor.[4] The international development community for all its rhetoric, with few exceptions, is still locked into *a priori* theorizing; narrow, fragmented, ideologically oriented solutions and "tool kit" approaches to development and poverty, which by and large help only the 10 percent less poor at best.

TOWARDS A NEW SCHOOL OF THOUGHT

The above shows that the mission of the South Asian Research Organization like SAPNA was not merely to critique the existing process of economic growth or the processes of centralized governance as it had been unfolding in the previous half a century. It was to systematically pursue a pioneering intellectual quest to identify critical micro–macro elements of a coherent conceptual framework, which could inform a relevant transitional response to the multifaceted crisis of governance and poverty in South Asia. To do this, it was necessary simultaneously, not only to question mainstream strategies but also some of the fundamental premises and certainties resulting from the social science discourse that was in use. The challenge was to develop, even in a rudimentary way, a *school of thought* pointing to a *vision* and a *transitional pathway* through practice. There are five interrelated fundamentals on which this "School of Thought" rests.

The Long Revolution and Social Transformation

The first premise that needs to be internalized is that a social transformation and structural changes are required. It had to go beyond not only the neo-classical thinking but also its marginally reformed and simplistic growth, redistribution, and human face models. Structural change was more than mere financial and budgetary discipline and ad hoc redistributive justice delivered from above. This social transformation has to be conceived as a long revolution, implying a complex chain of long and short time frames—not a one-shot "big bang" revolution. A corollary in the transformative process was the issue of self-reliance. South Asia had too long depended on external inspiration and hegemonies, which ended up with "soft" societies and near failed and dependent states.

Perspective and Values

The structural changes at the macro and micro levels outlined above have to start with a clear perspective and be value-led. This is fundamental for correct action. Before action is taken, the underlying values need to be made explicit. The perspective from which the search for the new underlying paradigm begins is that participatory democracy and development are two sides of the same holistic vision that has inspired human endeavor in different South Asian socio-cultural settings over the past 2,000 years, and more of recorded history. Several fundamental values, which existed in traditional South Asian societies, must be identified and re-examined in this connection. Some critical values relate to looking at life in its totality and all its richness, participation of the people, particularly the poor, in decisions that affected their lives; sharing and caring for the community, cooperative activities beyond individual self-interest; trust, innocence, simplicity, thrift; a work ethic with a fine-tuned balance between work and leisure; harmony with nature and a rational use of both natural and financial resources; communal ownership of the commons; and complementarity between men and women, as well as, gender equity.

Countervailing Power: A Political Approach to the Transition

Another fundamental in rethinking past paradigms of development and democracy relate to the question of participatory democracy. In this regard, devolution of power and empowerment of the poor and vulnerable groups, as opposed to representative democracy and highly centralized elite power is a critical element. Conventional thinking on both development and democracy was based on a harmony model. This needs to be demystified. The assumption of harmonious communities in a conflict-free social framework for change has no basis in reality, whether at local, national levels in South Asia, or at global levels.

Growth, Human Development and Equity: No Trade-offs

As the multifaceted crisis in South Asia deepened, the accumulation process set in motion either by means of private capital accumulation or of state capital accumulation—a process that was basic to the old concept of economic development and its reformist option—turned out to be insufficient, and the pressures mounted for an alternative accumulation process. It was not a matter of growth first and equity afterwards. A sustainable development strategy needs an alternative driving force for growth and change. It is also necessary for South Asian countries to adopt a more complex development strategy that combines development, growth, equity, and technological change with more creative use of local resources and knowledge. In this transition all countries, however, will need to pursue internally a basically two-pronged strategy that will permit them to maintain the gains from past attempts at modernization and industrialization and trade with appropriate damage limitation, and to make a direct attack on poverty in all its manifestations, an attack in which the poor themselves are the subjects and not the objects of the process. Initially the two prongs of strategy may have different time horizons and some contradictions, but over time they can be harmonized. South Asian regional cooperation can reinforce the national efforts. This kind of regional cooperation will also permit South Asian countries to adjust to the global system on more favorable terms.

Refocusing Praxis and Participation

Another fundamental that requires further elaboration is the methodology of praxis and management of the Knowledge System. Some systematic efforts are now being made to break out of the conventional social science methodologies into participatory action research by groups of South Asian scholars and activists working together. Social praxis and participatory action research (PAR) which goes with it, takes off from the cultural and historical experiences in South Asia. It critiques a predetermined universalism and stresses pluralism, including geocultural specificity. As has been stated in the past, social sciences have evolved through the study of Western societies. Hypotheses and value judgements have emerged from that historical cultural world and continue to influence a major part of the academic community and through it, the educational, technical, and administrative systems. The Knowledge System inherent in the culture must inform the whole process. The nature of knowledge and the method of the utilization of the wider stocks of knowledge and choice of technology have to be probed further. This, then, could help bridge the gap between real knowledge and wisdom and catalyze the process of social change and development action in new terms, linking knowledge with power and action.

These five interrelated fundamentals are critical to achieving social justice, self-reliance, and participation in this era of globalization.

KNITTING TOGETHER

As the contradictions in South Asian Societies sharpened further, clear warning signals were given from various quarters. In 1999, the Mahhub ul Haq Human Development Center in Pakistan stated in its Annual Report: "South Asia has emerged as one of the most poorly governed region in the world, with exclusion of voiceless majorities, unstable political regimes and poor economic management…the South Asian Region has the largest number of people living in poverty."

In his Republic Day Address, 2000, the President of India stated:

Fifty years into the life of our Republic we find that Justice—social, economic and political—remains an unrealized dream for millions of our fellow citizens. The benefits of our economic growth are yet to reach them. We have one of the world's largest reservoirs of technical personnel, but also the world's largest number of illiterates, the world's largest middle class, but also the largest number of people below the poverty line, and the largest number of children suffering from malnutrition. Our giant factories rise out of squalor, our satellites shoot up from the midst of the hovels of the poor. Not surprisingly, there is sullen resentment among the masses against their condition erupting often in violent forms in several parts of the country. Tragically, the growth in our economy has not been uniform. It has been accompanied by great regional and social inequalities. Many a social upheaval can be traced to the neglect of the lowest of society, whose discontent moves towards the path of violence.

These stark warning signals have been ignored. The challenge to the next SAARC Summit of Heads of State/Governments, in Dhaka, Bangladesh in January 2005, is to eschew the ceremonial and rhetoric and immerse themselves, even at this late date, in an in-depth discussion of the South Asian reality, and see how to move coherently through a value-led political process into core areas of regional cooperation, on the assumption that if they are serious, it can be done.

Three decades after the first SAPNA warning in the mid-1970s, and nearly a decade after the 1992 SAARC Poverty Commission Report's message to South Asian Heads of State, that the magnitude and complexity of the poverty contradiction in the widest sense not only puts democracy at risk, but also poses a risk to the very fabric of South Asian Societies—the paradigm has not changed.

The five interrelated fundamentals have been stated "simply" without being "simplistic" or dogmatic. At the same time, it has advocated strongly that without vigorous and informed/well researched *regional cooperation* based on core issues, no individual country could effectively manage the transition out of the unmanageable polity to which South Asia is descending.

An assertion that needs to be made is that a New Social Contract between the state and the poor in South Asia, based on the fundamentals outlined, is a prerequisite. The failures of the past and disarray in development thinking and action require a major new inspirational drive and dynamic, which can create a basis for bringing diverse social forces and communities into new partnerships. The social contract is the only instrument, which can help regenerate the trust between various stakeholders, which has been eroded. This social contract is premised on going beyond the old social contract between management and labor, the Keynesian Consensus, which led to the welfare state and the current discussion at the official level on a SAARC Social Charter. The new social movements can provide the material basis for both the New School of Thought and the New Social Contract. Herein lies the further challenge for thinking and practice.

Notes

1. The methodology of Praxis and PAR should be distinguished from pseudo methodologies in use like PRA, RRA, and Log frame analysis. Praxis and PAR are located outside the dominant framework of positivist knowledge and the fragmented Cartesian mold of knowledge management. (See Ponna Wignaraja, "Refocusing Development Praxis in South Asia: Critical Instruments," in *Participatory Development: Learning from South Asia*, Oxford University Press, Karachi/Oxford, 1991.

2. This was what the 1948 UN Universal Declaration on Human Rights was about. These underlying values for global governance were later supported by the Covenants on Genocide (1948), Covenant on Civil and Political Rights (1966), Convention on Elimination of All forms of Discrimination based on Religion or Belief, Declaration on Rights of Persons belonging to National or Ethnic Religious and Linguistic Minorities, and others.

3. The three messages are elaborated in great detail in chapters 1, 2 and 3 and the recommendation in Chapter 4 of the *Report of the Independent South Asian Commission on Poverty Alleviation*, 1992, SAARC Secretariat, Kathmandu, Nepal.

4. Latest estimates show that the number of poor are in reality much higher than the 40 percent indicated in the report of the 1992 SAARC Poverty Commission. See Utsa Patnaik, "Theorizing Food Security and Poverty in the era of Economic Reforms" (2005, New Delhi: JNU) and M. Guruswamy "Redefining Poverty—A New Poverty Line for a New India (2006, New Delhi: Centre for Policy Alternatives).

References

IGSAC. 1991. *SAARC: Moving Towards Core Areas of Co-operation*. Report of the Independent Expert Group on South Asian Co-operation. Colombo, Sri Lanka: IGSAC, September.

——. 1992. *Meeting the Challenge*. Report of the Independent South Asian Commission on Poverty Alleviation. Kathmandu: SAARC, November.

——. 1994. *Towards a Regional Monetary and Financial System in South Asia*. Report of the Expert Group Meeting on "South Asian Financial and Payments Cooperation". Proceeds from the Workshop organized by SAPNA and the Council for Social Development (CSD). New Delhi, August.

Annex: List of SAPNA publications

De Silva, G.V.S., W. Haque, N. Mehta, A. Rahman and P. Wignaraja. 1988. *Towards a Theory of Rural Development*. Lahore: Progressive Publishers.

Wignaraja, Ponna. 1990. *Women, Poverty and Resources*. New Delhi/Newbury Park/London: Sage.

——. 1993. *New Social Movements in the South*. London: Zed Books; New Delhi: Sage.

Wignaraja, P. and A. Hussain (eds). 1989. *The Challenge in South Asia: Development, Democracy and Regional Cooperation* (First Edition). New Delhi/Newbury Park/London: Sage; Second Edition, Oxford University Press.

Wignaraja, P., A. Hussain, H. Sethi and G. Wignaraja. 1991. *Participatory Development: Learning from South Asia*. Karachi/Oxford: Oxford University Press.

Wignaraja, P. and S. Sirivardana (eds). 1998. *Readings on Pro-Poor Planning through Social Mobilisation in South Asia: The Strategic Option for Poverty Eradication*. New Delhi: Vikas Publications.

——. 2004. *Pro-Poor Growth and Governance in South Asia: Decentralisation and Participatory Development*. New Delhi: Sage.

——. (forthcoming). *Role of the Facilitator in Social Mobilisation for Poverty Eradication*.

ABOUT THE EDITORS AND CONTRIBUTORS

EDITORS

Samir Dasgupta is Professor and Head, Department of Sociology at the University of Kalyani, West Bengal, India. He is the President of the Society for Applied Sociology in India. Professor Dasgupta has authored *Economic Sociology* (1983, in Bengali), *Sociology Through Objective Mirror* (1999), *A Short History of Western Sociology* (in Bengali), *Global Malady in the Third World— A Reflection* (2002, co-authored with Kaushik Chattopadhyay), and has edited *The Changing Face of Globalization* (2004) and *The Discourse of Applied Sociology* (with Robyn Bateman Driskell, forthcoming). Professor Dasgupta is currently working on a volume, *Understanding Global Environment*.

Ray Kiely is Reader in Globalization and Development, Department of Development Studies, SOAS, University of London, UK. His books include *Sociology and Development: The Impasse and Beyond* (1995), *The Politics of Labour and Development in Trinidad* (1996), *The Race to the Bottom and International Labour Solidarity* (2002), *The Clash of Globalisations: Neo-liberalism, the Third Way and Anti-Globalisation* (2005), *Global Myths, Imperial Realities* (2005), *The New Political Economy of Development* (forthcoming). Dr Kiely is currently working in the areas of US imperialism, cosmopolitanism and "anti-globalization".

CONTRIBUTORS

Elvira Del Pozo Aviñó is a doctoral student in the Department of Sociology at the University of Valencia, Spain. She received her Master's degree in Law in Sociology from Eastern Michigan University. She is currently doing research on collective action studies, social movements, and voluntary associations.

Sing C. Chew is Professor of Sociology at Humboldt State University, Arcata, California. His recent books include, *Underdevelopment and Development* (1999), and *Dark Ages over World History 2200 B.C.–A.D. 900* (forthcoming).

Robyn Bateman Driskell is an Associate Professor of Sociology at Baylor University. She received her Ph.D. in Sociology from Texas A&M University in 1998. Dr Driskell has been published in journals such as *City and Community* and *Michigan Sociological Review*. Her research interests include demography, globalization, race and ethnic relations, and issues of community.

Barry K. Gills is a Professor at the School of Geography, Politics and Sociology, University of Newcastle. He is also Editor of the journal *Globalizations*. Professor Gills' research interests include international political economy theory, historical analysis of social systems and social change, world economic history, globalization and the politics of resistance, globalization and reform in South Korea, and the political economy of development. His recent publications include, *Globalization and Global History* (2005), *Globalization and Politics of Resistance* (with J.K.Galbraith) (2002), and *Globalization and Politics of Resistance* (2000).

Tomás Mac Sheoin has been involved in anti-nuclear and anti-toxic campaigns in Ireland and the Bhopal Solidarity Campaign in India. His most recent publication is *Asphyxiating Asia* (2003).

Abbas Mehdi is currently advisor and board member for various local and international organizations including the International Research Foundation for Development (since 1999), The United Nations Association of Minnesota, The Minnesota International Center (since 1997), and Distinguished Resource Person, International Fellowship Programs, Hubert H. Humphrey Institute of Public Affairs, Minneapolis, MN, USA (1997–2002). Between 1996 and 1997, Dr Mehdi was also an advisor for the St. Cloud Chamber of Commerce, and a consultant on Middle East affairs for several American and European organizations. He is also Founder and Chairman of the Union of Independent Iraqis, an international organization that promotes democracy in Iraq. Dr Mehdi has been Professor of Organization and Sociology at St. Cloud State University, Minnesota since 1988. Between 1991 and 1997, he was also Adjunct Professor in the Department of Strategic Management and Organization in the Graduate School program of the Carlson School of Management at the University of Minnesota. His research interests include comparative management, and complex organization.

Jan Nederveen Pieterse is Professor of Sociology at the University of Illinois, Urbana-Champaign. He is associate editor of several journals and Fellow of the World Academy of Art and Science. Professor Pieterse's recent publications include, *Globalization or Empire?* (2004), *Globalization and Culture: Global Mélange* (2003), and *Development Theory: Deconstructions/Reconstructions* (2001). His research interests center around globalization, development studies and intercultural studies.

George Ritzer is Professor of Sociology, University of Maryland, USA, and has been Visiting Professor at the Associazione per l'Istituzione della Libera University' Nuorese, Sardinia, Italy (2002), University of Bremen, Germany (2001), and University of Tampere, Finland (1996). In 2004, Professor Ritzer received an Honorary Doctorate from LaTrobe University, Australia, and in 2001, he occupied the First Fulbright Chair at York University, Canada. He was awarded the American Sociological Association's Distinguished Contribution to Teaching Award in 2000, and in 1992, the UNESCO Chair in Social Theory, Russian Academy of Sciences. His recent publications include *The McDonaldization of Society* (2004), *Enchanting a Disenchanted World: Revolutionizing the Meaning of Consumption*, *Globalization of Nothing* (2003), and the *Encyclopedia of Social Theory* (forthcoming).

Kaxton Yu-Kwan Siu is a Master's student at the Division of Social Science at the Hong Kong University of Science and Technology and is also a teaching assistant in the Office of the University General Education at the Chinese University of Hong Kong. His research interests include looking at the new patterns of labor protest movement under flexible employment practices, focusing on case studies in Hong Kong.

Leslie Sklair is Professor of Sociology at the London School of Economics and Political Science. He was the Hans Speier Distinguished Visiting Professor at the Graduate Faculty, New School for Social Research, New York, in Spring 2002 and Visiting Professor at the University of Southern California in Spring 2004. Professor Sklair serves on the Executive Committee of the Global Studies Association, and on the editorial boards of the *Review of International Political Economy*, *Global Networks and Social Forces*. He is author of *The Transnational Capitalist Class* (2001; Chinese edition 2002, German edition forthcoming), *Sociology of the Global System* (1995 translated into Japanese, Portuguese, Persian, Korean and Spanish). He is currently researching iconic architecture and capitalist globalization.

Manfred B. Steger is Professor of Global Studies and Head, School of International and Community Studies at the Royal Melbourne Institute of Technology in Melbourne, Australia. He is also an affiliated faculty member with the Department of Political Science at the University of Hawai'i-Manoa. Professor Steger's research interests include ideologies of globalization, theories of nonviolence, comparative political and social theory, and international politics. His most recent publications include *Rethinking Globalism* (2004), *Judging Nonviolence: The Dispute Between Realists and Idealists* (2003), *Globalization* (2003).

Immanuel Wallerstein is a well-known and distinguished sociologist. He earned his Ph.D. from Columbia University and D.Litt. from York University. He was Professor of Sociology at McGill and Columbia universities. He was a Visiting

Professor at the Alicante, Amsterdam, Chinese, British Columbia, Illinois, Montepellier, Ottawa, and Texas universities. Professor Wallerstein's recent publications include *European Universalism: The Rhetoric of Power* (2006), *Alternatives: The U.S. Confronts the World* (2004), and *World-Systems Analysis: An Introduction* (2004).

Jarrod Wiener is Senior Lecturer in International Relations at the University of Kent at Canterbury, and (founding) Director of the University of Kent's Brussels School of International Studies. He is (founding) Editor of *Global Society: Interdisciplinary Journal of International Relations*. Dr Wiener has written *Globalization and the Harmonization of Law* (1999).

Ponna Wignaraja is Chairman, South Asian Perspectives Network Association (SAPNA). He was awarded the highest civilian National Honour in Sri Lanka—the *Deshamanya* – in 1993 for services to the Nation. Dr Wignaraja holds many important positions including Vice Chairman, SAARC Independent South Asian Commission on Poverty Alleviation, Member-Advisory Committee, BMZ/GTZ (Germany) Global Dialogue Network on Development, Development Advisor, Development Advisory Service, The World Bank, Development Advisor, International Monetary Fund, and Special Advisor, UN Research Institute for Social Development (UNRISD), among others. Amongst his recent publications, he has co-authored *Role of the Facilitator in Social Mobilisation for Poverty Eradication* (forthcoming), and *Pro Poor Growth and Governance in South Asia: Case Profiles of Participatory Development and Decentralised Reforms* (2004).

Nicola Yeates is Senior Lecturer in Social Policy, School of Sociology and Social Policy, Queen's University Belfast, Northern Ireland. Since September 2005 she has been co-editor of *Global Social Policy*. Dr Yeates' recent publications include *Globalization and Social Policy* (2001).

Jessica Young is currently reading International Political Economy at the Brussels School of International Studies, University of Kent at Brussels. Jessica Young's previous research includes a study of the language policies of the European Union, which was partly funded by a grant from the Monroe Scholar grant from William and Mary College.

Ernest M. De Zolt is an Associate Professor of Sociology at John Carroll University, Cleveland, Ohio, USA. His research areas include deviant behavior, corporate deviance, white-collar crime, and political sociology.

INDEX